FIELD MARSHAL SIR HE

Sir Henry Hughes Wilson, Bt., 1919, by Sir William Orpen

Field Marshal Sir Henry Wilson

Wilson

A Political Soldier

KEITH JEFFERY

OXFORD
UNIVERSITY PRESS

OXFORD
UNIVERSITY PRESS

Great Clarendon Street, Oxford OX2 6DP

Oxford University Press is a department of the University of Oxford.
It furthers the University's objective of excellence in research, scholarship,
and education by publishing worldwide in

Oxford New York

Auckland Cape Town Dar es Salaam Hong Kong Karachi
Kuala Lumpur Madrid Melbourne Mexico City Nairobi
New Delhi Shanghai Taipei Toronto

With offices in

Argentina Austria Brazil Chile Czech Republic France Greece
Guatemala Hungary Italy Japan Poland Portugal Singapore
South Korea Switzerland Thailand Turkey Ukraine Vietnam

Oxford is a registered trade mark of Oxford University Press
in the UK and in certain other countries

Published in the United States
by Oxford University Press Inc., New York

British Library Cataloguing in Publication Data
Data available

Library of Congress Cataloging in Publication Data
Data available

Typeset by Laserwords Private Limited, Chennai, India
Printed in Great Britain
on acid-free paper by
Biddles Ltd., King's Lynn, Norfolk

ISBN 978–0–19–820358–2 (Hbk.)   978–0–19–923967–2 (Pbk.)

1 3 5 7 9 10 8 6 4 2

For Jacquey, who was there at the start

Preface

Field Marshal Sir Henry Wilson (1864–1922) was one of the most controversial British soldiers of the modern age. Today, however, he is perhaps remembered more for the circumstances of his death than for the achievements of his career. On 22 June 1922, five months after he had retired as Chief of the Imperial General Staff, Wilson was assassinated by two Irish republicans on his doorstep in Eaton Place, London. By some accounts he drew his sword, and might therefore be described as the only British field marshal ever to have 'died in action'. A life-long unionist from southern Ireland (though with Ulster forebears), by 1922 he had become a symbol of 'repression' in Ireland and, as chief security adviser to the new Northern Ireland government, he was identified with the uncompromisingly unionist administration in Belfast. Wilson was accorded a state funeral and is buried in St Paul's Cathedral. He was celebrated as one of the greatest of British soldiers, and a man who had played a crucial role in the Allied victory in the Great War. Five years later his reputation was ruined by the publication of an official biography, *Field Marshal Sir Henry Wilson, His Life and Diaries*, by Sir Charles Callwell.

Callwell's biographical method was to quote very extensively from Wilson's voluminous diaries. The impression given by these all-too-quotable passages is that of an over-ambitious, self-serving monster, with such violent passions and prejudices as to appear at times actually unbalanced. Yet Wilson was admired and respected by many of his colleagues; and he served with distinction in a series of very senior and important positions in the British military hierarchy before, during, and after the First World War.

Wilson is frequently identified as a significant 'player' in the politico-military affairs of the time, though he rarely gets any extended treatment. A. J. P. Taylor describes him as 'an articulate military adviser' who 'knew how to cajole civilians in high places'.[1] Hew Strachan calls him 'the most effective and decisive voice in British strategic counsels before 1914'.[2] Niall Ferguson mentions 'the kind of huge armies dreamt of by men like Erich Ludendorff and Henry Wilson',[3] without in any way explaining who Wilson was, let alone why he might be spoken of in the same breath as Ludendorff. David Fitzpatrick categorises Wilson as 'Ulster's most ingenious and influential military ally',[4] while for Brian Bond he was 'one of Britain's most exuberant, flamboyant, exotic, outspoken and even perhaps preposterous generals'.[5]

---

[1] Taylor, *English History, 1914–45*, 140–1.
[2] Strachan, *The First World War*, i, *To Arms*, 202.   [3] Ferguson, *The Pity of War*, 105.
[4] Fitzpatrick, *The Two Irelands*, 46.
[5] Bond, *British Military Policy between the Two World Wars*, 28.

This biography seeks to assess Wilson's life and career in the light of more complete evidence than hitherto available, and to place him clearly in his social, national, and political context. The work also aims to illuminate many aspects of modern Britain, including civil–military relations, social and political linkages within the 'Establishment', the role of the Irish Protestant Ascendancy in the British military, Britain's strategic 'Continental commitment', coalition warfare in the 1914–18 war, and the problems posed by Irish nationalism and Ulster union-ism to the United Kingdom during the first quarter of the twentieth century. Wilson served as professional head of the British army at a time, moreover, when Britain's imperial power reached across the world and when there had been a mas-sive expansion of empire in the Middle East, with substantial British forces being deployed in what is today Israel, Jordan, Iraq, and Iran. Part of Wilson's task was to help match the increasingly limited military resources of post-First World War Britain with commitments inherited from the war, some of which were favoured by the more imperially visionary of his political masters. Wilson operated in cir-cumstances where policy was constrained by the limits—and limitations—of mil-itary power, a situation familiar enough to modern British (and, since 1945, American) decision-makers.

Nowhere was this clearer than Ireland in 1919–21, where a military security strategy was at first rejected by the government, and then—so far as Wilson was concerned—imposed too late and in too partial a fashion. In the meantime, and to Wilson's incredulous disgust, an officially unacknowledged and indisciplined counter-terror policy was applied at enormous political cost. The Irish context is central to an understanding of Wilson. He was Irish-born, felt himself to be an Irishman, and spoke with an Irish accent. Yet he came from a social class, and lived at a time, when he could also regard himself (and be regarded) as 'British', or even 'English'. He was a product of the 1801 Union (of Great Britain and Ireland), a citizen of the 'British Isles'—'these islands', as they are sometimes called in more politically correct language—and was possessed of a passionate unionism, embed-ded in his own sense of Irishness *and* Britishness.

For Irish nationalists, however, he became a unionist arch-bogeyman. His role during the 'Curragh crisis' in 1914 and his high-profile position as Chief of the Imperial General Staff (CIGS) from 1918 to 1922 gave him an understandable prominence and he was blamed for some of the Irish security policy excesses in a way, curiously, that Sir Nevil Macready, who was actually in charge, was not. In, for example, Padraic O'Farrell's *Who's Who in the Irish War of Independence* Wilson is credited with establishing the 'Cairo Gang', 'a group of British Intelligence Officers, so called because they met in Cairo at the behest of Sir Henry Wilson', and whose actions 'led to the Bloody Sunday executions' in 1920.[6] There is no evidence whatsoever for the allegation that Wilson was

[6] O'Farrell, *Who's Who in the Irish War of Independence*, 24, 156. This unfounded assertion is repeated in Foster, *Modern Ireland*, 507.

involved, nor even that the 'Cairo Gang' actually existed, but the reasonable supposition that there were British 'dirty tricks' in the Irish campaign, together with the fact that Henry Wilson, the professional head of the British army, was an undoubted unionist sympathiser, is enough for some writers to conflate the two, and posthumously damn him. Wilson's identification, moreover, with the Special Constabulary in the new Northern Ireland in 1922 (closer than was actually the case) and, by extension (though without any evidence), with Protestant sectarian attacks on Catholics, materially contributed to the circumstances of his own death. In fact, as was to be observed about his relationship with the Conservative Party, Wilson was *with* the new Northern Ireland regime, but never quite *of* it.

If we are to comprehend the modern and contemporary relationship between Britain and Ireland, we need to understand people like Wilson who were *neither* Orange *nor* Green, and appreciate that the relationships within and between the neighbouring islands cannot be reduced to a simple Manichaean duality. Wilson, for all his apparently simple, unswerving loyalty, was influenced by and possessed of plural allegiances, which the partitioned post-1922 Ireland could not readily accommodate. Ireland made him, and Ireland killed him. That he was also a successful servant of the British imperial system and sat in the councils of the great in the greatest empire, and during the greatest war anyone had ever known, makes him a fantastic subject for biography.

The principal source for this work is the huge Wilson archive preserved at the Imperial War Museum, generously deposited there by Major Cyril Wilson and Mrs Marjorie Stevenson. Modern historians owe a great debt of gratitude to people like Major Wilson and Mrs Stevenson for giving precious and nationally important family papers to institutions like the museum, where they will be preserved and made available to scholars in many different fields. The archive comprises forty-one volumes of manuscript diaries covering 1893 to 1922, with extensive and detailed daily entries. There is also a very considerable collection of official, semi-official, and personal correspondence and papers. I owe a huge debt to Roderick Suddaby and his staff in the Department of Documents for the marvellous job they do, and the friendly tolerance with which they have accommodated me for very many years. There are other important source materials in the United Kingdom National Archives (formerly the Public Record Office), the Royal Archives, and the Public Record Office of Northern Ireland. To the staffs of these institutions, and the other libraries and archives I have used, and which are named in the Bibliography, I offer my heartfelt thanks. Quotation from the Wilson papers is by permission of the Trustees of the Imperial War Museum. Quotation from the Royal Archives is with the gracious permission of Her Majesty Queen Elizabeth II. Crown-copyright material is reproduced by permission of the Controller of Her Majesty's Stationery Office. I also wish to acknowledge permission to use papers from the Trustees of the Liddell Hart Centre for Military Archives, King's College, London, the Churchill College Cambridge Archives Centre, the National Army Museum, the Bodleian Library, the British Library, and the House of Lords Record Office.

Over the long time during which I have been working on Henry Wilson I have incurred innumerable debts of gratitude. There have been so many people, over so long a time, that any list I provide here will inevitably (but inadvertently) miss some out, and to those omitted I apologise. At the Ulster Polytechnic, and later the University of Ulster, Professor A. J. A. (Tony) Morris, supported my work from the very beginning. His son, Tony, gave me a contract, in which, thankfully, neither he nor his successors at Oxford University Press were inflexible about the deadline for delivery of the text. Successive heads of department, Tom Fraser and Alan Sharp, have been consistently supportive, and I must also thank the university Faculty of Arts for research leave and financial support. External funding for completion of the work was received from the Arts and Humanities Research Board (as it was), under their research leave scheme. A large part of the book was written while I was Parnell Fellow in Irish Studies at Magdalene College Cambridge, and I must thank the Master and Fellows of the college for electing me to the fellowship, and the whole college community for making me so welcome during my time there. Early drafts of some chapters were written while I was a Visiting Scholar at the Australian Defence Force Academy in Canberra, and I must thank my colleagues there, especially Peter Dennis, Robin Prior, and Jeff Grey, for their congenial company.

Professional colleagues near and far have assisted in various ways: Joan Beaumont, Marie Coleman, Roy Foster, John Gooch (who alarmingly found the first typo on page 3 of the 'final' typescript), Alan Megahey, Eunan O'Halpin, Ferdinand von Prondzynski, Eileen Reilly, Mark Seaman, Peter Simkins, and Hew Strachan have all been especially helpful. Dr D. B. McNeill assisted with information about trains, and Dr James Riddell with medical matters on a number of convivial occasions. It was a great privilege to talk about Henry Wilson with two of his relations, his nephew Major Cyril Wilson, and his niece Bridget, Lady Blackburne. Both were generous with their time, and provided me with a rare and precious link back to the man himself. Colonel Robin Charley, Timothy H. S. Duke (Chester Herald), Jean Forbes, Sheila Lough, and Dr Brian Trainor also provided valuable information about the Wilson family. Geordie Fergusson gave me insights into the 'Curragh incident', and I treasure a conversation I had with his father about Wilson.

On a personal level, I must thank Lindsay Duguid and John Murray-Browne for unmatched hospitality in London, and much warm encouragement. My family have been amazingly patient about the 'Wilson project', although they have long been looking forward to its completion. Finally, I must thank many close friends who provided unbelievable support at a difficult time when the final text was being written.

K.J.

June 2005

Contents

Illustrations		xii
Maps		xiii
List of abbreviations		xiv
1.	The Irish context	1
2.	The making of a staff officer	11
3.	South Africa	26
4.	Work in the War Office	42
5.	At the Staff College	64
6.	Preparing for war	85
7.	Politics, the Irish question, and war	107
8.	With the BEF	131
9.	IV Corps	156
10.	Coalition warfare	179
11.	Winning the war	203
12.	Defending the empire	229
13.	Losing Ireland and saving Ulster	256
14.	Death and reputation	281
Bibliography		299
Index		311

Illustrations

FRONTISPIECE

Sir Henry Hughes Wilson, by William Orpen (National Portrait Gallery, London)

PLATES

1. Cecil, Lady Wilson (Hulton Archive).

2. Wilson in 'civvies' (*The Times*, Weekly Edition, 11 March 1922).

3. Lord Roberts, Sir Alfred Milner, and some staff officers, Cape Town, December 1900 (*from* Callwell, *Field-Marshal Sir Henry Wilson*).

4. Wilson's diary for 24 August 1914 (Imperial War Museum, HU 55854).

5. Members of the Allied Mission with the Emperor Nicholas II at Tsarkoe Selo, February 1917 (Imperial War Museum, HU 52750).

6. Military Section, British Delegation to the peace conference, March 1919 (Imperial War Museum, Q 113558).

7. Sir Henry Wilson, Sir William Robertson, and Winston Churchill during an Army Council visit to the Rhine, August 1919 (Imperial War Museum, Q 34708).

8. Four of the most powerful men in the British empire (*The Times*, Weekly Edition, 4 February 1921).

9. Wilson and Marshal Foch (*from* Callwell, *Field-Marshal Sir Henry Wilson*).

10. Wilson speaking at the unveiling of the war memorial at Liverpool Street station, 22 June 1922 (*The Times*, Weekly Edition, 29 June 1922).

11. Metropolitan Police handbill for Wilson's killers (Imperial War Museum).

Maps

1. South Africa: the Natal campaign of 1899–1900   41
2. Wilson's tours of the Franco-German frontier, 1908–11   106
3. The northern sector of the western front, 1914–18   155
4. The Middle East, 1918–22   255

List of Abbreviations

ADC	aide-de-camp
AG	Adjutant-General
BEF	British Expeditionary Force
CGS	Chief of General Staff
CID	Committee of Imperial Defence
CIGS	Chief of the Imperial General Staff
CinC	Commander-in-Chief
CO	commanding officer
CofS	Chief of Staff
DAAG	Deputy Assistant Adjutant-General
DMI	Director of Military Intelligence
DMO	Director of Military Operations
DMT	Director of Military Training
DSD	Director of Staff Duties
GOC(inC)	General Officer Commanding (-in-Chief)
GSO	General Staff Officer
IWM	Imperial War Museum, London
MGO	Master-General of the Ordnance
PRONI	Public Record Office of Northern Ireland, Belfast
QMG	Quartermaster-General
RIC	Royal Irish Constabulary
RMA	Royal Military Academy, Sandhurst
RMC	Royal Military College, Woolwich
SWC	Supreme War Council
TNA	The National Archives (United Kingdom), London
UVF	Ulster Volunteer Force
WO	War Office

1

The Irish context

On Monday 26 June 1922, the same day as Sir Henry Wilson's state funeral in London, a memorial service was held at the headquarters of the British forces occupying Constantinople (Istanbul) in the aftermath of the First World War. General Sir Tim Harington, the British commander, who had served as Wilson's Deputy Chief of the Imperial General Staff (CIGS), remembered his friend in the following terms: 'He died for Ireland. . . . His life has been taken by a cruel, dastardly cowardly act, at the instigation of an organisation directed against England and her King. England has lost a great patriot. . . . It may be that this sacrifice may save Ireland. . . . [Sir Henry] would have given his life cheerfully if he thought that England, the British Empire, and his beloved Ireland would gain.'[1] Also in the aftermath of Wilson's death, Lord Carson, the veteran unionist leader, sent a message to the Ulster Unionist Council which placed Wilson in an Irish and imperial context: 'We mourn the loss of Ireland's greatest son and one of the Empire's greatest citizens. He died for Ulster's liberty.'[2] An appreciation by a regimental colleague described Wilson as 'the very embodiment' of 'an English gentleman'.[3] No greater praise, perhaps, but scarcely an entirely satisfactory description of a man who regarded himself, and was widely regarded by others, as Irish.

Yet to characterise Henry Hughes Wilson simply as 'Irish' is not without its difficulties. Although he was born and reared in Ireland, he grew up at a time when the national identity of people living in the United Kingdom—'of Great Britain and Ireland'—itself was in a state of flux. This was especially true for Protestants in Ireland (and subsequently for many in Northern Ireland) whose nationality—'Irish'—and citizenship—'British'—sometimes appeared to be in conflict. J. C. Beckett has argued that following the Act of Union in 1800 the sense of being Irish which the Anglo-Irish community possessed 'though still deeply felt, had lost all political content. They were', he added, 'citizens of the United Kingdom.'[4] But while acknowledging the problem of national identity which perhaps confronted people of Wilson's class and time (and certainly

---

[1] As reported in *The Orient News* ('an independent British Daily Organ in the Near East'), 26 June 1922 (copy in Harington papers, box 1).   [2] *Belfast News-Letter*, 26 June 1922.
[3] Capt. R. C. Hargreaves, 'Field Marshal Sir Henry Wilson', in *Rifle Brigade Chronicle* (1922), 48.
[4] Beckett, *The Anglo-Irish Tradition*, 96.

confused any late twentieth-century observer of nineteenth-century Ireland), Beckett may have underestimated the extent to which 'Irishness' had a political meaning for both Protestant unionists and Catholic nationalists. It is doubtful, too, whether the concept of 'United Kingdom' citizenship actually had very much meaning to Irish people of whatever political persuasion. Indeed, the whole notion of nationality was only beginning to become well defined in legal terms during the second half of the nineteenth century, and not until 1914 did the law take its modern shape with the legislation which laid the basis for an official definition of nationality and that modern conventional token of national status, the passport.[5] Nationality, however, does not exclusively depend on legal definitions. This was certainly true of the nineteenth century, however much it may have come to dominate in more recent times. Factors such as family background, upbringing, education, career and, of course, self-perception are of central importance. Each of these will be considered in order to help us understand the universe—social, political, perhaps even emotional—within which Henry Wilson grew up.

Henry Wilson was born on 5 May 1864, at the family home of Currygrane, situated between Ballinalee and Edgeworthstown (Mostrim), county Longford in the midlands of Ireland. The Wilsons were an impeccably Protestant family of the middling sort who traced their ancestry back to a John Wilson who was reputed to have arrived at Carrickfergus, county Antrim, in the suite of King William III in 1690. Wilson almost certainly arrived in Ireland earlier, and there are lots of Wilsons in the vicinity before 1690, but it was socially more superior to claim an association with William of Orange than for the family to be mere 'Planters'.[6] Owning land at Rashee, not far from Carrickfergus, the Wilsons proved to be upwardly mobile. Towards the end of the eighteenth and into the nineteenth century, John's grandson and great-grandson, Hugh and William Wilson, made a considerable fortune in the Belfast shipping business. In a classic transition, William abandoned trade and, taking advantage of the Encumbered Estates Act of 1849 (which allowed indebted Irish landlords to sell their property), transformed himself into a country landowner, buying estates in counties Dublin, Westmeath, and Longford. When William died the property was divided between his four sons. Mostly situated in the rich agricultural lands of Leinster, the Wilson estates were clearly sufficient to provide a comfortable living for the whole family. But they were not great landowners. In the 1870s William's sons together owned approximately 17,500 acres, the lion's share of which was held by the three oldest. The youngest, James (Henry Wilson's father) inherited the Longford property of 1,200 acres with a valuation (in 1878) of £835.[7] In 1861

    [5] British Nationality and Status of Aliens Act, 1914.
    [6] Biographical details from Callwell, *Wilson*; Reilly, 'The Wilson Family'; and Sheila Lough, a member of the Wilson family, who has assembled a considerable amount of material relating to the family history.   [7] Figures calculated from Hussey de Burgh, *The Landowners of Ireland*.

James married Constance Hughes, the daughter of a successful Dublin barrister James Freeman Hughes.[8]

The Longford Wilsons were in many respects typical of their class and time. Socially something more than just large farmers, they did not, however, fall within the ranks of the 'Big House' families of Ascendancy landlords. For most of the nineteenth century people like them—characterised by nationalists as the 'English garrison' in Ireland—played a crucial role in the government of the country. Before reforms introduced in the 1890s, Irish local government lay in the hands of predominantly Protestant landowners and small-town professionals who dominated the county Grand Juries. All of William Wilson's four sons held the office of High Sheriff in their respective counties. James was additionally a Justice of the Peace and Deputy Lieutenant for Longford, as was his eldest son, James Mackay Wilson.[9]

James Wilson (1832–1907) had three daughters, and four sons, of whom Henry was the second.[10] Although the family estate was not very large, the Wilsons lived comfortably enough. Most of the property consisted of arable land, and in 1854 there were twelve tenants in the 600-acre estate around Currygrane. According to the 1901 Census, the house had 16 windows in the front and 28 occupied rooms. By this stage, 62 people lived on the estate, 49 Catholic and 13 Protestant (10 of whom were members of the Wilson family).[11] By all accounts the Wilsons were conscientious landlords. There are no records of Land League activity against them. Memories are long in Ireland, and it is significant that General Seán MacEoin, a war of independence IRA leader, whose family lived near Currygrane, in the 1960s described the Wilson family as 'people for whom I had the highest regard', and remembered them as 'good neighbours and good employers of Catholic and Protestant workers alike'.[12]

As well as Currygrane, the Wilsons rented a delightful eighteenth-century house called Frascati at Blackrock, county Dublin. This had been the seaside house of the dukes of Leinster, and, ironically, considering the Wilson family's passionate unionist sympathies, the boyhood home of Lord Edward Fitzgerald, a leader of the United Irishmen in 1798.[13] But it was particularly well located for the Wilsons to indulge their love of sailing, and several of the family, including Henry's father, himself, and two of his brothers, were members of the Royal

---

[8] Biographical information on the Hughes family provided by Dr Brian Trainor of the Ulster Historical Foundation.

[9] Patrick Buckland in *Irish Unionism 1*, his study of southern Irish unionists, took James Mackay Wilson as characteristic of the bottom stratum of southern unionism, who had primarily local interests, an important group, moreover, much under-studied by historians.

[10] The dates of birth of James Wilson's sons are as follows: James Mackay, 1863; Henry Hughes, 1864; Arthur John de Courcy, 1867; Cecil William, 1870.

[11] Reilly, 'The Wilson Family', 19.

[12] Notes of an interview with Seán MacEoin, 15 Jan. 1964 (O'Malley papers, P7.D3); *Sunday Independent* (Dublin), 28 July 1967.

[13] Bence-Jones, *Burke's Guide to Country Houses*, i, *Ireland*, 128. Despite attempts to have it preserved as a historic monument, it is characteristic of modern Ireland that the house was demolished to make way for a supermarket development (see *Irish Times*, 5 Nov. 1983).

St George Yacht Club at Kingstown (now Dun Laoghaire) Harbour.[14] Setting the family apart from the general run of Protestant minor gentry, both James and James Mackay Wilson were educated at Trinity College, Dublin, though there was no strong tradition of university education in the family as a whole. James Mackay Wilson had some 'gentleman scholar' inclinations. He joined the Royal Society of Antiquaries of Ireland in 1887, and immediately became its honorary secretary for county Longford, a position he retained until 1923. In the 1890s he contributed a few short pieces of the 'notes and queries' variety to the society's journal.[15] More typical, perhaps, was the fact that three of the Wilson sons were sent to public school in England: two to Harrow and Henry to Marlborough College in Wiltshire.

Henry Wilson was nearly 13½ years old when he arrived at Marlborough in September 1877. Up to this point he had been educated exclusively at home, by a succession of French governesses who planted in him a love of France and a knowledge of the French language, both of which were to be of considerable significance later in his life. Marlborough was an interesting choice of school. It had been founded in 1843, and, after a difficult start, including a celebrated school 'rebellion' in 1851, had gained a reputation both for athleticism and gaining scholarships at Oxford and Cambridge universities.[16] The education it provided, however, was not particularly 'modern' and among the boys (at least) anti-intellectualism held sway, as it did in many other English public schools.[17] In general the school offered 'a training in the style of a traditional leisured élite rather than the skills of an industrialised society', and, like other upper-middle-class schools of the period, it certainly emphasised what J. A. Mangan has called the 'secular trinity' of 'imperialism, militarism and athleticism'.[18]

Such a school environment would have well suited the young Henry Wilson who seems to have been set for a career in the army from an early age. But he displayed no evident aptitude or enthusiasm for academic work. His school reports recognised ability but not application, and he appears to have left little mark on the collective life of the school.[19] Preaching at Marlborough after Wilson's death, the headmaster remarked that as a schoolboy Wilson had been

[14] Information from the Secretary, Royal St George Yacht Club, 15 June 1994. James Mackay Wilson was a member from 1882 until 1924.

[15] Information from the *Journal of the Royal Society of Antiquaries of Ireland*. Wilson's contributions included 'Keenagh Old Church, County Longford' (ser. 5, vii (1897), 183–4) and 'Earthwork Fort or Rath in County Longford' (ser. 5, ix (1899), 67–8).

[16] Marlborough is treated extensively in Honey, *Tom Brown's Universe*, and Mangan, *Athleticism in the Victorian and Edwardian Public School*.

[17] See the reminiscences by E. F. Benson (Marlborough 1881–7), in *Our Family Affairs*, 137–57.

[18] Mangan, 'Athleticism: A Case Study of the Evolution of an Educational Ideology' (based on the history of Marlborough College), 154, 156–7.

[19] Callwell, *Wilson*, i. 2. Wilson occasionally returned to the school, e.g. in 1912 when he inspected the school Officer Training Corps, and for an 'Old Marlburians' day' in 1921 (Wilson diary, 24 June 1912, 5 Mar. 1921).

'whimsical, perhaps a little wild, full of wit, and what is rarer than wit, humour'.[20] Other school reminiscences appeared in 1922. Lord Askwith, whose time at the school overlapped with Wilson's, remembered him to have been 'a bright boy and extremely popular', and a correspondent to the *Daily Express* recalled as a very new boy being greeted by Wilson 'with a cheery "Come along, young fellow. I'll show you the way about." '[21] Whatever the status of these remarks, the image of him as 'a little wild' (and is there a hint here, too, of 'wild Irish'?) would fit in well with Wilson's later reputation as a slightly maverick character, prone to indulge in bouts of buffoonery and, certainly, addicted to whimsical facetiousness, if not actual humour.

Wilson stayed at Marlborough for less than three years. At Easter 1880, shortly before his sixteenth birthday, his father withdrew him from the school so that he might study with crammers at home in Blackrock for entry into the army. As Wilson left little mark on Marlborough, perhaps Marlborough, equally, left little mark on him. While as a Field Marshal the school was glad to claim him ('the greatest of living Marlburians'[22]), and he was willing to serve as president of the Old Marlburian Club (1920–1), he seems to have formed no lifelong friendships while a schoolboy. Although he was physically a very active youth, there is not much evidence of a particular enthusiasm for those traditional team sports which were reckoned to be so influential for inculcating the essential virtues of leadership, loyalty and corporate spirit.[23] In Ireland he rode, sailed, and played lawn tennis, considered by one expert to be an undesirable school game as it was 'not painful enough' to foster 'the spirit that faces hardship, the spirit of endurance'.[24] Although Wilson later played regimental polo, he always retained a special affection for the more individual pursuits of riding, sailing, and tennis.

Henry Wilson grew up at a time when the definition of 'Irishness' was by no means clear-cut. Although the Anglo-Irish, if only by habit, ordinarily referred to themselves as 'Irish' without qualification, this perception was increasingly being challenged during the nineteenth century with the rise of a distinctively Gaelic and Catholic notion of the 'Irish nation' and Irish nationality. Ironically, however, the same period saw a number of developments which undoubtedly tended to make the Anglo-Irish perceive themselves as more 'Irish' than hitherto. Terence De Vere White has argued that during the nineteenth century the Anglo-Irish became more 'Anglo' than Irish. One feature of this stemmed from the improvements in transport which enabled the fashion of Irish boys going to school in England.[25] Yet the very fact of going away to school could serve to confirm and reinforce an Irish identity, rather than to erode it. Claiming to be Irish as a

---

[20] *The Marlburian*, 50/829 (29 June 1922), 86.
[21] *Daily Telegraph*, 23 June 1922; 'By the Way' column, *Daily Express*, 27 June 1922.
[22] *The Marlburian*, 50/829 (29 June 1922), 87.
[23] See the stimulating discussion of these points in Best, 'Militarism and the Victorian Public School', 141–6.
[24] F. B. Malim (an assistant master at Marlborough and subsequently headmaster of Sebergh and Haileybury), 'Athletics', 153.   [25] White, *The Anglo-Irish*, 48.

schoolboy at Charterhouse, Robert Graves (who was born and brought up in Wimbledon) found himself being attacked by an *echte* (though undoubtedly Protestant) Irish boy already at the school.[26] In the mid-1920s, a couple of generations after Wilson, Brian Inglis went from Ireland to the Dragon School in Oxford. There he first became aware of his 'Irish identity'. Although he had no Irish accent, he found himself the 'butt of mild teasing' concerning his Irishness. 'For a time', he recalled, 'I was to begin to feel Irish in England more than I felt Irish in Ireland, where the "Anglo" element prevailed.'[27]

Religion was (and in Northern Ireland still is) a crucial 'signifier'. Although the equation of Protestantism with unionism, and Catholicism with nationalism, has never been absolute, Protestant religious belief has always been a central feature of the Anglo-Irish community. Beyond Ulster, where Scottish Presbyterianism is strong, by far the largest Protestant denomination is the Church of Ireland, which is part of the Anglican Communion. By the Act of Union in 1800 the Established Churches of England and Ireland were united. But in 1869 the Church of Ireland was disestablished and the 'United Church of England and Ireland' broken up. After 1 January 1871, when the Irish Church Act came fully into operation, the Church of Ireland began to develop an independent, distinct, *Irish* identity, emphasised, for example, by the preparation of an Irish Prayer Book. 'We are not,' averred Lord (later Archbishop) Plunket, 'as some would represent us, "the English Church in Ireland".... Let the word Anglicanism, as describing our faith and practice, be banished from our vocabulary.'[28] Even the name of the denomination, 'Church of Ireland', was a clear marker of a national status, and attempts by Presbyterians to call it the 'Episcopal Church' were robustly rejected. For regular members of the Church, like the Wilsons, the liturgical changes, albeit subtle, would at every service have confirmed the Irishness of their denomination. Family memorials in the church and graveyard of St John's Church of Ireland, Ballinalee, too, testify to the Wilsons' fidelity. James Wilson, moreover, was a prominent member of the denomination, serving on the Representative Church Body and several other committees, such as the Clergy Widows' and Orphans' Fund Board. After he died (in 1907) *The Times* said that 'since disestablishment, he held by election every post of honour which is open to laymen'.[29]

Although the evidence in these matters can never be absolutely reliable, Henry Wilson appears to have been a believer, and he was certainly a regular churchgoer. Like his father (who 'dreaded any departure in the Service of the Church from the old ways, and abhorred the introduction of innovations'[30]), he appears to have been theologically conservative and had rather evangelical, low-church tastes, more generally characteristic of the Church of Ireland than that of England. In 1899 Wilson complained to the army chaplain-general about a padre who 'was a

[26] Graves, *Good-Bye To All That*, 65.   [27] Inglis, *Downstart*, 27–8.
[28] Daly, 'Church Renewal', 23–38, 36.
[29] *The Times*, 15 Aug. 1907. See also e.g. the *Irish Ecclesiastical Gazette*, 25 Feb. and 24 Mar. 1888.
[30] From his obituary in the *Irish Times*, 14 Aug. 1907.

ritualist, of very advanced type'. Another entry the following year noted 'a very poor high church sort of thing'.[31] A communion service on Christmas Day, 1919, 'was so high and horrid that Cecil & I came out'.[32] The post-disestablishment constitution of the Church of Ireland, indeed, prohibited such 'Romish' practices as the wearing of vestments, the use of incense, and even the placing of cross and candles on the communion table (*not* an 'altar').[33] Attending a smart society wedding at the Catholic Brompton Oratory in 1910, Wilson noted: 'Beautiful music, but how I do hate all the R.C. farrago.'[34] On 12 July 1918 he went to a service in the Catholic Westminster Cathedral for 'the Dead French soldiers'. 'High Mass', he wrote, 'makes me positively sick, & wicked to a degree.'[35] Yet he was no Orangeman, prohibited by the association's rules from attending Catholic services.[36]

He also held sometimes quite forcefully expressed views about Catholics. Commenting on the appointment of his old friend Edmund Talbot as Lord-Lieutenant, and the first Catholic viceroy of Ireland since the reign of James II, he said: 'There isn't a decenter, honester Christian alive. But the poor man he is a Pope and he is in Ireland hinc illae lacrimae.'[37] Yet, while he might be critical of 'Papists' as a group, he does not seem to have been particularly prejudiced against individual Catholics, even, indeed, the Pope. On the death in 1903 of Leo XIII, who had been Pontiff for twenty-five years, he noted in his diary: 'The Pope died. A wonderful old man'; hardly the comment of a bigoted Protestant fanatic.[38] At an Allied conference in Rome in January 1917, Wilson toured 'the Vatican & Sistine Chapel. A wonderful place', he noted. 'I was sorry not to see the Pope.'[39] There is only one serious, specific allegation of religious prejudice against Wilson. In a memoir (written in 1947) about Sir George Macdonogh, Sir Walter Kirke asserted that Wilson, who 'had an intense dislike and distrust for what he called "Papists"', was prejudiced against Macdonogh because he had converted from Methodism to Roman Catholicism.[40]

From the 1870s the formation of an 'Irish Party' in parliament articulated and stimulated the growth of Irish nationalism as a popular political movement. On

---

[31] Wilson diary, 7, 8 May, 15 Oct. 1899, 4 Nov. 1900.   [32] Ibid., 25 Dec. 1919.
[33] Megahey, *Irish Protestant Churches*, 8.   [34] Wilson diary, 15 Oct. 1910.
[35] Ibid., 12 July 1918.
[36] In 1910 Wilson attended the Catholic wedding of Ferdinand Foch's daughter, and in 1911 he and Cecil (albeit as tourists) attended high mass at the Madeleine in Paris (ibid., 12 Oct. 1910; 26 Feb. 1911).
[37] 'Hence these tears', a quotation from the Roman writer Terence's play *Andria*, Wilson to Nevil Macready, 5 May 1921 (Wilson papers, HHW 2/2D/48). Perhaps the two and a half years at Marlborough were not entirely wasted.   [38] Wilson diary, 20 July 1903.
[39] Ibid., 9 Jan. 1917.
[40] Kirke, 'Lieut.-Gen. Sir George M. W. Macdonogh' (Kirke papers, IWM 82/28/1). Whatever the religious dimension to the relationship between the two men, it should be noted that Macdonogh's 'extremely taciturn and uncommunicative' (Kirke's words) personality contrasted sharply to Wilson's more sociable and gregarious nature. There is no corroborative evidence whatsoever for an allegation made by the family of Maj.-Gen. Sir William Hickie that Wilson blocked his further promotion because he was a Catholic (Dooley, *Irishmen or English Soldiers?*, 194).

the unionist side, the all-Ireland response to the growing threat of home rule, while opposing the demands of Irish nationalism, may paradoxically have actually heightened a sense of 'Irishness' among them. In 1885 the *Irish* Loyal and Patriotic Union was established, followed in 1891 by the *Irish* Unionist Alliance.[41] The founders of neither of these organisations chose titles which located them within the 'United Kingdom', or stressed any explicitly British allegiance. The unionist response which was, perhaps necessarily, sectional and geographically limited, clearly concentrated Anglo-Irish, Protestant Ascendancy, landlord minds in an *Irish* fashion.

The Wilson family played a prominent role in this movement. Wilson's father was 'for many years' an 'active and valued member' of the executive committees of both the Irish Landowners' Convention and the Irish Unionist Alliance. Wilson's elder brother, James Mackay Wilson—Jemmy as he was known in the family—who inherited the Currygrane estate, was a political activist. He stood in the Longford North constituency as a Conservative/Unionist in the 1885 and 1892 general elections. On both occasions he was soundly defeated by the Nationalist candidate, Justin McCarthy, by 2,549 votes to 163 in 1885 and 2,741 to 203 in 1892.[42] In 1885, moreover, his father stood in Longford South where he, too, was well beaten by the Nationalist.[43] Although the unionists chose to make a particular point by standing in every Irish constituency during the 1885 first home rule crisis, Jemmy Wilson's candidature in 1892 smacks of a certain obstinacy, not to say foolhardiness. As a unionist in the midlands of Ireland, he ploughed an increasingly lonely and bitter furrow, especially after the turn of the century, when it began to become clear that southern unionism was a lost cause. The Irishness—such as it was—of unionists like Jemmy Wilson (and there is evidence to suggest that Henry fully shared his brother's political opinions[44]), did not, however, extend to a conception of a legitimate and politically autonomous Irish nation. A clear distinction was made between Irishness and Irish nationality. 'You refer to Ireland by a "nation",' wrote Jemmy to the editor of the *Evening Standard*. 'Never was there such an error! That word implies a homogenous people. Ireland never was, and is not now, and never can be a Nation.'[45]

For Wilson, there was no difficulty in being identified as Irish. The problem perhaps lies with other people and the difficulty they may have in conceiving how he could reasonably regard himself as English, British, *and* Irish simultaneously. His Irishness was very important, both in his own self-perception and in the way other people regarded him. Socially, it may well have been a strength in

[41] See Buckland, *Irish Unionism 1*, for details of these organisations.

[42] Walker, *Parliamentary Election Results in Ireland*, 134, 147.

[43] Wilson senior got 321 votes to Laurence Connolly's 3046 (ibid. 134); obituary of James Wilson, *Longford Leader*, 17 Aug. 1907.

[44] The brothers kept up a regular correspondence, some of which has survived. A copy of a letter from Jemmy to Bonar Law (28 Apr. 1917) is endorsed by Henry 'Admirable letter' (J. M. Wilson papers, D.989A/8/7). See also Ch. 7 below.

[45] Letter by J. M. Wilson (TS copy), n.d. (*c*.1917) (ibid.).

England. Although he had attended an English public school, albeit briefly, he came to English social circles as something of an outsider, with not much more than his considerable native wit and sociable nature to carry him through. Wilson's comparative lack of 'background' and position as an outsider—as, perhaps, in Roy Foster's term, a 'Mick on the make'[46]—gave him opportunities which were maybe not available to his English and Scottish colleagues. Wilson's family were not rich. His relatively modest circumstances, moreover, seem to have acted as a powerful stimulus to his own ambition.

Wilson's Anglo-Irish background, however, did, it seems, provide him with some important social connexions. His father's committee work in the Church of Ireland, the Irish Landowners' Convention, and the Irish Unionist Alliance, together with his brother Jemmy's political activism brought them both into contact with powerful and well-connected members of the 'Ascendancy' class, providing him with a social 'network' which was to work to his advantage. This was a social class, moreover, which readily straddled self-perceptions of 'Irishness' and 'Britishness'. Many of them owned land in Great Britain as well as Ireland. Beyond the twenty-eight Irish representative peers, provided for by the 1800 Act of Union, a significant number sat in the House of Lords in their own right. Irish, English, and British upper-class families mixed freely at all the usual great events of the social calendar, and they certainly intermarried quite freely.[47]

In making his presence felt, Wilson was quite prepared to play the stage Irishman to a remarkable extent. As a rhetorical device he frequently adopted a dramatically 'Irish' pose and 'played the poor mouth'—the 'Begob, shure Oi'm only a puer Oirish fella' sort of thing. He could play a Flurry Knox (who, after all, represents an engaging and largely non-threatening Irish stereotype) to any 'R.M.' or similar English authority figure he encountered. And if the English were prepared to fall for this theatricality, more fool they (or should it be more clever he?). Good examples of this technique survive from his lectures. Speaking at the University of London in November 1913, he began a talk on 'Frontiers' by announcing: 'I am an Irishman. Now we Irish find it exceedingly difficult to understand you English.'[48] 'I am not an Englishman, I am Irish', he told an education conference in 1919.[49] He used this method, frequently laced with heavy irony, to the end of his life. And the theme of an Irish identity remained too. 'My country', he told the House of Commons in the spring of 1922, 'is supposed to be a savage and barbaric country, but really we have railways and roads and telegraphs and telephones, and even hotels.'[50]

---

[46] Foster, *Paddy and Mr Punch*, 281–305.

[47] See Cannadine, *Decline and Fall*, 472–87, for a consideration of Anglo-Irish aristocratic networks. [48] Lecture notes, 5 Nov. 1913 (Wilson papers, HHW 3/3/33b).

[49] *Proceedings of Imperial Education Conference, 11 & 12 June 1919* (HMSO) (ibid., HHW 2/67/90). By contrast, and further to confuse the issue, earlier that same year he returned from a visit to a horse show at Olympia to write: 'We English gave a disgraceful exhibition' (Wilson diary, 23 June 1913). [50] *Hansard*, House of Commons, 12 Apr. 1922.

Yet he could also be 'English'. 'On the whole then,' he wrote during the battle of Loos in September 1915, 'I am again satisfied as although we English did nothing much to-day, the French at Arras have got on.'[51] There is a parallel here with other parts of the 'Celtic fringe'. As Ged Martin has observed, 'until recent times, "English" was often used as a synonym for "British", even by upper-class Scots', and he quotes an observer in the 1930s being surprised by John Buchan referring to himself as 'an *Englishman*', adding, 'I have no use at all for the silly affectation of substituting Briton for Englishman when speaking of Scots'.[52]

But also, at the very end, there was not so much a confusion as a conflation of nationality, which Wilson evidently found to be quite natural. Unveiling a roll of honour at the Queen's University, Belfast, Officers' Training Corps in January 1922, we find in Wilson's speech a curious (to us) juxtaposition of province, land, and country, simultaneously clearly and ill-defined in the same passage. 'Scattered hither and thither over this dear country of theirs, of Ulster,' he declared, 'and that dear land of theirs, England, were memorials of those... who were not professional soldiers, the names of men who thought it was their duty to come forward to help their country when their country was in danger.'[53] Wilson, himself of course a professional soldier, certainly conceived it his duty to 'help his country' when it was in danger: Ireland, England, and ultimately, Ulster too.

---

[51] Wilson diary, 28 Sept. 1915.
[52] Martin, *The Cambridge Union and Ireland*, 76 and 303 n. 4. The observer was Hensley Henson.   [53] *Belfast News-Letter*, 20 Jan. 1922.

2

The making of a staff officer

Henry Wilson had some difficulty getting into the army. Even those regarded as ineffably stupid at school—like Winston Churchill—usually responded to the attentions of specialist crammers, but Wilson, despite individual tutoring at home, between 1880 and 1882 failed the entrance exams for the Royal Military College, Woolwich, twice and those for Sandhurst three times. The celebrated army historian, Sir John Fortesque, maintained that there was nothing surprising about this in Wilson's particular case. 'A very tall boy, such as he was,' he asserted (apparently seriously), 'needs time for his brain to develop.'[1] The competition, in any case, was quite stiff; in the late 1870s there were nine applicants for every place at Sandhurst.[2] But there was not much else for Wilson to do, other than join the army. In the long term, the family estate was only large enough to sustain his elder brother. Of the four Wilson brothers, the eldest, Jemmy, inherited Currygrane; Henry and the youngest, Cecil (known as 'Tono'), went into the army; the third son, Arthur, worked as a land agent for Lord Beauchamp. Many years after, Wilson reflected on 'the incalculable chances of life. "When I was a little boy in Ireland," he said, "who could tell what would become of me? One way (*crescendo*) Field-Marshal—Privy Councillor—G.C.B.—all the rest of it: the other way (*diminuendo*) just a little bit of bog-cotton." '[3] For the recently arrived Wilson family, too, army careers could help to confirm their social position within the local gentry. One historian of the late Victorian army has observed how the landed interest—who dominated the officer corps—was 'a relatively open group' which included 'newcomers, [who] having made their money in industry, commerce or speculation, moved on to the land'. For these people, 'military service was one method by which an aspirant or his descendants might seek the approval of local society'.[4]

Although the purchase of commissions in the army had been abolished in the 'Cardwell reforms' of the early 1870s, the old system had not been replaced by any comprehensive new method of selecting officers on the basis of ability. Happily for Wilson, the majority of candidates for commissions in infantry regiments, including those who failed to get into Woolwich or Sandhurst, were able to apply

---

[1] In a review of Callwell's biography of Wilson (*Observer*, 9 Oct. 1927).
[2] Spiers, *The Late Victorian Army*, 93.   [3] Marsh, *A Number of People*, 397–8.
[4] Spiers, *Late Victorian Army*, 94. See also Harries-Jenkins, *The Army in Victorian Society*, 24–5.

through the militia; 'what used in those days to be called the back-door'.[5] Following two periods of training, a militia officer could gain a regular commission by successfully completing a competitive examination. This system helped to maintain the social exclusiveness of the officer corps, since the admission of young men to be militia officers frequently depended as much on social status as any military aptitude. Militia officers, indeed, ran less risk of the sort of social embarrassment at Sandhurst remembered by one of Wilson's regimental colleagues, the perhaps typically snobbish Charles à Court Repington. There were 'of course, some dreadful outsiders amongst us, as could scarcely be prevented in an open competition'. He recalled 'that three or four of these were discovered by us to have dined with the commandant's cook one night, and we decided to punish them in our own way. We took them down to the lake and threw them in, and if they were not drowned it was not our fault.'[6]

Entry from the militia, however, was clearly a more individual route to the regular army than through either of the military colleges, and the instruction was certainly more cursory than even the rudimentary training offered at Sandhurst or Woolwich. Perhaps confirming his leaning towards being a 'loner' and something of a military free-thinker, Wilson missed the experience of studying with a group of like-minded colleagues at an important and formative point in his upbringing.

In December 1882 Wilson was gazetted a lieutenant in the Longford Militia (6th battalion Rifle Brigade). Over the next two years he received training in Ireland with that unit and the 5th Munster Fusiliers. Although the competitive examination was not reckoned to be very difficult, no chances were taken with his preparation and during the winter of 1883–4 he studied under crammers in England. Reflecting the enlightened attitude towards education held by his father, in 1883 Wilson was sent to Algiers, presumably to sharpen up his French, and also to Darmstadt to learn German, though apparently he spent more time there playing tennis than studying.[7]

Wilson sat the army examination in July 1884, passing fifty-eighth on the list of successful candidates. He was at first gazetted to the Royal Irish Regiment, but secured a transfer to the much more prestigious Rifle Brigade—perhaps the link with the Longford Militia helped here. Wilson's choice of the Rifle Brigade also no doubt reflected his military, and perhaps also his social, ambitions. This did not come cheap, and he was certainly stretched to meet the costs of his army career. Few officers in the nineteenth-century British army were able to manage without private means. After the Boer War an official committee reckoned that a junior infantry officer 'would need a private income of £100 to £150 upwards, though it should be possible for a careful subaltern to live on the lower of these amounts with comfort in a line battalion'. But the committee also recognised that there was

[5] Callwell, *Wilson*, i. 3. This was not an unusual route into the army, especially for those with an Anglo-Irish background. Other militia entrants who reached general officer rank included John French, Bryan Mahon, Oliver Nugent, Horace Smith-Dorrien, and Edward Spears.
[6] Repington, *Vestigia*, 38–9.   [7] Callwell, *Wilson*, i. 3–4; Buchanan, *Victorian Gallery*, 33.

a 'marked divergence in the expense of serving in different regiments of the same arm'.[8] The fashionable Rifle Brigade was undoubtedly an expensive unit, and regarded itself as 'a privileged caste'. From the beginning the regiment had an '*esprit de corps d'élite*', and 'could always handpick its officers, drawn from the leading public schools where they had been taught manners'.[9]

Manners or not, the Rifle Brigade evidently believed that Wilson had something to offer them and he seems to have been popular and well liked. He was, recalled one contemporary, 'a tall, gaunt youth, with very long, bony arms and legs, a merry eye, and a most delightful laugh that carried you with him'.[10] Early in 1885 he sailed to India to join the 1st battalion of the regiment. Here Wilson took up polo and enjoyed the local rough shooting and big-game hunting. In a reminiscence collected by Charles Callwell in the 1920s, Henry Yarde-Buller, who had joined the 1st battalion with Wilson, recollected his 'somewhat boisterous manner and unusually sunny disposition', but he also noted 'unbounded ambition', together with 'a rare quickness of perception and...his natural gift of Irish eloquence'. These were qualities to set Wilson apart, although they did not necessarily make him 'a man who was destined to make his mark in the world', as (with the evident benefit of hindsight) Yarde-Buller recalled. An additional recollection, that 'most of us in the 1st Battalion very speedily came to look upon him as a man of quite exceptional brain power',[11] carries with it a hint of that wariness with which the average Englishman (public schoolboy, or subaltern for that matter) regards a slightly-too-clever colleague.

Late in 1886 Wilson's battalion was posted to Burma to assist with imperial policing duties aimed at suppressing guerrilla activity along the upper reaches of the Irrawaddy river. On 12 November he arrived at Minbu on the Irrawaddy south of Mandalay.[12] Here Wilson remained for the next five months, enjoying some success in what was known as 'the Subalterns' war'. The soldiers were organised into mounted infantry, and were joined by men from the King's Royal Rifle Corps, including Lieutenant Henry Rawlinson, who was an almost exact contemporary of the Irishman. No doubt there was keen competition between the riflemen of different regiments, but Rawlinson recorded in his journal working with a section of the Rifle Brigade 'under a very good chap called Wilson'.[13] The two men were to become lifelong friends.

Wilson performed quite well during the campaigning. At the end of January 1887, he commanded the mounted infantry in a party of soldiers and 'Goorkha Police' who captured the camp high in the Arakan Hills of Boh Shwe, one of the local leaders, though he himself escaped. On 5 May, however, during the

---

[8] *Report of the Committee appointed by the Secretary of State for War to Enquire into the Nature of Expenses incurred by Officers of the Army*, p. 6, 8 [Cd 1421], H.C. 1903, x, 540, 542.

[9] Harvey, *The Rifle Brigade*, pp. ix–x, 122–3.

[10] Maj. H. A. N. Fyers, quoted in Callwell, *Wilson*, i. 5.   [11] Quoted in ibid.

[12] 'The 1st Battalion in Burma, 1886–9', *Rifle Brigade Chronicle for 1894*, 52.

[13] Maurice, *Rawlinson of Trent*, 16–17.

destruction of a further 'large entrenched camp', Wilson was quite seriously wounded over his right eye.[14] The injury, which left him disfigured for life, was bad enough for him to be sent to Calcutta on sick leave, but it refused to heal and he was invalided home in the autumn. He spent the period from November 1887 until nearly the end of 1888 convalescing in Ireland.

Despite the discomfort of the injury, which, among other things, may well have contributed to the intermittent attacks of neuralgia he suffered in later life, Wilson's time back home, especially at Frascati (which the family were shortly to give up), appears to have been filled by a near-idyllic round of riding, sailing, tennis, and socialising. In May 1888 Henry and his younger brother Arthur competed in the 'All Comers' Doubles' at the Fitzwilliam Square Irish lawn tennis championships, though they did not progress beyond the first round.[15] The two brothers clearly stood out in the Dublin society of the day. Years later, with a typical touch of gentle irony, William Orpen, the painter, gave a sketch of two self-assured and debonair young men-about-town travelling up on the suburban line from Blackrock:

I remember well how, when they appeared on the platform of the little railway station in the mornings to take the train to Dublin, a sort of hush spread over the little crowd waiting to be taken to the city to their daily tasks. Such perfect figures, such perfect clothes, spats to wonder at, boots to dream of! Sir Henry always with a rain-coat thrown over one shoulder, always with his yellow-gloved hands clasped behind him. Him we called 'Rake-faced Wilson,' and his brother was 'Droop-eye Wilson.' Yes, truly they were different from the little crowd; it was as if the Assyrian princes mentioned in Ezekiel had arrived amongst us, from the unknown world far beyond our ken. What a joyful creature Sir Henry was! His laugh even, made one laugh, though no one had any idea what he was laughing at. We kept our proper distance in those days.[16]

During this 'Irish interlude' Wilson began courting Cecil Mary Wray, whom he was later to marry. The Wrays and the Wilsons had a broadly similar family background, though the Wrays' experience more closely followed the fall of the Ascendancy landlord class. Cecil Wray's forbears had come over to Ireland towards the end of the reign of Queen Elizabeth I and had acquired land in counties Donegal and Londonderry.[17] During the first half of the nineteenth century the family fortunes waned somewhat. In the early 1830s Cecil's father, George Wray, established himself on a estate called Ardnamona on Lough Eske about seven miles from Donegal town, 'one of the loveliest rural estates in Ireland'.[18] But, as

---

[14] *Rifle Brigade Chronicle for 1894*, 64–6; Callwell, *Wilson*, i. 7.

[15] They were beaten 6–3, 6–2 by H. S. Mahoney and W. H. Boyd (*Irish Times*, 24 May 1888).

[16] Orpen, *Stories of Old Ireland*, 28. There is a similar description in a memoir of Wilson by Orpen in the *Empire Review*, 37 (1923), 573–6. The two families were acquainted. Orpen's elder brother, Richard Caulfield Orpen, later a well-known Dublin architect, stayed at Currygrane in 1893 while participating in some local amateur theatricals (Wilson diary, 6–11 Dec. 1893). The Orpens themselves were also keen tennis-players (see *Irish Times*, 5 July 1888).

[17] The family history is covered in Trench, *The Wrays of Donegal*.

[18] McQuillen, *Irish Country House Cooking*, 6. It is now a fine country-house hotel.

the family history notes, the Famine of 1845–9 caused the family 'serious financial loss. . . . Much of their prosperity went, never to return.'[19]

There was, too, some local trouble. During the night of 26 December 1849—a sort of late Christmas present—two kegs of explosive were set off outside Ardnamona. Although much damage was done, no one was hurt, but (with one exception) the family never spent another winter in the house, though they continued to use it for summer holidays until George Wray's death in 1878. In 1850 Wray became land agent for Lord Leitrim's Donegal estates. Leitrim was a notoriously bad landlord who was murdered, it is thought by tenants, in 1878. Wray resigned the job in 1857, apparently because he disagreed with Leitrim's way of doing things. He then took on the more agreeable agency of Lord Drogheda's estates in Kildare, which he held until his death.

Although George Wray unexpectedly inherited the bulk of the family property, after he died in 1878 there was not a great deal left for his widow and five surviving children (two sons and three daughters). The elder son, Charlie, was seriously in debt, having been living well beyond his means in Lord Drogheda's social circle. The other son, Kenneth, emigrated to Australia. One daughter, Leonora, had married, in 1874, John Townsend Trench—'Towney'—who was Lord Lansdowne's land agent and lived in Kenmare, county Kerry. George's widow, Charlotte, was left with little money and two unmarried daughters: Frances (who was 30) and Cecil (17). Ardnamona was sold, and the Wrays moved to a town house in Clarinda Park, Kingstown (now Dun Laoghaire), not so very far from the Wilsons in Blackrock. Although their circumstances were now 'very much straitened',[20] Cecil Wray, at least, continued to move in fairly smart Dublin society. She was presented at the viceregal court, went to balls at Dublin Castle, and took part in the social highlights of the Dublin year, including the Horse Show, the Fitzwilliam Square lawn tennis week, and the annual sailing regattas at Kingstown Harbour. Here she met Henry Wilson.

The Wray family history is a characteristic Irish Ascendancy story. Utterly dependent on the land, the land, it seemed, failed them. So, too, had the British government. From the 1860s onwards, and apparently in response to the sort of pressure characterised by the Ardnamona dynamiters of 1849, successive Liberal administrations undermined both their own title to land and a system of ownership which provided employment for land agents. Towney, an eccentric who abandoned the Church of Ireland for the Plymouth Brethren and became attracted to millenarian notions,[21] was 'near the end of his rope', noted Wilson in 1898.[22] From the mid-1880s, moreover, the possibility of home rule additionally threatened to take political power away from them and place it in the hands of the very people whom the Ascendancy system had exploited for generations. While there is no evidence that the Wrays were as politically active as the Wilsons, Cecil

[19] Trench, *The Wrays of Donegal*, 358. [20] Ibid. 374.
[21] Lyne, *The Lansdowne Estate*, pp. xlix–l. [22] Wilson diary, 21 Apr. 1898.

Wray's undoubted unionism was, if anything, more bitterly secured in her own family history than anything the Wilsons experienced, at least until the 1920s.

Henry Wilson's engagement to Cecil Wray affected his military ambitions. As a relatively impecunious junior officer in an expensive regiment, he could not afford to marry (especially someone of even more modest means) until he had secured some sort of advancement in the army. During 1888 he began working seriously for entrance to the Staff College. As Brian Bond has observed, 'the magic letters p.s.c. [passed Staff College] were seen to be worth having since they opened up opportunities not only of coveted appointments, but also of accelerated promotion'.[23] George Aston, a near-contemporary of Wilson, noted that while a private income was still necessary for an officer at the Staff College, the outgoings were lower than those in an expensive regiment (such as the Rifle Brigade). Aston, whose own means were modest, 'looked upon the Staff College course as a gamble'. He invested a small legacy 'in an education that would lead to an increase of income if I was given a Staff appointment at the end of the course, and I think many army officers, especially the married ones, had the same incentive'.[24] Wilson received a small allowance from his father, and, after his marriage, enjoyed the interest—of about £200 a year—from a £6,000 trust fund.[25]

At the end of the year Wilson was passed fit for regimental duty—though not overseas service—and in 1889 he joined the 2nd battalion at Dover. He told Hubert Fryers, a fellow subaltern, that he had determined on two things: 'The first is that I am going to pass into the Staff College, and the second is that I am going to marry Cecil Wray.' Fryers, who was remembering Wilson forty years afterwards, remarked on his cheerful charm and easy manner. But he also noted the striking impression which Wilson made on strangers as a somewhat unorthodox individual:

People who did not know him were perhaps disposed on first acquaintance to set him down as a wild Irishman of equally wild spirits. I remember, for instance, one day on the musketry ranges a staff officer coming to watch us, who presently drew me aside to ask 'Who is that officer standing over there, and what is his rank?' 'That is Mr. Wilson,' said I, 'a subaltern like myself.' The staff officer gazed at him with a puzzled countenance for a moment or two and then turned away with the remark, 'He seems a very comic fellow.' Wilson was perfectly well aware of the effect he had on others, especially on dull people, and, perhaps, he exploited this as a social device. Fryers' reminiscence continued: 'Henry gloated over it when I told him, and he used to refer to the incident years afterwards.'[26]

After a brief spell at Aldershot, the battalion was posted to Belfast in August 1890. Wilson continued working for the Staff College entrance and in May 1891 he passed fifteenth on the list of twenty-five successful applicants, with a handful

[23] Bond, *Victorian Army*, 153.
[24] Aston, *Memories of a Marine*, 98. Sir James Edmonds (who attended in the 1890s) calculated that it cost officers about £300–400 of their own money to attend the Staff College (Bond, *Victorian Army*, 161). [25] Wilson's will gives some details of the marriage settlement.
[26] Quoted in Callwell, *Wilson*, i. 9.

of marks more than Henry Rawlinson.[27] His best subjects were 'Tactics' and 'Military History and Geography'. Surprisingly—though he always spoke the language with more enthusiasm than accuracy—French was one of his poorer subjects and German was worst of all.[28] On 3 October 1891 Henry Wilson and Cecil Wray were married at her local Church of Ireland in Kingstown, county Dublin.[29] He was 27, she was 29.

Wilson began his two-year Staff College course in January 1892. The college had been established at Camberley in 1858 as part of the reforms following the army's patchy performance in the Crimean War. In the absence of a properly constituted general staff, or much official encouragement, the institution developed rather slowly. Many soldiers, suspicious as always of 'brains', regarded it as little more than a bolt-hole for over-ambitious colleagues, choosing a cosy billet away from regimental duties for a couple of years, avoiding uncomfortable foreign postings, and seeking preferential access to prestigious staff appointments. Wilson, however, arrived at a time of transition when the college was throwing off a reputation for pedantry and the excessively academic and theoretical study of military topics.

The change in command at the college during Wilson's course exemplified this transition. His first commandant was Brigadier-General C. F. Clery, an Irishman and author of a standard volume, *Minor Tactics*, but a distant character who was only rarely seen by the students. In August 1893 Clery was succeeded by Colonel H. J. T. Hildyard, who worked to make the course 'thoroughly practical' and succeeded, in Brian Bond's words, in transforming 'the College into a "mental gymnasium" for the Army just at a time when the future leaders of the First World War era were passing through'.[30] He reduced the importance of examinations, and introduced a system of more continuous assessment, based on practical exercises, both in the classroom and out of doors. This new emphasis was also applied by Colonel G. F. R. Henderson, a gifted military historian and teacher, who was Professor of Military Art and History, and clearly a very important figure: many military memoirs testify to his standing.[31] Henderson's method included an element of 'role playing'. When studying a military campaign, students were 'expected to replace the actors, to work out the operations step by step with map and compass, to investigate the reasons behind each decision, to ascertain the relative importance of moral and physical factors, and to deduce the principles on which the generals had acted'.[32] In later years, both as commandant of the Staff College and as a senior staff officer, Wilson frequently—and dramatically—adopted this technique in order to help his students and colleagues gain an imaginative insight into the problems presented to them.

---

[27] Wilson, 3,037 marks; Rawlinson, 2,947 (the highest score was 3,393), *The Times*, 1 Aug. 1891.
[28] 'Marks gained on entrance' in Staff College Roll 1858–1921 (Staff College Library, Camberley).   [29] *Daily Express* (Dublin), 5 Oct. 1891.
[30] Bond, *Victorian Army*, 154–5.   [31] See e.g. Maurice, *Rawlinson*, 26.
[32] Luvaas, *The Education of an Army*, 242.

Even with the curriculum changes, the college regime was not markedly strict, and there was plenty of time for play as well as work. All officers in the junior year had to pass a horse-riding examination, which presented no difficulty at all to Wilson, and hunting was virtually *de rigeur*. In the spring of 1893—during his second year—Wilson regularly hacked into lectures, hunted on average twice a week, and came third in the heavyweight section of the Staff College Point to Point. On gaining his place at the college, Wilson had taken the lease of a modest house, Grove End, about two miles from Camberley. Wilson's niece remembered the property as a 'horrid little house beside a railway',[33] but it evidently suited the Wilsons very well, since they leased it again in later years. Apart from being inexpensive, it had four acres of ground where Wilson could keep his horses and indulge his passion for gardening, especially vegetables. Indeed, if one judges from his diary for 1893, his most consuming interests while a Staff College student were his horses and his garden.

Despite not being noticeably well off, the Wilsons clearly enjoyed a full, if conventional, social life. In 1889 Wilson was elected to White's, 'the most exclusive club in London, with a list of members like a Debrett in Miniature'.[34] In 1894 his elder brother, Jemmy, was elected to Brooks's, another extremely exclusive club. How did these two young Irishmen, from a no more than middling family background, vault into such prestigious institutions? The explanation appears to lie in the political mobilisation of southern Irish Protestants. While the membership books for White's for this period do not survive, those for Brooks's do, and reveal that the elder Wilson's proposer was an Irish peer, Lord de Vesci,[35] who undoubtedly knew Henry and Jemmy's father, James Wilson, through his work on the executive of the Irish Landowners' Convention and the Irish Unionist Alliance. De Vesci was a founder member of the Irish Loyal and Patriotic Union, which became the Irish Unionist Alliance in 1891.[36]

At Camberley there was a busy round of lunches, teas, and dinners with fellow students and their wives. In June, all work ceased during the week of Ascot, where the Staff College had a luncheon and tea tent.[37] There was also plenty of leave. During 1893 Wilson spent three-and-a-half months back home in Ireland—January, December, and six weeks in the summer, during which he worked on a money-making exercise to sell hay from the Currygrane estate to various customers in England. At the end of the year he calculated a profit of £74 (from receipts of £435), but this did not take into account a loan of £200 which his father put up as initial funding.[38] Wilson and his manservant, Brown, had cut much of the hay themselves, but the game, evidently, was not worth the candle. The scheme was not repeated the following year.

[33] In conversation with the author, 8 May 1985.   [34] Colson, *White's*, 115, 197.
[35] I am most grateful to the late Nigel Clive, a member of Brooks's, for ascertaining this intelligence.   [36] Buckland, *Irish Unionism 1*, 1, 16.
[37] Aston, *Memories of a Marine*, 116.   [38] Wilson diary, memo. following 31 Dec. 1893.

An important part of the college course was the senior-year visit to the Franco-German War battlefields. For many this was as enjoyable as the '*bottle*field' tours enjoyed by more recent college groups. One officer, a year or two ahead of Wilson, recalled that the tour was 'very interesting, and I particularly remember some excellent burgundy we got in a delightful small spa in the Vosges'.[39] Wilson himself took the trip (led by Colonel Henderson in April 1893) very seriously, and in later years he was to visit and revisit the battlefields and the whole Franco-German frontier zone, becoming as familiar with the terrain as any man in the British army.

For many, the value of the Staff College lay as much in the fellow students as in the instruction. 'My experience', wrote John Adye, 'was that one learned more from one's fellow-students than from the professors.'[40] Certainly, enduring friendships were made at the college, especially between groups of men who had to work together on college exercises. Sir Aylmer Haldane remembered being part of a student syndicate with Wilson, Henry Rawlinson, and Thomas Snow.[41] Although in his memoirs (published long after Wilson's death) Haldane particularly recalled being 'good friends' with Wilson,[42] this is not confirmed by the evidence from Wilson's diary, which records his most regular companions as being 'Rawly' and 'Snowball', but not Haldane. Hubert Hamilton (who was killed in battle in October 1914), Walter Gaisford (who perished at Loos in 1915), and an officer from the year below Wilson's, Launcelot Kiggell (who became Douglas Haig's Chief of Staff in France, 1915–18), were other close college colleagues. Wilson, too, kept up with Rifle Brigade contemporaries, such as Jack Cowans, who had preceded him at the Staff College, and Henry Yarde-Buller ('Yardie'), who had joined the 1st battalion with Wilson in 1885.

Of all the friendships cemented at this time, that with Henry Rawlinson was the most significant. Wilson became Rawlinson's 'closest friend'. The two men worked jointly on essays and 'schemes'; they rode together; Wilson stayed at Rawly's house in London and went to the theatre with him. In April 1894 they cycled on their own round the Franco-Prussian battlefields (and toured Pommery and Greno's champagne vaults).[43] Rawlinson was just a couple of months older than Wilson and came from a secure, landed background, rather higher socially than the Irishman. Both were sporty, and especially keen on polo. Like Wilson, Rawlinson was notably quick-witted.

Both men were ambitious, and throughout their lives they competed keenly, but apparently amicably. They were frequently bracketed together; Ian Hamilton thought that they were 'each in their own line as selfish and cunning as foxes'.[44]

[39] Adye, *Soldiers and Others I Have Known*, 148–9.

[40] Ibid. 148. See also Bond, *Victorian Army*, 141–3, for some general reflections on memoirs of the college at about this time.

[41] Haldane, *A Soldier's Saga*, 60. By the time of writing, Haldane was the only one of the four still alive.   [42] Ibid. 206.

[43] Wilson diary, 3–12 Apr. 1894.   [44] In a letter *c*.1904, quoted in Lee, *A Soldier's Life*, 87.

Sir Edward May, Rawlinson and Wilson's superior at the War Office in the early 1900s, said the two men 'always hunted in couples, and no one could ever decide as to which was the cleverest'. Wilson, however, 'would certainly have won had wit and humour been the test'.[45] Wilson himself used to tell the story of how, when he and Rawlinson were stationed at Aldershot, they had each separately seen a desirable appointment advertised in the morning paper. Wilson hurried off to the station to catch an early train up to London to get his application in before his rival, but the first person he saw on the platform was Rawlinson, evidently on the same mission. 'We both pretended not to see the other,' said Wilson, 'and I hopped into a carriage close up to the front of the train in order to get out quickly at Waterloo Station and to the War Office before Rawly. Directly we arrived I got out of my carriage without a moment's delay just in time to see Rawly jump off the engine—he had beaten me by a short head!'[46]

In the mid-1880s Lord Roberts, then Commander-in-Chief in India, had taken on Rawlinson, as an aide-de-camp. When Lord 'Bobs' returned to England he came to stay with Rawlinson, who in May 1893 introduced him to Henry Wilson at a Staff College cricket match. As it happened, the two students were working on a 'defence of India' exercise and they seized the opportunity of testing out their ideas on Roberts.[47] Wilson made an extremely favourable impression on the Field Marshal, who proved in future years to be an important patron for him, as also for Rawlinson.

Wilson graduated successfully from the Staff College in December 1893.[48] Two days after he learned his result, Wilson went to the War Office to find that he was up for promotion to captain 'at once' and would be posted in March to the 3rd battalion of his regiment at Peshawar in India. 'This is a terrible upset,' he wrote in his diary. 'Went & saw Military Secretary who is afraid nothing can be done.'[49] Wilson went home to Ireland for Christmas and stayed on for most of January 1894. All the time he was worried about the proposed posting. He mobilised what assistance he could, but even the Duke of Connaught was 'not very hopeful'.[50] In the end help came from his doctor in Dublin, who told him that he could not go to India and supported him in a successful application to a medical board, which at the end of January gave Wilson four months' stay of travelling out east.[51]

Why did Wilson not want to rejoin his regiment in India? The medical reason has some plausibility. But, more importantly, banishment to the empire would leave him far away from the home staff appointments he coveted and in which he could undoubtedly shine. In February 1894 he learned that he had been posted to the 1st battalion, which was about to move from Calcutta to Hong Kong,

[45] May, *Changes and Chances of a Soldier's Life*, 276.   [46] Barrow, *Fire of Life*, 113.
[47] Wilson diary, 27–8 May, 13 Sept., 18 Nov. 1893; Maurice, *Rawlinson*, 25–6; James, *Lord Roberts*, 243.   [48] Wilson diary, 16 Dec. 1893; *The Times*, 23 Dec. 1893.
[49] Wilson diary, 18, 30 Dec. 1893.   [50] Ibid., 6 Jan. 1894.
[51] Ibid., 13, 30 Jan., 1 Feb. 1894.

where it would stay for two years before returning home.[52] Wilson seemed resigned to this, but when a fellow officer in the 2nd battalion in Dublin offered to swap places with him he jumped at the opportunity. 'Wonderful luck. Thank God', he wrote in his diary.[53]

Perhaps another factor in Wilson's apprehension about an overseas posting abroad lay in his domestic circumstances. His diary continually testifies to the pleasure he and Cecil had in creating a comfortable home and garden for themselves. In the absence of children, perhaps, the actual place which they shared became of especial importance. Wilson's public stance was to deny that his personal circumstances had any bearing on his professional life. The story was told years later that after Wilson graduated from the Staff College the commandant asked him if there were any suggestions he would like to make about the running of the institution. Wilson replied that married officers ought to be excluded from attending. The commandant naturally objected that Wilson himself was married. 'Yes, I know that,' he replied, 'but that fact has never been allowed to interfere with my duty or my work.'[54] For all this, Cecil Wilson remained a powerful influence throughout Wilson's life and had, as one of Wilson's obituarists put it, 'an almost blind faith in those marvellous qualities which she discovered long before others had recognized their existence'.[55] She played, too, a significant (and as it turned out, unfortunate) role in the construction of his memory after his death.

During September 1894 Wilson spent one of his very few periods of service with his regiment.[56] Throughout his career, although clearly alive to the importance of unit *esprit de corps*,[57] Wilson does not himself seem invariably to have been an outstandingly keen 'regimental man'. He did recognise, however, that the regiment had been good to him and believed that he owed much of his 'good fortune' to having been a Rifleman.[58] Nevertheless, as a subaltern he did not spend much time with his regiment. For almost two of his first six years in the regular army, between February 1885 when he joined his battalion in India, and January 1892 when he entered the Staff College, Wilson was away from his unit, either in hospital or on convalescent leave at home in Ireland. This compares, for example, with the eight years or so of regimental duty (also with the Rifle Brigade) served at home and abroad by his near-contemporary Charles à Court Repington, before he entered the Staff College.[59]

[52] Ibid., 28 Feb. 1894.
[53] Ibid., 23 Aug. 1894. The officer concerned, Capt. Hon. F. M. St Aubyn, unexpectedly died in Hong Kong in February 1895.
[54] 'Lady Wilson: An Appreciation', *The Democrat*, 1 July 1922, p. 7 (copy in Harington papers).
[55] Hargreaves, 'Sir Henry Wilson', 48.   [56] *Rifle Brigade Chronicle for 1894*, 163.
[57] See e.g. his observations in the *Civil & Military Gazette*, 1 Mar. 1901.
[58] Wilson diary, 1 Jan. 1907.
[59] For Repington, see his pre-war memoirs, *Vestigia*, and Ryan, *Lieut.-Col. Charles à Court Repington*. He was named 'Charles à Court' until 1903, when he took the additional surname of Repington.

Repington was another notably 'brainy' soldier, who as a staff officer and military intellectual was at the very least Wilson's equal. In 1894 he came to Wilson's aid. In July, Repington, then a staff captain in the War Office Intelligence Division, took Wilson for a week's tour of French military and naval manoeuvres. Wilson evidently performed satisfactorily—he had to write a report and provide sketches—for in November he was offered five months' unpaid attachment to the Intelligence Division, to be followed by a proper staff appointment in succession to Repington.[60] Wilson was overjoyed by this 'wonderful' opportunity. The problem of having to serve without pay, moreover, was solved by a cheque from his Uncle Bob, Robert Mackay Wilson, who had an estate of some 5,000 acres in county Kildare.[61]

For three years from November 1894 Wilson worked in the Intelligence Division. Vigorously promoted by General Henry Brackenbury in the late 1880s, the division had developed into 'a kind of substitute for a British General Staff'.[62] When Wilson joined there were six sections: one devoted to colonial defence; four 'foreign' sections; and a topographic and library branch. Each section had a staff of three: at the head was a deputy assistant adjutant-general (DAAG), who was assisted by a staff captain and a military clerk. Much of the information collated in the division came from open sources, such as newspapers and journals, supplemented by reports from military attachés and British officers travelling abroad. Information was shared on a regular basis with other government departments, principally the Admiralty, and the Foreign, Colonial, and India Offices. For the small staff involved there was plenty to do. Repington described the work as 'demanding, congenial, and stimulating'.[63] Wilson also found time to help Rawlinson with a publishing venture. In November 1894 he proof-corrected his friend's *Officers' Note Book* which brought up to date a pocket-book which Lord Wolseley had designed for active service. Rawlinson's effort was so successful that it prompted the authorities to produce their own *Field Service Pocket-book*.[64]

The Director of Military Intelligence (DMI) when Wilson went to the War Office was General Edward Chapman, who had succeeded Brackenbury in April 1891. Chapman, a protégé of Lord Roberts, had spent his entire career in India and was not especially well qualified to deal with the sorts of 'foreign political and other European matters' for which he was responsible.[65] But the momentum established by Brackenbury seems to have carried the department successfully through Chapman's time as DMI. Wilson was posted to 'Section A', responsible for information from France and its colonies, Belgium, Italy, Spain, Portugal,

---

    [60] Wilson diary, 7–10 Nov. 1894; Callwell, *Wilson*, i. 16–17.
    [61] Wilson diary, 24 Nov. 1894. Figures from Hussey de Burgh, *The Landowners of Ireland*.
    [62] Fergusson, *British Military Intelligence*, 107.
    [63] Repington, *Vestigia*, 89–90. The work of the Intelligence Division in the 1880s and 1890s is described in Fergusson, *British Military Intelligence*, chs. 5–6.
    [64] Wilson diary, 15 Nov. 1894; Maurice, *Rawlinson*, 29.
    [65] Gleichen, *A Guardsman's Memories*, 177.

Mexico, and Latin America.[66] Although Chapman had initially been 'very complimentary' to Wilson, he was to be disappointed in him the following year. In January he said that he wanted him to qualify as an interpreter in German. 'It's a great nuisance,' confided Wilson, 'though complimentary as apparently he wants to send me off and on to Berlin.' Despite intensive tutoring—three hours' lessons on some days—Wilson failed the examination in April. On 5 May, nevertheless, he took over from Repington as staff captain in Section A of the Intelligence Divison. It was his thirty-first birthday. 'I am the youngest Staff Officer in the British Army', he wrote in his diary.[67]

Wilson's duties were to collate the information coming into the office and generally to 'devil' for the head of his section, Major J. S. S. Barker. In his first year he was also sent abroad on intelligence-gathering missions, though in a perfectly open and above-board fashion. In June 1895, to check up on a French expedition to Borgu along the upper Niger river in west Africa, he went to Paris and interviewed both British diplomats and French officers. He also took the chance one night to go to the Comedie Française (' "*L'ami du femmes*" Excellent') and another to see the celebrated *chanteuse* Yvette Guilbert. In August, taking Cecil, he went to Brussels where he visited the embassy and lunched with the Belgian explorer, Baron Dhanis.[68]

The pace and direction of work varied with the international situation at any given time. 'Very busy day & unsatisfactory,' wrote Wilson in November 1895, 'as C. in C. asked about French use of high explosive, & Barker has gone away & I cannot find his "Gun" file.'[69] Wilson found the catastrophic Italian defeat by Ethiopian forces at Adowa 'very interesting', and on 11 March he briefed the Commander-in-Chief, Lord Wolseley, on the situation, which had implications for the British position in Egypt.[70] A twenty-one-page paper he prepared on Eritrea also illustrates the kind of work he was doing. It was based on 'a series of most interesting letters' by a British officer who had recently visited the region, noting military and colonial developments in the Italian colony.[71]

The War Office appointment meant that the Wilsons had to move from Grove End. After living in London for a few months, they took a lease on a spacious property, Selwood Park, at Stanwell, near Staines in Middlesex. Here they kept a variety of animals—cows and hens, as well as horses—and had room for a lawn-tennis court together with a sizeable vegetable garden. Cecil seems have liked the

---

[66] The other sections were B: British colonies and protectorates, Cyprus, Polynesia, South African Republic, Orange Free State; C: Germany, Netherlands, Sweden, Norway, Denmark, Switzerland, USA; D: Russia, India, Afghanistan, Burma, Siberia, China, Japan, Siam, Central Asia, Persia; E: Austria-Hungary, Balkan States, Ottoman Empire, Egypt, Independent African States; F: Maps and Library. Ibid. 85–6, 248. See also W. V. R. Isaac, 'History of the Directorate of Military Intelligence', 8 (Ministry of Defence (Central and Army) Library).

[67] Wilson diary, 26 Nov. 1894, 7, 10 Jan., 3–4 Apr., 5 May 1895.

[68] Ibid., 13–17 June, 9–11 Aug. 1895.   [69] Ibid., 9 Nov. 1895.

[70] Ibid., 4, 7, 11, 16 Mar. 1896.

[71] 'Notes on Eritrea', 20 Feb. 1896 (Milner papers, dep 440/7).

house greatly, and they both took part in local life. In 1896–7 Wilson served as secretary of the Stanwell Cricket Club, though he does not seem to have been much of a regular player. In a manner which was to become increasingly characteristic in later years, he was impatient with inconclusive committee meetings. In March 1897 he noted a small parish meeting 'to discuss what is to be done for this [Queen Victoria's Diamond] Jubilee. Much talk and nothing done.'[72]

The Wilsons' social life during the mid-1890s reflected a gently rising status. Their circle of friends included both army and Irish connexions. They were frequently invited away for house-party weekends, especially during the shooting season. Among others, in 1895–6 they stayed with Lord and Lady Lucan, Lady Elphinstone, and Lady Guilford, known as 'Gac', who was a particularly close friend. They spent Christmas at her house, Waldershare Park, near Dover, in 1894, 1896, and 1897. Lady Guilford was widowed in 1885 and she appears to have depended on Wilson as a 'role model' for her son 'Nipper', who, then a 19-year-old, lodged with the Wilsons for eight months between June 1895 and April 1896, while he prepared for the Sandhurst entrance exam, an ironic enough fact considering Wilson's own failure to pass it.

At the beginning of 1896 Wilson began to hear gossip that the twelve-year marriage of Jack Cowans was in difficulties. Cowans was a notorious womaniser, by some accounts with a penchant for 'rough trade'. Even his hagiographers, writing in the early 1920s, could not ignore the fact that he was 'by no means indifferent to all the colour and beauty women can bring into existence'. Cowans, they wrote in an elliptical though revealing fashion, 'found in women a source of refreshment and renewed energy, and if he did not always turn to the most refined and cultivated he shared that weakness, if it be one, with men even greater than himself'.[73] Shortly before he died in 1921, Cowans was received into the Catholic church. Alluding to his womanising, Sir Nevil Macready remarked to Wilson that he could not 'help thinking that he [Cowans] preferred a religion in which the Virgin takes the most prominent place'.[74]

The talk was that Cowans was separating from his wife, applying for a posting in Egypt, and giving up his position as a brigade major at Aldershot. In January 1896 General Swaine asked Wilson 'to be his Brigade-Major, in the event of Cowans going'. But Cowans (as he was to do in similar circumstances in the future) sat tight, and Wilson stayed on in the War Office.[75] During the summer, however, he temporarily joined General Clery's staff for manoeuvres in Kent.[76] But life in general seems to have been pretty relaxed, and he spent a month's leave in Ireland late in the year. At Currygrane he enjoyed the usual field-sports rituals, and occasional trips up to Dublin. With his father he went to a performance of

---

[72] Wilson diary, 11 Mar. 1896, 13 Mar., 1 Apr. 1897.
[73] Chapman-Huston and Rutter, *Cowans*, i. 92, 227.
[74] Macready to Wilson, 20 Apr. 1921 (Wilson papers, HHW 2/2D/32).
[75] Wilson diary, 17, 21, 30 Jan., 9–10, 21, 23 Mar. 1896.
[76] Ibid., 24 Aug.–12 Sept. 1896.

Charles Villiers Stanford's opera *Shamus O'Brien* at the Gaiety Theatre: 'an indifferent performance & indifferent music.'[77]

In June 1897 Wilson heard that he was 'at last' to succeed Cowans as brigade major of the 2nd Brigade, North Camp, Aldershot, and he took up the position at the beginning of September.[78] Here Wilson had the chance to sharpen his staff-work skills. At manoeuvres in June 1898, 'Plumer woke me at 3.40 [a.m.] I sounded the Assembly at 3.45 & the whole Bde, 5 battalions, 71 officers, 2610 men' were mustered two miles from the camp within an hour. 'We were the best.'[79] But this was a poor substitute for active service. At the end of 1896 he confided to his diary a hope, 'God being willing', that he might be posted to Egypt, where Kitchener was reasserting British control over the Sudan. A year later, having seen Rawlinson and other friends get the chance of 'real' soldiering, he noted his 'only loss' for 1898 'being that I did not get out to Egypt. This I trust may some day be remedied.'[80] In 1899 his wish was to be granted, but it was to be in South Africa, not Egypt.

---

[77] Ibid., 25 Nov. 1896.
[78] Ibid., 12, 29 June, 1 Sept. 1897. In 1955 Sir James Edmonds (then 94 years old) wrote that Wilson had been fired from the Intelligence Division by Sir John Ardagh (who became DMI on 1 April 1897) 'for being below the standard of education desirable in a staff officer' (note enclosed with Edmonds to the Librarian of the Staff College, 13 May 1955, quoted in Neillands, *The Great War Generals*, 11).   [79] Wilson diary, 30 June 1897.
[80] Ibid., 31 Dec. 1897, 31 Dec. 1898.

3

South Africa

There was a history of tension between the British colonies along the coast of South Africa at the Cape and in Natal, and the inland Dutch republics of the Transvaal and the Orange Free State. This had greatly intensified following the discovery of gold and diamonds in the Transvaal and the dramatic growth of a rumbustious British-dominated 'uitlander' community concentrated on Johannesburg. Imperialists at the Cape, notably Cecil Rhodes and his trusty supporter, Dr Frederick Jameson, Prime Minister of Cape Colony, desired the extension of formal British control over all of southern Africa. Ostensibly coming to the aid of oppressed uitlanders, in December 1895 Jameson led an armed band into the Transvaal, aiming to bring down the Afrikaner government. The adventure was a fiasco, but it exacerbated the progressive deterioration in Anglo-Afrikaner relations which eventually led to a final breakdown in 1899, and what was to be the last British war of imperial expansion.

Through the later 1890s Wilson followed the developing crisis in South Africa with quite close attention. He thought the Jameson raid 'very curious' and 'most extraordinary'.[1] By February 1897 he believed it 'very likely we will fight Kruger [President of the Transvaal], or else lose much prestige'. Of course, if there was going to be a fight, then there would also be opportunities for active service, and from the spring of 1897 Wilson began canvassing for a place in any expedition that might go out. He told General Clery that, if he went to the Transvaal in command of a brigade, 'he must take me. He doesn't think there will be a fight,' noted Wilson, 'I do.' In April Clery thought Wilson was 'safe for a billet if we go'.[2] In the meantime Wilson helped his colleague Major H. P. Northcott,[3] who headed the British empire section in the Intelligence Division, draw up a scheme 'for knocking Kruger's head off', and he invited Lord Roberts to lunch at White's to meet Northcott and discuss South Africa.[4] In his memoirs, Leopold Amery recounted that Roberts's main strategy in the South African War, 'of striking across country from the western to the midland railway system, cutting the

---

[1] Wilson diary, 2, 3 Jan. 1896.   [2] Ibid., 20, 27 Feb., 9 Apr. 1897.
[3] Erroneously identified as H. P. Northcote by both Callwell, *Wilson*, i. 22, and Collier, *Brasshat*, 37, 42–3, 48. Northcott, serving as Lord Methuen's 'much-valued chief of staff', was killed at the costly battle of the Modder river, 28 Nov. 1899 (Pemberton, *Battles of the Boer War*, 70).
[4] Wilson diary, 26 Mar. and 23 Apr. 1897.

enemy's lines of communication', had been worked out in 1897 'by him with two keen young officers, Henry Wilson and Hugh Dawnay'.[5] The Field Marshal, who had been sidelined to Dublin in 1895 while his old rival, Lord Wolseley, was Commander-in-Chief in London, seems to have been happy enough to exploit these junior officers (Wilson was only a captain) for both ideas and 'hot' intelligence. By this stage, moreover, Wilson had become something of a Roberts family friend, also socialising with the Field Marshal's son Freddie.[6]

In the summer of 1899 tension rose again, reviving Wilson's hopes for war service. Opinions varied about how large a force should be committed in South Africa. Facing an estimated 50,000 Afrikaners in the two Boer republics were some 10,000 British troops. Sir Alfred Milner, High Commissioner for South Africa, proposed the immediate despatch from Britain of an '*overwhelming* force' of 'perhaps 10,000 men'. Early in June Wolseley argued that Sir Redvers Buller's 1st Army Corps together with a cavalry division (about 35,000 men) would be needed to 'overawe Kruger'.[7] Wilson's view was 'that we should send *at least* 40,000 men to South Africa'.[8] Even this was a wild underestimate. In the end, some 448,000 British imperial and colonial troops, as well as perhaps 45,000 Africans, were mobilised to fight 87,000 Afrikaners.[9] During the summer arrangements were made to send Buller's corps out, but the government hesitated to act lest it should inflame the situation. On 8 September it was decided to reinforce Natal by 10,000 troops, drawn from India and various colonial stations. They were put under the command of Sir George White, the Quartermaster-General at the War Office, who sailed on 16 September with Rawlinson on his staff. Within three weeks—coincidentally on his eighth wedding anniversary—Wilson had received mobilisation orders and appointment as brigade major of the 4th or 'Light' Brigade (as the 3rd Brigade was now known), under the command of Major-General Neville Lyttelton.[10] Within another three weeks war had been declared (on 11 October) and he had set sail for South Africa.

Wilson's departure for South Africa provides us with a rare, personal glimpse of his wife. For thirty years, the relationship with her was central to Henry Wilson. Yet Cecil Wilson remains a rather shadowy character, who exists today only through comments in her husband's diary and a very occasional mention in the reminiscences of family, friends, and acquaintances. She was comparatively old when she married in 1891—just a fortnight short of her thirtieth birthday—and she may well have felt specially grateful to Wilson for rescuing her from the prospect of a spinster's life in reduced circumstances, like that of her eldest sister, Frances.[11] The Wilsons had no children, which seems to have been a particular

---

[5] Amery, *My Political Life*, i. 126. Dawnay was a Rifle Brigade lieutenant in 1897, who later served with the 2nd Life Guards and was killed in action on 6 Nov. 1914. His wife, Susan de la Poer Beresford, was Irish.   [6] See e.g. Wilson diary, 27 May–5 June, 1897.

[7] Pakenham, *The Boer War*, 71. This is the single best treatment of the conflict.

[8] Wilson diary, 6 July 1899.

[9] The great majority of the Africans served in non-combatant duties (Pakenham, *Boer War*, 572–3).

[10] Wilson diary, 3 Oct. 1899.   [11] See Trench, *The Wrays of Donegal*, 374–7.

disappointment to Henry, who always expressed a great fondness for young people, who in their turn readily responded to his playful character.[12] Eric Dillon, Wilson's private secretary for a few months in 1919, thought that the lack of children 'was a very real grief to him'. It was, he wrote, 'almost pathetic to see him with a child. He would go to almost any lengths to amuse and entertain any little boys or girls with whom he came in contact. With adults', he added, 'his behaviour was quite unpredictable.'[13] For Cecil Wilson the absence of a family, or, indeed, any career outside the home—she appears to have been a fairly typical Victorian middle-class woman—made her more than ever dependent on Henry. She was, too, ambitious for him, and could be fiercely strong in his defence.

A more intimate, almost pathetic, side of Cecil Wilson is revealed in Henry's diary which he left behind when he went to South Africa in October 1899. For the rest of the year Cecil kept the diary herself, regularly expressing concern for her 'beloved Henry'. When the likelihood of Wilson being mobilised was first raised in July 1899 he noted, 'Cecil is a good deal upset I'm sorry to say',[14] but he made no further mention of her feelings over the succeeding few months. This, though, was in keeping with the journal as a whole, which is not a notably senti-mental or reflective text. But, movingly and remarkably, the tone of the diary changed when Cecil took over. In common with thousands of other army wives she had to endure the heartache of separation. No doubt the rhetoric of 'national duty' helped some to bear the pain, but in the end, as poignantly shown by Cecil's own diary entry, the suffering was personal and individual: 'Henry and I had our parting in the dining room at 10 O'c. After he had left me I went into hysterics for the first time in my life. Few women in the world have ever had such a hard parting for he is <u>everything</u> to me . . . God grant I may soon begin to count the days of his c[o]m[in]g home.'[15]

Wilson, by contrast, was both excited and exhilarated by the prospect of action. Enviously he had watched contemporaries, including Rawlinson, take part in the Nile expedition of 1897–8 and other campaigns. When he was awarded a medal for riding in Queen Victoria's Diamond Jubilee procession he was pleased enough, 'tho' medals other than war medals are not to my fancy'.[16] Within just over a year of landing in South Africa, however, he had experienced plenty of action, and, at the end of 1900, improbably claimed that he had 'seen more fighting than almost any other living man'.[17]

Wilson's ship arrived at Cape Town on 18 November 1899. It had originally been intended to land the entire expeditionary force there, prior to a general advance on the Boer capitals of Bloemfontein and Pretoria, but enemy successes at

---

[12] These points were emphasised to the author by Henry Wilson's nephew, Maj. Cyril Wilson, and niece, Lady Blackburne, and further confirmed by a 1979 taped reminiscence of Nessie Hackett, a distant cousin who recalled Wilson's playfulness on a family visit when she would have been 10 or 11 years old (I am most grateful to Jean Forbes and Sheila Lough for this information). Legacies to children were provided for in Wilson's will, drawn up in January 1897.

[13] Dillon, *Memories of Three Wars*, 120.   [14] Wilson diary, 6 July 1899.

[15] Ibid., 24 Oct. 1899.   [16] Ibid., 10 July 1897.   [17] Ibid., 31 Dec. 1900.

the start of the war forced a change of plan. On 13 October Mafeking, in the far north of the Cape Colony, was besieged, followed the next day by the diamond capital, Kimberley. Early in November Boer forces began to penetrate south into Cape Colony, raising the dreadful possibility of a rising among the Boer population there. To the east, Sir George White, whose orders had been to secure Natal pending the arrival of the full expeditionary force, had unwisely—and contrary to Buller's explicit orders—pressed north of the Tugela river with 12,000 men. By 2 November he was beseiged at Ladysmith.

After consulting with Milner, Buller decided to divide his army in two. Leaving Lord Methuen and the 1st Infantry Division to attempt the relief of Kimberley, he despatched nearly half the force, including Henry Wilson's brigade, to Natal. By late November Wilson was encamped on the Mooi river, about 80 miles inland from Durban and 50 miles short of Ladysmith. 'Fair chaos reigns here', he noted. General Geoffry Barton, temporarily in command, seemed incapable of sensible action: 'Barton thought he would, thought he would'nt, thought he would, thought he would'nt advance. Result 2 Fus[iliers] Battns moved out 2 miles.'[18] Enemy resourcefulness was sharply emphasised by the Boer snipers' unsporting habit of picking off officers, prompting a message from the British headquarters in late November 1899: 'There is no objection to officers carrying rifles or sticks or in fact doing anything that they think will make them less conspicuous. Officers should remove any badges that would make them distinguishable from the men.'[19]

During the first week in December Buller himself arrived and took effective command of the Natal Field Force, although Sir Francis Clery was nominally in charge. Preparations began to force a crossing of the Tugela at Colenso, 16 miles south of Ladysmith. Buller had about 18,000 men, including four infantry brigades (the Irish (5th) Brigade under Fitzroy Hart; the Fusilier (6th) Brigade under Geoffry Barton; the English (2nd) Brigade under Henry Hildyard; and Lyttelton's Light Brigade, with Henry Wilson as brigade major), and field artillery under Colonel Charles Long. The plan was that, following an artillery bombardment, Hildyard would make a frontal assault on the village of Colenso. There would be a diversionary attack by Hart on the left, whose objective was to cross the river at a ford upstream of the village, while Barton and Lyttelton's brigades were held in reserve. Facing the British, and dug into the bluffs along the north bank of the river, was a force of 5,000 Boers under General Louis Botha.

On 15 December—'a lovely cool morning which turned into a blazing day in the Tugela valley'[20]—the British attack began well enough. Hildyard's brigade struck camp at 2.30 a.m. and Wilson noted in his diary that the force was in position by five o'clock and artillery began firing at 5.35 a.m. Ten minutes later, Hart, a 'fiery Irishman' who 'believed in the traditional virtues of close order and

[18] Ibid., 25, 26 Nov. 1899.
[19] 24 Nov. 1899, A.A.G. Pietermaritzburg to G.O.C. Mooi River (Wilson papers, HHW 3/1/2a, no. 11). [20] Wilson diary, 15 Dec. 1899.

dash',[21] set off. Sometime after six o'clock Colonel Long, another 'man of action'—he had a reputation in India as a tremendous pig-sticker—brought up two squadrons (twelve guns) of 15-pounders to within a thousand yards of the river, well ahead of Hildyard's infantry. Like Hart, he was determined to take the fight to the enemy, and, as with Hart's manoeuvre, the result was costly disaster. The idiocy of Hart's close-order, parade-ground advance, which made his men wonderfully easy targets for the hidden Boer gunners and riflemen, was compounded by a confusion as to his actual objective, so that he led the brigade into a loop of the river surrounded on three sides by the enemy, where they came under punishing fire. Hart 'began to retire at 7.15', recorded Wilson. 'We advanced with RB [Rifle Brigade] & DLI [Durham Light Infantry] & covered retirement from 7.40 to 12 noon. Hildyard attacked Colenso about 9 to 10 o'clock & fell back at 11.30. At 12 o'clock all rifle fire was over. Heavy guns went on till 4 o'clock.'[22] Commenting on the battle some time later for Leopold Amery, who was preparing *The Times History of the War in South Africa*, Wilson noted how Hildyard's advance, in contrast to that of Hart, had been 'in beautifully open formation, which led to small loss'.[23] Tactically, someone, at least, was thinking about how to approach an entrenched and well-armed enemy.

The field guns, in the meantime, were pinned down in the open under heavy fire. Valiant attempts were made to recover them. When Buller called for volunteers to help, two staff officers went out: Captain Walter Congreve, a regimental colleague of Wilson's, and Lieutenant Freddie Roberts, Clery's ADC. Congreve afterwards told Wilson how Roberts had cantered off 'laughing, talking and slapping his leg with his stick as though we were on the Mall at Peshawar again'.[24] Two guns were saved, while ten were lost to the Boers. Both Congreve and Roberts were wounded, the latter fatally. Six Victoria Crosses (including Congreve and Roberts posthumously) were awarded for the attempted rescue. Soon after, Buller gave the order to retire. Wilson's brigade 'fell back & camped at 3 p.m. on same ground we had left at 4 a.m.'.[25] Wilson's reputation for cheerfulness in adversity was certainly enhanced during the day. As wounded Irishmen from Hart's brigade withdrew, 'all pretty well played out', 'one big man with a bullet or two in him came by, and was highly amused by Harry Wilson saying to him, "This beats Athlone of a Saturday night, doesn't it, Pat?"'[26] After the battle Wilson wrote to his wife: 'We never got near the river, and although I was under fire for 5 hours, and sometimes brisk fire, I can only swear to having seen 5 Boers. It's quite marvellous. I doubt our having killed 100. More likely 50. And they remain complete masters of that side of the stream.'[27]

[21] Pakenham, *Boer War*, 213.   [22] Wilson diary, 15 Dec. 1899.
[23] 'Supplementary narrative, 25 Nov. 1899–18 Feb. 1900' (Wilson papers, HHW 3/1/6).
[24] Congreve to Wilson, 18 Dec. 1899 (quoted in Pakenham, *Boer War*, 235).
[25] Wilson diary, 15 Dec. 1899.   [26] Lyttelton, *Eighty Years*, 209.
[27] Wilson to Cecil Wilson, n.d. (quoted in Callwell, *Wilson*, i. 29).

Colenso anticipated some of the battles of the western front a decade-and-a-half later. Trusting to a heavy artillery bombardment, Clery and Buller expected that the enemy would be sufficiently softened up to allow their forces to advance across the Tugela relatively unscathed. But they underestimated the extent to which technological developments, especially magazine rifles and smokeless powder, had greatly enhanced the power of the defence This was 'the new, invisible war of the rifle-plus-trench'.[28] Well armed and entrenched, the Boers were able to see off their British attackers with comparative impunity. Buller lost 1,139 killed, wounded, and missing; Botha lost six killed and twenty one wounded.[29] 'A bad day's work', thought Henry Wilson.[30] So it was, and one for which Buller got the blame. Colenso came at the end of 'Black Week', during which Sir William Gatacre, leading a small formation in north-east Cape Colony, lost nearly 700 men missing and captured in the battle of Stormberg (10 December), and Lord Methuen was repulsed at Magersfontein in front of Kimberley the following day. As at Colenso, a frontal assault on entrenched positions had come to grief with heavy casualties. At home, the government decided that a change of command was required, and on 18 December Field Marshal Lord Roberts replaced Buller as Commander-in-Chief in South Africa, with General Lord Kitchener as his Chief of Staff. Wilson was delighted. 'Wonderful', he wrote in his diary. 'This makes Sir Redvers C. in C. of Natal only.' But there was sympathy too. 'Poor little Bobs. Of the four men he would have taken first for his staff, two are dead, Freddie & Jack Sherston [killed at Talana on 20 October], two are in Ladysmith, Johnny [Ian] Hamilton and Rawly.'[31]

Following Colenso, Buller withdrew his forces a few miles back down the railway to regroup and await reinforcement by General Sir Charles Warren and the 5th Division before attempting another crossing of the Tugela. Although the plight of the Ladysmith garrison continued to deteriorate—and at Colenso they could hear the exchanges of artillery fire at the siege—Buller, who was intermittently afflicted by 'a kind of reckless caution',[32] was perhaps understandably anxious not to try anything too adventurous. Wilson, however, was impatient for action, and on Christmas Eve proposed a plan for the Light Brigade and all the cavalry to cross the Tugela at Potgieter's Drift, 15 miles upstream. But Buller rejected the scheme as too risky.[33]

Buller's indecisiveness and apparent irresolution frustrated Wilson. 'There is no go or spirit about R. B.,' he wrote on 3 January. 'It's most curious. Constant chopping & changing & no scheming to throw the Dutchmen off their guard…à Court [Repington] who is an alarmist & has a perfervid imagination thinks very badly of things, & it is certainly difficult for anyone to be hopeful.'[34] The same day Lyttelton wrote to his wife that Buller's 'lack of enterprise' since

---

[28] Pakenham, *Boer War*, 335.   [29] Pemberton, *Battles of the Boer War*, 144.
[30] Wilson diary, 15 Dec. 1899.   [31] Ibid., 22 Dec. 1899.   [32] Collier, *Brasshat*, 53.
[33] Wilson diary, 24–5 Dec. 1899.   [34] Ibid., 3 Jan. 1900.

Colenso was 'deplorable'.[35] Reflecting later on his service in Natal, Wilson thought it 'hard to believe that with an energetic commander in the field we should have lain from December 16th to January 10th before making a move of any sort'.[36]

Even after the arrival of the 5th Division—to which the Light Brigade was transferred—when Buller began moving his forces upstream, Wilson continued to grumble. 'Things are not right here,' he wrote on 13 January. 'Buller never tells Wynne [one of his senior staff officers] a thing. Lyttelton is in equal ignorance...He is responsible, but has no power & knows nothing. It is quite impossible to get full value out of staff & troops in this way.'[37] A steady flank movement brought the British forces up to Potgieter's Drift, where the Boers were established along the hills overlooking the river, the most prominent of which was Spion Kop. 'The Boers' pos[ition]. is immensely strong', noted Wilson.[38] The actual crossing of the river was something of an anticlimax. On 16 January Lyttelton with two brigades crossed the Tugela unopposed at Potegieter's Drift and established a bridgehead. The next day the bulk of Buller's force under General Warren began slowly to cross the river at Trikhardt's Drift five miles upstream, just to the west of the Kop.

On 23 January the Light Brigade learned that Warren was to 'make a big attack' on Spion Kop at daylight, '& we are to help'. But no coordinated plan had been worked out, nor, as Wilson complained afterwards, had they 'been kept accurately informed of Buller's and Warren's plans and wishes'.[39] In part this was because (as at Colenso) the actual chain of command was confused. Although Warren was nominally in charge, Buller interfered from time to time. But it also reflected the absence of a proper staff at either Warren's or Buller's headquarters. During the night of 23–4 January 1,700 men secured what they believed to be the crest of Spion Kop. Unfortunately, when the mist cleared in the morning they found that they were left open to Boer fire from three sides. During the day the position was reinforced by a further 2,000 soldiers. For eleven hours in the blazing sun the British suffered continuous punishment, for the most part showing steadfast courage which soon became the stuff of legend. But, at the end of the day, they withdrew from the hill, leaving 243 dead behind them (a further 500 had been wounded), not knowing that the Boers had also crept away.

Lyttelton, meanwhile, had done his best to help. At four o'clock in the morning he had moved two battalions across the river to the east of Spion Kop in order to provide a diversionary 'demonstration'. But Buller, who wanted to keep the Light Brigade ready to break through the Boer lines once the enemy had been driven from the hill, ordered them back. In mid-morning, however, there was 'an urgent

[35] Quoted in Pakenham, *Boer War*, 280.
[36] 'Supplementary narrative, 25 Nov. 1899–18 Feb. 1900' (Wilson papers, HHW 3/1/6).
[37] Wilson diary, 13 Jan. 1900. Lyttelton was also becoming increasingly critical of Buller (see Pakenham, *Boer War*, 280).   [38] Wilson diary, 14 Jan. 1900.
[39] 'Supplementary narrative, 25 Nov. 1899–18 Feb. 1900' (Wilson papers, HHW 3/1/6).

appeal for help from Warren'. In an account written some time after the battle Wilson asserted that he wanted to send two infantry battalions—the Scottish Rifles (the Cameronians) and the 60th King's Royal Rifle Corps (of which Wilson's younger brother Cecil was adjutant)—together with Colonel Edward Bethune's Mounted Infantry (Bethune's Buccaneers), to occupy the 'Sugar Loaf', or Twin Peaks, two miles to the east-north-east of Spion Kop, in order to relieve the Boer pressure.[40] Twenty-five years after the event, Lyttelton told Charles Callwell a slightly different story. Wilson's 'most conspicuous service . . . in the field', he said, had been 'the suggestion to me to send reinforcements to assist Thorneycroft in the very critical condition he was in on the right of Warren's line on Spion Kop'.[41] In his diary, apparently written up in the evening of the battle, Wilson was silent about who originally proposed what. He merely recorded that, following Warren's appeal for help, 'we sent' two squadrons of Bethune's unit and the Scotttish Rifles to help the troops on Spion Kop, and 'the 60th' to take the Sugar Loaf. When, however, it appeared that the southern end of Spion Kop had become 'most dreadfully crowded' (as was certainly the case), 'I begged N.G. [Lyttelton] to let me change the order to the S.R. & send them on left of 60th & in support. But he did not like this plan.'[42] So the Scottish battalion continued to the Kop, and the 60th pressed on to their objective, where they met sharp Boer opposition.

Whatever the precise circumstances of the day, Henry Wilson did well at Spion Kop. Indeed, the Light Brigade as a whole confirmed its status as the best brigade in Buller's army, and Lyttelton as the soundest brigadier. The crossing of the Tugela at Potgieter's Drift on 16 January and the diversionary fire of Lyttelton's artillery (for which Wilson claimed credit[43]) over the following three days so successfully diverted the Boers' attention that Warren got his troops over the river at Trikhardt's Drift virtually unimpeded. Wilson's clear thinking during the battle itself, moreover, helped to relieve a very critical situation. Yet afterwards Wilson was left to reflect on the 'complete and absolute chaos' of the engagement and the significant British casualties, 'all to no purpose'.[44]

Following the battle the bulk of the British forces regrouped on the southern bank of the Tugela. Encamped by Potgieter's Drift on 27 January, Wilson reflected glumly, 'We stand once more where we did about 10 days ago, with a licking thrown in'. Not, apparently, discouraged by the reverse at Spion Kop, Buller resolved to have another shot at breaking through to the besieged garrison. On 29 January he announced that 'we would be in Ladysmith in 7 days. What he is going on', wondered Wilson, 'heaven only knows'. The prediction was 'a perfect puzzle unless he knows for certain that the Free Staters are off home'. Buller's plan was to

[40] Ibid. This may be the account prepared by Wilson in January 1902: 'The Chief [Roberts] got me to write some notes about Spion Kop emphasising the fact that NG only recalled the 60th on the representation of Buller through Miles' (Wilson diary, 21 Jan. 1902).

[41] Callwell, *Wilson*, i. 35.   [42] Wilson diary, 24 Jan. 1900.   [43] Ibid., 17 Jan. 1900.

[44] Ibid., 24 Jan. 1900.

make his push about five miles downstream from Spion Kop where a hill called Vaal Kranz on the north side of the river barred the way to Ladysmith. After an artillery bombardment, and a diversionary feint to the north of the target, the Light Brigade were to attack the hill. Wilson was cautiously hopeful: 'this being the only connected, thought out plan we have tried, [it] may succeed.' Buller's optimism—one of his most endearing traits, if not always absolutely justified—infected the troops. 'I never heard the men so cheery tonight,' wrote Wilson on 4 February, the night before the engagement. 'They were singing in masses.'[45]

The Light Brigade paraded at seven o'clock the next morning but, because of some delays in the diversionary movement, did not begin their assault on the hill until after two o'clock in the afternoon. But they had captured it by 4.30 p.m. and dug themselves in during the evening. 'We had', recorded Wilson,

a very disagreeable night. At 5.30 a.m. the Boers opened a very sharp fire, which was practically kept up until 7 p.m. when darkness stopped it. At 4 p.m. they had a try at our extreme left flank but were driven back after about 10 minutes. Hildyard relieved us at 9 p.m. our men having been under fire for 33 hours. Our loss was 16 Officers & 253 killed & wounded. We were glad to get back & Buller gave us each a horn of champagne than which I never drank anything I liked so much.[46]

Despite this success, Buller decided that the breakthrough could not be achieved and ordered a withdrawal on the evening of 7 March. 'Poor Sir RB,' wrote Wilson, 'it must be bitter work for him, & they won't like it at home, but Buller is right.' Wilson was certain 'that if we pushed on here we would probably have to lay down our arms. It's quite impossible with 15,000 men to turn 8, 10 or 12,000 out of lines & lines of entrenchments. We should have at least 50,000.'[47] It was an ominous anticipation of the battles of the First World War.

It is clear that during February 1900 even Wilson's own good temper and optimism were beginning to be tested by the lack of success. Writing from Chieveley, down the railway line from Colenso, he told his wife: 'It's exactly two months tomorrow since we came here before, and in those two months we have lost heavily, fought heavily, marched heavily, and are no nearer Ladysmith. And through no fault of the troops.' There were two causes for their failure: 'the first is that we have a quarter of the proper number of troops, and the other is bad generalship.' Amery told a story that so frustrated was Wilson at the appalling muddle on the Tugela that he 'called together the other brigade-majors and suggested their arresting the general in local command as *non compos mentis*'.[48] Lyttelton, however, had 'done better than any other general', and Wilson was 'not a little proud of this, as in some ways I may have helped him'.[49] Certainly the two

---

[45] Wilson diary, 27, 29, 30 Jan., 3, 4 Feb. 1900.   [46] Ibid., 6 Feb. 1900.

[47] Ibid., 7 Feb. 1900

[48] Amery, *My Political Life*, i. 192. Though Amery appears to have taken the story seriously, it has the air of a typically mischievous Wilson joke.

[49] 12 Feb. 1900, quoted in Callwell, *Wilson*, i. 34.

men got on well together, and Wilson was upset when Lyttelton was promoted temporarily to command the 2nd Division in place of Clery, who had gone sick. Wilson was left behind in the Light Brigade, under the command of General William Norcott.[50]

Wilson's frustrations are reflected in the increasingly critical tone of his diary before and during the February 1900 operations when Buller finally broke through to Ladysmith. The day before Buller began to attack Boer positions to the east of Colenso, Wilson, who thought 'the whole idea rather silly', grumbled that 'this aimless & purposeless wandering about' was 'very disheartening for all ranks'.[51] He told Rawlinson after the relief of Ladysmith that 'Buller and most of his generals' had been at loggerheads during the campaign.[52] He was also concerned about the condition of the men's kit, as they had not had a change since landing at Durban the previous November and were 'very badly in want of boots & clothes'.[53]

The push began quite well, and between 14 and 18 February the Boers were effectively cleared from the south bank of the Tugela. 'A real good day's work & NG was much cheered,' wrote Wilson on 18 February. 'Dutch are on the run, & we did damage.' But the advantage was not pressed home. The following day 'was practically wasted. There is no doubt the Dutch were on the run and we should have followed hot foot. These delays are miserable & lead to great loss of life as the enemy can collect again and dig.' 'Buller', he wrote on 20 February, 'is far too slow & doesn't gain any of the advantage his men lay open to him.'[54]

Over the next few days Wilson's criticisms fell more heavily on Fitzroy Hart, the commander of the Irish Brigade. Attacking the Boers on the heights north of the river (at a point which became known both as 'Hart's Hill' and 'Inniskilling Hill'), as at Colenso he again sent his men forward in close order, urging them impetuously onward. 'Hart had his usual slaughter', reflected Wilson mordantly. Two Light Brigade battalions, the Durham Light Infantry and the Rifle Brigade, were ordered to support the attack. On 24 February the Durhams were left in an exposed position 'under sharp front & flank fire'. In the evening Hart did not put out any outposts, 'though repeatedly asked by Billy Norcott & myself', and there was a troublesome Boer attack at nine o'clock which continued for much of the night. Only quick action by Wilson, alerting and deploying groups of soldiers around the camp, seems to have saved the situation. But when he reported to Hart, who was down by the river, what he had done he found that he 'had never been up & did not know in the least what was going on. He is', continued Wilson, 'a perfect disgrace & it's a scandalous thing that he should have command of a Brigade. He is quite mad & incapable under fire.'[55]

[50] Wilson diary, 9 Feb. 1900.   [51] Ibid., 3 Feb. 1900.
[52] Rawlinson South African War Journal, 1 Mar. 1900 (Rawlinson papers, 5201/33/7).
[53] Wilson diary, 10, 13 Feb. 1900.   [54] Ibid., 18–20 Feb. 1900.
[55] Ibid., 24 Feb. 1900.

A few days later, writing to his wife, Neville Lyttelton described Hart as 'a dangerous lunatic',[56] an opinion undoubtedly influenced by Wilson who had gone directly to him on 25 February to complain especially about the 'very trying' position the Durham Light Infantry had been left in (which Wilson had actually visited), 'with a large number of dead, dying & wounded all round whom they could not help & some of our shells coming in from behind'. Wilson thought that Warren (commanding the 5th Division), 'of course agrees with Hart that DLI are in an excellent position, most useful & very comfortable. A pair of d——incompetant fools.' Wilson's representations, although made through irregular channels bypassing the formal chain of command, were effective: 'About 5 o'c. came positive orders from Buller to Warren to withdraw the DLI.'[57] Two days later on Shrove Tuesday Buller outmanoeuvred the Boers with a coordinated attack which captured the main enemy positions above the Tugela. Encouraged by the news that General Cronje and his army at Paardeberg had surrendered to Lord Roberts, the Light Brigade took 'Inniskilling Hill'. They went into action at five o'clock in the afternoon: 'At 8 p.m. the Boers ceased firing quite suddenly & the night was perfectly quiet.'[58] At last the way was clear to Ladysmith, and the first of Buller's troops arrived there the following evening.

During the afternoon of 1 March Wilson himself rode in with Lyttelton and Yarde-Buller. He was 'struck by how well most of the men looked', and Rawlinson, who thought his old friend was 'very fit', told him that 'they could have held out another month'.[59] For the next few weeks, on Roberts's instructions, Buller remained on the defensive, taking stock and gathering strength for a further advance. It was not before time. On 4 March Wilson noted that, 'owing to shocking bad HQ staff arrangement our baggage was not up till to-day when camp was pitched. The Bde has been 18 days without tents or coats.' Four days later he wrote: 'We want a rest of 10 days, & our boots & clothes are deplorable.'[60] During March, when Clery returned to duties, Lyttelton was given command of the 4th Division. Wilson hoped to move with him, but Buller said that he 'could not be spared'. On 29 March Wilson lamented that he was now the only one left of the old Light Brigade staff who had arrived in South Africa four months before.[61] The halt on the Sunday river east of Ladysmith soon began to grate, and provoked Wilson to reflect further on the deficiencies of the high command. 'What we want', he wrote on 11 April, 'is a lot of M[ounted] I[nfantry] but Buller in the last 5 mos. has only raised 200 which are always kept in rear. Our regular Cav. are quite useless. Dundonald [who commanded a mounted brigade] a perfect fool & useless. We show such lack of enterprise that I would not be surprised if we were turned out of this.'[62]

[56] 3 Mar. 1900, quoted in Pakenham, *Boer War*, 357.   [57] Wilson diary, 25 Feb. 1900.
[58] Ibid., 27 Feb. 1900.
[59] Ibid.; and South African War Journal, 1 Mar. 1900 (Rawlinson papers, 5201/33/7).
[60] Wilson diary, 4 and 8 Mar. 1900.
[61] Ibid., 19–21, 28, and 29 Mar. 1900; Callwell, *Wilson*, i. 35; Lyttelton, *Eighty Years*, 233.
[62] Wilson diary, 11 Apr. 1900.

On 11 May Captain Sir Thomas Montgomery-Cuninghame joined Wilson's mess as brigade signalling officer. In his memoirs he vividly recalled encountering the Irishman:

I saw him first sitting bare-legged on a rock in the Sunday's River tending 'Bob'—a black, shaggy-coated, flop-eared remount of fatuous appearance—who had just come a cropper on the stony track. In a way which I came later to know so well, Henry cocked his eye at me as I rode up. 'Blemished, you see,' he said. 'What a calamity!' and then, pulling down one of the pendulous ears of the depressed animal, he added: 'Bob, what an ugly-looking brute you are.'

About six foot four in height, and gaunt at that, the bulk of Henry's weight was below the saddle, in his extraordinarily long legs. A colonial meeting him on the Laing's Nek accused him of being exactly like two schoolfellows of his. 'Yes, sir. We used to call one "skin" and the other "bone"!' His whimsical gargoyle face was deeply seamed with wrinkles and one eye had never recovered from a spear-thrust in the Burma War. His helmet was of a pattern invented by himself and, watching him mounted on Bob, with his stirrups deep below the animal's belly and his immense feet skidding along about two inches off the ground, he reminded me of the pottery caricatures of Don Quixote which are sold in Cordova.[63]

Leopold Amery's 'first glimpse' of Henry Wilson, at about the same time, was strikingly similar: 'An immensely tall figure standing in front of a tent in Natal with legs wide apart and a curiously rugged face unlike any other cheerily summoning me in to have a drink.'[64]

On the same day as Cuninghame arrived, the brigade moved off as part of the Natal army's move towards the Transvaal border. ('Orders as usual disgracefully late. Buller should be sent home.'[65]) In the meantime came the welcome news that Mafeking had been relieved and that Lord Roberts had taken Johannesburg and Pretoria. The main Boer forces were being broken up, and to Wilson, writing at the end of June, it 'certainly looks like shaping for guerrilla war'. A week later General Hart (who had been transferred to the western theatre of operations) 'rode into our camp, so at last the Natal Army & Cape Army meet. How long it has taken,' mused Wilson, '& how much it has all cost in lives and money.'[66]

Although Wilson had correctly predicted that the conflict would develop along guerrilla lines, he never anticipated that this phase of the war would eventually last until the spring of 1902. Like many of his colleagues he assumed that, with Roberts ensconced in the Transvaal capital, only the last remnants of the Boer forces needed to be mopped up and then everyone could go home. As it was, he deplored Buller's heavyhanded and inflexible tactics in dealing with the remaining Boer commandos. He should, he thought, 'be using cavalry to chase Boers', rather than cavalry, infantry, and ox transport. 'This escorting a huge convoy of 200 bullock wagons round the country,' he wrote, '& being sniped at

[63] Montgomery-Cuninghame, *Dusty Measure*, 30.   [64] Amery, *My Political Life*, 192–3.
[65] Wilson diary, 11 May 1900.   [66] Ibid., 26 June, 4 July, 1900.

all day is the most infernally idiotic thing that was ever done. It will prolong the war for months.'[67]

Wilson's position was about to be transformed. In August 1900 he was summoned to Pretoria to see 'the Chief'. Here he clearly confirmed the favourable opinion Roberts already held of him. After a spell helping Rawlinson in the Adjutant-General's branch, Wilson was offered the options of reverting to a brigade majorship, or remaining Rawlinson's assistant. 'I have chosen the latter,' he confided to his diary, '& hope I am right, in that it may lead to my getting home sooner.'[68] Rawlinson was delighted: 'Henry Wilson will now be my assistant permanently,' he wrote in his diary. 'I hope so; it will be good business.'[69] Wilson, however, was also sorry to leave the Light Brigade, but his responsibilities were transferred into the capable hands of his brother 'Tono' (Cecil), who had been adjutant of the 60th Rifles. 'Even more argumentative,' recalled Cuninghame, 'he was really more adaptable than his distinguished brother and quite as witty.'[70]

Part of Wilson's keenness to get home evidently stemmed from his desire to be reunited with his wife Cecil. His South Africa diary is punctuated by regular notes of writing to 'Cessie' and sharp pleasure at receiving letters from her. Other entries confirm her importance. One Sunday he went to '5.30 p.m. evening service which I enjoy very much as I sit all alone at the very back & think of Cessie'. Both their wedding anniversary and Cecil's birthday fell while he was in Pretoria on Roberts's staff. On the former: 'The moment I woke & all day long I thought of Cessie . . . Nine years married, & we are more to each other now than we were then.' A fortnight later: 'Cessie's birthday. God bless her. Dreadful to be away from her on such a day.'[71]

Wilson, nevertheless, had a great time in Pretoria. Happy to be at the centre of affairs, he shared a house with Rawlinson, General Sir William Nicholson (Roberts's military secretary and the Director of Transportation), and 'Eddie' Stanley (later Lord Derby), Roberts's private secretary. It was a jolly ménage, and the younger men—Wilson, Rawlinson, and Stanley were all in their mid-thirties—socialised with Roberts's two unmarried daughters, Aileen, who was not quite 30, and the 24-year-old Edwina. Roberts had a penchant for gathering round him a circle of bright young men, and Nora, Lady Roberts ('Ladyship' as she was known), took a close maternal interest in her husband's protégés. She was, recalled Rawlinson to Wilson on her death twenty years later, 'a really remarkable women and a very great friend to us both'.[72] After the loss at Colenso of their only son (who was 27 when he died) the presence of lively young officers must have been bittersweet indeed.

---

[67] Wilson diary, 15 and 19 July, 1900. [68] Ibid., 29 July–2 Aug. and 13–22 Aug. 1900.
[69] South African War Journal, 15 and 23 Aug. 1900 (Rawlinson papers, 5201/33/7).
[70] Montgomery-Cuninghame, *Dusty Measure*, 33.
[71] Wilson diary, 2 Sep., 3 and 16 Oct. 1900.
[72] Rawlinson to Wilson, 22 Dec. 1920 (Wilson papers, HHW 2/13C/8).

In a penetrating study of British defence policy during the years running up to the First World War, Nicholas d'Ombrain identified a 'Roberts "kindergarten"', a 'coterie of talent' gathered in South Africa, 'which was to dominate British military life for the next twenty years'. This group, which included John French, Douglas Haig, Henry Rawlinson, Henry Wilson, and William Robertson, 'were launched in careers as leaders of the "new army", on the strength of Roberts's support, and the acceptability of the "little chief's" advanced ideas—if not of his person—to the very few whose opinion mattered when it came to Army reform'. D'Ombrain went on to argue that these younger officers 'brought with them their own coteries of personal followers, of which [the] most elaborate and successful was probably Henry Wilson's Staff College and later General Staff group'.[73] While d'Ombrain's use of the term 'kindergarten'—explicitly drawing a parallel with Lord Milner's circle of able young imperialists—implies rather more coherence to the group of officers than was actually the case, both Lord Roberts's patronage and the collective experience of service in South Africa, which under-pinned a significant network of friends and acquaintances, were undoubtedly very important influences in Wilson's later career.

On 24 September Wilson learned that he was to succeed Beauchamp Duff as Roberts's assistant military secretary. 'I did not at first realize what this meant,' he wrote, 'which is that I go home <u>with</u> the Chief & perhaps have 2 months work at home with him. God be thanked for this wonderful thing.'[74] In fact, Wilson was now in considerable demand. Lyttelton said he would like him to stay in South Africa on his staff, while Kelly-Kenny, who was hoping to get the Southern Command back home, also wanted him.[75] In the meantime Wilson was assisting 'General Johnnie' (Ian Hamilton) in drawing up Roberts's list of honours and rewards for the South African campaign.

Lord Roberts, his family, and staff set off on the journey home at the beginning of December 1900. Their ship departed from Durban and on the way down to the coast the party stopped at Colenso to see where Freddie Roberts had been killed, and also at Chieveley 'for Chief and Edwina to see Freddie's grave'. On 5 December the SS *Canada* set sail. 'It is', wrote Wilson, 'truly delightful to feel at last I am on my way to Cessie.'[76] The ship called at East London and Cape Town, where Roberts landed to bid farewell to the High Commissioner, Sir Alfred Milner. A photograph was taken at Government House of 'Lord Roberts and Sir Alfred Milner with some staff officers', which neatly illustrates some of the social and professional connexions forged and reinforced by service in South Africa. Wilson is there, as is Rawlinson, the two flanking the cheery Eddie Stanley, who had retained his seat as a Conservative MP in the 1900 general election and subse-quently been appointed Financial Secretary to the War Office. Stanley and Milner, among others, were to give Wilson an entrée into Tory political circles.

[73] d'Ombrain, *War Machinery and High Policy* 143.   [74] Wilson diary, 24 Sep. 1900.
[75] Ibid., 19 Oct., 6 and 21 Nov. 900.   [76] Ibid., 1, 4, and 6 Dec. 1900.

Three of Roberts's four ADCs in the group remained significant for Wilson, Captain The Earl of Kerry (a Conservative MP, 1908–18, who succeeded his father as Marquess of Lansdowne in 1927), represented an Irish network which took in the Wilson family;[77] Walter Cowan, a naval officer who ended up as an admiral, remained close,[78] as did Hereward Wake, who asked Wilson to stand godparent to his son in 1916 and served under him in the Supreme War Council at Versailles in 1918. Included, too, was 'Archie' Murray, who was briefly CIGS in 1915.

On New Year's Eve during the voyage home, Wilson noted that he had 'lost many friends in action & thro' sickness, & have made many new acquaintances & friends'. As was his habit, he summarised his end-of-year financial position. After paying all outstanding bills he reckoned that on 1 February 1900 he would satisfactorily be in credit 'about £150'. But his chief thoughts were for his wife. 'Through God's Grace,' he wrote, 'I have kept well, & so has my poor Cessie, & now with His permission we are soon to be together again.... Please God the coming year will be happy for Cessie.'[79]

---

[77] Kerry's father was a leading member of the Irish Unionist Alliance along with Henry Wilson's brother. Cecil Wilson's sister Leonora married Lord Lansdowne's land agent.

[78] Dawson, *Sound of the Guns*, 139, 158.

[79] Wilson diary, 31 Dec. 1900.

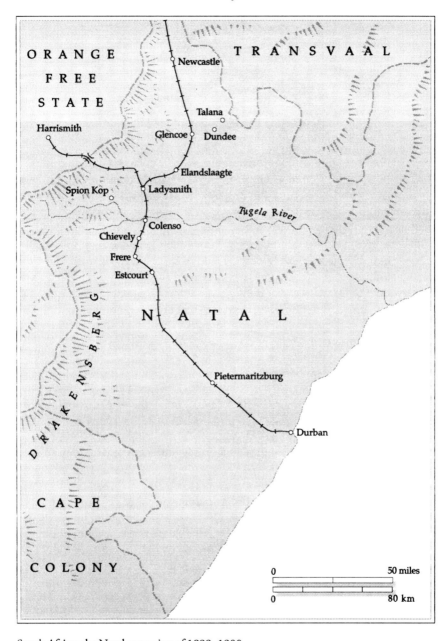

South Africa: the Natal campaign of 1899–1900.

4

Work in the War Office

It was quite a family reunion when Wilson arrived back in London. Not only was his beloved Cessie waiting for him, but also his parents, sister Eileen, and elder brother Jemmy and his wife Alice. Henry and Cessie were reunited at 2.30 p.m. on 3 January 1901, at the flat where she was staying in Lower Grosvenor Place, near Buckingham Palace. Scarcely a hint of emotion intruded in Wilson's diary entry: 'I found her looking a little pale, but well, & we are very happy.' Then the whole family went to the Grand Hotel for tea.[1] Wilson had a fortnight's leave, which he spent in London and at Frimley Lodge near Camberley, which Cecil had leased in his absence. Here Wilson returned to his precious gardening. On Sunday 10 February: 'I got a good bit of digging done and we got in two rows spinach, two rows broad beans, two rows lightning peas in bed next the green house . . . I am delighted with this little place.'[2]

Up in town, from the evidence of the diary, his—and Cessie's—chief cultural pleasure was theatregoing. Over a period of seven days, just a week after his return, he saw *Henry V* at Drury Lane ('a fine play'), *The Second in Command* (by the Scottish writer Robert Marshall) at the Haymarket, the Broadway musical *San Toy* at the Duchy (both described as 'a pretty little play'), and *Patience*, the Gilbert and Sullivan operetta, for which the whole family took a box at the Savoy Theatre ('very pleasant').[3]

As for work, Wilson was clearly a rising star and returned from South Africa with a greatly enhanced reputation. Enjoying the patronage of Lord Roberts, he was stimulatingly ensconced in the War Office, right at the centre of things. He spent his first nine months working as Ian Hamilton's assistant on honours and rewards for service in South Africa, work which included preparing individual citations where soldiers were 'mentioned in despatches' and drawing up lengthy lists of medal-winners.[4] It was a potential poisoned chalice. In a profession (and, indeed, society) so minutely hierarchical, army careers could be made or broken by the gaining—or not—of medals and distinctions.[5]

---

[1] Wilson diary, 3 Jan. 1901.   [2] Ibid., 10 Feb. 1901.
[3] Ibid., 11, 15, 16, and 18 Jan. 1901.
[4] The 'mention' despatch was published in the *London Gazette*, no. 27305, 16 Apr. 1901, 2597-613, and the lists of honours in nos. 27306 and 27353, 19 Apr. and 10 Sept. 1901, 2695-709 and 5927-969. Together there were over a thousand column inches of names.
[5] See the entertaining discussion of honours in Cannadine, *Ornamentalism*, 85–100.

Sir William Nicholson—'Nick'—Roberts's military secretary, who had returned to England to be Director General of Mobilisation and Intelligence, was 'very angry' about not getting a KCMG, and Kelly-Kenny, the Adjutant-General, complained to Wilson about not getting a KCB.[6] Kelly-Kenny had to wait until 1902 before getting a knighthood for 'services in the war'. Wilson himself got both a 'mention in despatches' and a gong. Lord Roberts's despatch of 2 April 1901 described Wilson as 'an officer of considerable ability' who had worked on the headquarters staff 'with energy and success'.[7] His medal was announced on 19 April. Two days earlier he had noted in his diary: 'About five o'clock I was over with the Chief when he said to me "What are your initials" then after I had told him he wrote something down & showing it to me said "I hope you won't mind that," & this was giving me a D.S.O. I really was breathless.'[8] Aylmer Haldane, whose grumpy memoirs are a rich source of malicious stories, told it differently in 1948. 'Sir William Nicholson', he wrote, 'to my surprise told me that Wilson had represented to Lord Roberts that as I was in possession of the D.S.O., he—not for any particular action—would like to have that decoration', and so he received it.[9] It is perhaps no wonder that Wilson, when reviewing the year 1901, reflected on personal relationships. Considering 'the part I had to play in bringing out Lord Bobs' large Gazettes of Mentions & Honours & Rewards', he noted that he had 'lost some of my old friends, but I hope not many'.[10]

Beyond the matter of honours, Wilson and his colleagues were consumed with the question of army reform. The decidedly patchy performance of both army and War Office during the South African crisis unsettled both politicians and people, who, basking in the recent celebration of Queen Victoria's 1897 diamond jubilee, generally took the imperturbable superiority of the British imperial system for granted. The reality of the South African War came as a nasty shock.[11] All aspects of the campaign went wrong, but there were particular weaknesses in supplies and logistics, there had been no prepared scheme for the sending of a sizeable expeditionary force overseas, and there were grave deficiencies in everyday staff work. The army had begun with no strategic appreciation or plan of campaign, it being thought that such matters were best left to the commander on the spot. Operations were severely handicapped by inadequate numbers of staff officers and, initially at any rate, the British were pitifully badly informed about their opponents and even the terrain over which they would have to march and fight.

In October 1900 a new Secretary for War, St John Brodrick, was appointed to oversee army reform. What he found on arrival at the War Office confirmed the need for change. 'I never in my life could have realized what a slough of despond I was tumbling into,' he wrote to Lord Curzon. 'The army is hopelessly disorganized

---

[6] Wilson diary, 22 Apr., 10 and 13 May 1901.
[7] *London Gazette*, no. 27305, 16 Apr. 1901, 2602.   [8] Wilson diary, 17 Apr. 1901.
[9] Haldane, *A Soldier's Saga*, 197.   [10] Wilson diary, 31 Dec. 1901.
[11] The general impact of the South African War on imperial defence is summarised in Jeffery, 'Kruger's Farmers'.

and used up; everyone is stale.'[12] Brodrick chose first to look at the army itself, postponing consideration of the War Office until Roberts had settled in as Commander-in-Chief. Early in March 1901 he presented a threefold programme to parliament. Arrangements had to be made so that a properly organised force of about 120,000 men could be sent abroad 'at any moment'. There had to be adequate provision for home defence; and deficiencies in various parts of the army, including artillery, mounted troops, transport, the Army Medical Service, and army training, had to be addressed.[13]

The most contentious of Brodrick's proposals concerned the 'expeditionary force', and the balance between it and the needs of home defence. Brodrick argued that not only might Britain need to defend its own possessions, but also 'if ever we should become unhappily entangled in a European war', it might need to send troops to the Continent. He proposed reorganising the army in the United Kingdom into six army corps of 40,000 men each, three composed wholly of regular troops, earmarked for foreign service, and three, including some part-time Militia and Volunteer units, for home defence. The number of regulars would be increased by 11,500. While he felt that this increase could be secured by more vigorous recruiting and increasing army pay, Brodrick raised the possibility that compulsory military service might have to be considered. The question of national service was to become a hot political issue in the years before the First World War. Traditional fears of a 'standing army', dependence on the navy for protection, and worries about the 'militarisation' (or even 'Prussianisation') of British society combined to underpin a powerful resistance to compulsion. Sir Henry Campbell-Bannerman, leader of the Liberal opposition, told Brodrick categorically that 'conscription in any form will not be endured by our people', and was concerned by 'cloudy talk about entanglements and commitments'.[14]

Wilson in the meantime had been asked by Sir William Rattigan (grandfather of the playwright Terence Rattigan) if he would write twelve letters on army reform for publication in the *Civil and Military Gazette* (the Lahore paper Rudyard Kipling once worked for).[15] Wilson had evidently impressed Rattigan, a Conservative MP, as an able and articulate commentator and he began writing the articles at the beginning of February. They were published between March and May 1901 and provide us both with a handy summary of the main issues facing the army reformers as well as the opinions Wilson was prepared to express in print (bearing in mind that they were published anonymously, 'by a Staff Officer').[16]

In his articles, which are rather well written, for the most part in an easy and accessible style, Wilson began by asserting the uniqueness of Britain's military

---

[12] 9 Nov. 1900, quoted in Satre, 'St. John Brodrick', 119. Curzon, an old friend, was Viceroy of India.   [13] 8 Mar. 1901, *Hansard*, Parl. Deb. H. C. 4s, vol. 110, cols. 1057–91.
[14] 14 Mar. 1901, ibid., cols. 1609–10.   [15] Wilson diary, 31 Jan. 1901.
[16] There are some slight inconsistencies in detail concerning the dating of the letters and equivalent notes in Wilson's diary, but it is clear that the twelve letters were written by him.

situation. It was difficult, he wrote, 'and in many cases quite impossible', to compare the British army and military system with Continental equivalents. Above all, the existence of a great maritime empire set Britain apart from her main rivals. Yet, although the maintenance of sea supremacy 'must always remain the foundation on which all schemes, naval and military, are built', the army was now of more importance than hitherto due to the existence of land frontiers with other great powers. It was, therefore, 'no longer safe for England (if, indeed, it ever was) to rely on her Navy alone'.[17] This was a challenge to the prevailing British defence orthodoxy, the 'blue water school', which assumed that the security of the state depended primarily on the maintenance of overwhelming British naval power.[18] The experience of the war in South Africa, however, had not only exposed deficiencies in the army, but was also a demonstration of how important the army might be for imperial defence, bearing in mind the 'immense increase in our Empire of late years'.[19]

Wilson's discussion of British military requirements began with a global *tour d'horizon*, starting, as it were, from defence 'first principles', and an assessment of the primary duties of the British army. This technique of moving from the general to the particular is an obvious enough teaching device, especially when dealing with non-specialists, and it was one which was to stand Wilson in good stead in the future. Here we see part of what made him attractive to politicians: a soldier, certainly with strong views of his own, but one able to set a military case in an intelligible wider political and strategic context.

There were, argued Wilson, three main duties which 'our soldiers' had to fulfil. The first was to guard the 'mother country' against invasion. Indeed this was an absolute imperative for both army and navy. Second was the defence of those important imperial possessions which were ostensibly threatened by other great powers. Third was colonial defence generally, especially that of the coaling stations and ports so essential for securing British naval mastery. The two main imperial possessions which needed to be protected were India and Canada, the former adjacent to and the latter contiguous with a major international rival. From about the mid-nineteenth century onwards, India was regarded by many as the central problem of British imperial defence. The threat of Russian troops marching inexorably on Britain's most valuable single possession was the greatest nightmare for Britain's imperial strategists. The threat to Canada was perhaps less apparent, but Wilson regarded the United States as a major imperial rival, especially following the American acquisition of former Spanish colonies during the Spanish–American War of 1898. While he thought that 'if there is one people with whom we ought to keep, and have every hope of keeping, on terms of friendship, it is the people of the United States', it would, nevertheless, 'be neither

---

[17] *Civil & Military Gazette* (henceforth *C&MG*), 1 and 10 Mar. 1901.
[18] The best introduction to British defence policy in the period is Michael Howard, *The Continental Commitment*. [19] *C&MG*, 10 Mar. 1901.

foolishness on our part, nor in the slightest degree insulting to our American cousins if we consider the best means of defending the Canadian frontier'.[20]

The only possible conflict that Wilson was prepared to contemplate in 1901 was an imperial one. Ironically (and unlike Brodrick), the one thing he categorically dismissed was the war that actually happened. 'The possibility', he wrote, 'of a European war may be ignored.' And by 'European war' he meant the invasion of a country in Europe by 'our' land forces.[21] He believed the chief danger to Britain was the loss of imperial possessions, and he asserted that it was 'easy to imagine England sinking to a second rate Power without a hostile foot being placed in the country itself'. With the loss of territories—he gave India, Canada, and Egypt as examples—and with a generalised notion of the actual foundation of British imperial power, he asserted that 'England's prestige would suffer accordingly, and with prestige would go her command of the money market; then her Fleet and then her Colonies, and the fate of Spain would be that of England'.[22]

It is interesting to compare Wilson's immediate reaction to the Brodrick proposals, as noted in his diary, with the more considered commentary in his newspaper articles. Among other things this illustrates the typically unrestrained way in which he used the diary. On Sunday 10 March he wrote that Brodrick's proposals 'appear to me absolutely futile. He ignores the question of increase in the Regulars... and puts his faith in Volunteers, Militia and Yeomanry, a fatal mistake.' The next day, at work, 'much discussion about Brodrick's proposal which is universally condemned amongst all of us at the office'.[23] In print, by contrast, Wilson welcomed both Brodrick's general commitment to reform and his particular argument for a stronger army. But Brodrick's estimate of the additional numbers required was far too low. The 120,000 earmarked for overseas service was 'quite insufficient for our needs'. The minimum needed, thought Wilson, was 200,000, 'and 250,000 better yet'. And, although Wilson thought that an increase in army pay would be sufficient to bring in the extra men, he also contemplated the possibility of conscription: 'if the country cannot pay in purse, then it must pay in person.'[24]

Wilson was worried about Brodrick's evident reliance on volunteer, part-time units to back up the regular army. These formations were all very well, but they were frequently ill-trained and could not be depended upon for anything more than short-term home defence. This was one of the 'lessons of the South African war'. 'To those who were in South Africa', he wrote, 'and saw heavy fighting the wisdom of employing Militia, Yeomanry and Volunteers in work absolutely unsuited to them was very questionable.'[25] His opinion was perhaps underpinned by the experience of the 13th battalion Imperial Yeomanry at Lindley in the Orange Free State at the end of May 1900. It included a company of Irish MFHs

---

[20] *C&MG*, 17 Mar. 1901.   [21] Ibid., 20 Apr. 1901.   [22] Ibid., 7 Apr. 1901.
[23] Wilson diary, 10, 11 Mar. 1901.   [24] *C&MG*, 19 May 1901.
[25] Ibid., 27 Apr., 4 and 19 May 1901.

(masters of foxhounds)—the 'Irish Hunt Contingent'—one of whom was the fifth Earl of Longford, and other Irish unionists of Wilson's acquaintance. However full of enthusiasm these men may have been, they were inadequately trained and badly led. Cut off from the main British army and overpowered by a superior Boer force in a sharp fight, some 80 volunteers were killed or wounded and 500 taken prisoner.[26]

Along with army reform, it was widely accepted that the organisation of the War Office itself needed a good shaking up. In the late nineteenth century hopes for the establishment of a modern and effective general staff to run the army had foundered on the rock of the conservative and autocratic Duke of Cambridge, who had been Commander-in-Chief since 1856. When he finally retired in 1895 a system was established which retained the post of Commander-in-Chief (initially Lord Wolseley, and Lord Roberts from 1901) while giving greater responsibilities—and direct access to the Secretary of State—to four other individuals: the Adjutant-General, responsible for discipline, military education, and training; the Quartermaster-General for supplies, such as food, uniforms, and housing; the Director-General of Ordnance for munitions; and the Financial Secretary, who dealt with money. This was neither fish nor fowl. For the reformers, although the resulting War Office board looked like an embryonic general staff, it had no collective responsibility, and therefore no power. For the traditionalists, the system represented a licence for the civilian minister to interfere in matters which were thought to be the preserve of professional soldiers. This was the crux of a question which was intermittently to trouble British civil–military relations for the next twenty years: in an increasingly democratic political environment, where did ultimate authority in the armed services lie?

Wilson's frustration with the inefficiencies of the War Office were intensified in the late summer of 1901 when serious work began on the detailed arrangements for the army corps scheme.[27] Even the revered Lord Roberts—who was over 70 and clearly feeling the pressure of work—came in for criticism. 'Every time I talk over a big question with the little man,' wrote Wilson on 15 August, 'I am horrified at his apparent incapacity to grasp fundamental facts.' Four days later: 'the Chief writes a lot of trivialities about things but never ever approaches big subjects. It is very disheartening, and in the end this incapacity will mean that Brodrick and the civilians will get all the power into their own hands.'[28]

The question of Wilson's future also came up. Brodrick laid down that any officer who had spent five years continuously on the staff would have go back to regimental service, a reasonable enough regulation to provide a turnover of officers, but an unwelcome development for Wilson who had been a staff officer

---

[26] Pakenham, *Boer War*, 436; Jeffery, 'The Irish Soldier in the Boer War', 147.

[27] Brodrick also had a temporary breakdown after his wife died in August 1901 (see Midleton, *Records and Reactions*, 135; and Satre, 'St. John Brodrick', 131).

[28] Wilson diary, 15, 19 Aug. 1901.

since 1894. Perhaps even beyond the clear pleasure he got from working in—or close to—the corridors of power, was the dismaying possibility that this might mean an overseas posting once again taking him away from his family. His 69-year-old father was seriously ill in the summer of 1901, with (among other things) what appears to have been dementia, though he was much better when Wilson got home to Currygrane ('the old place looking very green & very pretty') for a brief holiday in September.[29] When he learned that his brother Tono was being ordered back to South Africa, he thought it 'will be a great blow at home and I am much upset'.[30] The family outings in London, the holidays in Ireland, and the other domestic pleasures which Wilson so evidently enjoyed—the gardening and those wild nights when he and Cessie would share a bottle of champagne—reinforced his desire for a home posting.

We get another sight of the sentimental Wilson when his pet dog Paddles, which he was accustomed to bring to the office, 'fell down the lift shaft' and 'damaged himself terribly'. The vet was very pessimistic. 'It's a great blow to Cessie and me. We have had Paddles for 9 years.' The dog, happily, survived for another four years.[31] Childless themselves, the Wilsons lavished much affection on their household pets. But they had also provided a home for young Lord Guilford ('Nipper') in 1895–6, and after Cecil's elder sister died in December 1902, they took on her 17-year-old daughter Leonora—'Little Trench'—who was effectively to live with them for the next ten years.[32]

Wilson was also making his mark in the wider world. There were lunches with Arthur Balfour, who would become Prime Minister in July 1902, and the rising parliamentary star Winston Churchill, a South African acquaintance who had first encountered Wilson in February 1900 as 'a haggard but jocular Major emerging from a bloody night's work' at Inniskilling Hill,[33] and with whom Wilson 'sparred about Army Reform'. There was also dinner with Leopold Amery, where he met Leo Maxse, editor of the right-wing weekly, the *National Review*.[34] Both Wilson and Cecil continued to enjoy a steady round of entertainments and country house-parties. Christmas 1901, again at Waldershare Park with Lady Guilford, epitomises an Edwardian household at play. On New Year's Eve, a 'servants ball which was a great success & kept up to 4 a.m. We had a fine supper in the servants hall & North [Lord Guilford] made a couple of speeches & we sang the old year out & New Year in. Gac, Vidie, Muriel & North, the Jack Howards and ourselves & 98 servants.'[35]

At the end of 1901 Wilson was publicly involved in an embarrassing scandal which ruined the army career of his regimental colleague Charles à Court

[29] Wilson diary, 21, 23 July, 10 Sept. 1901.   [30] Ibid., 12 Nov, 1901.
[31] Ibid., 10 Dec. 1901, 5 Apr. 1905. Ten years later Wilson still had a note in his diary: 'Paddles died, 2 Wyndham Pl. 1905.'
[32] 'Little' Leonora was the daughter of John Townsend and Leonora (née Wray) Trench.
[33] Churchill, *The Great War*, iii. 1104.   [34] Wilson diary, 29 Apr., 9 May, 13 Nov. 1901.
[35] Ibid., 31 Dec. 1901.

Repington, who had given Wilson a hand up into the War Office Intelligence Division in 1894. Some years later Repington admitted that he was 'personally an enemy of this intriguing imposter Wilson', a 'low class schemer whose sole aptitude is for worshipping rising suns—an aptitude expressed by those who know him in more vulgar language'.[36] The two men, in fact, had been very close, professionally and socially. Indeed this closeness probably contributed to the bitterness and vehemence of Repington's subsequent feelings.

In August 1897 Repington was posted to Egypt to serve in General Francis Grenfell's army of occupation. He later went with Kitchener on the Omdurman campaign into the Sudan. By the end of the year Repington, himself married for fifteen years, had begun an affair with Mary Garstin, wife of Sir William Garstin, the British head of the Egyptian Ministry of Public Works.[37] Born Mary Isabella North, she was a cousin of Lady Guilford ('Gac'). At Gac's house, Waldershare Park, sometime probably in the late 1880s, Wilson had struck up a lively friendship with Mary's father (who died in 1893), his ready wit and cheerful company evidently paying social dividends. Between the two men, wrote Mary, there 'existed a queer attraction based on a mutual admiration for each other's alert mental ability'. Wilson 'addressed my father always as "Master", and Father replied to him as "My Disciple." They would argue by the hour—each delighting in the quick thrust and parry of the other's wit, which in Henry Wilson's case was apt to become decidedly Rabelaisian.'[38] Wilson, furthermore, as a brother Rifle Brigade officer, was an obvious choice to call in to try and help avoid anything so unpleasant as divorce. Apart from the social stigma, both parties had children, the Garstins two daughters and the Repingtons a son and a daughter.

The affair became public during the summer of 1898, when Mary and Repington, both temporarily back in London, spent a fortnight together in a suite at the famous Hotel Cecil off the Strand (scarcely, one would think, the best way to keep an adulterous relationship secret). Repington's wife Melloney threatened to inform the army authorities, which caused her husband briefly to break off the affair, and Garstin's sister also reported the matter to her brother. Mary confessed all and (despite being a Catholic) asked for a divorce.[39] Garstin refused, ostensibly for the children's sake. Over Christmas 1898, which the Wilsons spent at Waldershare Park, Lady Guilford got Henry involved. On Boxing Day he wrote to Repington specifically at her request. Perhaps she had asked him what would be

---

[36] Repington to Esher, 19 Aug. 1906 (Esher papers, 'Army 1906', vol. IV, quoted in Ryan, *Lieut.-Col. Charles à Court Repington*, 133).

[37] The details of the Garstin–Repington relationship are drawn from Ryan, *Lieut.-Col. Charles à Court Repington*; Lady Garstin's compelling and unusually frank memoir, Mary Repington, *Thanks for the Memory*; and the introduction to Morris, *The Letters of Lieut.-Col. Charles à Court Repington*.

[38] Repington, *Thanks for the Memory*, 154. The only corroborative evidence for Wilson's 'Rabelaisian' wit is in a note of a lecture he gave when he was GOC IV Corps on the Western Front: 'extraordinarily funny with many dirty stories!', Diary of Capt. L. Beaumont Tansley, 17 Apr. 1916 (Tansley papers). [39] *Daily Telegraph*, 13 Dec. 1901.

the impact on Repington's career, as on 28 December he 'called into W. O. and saw Cooper re Charlie à Court'.[40]

In November 1898 Repington had been appointed military attaché to the Low Countries, based jointly at Brussels and The Hague, a short train-and-ferry ride from London. With Mary Garstin also back in England, the affair resumed with renewed intensity. Repington set up a love-nest in Ravenscourt Park, west London. This was less central, to be sure, than the Hotel Cecil, but the couple were once more rumbled, just as Repington was about to depart for South Africa with a good job on Sir Redvers Buller's staff. Once again the families (with Henry Wilson) combined to force Repington to choose between his mistress and his army career. Repington immediately chose the army. 'The one solid unchanging devotion of his life', wrote Mary much later (and after witnessing Repington's serial infidelities), 'was really for England and England's Army. For the welfare of England he would make any conceivable sacrifice.... Otherwise', she added revealingly (and perhaps dismayingly for her), 'his standards were not very exacting.'[41]

Garstin evidently consulted Wilson—he and Colonel Horatio Mends, commanding officer of the Rifle Depot, stayed with him for a weekend in September 1899—and then gathered together a 'Council of War' (Mary Garstin's description) including himself, Melloney Repington, Lady Guilford, and Wilson. On 9 October Repington was forced to sign a statement about his relationship with Mary Garstin, promising 'on my word of honour as a soldier and a gentleman, to cease all communication with her whether by meeting or writing'.[42] The document was given to Wilson to hold as guarantor. Repington, meanwhile, had written to Lady Guilford (who was clearly a key actor in the drama) saying that his promise had been made on the understanding that Mary would be 'spared all further indignities and humiliations on my account'.[43] A few days later he left for South Africa.

With Repington safely off the scene, both Garstin and Lady Guilford apparently missed no opportunity to vilify him to Mary; Gac in particular accusing Repington of previous infidelities. That Garstin and Gac regarded Repington with contempt and sought to expose him as an incorrigible sexual predator was understandable. So, too, was the besotted Mary Garstin's utter rejection of a 'brutally unfair and underhand' attack 'on a man who was not in a position to reply'.[44] Mary wrote to Repington in South Africa to complain about the accusations, which allowed Repington both to assure the credulous Mary that they were untrue and also conveniently to assert that Garstin and Gac's behaviour

---

[40] Wilson diary, 26, 28 Dec. 1898. Maj. F. E. Cooper was head of the West European section in the Military Intelligence Division.   [41] Repington, *Thanks for the Memory*, 135.

[42] *The Times*, 13 Dec. 1901.

[43] 8 Oct. 1899, Repington to Lady Guilford, copy in Repington's statement of 19 Dec. 1901 (TNA, WO 138/7).   [44] Repington, *Thanks for the Memory*, 157.

now released him from his promise of 9 October. On 12 February 1900 he sought out Wilson at Chieveley near Colenso to tell him this. Wilson responded by saying, 'I suppose you know that this will end in the divorce court'.[45] So it was to be.

Over the next four months the other parties in the case also sought to involve Wilson. In March he noted a letter from 'Bill' Garstin (it had been 'Sir William' when they had met the previous September), and he regularly corresponded with Gac. On 27 June there was a letter from Repington's wife, evidently urging Wilson to help, for the next day he went to see Colonel Freddie Stopford, Redvers Buller's military secretary, 'about getting à Court a billet out here'.[46] Repington meanwhile had fallen ill with a variety of ailments, and perhaps his wife had heard that he might be returning to England. But Wilson's effort was in vain (Stopford was 'not very favourable') and Repington was invalided home the same month. He was not able to return to work until February 1901, when he resumed his military attaché duties. In the meantime, Mary Garstin had returned to Cairo to live with her husband, but came back to England in the summer of 1901. Predictably, perhaps, the affair picked up again. According to her memoirs, she tried to resist Repington (who, among other things, threatened suicide), and on 14 August 1901 even promised her husband in writing not to communicate in any way with him ever again. The very next day, after Repington had begged a final meeting, Mary capitulated and they spent the night together at the Great Eastern Hotel, Harwich, registered as 'Mr and Mrs Goodwin'.[47] This seems to have been the last straw for Garstin. 'Will Garstin came to see me', wrote Wilson in his diary on 16 August, 'and says the à Court business is going on the same as ever.' Wilson thought it 'an extraordinary thing',[48] testimony, perhaps, to his own apparently complacent monogamy.

Garstin v. *Garstin and à Court* was heard in the divorce court on 12 December 1901. Garstin was represented by two KCs (one of whom was the famous Edward Marshall-Hall). The night before, Wilson noted in his diary that he had 'to appear in Bill Garstin's and à Court's case. Very disagreeable.' He had been summoned 'to swear to' the letter Repington had signed in October 1899.[49] The petition was unopposed and the divorce was granted to Garstin, with custody of the surviving child. Repington (erroneously) appears to have believed that an unopposed action would attract little publicity and, moreover, that Garstin would not bring up in court the matter of Repington's promise to Wilson. But the very public assertion that he had broken his word 'as a soldier and a gentleman'—the adultery was evidently condonable—threatened to ruin his army career. He appealed to the

[45] Ibid., 157–8. This is confirmed by Wilson's recollection of the occasion in a memo to the AG, 21 Dec. 1901 (TNA, WO 138/7).   [46] Wilson diary, 27–8 June 1900.
[47] Repington, *Thanks for the Memory*, 177–84; *The Times*, 13 Dec. 1901.
[48] Wilson diary, 16 Aug. 1901.
[49] Ibid., 11–12 Dec. 1901. The most extensive report of the court proceedings is in *The Times*, 13 Dec. 1901, but see also *Daily Telegraph* and *Daily Mail* of the same date.

War Office, who asked him to explain why he had broken his word, 'before giving a decision in your case'.[50]

On 17 December he tried to get Wilson to sign a note of what he had stated at Chievely in February 1900, but Wilson 'wouldn't sign'. Having received Repington's explanation, Sir Thomas Kelly-Kenny asked Wilson to write an account of the crucial Chievely interview. For this purpose Wilson's assiduously written diary was no use, as he had made no mention whatsoever of the meeting. This, indeed, is an interesting indication of what Wilson (at this stage of his life) chose to record—and not record—in his diary. He regularly noted conversations as having happened, but rarely detailed their contents, and there is really very little of an intimate personal nature in the diary, or much tittle-tattle about friends and relations. The only written record he had made of the Chievely meeting was in a letter to Lady Guilford of 13 February 1900. Evidently aware of the importance of his recollection, he went to see her, but she told him she had destroyed it.[51]

In his memorandum for Kelly-Kenny, Wilson claimed that it had been 'a very hurried and interrupted interview in exceedingly busy times', that Repington had 'hinted at a possible return to his former relations' with Lady Garstin, but 'so far as I can recollect, the subject of his letter to me' (of 9 October 1899) was 'never alluded to in any way'. Wilson conceded that the matter 'certainly may have been present to his mind during our conversation but my memory is quite clear that no reference was made to it whilst talking on this subject'.[52] Thus he could not support Repington's argument that he had been released from his undertaking. It might not in any case have made much difference. Once the authenticity of the 9 October letter was established and confirmed by Repington, there was surely little he could say to exculpate his subsequent behaviour, especially bearing in mind the prevailing moral climate of the time, which treasured the sanctity of marriage (or at least its public maintenance) high above any animal passions. In the eyes of his army seniors he was sunk. Lord Roberts declared that he had given 'a solemn promise which he broke, he has not behaved like a gentleman', and he had to go. Repington thus was ordered to send in his resignation.[53]

Repington, it seems, was prepared to do or say virtually anything to save his career and reputation. He was, commented one critic, 'a clever man, marred by a colossal vanity',[54] and, understandably, considering this unshakable self-regard, was likely to blame anyone but himself for his misfortune. He was obviously a louse, charming and passionate no doubt, but a louse all the same, as is all too evident even in the memoirs of his poor, devoted doormat, Mary. But was Wilson also in the wrong? So far as Repington was concerned, Wilson had, literally, broken ranks and ratted on a fellow soldier. Army gossip in later years had it that

---

[50] See correspondence in Repington's personal file (TNA, WO 138/7).
[51] Wilson diary, 20 Dec. 1901.   [52] Memo by Wilson, 21 Dec. 1901 (TNA, WO 138/7).
[53] Minute by Roberts, 23 Dec. 1901 (ibid.).
[54] The Very Revd J. G. McCormick to Wilson, 27 Dec. 1921 (Wilson papers, HHW 2/91/89).

Wilson had dished Repington because of professional jealousy and to get rid of a rival.[55] Yet Wilson evidently had powerful ties with the families concerned: the warm relationship with the Guilfords, a growing closeness to William Garstin, and also a friendship with Repington's wife, Mellony, marked eight years on by Henry and Cecil Wilson's attendance at the wedding of her and Repington's daughter Kitty.[56] Wilson evidently subscribed to the conventional morality of the day, and as one divorce lawyer put it, 'the very fact of figuring in the Divorce Court as a co-respondent is a stigma against a man for life, whether he be found guilty or not'.[57] There is no indication in his diary of any satisfaction with Repington's fate, rather the contrary in fact. On 15 January 1902 he wrote: 'à Court was gazetted out today. It's a sad ending to what might have been a fine career.'[58] He had, nevertheless, to endure Repington's sustained obloquy thereafter, but as his career prospered Wilson could evidently take it, and enjoy the warm irony of his success. Advising Tim Harington in 1921 not to meet Repington, Wilson observed, not perhaps without some understandable *schadenfreude*, that 'the more he hates you, the more certainly does he make your career. He succeeded even in making me Field Marshal.'[59]

The matter of Wilson's future was solved in January 1902. In December he had been promoted to Major and 'brevet' Lieutenant-Colonel, 'in recognition of services in South Africa'.[60] This meant that he had sufficient rank to command one of the provisional battalions set up to supply drafts for South Africa. It was an attractive option. 'This would delight me,' he wrote. 'If I could get a Provisional Battn I would far rather have it than this DAAG [Deputy Assistant Adjutant General]ship.'[61] Given some choice as to which battalion he might take over, Wilson opted for one quartered at Colchester, 'as I hear such good accounts of the place for shooting, hunting and sport', and on 24 February he took command of the 9th Provisional Battalion.[62] In March and April he divided his time between Colchester and London, where he still had to help Roberts finish his final 'Addenda' Gazette.

Wilson seems to have enjoyed his interlude as a battalion commanding officer, settling quickly into a 'charming' house with an adequate kitchen garden. He smartened up the battalion, which had been rather neglected, so much so that at the Eastern District shooting championships in July his unit emerged 'carrying all

---

[55] James Edmonds told Basil Liddell Hart that Wilson 'did in Repington' (Liddell Hart TS diary notes, 16 Dec. 1935, 22 Apr. 1937, Liddell Hart papers 11/1935/117, 11/1937/30); see also Morris, *The Letters of Lieut.-Col. Charles à Court Repington*, 282 n. 38.

[56] Repington did not attend (Wilson diary, 10 Nov. 1910; *The Times*, 11 Nov. 1910).

[57] Mr Deane QC (appearing for Edwards in *Edwards* v. *Edwards and Wilson*), *The Times*, 20 July 1897.

[58] Wilson diary, 15 Jan. 1902. Wilson's attitude, moreover, does not appear to have stemmed from an intransigent moral disapproval of adultery *per se*. See e.g. uncensorious, and not unsympathetic, comments on marital breakdown in his diary, 5 and 7 May 1905.

[59] Wilson to Harington, 28 Jan. 1921 (Wilson papers, HW 2/58A/18).

[60] *London Gazette*, 3 Dec. 1901, 8563, 4. 'Brevet' rank gave the holder the status, but not the pay, of the higher rank.   [61] Wilson diary, 3, 4 Jan. 1902.

[62] Ibid., 22 Jan., 24 Feb. 1902.

before them'. He threw himself into battalion activities. On 30 September 1902, 'I ran with the recruits at 7 a.m. Inspected barracks, 7.30 a.m.'. A fortnight later there is a hint of firmness: 'went round all the barrack rooms. There is a very marked improvement since I began to be nasty.' In the autumn he played regularly on the battalion hockey team. 'After lunch', on 29 October, 'I played hockey for the Battn against Ipswich. We were beaten 5 goals to 0, but we had a capital game.'[63] In January 1903, visiting the soldiers' canteen, he played a game of billiards with a private, 'which I unfortunately won'.[64]

London was not far away, both for visits to the War Office and occasional outings to the theatre, the former sometimes after an early start. On 14 October Wilson was 'up at 4.00 a.m.' to see two drafts of troops off at 6.00 a.m. Then he wrote letters, saw battalion defaulters in the Orderly Room at 7.30 a.m., and caught the 10.33 train to London.[65] Cecil played her part, organising entertainments and various other charity fund-raising events. In December Wilson tried to get the celebrated singers Clara Butt and her husband Robert Kennerly Rumford down to Colchester for a concert. Wilson himself was part of a choir singing 'Plantation Songs' (spirituals). Although Butt and Kennerly Rumford did not respond, Princess Victoria, widow of Prince Christian Victor who had been an ADC to Lord Roberts in South Africa, did come, and with royal patronage 'Cecil's concert' was a great success.[66]

As Wilson had hoped, there was plenty of shooting around Colchester, though the 'sport' was not always first-rate. On 30 October (after an early 'Orderly Room') he shot at West Bergholt with a local landowner: 'A poor day's sport. 18½ brace partridge, 3 hares, 3 rabbits, 1 snipe.' The killing was better the following month at Thorington Hall, near Darsham in Suffolk, though Wilson himself 'shot most indifferently': '262 pheasants, 2 woodcock & 40 various.'[67] There were also people to be entertained. On 1 November, 'the Allenbys dined. A nice couple.'[68] Later that month Leopold Amery hosted Wilson for a weekend in Oxford at All Souls ('Lovely old College') and a month later Wilson had Amery down to Colchester, when they discussed 'his forthcoming letters about the state of the Army', which Amery was planning to publish in *The Times*. Amery recalled in his memoirs that at Colchester what he saw 'of the lamentable shortage of recruits, and of their physical and mental quality' only confirmed the need for army reform.[69] When he did publish his article, Wilson urged him on. 'By God's grace *you* have lit a fire... Now don't let the matter drop. Serve 'em up 'ot and serve 'ot like potatoes or chestnuts!'[70] Amery had also taken on the editing of *The Times*

  63 Wilson diary, 15 Mar., 14 Apr., 3 July, 30 Sept., 18 and 29 Oct. 1902; Callwell, *Wilson*, i. 47–50.
  64 Ibid., 3 Jan. 1903.   65 Ibid., 14 Oct. 1902.   66 Ibid., 6–17 Dec. 1902.
  67 Ibid., 30 Oct., 19 Nov. 1902.
  68 Ibid., 1 Nov. 1902. Edmund Allenby, nicknamed the 'Bull', had a well-deserved reputation for fierceness and a volcanic temper, but this evening he was obviously on his best behaviour. Next to this entry in Wilson's diary, in what looks like his own hand, is an 'X' with two exclamation marks.
  69 Amery, *My Political Life*, i. 193.
  70 Wilson to Amery, 26 Feb. 1903 (Amery, *Diaries*, i. 45).

history of the Boer War, and took the opportunity to pick Wilson's brains on the subject. During the Christmas holiday Wilson did some work 'putting my S. African papers straight', and on 2 January 'Amery's short hand writer came down & I dictated a lot of stuff to him about S. Africa'.[71]

In December 1902 Wilson was dismayed to learn that his battalion was to be abolished the following February. 'This throws us out in the world again,' he wrote, 'and is of course a great upset.'[72] There was talk of his going to be a staff officer at Aldershot, but in the end Lord Roberts's desire to have him back at the War Office prevailed, and in April he started work as Henry Rawlinson's assistant in a new department of military education and training under General Sir Henry Hildyard. During 1903 Hildyard, Rawlinson, and Wilson formed a committee, with Gerald Ellison as secretary, which worked on a *Manual of Combined Training* and a *Staff Manual*, aiming for the first time to establish some degree of coherent training 'doctrine' for the army. These works formed the basis of *Field Service Regulations Part II*, the manual in force when the army went to war in August 1914.[73] Rawlinson found the office hard going. 'This is a terrible place', he wrote in October 1903. He had 'never worked harder for six months with less result than I have here', and was delighted in November to be appointed Commandant of the Staff College.[74]

With £1,600 borrowed from his father, Wilson meanwhile bought a house in Wyndham Place, just off Marylebone Road, which he and Cecil did up themselves. Lord Roberts, on his first visit, found Wilson in his shirtsleeves hanging pictures. Princess Victoria came to tea and nicely declared that the house was 'the prettiest she had seen in London'.[75] Wilson reckoned it was about two miles to the office, which he walked ('quick work') in 25 minutes one May morning. 'I strolled back by Green & Hyde Park in 40 minutes.'[76] There was no garden, but there were parks nearby, and Wilson regularly went for a horse-ride, a cycle, or a run (accompanied by 'Paddles') before breakfast. He carried a morning paper with him when he ran, and he also usually wore an idiosyncratic Irish tweed suit (his 'Kerry suit') to the office. Callwell claims that on one occasion, having been mistaken for a newspaper-seller, he genially handed over his paper for the penny offered.[77]

Although his analysis of the deficiencies of the British army was basically sound, Brodrick's reforms never came to very much and they were overtaken by the devastatingly detailed report in August 1903 of the Royal Commission on the War in South Africa (the Elgin Commission), in which some of his own measures

[71] Ibid., 15–17 Nov., 18–20, 28 Dec. 1902, 2 Jan. 1903. On 18 Feb. 1903 Wilson had another session with Amery's shorthand secretary. In 1903 and 1904 he was correcting proofs of Amery's *History* (ibid., 30 Aug. 1903, 19 June 1904). [72] Wilson diary, 5 Dec. 1902.

[73] James, *Lord Roberts*, 383–4; Gooch, *Plans of War*, 28. Gooch's book is the best guide to the War Office and general staff reforms of this period. [74] Maurice, *Rawlinson*, 83.

[75] Wilson diary, 5, 27 May, 8 June 1903. [76] Ibid., 4 May 1903.

[77] Callwell, *Wilson*, i. 52.

were severely criticised.[78] Wilson thought the report 'absolutely damning' for both Brodrick and his predecessor Lord Lansdowne. They should both resign, he thought, 'but of course they won't'.[79] Brodrick, in any case, was becoming a political liability, attracting criticism in parliament from a group of 'Young Turk' Unionist MPs (of whom Leo Amery was the most prominent), clearly egged on by like-minded army officers including Wilson.[80] In October Brodrick was replaced as Secretary for War by Hugh Arnold-Forster, who was keenly interested in modernising the British defence organisation.

Although Arnold-Forster was to hold the office for the next two years, and to preside over considerable change, the real force behind the reforms was Reginald Balliol Brett, second Viscount Esher, a curious figure who for twenty years or so exercised enormous influence in Britain, especially in military and defence matters.[81] A combination of social position, good connexions, and bright intelligence fitted Esher well for the role of 'fixer', of a kind who occasionally emerges in the British political system (Lord Goodman springs to mind). In the proto-democratic Britain of the early 1900s (universal adult suffrage was a generation away), and in the military sphere where the monarch still asserted significant authority over such things as appointments, Esher's position as a trusted royal courtier magnified his usefulness for a Prime Minister like Arthur Balfour (a personal friend) looking for someone to sort out army and War Office reform. Naturally enough, some elected and accountable politicians resented his interference. Writing after Esher's death, Brodrick acidly observed that he 'shrank from taking personal responsibility, although in his converse with men highly placed, he was always shrewd and sometimes helpful'.[82] Esher, who had served on the Elgin Commission and was convinced of the need for reform, persuaded Balfour to let him head a three-man committee to oversee it.

What was officially known as the War Office (Reconstitution) Committee, and unofficially as the 'Triumvirate', comprised Esher, Admiral Sir John ('Jackie') Fisher (the Second Sea Lord), and Sir George Clarke, a distinguished engineer officer, author of a book on imperial defence, and currently Governor of the Australian state of Victoria. On Leopold Amery's suggestion, Wilson's colleague Gerald Ellison was appointed secretary. 'I am very pleased,' noted Wilson, 'as he & I have talked over this matter a hundred times.'[83] The committee worked with whirlwind speed, mostly because Esher knew exactly what he wanted to do from the start and was prepared to press on with scant regard for existing vested interests or personal feelings. Esher envisaged developing the existing Committee

---

[78] See the summary in Satre, 'St. John Brodrick', 136.

[79] Wilson diary, 29 Aug., 1 Sept. 1903.

[80] Between March and September 1903 Wilson (accompanied twice by Rawlinson and once by Ian Hamilton) dined with Amery on five occasions. Another MP he socialised with was George Kemp (ibid., 4, 11, Mar., 30 Apr., 26 June, 11, 18 Aug., 4 Sept. 1903).

[81] The best overall biography of Esher is Lees-Milne, *The Enigmatic Edwardian*, but Fraser, *Lord Esher*, is also very good.   [82] Midleton, *Records and Reflections*, 145.

[83] Gooch, *Plans of War*, 37–42; Wilson diary, 16 Nov. 1903.

of Imperial Defence (CID) into a powerful planning and co-ordinating staff for all national and imperial defence matters. This, however, was not yet practical politics (and, indeed, any remotely effective inter-service and inter-departmental defence planning had to wait until after the First World War). In the meantime, the War Office was to be reorganised with an 'Army Council', which would be the nucleus of a proper general staff, and fresh men brought in to run the new system.

While Henry Wilson generally sympathised with Esher's objectives, he was appalled by his methods. The committee began formal work at the beginning of January 1904 and published a first interim report on 1 February. Beyond recommending that the CID should be chaired by the Prime Minister and have an independent secretariat, the committee proposed to abolish the position of Commander-in-Chief and establish an Army Council of seven members, four military—Chief of the General Staff (CGS), Adjutant-General (AG), Quartermaster-General (QMG), and Master General of the Ordnance (MGO)—and three civilian—Secretary of State for War, Parliamentary Under-secretary of State, and Financial Secretary to the War Office. 'For the first time', as John Gooch observed, there was 'a system of collective responsibility for military policy.'[84] Before even detailing the distribution of duties within the reorganised War Office (outlined in a second report on 25 February) Esher moved smartly on to appointments, with an unsettling impact graphically recorded in Wilson's diary entries.

[On Wednesday 3 February:] I got here [the War Office] at 8 a.m. & the Chief [Roberts] came into my room when I was having a cup of tea & told me all sorts of gossip. Lyttelton, Douglas, Plumer & Wolfe Murray replace Nick, KK, Johnnie & Brackenbury. This is a sweeping change... During the day I saw Nick who is very sore, & I must say justly so.

[On 9 February:] I was working in my Office when about midday in walked Freddie Stopford saying he wanted to speak to me. We went up to Hildyard's room where he told us he had come up from Aldershot to take over Training, Mobilization & something else he didn't know what. Neither Hildyard nor I had been told a single thing about it. This is the new diplomacy.

[On 10 February:] At the Office I found matters getting worse and worse. The 'Triumvirate' are appointing Officers to billets here, there and everywhere, quite regardless of anyone... & when I went up to see the Chief before dinner I found that he knew nothing about it & had never been told. It really is most disgraceful treatment.

[Next day:] Our days pass like nightmares. The Triumvirate are carrying on like madmen. This morning I was in Nick's room talking over things with him, & his opinion is that all these sudden changes lead straight to chaos, when in walked Jimmy Grierson & said Esher had ordered him up from Salisbury to take over Nick's office. Nick himself had not been informed, nor had he been told to hand over... This is most scandalous work.

Wilson also learned that Roberts himself was 'dismissed & is more hurt & angry than I ever saw him, & no wonder'.[85]

---

[84] Gooch, *Plans of War*, 51–2.   [85] Wilson diary, 3, 9, 10, 11 Feb. 1904.

But Wilson himself was to be favoured in these wholesale changes. On 11 February he had lunch with Ellison, 'who asked me what I would like in the coming shuffle . . . I said on the whole I would like to be given the new Office of training Staff Officers & placing them.' The following day he was summoned before the committee, '& Esher asked me if I would undertake the new office which dealt with Staff College, Staff Officers their training & appointment, RMA & RMC and Promotion Exams. I said I would if I might have 3 DAAG's & other officers. He said there would be no difficulty about that.'[86] Wilson evidently impressed Esher (who was to be a very important ally in future years), for he soon found himself flatteringly being consulted by the committee about the distribution of duties in the reformed War Office. 'It is most interesting', he wrote, 'being so much in the swim.' In all, he was summoned before the committee five times, at the last of which Esher even enquired helpfully about the nomination of Wilson's superior, General Hutchinson: 'Esher asked me if I could get on with Hutchinson as my feelings & my work were all important. Very civil.'[87]

When the dust settled, Lord Roberts had been mollified by official apologies and a permanent salaried position on the CID.[88] Among the others who were cleared out, Hildyard indeed went to South Africa, where he became GOC, his last posting. Nicholson and Johnnie Hamilton went off to observe the Russo-Japanese War (from the Japanese side), representing the British and Indian armies respectively. They were both to return to senior British positions. As for the 'new blood', a decade before 1914 we begin to see soldiers moving into important jobs who were to hold high positions during the war (though not necessarily all with equal distinction). Of the 'Military Members' of the new Army Council, Charles Douglas, the AG, was Chief of the Imperial General Staff in 1914, and was succeeded by James Wolfe Murray (MGO in 1904). The ablest (and at 47 the youngest) member of the Council was the QMG, Herbert Plumer. Under Neville Lyttelton, the CGS, the three new 'Directors' (of Military Operations, Staff Duties, and Military Training) were Jimmy Grierson, Henry Hutchinson, and Frederick Stopford. Hutchinson and Stopford retired before the war, while Grierson was appointed to command II Corps, though died suddenly on his way to the front in August 1914. At the next level down, the assistant directors, was a group of ambitious colonels and lieutenant-colonels in their forties, all of whom went on to become generals. Edward May (assistant DMT) who commanded a division in India was the only one not to serve in the War Office or on the western front during 1914–18. William 'Wully' Robertson (assistant DMO) and Henry Wilson (assistant DSD) were successively CIGS. Charlie Callwell and Joey Davies (both assistant DMO) served in the War Office, the former as DMO, the latter as Military Secretary, while Alex Hamilton-Gordon (assistant DMT) commanded

[86] Wilson diary, 11–12 Feb. 1904.   [87] Ibid., 3 Mar. 1904.
[88] He was also offered, and refused, the Wardenship of the Cinque Ports (Wilson diary, 12–13 Feb. 1904).

IX Corps in France, 1916–18. Later that year Wilson reflected in his diary about the lack of ability at the major-general level in the army. In the 'younger school', however, he thought there were 'many able fellows', and, writing in November 1904, he had 'no fears for the Army ten years hence'.[89]

Encouraged by Esher, and evidently indulged by the easygoing Hutchinson, Wilson wrote his own job specification, including 'Organization, Formation, and Instruction of the General Staff. Appointments to the General Staff. Entrance into Staff and Cadet Colleges.'[90] Wilson began with considerable enthusiasm. In April 1904, as meetings got under way to plan the structure of the staff: 'Jimmy Grierson came over to compliment me on the way in which, in spite of many difficulties, I am engineering this General Staff.' This turned out to be a wildly optimistic assessment. The same day Wilson also noted that many officers were 'deadly opposed to me', including Stopford ('a 2nd rate ass') and Douglas.[91] The real debate was between those, like Esher and Clarke (and Wilson), who favoured a 'Blue Ribbon' staff organisation with a coherent identity and distinct career path, including accelerated promotion, and the more conservative side, who would countenance little more than some mildly incremental development of staff work.

It took over two years, and a change of government, before any general staff organisation, as sketched out by Esher, was formally established. Throughout 1904 Arnold-Forster took little interest, being fully occupied with a complex and ultimately abortive scheme to replace the existing regular army and part-time Militia with a long-service force for overseas duties and a short-service one for home defence. Late in October 1904, after the Russian fleet en route to fight (and be defeated by) the Japanese in the Far East had fired on British fishing boats in the 'Dogger Bank incident', there was a brief war scare which exposed the continued unpreparedness of the army for war. 'We know nothing', wrote Wilson, 'about transports, remounts, ordnance, etc.' For home defence, he added, 'we can man coast defences, & mobilize, & call out the militia, but there is no scheme for Brigading the militia, etc, no reserve of regulars or Auxiliary officers'. Early in December Wilson tackled Lyttelton about the General Staff 'and pointed out that practically speaking nothing had been done since he came into office last March'.[92]

External lobbying in favour of a general staff came from Repington, who by now was military correspondent of *The Times* and pressed the reform in two articles in May 1905. It was essential, he wrote, to attract to the General Staff 'the best men in the Army, ... to establish sound and settled doctrines upon all questions of military policy ... and to provide the country with that aristocracy of talent, independent of birth, influence or means, which is indispensable for

[89] Ibid., 19 Nov. 1904.
[90] 'Distribution of business in the War Office', *War Office List 1905*, 67.
[91] Wilson diary, 13, 5 Apr. 1904.   [92] Ibid., 28 Oct., 6 Dec. 1904.

success in modern war'. Wilson thought this 'most excellent'. Repington's proposals, he added, 'are really identical with mine of 15 mos. ago'.[93] *The Times* articles provoked Arnold-Forster into action and, completely bypassing the War Office hierarchy, he asked Wilson privately for his views on the subject. Wilson's memorandum for the Secretary of State encapsulated the 'blue ribbon' view of a general staff system, which, he said, should have two objects: the gathering together of 'the ablest men in the army' and 'by means of these men, to form a school of military thought which shall be abreast, or ahead, of that of any other army'. Wilson argued that the military advice tendered to the government should be 'the carefully balanced opinion, after mature thought and deliberation, of a collective body of experts', but that this advice should be transmitted through the Chief of the General Staff, a powerful figure, who would be the sole adviser of the Secretary of State on all matters of strategy and military operations.[94] It was not until the First World War (when Sir William Robertson was CIGS) that this central and exclusive function for the Chief of Staff became established. But, as John Gooch has observed, by this stage Wilson 'was quite ready to abandon the notions he had propounded twelve years earlier'.[95]

Despite further urgings by Repington, as well as pressure in the CID from Esher and Sir George Clarke, progress on the General Staff was extremely slow. In August Arnold-Forster issued a memorandum effectively embodying Wilson's minute of three months earlier. The CGS, Lyttelton (not knowing of Wilson's role in the matter), told Wilson (to his amusement) that he thought it 'a "most able minute" ', and that he proposed 'to carry it out in its entirety'.[96] Further progress, however, got bogged down in the War Office, until Arnold-Forster tried to push things on in November. In slightly obscure circumstances his memorandum was released to the press—Wilson claimed he had been instructed to do so, Arnold-Forster professed 'amazement' at the publication. But the memorandum was generally well received (especially so by Repington) and Arnold-Forster afterwards told Wilson that he thought the publication had 'done nothing but good'.[97]

Arnold-Forster's highly irregular enlistment of the comparatively junior Wilson to advise on the general staff question was just one example of the propensity of more senior figures to seek out his fluent and articulate opinions. Of course, it takes two to tango, and Wilson was undoubtedly flattered, and more than willing, to respond. In the years following the Boer War the closest such relationship was that with Lord Roberts. Although it is probably going too far to suggest that Wilson acted as a sort of surrogate son after Freddie Roberts died in South Africa, the 'old chief' certainly came to rely very heavily on Wilson, who, with Cecil,

[93] *The Times*, 18 and 25 May 1905 (quotation from 25 May article); Wilson diary, 25 May 1905.
[94] Callwell, *Wilson*, i. 62–3.   [95] Gooch, *Plans of War*, 80–1.
[96] Wilson diary, 24 Aug. 1905.
[97] Ibid., 21–3 Nov. 1905; Callwell, *Wilson*, i. 64; Gooch, *Plans of War*, 88–92.

effectively became part of the family: father, mother, and two unmarried daughters, Aileen and Edwina. The Wilsons, for example, regularly took meals at the Roberts's homes in London or Englemere, including Christmas dinner in 1904 and 1905. The Roberts, for their part, frequently came to the Wilsons, and Lord Roberts was relaxed enough with Wilson to discuss both his will and his anxiety for his daughters to marry so that his name would be handed down to posterity.[98]

The closeness to Lord Roberts was to cause Wilson some bother. On New Year's Eve 1904 Lyttelton told Wilson 'that several people "not otherwise hostile" had been commenting on my frequent visits to the Chief'. Wilson reckoned one of these was probably Johnnie French. But the rebuke had no effect on Wilson's socialising. The same day, 'the Chief and Edwina were here for tea', and on New Year's Day both Wilsons had lunch with the Roberts.[99] Towards the end of May 1905 Lyttelton told Wilson that the Secretary of State had spoken to him about Wilson's 'friendship with Lord Bobs & that he (S. of S.) took such exception to it that he wished me removed from the W.O. at once'. According to his diary, Wilson 'flatly refused to allow the S. of S. to dictate my friends to me', which was a little disingenuous. Wilson's relationship with Roberts went beyond a mere private friendship. He regularly gave Roberts help with speeches for the House of Lords and elsewhere, and, as a War Office subordinate, this was a legitimate concern for his superiors. Yet in May 1905 Lyttelton seems to have been dissembling, since it was the very next day that Arnold-Forster, far from wanting Wilson kicked out, himself asked for advice on the general staff question.[100]

Relations with Lyttelton became progressively more strained in 1905–6. It may be that Lyttelton resented Wilson's rising reputation, especially among the supporters of army reform, and his apparently ready access to powerful and influential circles. Lyttelton was sensitive to Repington's opinions, and there is a possibility that the journalist, now an implacable enemy of Wilson's, was colouring Lyttelton's views. Certainly, in May 1905 William Nicholson—Nick—told Wilson 'he thought à Court [Repington] was actively hostile to me'.[101]

Among Henry Wilson's other responsibilities was the 'higher training of officers and their examinations for promotion', which gave him the opportunity to travel about the country supervising local sessions. During 1904 he went to York for a staff ride, and Cork for a war game. 'Paddles glad to see me back', he recorded on his return.[102] In May there was a visit to the Waterloo battlefield with Lord Roberts, and another weekend (this time along with Neville Lyttelton) at

---

[98] Wilson diary, 12 Oct. 1905, 16 Dec. 1904. Roberts's younger daughter Edwina (b. 1875) married in 1913 and had a son, Frederick, in 1914. He was the only grandchild and, since Roberts had arranged for his title to pass down through the female line, would have succeeded to the title of Earl Roberts had he not been killed in action in Norway in 1940.

[99] Wilson diary, 31 Dec. 1904, 1 Jan. 1905.   [100] Ibid., 29–30 May 1905.

[101] Ibid., 29 May 1905. A year later Wilson wrote that he had heard à Court 'is crabbing me for all he is worth' (ibid., 24 July 1906).   [102] Ibid., 28–30 Mar., 23, 26, 29 Apr. 1904.

All Souls in Oxford hosted by Leo Amery. Wilson and Amery went punting before breakfast, 'his pole sticking in the mud & having no paddle he had to stop & swim for it'. At the beginning of July he accompanied Rawly on exercises with the Staff College students in Wales.[103] Herbert Austin, a Staff College student in 1903–4, recalled Wilson taking part 'with the Directing Staff in the "pow-wows" held during the Staff rides away from the College. He was always bright and sparkling in his criticisms, and a *persona grata* with all, by reason of his never-failing cheeriness and quick Irish wit.' Writing after Wilson's death, and (perhaps more significantly) after Callwell's *Life* had been published, Austin added: 'Yet one did not always feel sure that his judgment was sound, perhaps because the Irish temperament is often credited with a tendency to volatility.'[104]

Wilson's work on what could be called 'in-service training' continued into 1905. The year began with the first ever Staff Conference and General Staff Ride, held at the Staff College in January. This was 'an immensely important innovation',[105] which brought colleagues (including Lyttelton and other senior officers) out of the War Office for a week of lectures, practical exercises, and the writing of appreciations and orders. Although Wilson thought some of the work 'rather poor stuff', on the whole he felt the event had been 'most successful.... It was entirely my idea, carried out entirely on my lines, with my criticisms etc throughout & I was a little nervous as to how it would go, but I am very pleased with the result.'[106] This became an important annual event, and, with its combination of practice, theoretical work, and critical self-reflection, contributed both to the 'team-spirit' of the staff and its increasing professionalisation in the years leading up to the war.

The second annual Staff Conference and Ride was also a success, and Wilson rewarded himself with a month's Continental holiday for himself, Cecil, and Little Trench. They spent three weeks in Adelboden, Switzerland, the women sharing a double room in the Grand Hotel, Henry staying in the *Pension*. It was Wilson's first time skiing, and he thoroughly enjoyed the experience ('very fine exercise', 'enchanting work').[107] While on holiday he noted the final results of the British general election. The Conservative government having run out of steam during 1905, Balfour resigned in December, to be replaced by a Liberal administration under Campbell-Bannerman, a politician regarded with much suspicion by many soldiers because of his opposition to the war in South Africa. Wilson gets no marks for electoral prediction. 'I cannot think', he wrote, 'that that traitor C.B. will get a majority', without the assistance of the 'Johnnie Redmonds' (Irish nationalist MPs). But the result was far, far worse than he anticipated. The Liberals won a landslide victory, with a three-figure majority over all the other parties combined. 'The Elections at home are dreadful.... Socialism is coming

103 Wilson diary, 14–15, 21–3 May, 4–6 July 1904.
104 Austin, *Some Rambles of a Sapper*, 210.   105 Gooch, *Plans of War*, 72.
106 Wilson diary, 6, 11 Jan. 1905.   107 Ibid., 25, 31 Jan., 11 Feb. 1906.

more to the front than I could have thought possible.' The only redeeming feature was the old warhorse Joe Chamberlain, Liberal Unionist and Imperial Free Trader, being returned 'with an immense majority'.[108]

Richard Burton Haldane, the new Secretary of State for War, was determined to see army reform through. In order to meet Liberal requirements, this had to combine economy with efficiency, and had also to avoid any hint of 'militarism'.[109] During 1906 he began to make systematic plans for an Expeditionary Force, to lay the basis for a thoroughgoing reorganisation of the Militia and Volunteers (which was eventually embodied in the Territorial and Reserve Forces legislation of 1907), and finally, to establish a General Staff.

What Wilson called the 'chaos' of the existing system was illustrated when there was another war scare in May 1906, after Turkish forces occupied an old Egyptian fort at the head of the Gulf of Aqaba in Sinai. A scheme for military action was 'drawn up by some Captain in Grierson's office'. Both Grierson (the DMO) and Lyttelton ('absolutely incapable... positively a dangerous fool when anything has to be done') had approved it, but neither the AG nor the QMG had been 'consulted as to Establishments, Peace or war, transport etc., nor have we been asked anything about Staff etc.'.[110] Late in 1905 Wilson had drafted an Army Order for the formal creation of a General Staff, but it was held up while responsibility for actually appointing staff officers was sorted out between the Chief of the General Staff (as favoured by Wilson) or the eleven-member Selection Board, which he anticipated would lead to a much diluted system. Eventually, on 12 September 1906, Army Order 233 was published, constituting the General Staff, whose duties were clearly laid out as: 'to advise on the strategical distribution of the Army, to supervise the education of officers, and the training and preparation of the Army for war, to study military schemes, offensive and defensive, to collect and collate military intelligence, to direct the General policy in Army matters, and to secure continuity of action in the execution of that policy.'[111] Not only did this paragraph effectively implement (at last) the recommendations of the Esher Committee, but it also covers almost precisely the tasks which Henry Wilson was energetically to address over the next eight years.

---

[108] Ibid., 13, 19, 20 Jan. 1906. The results of the election were: Conservative, 157 MPs; Liberal, 400; Labour, 30 (up from 15 in the previous election), Irish Party, 83.
[109] The best account of Haldane's work will be found in Spiers, *Haldane*.
[110] Wilson diary, 11 May 1906.
[111] TNA, WO 123/48, quoted in Gooch, *Plans of War*, 107.

5

At the Staff College

Late in October 1906 Henry Wilson learned that he was going to succeed Henry
Rawlinson as Commandant of the Staff College.[1] It was a significant step up
for the 42-year-old Wilson. He was now to be in a position to put theory into
practice, and, potentially, influence the staff 'doctrine' of the army. As his
successor as Commandant, Wully Robertson, believed, there was 'no position in
the army where greater influence for good or evil can be exerted over the rising
generation of officers'.[2]

The possibility of Wilson winning the job had, in fact, been in the air for more
than eighteen months. In March 1905 Rawly had told him he had been offered a
brigadier-general's staff job at the Aldershot Command. 'This leaves the S.C.
open', noted Wilson, '& I may possibly tho' not probably succeed him.' When
Rawly's move was postponed to the end of the year, Wilson resigned himself to yet
another period of uncertainty about his future. In June, however, Arnold-Forster's
private secretary told Wilson that the Secretary of State thought very highly of
him and 'had again & again said that I was the man for the Staff College'.[3]
Whatever this meant, Wilson's hopes for the job were apparently dashed in July
when, on Lyttelton's proposal, the commandantship was raised to a brigadier's
post, thus excluding Wilson, who as yet was insufficiently senior in rank.[4]

In July 1906 Rawlinson, who had resolved to move on at the end of the
year, told Wilson that he should succeed him,[5] and during August a number of
newspapers announced Wilson's appointment as an established fact. There is no
evidence that Wilson told the story to the press. A reference in the *Daily Mail* to
Rawlinson's tenure as Commandant having been 'so brilliant a success' might, to a
cynic, suggest 'sources close to' Rawly.[6] Wilson, by no means a public figure at this
stage, was non-committally described as a 'capable officer' who 'did much useful
work in South Africa'.[7] 'Letters of congratulation pour in,' he noted, '& really it's
very tiresome.'[8] Yet it was still quite uncertain that he would get the job. Lyttelton,

---

[1] Wilson diary, 24 Oct. 1906. The entry is marked in red ink.
[2] Robertson, *From Private to Field Marshal*, 169   [3] Wilson diary, 2 June 1905.
[4] Ibid., 12 July 1905.   [5] Ibid., 27 July 1906.   [6] *Daily Mail*, 20 Aug. 1906.
[7] *Daily Telegraph*, 22 Aug. 1906. On the same day a similar notice appeared in the
Scotsman. Wilson noted the story as being in the papers also on 1 August.
[8] Wilson diary, 23 Aug. 1906.

in a term that Wilson's Ulster forebears would have readily understood, appeared to have 'taken a scunner'—an active dislike—to him, and seemed determined to place someone—anyone—else at the Staff College.

During September and October 1906 the Staff College succession dominated the army rumour-mill. Lyttelton appeared to be favouring Colonel Edward May ('Edna'), the assistant Director of Military Training. Spencer Ewart (the DMO) told Wilson that May's candidature was 'ridiculous', and Douglas Haig was also reported as being 'deadly opposed to Edna going to the S.C. & in favour of me'.[9] By this stage, however, powerful support had moved behind Wilson. On 3 October Roberts, who regarded the commandantship as of 'supreme importance to the future of the Army', asked Esher to raise the matter with Haldane. Esher said that the 'only candidate' Haldane had 'ever discussed with me is Henry Wilson, whom personally I think qualified perfectly to hold that post, by intellectual attainments and general capacity'. Esher, who dismissed May as 'a worthy but stupid officer', hoped that Wilson would get the job.[10] Roberts replied, expressing his full agreement, and saying that he had written to Haldane to recommend Wilson.

Since most of the contemporaneous evidence we have for the Staff College appointment comes from Wilson's own diary, it is worth quoting at some length from Roberts's second letter to Esher, as it is an impressive character reference and throws light on the decidedly high opinion the Old Chief had of his protégé:

I know that Wilson has enemies at the W.O., and that they are trying to make out he is generally unpopular in the Army. So far from this being the case, I should say that Wilson is perhaps the best known and the most popular man in the Army. He is looked up to as a very promising officer, chiefly I believe on account of the excellent manner in which he performed his Staff duties in South Africa, and I know that the officers now at the Staff College are looking forward with great hopefulness to his being Rawlinson's successor.

The Staff College has suffered in the past from not having had practical men at its head. Hildyard did much to improve matters. It fell off under Miles,[11] Rawlinson has raised it up again. And now a good man—above all a man of character is needed to keep it up to the mark. None of the possible men I have heard mentioned can, in my opinion, and I feel sure I am expressing the opinion of the Army generally, be compared to Henry Wilson for the post.

The fact is that Wilson has too much character for some of the men with whom he is associated at the W.O.[12]

Wilson eventually learned of his appointment to the Staff College in a typically indirect fashion. On arrival at the office on 24 October he found on his desk a letter of congratulations from his Staff College contemporary Aylmer Haldane—a cousin of the Secretary of State. As soon as he had heard the good news, Wilson quickly wrote to Roberts to thank him for his support: 'I know well how much I

[9] Ibid., 15, 24 Sept. 1906.
[10] Roberts to Esher, 3 Oct. (Esher papers, ESHR 10/27), and reply, 5 Oct. 1906 (Roberts papers, NAM, 7101/23/29).   [11] Hildyard was Commandant 1893–8, and Herbert Miles, 1898–9.
[12] Roberts to Esher, 11 Oct. 1906 (Esher papers, ESHR 10/27).

owe you Sir . . . & if I can pay you back by doing my best while there you may trust me to do so . . . It has', he continued, 'been due to your quite extraordinary kindness in the past that I have become senior enough to be able to take up this new duty and so it is no exaguration [*sic*] to say that the whole of my career and future prospects have been of your making.'[13]

In the late 1930s James Edmonds, the official historian, told Basil Liddell Hart what purported to be the 'true story' of Wilson's appointment. Edmonds claimed that Wilson, who 'was at the time acting as Director of the new Staff Duties Branch, which dealt with staff and educational appointments', had been in a position to get rid of likely rivals to various postings. When the Staff College appointment came up, therefore, 'and Henry Wilson was asked about it, he was able to say that May—a really stupid Irishman—was the leading candidate. He was obviously no good, and was promptly turned down, whereupon Henry Wilson deprecatingly remarked: "The next name on the list, Sir, is mine." "You had better go there then." '[14] In his (unpublished) memoirs, which Edmonds wrote in the late 1940s, he told substantially the same story, that Wilson had effectively fixed it to ensure that he got the commandantship.[15]

Liddell Hart noted Edmonds's observation that 'the Army suffered above all, and always had done, from the system. The careers of promising officers', he added, 'were too much at the mercy of one man', particularly successive Chiefs of Staff. This idea of 'the system' was taken up by Tim Travers in his study of the British army in the First World War. Drawing quite extensively on the evidence provided by Edmonds and Liddell Hart (and using Wilson's appointment to the Staff College as one of his examples), Travers has argued that there was 'an idiosyncratic promotions and removals system based on arms rivalry and personal favouritism as much as merit'. This situation, which extended into the First World War and, he argued, had a negative impact on the army's performance, in part stemmed from the fact that the institution was 'caught in a transitional stage of development when the First World War broke out'. The army, indeed, was 'really a faithful reflection of Edwardian society'.[16] Britain, too, was at 'a transitional stage', caught as it was in a 'crisis of modernisation', with symptoms extending well beyond the armed services.

Although a counter-narrative which supposes an appointments system which did *not* involve favouritism, unit loyalties, or other intangible personal factors seems wholly fanciful, there is much power in Travers's argument. Part of the fascination with Henry Wilson's career stems from it lying precisely across a transitional period, when the old amateur military tradition of the British army was giving way to more modern standards of 'military professionalism'. Far from Wilson's appointment to the Staff College demonstrating the negative features

---

13 Wilson to Roberts, 24 Oct. 1906 (Roberts papers, NAM, 7101/23/88, no. 14).
14 'Talk with General Edmonds', 22 Apr. 1937, Liddell Hart TS diary notes, 23 Apr. 1937 (Liddell Hart papers, 11/1937/30).   15 Hussey, 'Appointing the Staff College Commandant'.
16 Travers, *The Killing Ground*, 3–4, 26–7.

of the old system, it may be that Lyttelton's inability to impose a 'personalised' candidate in the face of a well-qualified but (for whatever reason) disliked alternative actually reflected rather well on the selection process. This is the finding of John Hussey in an impressively careful examination of the circumstances of Wilson's selection. It was, he maintains 'debated, disputed, referred back and forth between senior officers (including at least one other Army Council member) and kept under review by two successive Cabinet Ministers, Arnold-Forster and R. B. Haldane', and he concluded that 'in essence it was a collegiate decision about a difficult but suitable man'. Edmonds's story, moreover, was 'worthless as evidence to prove anything about the structural defects of the old Army'.[17] Edmonds, for his part, never had anything good to say of Wilson, waxing eloquent on the topic of his 'intrigues' to Liddell Hart and also in his memoirs. On the evidence of the Staff College story, however, the historian Charles Cruttwell's dismissal (in 1936) of Edmonds as 'just a spiteful old gossip' carries some weight.[18]

For Wilson, the appointment to the Staff College at Camberley was a wonderful promotion. 'I will have gone (tomorrow)', he noted in his diary at the end of 1906, 'from Captain to Brigadier General in 5 years & 1 month.'[19] But the new job also brought with it some concerns about money. Wilson was not a rich man, and for most of his career he had to subsist principally on his army pay. At one of his less optimistic moments 'Bungo' (Julian Byng) told him that he should get out of the War Office. 'I quite agree,' reflected Wilson, 'but for a pauper it's not so easily done.'[20] In his classic and indispensable study of the Victorian army and the Staff College, Brian Bond discusses Wilson's hopes for the commandantship and asserts wrongly that Wilson, 'who in these years was extremely hard up, gambled on returning to Camberley by again taking the lease of a charming cottage, Grove End, two miles from the College'.[21] But the Staff College position came with its own house and Wilson still held a lease on Frimley Lodge (also near Camberley).[22] The move to Grove End was unrelated to Wilson's professional ambitions and was, in fact, a money-saving exercise, reinforced by Wilson's desire to get out of the city. He found someone to take Wyndham Place off his hands, and following the move hoped 'to have £150 in my pocket when everything is settled up'.[23]

Summing up his financial position at the end of 1906, Wilson calculated that he would need to borrow £350 to cover anticipated expenses associated with moving to the Staff College, and also the purchase of his first motor car. The new position also involved a considerable amount of entertaining, not all of which was covered by expenses. On the other hand, once settled in Camberley, there were many fewer outings to the London theatre. Holidays, too, were restricted.

---

[17] Hussey, 'Appointing the Staff College Commandant', 104–5.
[18] 'Cruttwell's opinions', Liddell Hart TS diary notes, 2 Oct. 1936 (Liddell Hart papers, 11/1936/80). For a more nuanced view of Edmonds, see Green, *Writing the Great War*, 21–3.
[19] Wilson diary, 31 Dec. 1906.   [20] Ibid., 3 Jan. 1905.
[21] Bond, *The Victorian Army and the Staff College*, 245–6.
[22] Frimley Lodge had been sublet to people called Blacker who, moreover, moved out in the spring of 1905 (Wilson diary, 29 Apr. 1905).   [23] Ibid., 18 Apr. 1905.

Following the successful skiing holiday in Switzerland in January 1906, the Wilsons had no more than a few days away at any one time until the summer of 1907 when they spent a month in Ireland on account of Wilson's father's death in August. A legacy from him of £1,300 certainly eased Wilson's financial concerns, so much so that he could afford to spend £125 on two polo ponies in May 1908, and £325 on a second car a year later.[24]

From January 1907 to July 1910 Wilson's life followed the rhythms of the Staff College year. There were three ten- or eleven-week terms: late January to mid-April, followed by a month's break; mid-May to the end of July; and the beginning of October to mid-December. The course lasted for two years ('Junior' and 'Senior'). When Wilson arrived there were thirty-nine soldiers in each 'Division', as well as seven naval officers who only came for a year.[25] The bulk of the teaching was handled by seven 'Directing Staff', who taught strategy, tactics, staff duties, and military history. Under Rawlinson the number of formal examinations the students took had been effectively reduced to one at the end of the first year. Most of the work was continuously assessed, and the students mainly worked together in 'syndicates', stressing and developing 'team-building' rather than purely individual skills. Another of Rawlinson's innovations (and one strongly supported by Wilson) was to have Royal Navy officers seconded to the college, so that training for 'combined operations' became a credible exercise.[26]

In his memorandum on the General Staff for Arnold-Forster in May 1905, Wilson had argued the need to form a 'school of military thought', and he undoubtedly had a pretty clear idea of what he wanted to achieve at the college. In December 1906 he had a talk with Hutchinson in the War Office 'about training the General Staff & forming a school of thought neither of which things he understands in the faintest degree'. Hutchinson's mind, he wrote, 'never rises above examinations & circulars'.[27] Wilson's broader conception involved both professional and policy-related aspects. In common with other army 'progressives' (a group which included Esher, Ellison, Nicholson, and Haig), Wilson wanted to establish a coherent system of higher education and training for the army. It was vitally important for the professional skills of staff officers to be improved, and that the Staff College should work towards producing a corps of officers 'imbued with uniform methods of work and a common approach to staff problems'.[28]

Wilson set out his priorities clearly in his opening address, in which he stressed the overwhelming importance of 'administrative knowledge'. This requirement, he thought, had been 'quite ignored by Rawly very much to the detriment of the

    [24] Wilson diary, 16 Aug. 1907, 23 May, 14 Nov. 1908, 4 Mar., 13 Apr. 1909.
    [25] 'Statement of number of Students, Naval Officers & Directing Staff, 1 Jan. 1907 to 12 July 1910' (Wilson papers, HHW 3/33/1).
    [26] Bond, *The Victorian Army and the Staff College*, 196–8. Bond's thoughtful chapter, 'A School of Thought' (ibid. 244–73) on Wilson's tenure of the commandantship is an essential commentary, upon which I have drawn for the following discussion.   [27] Wilson diary, 21 Dec. 1906.
    [28] Bond, *The Victorian Army and the Staff College*, 259.

training of the officers'.[29] Wilson's notes for this address have survived (as have all his Staff College lecture notes) and we can, therefore, get both an indication of the general content and a flavour of his actual words. The Staff College, he began, was 'a training school for <u>war</u> & incidentally for peace. The war training taking the shape of fitting Officers to perform the two duties of Staff & Command, and the peace training to fit Officers to train troops & administer them.' He made quite clear his belief in administrative competence, and urged his listeners

to put quite out of your head the childish idea that a man can be a good General Staff Officer and at the same time be ignorant of, or superior to, all the drudgery of Administration.... So strongly do I feel on this matter that it would be quite impossible for me to report on an Officer as being fit for the General Staff however brilliant he might be in imagination (one of the most essential qualifications for General Staff work) unless he is firmly based on sound Administrative knowledge.

But having begun with this stern, and perhaps rather intimidating, admonition, Wilson then smartly reassured the students that 'to be a good Administrator within the somewhat narrow limits conceded to soldiers in this country by a militarily suspicious & ignorant H. of C. [House of Commons] is <u>not</u> a very difficult business'.

Following a side-swipe at the propensity of British politicians to propose schemes for the army which were only really suitable for conditions of peace ('War as we soldiers know it', he declared, 'is quite unknown to S[ecretarie]s of S[tate] & the H. of C.'), Wilson remarked on the extent to which 'we adhere to the Voluntary principle for the creation of an Army'. While he was careful not to criticise this ('I am not going to say whether this is a good plan or a bad') and, indeed, also emphasised the proper constitutional situation whereby the Secretary of State was 'absolute master at the W.O.', we can see in this first Staff College lecture that he began, at least inferentially, to trespass on political matters.

He ended the lecture with some general remarks on the qualities he believed essential for a 'General Staff Officer or Superior Commander'. Although the first of these was 'administrative knowledge', onto this had to be superimposed 'the necessary soldierly & field qualities which the Administrator pure & simple does not possess'. In the order listed by Wilson, these were physical superiority, imagination, 'sound judgment of men & affairs', and 'constant reading & reflexion on the campaigns of the great masters'.[30] This, then, was Wilson's manifesto for the Staff College students, and he repeated the lecture, more or less unaltered it seems, in 1908 and 1909. In his notes for 1909 is an additional page on 'How to obtain a School of Thought'. It is clear from this that his main conception of the 'School of Thought' was simply to establish common, and constructive, habits of thinking and working throughout the staff. This was important enough in itself, but, as we shall see, there were also specific policy preferences which he (and others) wished to promote, both within the army and, indeed, in Britain generally.

[29] Wilson diary, 21 Jan. 1907.
[30] 'Opening remarks', 23 Jan. 1907 (Wilson papers, HHW 3/3/8).

The development of administrative skills was principally done on a severely practical basis. Particular emphasis was placed on collaborative work on 'Tactical Days', which involved working out schemes on paper, together with 'Staff Rides' and other outdoor exercises. At the end of Wilson's first term there was a two-day 'staff exercise' based at Worthing in Sussex, and in May the senior division went to Portsmouth for a joint 'Naval and Military Staff Ride', which included a night-time amphibious landing. The seniors had another staff ride around Chipping Sodbury in Gloucestershire, and their summer term's work finished with a week-long ride in North Wales, where the mountains of Snowdonia were supposed to replicate the North-West Frontier of India. Once that was finished, the junior division started on their first staff ride, this one based in the Camberley area.[31]

Archibald Wavell, who was successively to be CinC Middle East and CinC India during the Second World War, cast some doubt on the success of the training regime. Although he felt that the standard of instruction had in recent years improved, it was still rather 'too academic and theoretical and aimed too high. Its main object should surely have been to turn out good staff officers and not to train commanders of corps and armies.' What seemed to him 'weak was the administrative side, especially supply and transport. It was never rubbed into us that all operations were entirely dependent on transportation.' He thought, too, that they were not given enough training at producing clear orders or instructions under pressure, yet he also remarked on Wilson's '*Allez-Allez*' schemes, which would have provided at least some practice at quick, clear thinking and expression.[32]

'Physical superiority', the second of Wilson's officerly qualities, was to a very great extent taken for granted. The students were expected to be fit and to partici-pate in all sorts of sports and games. 'It was not all work and no play at the Staff College,' wrote Berkeley Vincent, a student in 1907–8. 'We had the Drag [Hunt] twice a week in the Winter, cricket and tennis in the summer, and two or three others besides myself played polo.'[33] 'Much importance', recalled Brudenell White, an Australian officer a year ahead of Vincent, 'was placed there on cross-country riding as a test of character.'[34] Another student, indeed, saw the Drag as directly relevant to Wilson's conception of the college as 'a training school for war'. 'What fun the drag was,' he wrote, 'and what a training for war!'[35] Wilson certainly approved of the hunt. When Hastings Anderson was charged with reopening the Staff College early in 1919, after wartime closure, the only specific instruction he received from Wilson (by this time CIGS) was: 'Well, Hastings, mind you start the Staff College Draghounds as soon as you can!'[36]

Part of Wilson's success at the college came from his enthusiastic participation in all these activities. Although in his mid-forties, he was well able to match, and even surpass, his juniors in virtually any physical activity. His diary during the

[31] Wilson diary, 8–10 Apr., 13–16, 28–31 May, 1–4, 23–5 July 1907.
[32] Connell, *Wavell*, 62–3.   [33] Vincent TS memoirs, vol. ii, 586 (Vincent papers).
[34] Bean, *Two Men I Knew*, 84.   [35] Dillon, *Memories of Three Wars*, 27.
[36] Neame, *Playing with Strife*, 83.

early summer of 1908 reveals impressive and intimidating energy. On 21–2 May he was in Swanage for a joint army–navy 'Disembarkation Scheme', which started at 11.20 p.m. and ran through the night until 6.30 a.m. The re-embarkation was between 6.30 and 10.00 p.m. the following evening, with only a two-hour lie-down to recover. Next day (23 May) Wilson played his first game of polo for nine years. On 24 May 'several games of tennis on own court'; 26 May saw both Wilsons at Buckingham Palace for a state ball for the French President Faillières, returning home at 3.00 a.m. The next day there was a 'Soldiers' and Sailors' dance in village hall', and on 29 May another dance (at the college) which again kept him up until 3.00 a.m. Perhaps it is not surprising that at polo on Saturday 30 May he ran out of steam a bit. 'I played a most miserable game getting dreadfully blown. I want practice badly.'[37]

A year later we find Wilson on a tour of the 1870–1 Franco-Prussian War battlefields, getting his staff and students to run the course of the Prussian General Claus von Bredow's charge at Mars-la-Tour, east of Metz: 'I took the extreme left, & so had much the furthest to go, & yet was easily in first, Perks [Colonel Percival] coming next. Not bad on my 45th birthday; 2 miles over plough & young seed.' The following month with the senior division at Capel Curig in Snowdonia he set a similar cracking pace. 'To-day we walked up Moel Siabod & altho' I stayed back at first talking to Irby [his driver] I caught the others up & got on top first. I went from Hotel to top [about two miles and 2,000 feet] in 63 minutes & I could have done it in about 55 if I had not hung back.'[38]

Wilson's third and fourth criteria, the rather more intangible 'imagination' and 'sound judgment of men & affairs', are perhaps easier to assess than to teach. Regarding the former, however, the students were in turn required to give a lecture on some subject of their own choosing. Here Wilson encouraged them to think widely, even venturing into political matters. In February 1908 'our first students' lecture of the year' was a three-hander on 'Socialism'. 'Only fairly good', noted Wilson.[39] Despite his own conservative political opinions, Wilson evidently valued a student's intelligent engagement with ideas more than any slavish toeing of some conventional political line. C. B. Thomson, the Labour Secretary of State for Air who perished in the R.101 disaster in 1930, was at the Staff College in 1909–10, when his early socialist sympathies were 'said to have pleased more than it displeased' Wilson, 'because the clash of opinion between him and his brilliant pupil was the occasion of slashing arguments'.[40] The Labour Prime Minister Ramsay MacDonald observed that Thomson possessed 'just those qualities likely to commend him to that clever, witty, and wayward soldier'.[41]

[37] Wilson diary, 21–4, 26–7, 29–30 May 1908.   [38] Ibid., 5 May, 30 June 1909.
[39] Ibid., 1 Feb. 1908.   [40] Obituary of Lord Thomson, *Spectator*, 11 Oct. 1930.
[41] Introduction by J. Ramsay MacDonald to Thomson, *Smaranda*, p. xii. Wilson later took Thomson onto his staff in the War Office in 1911–14, and at the Supreme War Council at Versailles in 1918.

The final criterion, 'constant reading & reflexion on the campaigns of the great masters', was taught through formal lectures and class instruction at the college, as well as by the senior division tour to the battlefields around Metz, where in August 1870 the Prussians won important victories. For Wilson the explanation for French failure was clear. 'The same thread of disaster & victory', he told the students in May 1909, ran through all the battles, '& for the same cause, i.e. want of purpose on one side & purpose on the other due to a <u>School of Thought</u>'.[42] Wilson also took the opportunity on these tours to discuss tactics, and we find him favouring what appears to be a 'defensive-offensive' approach. In April 1907 he suggested that on the battlefield 'tactical knowledge' could be acquired either 'by attack in the shape of Reconnaissance in force which might bring on a premature action & moreover expose the fact of want of knowledge', or 'by defence & luring on the enemy by advanced posts & false fronts & thus make him show his hand'.[43]

Brian Bond has suggested that for Henry Wilson the term 'School of Thought' consisted of two distinct but related aspects: the development of uniform professional practice (as outlined above) and also the establishment of two specific policies, 'first, the need for a close relationship with France against Germany and, second, the introduction of conscription'.[44] In his various writings, however, Wilson never linked these policy objectives with the term 'School of Thought', which he only used in the purely professional sense. This he made clear in his 'final address' to the seniors. 'We, who are on the Staff,' he said, 'do our utmost to form & to foster this School of Thought. As far as can humanly be done, we think alike, work alike, & teach alike.'[45] Although Bond is wrong to inflate the extent of the 'School of Thought', Wilson's views on Britain's alignment with France, as well as the desirability of conscription, were certainly shared by many fellow officers.

A life-time Francophile, Wilson welcomed the 1904 Entente Cordiale with France, which was part of the general British strategic reassessment which followed the end of the Boer War. 'I have for many years advocated friendship with the French as against the Germans', he reflected during the state visit of the French President Joubert in July 1903. There was, he thought, 'no legitimate cause to quarrel with the French, on account of their not wanting Colonies owing chiefly to no overflow population'. The Germans, on the other hand, 'who have an increasing population & no political morals <u>mean</u> expansion & therefore aggression'.[46] By the time he arrived at Camberley, the alliance with France was well established, and the possibility of Britain getting involved with the French in a war against the Germans was widely accepted.

In 1908 and 1909 he set the senior division an exercise called the 'Belgian Scheme', 'a study of operations involving the employment of the British

---

[42] Wilson diary, 7 May 1909.
[43] Ibid., 30 Apr. 1907.   [44] Bond, *The Victorian Army and the Staff College*, 259.
[45] 'Notes on final address to seniors, 16 Dec. 1908 and 20 Dec. 1909' (Wilson papers, HHW 3/3/19).   [46] Wilson diary, 6 July 1903.

Expeditionary Force on the Continent of Europe'. It began with the warning that 'there are many sets of circumstances which might necessitate' this kind of deployment, but in order to make the exercise realistic 'certain policies' were 'ascribed to various Powers, but it is not to be assumed that these policies in any way represent present day conditions'. In fact, the scenario involved worsening relations between France and Germany, and an assumption that Germany, having 'aggressive designs ... intends to break up the understanding between France and England and is attacking France primarily with that idea'. It was considered, moreover, that Germany would 'violate Belgian neutrality if such a step will assist her ultimate designs against England'. The students, who were divided into seven syndicates of five or six officers, were instructed to provide for the Cabinet a memorandum setting forth the views of the General Staff 'as to the most effective means of employing the British Expeditionary Force, when its mobilization is completed'. In 1908 the exercise was handed out on Monday 23 November, and the finished work had to be handed in at 9.30 a.m. on the following Saturday morning.[47]

This exercise, while strikingly prescient, was also politically very sensitive. Although one of the necessary tasks of armed services and general staffs in any country is to plan for possible international conflict, governments rarely like this to be widely known. One member of the Wilson's teaching staff recalled that the scheme 'came to the ears of some M.P.'s and questions were asked in the House whether we were to be permitted to hatch malicious plots against the harmless, peace-loving Germans'.[48] These criticisms obviously had an impact. In the 1909 instructions no suggestion was made that Germany might violate Belgian neutrality, and the students were sternly warned that the whole scheme 'and all work connected therewith, must be regarded as SECRET'.[49]

Wilson underpinned his own commitment to closer Anglo-French relations by engineering a visit in December 1909 to the French equivalent of the Staff College, the École Supérieure de Guerre. Although it had apparently been arranged for Wilson to spend just a morning at the college, he hit it off from the start with General Ferdinand Foch, his French counterpart. Foch was attracted by Wilson's enthusiastic command of the French language, and untypically (at least in French perceptions of the British) cheery openness. He was also, no doubt, flattered by Wilson's extremely complimentary assessment of what he saw at the École. 'The teaching I saw to-day', he wrote, 'could scarcely be bettered. Very fine.' Foch, moreover, agreed with Wilson about the German threat. 'His appreciation of the German move through Belgium is exactly the same as mine, the important line being between Verdun & Namur.'[50] Travelling home from a skiing holiday in Switzerland in January 1910, Wilson again went to see Foch. 'He was

[47] Senior Division 'Belgian scheme' notes, Nov.–Dec. 1908 (Wilson papers, HHW 3/3/17 (i)).
[48] Barrow, *The Fire of Life*, 115.
[49] Senior Division 'Belgian scheme', notes, Nov. 1909 (Wilson papers, HHW 3/3/17 (ii)).
[50] Wilson diary, 2–3 Dec. 1909.

most open,' noted Wilson. 'Explained the whole working of the College again to me.... Also told me much of the Russian unpreparedness, & we talked at great length of our combined action in Belgium. Most interesting.'[51]

An immediate result of Wilson's visit to Foch was his introduction at Camberley of what became known as '*Allez-Allez*' schemes. Based on what he had seen in France, he introduced 'frequent small outdoor exercises with answers given unprepared, on the ground, by the students'. In order to simulate the pressures of a war situation, the directing staff would harass the students with cries of '*Allez-Allez*' and '*Vite, vite*'.[52] Ten years on, these 'high-pressure tactical exercises' were still known as 'Allez! Allez! schemes'.[53] Foch was also invited to come to England, and in June 1910 Wilson set up a first-class programme of tours and meetings for him. Foch and Colonel Victor Huguet, the French military attaché in London, spent a day at the Staff College, and another out on an exercise with the students. Wilson brought him to Lord Roberts's house at Englemere for tea, '& the Chief & Foch made great friends, neither understanding a word the other said'. Wilson brought his guests to meet the Secretary of State, Haldane, and various senior officers in the War Office. Then he took him to the Royal United Services Institution (RUSI) where, according to Callwell, he introduced Foch to the secretary, Arthur Leetham, telling him that 'this fellow's going to command the Allied armies when the big war comes on'.[54]

While he was commandant of the Staff College, Wilson began going on a series of trips to the Continent, during which he explored the Low Countries and the Franco-German frontier from the Channel to Switzerland. In August 1908, with two of his directing staff, George 'Uncle' (or 'Daddy') Harper and Edward Percival ('Perks'), he set off south from Namur in southern Belgium, travelling by train and bicycle. 'Splendid roads & perfect country for troops', wrote Wilson. They had some trouble getting into a hotel at Dinant sur Meuse, 'as they thought we were tramps without luggage [it had been sent on by rail]. Luckily Rawley had written to me here, & when they found I was a General all was smiles.' Along the way he made notes about the topography, and further south, near Mézières in the Ardennes, he estimated that it would be difficult country for the French to defend.[55] In December, on his way to Switzerland for a skiing holiday, he inspected the fortifications around Belfort in Alsace, and the following May after the Staff College tour of the 1870 sites near Metz, he looked at battlefields from Napoleon's 1814 campaign south of the upper River Marne, concluding with a visit to a couple of champagne houses in Rheims.[56] In August 1909, again with Uncle Harper, and travelling by train and bicycle, he went from Mons in Belgium into France, and then down the French frontier nearly to Switzerland. The following

[51] Wilson diary, 14 Jan. 1910.

[52] Connell, *Wavell*, 63; Callwell, *Wilson*, i. 79; Bond, *The Victorian Army and the Staff College*, 261.

[53] Marshall-Cornwall, *Foch as Military Commander*, 32. Marshall-Cornwall was a Staff College student in 1919.   [54] Wilson diary, 6–10 June 1910; Callwell, *Wilson*, i. 79–80.

[55] Wilson diary, 11, 14 Aug. 1908.   [56] Ibid., 29 Dec. 1908, 10–13 May 1909.

spring, before joining the senior division east of Metz, he and Harper motored from Rotterdam into Germany, and worked their way down the German side of the frontier. At St Vith, just north of Luxembourg, he noted a new railway station '& 9 sidings', and at Bitberg a little further south, 'a new double line running west with many sidings'.[57]

German preparedness for war was one of the yardsticks Wilson presented to his students against which they could measure the British position. His annual lecture on 'Standard of Efficiency' mostly comprised a generally unfavourable comparison between the British and German nations and armies.[58] The German army, more-over, like that of every other major Continental power, was a conscript one, and Wilson, as he had indicated in his *Civil and Military Gazette* articles, believed that Britain, too, would need to adopt conscription in order to keep up militarily with its great-power rivals. Many fellow officers shared this opinion. In April 1905 William Nicholson told Wilson he thought 'that compulsory service was essential to the safety of the Empire. I quite agree with him,' wrote Wilson, 'tho' I fear it's still 10 years away from us.'[59] Wilson was nearly right. Conscription was introduced in Great Britain in 1916.

British political opinion, however, and especially that of the Liberals, in power from December 1905, was firmly opposed to conscription. But successive war secretaries still had to grapple with the problems of establishing a credible and gen-uinely useful reserve for the army, and it fell to Richard Haldane to formulate a peculiarly British 'nation in arms' concept based on voluntary service and traditional institutions.[60] Throughout 1906 Haldane worked on a scheme which was to sweep away the old ramshackle structure of Militia, Yeomanry, and Volunteers and replace it in Great Britain with a single 'Territorial Army', organised on the same basis as the regular army. There would be sixteen divisions of part-time volunteers, which would be deployed for home defence on the outbreak of war, although the soldiers would also be asked if they were prepared to serve abroad.

Wilson was not impressed. Haldane's schemes 'are quite the worst & most impracticable of any that I have ever read', he wrote in December 1906. The 'only solution' was '<u>compulsion</u>'.[61] This was also the view of Lord Roberts, whose 'last glorious campaign' was an ultimately unsuccessful one to introduce conscription in peacetime Britain.[62] Wilson, seeing Roberts off on a journey to Balmoral, where he hoped to persuade the King (and Arthur Balfour, who was also going) of the merits of conscription, thought it was 'quite possible we saw the Little Chief start on an historic mission carrying with it the seeds of compulsion. I sincerely hope this may be so. It would be the saving of the Empire.'[63] In 1905 Roberts had

[57] Ibid., 3–11 Aug. 1909, 26–9 Apr. 1910.
[58] 'Standard of Efficiency: Lecture I' (Wilson papers, HHW 3/3/5).
[59] Wilson diary, 26 Apr. 1905.
[60] Spiers, *Haldane*, 95; and for the background and introduction of the reforms, pp. 92–115.
[61] Wilson diary, 31 Dec. 1906.   [62] Forrest, *The Life of Lord Roberts*, 336–50.
[63] Wilson diary, 1 Oct. 1905.

become president of the National Service League, whose membership grew from 2,000 in 1905 to over 60,000 in 1910. The league attracted support from many conservative and imperialist friends and acquaintances of Wilson, including Leo Amery, William Garstin, Leo Maxse, and Lord Milner.[64] But Wilson's main link with the league was through Roberts, to whom he remained very close. Each year from 1905 to 1909 Henry and Cecil had Christmas dinner with the Roberts, and in May 1909 they were among the select two-dozen guests invited to Englemere for the Roberts' golden wedding celebration.[65]

One of the things which Wilson did in his 'Standards of Efficiency' lecture was to contrast the effective training of French and German conscripts with the much less rigorous approach of the British voluntary system. Wilson was not so much against the Territorial Army as it emerged after 1907, as frustrated that the reform did not nearly go far enough. 'The Territorial Scheme', he wrote to Roberts, 'is a vast improvement, and the Territorials themselves are the best & most patriotic men in England because they are trying to do something', but they could not match German standards of education and training. The 'necessity of being at least as good as enemy', he thought, 'forces all thinking men to conclusion that compulsion is necessary.'[66] In the meantime Wilson's championing of conscription prompted adverse comment (for which Wilson thought Repington was responsible) in the Liberal *Westminster Gazette*. In an editorial backing Haldane's reforms, it was remarked that 'the brains of the Army . . . as represented by the Staff College, are having it assiduously dinned into them by their present commandant' that two years' military service on the Continental model was 'the right option'.[67] Wilson had to see Haldane to explain himself, and evidently did so satisfactorily, and although his private opinion (and that of Cecil, who herself organised a National Service League meeting in Camberley in November 1909[68]) was clearly pro-conscription, the notes he made for a college lecture entitled 'Is conscription necessary?' reveal a more open-minded approach than the *Westminster Gazette* alleged.

Wilson began with a summary of the arguments for and against conscription. 'On the whole,' he said, 'I plunge for the Voluntary Service, thinking that where things are so nearly balanced it will be inadvisable to revolutionize society for an uncertain gain.' Voluntarism was, moreover, the government's policy, and 'we are all agreed at this College that the statesman is the master of the soldier'. Observing, however, that Britain's traditional policy was the maintenance of a 'Balance of Power' in Europe, he said that with the growth of mass, conscript armies on the

[64] Adams, 'The National Service League', 62–3. See also 'General Committee' list, *National Service Journal*, Sept. 1904 (Wilson papers, HHW 3/3/5).

[65] Among the other guests were Henry Rawlinson, Bill Furse, Neville Chamberlain (with their wives), 'Johnnie' Hamilton, and Lady Lansdowne (Wilson diary, 17 May 1909).

[66] Wilson to Roberts, 19 Apr. 1910 (Roberts papers, TNA, WO 105/45); undated note, with 'Standard of Efficiency' lecture (Wilson papers, HHW 3/3/5(i)).

[67] *Westminster Gazette*, 1 Mar. 1909, itself quoting an article in the journal *National Defence*.

[68] Wilson diary, 17 Nov. 1909.

Continent, Britain might need more men than could currently be provided by voluntary means. 'The logic of the thing is irresistible', he argued. 'If our present numbers in the Regular Army are not sufficient to keep the balance we must increase those numbers or alter our policy.' Having begun with an explicit, if only rather lukewarm, statement in favour of voluntarism, the thrust of Wilson's lecture thereafter was very much towards compulsion, though in the end he left the question open for the students themselves to make up their own minds. In November 1909 he noted that the lecture had caused 'a tremendous lot of "chat" '.[69]

One worry which Wilson had about the Territorial Army was the provision of staff officers for the new organisation. Dining with Haldane at Lord Roberts's house in November 1907, Wilson took the opportunity to raise the matter, with the result that Haldane, after a visit of inspection, sanctioned an increase of both staff and students.[70] A further expansion in 1910 meant that during Wilson's time as Commandant the number of staff rose from 7 to 16, and students from 64 to 100. In all, during his time as commandant, 224 army and 22 navy officers passed through the college.[71] In 1909 Nicholson secured a welcome increase in the Commandant's pay, which by 1910 had risen to £1,350 from £1,200 in 1907.[72] Clearly, whatever Wilson's political views, Haldane, who was under great parliamentary pressure to keep army expenditure down, was sufficiently impressed with the work he was doing to approve these increases. There were further public marks of esteem. In June 1908 he was appointed Commander of the Order of the Bath (CB) in the Birthday Honours, and in July 1910 ('Quite successful. Lovely day', he noted) King George V, just three months after succeeding to the throne, came to visit the college.[73]

By the time of the King's visit Wilson's days at the college were numbered. The appointment was officially for four years, which would have taken him to January 1911, but in the early summer of 1909 there was talk that he might succeed Douglas Haig as Director of Staff Duties. Wilson, however, did not at all want to return to the War Office, and hoped to get command of a brigade.[74] Nothing happened for a year, until April 1910, when to Wilson's dismay Nicholson hinted that he wanted him back in the War Office, probably as Director of Military Operations. Although he told Horace Smith-Dorrien, who wanted Wilson for his Aldershot Command, that he 'would love to have' the Borden brigade 'more than any other billet', he could not accept the offer 'without Nick's permission'.[75] When Smith-Dorrien told him that Nicholson had refused to let him go to Aldershot, Wilson was 'dreadfully disappointed as I suppose this means I am to

[69] 'Is conscription necessary?', 3 Nov. 1909 and 11 July 1910 (Wilson papers, HHW 3/3/22); Wilson diary, 4 Nov. 1909.   [70] Wilson diary, 3 and 5 Nov. 1907, 2 and 6 Feb., 31 Mar. 1908.
[71] Memo to Director of Staff Duties by Henry Wilson, 31 July 1910, and 'Statement of number of students', 1 Jan. 1907 to 12 July 1910 (Wilson papers, HHW 3/3/31–2).
[72] In his diary (3 Feb. and 19 Mar. 1909) Wilson records the increase as £200; figures from *Royal Warrant for the Pay* [etc.] *of the Army, 1907* and *1913*.
[73] Wilson diary, 26 June 1908, 13 July 1910.   [74] Ibid., 21 and 25 May, 9 June 1909.
[75] Ibid., 18, 21, 29 Apr., 12 May 1910.

succeed Spencer Ewart' (DMO). 'I dread rather going to London', he wrote, '& all the Office work again, but of course I will do what I am ordered.' So it was to be, and on 17 June 'Old Nick' told him he was to take over as DMO 'probably in about a fortnight', though eventually the appointment was settled for 1 August.[76]

Naturally Wilson was interested in who might succeed him at the college. On 8 June: 'long talk with [Sir Charles] Douglas about my successor. It looks like Robertson & I confess I am nervous.' Ten days later Nicholson told Wilson he opposed Robertson (whose background was humble, and who had risen from the ranks) 'because of want of breeding'. Wilson suggested Lancelot Kiggell. But on 4 July he learned that it was to be Robertson. 'This is a tremendous gamble,' he wrote, 'with the chances against him. I am very sorry.' When Robertson came over to the Commandant's house to discuss the handover, Wilson was still pessimistic: 'My heart sinks when I think what it all may mean to the College & this house.'[77]

Wilson's attitude is difficult to explain. There is no hint before this time of any particular antagonism between the two men. Though they were by no means close friends, they met regularly, and the Wilsons had had the Robertsons to dinner on more than one occasion. Wilson, too, had invited Robertson to lecture at the college, and they had cooperated on the work for various staff rides. It may be, as Brian Bond has suggested, that Wilson's concern was for the social side of the job, which included entertaining, much of which the Commandant had to pay for himself.[78] Robertson had no private means whatsoever, and, indeed, briefly hesitated over accepting the post on the grounds that it was 'greatly underpaid'.[79] There is some suggestion, moreover, that Robertson himself had hoped to become DMO, and he undoubtedly felt himself to be less favoured than colleagues like Wilson. 'There is now such a pestilential circle that there is no chance for the ordinary man', he complained to Alex Godley. 'Wilson DMO, Ewart AG, Stopford Cmdt RMC is enough to make one sick.'[80]

Robertson, however, had his own ideas as to what he wanted to do at the Staff College, and he was determined to shift the balance of instruction away from what he saw as an over-theoretical approach to a much more practical basis.[81] No doubt he had discussed this with Lord Kitchener, when they came over together from Aldershot to visit the college a couple of days before Wilson was to leave. 'He [Kitchener] attacked me', recorded Wilson, 'about trying to form a "School of Thought," but he got no change out of me, & he really talked a great deal of nonsense & imputed all sorts of things here which simply are not so.'[82]

In the light of the future relations between Wilson and both Kitchener and Robertson, this disagreement may have the significance Callwell ascribes to it, and

[76] Wilson diary, 4 and 17 June, 16 July 1910.   [77] Ibid., 8 and 17 June, 4 and 18 July 1910.
[78] Bond, *The Victorian Army and the Staff College*, 268.
[79] Robertson, *From Private to Field Marshal*, 168.
[80] Robertson to Godley, 12 May and 25 June 1910 (Godley papers, Liddell Hart Centre for Military Archives, 3/542, 544–5).   [81] Robertson, *From Private to Field Marshal*, 175.
[82] Wilson diary, 28 July 1910.

it also may throw light on a story which James Edmonds told about the end of Wilson's time at the Staff College. According to Edmonds, on his arrival at Camberley Robertson 'found on the hall table a bill from Henry Wilson for £250 for various items he was leaving behind'. Robertson was completely unable to pay such a sum, and he wrote to Rawlinson to ask what had happened when he took over in 1903. Rawlinson treated the whole thing as a terrific joke: 'That fellow Henry! My wife put in those rose trees and gave them to Lady Wilson. The furniture is a gift of past Commandants and goes with the house. You had better dig up the potato patch and see if the seed potatoes are still there.'[83] It is possible that Wilson, who had been an enthusiastic admirer of Kitchener, thought that Robertson had prompted the great man to attack his Staff College methods. Perhaps, then, the bill, if it existed at all, was drawn up in a spirit of petulant irritation, designed principally to demonstrate that a man with no means was unsuited to lead the college. Perhaps, even, it was a joke (which badly misfired). Whatever the truth of the matter, the two men were never close thereafter.

Robertson in his turn made rather a success of the commandantship, and there is general agreement that the commandants of the college from 1903 to 1913, Rawlinson, Wilson, and Robertson, transformed the place into something approaching an effective, modern 'war school' whose contribution helped to make the British army much more adequately prepared to go to war in 1914 than had been the case in 1899.[84] A series of memoirs have survived of contemporary students, and they all reflect the power of Wilson's personality and the impact he had.[85] Thomas Montgomery-Cuninghame, who so admired Wilson that he asked him to be godfather to his son[86] and also used a photograph of him for the frontispiece of his 1939 autobiography, attended the college in 1906–7, during Rawlinson's last year as commandant and Wilson's first. Under Rawlinson, he recalled, 'the training was not in any way special. Our task was to learn the arts of lubrication. We were learning to be greasers of the army machine, normal functionaries and not disciples specially selected for a rescue campaign.' When Wilson arrived, however, the atmosphere changed, as Wilson began to preach the likelihood of a European war, and 'bent all the resources of his fertile mind' to establishing that Britain's only option was 'to join the French and with them fight the Germans. The students at the Staff College', added Montgomery-Cuninghame, 'were obvious and handy instruments, and he got to work on us at once.'[87]

---

[83] Bond, *The Victorian Army and the Staff College*, 268–9; Bonham-Carter, *The Strategy of Victory*, 74. Long afterwards Rawlinson was still teasing Wilson about this. When Gen. Lord Cavan was about to take over the Aldershot Command from him, Rawlinson wrote: 'I must get Fatty [Cavan] over next week to take over the potatoes etc!!' (Rawlinson to Wilson, 23 Sept. 1920, Wilson papers, HHW 2/13B/32).

[84] See Brian Bond, *The Victorian Army and the Staff College*, and the remarks of Sir Harold Franklyn (who gives Wilson and Robertson more credit than Rawlinson) in Young, *The Story of the Staff College*, 23.

[85] None of the memoirs quoted below appear to have been written before 1930.

[86] Wilson diary, 14 Dec. 1906.   [87] Montgomery-Cuninghame, *Dusty Measure*, 50–1.

Montgomery-Cuninghame remembered disagreeing with Wilson on the inevitability of war. Responding to his belief 'that nothing but inconceivable stupidity on the part of statesmen' would bring about war, Wilson 'used to laugh, in his cheery way, at this objection. "Haw! Haw!! Haw!!! Inconceivable stupidity is just what you're going to get." ' What comes through powerfully in Montgomery-Cuninghame's recollection is the strength of Wilson's personality, the practicality of his approach—'his mind did not stray into the fields of academic abstraction'— and the fertility of his 'positive, pragmatic, constructive and above all, political' analysis. As Commandant, moreover, 'he found scope for action, for he was essentially a man of action. "It's no use thinking a thing if you don't say it," was one of his favourite maxims.'[88] Montgomery-Cuninghame concluded that 'the eager impetuosity' of Wilson's character 'carried him far, and with him simultaneously—willy nilly—many influential men, including some who were not wholly convinced that his premises were sound nor that his reasoning was justified'.[89]

Officers who attended the college under both Wilson and Robertson invariably noted the contrast between the expansive Irishman and his more taciturn successor. Writing in the 1940s, Arthur Green, a student in 1909–10, described Wilson as 'an Irishman with a brilliant brain and of a versatility that establishes him as one of the outstanding personalities in the history of the British Army'. He was 'an eloquent and persuasive teacher and lecturer whose every utterance was an entertainment; he was a tall and commanding figure with one of the most attractive ugly faces I have ever seen'. At the college, Wilson 'taught us to think big. He talked in very big terms himself, and he did not mind a student spreading himself on the subjects of policy or strategy.' But Wilson and Robertson were like 'chalk and cheese', and Robertson was emphatically *not* keen on students adopting the grandiloquent Wilson approach.[90]

Walter Nicholson, a year behind Green, also noted how 'Wilson fascinated us by his sparkling brilliance, his interest in outside affairs, his personality. He lifted us bodily out of the rut of everyday soldiering and let us air our twopenny-halfpenny views on the world at large. We throve', he said, 'under the treatment; blowing bubbles of great size and of marvellous colour.' Robertson arrived at the college 'in time to hear one of our weekly students' lectures; prepared, incidentally, for his predecessor's hearing'. After the lecture, which included 'several political sallies', Robertson rose 'and brought us all down to the ground with a bump, good and proper. What business', he asked, 'had we to say this and that should be done, when we were the servants of the government, whatever the government

[88] It is tempting to speculate that this particular recollection of Montgomery-Cuninghame's had been coloured by the publication in the late 1920s of Wilson's serial diary indiscretions.

[89] Ibid. 51, 53–4. Montgomery-Cuninghame says that he was living near what appears to have been Grove End, and that he and Wilson 'used then to bicycle part of the way home together every day'. This is clearly wrong, as Wilson lived in the Staff College House throughout his time as Commandant. It may also be that Montgomery-Cuninghame's other recollections are unreliable.

[90] Green, *Evening Tattoo*, 31–2.

might be?' 'Wullie', said Nicholson, 'brought us back to soldiering—good practical problems, with never a hint of theory.' He was 'a great man and a great commandant. He taught us to be practical staff officers; an end that Henry Wilson could never have achieved.'[91]

Although Nicholson's story of the student lecture cannot have been quite as he remembered it,[92] Archibald Wavell, whose final term at the college coincided with Robertson's first, told a similar tale in his 'Recollections'.[93] Wavell was summoned to the Commandant's office one day, to find Robertson with an essay Wavell had written for his precedessor, and which contained a reference 'to the relations between soldiers and statesmen which would have delighted Wilson'. Robertson was not at all impressed. 'What do you mean by writing nonsense like this?' he asked Wavell. 'What have you to do with statesmen and their affairs? Your job is to learn the business of a staff officer, not to meddle with political matters.'[94]

Eric Dillon, a student in 1910–11 (and who served as private secretary to Wilson in 1919–20, and to Robertson in 1920), described 'that unique and curiously attractive person Henry Wilson' as combining 'a brilliant brain, a marvellous sympathy, especially with the young, a complete disregard of convention and a wonderful sense of humour'. Wilson, he wrote, was 'succeeded by his direct antithesis, Sir William Robertson. Whereas "H.W." was a chameleon, "Wolly" [sic] was a rock.'[95] George Barrow, a member of the directing staff under the two commandants, observed how Wilson, 'the most original, imaginative and humorous man I have ever known', 'riveted the attention and made the dullest subjects bright'. He brought 'something new, something nobody else had thought of into the discussions of lectures and problems, and his summings-up at conferences and on Staff tours were models of well-balanced judgments'. Barrow, who venerated both men, reflected eloquently on their differences:

One would have to go far to find two men, with working lives passed in the same milieu and brought up in the same doctrines, belonging to the same profession in which both reached the highest post, and chosen in turn to be commandant of the Staff College, more unlike in body and mind than Henry Wilson and 'Wully' Robertson. It was the difference between the agile greyhound and the tenacious bull-dog—Wilson, expansive, giving himself out to those above him; Robertson, repressive, drawing others in towards himself; Wilson's eyes searching the horizon, Robertson's closely scanning the objects at hand.[96]

[91] Nicholson, *Behind the Lines*, 169–70.
[92] Wilson finished his tenure at the end of the summer term (27 July). Robertson would have met the 1909–10 class (including Nicholson) for the first time at the beginning of October 1910, after a two-month vacation. It seems unlikely that any student lecture given in the autumn term had specifically been prepared for Wilson's ears.
[93] These appear to have been prepared in the 1940s, and are quoted extensively in Connell, *Wavell*.
[94] Ibid. 64–5. It will be recalled that Robertson himself wrote a two-volume work entitled *Soldiers and Statesmen*. [95] Dillon, *Memories of Three Wars*, 26.
[96] Barrow, *The Fire of Life*, 112, 120. Barrow was writing in the light of considerable staff experience, An Indian Army officer, he served as Maj.-Gen., General Staff, in the First Army on the western front, and later under Allenby in Palestine, ending up (1923–8) as GOC Eastern Command in India.

Among these recollections only that by Berkeley Vincent (a student in 1907–8) is keenly critical of Wilson and of his ambitions to create a 'School of Thought'. Bearing in mind the vehemence of Vincent's criticisms (but also noting the fact that they appear to date from the 1930s), it is worth dwelling on them as they provide an alternative to the eulogies left by others. Vincent had accompanied Sir Ian Hamilton as an observer with the Japanese army in the Russo-Japanese War of 1904–5 and (by his own account) had very considerably assisted Hamilton with his successful book on the war.[97] Hamilton, however, ran into trouble with the volume on the grounds that he had no right to profit personally from his experiences, and Vincent certainly believed that the difficult time he had at the Staff College arose from his association with Hamilton. He believed that an 'order' had gone forth 'to "down" me', and 'no better agent could have been chosen for this than the new Commandant of the Staff College, Henry Wilson'. There was, wrote Vincent, 'no love lost' between Hamilton and Wilson, who, he thought, 'was probably also jealous of Sir Ian's recent experience in modern warfare, and quite possibly even of mine'. [98]

Vincent described the War Office reforms leading to the creation of a General Staff as embodying the idea of forming a 'school of thought' with a 'doctrine'. Wilson, he maintained:

had determined that it was to be his 'doctrine' and his 'school of thought', in fact he would be the von Moltke of the British army. Whenever he addressed us he told us to think alike, which meant to think as he did. His Staff, carefully chosen by himself, were eager enough to follow him, in fact had to or clear out. They and most of the students felt that he was the 'coming man', and therefore one to be in with. The General Staff was to be a sort of Jesuit community with Henry Wilson at the top and the rest nowhere.

Vincent's principal criticism of Wilson was that the 'doctrine' he espoused was fundamentally unsound. 'He continually preached the "Defensive–offensive" rather than the "offensive" form of war.' To Vincent, 'fresh from the Manchurian battlefields, his teaching was anathema. I had seen the value of the "Offensive" and its moral effect.'[99] This is an astounding criticism coming from a western front veteran (who had, moreover, done well as a brigade commander) writing fifteen or so years after the end of the Great War, during which a touching faith that the 'moral' value of the offensive spirit, the 'bravery and determination of officers and men' (Vincent's words), could triumph over artillery, barbed wire, concrete, and machine-guns had resulted in industrial-scale slaughter. [100] If criticism on this subject be offered of Wilson, it should be *not* that he favoured a

---

[97] 'My diaries, sketches and maps were the foundation of the book.' (Vincent TS memoirs, vol. ii, 574, Vincent papers.)   [98] Ibid. 583.
[99] Ibid. 584.
[100] For a commentary on views such as Vincent's, see Travers, *The Killing Ground*, ch. 2, 'The Cult of the Offensive and the Psychological Battlefield'. As GOC of 35th Brigade, 12th Division, nevertheless, Vincent did particularly well on the first day of the battle of Arras, 9 April 1917.

more sophisticated and thoughtful doctrine, but that during the Great War he in fact appeared to accept the costly application of a purely 'offensive' strategy in France and Flanders.[101]

For good measure, Vincent also took objection to Wilson's lecturing style: 'As a lecturer he depended for success on a sort of witty buffoonery, which often carried the audience with him. He always posed as an Irishman, a sort of English stage Irishman, which may have taken in the English, but not anyone coming from the South of Ireland like me. One saw at a glance that he really was nothing more than a canny North of Ireland schemer.' On the other hand, Vincent did concede that while at the college he remained socially on 'quite friendly terms' with the Commandant and staff. 'Henry Wilson', he wrote, 'used to clap me on the back in his playful manner and call me by my Christian name.'[102]

The contrast between Wilson and Robertson is striking, but looking at the actual evidence there seems to have been less of a substantive difference between the two men than some of the memoirs would suggest. Certainly they had sharply different personalities, and it is not surprising that what people remembered was more style than substance. The persistent recollection of Wilson's gripping speaking style is actually based on only a relatively few instances, as he did not lecture very frequently at the college. Over the three-and-a-half years of his commandantship he gave thirty-three formal lectures on sixteen different topics, and never more than ten in any calendar year.[103] But evidently these were memorable occasions. He was 'a spell-binding lecturer—always joking & amusing & informal'.[104]

Drawing on his surviving lecture notes, moreover, it is clear that, while making sweeping and challenging political and strategic generalisations, Wilson also strongly emphasised the importance of administrative work. He and Robertson at one time appear generally to have agreed about the role of the college and the general thrust of the instruction there. While he was Commandant, Wilson consulted Robertson, then on the staff at Aldershot, about the summer staff ride in 1908,[105] and he invited Robertson to lecture at the college on several occasions. In October 1907 Robertson 'gave us a most excellent lecture on Belgium and the certainty of Germany violating her territory in a war with France, & our position when we joined in as Allies to France'. This lecture, which hardly smacks of micro-cosmic, detailed staff work, was such a success that Wilson had Robertson back to repeat it the following year.[106] In 1908 Robertson also 'gave us a most admirable lecture on the Canadian frontier and military problems', another topic with a

---

[101] In October 1916, for example, Wilson told Lord Esher that what was required in 1917 was a huge offensive equating to '2 Sommes' (Wilson diary, 28 Oct. 1916).

[102] Vincent TS memoirs, vol. ii, 584–6 (Vincent papers). Vincent's family home was Summerhill, County Clare.

[103] As recorded in Wilson's apparently complete lecture notes (Wilson papers, HHW 3/3).

[104] Note by Launcelot Kiggell on file of letters from Henry Wilson (Kiggell papers, III).

[105] Wilson diary, 15 Apr. 1908.   [106] Ibid., 23 Oct. 1907, 14 Nov. 1908.

political dimension, and in December 1909 he spoke on the Balkans.[107] Around about the same time Robertson was giving this general lecture, Wilson was commending one student's work for its 'good, hard, soldierly common sense', values more commonly associated with Robertson than Wilson. To the same student Wilson also revealingly urged him to work on his style of expression. 'Style counts for so much,' he wrote, 'in my judgement it counts for far too much, and as this is so it is wise to realize the fact & make as much of it as we are able.'[108]

Wilson's final days at Camberley were marked by a series of extraordinarily warm tributes to his stewardship of the college. At his 'farewell dinner' on 29 July, 'I got the most extravagant praise from everyone'. He himself was sentimental and self-deprecating in his speech. The story of his four years was that 'of a man who had great opportunities & never made full use of them', who 'with all his faults & all his shortcomings tried, and tried hard to do his best', and who felt more than he could tell 'the comradeship & friendship so freely given' to him. 'I am so glad it is over,' he wrote in his diary that night. 'It was a great ordeal.'[109]

Some years later Lord Esher wrote an eloquent assessment of Wilson's time at the Staff College:

From the Surrey village where, as Head of the Staff College, he taught the principles of war, his pupils went forth imbued with a sense of its cataclysmic imminence. Below the ascending woods where he so often stood, there lay before his mind's eye, in lieu of cricket-fields and polo-grounds, curving reaches of the Meuse and bloodstained flats of Flanders. Day by day he visualized a German inrush, and calculated to an hour the crucial moment at which six British Divisions could be brought shoulder to shoulder with their French Allies between Mons and Namur.

When others prattled of peace, he prepared young men's souls for war, not for an indefinite war, as men barricade their doors against imaginary thieves, but for a specific struggle with the German nation, the early stages of which he foresaw in detail with a soldier's insight. [110]

This passage is significant, published as it was while Wilson was still alive and, indeed, serving as CIGS (though it had been written during the war).[111] Not only did it vindicate Esher's own part in securing Wilson's appointment to the Staff College, but it also embedded one view of the role Wilson played, both at Camberley and subsequently as DMO in the War Office, in preparing the United Kingdom for war in 1914.

[107] Wilson diary, 28 Nov. 1908, 11 Dec. 1909.
[108] Comments by Wilson, dated '11.09', on Military History 'Memoir' kept by Maj. Douglas Loch, Senior Division (Loch papers, 71/12/1).
[109] Wilson diary, 29 July 1910; 'Farewell speech at Staff College' notes (Wilson papers, HHW 3/3/31).
[110] Esher, *The Tragedy of Lord Kitchener*, 84–5. Bond describes this as 'flowery, but essentially accurate prose' (Bond, *The Victorian Army and the Staff College*, 245).
[111] In January 1916 Esher sent Wilson a three-page draft of this passage, which he described as 'An extract from a history of the War' (Wilson papers, HHW 2/82/11).

6

Preparing for war

Fifty years after the end of the First World War, Sir Charles Deedes, who had served under Henry Wilson in the War Office before 1914, firmly stated that it was through Wilson's 'energy, determination & foresight' that the British army 'was brought to a state of readiness to proceed overseas in August 1914'.[1] Allowing that the British commitment to war alongside France was (as Wilson fervently believed) both morally and politically the right thing to do, it may be that Wilson's four years as DMO constituted the most productive and successful of his whole career. An alternative view, however, is that Wilson's achievements during these years were disastrous for Britain. One inter-war critic noted that Wilson, having 'captured' the British General Staff and 'swallowed wholeheartedly the gospel of the French General Staff', created a situation where Britain's strategic freedom on the eve of the war was seriously compromised and the British Expeditionary Force committed 'merely as an appendage to the French Army'.[2] Lord Kitchener, wrote another, 'would never have consented' to the 'summary despatch' of the British Expeditionary Force to France 'had it not been long previously bespoke for the ranks of death by the egregious optimism of Sir Henry Wilson'.[3] 'From the very beginning', what Nicholas d'Ombrain has called 'the new British Army' (which emerged in the post-Boer War years) 'committed the cardinal error of failing to have an alternative to their policy of Continental adventure'.[4]

As a result of the Tangier (or 'first Moroccan') crisis in 1905, when rival French and German ambitions in north-west Africa appeared to threaten war between the two, one of the first tasks of the new General Staff had been to explore the feasibility of British military deployment on the Continent in keeping with the Entente Cordiale.[5] The then DMO, James Grierson, organised a 'strategic war game' to work out the possibilities and he also started to liaise with the French military attaché in London, Colonel Victor Huguet, and begin some direct talks with the French General Staff. Under Grierson's successor, Spencer Ewart, the pace of

[1] Deedes to John Gooch, 19 Sept. 1968 (I am obliged to Professor Gooch for this reference).
[2] Germains, *The Tragedy of Winston Churchill*, 51, 72.
[3] 'Translator's Preface' (by Gerald Griffin), to 'Arminius', *From Sarajevo to the Rhine*, 13.
[4] d'Ombrain, *War Machinery and High Policy*, 150.
[5] Howard, *The Continental Commitment*, 35–6. A very full account of the crisis and its military consequences will be found in Williamson, *The Politics of Grand Strategy*, 30–88.

consultation slowed down somewhat, but in July 1909 the Committee of Imperial Defence (CID) agreed that the War Office should continue to 'work out the necessary details' for the despatch of a force 'in the event of an attack on France by Germany'.[6] When Henry Wilson became DMO, he 'conceived it to be my most important duty to continue this work and so far as human foresight was possible to complete a scheme which would be at once useful & practical'.[7]

This scheme for the deployment of an 'Expeditionary Force' had been part of the army reforms planned by successive secretaries of state since St John Brodrick in 1900–3. From the start, Haldane had put a particular priority on organising the army so that it would be prepared for an overseas strategic role. Along with soldiers like Wilson, he envisaged that this would be a 'Continental commitment', though the effective adoption of this new strategy—anathema to anti-militarists on the Radical wing of the Liberal Party—was never made explicit to his Cabinet colleagues, let alone the British public at large. The army organisation which emerged in 1906–7 comprised six divisions, each containing three infantry brigades, and one cavalry division (of four brigades). Although Haldane asserted in his (post-war) memoirs that the particular size of the force had been the result of 'a careful study', Edward Spiers has shown that this claim 'was an utter fabrication', and the formation merely 'represented the maximum number of divisions which could be formed out of the force retained at home for draft-finding purposes'.[8] Henry Wilson was not fooled by 'Haldane's 6 Divn & 4 Cav. Bdes Scheme... There is', he commented, 'really nothing in it except a re-shuffle', and he was wont to tell people at the Staff College that there was actually no military question to which the answer was six divisions.[9] Yet the *fact* of an expeditionary force existing at all was more important than its specific size. This is reflected in an anecdote of Victor Huguet's. 'It doesn't matter what you send us,' Foch is cynically supposed to have told Wilson. 'We only ask for one corporal and four men, but they must be there right at the start. You will give them to me and I promise to do my utmost to get them killed. From that moment I will be at ease since I know that England will follow them as one man!'[10]

Military Operations was, with Staff Duties and Military Training, one of the three directorates set up under the 1904 reforms within the department of the Chief of the General Staff (Chief of the *Imperial* General Staff from November 1909). In 1910 the responsibilities of Wilson's 33-man strong directorate covered both war planning and the 'collection of intelligence'. It was divided into five main sections: 'strategical and colonial' (M.O.1), 'European' (M.O.2), 'Asiatic'

   [6] Memo on the 'W.F.' Scheme by Sir W. Nicholson, 6 Nov. 1911 (TNA, WO 106/49A/1); MacDairmid, *Life of General Grierson*, 212–15.
   [7] 'Minute to CIGS reporting progress on scheme of E.F.', Apr. 1913 (Wilson papers, HHW 3/7/2).   [8] Haldane, *Before the War*, ch. 4 (pp. 156–82); Spiers, *Haldane*, 80–1.
   [9] Wilson diary, 14 Jan. 1907; Montgomery-Cuninghame, *Dusty Measure*, 52.
   [10] Huguet, *Britain and the War*, 26.

(M.O.3), 'geographical', and 'miscellaneous'.[11] Only the 'mapping section' pleased him and 'seemed to be in excellent order'.[12] Indeed, one of his first actions as DMO was 'to have an immense map of the German frontier with France and Belgium hung upon one of the walls of his room at the War Office'. Not surprisingly, Huguet when he came to see Wilson in November 'was delighted by my big map'.[13]

Along with his two fellow-directors, Launcelot Kiggell (DSD) and 'Archie' Murray (DMT), Wilson was keen to shake things up. 'We are determined to combine & push matters a bit', he wrote, especially 'about getting rulings from C.I.D. & Admiralty' concerning the expeditionary force plans, '& about getting out a scheme for Conscription'.[14] Despite his hopes for compulsory service, which were evidently shared by his colleagues, little progress was made on that front, and Wilson found himself increasingly engaged with the expeditionary force. The priorities and balance of his work at the War Office are usefully illustrated in a file where he collected some papers he wrote as DMO between November 1910 and July 1914.[15] Of the thirty-six papers, twenty-one were devoted to the expeditionary force and related matters. Of the remaining fifteen, moreover, over half (eight) were written during his first year as DMO.

But it was an uphill task. Three months into the job he reflected on how much there was to do: 'I am very dis-satisfied with the state of affairs in every respect. No real arrangements for concentration & movements of either Expedy Force or Territorials. No proper arrangements for horse supply. No arrangements for safeguarding our arsenal at Woolwich. A lot of time spent in writing beautiful and useless minutes. I'll break all this up somehow.'[16] This was a strikingly ambitious intention from a comparatively junior officer. When he became DMO Wilson was still only a colonel temporarily made up to brigadier-general, and would not be promoted major-general until November 1913. His advice, however, was sought (and for the most part, it seems, valued) by his CIGS, Sir William Nicholson, though, inevitably, Wilson came to grumble in his diary about 'Old Nick's' shortcomings and feet-dragging.

Between August 1910 and January 1911 Wilson reorganised his directorate to make it more effective for war planning. M.O.1, 2, and 3 were recast into an 'Expeditionary Force section in which were included India & the Dominions, i.e. the whole of the military forces of the Crown except the Terr[itorial] Army' (which being earmarked for home defence was the responsibility of the DMT),

---

[11] *War Office List, 1910*, 46–8. These were designated M.O.1–M.O.5 respectively. There was also a one-man 'Medical Section' (M.O.6), which collected foreign medical information and statistics. For the general organisation of military intelligence, see Fergusson, *British Military Intelligence*, 220–1. [12] Wilson diary, 2 Aug. 1910.

[13] Adye, *Soldiers and Others I Have Known*, 220 (Col. John Adye was head of M.O.1 when Wilson became DMO); Wilson diary, 3 Nov. 1910. The following March Jimmy Grierson 'came to see me & was delighted with my big frontier map' (ibid., 16 Mar. 1911). [14] Wilson diary, 1 Sept. 1910.

[15] Wilson papers, HHW 3/5 and HHW 3/7/2 which contains some papers extracted from 3/5.

[16] Wilson diary, 25 Oct. 1910.

and two sections devoted respectively to studying the Dual Alliance (France and Russia), and the Triple Alliance (Germany, Austria, and Italy). Over his first autumn and winter as DMO, 'almost the whole of my Directorate was employed in working out a great strategical War Game' with the object of determining 'how the Great Powers would go to war with each other, what forces they would employ and when & where these forces would meet'.[17] Not until this exercise had been completed could detailed planning begin for the organisation and deployment of the expeditionary force.

The move to London brought a new house. He and Cecil quickly found a 'very nice' property at 36 Eaton Place in Belgravia, which they agreed to take on a thirteen-and-a-half-year lease for £2,100.[18] But, perhaps reflecting the perennial fragility of his finances, and also the fact that he largely depended on his army pay (now £1,500), Wilson's own bank, the National (despite the manager being 'most civil') refused him a mortgage. He eventually raised £2,500 from Drummond's Bank, to whom he transferred his account.[19] It is clear, however, that the purchase stretched the Wilsons financially, for they let the house in January 1911 while they went on a skiing holiday, and Wilson investigated the possibilities of letting it again for the opening of the London 'season' in April.[20] The house, nevertheless, was a great success and Wilson was to live there for the rest of his life. It was close enough to Whitehall for him to walk—or run—across the park to work, and it was conveniently located for the entertaining that he so enjoyed. His growing circle of contacts included Sir Arthur Nicolson (Permanent Secretary at the Foreign Office from 1910 to 1916), who lived close by and shared Wilson's conviction that the British army might have to intervene across the Channel. 'While walking to the Office this morning,' wrote Wilson in his diary in November 1911, 'I overtook Sir Arthur Nicolson & went with him to his room at the F.O. & was much pleased with a long talk I had with him. He is fully alive to the fact that we have no army & can do little on the Continent & he is quite prepared to help in remedying this.'[21]

Wilson, however, also had enemies, most notably his former friend Charles à Court Repington, military correspondent of *The Times*. Out of the blue, in September 1911, Repington 'made a nasty covert attack on the S. C. [Staff College] & me... Dirty brute.' Commenting on some inadequate staff work at the recent army manoeuvres, Repington observed that it was 'a comfort to think that such a first-rate man as Brigadier-General Robertson has taken the Staff College in hand'. 'Judging by this year's experience,' he continued, 'the minds of our young staff officers have been in cloudland, and the daily work of the Staff

[17] 'Minute to CIGS reporting progress on scheme of E.F.', Apr. 1913 (Wilson papers, HHW 3/7/2). See also Gleichen, *A Guardsman's Memories*, 340–1.

[18] There was a curious prescience here, as the lease ran to mid-1923. Wilson, of course, had no use for the house after mid-1922.   [19] Wilson diary, 20–3 June, 18 and 20 July 1910.

[20] Ibid., 16 Jan., 21 Mar. 1911. By letting the house Wilson managed to reduce his mortgage in 1911 to £1,600 (ibid., 31 Dec. 1911).   [21] Ibid., 17 Nov. 1910.

officer in the field has been much neglected. We do not want to educate sucking Napoleons at the Staff College.' This stung old Colonel Lonsdale Hale into a defence of both Rawlinson and Wilson's stewardship of the college, both 'first-rate' men, who had 'kept the minds of the young officers in this practical and mundane world, declining to utilize "Cloudland" as a hall of study'. Wilson hoped that 'the lying brute', Repington, had 'over-reached himself this time'.[22] Although Wilson dined, apparently quite amicably, with Robertson at Lord Roberts's house ten days later, an incident at Camberley clouded the end of the year. Just before Christmas, when Wilson accompanied Nicholson and other general staff officers on the CIGS's annual inspection of the Staff College, Robertson cut him dead. He 'never took the slightest notice of me, & never asked me inside his room. I must say', he wrote, 'I was rather hurt.'[23]

In Robertson's defence, gruff, inarticulate, and perhaps a little socially insecure, he must have found it appallingly difficult to follow the effortlessly confident and gregarious Wilson. He might, too, reasonably have resented Wilson's turning up with the CIGS's party when his responsibilities at the War Office did not actually extend to the Staff College. Wilson, for his part, was much more than 'rather hurt' by the slight. The following day, back in London, he 'let fly' at 'Nick' about 'Robertson's most rude & unpardonable behaviour', and a week later he was still complaining about the incident.[24] The next time he ran into Robertson, in March 1911, the latter 'was not effusively civil', and at the Staff College point-to-point races 'Robertson never even spoke to me. He is an ill mannered swine though,' added Wilson with perhaps some sympathy for Robertson's social inadequacies, 'I don't think he means to be rude.'[25]

Repington, on the other hand, certainly meant to be rude, and for Wilson remained as a sort of nemesis (or, at least, that appears to have been his ambition). The feeling was mutual, though Wilson generally affected an airily dismissive attitude to Repington's criticisms, telling one friend: 'we can comfort ourselves with the reflexion that to be abused by Repington is the highest praise an honest man can get.'[26] In February 1911, Wilson 'told Foch a good deal about Charlie à Court' and 'put him on his guard ag[ains]t him', and in May he appears to have attempted the same with Geoffrey Robinson, a new deputy editor at *The Times*.[27] But Repington had the ear of the Secretary of State, who nominated him to edit a new General Staff quarterly, the *Army Review*. Wilson was incandescent when Nicholson told him that Haldane 'was anxious that I should make matters as smooth as possible'. Repington, he spat, 'was a man devoid of honour, & a liar'. He declared 'that he was absolutely untrustworthy & that the appointment would be loathed by all of us'. While Wilson 'would, of course, do all he could to help

[22] *The Times* and Wilson diary, 27 and 28 Sept. 1910.   [23] Wilson diary, 20 Dec. 1910.
[24] Ibid., 23 Dec. 1910, 1 Jan. 1911.   [25] Ibid., 25 Mar. 1911.
[26] Wilson to Lord Loch, 27 Sept. 1910 (Loch papers, 'Other correspondents' box).
[27] Wilson diary, 26 Feb. and 24 May 1911. Robinson, who later changed his surname to Dawson, became editor of *The Times* in 1912.

him (Nick)', he 'absolutely refused to make a friend of à Court'.[28] The irony of the situation was that Wilson was broadly sympathetic to the modernising developments encapsulated in the new journal. Writing in the second volume, Sir John French asserted that it was 'of incalculable benefit to the Army that all its leaders, and especially all its higher leaders, should act on the same inspiration, should be guided by identical principles . . . and seek to attain by common action a common end'.[29] As a summary of Wilson's own idea of a 'School of Thought', this could hardly be bettered.

Wilson's move to the War Office did not restrict his European travels. In fact, the day after he took over as DMO, at Foch's invitation he joined a French Staff tour north-east of Paris, where they were rehearsing a response to a German invasion. In October he returned to Paris to attend the wedding of Foch's daughter. Though an invitation to a family occasion such as this could be taken to mark a significant stepping-up of his relationship with Foch, the fact that Colonel Fairholme, the British military attaché in Paris, was also invited suggests that Foch might have had an ulterior political motive. In any case, the next day Wilson spent two hours at the École Supérieure de Guerre. Foch had just returned from a visit to France's ally, Russia, and told Wilson that France could not depend on Russian support in the event of a war with Germany. France, therefore, 'must trust to England & not to Russia, & that all our plans must be worked out in minutest detail so that we may both be quite clear of the action & line to take'. In December Foch came to London for more talks, and Wilson took him to see Nicolson at the Foreign Office.[30]

Early in 1911 Wilson had an opportunity to check out the Germans for himself, when he visited Munich, Nuremberg, and Berlin on his way home from his skiing holiday in Switzerland. At dinner in the British embassy he met both Theobald von Bethmann-Hollweg (the German Chancellor from 1909 to 1917)—'a big powerful man with strong face'—and Admiral Alfred von Tirpitz (who was to command the German navy on the outbreak of war in 1914), whom he found less impressive: 'a big fat soft looking man without much power in his face or figure.' Travelling on to Paris on the overnight train from Berlin, he did not neglect the intelligence-gathering possibilities. At Herstal on the Belgian frontier he noted the Germans were 'making many sidings . . . about 8 or 10'. In Paris he had dinner with Foch and the French Chief of Staff, General Laffort de Ladibat, and the following day de Ladibat came to see him at the Crillon Hotel, where 'we had ½ an hour's talk on secret affairs'.[31]

Wilson got home to London to find his enthusiasm for Continental military operations was beginning to attract public notice. A rather flattering pen-portrait in the *Army and Navy Gazette* noted his 'passion for the scenery along the

[28] Wilson diary, 28 Mar. and 12 Apr. 1911.
[29] 'Memorandum' by Sir John French, *Army Review*, 2/2 (Apr. 1912), vii. French had become CIGS in March 1912.   [30] Wilson diary, 3–5 Aug., 11–13 Oct., 6 Dec. 1910.
[31] Ibid., 17–27 Feb. 1911.

Franco-German frontier'.[32] Navalists were less impressed. 'Jacky' Fisher complained to J. A. Spender 'that the whole War Office is permeated and saturated with the idea of our being in collision with Continental armies on their own ground. General Wilson, the Director of Military Operations, preaches this doctrine day and night.'[33] Later in the year Maurice Hankey, Assistant Secretary to the CID and himself not very keen on any Continental commitment, observed to the First Lord that Wilson 'has a perfect obsession for military operations on the Continent. He spends his holidays bicycling up and down the Franco-German frontier; he has preached this gospel at the Staff College for years; has packed the War Office with staff officers who share his views.'[34]

At the beginning of 1911 Wilson formally took up with Nicholson the deficiencies of what was becoming known 'for purposes of secrecy' as the 'W.F.' (With France) scheme.[35] One problem was War Office interdepartmental co-operation. On 9 January 'I told Nick he must support me in my endeavour to force Miles [the QMG] to make detailed arrangements for railing the Expy Force to ports of embarkation. At present <u>absolutely nothing</u> exists, which is scandalous.' Later on, Wilson 'spent the afternoon going over the papers re the W.F. Scheme. They are disgraceful. A pure academic, paper arrangement of no earthly value to anyone.'[36] He drew up a minute for the CIGS summarising his concerns about the state of horse supply, the lack of liaison with the railway companies, the absence of staff or naval arrangements at the embarkation ports, and the failure to work out protection schemes for arsenals and fortresses. 'In short,' he wrote, 'the present state of affairs in regard to the Expeditionary Force is so unsatisfactory, incomplete, and confusing that as far as my judgment goes it is not possible to make any accurate forecast of when the Army would be ready to take the field; and this remark', he added pointedly, 'applies with special force if the theatre of operations is over the seas.'[37]

Although Wilson was a little worried about the impact this trenchant minute might have on Nicholson, in fact it had completely the desired effect. Nicholson showed it to Haldane who invited Wilson to a private tête-à-tête lunch at his house in Queen Anne's Gate. According to his diary, Wilson spoke frankly to Haldane about the 'state of unpreparedness we were in'. Haldane told him he had consulted Sir Edward Grey (the Foreign Secretary), who had agreed that the army could now start discussing plans with the railway companies. In a neat bit of

---

[32] *Army and Navy Gazette*, 4 Mar. 1911.
[33] Fisher to Spender, 27 Feb. 1911 (Marder (ed.), *Fear God and Dread Nought*, 359).
[34] 15 Aug. 1911, Hankey to McKenna (Hankey papers, HNKY 7/3).
[35] The quote is from the unpublished memoirs of Gen. Sir Charles Deedes, who worked in M.O.1 in 1914 (Scott, 'The View from the War Office', 15). Sometimes 'W.F.' was incorrectly taken to mean 'Wilson-Foch'. In the French staff papers, the BEF was alluded to as 'L'armée "W"', which did stand for Wilson ('W.F. Scheme 1914', address by Sir Percy Radcliffe, n.d. (but, from internal evidence, written after the 1922 publication of Vol. 1 of the official history, *Military Operations: France and Belgium, 1914*) (TNA, WO 106/49A/1)).   [36] Wilson diary, 9–11 Jan. 1911.
[37] Spiers, *Haldane*, 154; Wilson to Nicholson, 12 Jan. 1911 (TNA, WO 106/49/WR/4 (ii)).

empire-building, Wilson got Haldane to agree that two officers from the QMG's department would temporarily be transferred to his directorate. Wilson was (with some justification) pretty pleased about the meeting. Haldane, moreover, assured him that 'before he would reduce another regular soldier he would abolish the whole of the Territorials'. While it seems improbable that Haldane spoke in quite such categorical terms about the Territorial Army in which he had invested so much of his political reputation, for Wilson it looked 'like a glimmer of light in the poor man's mind at last'.[38] The pace of planning picked up a little in the spring of 1911, after the 'French & German campaign' exercise was finally concluded. On 21 March Wilson held his first meeting 'about accelerating mobilization'. It was decided that the six infantry divisions 'would embark on the 4th day', the cavalry on the seventh, and the artillery on the ninth day.[39]

In the summer of 1911 a serious international crisis provided for Wilson his greatest personal and professional opportunity yet. In July 1911 the Agadir, or 'second Moroccan', crisis again raised the spectre of war between France and Germany.[40] In Britain it precipitated an intense examination of both grand strategy and actual war plans, which by the end of the summer had irrevocably, it seems, confirmed the 'Continental commitment' on the side of France, effectively dismissed the navy's war plans in favour of those of the army, significantly advanced the pace and scale of Expeditionary Force planning, and powerfully established Henry Wilson's reputation among leading politicians, in particular Winston Churchill and David Lloyd George.

The immediate cause of the crisis was the arrival of the German gunboat *Panther* at Agadir on Saturday 1 July. The following Monday *The Times* promised that Britain would 'not be disloyal or unfaithful' to the Entente, and the Cabinet resolved to back up France, though there was no suggestion that anything more than diplomatic support would be given. Henry Wilson, in the meantime, 'was up to midnight drafting a long minute to CIGS on the present most unsatisfactory state of the Exped. Force'.[41] Wilson and Huguet met three times within a week, and it became clear that the haphazard and incomplete British plans were of no use to the French. Wilson, as ever, was keen to force the pace, and on 19 July, apparently with the tacit support of Haldane and Nicholson, he went to Paris for talks with the French General Staff. There, with the French Chief of Staff, General Auguste Dubail, and the War Minister, Adolphe Messimy, he discussed 'the conditions of eventual participation of an English army with operations of French armies in the North East, in a war against Germany'.[42]

[38] Wilson diary, 20 Jan. 1911; Spiers, *Haldane*, 154–5.

[39] Wilson diary, 9, 13, 21 Mar. 1911; see also 'Minute to CIGS reporting progress on scheme of E.F.', Apr. 1913 (Wilson papers, HHW 3/7/2).

[40] The best general account is in Williamson, *The Politics of Grand Strategy*, 141–66, and I have drawn on it for the political and diplomatic background in the following paragraphs.

[41] Wilson diary, 4 July 1911.

[42] Ibid., 20–1 July 1911; Memorandum of meeting held on July 20, between Gen. Dubail and Gen. Wilson, 21 Aug. 1911 (Gooch and Temperley (eds.), *British Documents*, vii, no. 640, p. 629).

The resulting 'Dubail–Wilson' memorandum formally (though only rather sketchily) summarised the British military commitment envisaged within the Entente Cordiale. Wilson affirmed that the whole expeditionary force of six infantry divisions and one cavalry division, comprising 150,000 men, would be sent. He assured Dubail that cross-Channel transport would be handled by the British Admiralty. The force, which was to be landed at the French ports of Rouen, Le Havre, and Boulogne, would concentrate between Arras, St-Quentin, and Cambrai, and was expected to be ready for operations on the thirteenth day after mobilisation.[43] Much of this was moonshine. As Wilson had repeatedly complained in the War Officer (and to his diary), there were no detailed British arrangements to mobilise the expeditionary force, and, despite some desultory conversations with railway companies and colleagues in the Admiralty, no plans existed for the transport of the force either to the British ports of embarkation or across the Channel. It is not clear, moreover, how much of the British unprepared-ness Wilson revealed to the French, though his regular meetings with Huguet (who frequently came to tea at Wilson's house) suggest that they were kept quite well informed. And, although the memorandum specifically laid down that the staff talks in no way committed either government to action,[44] by formalising the anticipated British deployment so categorically—in a document which, as Samuel Williamson has argued, 'resembled a de facto military convention'—it is clear that Wilson was making intervention on the Continent much more likely than hitherto.[45] It is also clear that, while he may have been among the most active and energetic proponents of the Anglo-French military alliance, he was not actually exceeding the limits of British policy, as already established within the broad contours of the Entente.

The day Wilson returned to England, Lloyd George made a speech at the Mansion House in London in which he firmly placed Britain at the side of France in any dispute with Germany. This, Wilson thought, was more likely to prevent war than the more cautious policy favoured by the Foreign Secretary. 'Every day the funk Edward Grey procrastinates', he wrote, 'brings us nearer to a possible war.' All through late July and early August—days of 'semi-scare and hasty prepa-ration & scramble', he called them—Wilson and his colleagues worked to sort out the expeditionary force scheme. The apparent seriousness of the crisis, however, should not be got out of proportion. For all the urgency of the War Office work, Wilson managed to enjoy a pretty normal social life. On 28 July he and Cecil went to the opera (the *Barber of Seville*), and the next day they went off to Cowes where they spent a week on Albert Brassey's 560-ton yacht *Czarina*. He stayed the fol-lowing weekend with Rawly, and when he got back to London he 'found in the Office that nothing much had happened in the last week'.[46]

---

[43] Ibid., 629–31.
[44] 'Les pourparlers engagés . . . ne pouvaient lier en rien les Gouvernements anglais et français' (ibid. 629). [45] Williamson, *The Politics of Grand Strategy*, 177.
[46] Wilson diary, 25, 27–9 July, 1911.

It is clear, however, that the government was increasingly contemplating the military options. On 9 August Haldane had Wilson to lunch with Sir Edward Grey and Sir Eyre Crowe (Assistant Under-secretary at the Foreign Office). Wilson pressed on them three main points; 'First, that we <u>must</u> join the French. Second, that we <u>must</u> mobilize the same day as the French. Third, that we <u>must</u> send the whole six divisions.' Wilson (as usual) was not impressed by

the grasp of the situation possessed by Grey and Haldane, Grey being much <u>the most</u> ignorant & careless of the two. He not only had no idea of what war means but he struck me as not wanting to know, although he admitted, indeed, volunteered the opinion, that it was quite possible the present situation might at any moment develop into war. Grey seemed to me to be an ignorant, vain & weak man quite unfit to be the Foreign Minister of any country larger than Portugal.[47]

This is a typical Wilson diary comment, warmly dismissive of anyone who did not wholly share his world-view, or appear to understand his impatient desire to perfect British war planning. Grey, for his part, was anxious to steer a peaceful way through the crisis, and he no doubt appreciated that, while a well-prepared military machine could usefully back up his diplomatic endeavours, by making war more feasible it might also make it more probable. Finally—and this was not a consideration likely to cut much ice with Wilson—Grey had to bear in mind the wider political context. Apart from the Agadir crisis in the summer of 1911, the government had some domestic political problems, which together might have muted any temptation to indulge in an adventurous foreign policy. The 'Veto Bill', finally restricting the powers of the House of Lords, was working its way through parliament in the face of bitter (but ultimately vain) Conservative opposition, and a wave of quite serious labour unrest swept across the country, requiring troops to be ordered out in aid to the civil power in Liverpool (where two demonstrators were shot dead), South Wales, and London.[48]

At Nicholson's request, Wilson prepared an extremely important paper 'on the pros & cons of our joining with France in a war with Germany'.[49] It carefully articulated Wilson's own belief that 'we <u>must</u> join France', and was adopted by Nicholson as embodying the views of the General Staff as a whole.[50] Over the ten years since his *Civil and Military Gazette* articles ten years earlier Wilson had developed and refined his ideas. His paper was the culmination of this process, and an occasion when he could connect concrete military proposals to the broad thrust of Britain's foreign-policy requirements. It was, moreover, written at a time when he was in a position to influence high-level decision-making, and was the basis of the army's submission (as presented by him) to a strategic review

---

[47] Wilson diary, 9 Aug. 1911.   [48] Morgan, *Conflict and Order*, 164–75.
[49] Wilson diary, 11 Aug. 1911.
[50] Wilson's draft, dated 12 Aug. 1911, is in the Wilson papers, HHW 3/5/13; copies of the General Staff Memorandum, 'Military aspect of the Continental problem', dated 15 Aug., are in TNA, CAB 4/3/2 and 38/19/47.

conducted by a full-scale meeting of the Committee of Imperial Defence on 23 August.

Following a classical statement of British strategy, the 'axiom' that 'the policy of England is to prevent any Continental Power from attaining a position of superiority that would allow it to dominate, and dictate to, the rest of Europe', Wilson moved on to the two British policy options in the event of Germany, 'in pursuance of a policy of domination', attacking France: first 'England remains neutral'; and second, 'England becomes the active ally of France'. In the first case, he argued, 'the result of such a war can scarcely be doubted'. Even if France had 'the active assistance of Russia', this would be 'more imaginary than real'. It would have no value on the sea, 'and on land it could easily be met by German and Austrian troops with no sensible diminution of the German troops on the French frontier'.[51] Since Germany would win, and become dominant in Europe, it was, he asserted, 'impossible for England to remain neutral'.

Moving on to consider England as an 'active ally', Wilson made three main points. He began with an acknowledgement of the traditional 'blue water' strengths of British strategy. The English and French fleets, he suggested, would command the sea, with the result that 'the chief fiscal dislocation and commercial loss will fall upon Germany. The longer the war lasts the more this strain will be felt by that country.' Second, he asserted that, with British support, the disparity in numbers between the opposing armies would crucially be reduced and that 'the numbers of the opposing forces at the decisive point would be so nearly equal during the opening and early actions of the war that it is quite possible for the Allies to win some initial successes which might prove invaluable'. Third, allowing that 'perhaps this is the most important consideration of all', he argued that the moral effect on the French of British intervention 'would be of incalculable value'. Together, these last two points could be persuasive to both hawks and doves in the British policy-making community. The hawks could be taken with the deployment of force 'at the decisive point' argument, while the doves might be persuaded that the 'moral effect' of credible joint planning with the French could underpin the deterrent value (on Germany) of the Entente. It was, moreover, a version the *si vis pacem, para bellum* argument so beloved of soldiers (and some statesmen) through the ages: if you wish for peace, then prepare for war.

The most striking and dramatic part of Wilson's argument related to the deployment of the expeditionary force and was plausibly backed up with a detailed analysis of French and German mobilisation. If both countries mobilised at the same time, by the thirteenth day the Germans would have 57 divisions and the French 63 along the frontier. By the seventeenth day, however, the Germans would have 96 as against the French 66. But geographical factors had also to be

---

[51] This point was backed up by various calculations about Russian and Austrian mobilisation, and possible deployments between Germany, Austria, and Russia, Wilson arguing that 'the intervention of Russia does not materially affect the French and German frontier, at all events during the early days of the war' (ibid.).

taken into account. Here Wilson, of course, could speak with personal authority. He argued that only about half of the 230-mile frontier was 'passable', and 'in the 110 miles of open frontier there are not more than 17 or 18 through roads' which the Germans could use. Asserting that it was practicable for only three divisions to use each road, 'we find that the Germans cannot employ more than 51 to 54 Divisions' in the opening phase of the war.[52] This was his key point. 'The very marked superiority in German numbers' could not 'be brought into play at the commencement of the campaign', and this, in turn, enhanced the importance of the rapid deployment of the British force. 'The early intervention of our six Divisions', he wrote, 'would be more effective than the tardy presence of double their number', and thus Britain must mobilise at *exactly* the same moment as France. Although conceding that the decision for war, and the date and hour of mobilisation, lay with the politicians, he portentously concluded it to be 'essential that the Secretary of State for War should be fully aware of the difference it will make to the course of the campaign whether we mobilize early or late. It is scarcely too much to say that the difference may be that of victory and defeat.'

Haldane's response was to have Wilson argue his case in person to a meeting of the CID, which turned out to be of extraordinary importance in the evolution of British strategic planning before 1914. As Zara Steiner has observed, it was the only time the CID 'actually reviewed the over-all pattern of British strategy before 1914'.[53] Wilson's paper was circulated in advance, as was one by Sir Arthur Wilson (the First Sea Lord), which Henry Wilson dismissed as 'one of the most childish papers I ever read about the use of our Exped. force in a Continental war. Absolutely hopeless. It appears that 5 Div. are to guard the east coast & one Div. is to land in Germany! I never heard such a thing.'[54]

Chaired by the Prime Minister, the CID meeting was attended by Haldane, Churchill, Grey, McKenna (First Lord of the Admiralty), and Lloyd George. Nicholson, Sir John French, and Wilson represented the War Office; Sir Arthur Wilson and Alexander Bethell (Director of Naval Intelligence) the Admiralty. Beginning at 11.30 in the morning, the War Office batted first. Nicholson left Wilson to put their case. 'I had all my big maps on the wall,' he wrote, '& I lectured for 1¾ hours. Everyone very nice. Much questioning by Winston and Lloyd George, especially.' After a break for a late lunch, Arthur Wilson led for the Admiralty. 'It soon became apparent', recalled Churchill, 'that a profound difference existed between the War Office and the Admiralty view.' Insofar as any coherent navy plans existed at all, they depended on the traditional enforcement of a maritime blockade on the enemy, coupled with the limited use of the army for

[52] Wilson's calculations of the numbers of French and German divisions has been sharply criticised by Ernest R. May, giving the impression that the figures were 'cooked' to support the argument in favour of military intervention (May, 'Cabinet, Tsar, Kaiser', 11–17). Edward W. Bennett's detailed and devastating critique of May, however, suggests that Wilson's figures were not seriously out of line (Bennett, 'Intelligence and History', 324–9).

[53] Steiner, *Britain and the Origins of the First World War*, 200.

[54] Wilson diary, 21 Aug. 1911.

raids on the German North Sea coast. Asquith called the navy's half-baked plans 'puerile' and 'wholly impracticable'. But Churchill's 'profound difference' was one of style as well as substance. In the 'battle of the Wilsons' the admiral was no match for the general, and Henry Wilson carried the day as much through the 'remarkable brilliance' (Hankey's description) of his exposition as the depth and completeness of his plans. After the meeting, indeed, he 'got a nice note from Haldane. It ran: "My dear General. You did admirably to-day. Lucid & of real grip, your exposition made a real impression." '55

There were gaps and deficiencies in the army's case as put by Henry Wilson, not least because his planning depended so heavily on the French. But the navy's view was put so badly and incompetently by Arthur Wilson that it obscured the weaknesses in the army plans. Asquith was indeed no great supporter of the 'Continental commitment', but he had to agree that 'in principle the General Staff scheme is the only alternative', though he wanted it in the first instance to be limited to the despatch of only four divisions.56 The 23 August meeting was important, not so much (as some have argued) because this was the moment when the commitment to France was made. This had been agreed by 1906, and military planning had proceeded accordingly. Yet the CID meeting was a moment when Henry Wilson could have *lost* the case (as his naval namesake did). Wilson's brilliance as a lecturer, with his evident mastery of facts, figures, and the geography of the Franco-German frontier, carried him through, and left an indelible impression on his audience of politicians. Victor Wallace Germains, a journalistic commentator in the 1930s, made a similar point, though he cast Wilson in a rather less favourable light. Wilson, he wrote, 'was a soldier who brought to the study of military problems the jolly wit of the "commercial room" of a small hotel, and to the council chamber, the flowing, forceful "patter" of the salesman pushing his wares'.57 Arthur Wilson's incompetence, by contrast, ensured that thereafter no one seriously considered any alternative to the army strategy. The military view afterwards, as expressed by Sir Percy Radcliffe, who served in M.O.1 in 1913–14, was that even after the 23 August meeting 'there was still no definite agreement with France to come in with her, nothing but a very grudging authorisation by our Government to the General Staff on the theory of eventual co-operation'. It was, he asserted (sometime after 1922), 'only the ardent spirit of Sir Henry Wilson, his tireless energy, wide vision and dauntless perseverance that got those conversations translated into definite practical arrangements'.58

One of the people whom Wilson most impressed was Winston Churchill, at 37 the youngest member of the Cabinet. Churchill was concerned about what Keith Wilson has called the 'Belgian option', and wanted to explore the choices and

55 Ibid., 23 Aug. 1911; CID 114th meeting, 23 Aug. 1911 (TNA, CAB 2/2/2); Churchill, *The World Crisis*, 58; Asquith to Haldane, 31 Aug. 1911 (quoted in Williamson, *The Politics of Grand Strategy*, 193); Hankey, *Supreme Command*, i. 79.   56 Asquith to Haldane, 31 Aug. 1911.
57 Germains, *The Tragedy of Winston Churchill*, 51.
58 Radcliffe, 'W.F. Scheme 1914' (TNA, WO 106/49A/1).

opportunities available to the British army, not just alongside the French, but the Belgians as well.[59] At the 23 August meeting Wilson had stated that the expeditionary force would concentrate around Maubeuge on the Franco-Belgian frontier (a little further forward than the Arras–Cambrai–St Quentin zone envisaged in the Wilson–Dubail agreement). The assumption was that in an invasion of France the German forces would only cross Belgian territory south of the River Meuse. Wilson argued that there were three reasons why the Germans would not extend their right wing any further north. First, to do this they would have to infringe Dutch neutrality in the 'Maastrict appendix'. Second, they would need to divert too many troops to reduce the Belgian fortresses at Liège, Huy, and Namur. Finally, while the Belgians would most likely accept 'the violation of their southern provinces, they would almost certainly fight if the Germans were to invade northern Belgium as well'.[60]

Prompted by Lloyd George, who considered that co-ordinated Anglo-Belgian operations should be encouraged, Churchill came to Wilson's office and stayed for three hours discussing the possibilities. Over the next fortnight or so the two men had several more meetings, and Wilson also had private sessions with both Grey and Lloyd George.[61] What emerged from this was broad agreement between Wilson and Churchill on the high importance of securing, if possible, a British alliance with Belgium which could underpin Anglo-Belgian military operations on the flank of an invading German force. But Wilson's support for a Belgian alliance provoked a sharp reaction from both Haldane and Nicholson. Haldane told Churchill that Wilson was 'a little impulsive. He is an Irishman &, while good, knows little of the Belgian Army.'[62] This was certainly over-dismissive. It was, of course, precisely Wilson's job to know about the Belgian army. In January 1911 he had visited Brussels, dined with members of the Belgian General Staff, and motored across the southern part of the country, from Namur to Luxembourg, with Colonel Tom Bridges, the British military attaché in Brussels.[63] Nicholson was no more enamoured than Haldane of this 'fresh proposal', which would, he claimed, 'involve a radical change in our scheme for supporting France'.[64] Nicholson, moreover, suppressed a lengthy paper by Wilson on 'the political and military situation in Europe', which argued the potential high importance of Anglo-Belgian military action on the German flank.[65]

What is interesting about this discussion is that, while we find Nicholson supporting the 'pure' British commitment to France, Wilson is arguing for a more

[59] See Wilson, *Empire and Continent*, 126–40.

[60] CID 114th meeting, 23 Aug. 1911 (TNA, CAB 2/2/2).

[61] Wilson diary, 28, 31 Aug., 4–5, 12–14 Sept. 1911.

[62] Wilson to Churchill, 29 Aug.; Haldane to Churchill, 31 Aug. 1911 (TNA, ADM 116/3474). Haldane was a Scot.   [63] Wilson diary, 27–8 Jan. 1911.

[64] Nicholson to Churchill, 2 Sept. 1911 (TNA, ADM 116/3474).

[65] 'Appreciation of the Political and Military situation in Europe', 20 Sept. 1911 (Wilson papers, HHW 3/5/18a). Nicholson's successor as CIGS, Sir John French, had this paper printed and circulated to the CID in April 1912.

flexible, and less exclusively French, position. This, in turn, might modify the easy assumptions of some historians about Wilson's apparently simplistic and unvarying 'devotion to all things French'.[66] Zara Steiner characterises Wilson as 'a one-man propaganda team for the Anglo-French connection', and the underlying supposition in her study of British diplomacy before the First World War is that Wilson was an uncritically pro-French and rather malign influence on British decision-making.[67] In the light of the 'Belgian option' evidence, moreover, Gerhard Ritter's magisterial and categorical assertion that Wilson was 'a man, who may without reservation be described as wholly in thrall to French aims and ideas', is wrong.[68]

Three points, however, need to be made. The first is that Wilson was and remained a keen and powerful proponent of the French alliance and the Continental commitment. What is being argued here is that his position was less automatic and rigid than has sometimes been asserted. The second point is that, in any case, Wilson was not some sort of 'one-man band' forcing a policy on the country which it would not otherwise have adopted. His general strategic attitudes were shared by most of his army colleagues, and, certainly after August 1911 (if not also before), by the most influential men in the government. The third point (and this might help explain both contemporary and subsequent assessments of Wilson) is, as was strikingly demonstrated at the 23 August meeting, that his very facility and success as what might be called a 'policy entrepreneur', his presence and his verbal plausibility, all combined greatly to magnify his role in the policy-making process. In this pre-war period (and not just then), he was so bright a star (in what admittedly were often pretty dull constellations) that it is sometimes difficult to perceive the other players on the stage.

One reason why Wilson (who was still only a brigadier-general) received such flattering attention from senior politicians during the summer of 1911 was the apparent quality of the information he possessed. Politicians are often attracted by the ostensibly intriguing world of intelligence. Throughout his career Churchill, for one, found secret sources to be seductive, and we can see at one stage of the Agadir crisis how readily he responded to 'hot' intelligence provided by Henry Wilson. On 4 September Wilson had heard from an agent in Belgium called Charrier (who had been turned back at the German frontier) that two German divisions had been deployed in Malmédy just across the border. Wilson thought this 'ominous'. Another report described how the Germans were buying up extra stocks of wheat. Late that evening at home he received a letter from Major Twiss (an officer in M.O.2) in Bavaria 'describing the present warlike temper of the German people'. Wilson was sufficiently alarmed by the cumulative effect of these pieces of information that he telephoned Churchill at the Café Royal, where

[66] Kennedy, 'Great Britain before 1914', 191.

[67] Steiner, *Britain and the Origins of the First World War*, 197, and *passim*. This assumption remains the same in the second edition of this work, by Steiner and Neilson.

[68] Ritter, *The Sword and the Scepter*, 71.

he was having dinner with Sir Edward Grey. Churchill and Grey, in their turn, were concerned enough to call in at Wilson's house at eleven o'clock and stay on discussing the situation until after midnight.[69]

Wilson got information from a variety of sources. One was fellow officers, like Twiss, travelling on the Continent (as Wilson did himself). Military attachés, especially those in Paris (Fairholme), Brussels (Bridges), and Berlin (Russell) were also important.[70] On 6 September Jimmy Grierson, who had been in France, told Wilson that the French (improbably) were 'going to attack'. There were also secret service agents. On 18 September Wilson received 'no less than four reports of our S.S. from the frontier saying German troops were massing along Belgian frontier'.[71] Wilson was responsible for military intelligence at a time when the modern British intelligence community was being established. In February 1909 James Edmonds, head of the 'special section' in M.O.5, produced an alarmist report about German espionage in Britain. Across the country, it seemed, German clerks, waiters, and barbers were gathering intelligence for the enemy.[72] Even Wilson, though by no means as gullible and credulous as Edmonds, was affected by 'espionage fever', and in 1908 had excluded two German barbers from the Staff College.[73] By the time Wilson became DMO, Colonel George Macdonogh had taken over M.O.5, and embryonic separate agencies for counter-espionage (M.I.5) and foreign intelligence (M.I.6) had been established, headed by Colonel Vernon Kell and Commander (RN) Mansfield Cumming respectively. The documentation is sparse for these inchoate, early days, and although the organisations were by no means integrated into Wilson's directorate (or that of his naval counterpart, Admiral Bethell), Wilson certainly met the intelligence chiefs from time to time. Kell had a 'biennial meeting' with the DMO, and reported specific matters to him.[74] In November 1911 Wilson dined with Lord Haldane, 'Cumming & Kell also'.[75]

Wilson, meanwhile, continued to go intelligence-gathering himself. In October 1911, when the international crisis had eased, he set off for Belgium, where he spent a week with Major 'Fanny' Farquhar, an officer in M.O.3, mostly cycling around the zone south of the Meuse where Wilson expected the German right wing to be. They also explored the French side of the frontier between Avensnes and Hirson. Wilson continued on his own further south, to Verdun and the 1870 battlefield at Mars-la-Tour which he used to visit with the Staff College

[69] Wilson diary, 4 Sept. 1911. For Churchill's attitude towards secret sources, see Andrew, 'Churchill and Intelligence'; and Stafford, 'Churchill and Intelligence'.
[70] Wilson diary, 20 Mar. 1911.
[71] Ibid., 6, 18 Sept. 1911. Wilson also noted secret agent reports on 12 and 19 Sept.
[72] For 'invasion fever' and the early history of the intelligence community, see Andrew, *Secret Service*.   [73] Wilson diary, 9 Mar. 1908.
[74] See '10th report on Secret Service', Apr.–Oct. 1913, 'copy submitted to DMO' (TNA, KV1/9); Kell diary, 29 July, 15 Nov., 1, 22 May, 8 June 1911 (TNA, KV1/10). There is no mention of these meetings in Wilson's diary.
[75] Wilson diary, 26 Nov. 1911. Haldane accepted a peerage in March 1911.

students. Here there was a statue representing 'France', and on 16 October, in a sentimental (if not also sacramental) gesture, he 'laid at her feet a small bit of the map I have been carrying showing the areas of concentration of the British forces on her territory'. The next day he visited Fort St Michel at Toul, east of Nancy: 'an immensely strong place, quite impregnable except by siege.' He ended the tour with a couple of days' break based in Neuchâtel in Switzerland. Returning back through Brussels, where he stayed with the attaché, he was still thinking of the possibilities of an alliance. 'I think', he wrote on 24 October, 'we ought to be able to snaffle these Belgians.'[76]

In the middle of November, Wilson's valued position in the General Staff was confirmed when he came under criticism from some Radical Cabinet ministers. The 'Peace party', as Wilson put it, began to call for his removal, arguing that he had 'forced the pace during the crisis, & they quote all my teaching at the S.C. as evidence of my villainy'. But Haldane told him 'there was no question of my being asked to leave the W.O., on the contrary he twice told me how "amazingly" well I had done & how I had impressed his colleagues at the meeting of Aug. 23rd'. There was, noted Wilson the next day, a 'grave difference between the good members of the Cabinet (Asquith, Haldane, Winston, Lloyd George & possibly Grey) and the wasters (Morley, McKenna, Harcourt, Crewe & the like)' as regards the 23 August decision.[77]

During the Agadir crisis Douglas Haig, in one of a series of friendly letters written from India where he was Chief of Staff, remarked to Henry Wilson: 'What times you seem to be having at home. But these war scares should do good if the lesson of unpreparedness is driven home in the right quarters.'[78] He was correct, and after the crisis had passed, detailed and effective planning for all aspects of the expeditionary force was finally begun. Reflecting in April 1913 about progress on the scheme, Wilson noted the significance of the 1911 crisis in changing the atmosphere and accelerating the planning process. In his post-war account, Percy Radcliffe added that the key branch in Wilson's directorate was M.O.1, which Colonel George 'Uncle' Harper headed from June 1911. 'From having been a rather academic and sterile branch, living in a rarefied atmosphere of its own,' wrote Radcliffe, it 'became the mainspring of all our preparations for war.'[79] Matters were additionally helped when Winston Churchill moved to the Admiralty (in a straight swap with McKenna), where he pepped up the navy staff and offered Wilson cooperation between the navy and the army. Early in 1912, when Wilson was receiving reports that war with Germany was likely in the spring, he found William Nicholson dilatory about 'getting ready for war'.

[76] Ibid., 4–24 Oct. 1911.   [77] Ibid., 16–18 Nov. 1911.
[78] Haig to Wilson, 7 Sept. 1911 (Wilson papers, HHW 2/70/17). There are six other letters from Haig, Mar.–Nov. 1911 (ibid. 2/70/1, 3–4, 6–7, 19).
[79] 'Minute to CIGS reporting progress on scheme of E.F.', Apr. 1913 (Wilson papers, HHW 3/7/2); Radcliffe, 'W.F. Scheme 1914' (TNA, WO 106/49A/1). Harper had been on the directing staff at the Staff College from May 1908 to December 1910.

By contrast, Churchill (who continued to consult Wilson on a regular basis) 'at all events, is alive to the German danger'.[80]

In March 1912 Nicholson retired. Wilson's assessment of his time at the War Office was typically sweeping: 'I doubt if, in the whole time he has been C.I.G.S., he has done a single thing to prepare the Army for war.' He had higher hopes for the new CIGS, Sir John French, who on his first day in the office told his three directors, Wilson, Murray (DMT), and Kiggell (DSD) 'what he hoped to do. In effect it was that he intended to get the Army ready for war. This', noted Wilson, 'is good news.'[81] French, who was no brain-box, generally proved receptive to Wilson's ideas. He was, for example, persuaded to explore the possibility of a military alliance with Belgium, though in the end Belgian nervousness about upsetting Germany, coupled with suspicions of British motives, caused them to maintain a strictly neutral position up to the outbreak of war.[82] By November 1912 Wilson felt able to note some good news about his war planning. 'At last,' he wrote, 'after 2 years we got off our railway time tables to the Commands.' Indeed, as Samuel Williamson has observed, no part of the mobilisation arrangements 'was so carefully studied and computed' as the rail movements.[83] The eventual despatch of the expeditionary force from just three English ports—Southampton for troops, Avonmouth for mechanical transport, and Newhaven for stores—ran very well. 'As a matter of fact,' recalled Sir Charles Deedes, 'the running of trains in and out of Southampton docks worked perfectly and was a model of railway organization.'[84]

But it still took time. Despite Churchill's presence the Admiralty were slow to get going, though eventually a joint committee with the War Office, including representatives of the merchant-shipping industry, was set up which met twice a week from February 1913, and finally produced a workable scheme in the spring of 1914. The General Staff co-ordination was handled by M.O.1, under Harper, with three officers seconded from the QMG's department. Rather like the Intelligence side, the branch was small, and included no more than ten officers in all. Because of the necessity for secrecy, 'the clerical work was done by officers, no clerks having access to any of the most secret papers', and the original railway timetables were personally typed out by one officer before being 'printed off in the secret War Office Press'.[85]

During 1911 and 1912 Henry Wilson continued to visit the Continent, combining business with pleasure. En route to his annual skiing holiday in February 1911, he inspected the docks at Rouen, had meetings in Paris with the French Chief of Staff, Joffre, his principal strategic adviser, General de Cuières de Castelnau, and the War Minister, Alexandre Millerand, and dropped in on Foch,

[80] Wilson diary, 8 Jan. 1912.   [81] Ibid., 14, 16 Mar. 1912.
[82] Gooch, *Plans of War*, 292–3.
[83] Wilson diary, 14 Nov. 1912; Williamson, *The Politics of Grand Strategy*, 312.
[84] Scott (ed.), 'The View From the War Office', 15.
[85] Radcliffe, 'W.F. Scheme 1914' (TNA, WO 106/49A/1).

now commanding a division at Chaumont. At the Hotel Europe in Montreux the next day he encountered a party of English lady travellers: 'I never saw so many "frights" as there are in this hotel. Old Girton girls I should think.'[86] At the end of the holiday he spent a few days with his friend and colleague (he worked in M.O.2) 'Tit Willow'—Major Charles Sackville-West—once again investigating southern Belgium and the Maastrict 'appendix'.[87] In April he spent two days in Ostend playing golf with Tom Bridges and briefing him for talks to try to secure an understanding with Belgium. 'The Belgians', he thought, 'really must strengthen Liege & Namur as if the Germans stretch north the problem is much more difficult.'[88] How right he was.

In the autumn of 1912 Wilson went to Russia, taking in Paris (where he was introduced to the French Foreign Minister) and the French army manoeuvres on the way out. In Paris he ran into his old colleague Jack Cowans, by now QMG, who had checked into the hotel with a Mrs McCalmont, posing as her husband. Evidently this was not much of a surprise, as it elicited no special comment in his diary.[89] With Alfred Knox (the British military attaché) he went round Warsaw and discussed 'the Polish and E. Prussian problem which, now that I have seen something of the country, has become alive to me'. Two days later, he met General Zhilinski, the Russian Chief of Staff, who 'was very civil but exceedingly non-committal', and 'very anxious to know what I was doing in St Petersburg'. In fact, it seems that Wilson's visit was more of a 'jolly' than a serious intelligence-gathering exercise. From Moscow he visited the 1812 Napoleonic battlefield of Borodino.[90] After visiting Kiev, Lemburg, Cracow, and Vienna he had intended to travel on to Constantinople (Istanbul), but tension between Bulgaria and Turkey, which erupted into the 'First Balkan War', prevented this and he went on to Venice before returning home through Paris. As with the Moroccan crisis the previous year, the Balkan situation added point to war planning at home. Wilson felt his constant emphasis on the importance of a speedy mobilisation was vindicated by reports of a Bulgarian victory over the Turks 'exactly a month after mobilization was ordered. It must be a warning', he wrote, 'for fools like Haldane' who thought they would have '6 mos. preparation after declaration of war'.[91]

British liaison with the French also intensified. During 1913 Wilson made seven visits to France, regularly seeing Joffre, Castelnau, and Foch. In August he went with Sir John French and Jimmy Grierson to the French manoeuvres near Châlons on the Marne east of Paris, and in September to the manoeuvres of the XXᵉᵐᵉ Army Corps of which Foch was now GOC. We get an indication of Wilson's facility in the French language from this latter visit in his notes for an after-dinner speech. Much is made of Wilson's fluency in French, and of

[86] Wilson diary, 2–5 Feb. 1912.
[87] Ibid., 27 Feb.–3 Mar. 1912. Sackville–West had been one of Wilson's directing staff at the Staff College. [88] Ibid., 5–7 Apr. 1912.
[89] Ibid., 7 Sept. 1912.   [90] Ibid., 24, 26, 29 Sept. 1912.
[91] Ibid., 1 Nov. 1912.

the importance this had in cementing Anglo-French relations. What these notes indicate is that while he was evidently fluent, his French was not always absolutely accurate, yet he spoke it with a characteristic and engaging enthusiasm, which his French listeners clearly and understandably found attractive:

M Général et Messieurs je vous remercie de pleine cour pour l'acceuil si bienfaisant que vous m'avez faites. J'ai souvant vu les soldats francais en campagne, et chaque fois que je les ai vu, je les aime et je les admire le plus. L'année derniére à vos Grands Manoeuvres j'ai dit que 'je prefererai infinitement me battre avec eux que contre eux'. En causant un jour avec Le Général Lanrezac je lui ai demandé s'il parlait Anglais. Il m'a dit que oui—un peu— c'est à dire qu'il savait l'Anglais pour 'beautiful woman' (Dame charmante), 'Kiss me quick' (Embrassez moi vite) ['Donnez moi un baiser vite' crossed out], et 'Beefsteak and potatoes' (Bifsteak et pommes de terre)—et il ajouta qu'avec ces brefs ['trois' crossed out] mots 'on peut faire le tour du monde'. Je crois, mon Général, qu'avec quelques Corps d'Armée comme le Vingtième vous pourriez faire sinon le tour du monde au moins le tour d'Europe.

Je léve mon verre à le Vingtième Corps d'Armée et à l'Armée glorieuse de la France.[92]

Maxime Weygand, Foch's faithful Chief of Staff, recalled that Wilson 'talked French fairly well and could keep up a conversation on any topic, serious or comic'. He would only revert to English 'when discussing an important matter', when he 'did not want to risk using an expression which might be inappropriate'.[93]

In October 1913 Wilson finally reached Constantinople, travelling with his old regimental friend Charlie Hunter, who had been Conservative MP for Bath since 1910. Wilson and Hunter inspected the Charaldhza lines of defence just west of Constantinople and, a few days later, the Lüle Burgaz battlefield where the Bulgarians had defeated the Turks in October the previous year, and the fortress of Adrianople where they were 'shown <u>everything</u>'.[94] Wilson's overall assessment of Turkey was not very optimistic. He thought that the recent introduction of a constitutional, party system of government would probably be 'fatal' to the country. The Turkish army, he noted, 'is <u>not</u> a serious modern army', and the country was poorly developed: 'no roads, only single railways & very few of them, & in fact no sign of adaptation to Western thought & methods.' The army, he concluded, 'is ill

---

[92] Handwritten notes for a speech, Sept. 1913 (Wilson papers, HHW 3/7/5). 'General and gentlemen, I thank you from the bottom of my heart for the warm welcome you have given to me. I have often looked at French soldiers in the field, and each time that I have seen them, I like and admire them more. Last year at your Grand Manoeuvres, I remarked that "I would infinitely prefer to fight with them than against them". Chatting one day with General Lanrezac, I asked if he spoke English. He told me yes—a little—that is to say he knew the English for "beautiful woman", "kiss me quick" and "beefsteak and potatoes"—and he added that with these few words "one could go round the world". I believe, General, that with several Army Corps like the Twentieth you would be able to go round Europe, if not the world. I lift my glass to the Twentieth Army Corps and to the glorious French Army.' A diary note in more accurate French of a brief speech proposing Gen. de Castelnau's health suggests (not implausibly) that his command of the language improved during the war (Wilson diary, 25 Feb. 1917).

[93] Weygand, quoted in Marshall-Cornwall, *Foch as Military Commander*, 147.

[94] Wilson diary, 13, 15–18 Oct. 1912. For the first Balkan War, see Hall, *The Balkan Wars*, ch. 2.

commanded, ill officered & in rags. I cannot think Turkey in Europe will survive another shaking.'[95] In the long term Wilson was, of course, broadly correct, though his dismissive opinions also, no doubt, contributed to the perilous underestimation of Turkish resilience which underlay the disastrous Dardanelles campaign of 1915.

Each year when Wilson went with Cecil to Switzerland—he skiing, she occasionally skating—they let their Eaton Place house. In 1913 they also let it during the early summer London 'Season', and in 1914 for a whole year. When they were not abroad they moved into lodgings, or rented cheaper accommodation. It was, wrote Wilson, 'a bore & yet one can't refuse'.[96] Evidently it made financial sense. In January 1912 they accepted £170 for a nine-week let, and in May–July 1913 the Anglo-Irish Lord Dunsany paid over £250 for seven weeks.[97] In April 1914 they rented out their 'dear 36' for a year, moving to a more modest house at 7 Draycott Place, off the King's Road.[98] At the end of 1912 Wilson calculated that, even after spending £200 putting in two bathrooms at Eaton Place, he had managed to save £500 over the year and pay off some of his mortgage.[99]

During the 1913 Christmas holiday Lord Roberts told Wilson he ought to be promoted to major-general, as his DMO predecessors had been, and said he had written to Johnnie French to say so. Wilson was naturally gratified by the old man's continued support, but worried that if he were promoted it would make him ineligible to command a brigade. This, in turn, might prevent him getting a division, which he hoped the next move would bring. In April (since a brigade command was about fall vacant) he raised the matter with French, who reassured him that he hoped to promote Wilson to major-general before the end of the year, and that lack of a brigade command would not disadvantage him in the matter of a division.[100] In November 1913 Wilson got his promotion. Later that month French revealed to him, 'in utmost secrecy', some ideas for future General Staff appointments. French himself was to have an extension of two years as CIGS, taking him to March 1918. Murray would become 'Sous Chief', and succeed French as CIGS. Wilson, meanwhile, was to get a division when his term as DMO ended, and in 1918 succeed Murray. 'This of course is delightful,' noted Wilson, 'but except for the Division it is looking much too far ahead for our funny little army.'[101] Indeed it was, and more so than either French or Wilson could have anticipated. Wilson was never to get his division, and by August 1914 (when his stint as DMO was due to run out), French was no longer CIGS.

[95] Wilson diary, 9, 18 Oct. 1912.   [96] Ibid., 20 Nov. 1913, 27 Apr., 2 May 1914.

[97] Jan.–Mar. 1912: 9 weeks at 18 guineas (£18.90) per week; May–July 1912, 7 weeks at 35 guineas (£36.75).   [98] Wilson diary, 27 Apr., 2 May 1914.

[99] The Wilson's financial position was also improved by a £1,000 legacy Cecil received in 1911 from her Aunt Juliet (Wilson diary, 12 Dec. 1911, 1 May, 31 Dec. 1912).

[100] Ibid., 4–5 Jan., 31 Mar., 1 Apr. 1913.   [101] Ibid., 22 Nov. 1913.

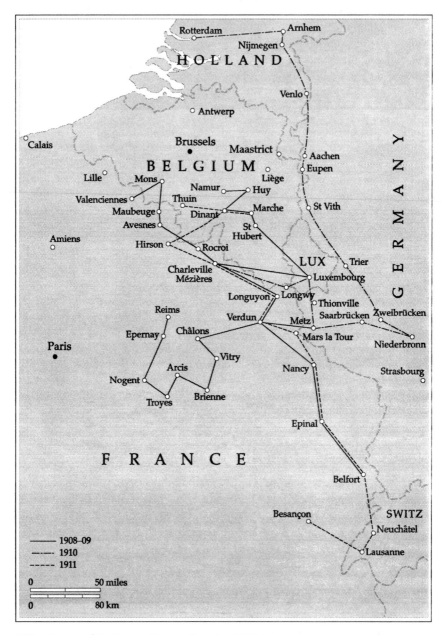

Wilson's tours of the Franco-German Frontier, 1908–11

7

Politics, the Irish question, and war

Henry Wilson's reputation as a 'political' general, with an unrivalled name for mischievous intrigue, very substantially stems from the years 1912–14, when the balance of British politics, the continuing campaign for conscription, and the Irish question combined to intensify his engagement with party politics. Wilson was an up-and-coming officer, to whom the highest ranks of the army were beginning to beckon. Johnnie French had suggested that he might be sub-Chief of the Imperial General Staff by 1918 which, at the age of 53 or 54, would put him next to the very top. Nicholson had been 63 before becoming CIGS, and French 59. Increasingly, too, Wilson was coming into contact with senior politicians. He was regularly consulted by the Secretary of State for War and attended meetings of the CID. His performance at the meeting on 23 August 1911, moreover, had catapulted him into closer relations with Cabinet ministers than most of his fellow General Staff officers enjoyed. Writing fifteen years after Wilson's death, Sir Sam Fay, a railway executive who worked in the War Office in 1917–19, acidly quoted the opinion of an unnamed senior general that 'whenever Wilson came within a mile of prominent politicians he suffered from a sexual disturbance'.[1] Be that as it may, it is undoubtedly true that Wilson enjoyed the attention of ministers like Churchill and Lloyd George, and, increasingly after 1910, that of opposition Conservative and Unionist politicians as well.

The landslide election victory of 1906 which gave the Liberals a huge parliamentary majority sustained a programme of reformist legislation which laid the foundations for the modern welfare state in Britain. But the introduction of a broadly based national insurance scheme, old-age pensions, and labour exchanges, together with other education, housing, and health reforms (not to mention increased naval expenditure to keep ahead of the Germans), all cost money, and David Lloyd George, the Chancellor of the Exchequer, sought to raise taxes to pay for the reforms. In 1909 his so-called 'People's Budget' was rejected by the House of Lords, precipitating a constitutional crisis which turned on the

---

[1] Fay, *The War Office at War*, 100. Fay added that the general 'did not put it in these words, his language was vulgar and obscene'. In contrast to this colourful observation, the surviving exchange of letters between Fay and Wilson on the former's retirement from the War Office is entirely friendly. Fay thanked Wilson for the 'consideration' he had given to him, and Wilson wrote that 'it was always a real pleasure to me to see you come into my room.... "Happy go you" as the Dutch say' (Fay to Wilson and vice versa, 3 and 7 May 1919 (Wilson papers, HHW 2/67/84).

relative powers of the Commons and the non-elected Lords, where the Conservatives were in an overwhelming majority. The Liberals' response was to introduce a bill abolishing the Lords' traditional veto, replacing it with the power merely to delay legislation approved by the Commons. In 1910 two heated elections were fought on the issue, which the Liberals won, though with a much reduced majority, and in 1911 the Parliament Bill was forced through the Lords, against Asquith's threat to flood the House with enough new Liberal peers to ensure the bill's passage.

The party battle over the 'Veto Bill', as it was known, was extremely intense and bitter. The Conservatives claimed that the Liberals were out to destroy the constitution, undermine all traditional authority, and would plunge the country into political and social chaos. For them the increasing number of Labour MPs (thirty in 1906, forty-two at the end of 1910), the growing incidence of industrial unrest, and the emergence of a militant 'votes for women' campaign represented further challenges to the established order. Part of the domestic political agenda of the National Service League, indeed, was the assertion that compulsory national service might help to regenerate the nation by taming and channelling turbulent social energies (though presumably not, or not directly, those of women). Although there was some attempt to make the campaign an all-party one, leading Liberals were reluctant to offer any public support. Both Churchill and Lloyd George, nevertheless, occasionally expressed support for conscription in private.[2] For the most part, the leadership of the League was dominated by unambiguously conservative property-owning types.[3]

These were the sort of people Wilson increasingly began to move among, at first mainly through his close relationship with Lord Roberts, but also after he moved back to London in 1910 and developed his own social networks. His friendships with Conservative MPs like Leo Amery, Arthur Lee, and Charlie Hunter (who passed on Wilson gossip to party colleagues[4]), and aristocrats such as Earl Percy and Simon Lovat, reinforced his own political predilections. In January 1910 he 'voted for the first time in my life in a Parliamentary Election' for a Conservative and Unionist candidate.[5] Amery and Hunter introduced him to Conservative writers and publicists like J. L. Garvin (editor of the *Observer*), H. A. Gwynne (editor of the *Morning Post*), and F. S. Oliver, an especially keen conscriptionist, owner of Debenham and Freebody's department store, and described by one historian as 'the most intellectual draper in the country'.[6]

Wilson provided much 'off the record' support for the National Service League. He briefed publicists like Oliver and Percy, and helped to co-ordinate press

[2] Wilson diary, 5 Nov. 1912; Williamson, *Politics of Grand Strategy*, 305.

[3] Adams, 'The National Service League', 64–5.

[4] Such as Robert Sandars, a Conservative whip, 1910–14 (see Ramsden (ed.), *Real Old Tory Politics*, 31, 67, 80).   [5] Wilson diary, 26 Jan. 1910.

[6] Morris, *The Scaremongers*, 484. This is an excellent guide to the political debates and journalism about British foreign and strategic policy in the pre-war period.

campaigns. In December 1912, for example, Wilson, Oliver, and Gwynne worked together on a campaign first to destroy the Territorial Force, and then 'force the Govt. to go to the Opposition about compulsory service'.[7] The following May he helped Percy with an article demolishing 'the voluntary principle' for the *National Review*. 'This was entirely my idea,' recorded Wilson, '& I gave him a lot of my notes.'[8] Wilson continued to draft national service speeches for Lord Roberts, even though the two men did not entirely agree on the degree to which compulsion should be applied. Wilson was a 'whole hogger', favouring the imposition of full conscription along the Continental model, while Roberts was only prepared to propose it to create a 'citizen army' for home defence. Roberts believed that overseas service should remain voluntary. Wilson, well aware of the unique value of the Chief's support for the campaign, firmly ruled that 'we (the whole hoggers) should not quarrel with Lord Bobs'.[9]

For Wilson, as DMO and conscriptionist, the Territorial Force raised difficulties which exposed his shortcomings as a truly 'political' operator. It was the perennial political issue of achievability, the 'art of the possible'. On the one hand, Wilson was faced with the existence of the force, which, while imperfect and under-strength, had regularised the voluntary military effort in Great Britain, and did provide some basis for home defence organisation. On the other, he was so committed to the ideal of full national service that he simply dismissed any other option as quite useless. His tendency to focus, perhaps obsessively, on specific targets, which was a strength when directed towards the minutiae of perfecting a detailed mobilisation scheme, was a considerable weakness in other spheres of wider national policy, where his political prejudices tended to blind him to the possibility of any alternatives. His success in promoting the Continental commitment at the CID, moreover, seems to have persuaded him that simply by force of argument (and brilliance of presentation) he could advance the cause of so self-evidently the right policy as conscription. But persuading a group of senior decision-makers, already generally disposed towards the matter in question, was a very different matter to selling a radical new policy to the country at large.

Haldane had correctly judged that British public opinion would not easily accept compulsory military service, a conclusion shared by his Under-secretary of State, J. E. S. Seely, who became War Minister in June 1912, after Haldane was appointed Lord Chancellor. 'I suppose we shall get Jack Seely', wrote Wilson. 'Ye Gods.'[10] Seely, a rather flamboyant figure, who had served in South Africa, been elected as a Conservative MP, but (like his friend Churchill) crossed the House to the Liberals, was regarded as a bit of a lightweight in the War Office.

[7] Wilson diary, 5, 8, 10 Dec. 1912.

[8] Ibid., 2, 14 May 1913; Earl Percy, 'The Voluntary System in History', *National Review*, 41 (June 1913), 629–51.

[9] Wilson diary, 16 Nov., 7 Dec. 1912, 9 Mar. 1913; Earl Roberts, 'National Service Ideals' (speeches given at Leeds, 18 Apr., and Glasgow, 6 May 1913), *National Review*, 41 (June 1913), 658–73. [10] Wilson diary, 10 June 1912

Besides, 'a madly enthusiastic yeomanry colonel was exactly what Wilson and the other generals did not want'.[11] In April 1913, to Wilson's amazement, Seely told the House of Commons not only that the existing Territorial Force could see off an invasion force of 70,000 men, but also that the General Staff were 'against compulsory service'. Wilson told French that he and his two fellow directors would resign if Seely did not correct this 'lie'. French secured a partial retraction, but was less firm with the minister than Wilson desired. French had just been promoted Field Marshal, which 'made him anxious not to be more nasty to Seely than he could help', and even Wilson recognised that this was a 'very natural' attitude.[12]

A further problem concerning the Territorial Force was that if, as Wilson asserted, it were wholly useless, then home defence might have to be provided by some of the regular formations earmarked to be part of the expeditionary force, an issue which came up in an 'invasion inquiry' run by the CID during 1913 and early 1914, and which explored the possibilities of German raids, or even a 'bolt from the blue' (a recurring worry of the 'blue water' school), and the efficacy of the Territorial Force. To give him his due (which Wilson did not), Seely sought the committee's approval for the despatch of the whole Expeditionary Force on the outbreak of war, and when Wilson gave evidence to the CID in November 1912, Seely backed up his reiteration that the presence of British divisions on the Continent could play a decisive role.[13]

One ironic result of the conscription campaign was that it brought about a brief quasi-reconciliation between Wilson and Repington. For years they had maintained unremittingly hostile relations, and whenever they chanced to meet, cut each other dead.[14] In November 1912 Repington told Haldane that Wilson's 'constant intrigues threaten the existence of the TF' (which Repington thought could provide a framework for compulsion), and that he should be replaced by Wully Robertson, 'who would give you the ballast now wholly lacking'.[15] In the spring of 1913, however, Simon Lovat said 'it was absolutely essential' that Wilson should meet Repington. Wilson refused point blank until Roberts also asked him, and the two men subsequently dined together (among others), and had lunch at Lovat's house with Roberts to discuss what Repington and Roberts should say to the invasion inquiry. Wilson even noted an 'excellent letter' by Repington in *The Times*, asking why 'the Director of Military Operations, who is best qualified to explain the military resources which foreign countries possess for invading us', was not on the inquiry committee ('Just as glad I am not', he thought).[16]

[11] Scott, *Galloper Jack*, 134. This racily written book is not to be relied upon for matters of fact.
[12] Wilson diary, 12, 14–18, 20 Apr. 1913.
[13] Ibid., 12 Nov. 1912; Williamson, *Politics of Grand Strategy*, 307–10.
[14] See e.g. Wilson diary, 3 June 1912.
[15] Repington to Haldane, 27 Nov. 1912 (quoted in Morris, *The Scaremongers*, 322).
[16] Wilson diary, 26, 31 Mar., 10, 14 Apr., 28 June 1913; *The Times*, 14 Apr. 1913. The two men do not appear to have met again after June 1913. The following year, however, when the 'Curragh

Wilson's political activities in the years immediately preceding the First World War were increasingly suffused by the growing crisis over Irish home rule. The 'Irish question' was one of the great political issues of nineteenth- and early twentieth-century British politics.[17] Aiming to satisfy growing Irish nationalist calls for the repeal of the Act of Union, and the revival of an Irish parliament in Dublin, the great Liberal leader Gladstone had introduced Irish 'Home Rule' bills in 1886 and 1893. Neither passed into law. The first split his party, with Liberal Unionists led by Joseph Chamberlain, breaking away (and eventually joining the Conservatives). The second was passed in the Commons, but soundly rejected by the Conservatives in the Lords. After 1906 it seemed extremely likely that the Liberals, back in power with a comfortable majority, would again address the question. This became certain once the House of Lords' veto was abolished, and a third Irish Home Rule Bill was introduced in the spring of 1912.

In Ireland political opinion divided principally (though by no means exclusively) along sectarian lines: most Protestants were sympathetic to unionism; most Catholics to nationalism. Catholics, moreover, were in a clear majority across the island. Over the nineteenth century the Irish nationalist movement assumed an increasingly Catholic character, raising among Protestant unionists old fears of religious domination, more suited, perhaps, to the seventeenth than the nineteenth or twentieth century, but certainly very real all the same. For them, home rule threatened to be 'Rome rule'. In the province of Ulster, comprising the northernmost nine counties of the island, Protestants were in a majority, and here the resistance to home rule was strongest. Not only was there strength in Protestant numbers, but the commercial and industrial success of the north— textiles (especially linen), engineering, and shipbuilding—in contrast to the comparative economic stagnation of the predominantly agricultural south, underscored Ulster unionist beliefs in their general superiority and demonstrated an economic rationality to the Union. Belfast, in short, was a more demonstrably 'British' city than Dublin or Cork, and the interests of Ulster's prosperous capitalists (as well as the industrial working class) clearly (it was argued) lay in a British and British imperial sphere much wider than anything which could be offered by a home-rule parliament in Dublin. In the south and west, unionists, for the most part, were more widely spread and socially privileged than in the north, and the leadership of Irish unionism was dominated by landowners and grandees of the so-called 'Ascendancy class'.

With their Ulster roots and southern estates, the Wilson family had a foot in both unionist camps. Passionate unionists, Henry Wilson's father and his elder brother, Jemmy, as we have seen, both vainly stood for parliament in the 1880s. In 1903 Wilson's father was selected by the Landowners' Convention to be part of a deputation sent to London to monitor the progress of Irish land legislation

incident' was being discussed in parliament, Repington telephoned Wilson for guidance about what line *The Times* should take (Wilson diary, 21 Apr. 1914).

[17] A good general account, upon which I have drawn, is Jalland, *The Liberals and Ireland.*

through parliament.[18] In 1906 Wilson's younger brother Tono worked in Swindon as a Conservative Party agent.[19] Among their political heroes was Joseph Chamberlain. In February 1895, for example, Henry and Cecil went to a mass meeting in Stepney, East London, 'at which Joe Chamberlain made a very fine speech, which we all enjoyed immensely'.[20] The attractions of Chamberlain's heady mix of unionism, imperialism, 'improvement', and progress perhaps reflected the Wilsons' Belfast mercantile past more than their more recent landed squirearchical pretensions. Henry Wilson, the keen military moderniser, was no conservative for conservatism's sake. Indeed, it might be hazarded that he was mainly a conservative for *unionism's* sake, since a central tenet of Conservative Party faith from the late 1880s to 1922 was the maintenance of the legislative union between Britain and Ireland.

Wilson kept a keen weather eye on political affairs. During the first general election of 1910 he remarked that 'the lies told by the Radicals from Asquith down are revolting'. After the results began to come in he thought the elections had been 'going well....We are only three votes behind Liberals & Labours combined.'[21] In the second 1910 election he again hoped the Liberals would be defeated: 'We [Wilson had been talking to his brother Arthur] all feel we are going to knock Asquith hard & sensibly reduce his majority.'[22] Alas not. Asquith took the Liberal victory, however narrow, as sufficient of a mandate to force through the Parliament Act, and when the final stages of its passage coincided with the Agadir crisis, Wilson extravagantly thought it 'one of the most momentous weeks of our history'.[23]

He was probably not very wrong so far as the Ulster unionists were concerned. The certainty of a measure to apply home rule in Ireland powerfully galvanised unionist opposition in the North, to such an extent that by 1914 the issue was accompanied by a very real threat of civil war in Ireland.[24] Irish unionists had been contemplating organised, military ways of resisting home rule since the 1890s. Tipped into Wilson's diary for 1893 are two pages of notes he wrote about a proposal 'to force Gladstone's hand by showing beyond doubt that the loyalists of Ireland are determined to fight ag[ains]t all government set over them, other than the Imp[eria]l Govt.'. Concerned that the generally law-abiding nature of Irish loyalists (in contrast, of course, to nationalist troublemakers) had led the British to assume that they would meekly accept any home-rule legislation passed

---

[18] *The Times*, 15 Aug. 1907.   [19] Wilson diary, 16 Nov. 1906.

[20] Ibid., 6 Feb. 1895. The speech was devoted to London municipal questions (*The Times*, 7 Feb. 1895). Wilson went to other Chamberlain political meetings (see his diary for 22 May 1895).

[21] Wilson diary, 6, 27 Jan. 1910. This was an optimistic underestimate. By the end of the election (9 Feb.) the Conservatives (273 seats) were 42 behind the Liberals (275) and Labour (40). The Irish Party won 82 seats.

[22] Ibid., 30 Nov. 1910. This was another overestimation. The final result was; Conservative, 272 seats; Liberal, 272; Labour, 42; Irish Party, 84.   [23] Ibid., 23 July 1911.

[24] The classic, and still indispensable, account of these developments is Stewart, *The Ulster Crisis*, but see also Foy, 'The Ulster Volunteer Force'.

at Westminster, Wilson aimed 'to <u>force</u>' the government 'to take notice, & a very serious notice'. He proposed that 'a number, say 2,000, or 4,000 men enlist & commence drill at once' in a number of towns and villages across Ulster. 'Let them look upon themselves as soldiers', he wrote, and 'let them <u>so far as possible</u> [but this was a fantastic ambition] be both Protestants & R.C.s'. He said that the men should not in the first instance wear uniforms or carry arms, and that they should maintain that they were 'drilling for self defence in case of need', and had 'no quarrel with the Queen'. Sound military organisation on these lines would provide 'in case of war, a <u>very</u> material advantage'.[25]

But if these dramatic and, as it were, rhetorical methods did not convince English public opinion that 'Ulster' was serious, then more definitely practical measures would have to be taken. Towards the end of 1910 Wilson noted Walter Long, an English MP who was leader of the Irish Unionist MPs, asserting that 'the north of Ireland would fight'. A week later Charlie Hunter told Wilson that he looked 'to Ulster to save the situation by threat of arms if necessary'.[26] While Irish and Ulster unionists might have been expected to take an extreme line on the question of home rule, what needs to be explained, however, is why the British Conservatives, a party of social and constitutional propriety, and of law and order, toyed with clearly unconstitutional methods, extending even to violence (or at least the threat of it), against a lawfully constituted government.

British support for the Union was sustained by a powerful mixture of high moral principle and low political advantage. The unionists marshalled constitutional arguments—for example, that the abolition of the ancient powers of the House of Lords was unconstitutional—and asserted 'British rights'—arguing that the government simply could not expel loyal citizens from the United Kingdom. With a kind of electoral legerdemain, they further asserted that the Liberals, despite their clear majority in the House of Commons, had no democratic mandate to break up the kingdom. After the December 1910 election the numbers of Liberal and Unionist MPs in the House of Commons were exactly equal, at 272. The Unionists asserted that the passage of the measure would depend only on the 84 Irish Party MPs, who, as representatives of a purely sectional interest, had no right to impose their views on the kingdom as a whole. This calculation glossed over the fact that 17 of the Unionist MPs were Irish, and, more importantly, that the 42 Labour MPs were likely to support home rule. Even if the Irish MPs abstained, the government could command a majority for the measure. But the electoral balance was apparently narrowing, coming close enough for the Conservatives to nurse hopes that they could win the *next* general election.

A key figure in the definition of Conservative Party strategy during these years was Andrew Bonar Law, who took over from Balfour as party leader in the Commons in November 1911. Bonar Law had Ulster Scottish roots, and to this

---

[25] Undated notes (Wilson papers, HHW 1/1).   [26] Wilson diary, 29 Nov., 7 Dec. 1910.

has been ascribed his passionate support for the unionist cause.[27] His father was an Ulster-born Presbyterian minister who returned to his home district of Coleraine, where his son was a regular visitor. While Bonar Law's background undoubtedly coloured some of his responses, his policy as a stronger and more determined party leader than has sometimes been recognised seems chiefly to have been directed towards forcing the Liberals into calling another general election.[28] In April 1912 he came to a monster protest meeting in Belfast, scheduled for the day before the first reading debate began on the Home Rule Bill. *The Times* estimated that 80,000 to 100,000 men marched 'in military order' past Bonar Law, who spoke warmly in support of a motion that: 'We will never, in any circumstances, submit to Home Rule.' On the platform with Law, representing southern unionists and also speaking, was Henry Wilson's brother, Jemmy. 'A great honour', noted Wilson in his diary. A couple of days later Leo Amery (who had also been at the Belfast meeting) reported to Wilson Bonar Law's opinion 'that if the North of Ireland resort to fighting so might all loyal men in this country'.[29] As the Home Rule Bill continued its stately progress through parliament, some sort of 'direct action' seemed increasingly likely.

Charlie Hunter, who had also been to Belfast, was one of a number of prominent British Conservatives who formed the 'Ulster Defence League', under Walter Long's chairmanship, to promote propaganda work in Britain. During the summer of 1912 Jemmy Wilson came over for this, and told his brother he was 'enjoying himself hugely' working for Long.[30] Over dinner at Charlie Hunter's house one Sunday night, according to the diary, Cecil Wilson suggested that Henry should meet Bonar Law, and Hunter arranged it a few days later. Wilson, who was impressed by Law's 'quiet unostentatious manner, & his exceedingly logical & practical mind',[31] spent an hour and three-quarters discussing not Ireland but Britain's general strategic position. Over the next few weeks Wilson also had several sessions with Walter Long, again devoted to wide strategic matters. Long was keen to establish a cross-party understanding on defence matters and, curiously, used Wilson to pass messages on to Winston Churchill.[32]

The peculiar thing about this matter is that none of the men involved seems to have thought that the use of a senior serving General Staff officer by a leading member of the opposition to act as an intermediary with the First Lord of the Admiralty was at all an odd way of going about things. But it does reflect the permeability of the political and military elites in early twentieth-century Britain, and the interconnecting social networks into which Wilson had already been drawn through his closeness to Lord Roberts and friendship with (among others) Leo Amery and Charlie Hunter. The personalities of those concerned (though this

---

[27] Blake, *The Unknown Prime Minister*, 19, 22, 125–30; Adams, *Bonar Law*, 98–100.
[28] This is the argument of Smith, *The Tories and Ireland*, 5.
[29] *The Times*, 10 Apr. 1912; Wilson diary, 10, 12 Apr. 1912.   [30] Wilson diary, 7 July 1912.
[31] Ibid., 23 June 1912. The Wilsons and Hunters dined together on a fairly regular basis.
[32] Ibid., 27 June, 9, 14–17, 23 July 1912.

applies more to Churchill and Wilson than Walter Long) was another factor. Both men had maverick tendencies, and were wont to operate with scant regard for the propriety of their actions. Imperial defence, moreover, was widely regarded as a subject of such importance that it transcended party divisions, hence the original conception of the Committee of Imperial Defence, to include members outside the government of the day, or the National Service League's efforts to secure multi-party representation among its patrons. The notion that there might be subjects which were above party, or indeed, even government, of course applied with particular force concerning Ireland.

In September 1912 Bonar Law raised the stakes further in a famous speech at a great unionist demonstration at Blenheim Palace. The government, he said, was a 'revolutionary committee which has seized by fraud upon despotic power'. He pledged his support to the Ulster unionists, even apparently to the point of civil war. 'I can', he declared, 'imagine no length of resistance to which Ulster will go in which I shall not be ready to support them and in which they will not be supported by the overwhelming majority of the British people.'[33] Later the same month Ulster unionist solidarity was powerfully affirmed by the carefully choreographed mass signing of a 'Solemn League and Covenant' by over half-a-million people. But none of this held up the Home Rule Bill, which was finally passed by the Commons in January 1913. After the Lords threw it out, the provisions of the Parliament Act allowed for it to become law after the bill had passed through the Commons in two more parliamentary sessions, 1913 and 1914.

Faced with this legislative *fait accompli*, the Ulster unionists embarked on a more definitely military campaign. On 13 March Jemmy, who had come to London in a deputation to meet Bonar Law, told Wilson about Ulster plans to raise a force of 25,000 armed men, with another 100,000 'to act as constables', and to form a provisional government, taking control of banks and railways. 'As far as I could judge,' wrote Wilson, 'all very sensible', a stupendous comment for any law-abiding citizen (let alone a serving soldier) to make about what was in effect a scheme for armed rebellion. What can have brought him to this state of mind? Either (as the Liberals optimistically assumed) it was simply bluster and bluff, in which case sabre-rattling of this sort was a sound policy, or the Unionists were so convinced of the rightness of their cause, and so backed into a political corner, that they could actually contemplate the possibility of civil war. The very matter-of-factness of Wilson's attitude suggests the former, and a parallel could be drawn with his wider, British military view that adequate preparation for war made open conflict with Germany less, rather than more, likely. But the evidence of his behaviour in 1913–14 suggests that he did take seriously the possibility of armed conflict over the home-rule issue. On 16 March Lord Roberts told him he had been asked if he would take command of the 'Army of Ulster', and take

[33] *The Times*, 29 July 1912; Smith, *The Tories and Ireland*, 67–8. There is some ambiguity in the use of the verb 'imagine'.

Wilson as his Chief of Staff. 'I said that if the alternatives were to go & shoot down Ulster or shoot for Ulster I would join him if he took Command. Imagine', he wrote, 'our having come to such a state.'[34]

The 80-year-old Roberts was too old for any sort of active command—a point which adds some weight to the argument that the military mobilisation of Ulster was more symbolic than real—but he enlisted a retired Indian Army general who had settled in Ireland, Sir George Richardson, to take charge of what became the Ulster Volunteer Force (UVF). Organised along British army lines, by the end of 1913 it had 100,000 members and had begun to make a public impact with parades and drills throughout Ulster. It also started to import arms, if as yet on a modest scale. In England a 'British League for the Support of Ulster' was formed to organise and drill young men for service in the Ulster cause, a development which added to the sense of potential civil war.

As the political tension over home rule increased, Sir John French, as CIGS, justifiably became worried that if the army were deployed to keep order in Ireland, it could severely strain the loyalties of individual soldiers. The British officer corps naturally tended to be a conservative body, and the instinctive position of most officers was to be strongly unionist, reinforced in many cases by Irish family links. Indeed French himself was an Anglo-Irishman. In September 1913, 'in utmost secrecy', he had been sounded out by the King 'as to the effect which would be produced in the Army if the Troops were called upon to oppose an Armed Resistance by Ulster to Home Rule'. While French assured the King that 'the spirit of discipline' in the army was 'of the highest order', he also felt that there were 'many good officers & men, not possessing any logical minds, who would be led to think they were best serving their King & country either by refusing to march against the Ulster men or openly joining their ranks'.[35]

Early the following month French had a long talk about the situation with Wilson. The CIGS was

evidently nervous that we are coming to Civil War & his attitude appears to be that he will obey the King's Orders. He wanted to know what I would do. I told him that I could not fire on the North at the dictates of Redmond & this is what the whole thing means. England quâ England is opposed to Home Rule, & England must agree to it before it is carried out. I was much struck by his seriousness. I cannot bring myself to believe that Asquith will be so mad as to employ force. It will split the Army & the Colonies as well as this country & the Empire.[36]

This was the first time Wilson reflected at any length in his diary about the impact of the growing 'Ulster crisis' on the army, and he evidently felt very strongly about

---

[34] Wilson diary, 13, 16 March 1913.

[35] French to Lord Stamfordham (private secretary to the King), 25 Sept. 1914 (quoted in Beckett, *The Army and the Curragh Incident*, 39–40). Beckett's volume is the best single source for the circumstances and course of the 'Curragh Incident'. Two other useful accounts are Ryan, *Mutiny at the Curragh*, which is primarily narrative, and Fergusson, *The Curragh Incident*, which was written by the son of a senior army officer involved, and is sympathetic, though not uncritically so, to the soldiers' predicament.   [36] Wilson diary, 4 Nov. 1913.

the matter. But his comments here embody an unhappy mixture of confused assumptions and shaky logic. John French is often dismissed as being not very bright, but on this evidence he seems precisely to have anticipated Wilson as being among those who did not posses a 'logical mind', or at least a clearly rational appreciation of the situation. To be sure, French's position, that soldiers had a duty to obey the 'King's Orders', left the question open as to who precisely would formulate these instructions. The proper constitutional line gave that authority to the elected government of the day, but Wilson chose to assume that any orders to act against Ulster would be 'at the dictates of Redmond' and 'disloyal' Irish nationalists. Thus they would in some way be illegitimate, and therefore not binding on 'loyal' soldiers of the Crown. Wilson furthermore asserted a democratic basis for his stance, believing that 'England quâ England' (whatever that precisely meant) was opposed to home rule. He clearly also felt that home rule could not be introduced until the government had fought a general election on the issue, which he believed the Liberals would lose. Unionist advances in two by-elections in November 1913 lent some strength to this argument, though the position was by no means as clear-cut as Wilson (and Bonar Law and the rest of them) chose to believe.[37]

In addition to these political considerations, Wilson appeared emotionally to be in denial as to what Asquith might do. The consequences of forcing through home rule were so grave that even Asquith would not 'be so mad as to employ force'. This being the case, unionists were justified in adopting increasingly extreme measures, *precisely* in order to dissuade Asquith from plunging the country into disaster. But the growing militarisation of the unionist campaign in late 1913 and 1914 made a government resort to the forceful maintenance of law and order increasingly likely. The fact that each set of opponents tended to believe that the other was fundamentally bluffing also raised the stakes. Not much of this was entirely rational. As Wilson himself exemplified, there was a visceral, emotional component to support for the unionist cause (and of course, *mutatis mutandis*, on the nationalist side), which made an already dangerous situation extremely volatile indeed.

A few days after his conversation with French, Wilson, who thought the 'Ulster business' was 'getting serious', went to see Bonar Law to tell him 'that if we were ordered to coerce Ulster there would be wholesale defections'. Law told him that Lord Stamfordham, the King's private secretary, thought that 40 per cent of officers and men would leave the army. 'Personally I put the p.c. much lower but still very serious.' Wilson went on to tell Law of Cecil's idea 'that [the unionist leader Edward] Carson should pledge the Ulster troops to fight for England if she was at war', aiming thereby to stress the continuing, higher national 'loyalty' of the Ulster unionists.[38]

---

[37] On 6 Nov. 1913 the Unionists won Reading from the Liberals, and reduced a Liberal majority of 2,000 to 500 at Linlithgow. See also Smith, *The Tories and Ireland*, 137, who, however, erroneously states that the Tories won Linlithgow.   [38] Wilson diary, 6, 9 Nov. 1913.

Noteworthy here is the explicit appearance of Cecil Wilson in the narrative. Taking the evidence of Wilson's diary, her role in the household appeared generally to match the classic 'two spheres' model of Victorian and Edwardian gender roles. While men dealt with 'public' affairs, women occupied themselves purely with domestic matters. So it appeared to have been with the Wilsons, where, beyond a bit of light charity work, Cecil's concerns were mainly limited to conventional 'homemaking'. But twice in 1912–13 in Wilson's diary she emerges to take a significant part in discussions about Irish home rule. So unusual is this that it suggests not only that she had very strong views on the issue, but also that she participated on a regular basis when the topic was discussed, and furthermore, that her policy advice was valued by her husband. It is possible that Cecil Wilson actually felt more strongly about the matter than Wilson himself. Her family were always less well off than the Wilsons, and the seismic changes of nineteenth-century Ireland, which effectively swept away the old landed ascendancy, had robbed them of their livelihood as land agents. She could, moreover, hardly have relished handing over power in Ireland to people she may have identified with the Ardnamona dynamiters of Christmas 1849.[39]

The growing air of crisis during November and December 1913 is vividly charted in Wilson's diary. On 13 November he discussed the situation with Nevil Macready, the Director of Personal Services, whose responsibilities included 'duties in aid of the Civil Power'. Macready said that he was being sent over to Ireland 'to watch the North', but assured him that the Cabinet had 'settled not to try & employ troops as they realize at last the temper of Ulster & of the Army'. On 14 November Wilson dined with Charlie Hunter and Lord Milner, who told him that any officers who resigned over Ulster would be reinstated 'when the Conservatives came into power'. The next day he lunched with Edward Sclater, one of the Ulster unionist leaders, and warned him that the UVF should firmly avoid taking 'any action hostile to the Army'.[40] Wilson was evidently reassured by Macready's opinion that the government were stepping back from the brink. But things took a turn for the worse when Asquith made an uncompromising speech in Leeds in which he said that the government, while happy to contemplate any 'reasonable and honourable way of peace', would 'see this thing through' without submitting the matter to a general election.[41] Wilson thought this 'ominous' and interpreted it as meaning that Asquith would now use the army 'to coerce the North'. Johnnie Du Cane (who had taught at the Staff College under Wilson and was currently commanding a brigade) turned up in the War Office 'very angry with Asquith', and asserting that Ulster would have to be granted 'belligerent status', as the situation was comparable to the American Civil War.[42]

---

[39] Henry and Cecil also opposed votes for women. In 1913 and 1914 they together attended the annual meeting of the Anti-Suffrage League (Wilson diary, 25 June 1913, 26 June 1914).

[40] Wilson diary, 13–15 Nov. 1913.   [41] Jalland, *The Liberals and Ireland*, 178.

[42] Wilson diary, 28 Nov. 1913. The American Civil War was an important topic on the Staff College syllabus, and it is reasonable to suppose that, for those officers who had studied it, their

Over Christmas, which both the Wilsons and the Rawlinsons spent with the Roberts at Englemere, there was much talk of the Irish situation. On Boxing Day Wilson and Rawly played golf with Brigadier-General Johnnie Gough, a senior staff officer at Aldershot, and an Anglo-Irishman with a family home in county Tipperary. Gough declared that he 'had definitely made up his mind to join Ulster if the crash came'. Lord Roberts said that when the Home Rule Bill had passed the Commons for the third time he would go to the King, whom he hoped could be persuaded not to sign the legislation. If the King refused, Roberts was going to write to the papers pointing out that the bill had been passed while the constitution was 'in abeyance' and 'by the vote of the Irish who never lost an opportunity of deriding the Army & cheering its enemies & therefore no Officer or man ought to demean himself by obeying the orders to coerce Ireland'. Reviewing the past year on New Year's Eve, Wilson wrote that Ulster was 'rapidly becoming the sole & governing & Immediate factor in the national life'.[43] On New Year's Day he lunched with Leo Amery at White's Club, 'very pessimistic about the whole political situation and above all anxious that the army should not be drawn in'.[44]

Early in January 1914 Wilson discussed the question with his two fellow directors: Joey Davies, who had become DSD in October 1913, and Wullie Robertson, who had left the Staff College at the same time to become DMT. The three men 'had a long and serious talk about Ulster, & whether we could'nt do something to keep the Army out of it'. According to Wilson, they agreed that the main difficulty lay with 'poor Johnnie French', who had assured Seely 'that the Army will be solid in obeying orders'. The three men resolved to take soundings about army opinion during the annual Staff Conference at Camberley the following week. Wilson pronounced himself 'pleased' with colleagues' attitudes '& the feeling against the Govt. policy'. He was also cheered by a tea-party hosted by the new Commandant, Lancelot Kiggell. 'It's so funny', wrote Wilson, being back in the Staff College house 'as a welcome guest after 4 years of absence owing to Robertson never once having asked me near the place'.[45] At the end of February Wilson went to Belfast, ostensibly to inspect the 3rd battalion Royal Irish Rifles, of whom he had recently been appointed honorary colonel, and to give a lecture on 'the Balkans' at Victoria Barracks. But he visited the Unionist headquarters at the Old Town Hall and noted that 'the arrangements of the Ulster Army are well advanced & there is no doubt of the discipline & spirit of the men & Officers'. While Wilson had apparently not gone to Belfast on official business (though there was also some speculation in the press that it 'had relation to the present political situation'), it was in no way a secret visit, and he reported his impressions to both the Secretary of State and Sir John French. In Ulster, he said, there were '100,000 men who are in deadly earnest'. But he also continued to see opposition

---

attitudes towards the Irish crisis might have been coloured by their knowledge of the painful Civil War fracturing of the American officer corps.

[43] Ibid., 26, 31 Dec. 1913.   [44] Amery, *The Leo Amery Diaries*, 97.
[45] Wilson diary, 7, 12 Jan. 1914. Robertson was apparently not invited to the tea-party.

MPs, including Charlie Hunter, John Baird (Bonar Law's parliamentary private secretary), and Bonar Law himself.[46]

There was some talk of compromise, and a scheme was proposed to allow Ulster counties to 'opt out' of home rule for up to six years, but Carson memorably declared that Ulster did 'not want sentence of death with a stay of execution for six years'.[47] The Cabinet, tiring of Ulster's posturing (as they thought), resolved to take a firm line, and matters came to a head in what Ian Beckett has called the 'March Days'.[48] In Bradford on 14 March, Winston Churchill issued a clear public challenge when he declared that there were 'worse things than bloodshed, even on an extended scale', and that if the opponents of home rule continued to be obdurate, 'let us go forward together and put these grave matters to the proof'.[49] Worrying that the UVF might raid army barracks for guns, the government decided to deploy troops across Ulster in what was described as a 'precautionary' move, and Sir Arthur Paget, the army commander in Ireland, was brought over to London for instructions on 18–19 March. In the House of Commons the final parliamentary circuit of the Home Rule Bill had begun on 9 March, and there was a particularly bitter debate on 19 March, at the end of which Carson dramatically left for Belfast, amid rumours that he was about to be arrested and a provisional government declared in Ulster.

Between noon on 18 March and eight o'clock the following evening a series of meetings took place involving Cabinet ministers (notably Seely and Churchill), Paget, French, Sir Spencer Ewart (the Adjutant-General), and Sir Nevil Macready (Director of Personal Services), during which the deployment of troops in Ireland was discussed. Regarding what Seely called 'the question of officers' resignations', it was decided that those who had a 'direct family connection' with Ulster would be permitted to 'remain behind', while all other officers who refused to take part would be 'removed' from the army.[50] No provision was made for enlisted men who had conscientious objections about 'coercing Ulster'.

On 18 March Sir John French told Wilson in general terms what had been decided, that the government was 'contemplating scattering troops all over Ulster, as though it was a Pontypool coal strike'. French asked if the General Staff had made any plans, a reasonable enough question, seeing that that was their purpose. Wilson told him that since it would be 'Home Defence', it was not his responsibility as DMO, but that of the DMT, Robertson. Wilson did predict, however, that any trouble in Ulster would be accompanied by unrest elsewhere in Ireland and England, '& the Continent would not look on unmoved'. The next day French called in both Wilson and Robertson. Wilson expanded on the difficulty of using

[46] Wilson diary, 2–4, 13, 15, 19 Mar. 1914. Baird, who became an MP in 1910, had been Sir William Garstin's private secretary in Egypt in 1900–2. For press comment on Wilson's visit to Belfast, see *The Times* and *Irish Times*, 3 Mar. 1914.   [47] Jalland, *The Liberals and Ireland*, 203.
[48] Beckett, *The Army and the Curragh Incident*, 79–259.
[49] Jalland, *The Liberals and Ireland*, 219.
[50] Note by Seely to Asquith, 19 Mar. 1914 (quoted in Beckett, *The Army and the Curragh Incident*, 62).

the army to coerce Ulster. The 'whole Army' would need to be mobilised, and 'even then I much doubted if it could be done owing to the character & determination of the Ulstermen'. He reiterated the likelihood of trouble all across Ireland, 'the further certainty of riots in Liverpool, Manchester, Glasgow, etc', adding for good measure 'the hostility of the European Powers as well as the dangers in Egypt, India etc', and, of course, 'serious disaffection in the Army'. In what was a familiar Wilsonian debating technique, conceding the possibility of a certain course of action but only with ruinous consequences, he said 'it would take 12 or 18 months to knock Ulster out, & that it will be the end of the Empire'.[51]

Arthur Paget was not the man for the extremely delicate job of steering a path which would meet the government's legitimate concerns for the maintenance of law and order in Ulster (as well, perhaps, as their desire to match the 'theatrical' manoeuvres of the UVF with a demonstration of strength of their own), while negotiating the deeply held, and sometimes very passionate, unionist sympathies of many army officers. Out of his depth, he flapped and blustered, apparently believing that the army would be plunged into widespread turmoil. At one of the London meetings he wildly declared, 'I shall lead my army to the Boyne', at which French sensibly told him 'not to be a "bloody fool" '.[52] On 20 March the storm broke. Back in Dublin, Paget summoned his senior commanders and, in an emotional and tense meeting, announced the likelihood of 'active operations' in Ulster. Any officer whose home was 'actually in the province of Ulster' would be permitted to 'disappear' for the duration, with no loss to his career; any other officer who, for whatever reason, was 'not prepared to carry out his duty as ordered' would be 'dismissed from the Service'.[53] Among Paget's officers was the charismatic but combustible Hubert Gough (Johnnie Gough's brother), commanding the 3rd Cavalry Brigade at the Curragh Camp. With tempers running high, Gough and sixty fellow officers chose to accept dismissal.[54]

This was the so-called 'Curragh mutiny', which precipitated the most serious crisis of civil–military relations in modern British history. It was not, in fact, a 'mutiny', since no one actually disobeyed orders, but the scale of the protest did raise the possibility of potentially mutinous disaffection in the army as a whole, and the result of the affair was seriously to limit the government's policy options with regard to Ireland. Numbers of other officers (up to perhaps a hundred) in the Irish Command offered to resign, and there was widespread support for Gough elsewhere. The news of the protest travelled extremely fast. Wilson, who had spent

[51] Wilson diary, 18–19 Mar. 1914.

[52] French's account, as told to H. A. Gwynne, editor of the *Morning Post* (quoted in Beckett, *The Army and the Curragh Incident*, 74).

[53] Orders by Gen. Sir Charles Fergusson, 20 Mar. 1914 (quoted in Beckett, *The Army and the Curragh Incident*, 81).

[54] The erroneous total of 58 officers is frequently cited, but, according to Gough, 60 (a figure which probably does not include Gough himself) officers in the 3rd Cavalry Brigade resigned. For a discussion of the figures, see Beckett, ibid. 14. One colleague described Gough as 'hot headed & very Irish' (Sir Philip Chetwode, see ibid. 286).

the morning of 20 March drafting a letter for French 'to send to Asquith begging Asquith to pause before employing the Army as it would split the Army from top to bottom', was telephoned at the office by his wife 'for me to come home to see Johnnie Gough', who had come up from Aldershot, having received a wire from his brother outlining the situation. Wilson, who thought that Paget had evidently 'made a d—— fool of himself' (how right he was), at once telephoned French with the sensational news, but the only reaction he got was 'windy platitudes till I was nearly sick'. Wilson's immediate response was to counsel calm, and 'with much difficulty' persuaded Gough 'not to send in his papers till tomorrow when we must find out if this is all true. . . . We must', he wrote, 'steady ourselves a bit.'[55]

Hubert Gough was summoned to the War Office to be carpeted by Seely and French. Backed up (and advised throughout the day) by his brother and Henry Wilson, he refused to withdraw his resignation (or that of his officers) without some kind of written assurance that the army would not initiate active operations against Ulster. After meetings on 22 and 23 March, and a lot of toing and froing, a statement authorised by the Cabinet was offered to Gough. It asserted that the resignations in his brigade had been due to a 'misunderstanding', and reiterated the 'duty of all soldiers to obey lawful commands' for the protection of lives and property. But nothing specific was said about operations in Ireland. Henry Wilson worried that 'lawful commands' to coerce Ulster might be issued by a Dublin government after the Home Rule Bill had been introduced. Gough asked for clarification to be included on this point, and Seely, on his own authority (though he consulted Lord Morley), added two paragraphs. The first affirmed the government's right 'to use all the forces of the Crown in Ireland, or elsewhere, to maintain law and order and to support the civil power in the ordinary execution of its duty', while the second stated that the government had 'no intention whatever of taking advantage of this right to crush political opposition to the policy or principles of the Home Rule Bill'. This still seemed unclear, so Gough added a note on the memorandum to the effect that his understanding of the last paragraph meant that his troops would 'not be called upon to enforce the present Home Rule Bill on Ulster'. After a little hesitation, Sir John French, in turn, added 'this is how I read it'.[56]

At the top of the diary page for Monday 23 March 1914, Henry Wilson wrote: 'We soldiers beat Asquith & his vile tricks.' The document which Gough had secured, signed by Seely, French, and Sir Spencer Ewart, with French's further endorsement, greatly restricted the government's freedom of action concerning Ireland. Although military action had only ever been an option of last resort, the political costs of the concession to Gough and his fellow officers were extremely high. It appeared that the Ulster unionist threat of military action had worked, a lesson not lost on their nationalist compatriots, who were in any case angered,

[55] Wilson diary, 20 Mar. 1914.

[56] This document, and the Gough brothers' accounts, are in Beckett, *The Army and the Curragh Incident*, 218, 244–5, 248–54; Wilson diary, 23 May 1914.

dismayed, and demoralised in equal measure by the events. In Britain, Labour and the Radical wing of the Liberal Party were outraged by a contest between 'army' and 'people', in which the people appeared to have conceded without very much of a fight. Although not, perhaps, along the same lines of cleavage as Henry Wilson envisaged, the potential for widespread national conflict seemed scarcely much reduced after the 'March days' than before.

Gough's document, however, had not actually been authorised by the government. Seely's two 'peccant paragraphs', and French's endorsement were both repudiated by Asquith. But the damage was done, and Asquith could never return to the *status quo ante*. The three signatories, Seely, French, and Ewart, were obliged to resign. Seely's hitherto promising political career was fatally blighted, and Ewart was to sit out the war in the relative backwater of Scottish Command.[57] Only French bounced back. Many in the army felt he had 'done the right thing' by resigning, having been put in an impossible position by the government, though at the height of the crisis Lord Roberts had told Wilson he did not think he could 'write or ever speak again to French', on the grounds that 'he must have known and agreed to the wicked plans of Government to quietly assemble troops in Ireland, and then proceed against Ulster as if it were inhabited by a rebellious enemy, instead of our own kith and kin'.[58] Early in April, while the dust was still settling after the crisis, and French was sorting out some papers for his successor as CIGS, Sir Charles Douglas ('Sunny Jim'), he told Wilson that Asquith had nominated him to be commander of the expeditionary force.[59] Asquith, of course, cannot have anticipated how soon that position would arise; he may simply have been offering the potential command as a consolation to French.[60]

Wilson's diary provides a especially vivid and detailed narrative of the crisis, and documents the extent to which he worked behind the scenes in support of the Ulster cause. In addition, his own file of 'Curragh' correspondence, containing over fifty letters, is one of the best single sources for the army side of the affair.[61] The crisis saw a sharp intensification of Wilson's contacts with leading Opposition figures. Over a ten-day period, from 21 March until the end of the month, he saw Bonar Law six times at home (on 29 March having lunch with Carson), and Law came to Wilson's house three times. He also saw H. A. Gwynne three times, Milner and Arthur Lee twice, and Geoffrey Robinson once. Amery (who lived round the corner) came round four times in the evening after dinner, keen, like all the others, to catch up on the latest news from the War Office. There is no

---

[57] Seely did have a 'good war' commanding the Canadian Cavalry Brigade, and held junior ministerial office in 1918–19. He became Lord Mottistone in 1933, when he was chairman of the National Savings Committee.

[58] Roberts to Wilson, 24 Mar. 1914 (Wilson papers, HHW 2/74/12). Roberts, in fact, did not stick to this opinion of French; see Wilson diary, 12 Nov. 1914.   [59] Wilson diary, 3 Apr. 1914.

[60] French, however, remained uncertain as to whether he would actually command the BEF until formally appointed in late July 1914 (Holmes, *The Little Field-Marshal*, 193–6).

[61] There is extensive transcription of this material in Beckett, *The Army and the Curragh Incident*. The 'Letters re the Gough Incident, March 1914' are in Wilson papers, HHW 2/74/1–54.

indication in the diary that Wilson kept these meetings particularly secret, though on 22 March he thought it 'wiser not' to accept Bonar Law's invitation to dine at Lansdowne House to meet Balfour and Austen Chamberlain.

Wilson was not the only officer 'leaking' information. Lord Roberts (fed news by Wilson, Johnnie Gough, and others) was an important conduit. But, above all, French consulted H. A. Gwynne, and kept him informed at every stage of the crisis. He saw Gwynne twice on 23 March, once the following day, twice on 25 March (one meeting at French's room in the War Office, so not much secrecy there), twice on 27 March, and once on the 29th.[62] One of the issues afterwards which disturbed Spencer Ewart (an officer whose conduct was wholly admirable throughout) concerned who immediately leaked details to the press of the 'celebrated treaty' of 23 March (which Gough had promised to keep confidential). In Ewart's opinion, it was 'a melancholy story of Army disloyalty to its own Chiefs'.[63] The evidence points primarily to Gough and French. At Euston Station, on his way back to Ireland, Gough himself told H. A. Gwynne (who, it must be remembered, was the editor of the most Conservative and Unionist major national newspaper). The same day John French also told Gwynne about the letter he had signed. Late that evening Henry Wilson told Amery about it when he called round, and when Bonar Law telephoned the next morning he told him as well.[64] Far from 'Army disloyalty to its own Chiefs', it seems more to have been the chiefs being disloyal to the army, or at least that part of it which remained true its proper duty.

It is indisputable that the impetuous Goughs, and Wilson, were wrong to take the line they did. Although they claimed correctly that no orders had been disobeyed, the declaration wrung from Seely and the others in practice limited the government's legitimate freedom of action. It was a kind of pre-emptive mutiny. Many other officers, however, some with strongly conservative political sympathies, took the correct line that it was no part of their duty to pick and choose what orders they might obey.[65] One general, an Irishman sympathetic to the Gough position, said his view was 'that I carry out all orders that I receive from the Govt. with the King at its head, orders however repugnant they may be—Anything else to me spells anarchy.'[66] Sir Philip Chetwode, who was nominated to go to Ireland to replace Gough when news of his resignation first came in, knew he would be 'looked upon by all his brother officers as a scab', yet believed it was 'his duty as a soldier to do as he was ordered & not to meddle in politics'.[67]

[62] Memorandum by H. A. Gwynne, 2 Apr. 1914 (reproduced in Beckett, *The Army and the Curragh Incident*, 236–9).   [63] Ewart diary, 18 Apr. 1914 (in ibid. 366).
[64] Ibid. 219, 220, 236; Note of conversation with Brig.-Gen. Gough, Euston Station, 23 Mar. 1914 (Gwynne papers); Wilson diary, 23–4 Mar. 1914.
[65] This position, however, is not absolute, since moral considerations may limit what orders a soldier may legitimately follow.
[66] Gen. Granville Egerton (GOC Lowland Division, Scotland) to Gen. Sir Alexander Godley (GOC, New Zealand), 29 Apr. 1914 (Godley papers (IWM)).
[67] Capt. Richard Stapleton-Cotton (Chetwode's brother-in-law) to Admiral R. E. Wemyss, 25 Mar. 1914 (Beckett, *The Army and the Curragh Incident*, 285). Although he never reached the Curragh, Chetwode did attract some opprobrium. Hubert Gough dismissed him as 'a poor creature'

Although Lord Milner extravagantly claimed that Henry Wilson had 'saved the Empire' (which Wilson thought 'much too flattering'),[68] his role in the affair was not so clear-cut as was sometimes subsequently asserted. A month after the crisis Hubert Gough told Alex Godley that Wilson 'talked a lot about resigning etc. previously, but never raised a finger, till everybody else did. He was however useful in various ways, but did not mean to risk his own skin, & was very glad to help us pull out the chestnuts for him!'[69] In his diary on 21 March Wilson (who had already counselled Johnnie Gough to wait before sending in his resignation) had declared himself 'more than ever determined to resign, but I <u>cannot</u> think of a really good way of doing it'. The next day, after Hubert had got his assurances (as he thought from the government), there was no pressing need for anyone to resign. And perhaps the main thing to ensure at that moment was the unity of the army, which meant withdrawing the threat of resignations. On 25 March he told Hubert Gough to 'stand like a rock. . . . So long as we hold the paper we got on Monday we can afford to sit tight.'[70] Once Wilson felt the immediate crisis had passed, his concerns moved on from the danger of the army splitting to the political advantages which could accrue from the situation. He thought, for example, that the resignations of Seely and French would only be the start, that Morley and Haldane (who had been advising John French) would also go, which would in turn 'break' the Cabinet.[71]

Wilson had thought about the problem of military loyalty long before the Curragh crisis. In a lecture at the Staff College in March 1907 he had laid down that 'we owe allegiance to the King as citizens & soldiers, to the Cabinet only as citizens and to our military chiefs as soldiers. Only in the case of the King do we see the maximum allegiance.'[72] But this formulation ignored the requirements of a democratic (or partially so), constitutional monarchy of the British type, whose sovereign could only rule through parliament and the elected political executive. It is an irony that Wilson, who held distinctly reformist ideas of modern military organisation, should in the Irish case find himself championing, with a kind of atavistic fervour, the cause of the most hidebound and reactionary elements in military and political life. Perhaps it was due to his Irish background. The Englishman, Lord Esher, certainly thought so, and his judgment (as with his estimation of Wilson's Staff College role) is worth quoting. Wilson's

---

(ibid. 359). Henry Wilson does not seem to have held any grudge, as he appointed Chetwode to be his DCIGS in 1920.

[68] Wilson diary, 29 Mar. 1914.

[69] Gough to Godley, 29 Apr. 1914 (Godley papers (IWM)). In his memoirs, Gough alleged that Wilson was 'aware all along of the Government plans for the invasion of Ulster' but did nothing 'until "the gaff was blown" so to speak' by the resignations at the Curragh. As a result, Johnnie Gough 'refused ever to speak to Wilson again'. While there is no evidence at all for the allegation, Johnnie Gough and Henry Wilson were certainly estranged after March 1914 (Gough, *Soldiering On*, 171; see also Beckett, *Johnnie Gough*, 170).   [70] Wilson diary, 25 Mar. 1914.

[71] Ibid., 29 Mar. 1914.

[72] 'Lecture on optimism and pessimism', 14 Mar. 1907 (Wilson papers, HHW 3/3/4).

Irish blood, exuberant with combative malice, in an unfortunate moment seduced him from the arid paths of military science. He plunged with delight into an Irish quarrel, which earned for him from politicians the appellation of 'a pestilential fellow,' and was destined to cripple his chances of obtaining the highest Staff appointment in a war which he had correctly appreciated. The implacable wrath of political partisans stood between him and the fullest use of his faculties in the war of his waking dreams. For this he had himself and his Irish ancestors to blame.[73]

Whatever the motivation, it turned out that Wilson's actions during the crisis, whether they 'saved the Empire' or not, markedly damaged his career prospects.

As for the 'Ulster crisis', while the Home Rule Bill proceeded slowly, but inexorably, towards the 'Statute Book', the government (with force having been ruled out by the Currragh incident) haphazardly moved towards negotiating with the unionists, and began to consider more seriously schemes for the exclusion of part or all of Ulster. In the meantime, both the Ulster unionists and the Irish nationalists imported considerable quantities of arms, the former more efficiently than the latter. In June, Wilson proposed to Charles Douglas that 'Ireland ought now to be flooded with troops, impartially N. S. E. & W. & thus escape any murders, burnings etc.'[74] The CIGS did not agree, but Wilson's suggestion, albeit involving the whole of Ireland, bears an ironical resemblance to the proposed 'precautionary' deployment which had sparked off the Curragh incident. At the end of the month, very concerned about the fact that 'between 200,000 & 300,000 men' were 'drilling & arming in Ireland', and that the army might be called in to support the civil power, Wilson drafted a paper for the Army Council to submit to the Cabinet, pointing out the dangerous situation and asking for guidance 'in regard to their coming policy in Ireland'.[75] But the international political situation was about to overshadow Irish affairs. The day before Wilson submitted his memorandum on Ireland he noted in his diary an 'awful tragedy at Sarajevo': the assassination of the Austrian Archduke Franz Ferdinand and his wife on 28 June 1914.[76]

Henry Wilson's personal concern with Irish matters did not greatly affect his continuing work as DMO. When in April 1914 the report of the CID invasion committee recommended that two of the expeditionary force's six divisions should be held back in the event of war, Wilson complained in person to Asquith ('the first time I have seen him since he became S. of S.') that this would 'entirely abolish the Exp. Force'. Without consulting the CID, Asquith decided that five divisions could 'go at once'. 'This is **good**', wrote Wilson.[77] Liaison continued with the French. Between the start of 1914 and the end of May, Wilson visited

---

[73] Esher, *The Tragedy of Lord Kitchener*, 85.   [74] Wilson diary, 22 June 1914.
[75] Minute re Government Policy towards Ireland, 30 June 1914 (Wilson papers, HHW 3/5/30). Wilson and Robertson drew up a longer, more detailed, paper on the same topic on 1 July (ibid.).
[76] Wilson diary, 29 June 1914.
[77] Ibid., 6 May 1914. For the invasion inquiry report see Williamson, *The Politics of Grand Strategy*, 310–11, and Gooch, *Plans of War*, 294–5.

France four times. In January he had wide-ranging discussions about the arrangements for the expeditionary force and the broader strategic situation. On his way back in February from skiing at Gstaad he saw General Belin (Joffre's deputy Chief of Staff) and 'did some work'. In mid-April he (of all people) was sent to Paris to reassure the French high command that, despite the Curragh crisis, the British army could still be relied upon, and in May he and Ivor Maxse spent three days observing a French staff tour in the country south of Nancy, not far from the German frontier.[78] Wilson's staff continued with detailed planning for the expeditionary force, and officers from his M.O.1 section also visited France. By 4 July, in fact, British and French officers had agreed that the plans were just about as complete as possible.[79]

During most of July 1914 Henry Wilson's principal worry was the possibility of civil war in Ireland. While the Conservatives were attempting to exclude Ulster from home rule with an 'amending bill' in parliament, London was full of rumours that Carson would declare a 'provisional government' in Belfast. At a Court Ball on 16 July, Wilson 'had much talk' with Lord Derby, the Duke of Westminster, and others, 'and they were all of opinion we were into Civil War. It's appalling.' On 20 July the passage of the amending bill was postponed and an all-party conference organised at Buckingham Palace. 'What this all means I don't know,' wrote Wilson, 'but I suppose it's another filthy trick of Asquith's to gain time.' On 24 July the conference broke down, ending 'a perfectly useless attempt to come to an Agreement on a subject which is not agree-able'. And there, for the moment, the Irish question rested. From the next day, when Wilson noted that the 'Austro-Servian news' was 'very serious', the wider European crisis began to command his attention.[80]

Austria (not without justification) blamed Serbia for the assassinations at Sarajevo, and, having secured German support, resolved to punish the Serbs and thus reassert its power in the Balkans. The Serbs, however, confident of backing from Russia, refused to meet all of Austria's demands, and by 25 July the two states were at war.[81] There was never any real possibility that the conflict could be restricted to the Balkans. As Henry Wilson's diary entry for 25 July indicates, the interlocking pattern of European alliances and rivalries immediately magnified the Austro-Serbian quarrel into something much more threatening. Following his customary morning walk, Wilson called in on Arthur Nicolson at the Foreign Office. Nicolson showed him a telegram from Sir George Buchanan, the British ambassador at St Petersburg: 'Buchanan said that Russia would not tolerate Austria attacking Serbia & would go to war to prevent it.' Poincaré, the French

[78] Wilson diary, 14, 17 Jan., 20 Feb., 18–19 Apr., 25–7 May 1914.
[79] Scott (ed.), 'The View From the War Office', 15–16.
[80] Wilson diary, 16, 20, 24–5 July 1914.
[81] There are numerous accounts of the outbreak of the First World War. The best is Strachan, *The First World War*, i, *To Arms*. A good and accessible one-volume recent treatment of the origins and course of the war is id., *The First World War*.

President, 'had pledged the French Army to support Russia'. Both Russia and France wanted to know 'what part we would play'.[82]

No one was sure what line the government would take, and there were worries that they might, in Wilson's words, 'run away'.[83] Lord Milner was particularly vehement. Writing to Wilson on 27 July, he noted that the 'nightmare' of British troops being used against Ulstermen 'seems to be vanishing', but 'everything else is as black as possible.... The Army may have to take charge yet, to prevent a general relapse into anarchy.'[84] We can also see the mounting tension from a handwritten note Wilson made on a copy of a telegram from Buchanan reporting general mobilisation in Russia: 'Eyre Crowe brought this over at 5.45 p.m. 31. 7.14. He told me that he had had ¾ of an hour with Grey & he thought the case was hopeless. Grey spoke of the ruin of commerce, etc, & in spite of all Crowe's arguments appeared determined to act the coward. Crowe begged me to see Asquith or Grey, but of course they would not see me. Crowe was in despair.'[85] In the event, the Russian mobilisation provoked the Germans into declaring war on 1 August, which brought France in. Two days later France and Germany were also at war, and Berlin had issued an ultimatum to Belgium demanding unimpeded passage for its army. This, for Britain, was the precise *casus belli*, the violation of Belgian neutrality, which had been guaranteed by all the European great powers in the Treaty of London of 1839.

On 3 August the British government ordered mobilisation, and the next day Britain and Germany were at war. For Wilson the problem now was the urgent need to set in motion his carefully constructed scheme for the deployment of the Expeditionary Force. 'Grey's delay & hesitation in giving orders for embarkation', he complained, 'is sinful.'[86] The crucial decision was taken during the late afternoon of 5 August at a 'War Council', the importance of which 'in the formation of British war strategy', wrote Samuel Williamson, 'cannot be overexaggerated'.[87] Chaired by the Prime Minister, those present included three other Cabinet ministers (Grey, Churchill, and Haldane), as well as Lord Kitchener, who was to become War Minister the following day. Battenberg (the First Sea Lord) represented the Navy, Maurice Hankey the CID, and there were nine soldiers, including Lord Roberts, Charles Douglas, John French, Ian Hamilton, Douglas Haig, and Henry Wilson. All the planning and discussions of the past decade or so, by Wilson, the General Staff, the CID, and the rest, came to a head at this historic gathering. And despite the apparent perfection of Wilson's plans, as well as (to his mind) the unassailably compelling need to despatch the British Expeditionary Force *immediately* to France, various other options were raised before any decision was taken.

---

[82] Wilson diary, 25 July 1914.   [83] Ibid., 31 July 1914.

[84] Milner to Wilson, 27 July 1914 (Wilson papers, HHW 2/73/32 & 39).

[85] Notes on telegram from Sir George Buchanan to Foreign Office, 31 July 1914 (Wilson papers, HHW 3/8/4).   [86] Ibid., 4 Aug. 1914.

[87] Williamson, *The Politics of Grand Strategy*, 364.

French, who was to command the BEF, 'dragged in the ridiculous proposal of going to Antwerp'.[88] Douglas Haig queried whether the force should not be held back for a while. That morning he had shocked Wilson by proposing 'not to go over for 2 or 3 months', during which 'the immense resources of the Empire' would be developed. Then there was the matter of where the BEF should go. It had already been agreed with the French that the BEF would concentrate between Le Cateau and Maubeuge, but fears were raised that this area might no longer be 'available'. After a discussion of 'desultory strategy (some thinking that Liege was in Holland!) & idiocy', Kitchener 'plumped for Amiens', but the general sense of the meeting was that the precise location of the BEF should be left to the French. With Churchill's assurance that the naval situation was 'most favourable', it was decided to send five of the six divisions to France.[89]

And so Britain's Continental commitment was finally made, and Henry Wilson's years of planning and lobbying apparently vindicated. Despite the introduction of alternative possible courses of action (by French and Haig, for example), Wilson's plan was the only practicable option if the British government wished to offer any immediate support to their French allies (not to mention the Belgians). Even Maurice Hankey, who rather tended towards 'blue water' attitudes, recognised that 'the plan for co-operation by our Expeditionary Force on the left of the French Army had been worked out by the two Staffs in great detail, and this could not be said of any other plan'.[90] Thus the very completeness of the 'W.F. scheme' (which had, moreover, been approved in outline by the government) reinforced (at the very least) the government's decision to adopt it.[91]

What of Ireland? On 26 July Wilson's old friend Huguet wrote from France that war seemed 'inevitable'. But there was a silver lining to this particular cloud. It may be, he wrote, 'good for you, should you decide to join us as you will never find a better diversion to your internal difficulties'.[92] The notion that the onset of the First World War 'prevented the outbreak of a bloody civil war in Ireland' was widely asserted at the time and since.[93] But what the Great War prevented may merely have been the particular type of civil war anticipated and feared in the summer of 1914. What the outbreak of war may actually have done, by interrupting the intense political efforts to find an accommodation in Ireland, and by

---

[88] Wilson had already dismissed this on practical grounds: 'we can't cross North Sea, north of Scheldt is Dutch, & no arrangements made for transportation so quite hopeless' (Wilson diary, 3 Aug. 1914).

[89] Williamson, *The Politics of Grand Strategy*, 364–7; Wilson diary, 5–6, 12 Aug. 1914.

[90] Hankey, *The Supreme Command*, i. 170–1.

[91] It has been argued that there was, however, a breakdown of civilian political control in the matter of war planning, in part because 'none of the British ministers showed any appreciation of how the conjunction of railroads and mass armies had tied modern warfare to elaborate timetables prepared years in advance' (Coogan and Coogan, 'The British Cabinet and the Anglo-French Staff Talks', 129–30).   [92] Huguet to Wilson, 26 July 1914 (Wilson papers, HHW 2/73/31).

[93] The quotation is from Denman, *Ireland's Unknown Soldiers*, 19, but see also (for example) a similar assertion in Beckett and Jeffery, 'The Royal Navy and the Curragh Incident', 69.

suspending 'normal' political activities (in Great Britain as well as Ireland), was to favour the further radicalisation of Irish separatism, and make a republican-led revolution more likely than before, precipitating and intensifying violent civil and intercommunal conflict in Ireland, and postponing any kind of political settlement for at least eighty years.[94]

[94] These points are in part based on arguments put forward in Jeffery, *Ireland and War in the Twentieth Century*.

8

With the BEF

Brian Bond has argued that perhaps Wilson's 'greatest achievement' as DMO 'was in the innumerable practical arrangements—such as the provision of horses and transport—which made the mobilization of the B.E.F. an outstanding success, when four years earlier it would certainly have been a shambles'.[1] Lord Roberts, generous as ever, told Wilson that he had 'laid the foundation for the success which—with God's help—we firmly believe will be achieved by our troops'.[2] Contemporary accounts confirm the efficiency of the operation. C. R. Woodroffe, a junior officer at GHQ, noted in his diary on 22 August 1914: 'By midnight tonight the complete force of 4 Divisions will be here in its appointed place. That is to say 16 days after mobilisation—a wonderful performance.'[3] One participant, writing in a 1916 'pot-boiler' publication, told how the organisation of the Channel crossing had been run 'with never a single hitch'; so much so that he described it as 'German-like efficiency'.[4]

But the period between the decision having been made to send the Expeditionary Force and its actual despatch was one of considerable strain for Wilson. For years he had told the French that British soldiers would be at their side if the Germans invaded, and his devotion to the French alliance had informed and sustained his planning work over the past four years. It had powerfully contributed to the completeness and excellence of the plans, but it also affected his judgment when it seemed as if 'his' plan and 'his' commitment to the French might be modified or even (heaven forbid) abandoned. On 1 August, when the government was vacillating about supporting France, Wilson went to the French embassy to discuss the military situation with de la Panouse, the French military attaché. The ambassador, Paul Cambon, 'came in to see me. He was very bitter though personally charming.' Two days later, with British mobilisation ordered, he met Cambon in the Foreign Office: 'He held out both his hands to me. So different to day before yesterday.'[5]

Once the crucial decision for war had been taken, Wilson himself began to try to force the pace. Relying on Asquith's decision of 6 May (and taking it as more

[1] Bond, *The Victorian Army and the Staff College*, 258.
[2] Roberts to Wilson, 7 Aug. 1914 (Wilson papers, HHW 2/73/45).
[3] C. R. Woodroffe personal diary, 22 Aug. 1914 (Woodroffe papers).
[4] Corbett-Smith, *The Retreat from Mons*, 26.   [5] Wilson diary, 1, 3 Aug. 1914.

definitive than Asquith perhaps intended), he told de la Panouse that Britain *would* send five divisions. This was the decision made at the War Council on 5 August, but the next day Lord Kitchener, now Secretary of State for War, persuaded the Cabinet to send only four divisions, though the others would follow 'as soon as possible'.[6] Field Marshal Earl Kitchener of Khartoum was a new factor in the situation. An imperial soldier and proconsul, he had been Commander-in-Chief in South Africa (during the latter stages of the Boer War) and later in India. Temporarily in London in the summer of 1914, he seemed the ideal man to lead the war effort. In his appointment as War Minister he straddled the military and political spheres, giving him, for a while at least, effectively unassailable power. At the start of the First World War governments everywhere, democratic or not, handed over power to the military, subcontracting (as it were) the generals to get on and win the war. No one really anticipated the struggle to be as long, or as 'total', as it turned out to be, and once the generals failed to deliver a quick result, the pattern of civil–military relationships in each of the major belligerents became one where the politicians strove to gain (or regain) supremacy over the military.[7]

But in August 1914 what Britain apparently needed was the powerful, iconic, and decisive figure of Lord Kitchener as leader, emblematically commemorated for ever in the famous recruiting poster 'Your Country Needs You'. As a figurehead, Kitchener was marvellous, and his insistence that the war would be a long one (and that Britain therefore needed to raise a mass army) was an important corrective to the prevailing military wisdom, but he was hopeless as a Cabinet minister, with no sense of collective responsibility or the wider public environment within which politicians have to work. Within the military hierarchy, too, his impact was mixed. He had no real confidence in (or, in fact, experience of) the British General Staff system. One of the deficiencies, moreover, of British war planning before 1914 was a failure to anticipate what should happen to the staff in time of war. Partly this was due to the 'short war' assumption, and when war broke out virtually the entire General Staff was broken up and scattered to all parts of the army. Most went off with the BEF, including Wilson, Joey Davies, and Wully Robertson, as did Johnnie French as Commander-in-Chief. This left what Ian Beckett has called a 'policy vacuum' in London, filled in part by Kitchener.[8]

The BEF appointments initially left Wilson in a distinctly subordinate position. When Sir Charles Douglas told him that French would be Commander-in-Chief, Sir Archibald Murray Chief of Staff, and Robertson QMG, Wilson was 'reduced to B[rigadier] Genl. of Operations!' As he had been a substantive major-general since November 1913, this was a bit rough. A few days later Wilson noted in his diary that he had 'got my appointment turned into Sub-Chief'.[9] The story told afterwards (though there is no absolutely contemporaneous evidence for this)

  6 Wilson diary, 5–6 Aug. 1914.
  7 This process is usefully summarised in Gooch, *Armies in Europe*, ch. 6.
  8 Beckett, 'King George V and His Generals', 257.
  9 Wilson diary, 30 July, 3 Aug. 1914.

was that French had wanted Wilson, but, because of his role during the Curragh incident, 'government opposition had prevented his selection as CGS'.[10] Whatever the truth of the story, Murray was senior to Wilson, he had gained a reputation as an efficient staff officer in South Africa, and had served as French's Chief of Staff at Aldershot, so was apparently well qualified for the post.

Wilson and the autocratic Kitchener soon clashed. After the War Council decision of 5 August, Kitchener requested that the French be asked to send over a 'specially accredited' officer to discuss Anglo-French co-ordination. Huguet arrived the next day but, according to Wilson, 'he had come so hurriedly that he had no secret information or French dispositions or intentions'. Following a 'long talk' with Wilson on the morning of Friday 7 August, Huguet went back to France, agreeing to return the following Wednesday having seen Joffre.[11] Wilson evidently felt that there was no point Huguet seeing anyone else, but when Kitchener discovered that he had been and gone he summoned Wilson and they had the most terrific row, as is obvious from Wilson's diary account of the meeting:

> Lord K. sent for me 1.45 pm & was angry because I had let Huguet go & angrier still because I had told everything to Huguet about our starting on Sunday. I answered back as I have no intention of being bullied by him especially when he talks such nonsense as he did to-day. The man is a fool. He is now bringing the 6th Div. to England & sending troops from Aldershot to Grimsby, thus hopelessly mixing up our plans. he is a d——fool.[12]

Wilson was also clearly driven to distraction by Kitchener's messing up the deployment scheme, by proposing that part of the two Aldershot divisions be sent to the east coast against the possibility of a German raid there, a change he later rescinded.

The next issue to strain relations between Kitchener and Wilson was the question of exactly where the BEF should concentrate. Huguet returned to London on 12 August and reported 'all the German & French dispositions' to a meeting of Wilson, French, and Murray. They decided to stick with a concentration about Maubeuge. But when they went to Kitchener he wanted to go to Amiens, as he thought the Germans were 'coming north of the Meuse in great strength'. He only reluctantly changed his mind after a three-hour meeting, 'which was memorable as showing K's colossal ignorance & conceit'.[13] There was certainly conceit on both sides, insofar as each man believed that he knew better than the other. Kitchener had a deserved reputation for unsympathetic hardness, and he was not a man to allow a junior like Wilson to contradict him. Besides, the two men had already crossed swords when Kitchener and Robertson visited the Staff College in

---

[10] Gardner, *Trial by Fire*, 5. Gardner cites Walter Kirke's post-war memoir of George Macdonogh, a December 1930 letter by Murray, and Edmonds's memoirs for this story. There is nothing at all in Wilson's August 1914 diary to match his quite heated complaints in December that he was being disadvantaged because of his 'Ulster' activities.

[11] Callwell, *Wilson*, i. 159; Wilson diary, 6–7 Aug. 1914.

[12] Wilson diary, 7 Aug. 1914. Most of the 6th Division was stationed in Ireland.

[13] Ibid., 12 Aug. 1914.

July 1910. Kitchener was slow to forgive, and relations between the two men remained distinctly chilly until well into 1915.

On 13 and 14 August Wilson said his goodbyes before setting off for France. He specially went to see Winston Churchill and told him that, while they had had their differences (Churchill, as one of the 'plotters' against Ulster, was a particular unionist *bête noir*), he thought Winston 'had behaved like a hero on Aug. 5th & I wished to shake hands with him & say Goodbye'. Churchill began to tell Wilson he believed he would 'lead to Victory', but then 'completely broke down & cried so that he could not finish his sentence. I never liked him so much.' There were family farewells too; his mother, and 'poor Cecil . . . She was in great distress. God guard her.'[14]

Wilson, French, and Murray travelled over to France on 14 August, first to Amiens then to meetings in Paris, and on to GHQ at Le Cateau on 17 August. 'We are getting on all right,' he wrote to Cecil, 'and all the plans of the last four years are working smoothly and quietly, but it is <u>criminal</u> and <u>sinful</u> to keep 2 splendid divisions back in England, when they are badly wanted here.'[15] But the question now was, where would they fight? Motoring through southern Belgium in August 1913 with 'Uncle' Harper, Wilson had run along 'the position on which I want to fight', a 25-mile or so line north from Rochefort to Andenne on the River Meuse, just east of the fortress of Namur.[16] While Belgium remained strictly neutral, this could never be more than a purely paper scheme. Once the Germans invaded, however, it was possible that a co-ordinated Anglo-French advance into Belgium forming a defensive line from Verdun north to the Meuse might have held the German armies driving westwards south of the river, and even threatened the flanks and communications of the two German armies which (as Kitchener had anticipated but Wilson had not) were swinging through Belgium north of the Meuse.[17] But there was no co-ordinated defensive strategy, the French armies to the south went (disastrously) on the offensive, while the BEF concentrated at Maubeuge, expecting to take on the Germans in conjunction with the French Fifth Army under General Lanrezac. By 23 August they had moved 10 miles or so northwards into Belgium, nearly to Mons, where they clashed with the Germans for the first time.

The experience of the famous 'retreat from Mons' which followed is well illustrated in Wilson's diary. He began optimistically. Believing there were no more than two enemy corps opposite, Wilson spent the afternoon of 23 August drafting orders for an attack the following day. By early next morning, however, with intelligence indicating rather greater numbers of Germans, and Lanrezac falling back on the British right, 'we drafted orders & made arrangements for retirement to the line Maubeuge–Valenciennes'. It had been, he wrote, 'a day of

[14] Wilson diary, 13–14 Aug. 1914.
[15] Wilson to Cecil Wilson, 18 Aug. 1914 (quoted in Callwell, *Wilson*, i. 164).
[16] Wilson diary, 21 Aug. 1913.
[17] This optimistic argument is put forward in Ash, *Brasshat*, 170–3.

sharp fighting & severe disappointment'. On 24 August: 'heavy fighting all day till 4.30 pm., & some moments of great anxiety.' Although a fifth British division began to arrive, it was, thought Wilson, too late. 'If only we had our 6 Divs & had been sent in time,' he wrote, 'this retirement would have been an advance & this defeat a victory.'[18] By 26 August things were looking very bad indeed. French had instructed the two British Corps commanders, Douglas Haig (I Corps) and Horace Smith-Dorrien (II Corps)—each corps containing two divisions—to withdraw together, but Haig had moved without Smith-Dorrien, who had resolved to hold his exhausted troops and make a stand at Le Cateau. This caused consternation at GHQ. Wilson thought it would 'lead to a disaster, or it ought to'. French seemed 'quite incapable of understanding what it means', and refused to wake up Murray (it was about 6.30 a.m.). According to Charles Deedes, a subordinate of Wilson's at GHQ, Murray 'had completely broken down' and had been given 'morphia or some drug' rendering him 'quite incapable of performing his duty'. When he was given the news at seven o'clock, 'he promptly got a fainting fit'.[19]

Smith-Dorrien's stand did not end disastrously, and he managed to extract his corps more or less intact, but the BEF remained in 'great disorder'. The retreat, however, slowed down a little, and GHQ remained at Compiègne for three days. Joffre wanted Lanrezac to attack, which Wilson thought 'mad', as he was opposed by clearly superior German forces, and the only thing to do was continue to retire, regroup, and bring French reinforcements up from Alsace before contemplating a counterattack. During the afternoon of 29 August he 'had 2½ hours with Belin and Berthelot', and at 7.30 that evening he caught up with Joffre at the Lion d'Or hotel in Rheims. 'Under the electric light of the archway I had a long talk with him . . . urging him not to commit Lanrezac.' When Wilson got back to GHQ he found that there had been a wild panic—'a perfect debacle' he called it—with 'Murray leading the fright'. But his entreaties with Joffre had been successful and the more-or-less co-ordinated retreat continued. As the Germans began to run out of steam, this was happily at a slightly less frenetic pace. They crossed the Marne on 3 September and finally stopped to the east of Paris, south of Meaux.[20]

During the retreat from Mons, Wilson's contribution can be assessed in three distinct areas: process, advice, and liaison. The first concerns how the staff of GHQ as a whole operated, and the judgment must be that the system did not work very well at all. Based on a penetrating examination of the opening weeks of the war, Nikolas Gardner has concluded that 'while the "Old Contemptibles" performed well throughout the retreat from Mons, their commanders often proved unequal to the strains of the 1914 campaign'.[21] No doubt the circumstances of an unanticipated and confused withdrawal did not help, but there were systemic

18 Wilson diary, 23–4 Aug. 1914.
19 Ibid., 26 Aug. 1914; Scott (ed.), 'The View From GHQ', 10.
20 Wilson diary, 27, 29 Aug., 3–4 Sept. 1914.
21 Gardner, *Trial by Fire*, 65. The nickname 'Old Contemptibles' was taken on by the BEF after they were allegedly dismissed by the Kaiser as a 'contemptible little army'.

problems as well. No effective arrangements had been made before the war for the BEF staff, which only began meeting together from about 3 August. None of the BEF staff had actually rehearsed their precise wartime roles. Nor had any BEF officer commanded anything larger than a division in active operations. There were personality problems too. Sir John French, while quite a dynamic and inspiring leader, was inclined to flap and proved ill-equipped for the more managerial side of command. Murray's uncertain health and indecisiveness, together with Wilson's rivalry and much more dominant personality, further undermined the potential cohesion of the staff.

Writing in his diary on 26 August, C. R. Woodroffe described French as 'fit & quite cheery', Murray as 'dead beat', and Wilson as 'splendid, he is up & cheery all the time'.[22] Nevil Macready, AG of the BEF, recalled in his memoirs that Wilson 'never lost his cheery optimism'.[23] Frederick Sykes wrote that he 'saw a good deal of Henry Wilson during the retreat. He was a tower of strength to us all. He was never depressed, always optimistic, and was practically the only member of the Staff who could inspire our Allies with any degree of confidence.'[24] C. D. Baker-Carr, a civilian army driver, remembered Wilson's *sang froid* at Dammartin, where GHQ was based on 31 August–1 September: 'I shall never forget the sight of Henry Wilson . . . clad in a dressing-gown, riding-breeches, and carpet slippers, standing on the steps of the *château* where General Staff was established, waiting for his car. As usual he was perfectly calm and collected, though many of the other members of the staff appeared somewhat 'rattled'. As, also, was his custom, he kept firing off sardonic little jests at all and sundry within earshot.'[25]

But there were also indications of less sanguine behaviour. When Wilson's old Staff College friend 'Snowball' (Sir Thomas Snow, GOC of the 4th Division) arrived at Le Cateau on 25 August, the seriousness of the situation was outlined to him by Wilson 'in that half chaffing, half serious way, which was peculiar to him'. Coming thus 'from a man who was the greatest optimist I have ever met, it was not quite so overwhelming as it might have been if unfolded by others, but in all conscience it was bad enough'. Two days later Wilson issued what became known as the *sauve qui peut* order (which Snow thought was very bad for morale), instructing troops to dump all ammunition 'not absolutely required and other impedimenta such as officers' kits etc.', to allow transport wagons to carry tired soldiers.[26] The impulse, though, appears to have been as much out of concern for

---

[22] Woodroffe personal diary, 26 Aug. 1914 (Woodroffe papers). Woodroffe, however, significantly wrote that he thought William Robertson (the QMG of the BEF, and his immediate superior) was 'the only man capable of getting us safely out of this'.

[23] Macready, *Annals of an Active Life*, i. 206.

[24] Sykes, *From Many Angles*, 134. Sykes was Chief of Staff of the Royal Flying Corps.

[25] Baker-Carr, *From Chauffeur to Brigadier*, 29. James Edmonds told another story in his unpublished memoirs, that the sight of a single German soldier (who was, in fact, a prisoner) was enough to make Wilson 'tumble out of the chateau', jump into a car, and order the driver to 'drive to Paris like hell' (quoted in Green, *Writing the Great War*, 40).

[26] TS story of 4th Division BEF, Aug.–Sept. 1914 (Snow papers, 76/79/1).

the soldiers' plight as through panic. Ernest Swinton, who came out early in the campaign as the official British war correspondent, noted how Wilson was visibly affected 'by the inadequacy of the arrangements for dealing with casualties' and wanted the journalist to raise the matter in his reports. Though this showed Wilson's 'sensibility', wrote Swinton (with considerable hindsight concerning First World War casualties), it also 'exhibited a certain blindness to realities and a lack of sense of proportion'.[27]

The advice Wilson gave at any one time was obviously coloured by his state of mind. Although he appears to have kept a more optimistic attitude than many of his colleagues (though it must be said that the impression given by his diary entries tends to be pretty pessimistic), at times he, too, seems to have faltered. There were, nevertheless, three moments when Wilson's advice had an important influence on the fate of the BEF. The first, and arguably the most important, was in the aftermath of Le Cateau, when the 'auspicious' decision was made to continue to withdraw southwards, rather than south-west towards the Channel coast.[28] The Germans, believing that the BEF was shattered, worked on the latter assumption, which enabled Smith-Dorrien to withdraw largely unmolested. Discussing Le Cateau after the war, William Bartholomew, who had been a staff captain in the Operations branch of GHQ, told Basil Liddell Hart that 'Henry Wilson was the man who saved the British Army'.[29] The second moment was on 29 August, when Wilson persuaded Joffre not to commit Lanrezac to a major attack, to which the British could not have contributed, and which would have left the BEF even more up in the air than it already was. The third was in early September after the BEF had crossed the Marne. John French wanted to continue to withdraw south (and had given orders to do so), at precisely the time Joffre proposed to move onto the offensive. 'It is simply heartbreaking', wrote Wilson on 4 September, but the next morning he persuaded French 'to retrace his steps & join in offensive movement', and although there was inevitably some confusion, the BEF was able to take its part in the momentous battle of the Marne which began on 6 September.[30]

What these three key moments had in common was that in each case Wilson's advice reinforced the position of the BEF alongside their French allies. This was obviously of a piece with his Francophile sympathies, but he was not the only person sustaining the alliance. When, after Le Cateau, John French wanted to take the BEF completely out of the line and withdraw behind the River Seine, Kitchener (with the backing of the Cabinet) had vetoed it. On a day-to-day basis, nevertheless, Wilson was the single most important senior British soldier liaising with the French on the battlefield in the early weeks of the war. The confused early

[27] Swinton, *Eyewitness*, 50.   [28] Gardner, *Trial by Fire*, 57–8.

[29] 'Conversation with Gen. Bartholomew', 24 Mar. 1927, Liddell Hart TS diary notes (Liddell Hart papers, 11/1927/1b). Gardner (n. 28 above) suggests this refers to the decision to withdraw south. In context, however, it could reflect generally on Wilson's role during the retreat as a whole.

[30] Wilson diary, 4–6 Sept. 1914.

days of the retreat had left John French suspicious of the French and resentful that they had not supported him as he thought they should. Joffre's autocratic manner, and his assumption that the British should do what he told them to do further alienated him. Touchy and irascible as both French and Joffre were, it fell to Wilson to help smooth ruffled feathers and facilitate meaningful communication both between these two leaders and the British and French in general, a role which he was to play (albeit with varying success) for much of the war.[31]

At a dinner party in London in March 1920, Henry Wilson (clearly aiming to stir things up) 'said that had he been a German he would have advised them to go to war at the time they did since it seemed as good a moment as they could have selected; that they ought to have won but for bad luck'.[32] Bad luck or not, the opportunity for a quick German victory in the west had passed by the first week of September 1914, when Franco-British forces went on the offensive at the Marne, the Germans began to retire, and there was a 'race to the coast' which, when the positions of the opposing armies stabilised, resulted in a line of entrenchments from the Channel to Switzerland. By the end of October the BEF had deployed to the left of the main French armies. Wilson, having discussed the move with Huguet, had suggested it to French. Joffre was at first reluctant to agree. He and his staff did not trust French and Murray 'to act with energy', and were reluctant to let the BEF move closer to the Channel ports, but in the end agreed.[33] The new British position, moreover, was adjacent to French troops under Foch's command, which further enhanced Wilson's significance as a link between the two allies. Wilson's closeness to Foch was confirmed when he, John French, and Murray arrived at Foch's headquarters at Doullens. Foch 'shook hands with Sir John and Murray but when he saw H.W. he threw his arms round his neck and gave him a big smacking kiss on each cheek—It was not resented in some quarters but it may have been.'[34]

Agreeing with Foch, in the late autumn of 1914 Wilson thought the war could still be won in a relatively short time. There were hopes (though vain) that the Russians could draw off German troops from the western front. 'I still think', he wrote to his wife, 'the campaign will be over in the spring, that is to say if the Russians do moderately well, and I know of no reason why they shouldn't.'[35] But because of Kitchener's decision to raise a mass volunteer army, the BEF were being denied adequate replacements for the casualties it had suffered, thus jeopardising the possibility of success. 'K.'s "shadow armies," for shadow campaigns, at

[31] For a sustained acknowledgement of Wilson's role in maintaining good Anglo-French relations, see Huguet, *Britain and the War*, which Huguet dedicated to Wilson's memory.
[32] John Davies diary, 3 Mar. 1920 (Davies papers, MS 170/13). Wilson did get a response: 'Hugh Cecil argued against this, praising Foch etc.' Davies was the American ambassador in London 1918–21. I am most grateful to Eunan O'Halpin for this reference.
[33] Wilson diary, 24–30 Sept. 1914.
[34] Lord Loch to his wife (TS copy), 11 Oct. 1914 , letters 1914–15 box (Loch papers, 71/12/1). Loch (a Staff College student when Wilson was commandant) was liaison officer between GHQ and II Corps.   [35] Wilson to Cecil Wilson, 19 Sept. 1914 (quoted in Callwell, *Wilson*, i. 183).

unknown and distant dates', asserted Wilson, 'prevent a lot of good officers, N.C.O.s and men from coming out.' These armies, he argued, could not be trained and take the field for two years; what was needed was for the BEF to be at 'full strength' *now*.[36] Writing to Charlie Hunter, Wilson argued, 'we have to balance the problematical advantages of "shadow armies" wh. can <u>never</u> take the field, against the clearance of the Germans out of northern France before winter sets in. Which', he asked, 'is the more important?'[37] The month-long German offensive which began on 21 October (the 'First Battle of Ypres'), however, suggested that victory might not be very swift, or in any way easy. First Ypres, indeed, provided a kind of pattern for the grim war of attrition which was to prevail along the western front for the next four years. While remaining optimistic, Rawlinson got it broadly right towards the end of the year. 'There is no manner of doubt', he wrote, 'that we are going to succeed in crushing the German Empire. It may be a war of exhaustion, it may take one, two or three years to complete, but we shall be daily gaining wealth & strength, whilst Germany will be daily losing theirs.'[38]

In November 1914 the 82-year-old Lord Roberts came to France to visit the troops. Wilson thought he 'seemed very well', and he 'told me all about K. & invasion [scares] & the chaos there is at home'. But Roberts caught a chill on a Friday and died on the Saturday evening. Wilson was at his bedside, and wrote that his life was 'thus completed as he would have wished himself; dying in the middle of the soldiers he loved so much & in the sound of the guns'.[39] Wilson accompanied Roberts's body back to England for the funeral at St Paul's Cathedral in London. He was at home for four days, where he found Cecil not very well, suffering from gallstones. At the War Office he had '1¼ hours with K. who talked some sense & much nonsense', but he also saw a number of Opposition leaders: Bonar Law, Milner, Walter Long, and Austen Chamberlain.[40]

The stabilisation of the battle-lines along the western front, and the growing appreciation (by politicians as well as soldiers) that the war would not be 'over by Christmas', brought on the first serious re-examination of the BEF higher command. In the battle zone the two main considerations were the capabilities of the commanders themselves and their relations with the French armies fighting alongside them. The first had already been sorely tested during the early weeks of the war, and the uneasy relationships between French, Murray, and Wilson continued into the autumn. Lord Loch, the liaison officer between GHQ and II Corps, told his wife that 'Mons, Le Cateau and the whole retreat were not actually caused but intensified by the want of pulling together of the whole show'. There

[36] Wilson to C. Wilson, 15 Sept. 1914 (ibid. 178). See also Wilson to Kiggell, 15 Sept. 1914 (Kiggell papers, 3/1). The first New Army divisions in fact arrived in France and Flanders in May 1915.

[37] Wilson to Hunter, 18 Oct. 1914 (copy) (Milner papers, MS Milner dep. 349, fos. 336–7).

[38] Rawlinson to Lord Derby, 24 Dec. 1914 (Rawlinson papers, NAM 5201/33/17).

[39] Wilson diary, 13–14 Nov. 1914.   [40] Ibid., 17–20 Nov. 1914.

was no clear central control, 'no master hand pulling all the strings and taking a grip of the situation'.[41] Early in October Huguet told Wilson that Murray had 'proceeded to denounce me...saying I considered myself as superior'. Huguet said 'he showed a jealousy & a dislike which was quite remarkable'. Wilson put this down to Murray's shame at breaking down during the retreat, but Murray was also irritated by Wilson usurping his position. In November, for example, Wilson rewrote 'an ambiguous & badly worded order' of Murray's, 'to something more definite'. When, the next morning, he 'showed Murray how I had amended his order there was a scene, & he threatened to resign!'[42] That Wilson was surprised about this (note his exclamation-mark), is surely more remarkable than that Murray was annoyed.

Wilson raised the matter of 'Murray's explosion to Huguet' with Billy Lambton, John French's military secretary. Lambton (according to Wilson's diary) thought that Wilson should replace Murray, to which Wilson rather piously commented that 'this was a thing I cared very little about; my chief concern being to keep the show going for Sir John as best I can'. A couple of days later Murray confided in Wilson that 'it was becoming very difficult, Sir John getting more unreasonable'. He asked Wilson if he should resign. Murray had his weaknesses, but he was no fool and perhaps he was trying to flush out Wilson's real opinion. Wilson, however, told him not to, and said 'that I knew of no one who could take his place with greater success'. Perhaps disingenuous in turn, and certainly dodging the issue, Wilson argued to himself, 'I could not tell him that I thought I could do better than he, so I had no option. I was sorry for him. I told Billy of our talk, & he agreed it was the best thing.'[43]

At the end of November and again in mid-December John French himself told Wilson that he should replace Murray. On both occasions Wilson asserts that he did not press his own cause but told French to look round the whole army and 'pick the best man he could find'. French, in turn, said he was resolved to give Murray a Corps and install Wilson as Chief of Staff: 'he said he would have me or nobody for C. of S., & had so written to K. & that if Murray left & K. gave him anyone else he would resign.'[44] But French had reckoned without Asquith, who summoned him to London as soon as he heard of the proposed change. French wanted to replace Murray, wrote Asquith to his confidante Venetia Stanley, 'by that poisonous tho' clever ruffian Wilson who (as you remember) behaved so badly at the W.O. this spring about Ulster & c. I am glad to say', he continued, 'that after a little talk he quite dropped it, and Murray (who is an excellent tho' slightly jumpy man) will go on.'[45] French returned to St Omer and, clearly embarrassed,

---

[41] Loch to his wife (TS copy), 11 Oct. 1914 , letters 1914–15 box (Loch papers, 71/12/1).

[42] Wilson diary, 6 Oct., 4–5 Nov. 1914.   [43] Ibid., 7, 10 Oct. 1914.

[44] Ibid., 29 Oct., 16, 18 Dec. 1914.

[45] Asquith to Venetia Stanley, 20 Dec. 1914 (Asquith–Venetia Stanley letters, MS Eng. c.7095, fo. 42). From a letter from Asquith to Kitchener, 18 Dec. 1914 (of which, oddly, there is a copy in Robertson's papers), it is clear that Kitchener did not favour Wilson either (Robertson papers, I/13/1).

explained to Wilson that 'neither K. nor Squiff [Asquith] will have me'. French spoke warmly of Wilson's valuable work, and how he was 'absolutely necessary to the rest of the staff'. He added that 'this Government would soon be out & then it would be all right', to which Wilson noted in his diary 'So there is politics in our Army!', a fact which he, more than most, should have known well.[46] Wilson was evidently very disappointed. Later he told French that he *ought* to offer the job to him, but that, to help him out, Wilson would refuse to accept. It was, nevertheless, an appointment he had 'worked for & dreamt of for years'.[47]

Murray was not the only British general whose position was being discussed. In November Foch came to see Wilson to tell him that Kitchener had proposed to Joffre that he might replace Sir John French with Sir Ian Hamilton, but Joffre would not agree. Encouraged by Foch, Wilson told French who was naturally upset, and wanted to get H. A. Gwynne to 'start a Press campaign ag[ains]t K.'.[48] In his memoirs Joffre described French as a 'loyal soldier' unfortunately 'rent between two influences': Wilson, 'a man of keenest intelligence, with a sound appreciation of every situation, and, in addition, accustomed to French methods and thoroughly knowing France', and Murray, 'who spent his time exhorting the Field Marshal with counsels of extreme prudence'.[49] On 27 December, when French and Wilson went to Joffre's headquarters at Chantilly, Wilson 'heard Joffre say "General Murray va-t-il partir"? & when Sir J. said no, Joffre said "Ah c'est dommage".'[50] When Asquith was told that Joffre was complaining about 'want of energy' on Murray's part, he said that both he and Kitchener believed this 'to be another proof of the constant intriguing of that serpent Wilson, who is just under Murray and wants to supplant him'. He and Kitchener were 'quite determined' that Wilson should 'not succeed'.[51]

In London for a week's leave in January 1915, Wilson was told by Clive Wigram (the King's assistant private secretary) that Kitchener 'was not really hostile to me, but it was Squiff who knocked me out'. Bonar Law and Carson told him they were anxious that he should succeed Murray, so perhaps there was hope yet.[52] Back in France on a Sunday afternoon he told Robertson he thought that he (Robertson) would now be offered the job. Robertson 'said he would not accept it, he could not manage Johnnie who was sure to come to grief & would carry him with him'. As the two were going up to church by car, Robertson 'begged' Wilson to 'put Johnnie off offering it to him, because he must refuse. The chance of a lifetime', mused Wilson, 'and two men in a car, both refusing it'.[53]

But Robertson *was* offered the job and he *did* take it. The change was precipitated by Murray's doctor saying he would be unfit for duty for about a month,

[46] Wilson diary, 24 Dec. 1914.   [47] Ibid., 30 Dec. 1914.   [48] Ibid., 5, 8 Nov. 1914.
[49] Joffre, *Memoirs*, i. 277.
[50] Wilson diary, 27 Dec. 1914. 'Is General Murray departing?' 'A pity'.
[51] Asquith to Venetia Stanley, 28 Dec. 1914 (Asquith–Venetia Stanley letters, MS Eng. c.7095, fo. 91).   [52] Wilson diary, 9, 11–12 Jan. 1915.
[53] Ibid., 17 Jan. 1915.

whereupon French offered Robertson the post.[54] In his memoirs Robertson said that, although 'the offer was a tempting one, as it meant an increase of pay as well as of position', he did not at first wish to accept it as he knew he was not French's first choice. In the end, however, 'I realised that it was my duty to put personal considerations aside', and on 25 January he took up the position.[55] Wilson, who was in Belfort, well to the south, on a tour of the French line, received the news in a telephone message from Robertson: 'Commander in Chief wishes me to tell you that Murray is going home on account of his health and that I have taken his place.' Wilson had been made 'Principal Liaison Officer with French Army'.[56]

Back at GHQ, Wilson, who clearly felt slighted by the changes, suggested to French and Robertson that there were three possible options: he could remain as Sub-Chief (under Robertson), but 'devoting myself to the French'; he could, with promotion to temporary lieutenant-general (to establish his seniority), 'work with the French'; or, finally, he could be sent home. French told him that Robertson would not have the first option, and he himself 'would not hear' of the third. Clearly aiming to mollify Wilson, he told him 'he trusted me more & looked to me more & liked me more than all the others & in consequence I must always remain with him'.[57] In a letter to Cecil, Wilson made the best of the situation. He told her of French's flattering remarks, and assured her that 'all this fuss' had 'ended in making me much bigger and more powerful than I was before'.[58] This is the impression Loch got when he discussed the changes at GHQ. Wilson, he wrote to his wife, is not 'in anyway displaced if he plays the game in fact he is in a stronger position'.[59]

Repington, who could be counted upon to place the worst possible construction on Wilson's actions, told Haig that Wilson 'had got Huguet . . . to get Joffre and the French government' to ask Asquith to make him Chief of Staff. 'Such an intrigue greatly astonished me', mused Haig. 'What an intriguer the man is!' wrote John Charteris, Haig's ADC and later his chief intelligence officer. 'For a soldier of his rank,' he added, employing a curious metaphor, 'to descend to intrigue is mental adultery.'[60] Part of the thinking behind Wilson's new position was apparently to curb his trouble-making proclivities. French 'knows that he [Wilson] is an intriguer', noted Haig early in February, 'but he thinks he can do no harm in his present appointment'.[61] 'Wilson (I rejoice to say)', wrote Asquith, 'is put out of the reach of mischief making by being appointed chief officer of <u>liaison</u> at the French Headquarters.'[62]

[54] French diary, 24 Jan. 1915 (French papers, 75/46/2).
[55] Robertson, *From Private to Field Marshal*, 218.
[56] Note of telephone message, 26 Jan. 1915 (tipped into Wilson diary).
[57] Wilson diary, 29–31 Jan. 1915. In his own diary (1 Feb. 1915) French noted 'another talk with Wilson. He seems quite happy and contented now' (French papers, 75/46/2).
[58] Wilson to Cecil Wilson, 31 Jan. 1915 (quoted in Callwell, *Wilson*, i. 204).
[59] Loch to his wife (TS copy), 28 Jan. 1915, letters 1914–15 box (Loch papers, 71/12/1).
[60] Haig TS diary, 22 Jan. 1915 (TNA, WO 256/3); Charteris to his wife, 22 Jan. 1915, quoted in Charteris, *At G.H.Q.*, 73.   [61] Haig TS diary, 5 Feb. 1915 (TNA, WO 256/3).
[62] Asquith to Venetia Stanley, 26 Jan. 1915 (Asquith–Venetia Stanley letters, MS Eng. c.7095, fo. 56).

There is actually not much evidence that Wilson systematically 'intrigued' either against Murray or on behalf of himself. What we do have is evidence (mostly in his own diary) of considerable dissatisfaction with Murray (and French), which (as was his way) he frequently shared with all and sundry. It is clear, too, that individuals in both England and France were lobbying in his favour. His conservative political friends at home both valued his abilities (perhaps even genuinely wanting them employed to best effect in the war effort), and no doubt desired the promotion of a potential ally within the military hierarchy. Above all, and for obvious reasons, the French—especially Huguet, Foch, and Joffre—took every opportunity to praise Wilson and urge his promotion. He was regarded by the French as so valuable and apparently amenable a colleague that they pushed his case without him necessarily having to encourage them very much.[63] In January 1915, for example, Lord Bertie, the British ambassador in Paris, had dinner with François Flameng the painter 'who has been much at the Front'. Flameng 'praised French's Chief of Staff, which is the reverse of what I had heard from the French point of view. I discovered, however, that it was the Assistant Chief of Staff—Henry Wilson—whom Flameng had in mind and not Sir A. Murray.'[64] Of course, the more the French praised Wilson, the more some British fellow officers suspected him, not only, perhaps, for 'intriguing', but more generally as being insufficiently loyal to Britain.[65]

The events of December 1914–January 1915 also serve to illustrate military attitudes towards politicians. Wilson put his failure to succeed Murray down to an 'infernal political intrigue', based on Asquith's resentment at his actions during the Curragh crisis. Wilson, paradoxically (and perhaps over-optimistically), thought that his position within the army was strengthened ('impregnable', he called it) by the transparently biased decisions of the Cabinet.[66] For soldiers, 'political' was evidently a term of abuse. Early in the war, Charteris had recorded Haig's low opinion of Wilson: 'D.H. thinks Wilson is a politician, and not a soldier, and "politician" with Douglas Haig is synonymous with crooked dealing and wrong sense of values.'[67] This observation is significant as much for what it says about Haig's opinion of politicians as for his estimation of Wilson. The ostentatious, and even contemptuous, rejection of politics and politicians as inherently dishonest was (and perhaps still is) a familiar enough opinion voiced by soldiers, confident in their apparently straightforward duty to Crown and Country. Wilson himself, that most 'political' of generals, rarely had anything good to say about those whom he dismissed as 'Frocks' ('Frock-coats', as opposed to 'Brasshats'—soldiers). Talking to Liddell Hart in the 1930s, Lloyd George

---

[63] This is the sense in Prete, 'Joffre and the Question of Allied Supreme Command', 330–1.

[64] Bertie diary, 18 Jan. 1915, quote in Bertie, *The Diary of Lord Bertie*, i. 100. Flameng was an official French war artist.

[65] This could happen on the French side too. Joffre wrote a letter to Foch giving 'Huguet a nasty swipe for being too pro-English' (Wilson diary, 28 Feb. 1915).   [66] Wilson diary, 30–1 Jan. 1915.

[67] Charteris to his wife, 16 Aug. 1914 (quoted in Charteris, *At G.H.Q.*, 11).

remarked 'about soldiers' incurable prejudice to politicians; that even Henry Wilson, who owed everything to politicians, was always jeering at the frocks'.[68] But for all their professional expertise, and undoubted loyalty to what they conceived to be their proper duty, all soldiers in early twentieth-century Britain also had an obligation to obey the instructions of their democratic masters. As Hew Strachan has observed, moreover, 'those feelings against party politics which soldiers were apt to cite as evidence of their political neutrality...in essence constituted a contempt for parliamentary government'.[69]

The irony, so far as Henry Wilson was concerned, was that as the 'political dimension' became increasingly significant in the wider prosecution of the war, so too did the value of his own talents. In his memoir-cum-history *Politicians and the War*, Lord Beaverbrook wrote that Wilson 'possessed throughout the war an importance quite disproportionate to his military status'. Beaverbrook ascribed this to the fact that Wilson was 'a schemer and intriguer both', who 'was endued with the political mind, and could and did talk the language of politicians'.[70] In 1914–15 Wilson's importance was considerably amplified by his position as '*persona gratissima* in French military circles'.[71] But as the Franco-British military alliance moved from the ad-hocery of the early weeks of the war, Wilson's position became increasingly anomalous. *Either* he could be Chief (or Sub-Chief) of Staff, with the responsibility to inform, interpret, and communicate the Commander-in-Chief's decisions to the BEF at large, *or* he could superintend and facilitate high-level liaison with the French. At times, both during the retreat from Mons and afterwards, he effectively performed both roles, arguably to the detriment of each. After the front had stabilised, reciprocal military missions were established in both French and British headquarters, with Colonel Victor Huguet heading the French mission at GHQ and Major Sidney Clive the British at Joffre's headquarters.[72] Wilson and Huguet, old friends, worked together extremely closely, leaving Clive rather outside the loop. Wilson's appointment as principal liaison officer in January 1915, together with Robertson's replacement of Murray as DMO, to some extent regularised the situation at GHQ, though, as we shall see, personal considerations continued to influence matters.

For Sir John French and the BEF a central question (as in any kind of coalition warfare) concerned who was in charge? French's original instructions from Lord Kitchener in August 1914 had reflected the ambiguities of the Franco-British alliance. He had been told that 'the special motive of the force under your control is to support and co-operate with the French Army against our common enemies'.

---

[68] 'Talk with Lloyd George', 24 Sept. 1932, Liddell Hart TS diary notes (Liddell Hart papers, 11/1932/42a).   [69] Strachan, *The Politics of the British Army*, 101.
[70] Beaverbrook, *Politicians and the War*, i. 198. Lord Beaverbrook (Max Aiken until 1917), owner of the *Daily Express*, was the Canadian government representative at the front, 1916–17, and British Minister of Information, 1918. Bonar Law told Wilson in 1916 that Aiken wanted him to become GOC of the Canadian Corps (Wilson diary, 27 Apr. 1916).   [71] Collier, *Brasshat*, 205.
[72] Philpott, *Anglo-French Relations*, 95–6. This book is a useful study for Anglo-French relations generally.

But Kitchener also explicitly reminded French that the BEF was an autonomous force: 'I wish you to distinctly understand that your command is an entirely independent one, and that you will in no case come under the orders of any Allied General.'[73] French, by and large—and this was broadly true for the BEF as a whole—firmly placed the independence of his command well above support and co-operation with the French army. Even Henry Wilson did not (at this stage) envisage British units serving under French command. In November 1914, when Foch wanted 'Allenby & 2 Batt[alion]s to help' in an attack, French 'went so far as to say he would put Allenby under Foch', but Wilson 'was opposed to this'.[74]

Sir John French's uneasy relations with his French counterparts primarily stemmed from the difficulties of reconciling British national interests with the alliance priorities of the western front, but they were powerfully exacerbated by at least three other factors. Temperamentally, he was inclined to drastic swings of mood and outbursts of violent temper. He also resented it if he thought he was being dictated to, which did not assist relations with either Kitchener or Joffre, who were both markedly decisive in manner. In the second place, French was clearly under considerable strain, not only during the panicky days of August and September. He was in command of a force larger than anything he had experience of, and in novel conditions of modern, industrialised war. This was nothing like the dashing cavalry campaign of the South African veldt with which he had made his name, but an increasingly grim, mechanised struggle in which every action appeared to be accompanied by appalling casualties. Last, and by no means least, French could not speak the French language, or scarcely so, which, apart from the inevitable misunderstandings and confusions which could occur, enhanced any frustrations he might already feel about working with a problematic ally.

Wilson, both before and after January 1915, was perfectly placed to record the mutual frustrations of the two allies. In October 1914, after Foch, worried that the Belgians on the extreme left of the line might collapse, was looking for support from the British and had written to French for support, Sir John told Wilson 'he would be d——if he would be dictated to by Foch who had better mind his own business etc etc'. In April 1915 French was 'again very angry with Joffre who, with Millerand' (the French Minister of War) was 'trying to get him (Sir J.) under his command'.[75] French dismissed Millerand as 'a d——d little socialist cad'.[76] Joffre for his part did not help matters by writing directly to Kitchener from time to time when he thought French was being particularly unhelpful. In April 1915, when French troops broke under the first serious German gas attack north-east of British positions near Ypres, there was an especially vehement outburst. French was 'furious with Foch & Joffre & all Frenchmen! He says they always let them in (at Mons, on the Aisne & now) & that our Ministers are right & we ought to clear out of France bag & baggage & go elsewhere! Where he did not know!' Wilson

---

[73] Theses instructions are reproduced in full in Edmonds, *History of the Great War: France and Belgium*, 1914, i. 499–500.   [74] Wilson diary, 4 Nov. 1914.
[75] Ibid., 16 Oct. 1914, 2 Apr. 1915.   [76] Clive diary, 7 June 1915 (Clive papers, II/1).

noted that Joffre was expected at GHQ, and 'Sir J. says he is going to tell him what he thinks of him! He had better not,' added Wilson, '& of course won't.'[77] Sidney Clive thought the meetings between French and Joffre had 'no good effect for the former is irritable & the latter silent'. Any 'good understanding' had to be sorted out by their respective staffs before plans were put before the commanders.[78]

The French had equally strong views about the British GOC. 'Comme il aime pleurir, ce Bébé', remarked Foch of French after one meeting.[79] In March 1915 Sidney Clive reported that Joffre had called French a 'menteur' and a 'mauvais camarade'.[80] These were the kinds of remarks that Wilson had to try to keep from French in order to smooth relations between the commanders. There was an obvious linguistic barrier, and here Wilson's command of the French language was crucial. Wilson personally did quite a lot of interpreting. This could be done creatively, as at a meeting in May 1915 when Joffre was again looking for support from French, who was again holding back. Joffre, wrote Wilson, 'hinted at Govt. action [evidently a direct appeal to Kitchener] which luckily Sir J. did not quite catch & I got the chance of interpreting wrong, but as both were getting hot I got Sir J. to go away saying he would send an answer by me later'. Wilson took a similar line in July with 'a rather abrupt letter from Joffre' asking 'that Sir John should put, at least, 10 Divs into the coming fight', which he toned down in 'a very free translation'.[81]

A man of Wilson's seniority, however, could not continue indefinitely to perform interpreting duties, nor the comparatively routine work of translating documents. But for a while after he became principal liaison officer (with promotion to temporary lieutenant-general) he tried to carry on as before, in the process upsetting both Sidney Clive and Wully Robertson. At the end of January 1915 Clive doubted whether Wilson 'will find enough work to do', but felt 'quite sure that Gen. R. will not allow him to have the slightest independent access to Sir John'. In fact, until the late summer of 1915 Wilson, who exploited his close personal relations with both Foch and French, effectively bypassed Clive. He was at his busiest as a 'go-between' during the spring, when on average he saw Foch every two or three days, though Joffre rather less often. In late August, however, Clive suggested to Wilson that 'the time ought to come when the heads of the different armies could communicate direct, without doing it through a solicitor, but H.W. thought that day is still far off'. Wilson was wrong, and the following month Clive was confirmed as the sole conduit of communications between French and Joffre.[82]

The new arrangement clearly suited Robertson whose relationship with Wilson remained distinctly uncomfortable during 1915. Although Wilson told Foch he 'thought Robertson would do very well', his private comments on the new CGS

[77] Wilson diary, 25 Apr. 1915.   [78] Clive diary, 6 June 1915 (Clive papers, II/1).
[79] Wilson diary, 8 Dec. 1914. 'How he likes to cry, this Baby.'
[80] Ibid., 6 Mar. 1915. 'Liar' and 'bad comrade'.   [81] Ibid., 12 May, 15 July 1915.
[82] Clive diary, 26 Aug., 1, 20 Sept. 1915 (Clive papers, II/2).

were far from favourable. 'He is secretive,' he wrote on 8 February, '&, like all underbreds, suspicious; also his manners are somewhat repugnant.' Later the same month he described him as 'a slippery old boy & hostile to me now, out of jealousy'.[83] In May, when planning for a co-ordinated attack was being discussed with Huguet, Robertson mightily annoyed Wilson by accusing the French of breaking their word. Once again, the CGS's humble origins came in for remark: 'It is d[amnable?] to work with a man who is not a gentleman. The moment the strain comes so does the hairy heel.'[84] Despite Clive's confident prediction in January 1915, Robertson had to tolerate French regularly consulting Wilson about all areas of military policy. In April, indeed, French insisted that Wilson come to dine in his mess on a regular basis.[85] Wilson, of course, was a much more congenial personality than Robertson, and, whatever his formal status, was a lot more fun to be with than the sombre and rather saturnine CGS.

Wilson's cheery sociability was pretty much a constant feature of his relationships. In March 1915 Billy Congreve dropped in on his father Walter (then commanding the 6th Division). 'Henry Wilson turned up for tea and was like a sort of delightful whirlwind,' he wrote in his diary. 'I do admire him, more than anyone I know.'[86] 'During the war,' wrote Arthur Green (who had been at the Staff College under Wilson), 'the effect of his sudden appearance at some headquarters, arrayed in an exotic poshteen or embroidered coat, would be stupendous. There was', he added, 'something theatrical and spectacular about him.'[87] There was public recognition, too, though only grudgingly bestowed. On 13 February Robertson (on behalf of French, who was 'very angry' about the matter) told Wilson that he 'had been cut out of the KCBs in the forthcoming Honours Gazette'. It is not clear who denied Wilson the award he was probably due, but he affected not to care, except for 'poor Cecil', who would have become Lady Wilson. In June, however, despite a scare that he might 'be cut out again', he finally became *Sir* Henry Wilson.[88]

The British fought a number of battles on the western front during 1915, each more-or-less co-ordinated with bigger French offensives. Hopes were still high that the war could be won—or at least major success achieved—in the near future. Joffre told Wilson in March that 'by the end of Apr. he would be in a condition to attack & break the line'. In May 'he talked of getting to Namur & the war being over in 3 mos.'. Later that month, between the disastrous British battle of Aubers and the scarcely less damaging attack at Festubert, Wilson asserted in his diary that this could be 'one of the decisive actions of the war', and on 17 May complained that Kitchener was holding back troops when 'we are on the edge of

[83] Wilson diary, 4, 8, 26 Feb. 1915. Wilson also told Clive Wigram (assistant private secretary to the King): 'Robertson will I feel sure do very well as C.G.S.' (Wilson to Wigram, 1 Feb. 1915, Royal Archives, RA PS/GV/Q 832/362).   [84] Wilson diary, 16 May 1915.

[85] Ibid., 26 Mar., 2, 5 Apr. 1915.

[86] Congreve, *Armageddon Road*, 105. Both Billy and Walter were fellow Riflemen.

[87] Green, *Evening Tattoo*, 31–2.   [88] Wilson diary, 13 Feb., 29 May, 24 June 1915.

great things here'.[89] This was all very over-optimistic. Neither in 1915, nor in 1916 (even with massively greater resources), was there any realistic hope that the British or the French would dramatically break through the German front.

Wilson (and French) blamed the failures of 1915 not only on the 'holding back' of troops, but also on shortages of munitions, the former reflecting a British strategic focus away from the western front, and the latter the failure of British pre-war planning to anticipate the scale and demands of modern war.[90] The apparent and costly stalemate on the western front by the end of 1914 led some British policymakers to consider where else the 'Central Powers' (Germany and Austria-Hungary had been joined by Turkey in November 1914) might be attacked. Early in 1915 the government approved a plan for a naval operation against the Dardanelles, the narrow straits between the Mediterranean and the Black Sea.[91] Not only would this strike close to the Turkish capital of Constantinople (Istanbul), but it would provide strong encouragement, and enable practical support, for Russia. The scheme, which seemed to offer a relatively low-cost opportunity to make a dramatic difference to the balance of power, had wide support at home. Churchill, seeking to exploit Britain's naval strength, was an especially powerful proponent, but there was backing too from Lloyd George and Opposition leaders, including Bonar Law. Faced with the alternatives of a continuing high 'butcher's bill' in France and Flanders, or an imaginative operation which might materially shorten the war, it is not difficult to see why individuals plumped for the latter. But there was a strong body of opinion, mostly within the army, which asserted that the war against Germany could only be won by success on the western front—'the old principle of decisive numbers at decisive theatre'.[92] It was a debate which was to continue for most of the war, sometimes characterised as 'Easterners' against 'Westerners', with the latter dismissing operations elsewhere as no more than 'sideshows'.

The original conception had been purely naval, but when in March 1915 Churchill's battleships failed to break through, it was decided to land troops on the European side, along the Gallipoli peninsula. From the start Henry Wilson feared (with some reason) that the venture would draw resources away from the western front. He could see no point in it anyhow, as success would simply mean 'putting Russia in C-ople'. A week after the 25 April landings, he wearily noted, 'we gain ground & lose men (8000)'. A month later Wilson had an argument with Eddie Derby, who 'saw no harm in the Dardanelles'. Wilson, by contrast, reflected that if the 100,000 troops now out there had been available in France, Neuve Chapelle (the first major British offensive of the war) 'might have been a success'.[93] On 10 June he was told that another four divisions were being sent out to Gallipoli. 'How they will laugh in Berlin', he commented. And when new

[89] Wilson diary, 23 Mar., 4, 13, 17 May 1915.
[90] This is the theme of French, *British Economic and Strategic Planning*.
[91] French, *British Strategy and War Aims*, 68–74.   [92] Wilson diary, 1 Feb. 1915.
[93] Ibid., 3 Apr., 1 May, 6 June.

landings were bungled at Suvla Bay in August, he wrote that it was 'all a cruel waste of men & Winston first & others after should be put on their trial, for this mad enterprise is sheer murder nor can success lead to anything except further disaster'.[94] In this case Wilson, happily, was wrong. Against all expectations, although it was undoubtedly itself a defeat, the Gallipoli campaign did not end in 'further disaster'. Between December 1915 and January 1916 the allied forces on the peninsula were evacuated with minimal casualties.

The battle of Aubers (close to Neuve Chapelle) in May 1915 went badly wrong. John French claimed that its failure was principally due to a shortage of munitions, an opinion he leaked to Repington who promptly published it in *The Times*, precipitating a major political crisis.[95] Munitions shortages, exacerbated by instructions from London to send supplies already in France to the Dardanelles,[96] had been affecting the BEF for some time. In February 1915 Johnnie Du Cane, French's artillery adviser, told Henry Wilson that he did not think there was enough high-explosive ammunition to carry out a major attack until the middle of May. This propelled Wilson into a more-than-usually acid comment: 'It is not a bad commentary on our state of preparations & our power of production to say that 6 mos. after war breaks out we have only 12 Div. in the field of which 2 are Indian, & that with this force we cannot attack (with say 4 Div.) until 3 mos. later on account of lack of H.E. Ammun! Somebody ought to hang.'[97] As it turned out, there was not even enough in May, though it has to be said that the failure at Aubers cannot entirely be blamed on the 'shell scandal'. Nevertheless, the suggestion was enough to precipitate a heated public debate back home.

In March 1915 Wilson had hoped that the 'whole Dardanelles affair may prove a fiasco', as it would help 'get rid of Winston'.[98] Indeed it did; Churchill resigned in November 1915, but the combination of failure at Gallipoli and the 'shell scandal' accelerated more profound political changes. In the spring of 1915 Asquith had come to realise that the political and administrative demands of what was becoming a 'total war', and the need to ensure the full economic, social, and industrial mobilisation of the 'home front', required an all-party coalition government. In May, after some jockeying for position, the first coalition government of 1914–18 was formed. Bonar Law, Balfour, Carson, Austen Chamberlain, Lord Curzon, and other Conservatives joined the government. Arthur Henderson became the first-ever Labour Cabinet minister. Only the Irish Party (and some Labour pacifists) refused to join.[99]

The arrival of Conservative friends and admirers in government boosted Wilson's prospects. From the beginning of the war he had kept a voluminous

[94] Ibid., 10 June, 11 Aug. 1915.

[95] *The Times*, 14 May 1915, 'Need for shells'; see also Repington, *The First World War*, i. 34–40.

[96] Wilson diary, 11 May 1915.   [97] Ibid., 9 Feb. 1915.

[98] Ibid., 18 Mar. 1915.

[99] The price of this rejection was to tip the political balance further against the Redmondite constitutional nationalists (see Mansergh, *The Unresolved Question*, 87).

correspondence going with what Earl Percy called 'the old gang'.[100] They were pleased to get hot news and opinions from the front, while he was equally keen to keep up with the latest political gossip from home. Wilson's friends assured him that his proper place was back in London, ideally as CIGS.[101] After Sir Charles Douglas had dropped dead of overwork, the 'notoriously incompetent' Sir James Wolfe Murray had been made CIGS in October 1914.[102] Wolfe Murray was incapable of standing up to Kitchener, and the General Staff at the War Office served little useful function until he was replaced by Sir Archibald Murray (whom Asquith had always rather admired) in September 1915.[103]

In the meantime, as his star rose in London, there was an easing of relations with both Kitchener and Asquith. By September 1915 Wilson thought that there were 'three things we must do forthwith if we want to beat the Boch:— 1. Conscription. 2. Make some ammunition. 3. Clear out of Gallipoli.'[104] He pushed them hard in private interviews with both Kitchener and Asquith, the latter 'most cordial & appreciative'.[105] Although Wilson changed his mind about the quality of Kitchener's 'New Armies'—when he inspected the 12th (Eastern) Division in April 1915 he 'was very agreeably surprised' and found the 'men all much better class than our regulars heretofore'[106]—he did not believe the war could be won without conscription, an opinion naturally shared by old National Service League allies like Leo Amery, F. S. Oliver, and Earl Percy. Unexpected support came from Josiah Wedgwood MP, 'radical & socialist' and 'an ardent conscriptionist', who came to see Wilson in September 1915 to discuss the situation, '& also to ask me to go back & be C.I.G.S.! which rather astonished & amused me!'[107]

By the summer of 1915 Robertson and others had decided that French ought to be removed from his position at the head of the BEF. Several of them began lobbying the King. On 1 July, after a 'long talk' with Robertson 'about the position of affairs at the front', the King became 'convinced it would be better for all concerned if the CinC were changed'. When George V toured the front in October, Hubert Gough and Richard Haking assured him 'that everyone had lost confidence in the CinC'. Douglas Haig told him that French was 'a source of great weakness to the army', and that Robertson, moreover, 'ought to go home to England as CofS at once'.[108] Robertson had already complained to Wilson that French 'chopped & changed every day & was quite hopeless'. He was, wrote

---

[100] Percy to Wilson, 18 July 1915 (Wilson papers, HHW 2/77/14). In the Wilson papers, for example, between November 1914 and December 1915 there are 29 letters from Percy, 10 from Charlie Hunter, 7 from Leo Amery, and 6 each from Geoffrey Robinson and H. A. Gwynne.

[101] See e.g. Leo Maxse, H. A. Gwynne, and Earl Percy to Wilson, 17, 22, and 23 July (Wilson papers, HHW 2/77/14, 24, and 27).

[102] Churchill nicknamed him 'Sheep Murray' (Gooch, *Plans of War*, 303).

[103] Ibid. 316–19.

[104] Wilson to L. J. Maxse, 4 Sept. 1915 (Maxse papers, 471, fo. 209). I am most grateful to Professor A. J. A. Morris for this reference.   [105] Wilson diary, 30 July and 4 Aug. 1915.

[106] Ibid., 17 Apr. 1915. Two days later he thought the 17th (Northern) Division a 'fine body of men but very short of equipment'.   [107] Ibid., 5 Sept. 1915.

[108] RA GV/King George V's diary/1915: 1 July, 24 Oct.

Wilson on 12 August, 'very sick with Sir J., he cannot manage him, nor influence him . . . & altogether it seems to me these two are drifting into a relationship which will become very difficult'. Wilson suspected (correctly) that Robertson was 'trying to get rid of him [French] by writing home, & sending copies of Appreciation notes on Ammn. supply etc which he drafted for Sir J. but which the latter would neither read nor sign'.[109]

These manoeuvrings appeared to have met with some success during the last two months of 1915. French, it was rumoured, was definitely to be replaced, though it was not clear by whom. Archie Murray's position as CIGS was also precarious. While in London for ten days at the beginning of November, Wilson encountered much talk of his replacing Murray: French, Milner, Lloyd George, and Arthur Lee all raised the possibility.[110] Wilson noted these views with scarcely any personal comment. If he fervently desired promotion for himself, there is no explicit sign of it in his diary. Back in France when it was reported to him that Joffre thought he should replace Kitchener as Secretary for War, he merely commented, 'very friendly, but how little he knows'.[111]

Robertson did indeed succeed Murray. There was never any real likelihood that Asquith would favour Wilson for the post. Even Rawlinson preferred Robertson as CIGS, and he also thought that Haig should replace French.[112] So it was to be, though at one point it seemed that Robertson might actually replace French. All through the period of uncertainty over who was going to replace whom Wilson appears to have stuck by French. There is nothing in his diary or correspondence to suggest that his loyalty was anything other than genuine, though some element of self-interest cannot be ruled out. French had been an important patron for Wilson, valuing his abilities and relying on his advice. The coming men, Haig and, especially, Robertson, would hardly show any similar confidence. On 4 December Wilson resolved that if French were to go so would he, as he 'could not serve under either Haig or Robertson'. Six days later he handed French his resignation. 'The moment has now come when in my opinion I will best serve the public interest by resigning my appointment', he wrote. His political friends were appalled. Bonar Law urged him not to resign as it would seriously damage his prospects, Anglo-French relations, and 'the cause'. Wilson expressed both high and low reasons for going. He thought 'that though it might be fatal for my career I felt it was the right thing to do to give Johnnie's successor an absolutely free hand when he takes over CinC and furthermore that as nobody ever takes my advice it is obviously no good my staying on'.[113]

[109] Wilson diary, 29 July, 12 Aug. 1915.   [110] Ibid., 4, 5 Nov, 1915.
[111] Ibid., 17 Nov. 1915.
[112] See Rawlinson to Lord Derby, 12 Nov. 1915, and to Clive Wigram, 29 Nov. 1915 (Rawlinson letter-book, NAM 5201/33/17).
[113] Wilson diary, 4, 12 Dec. 1915; Wilson to French (draft), 9 Dec. 1915 (Wilson papers, HHW 2/77/101). Charles Callwell also advised Wilson not to resign: 'Resignations on active serve are a little unusual and your action would give a handle to anybody who happened to want to "down you" ' (Callwell to Wilson, 13 Dec. 1915, ibid., HHW 2/75/74).

Although Wilson apparently did not know it, by this time it had already been decided that Robertson would go to London as CIGS and Haig would replace French as commander of the BEF. Indeed, on the very day Wilson was contemplating his resignation, Haig and Robertson were discussing 'the difficulty of finding a place for General Henry Wilson'. The CIGS-designate, no doubt bearing in mind that he would be based in London, thought that Wilson 'would do less harm in France than in England'. Haig had a field command in mind, but considered that Wilson should 'command a Divison before being given a corps'.[114] Rawlinson, meanwhile, seems to have been doing his bit for Wilson. Anticipating, as did Haig and Robertson, that he might follow the new CinC as the head of First Army, Rawlinson enquired (to Wilson's surprise) 'if I had thought of succeeding him' in command of IV Corps. Interestingly, Wilson thought he 'would rather not be under Rawly'. It may be that the rivalry between the two old friends was not quite so light-hearted as they publicly liked to make out. Perhaps, too, Wilson did not wholly trust Rawlinson's loyalty to colleagues, and he may have got wind of his machinations against French during the late autumn of 1915. Rather than taking over IV Corps, Wilson thought on reflection he would prefer to have the new XIV Corps (including the Ulster Divison) he had heard was being formed for the Third Army under Allenby.[115]

Haig was not impressed when he heard that Wilson was contemplating resigning and going on half pay. He told Rawlinson that an officer of Wilson's standing should not do that and that he 'was willing to help him [Wilson] in every possible way to find a suitable appointment'. But he was not prepared to offer more than a division, influenced perhaps by the fact, as he confided to his diary, that 'I knew H.W. had been abusing me and other British Generals and that he instigated an article in the "Observer" suggesting that the British Army in France should be placed under the command of General Foch!'[116] Asquith, curiously, came to Wilson's assistance. He summoned Wilson to London, where he—'evidently anxious to please'—offered him a corps himself. ('Never were my eyes so blue, or my hair so curly', Wilson told Clive on his return to France.[117]) Kitchener, who 'was very nice', told Wilson that the corps 'would be only temporary pending something better'. In the meantime he seemed to think Wilson could also continue liaising with the French, but Wilson told him that he 'was now in command of a Corps & could not go racing to Paris etc'.[118]

Why were Asquith and Kitchener suddenly so nice to Wilson? Whatever the circumstances, getting a corps was pretty good going considering that Wilson had no experience whatsoever of field command. Asquith, having clipped Kitchener's

---

[114] Haig TS diary, 12 Dec. 1915 (TNA, WO 256/6). French had offered Wilson a corps in August, which Wilson had refused, in part 'because I thought it was hard luck on some Divisional Commanders' (Wilson diary, 20 Aug. 1915).   [115] Wilson diary, 13 Dec. 1915.
[116] Haig TS diary, 14 Dec. 1915 (TNA, WO 256/6). This was in an editorial: *Observer*, 21 Nov. 1915. J. L. Garvin was editor of the *Observer*.   [117] Clive diary, 18 Dec. 1915 (Clive papers, II/2).
[118] Wilson diary, 13, 16, 17 Dec. 1915.

wings with the appointment of Robertson as CIGS, no doubt was glad to see a loose cannon like Wilson tied down with a comparatively senior position at the front, and the seniority of the command could also serve to mollify Wilson's political friends. Kitchener, for his part, may have thought that, with Robertson ensconced in the War Office, Wilson might yet prove to be a useful ally.

The circumstances surrounding the changes in the British high command of December 1915 help illuminate the climate of gossip and intrigue, real and imagined, which permeated the higher levels of the British officer corps, as no doubt elsewhere in the army. It also provides an opportunity to examine Henry Wilson's reputation for disloyalty in context. This was based on three factors: his role during the 'Ulster crisis' in 1914; his closeness to the French; and his well-known propensity for sharing his opinions with all and sundry, but especially politicians. The first of these clearly counted most in Downing Street, and Asquith's antipathy had helped prevent Wilson from succeeding Murray at the beginning of the year. Maurice Hankey, who was well placed to know, considered that Wilson might have become CIGS in December 1915, 'but for the mistrust he had awakened at the time of "the Curragh incident" '.[119] Wilson's undisguised Francophile sympathies were not much reciprocated among his British colleagues. In October 1915 Robertson complained that 'Wilson has the reputation of leaning too much to the side of the French and not sufficient to the side of the Army to which he belongs',[120] an aspersion on Wilson's loyalty (albeit cautiously worded) which Kitchener was unlikely to overlook when considering him for promotion. John Charteris, Haig's head of intelligence, noted: 'Apparently there is great difficulty in placing Wilson. Neither D.H. nor Robertson wants him anywhere near them. He has been instigating articles recommending that the British Army should be put under Foch, and has been belittling everybody except himself and Foch.'[121]

Haig (no doubt with the best of intentions) had been criticising his own chief, Sir John French, for some time. As early as August 1914 he had told Charteris that French was 'quite unfit for high command in time of crisis',[122] but the complaints grew increasingly strident after the battle of Loos in September 1915, when first Rawlinson and then Haig claimed (erroneously, in fact[123]) that the opportunity for a great victory had been lost through French's handling of the reserves. Haig felt so strongly about the matter that he told Rawlinson (who agreed that French should be replaced) that while he had 'been very loyal to Sir John all along... over the last show he cannot be so'.[124] In October Robertson told the King that French should be removed, Haig 'would make an excellent C.inC.', and that Wilson

[119] Hankey, *The Supreme Command*, ii. 445.
[120] Robertson to Brinsley FitzGerald (Kitchener's military secretary), 19 Oct. 1915 (Robertson papers, I/13/26).   [121] Charteris to his wife, 12 Dec. 1915 (quoted in Charteris, *At G.H.Q*, 125).
[122] Charteris to wife, 16 Aug. 1914 (ibid. 10).
[123] See the discussion of this point in Prior and Wilson, *Command on the Western Front*, 130–2.
[124] Rawlinson diary, 10 and 22 Oct. 1915 (quoted in Prior and Wilson, *Command on the Western Front*, 133).

'ought to go at once [as] he is not loyal'.[125] During the late autumn Haig became keenly anxious for politicians back home to be informed about the situation. Robertson assured him from London (where he spoke to the King, Asquith, and others) that he would try his best 'to put things straight.... I think', he added, 'the first thing is to get you in command.'[126] Although from the evidence of his own diary Haig hesitated to criticise French openly to some politicians (for example, Asquith and Bonar Law), he certainly unburdened himself to the King when he visited the front in October, and also made his views clear to Robertson who promptly passed them on to London.[127] He does not seem to have minded other soldiers passing on critical views. When Hubert Gough asked him if he should see Lord Milner when he was home on leave, Haig said 'certainly he ought to do so', in order to explain 'the faulty working of the military machine in France'.[128] French, inevitably, got wind of these machinations and asked Wilson 'if Haig & Rawley & Gough had been disloyal to him'. Wilson replied 'that I knew nothing about this nor if I did would I say anything. It would not be fair, but that I thought Haig was too good a fellow to do such a thing.'[129]

This is an irony indeed: Wilson, the 'arch-intriguer', admittedly by his own testimony, reassuring French that Haig remained loyal to him, when actually the very opposite was true. Haig, with some justification, no doubt felt that criticising his immediate superiors to the King, as constitutional head of the armed forces, was no disloyalty, but it would have been disingenuous to imagine that the action would be without consequences. In fact the King himself told Haig afterwards that as a result of his (and other) representations he had insisted to Asquith that French be replaced as Commander-in-Chief of the BEF.[130] The combined effect, of course, of the Haig–Robertson–Rawlinson–Gough activities was an intrigue against Sir John French. The difference between the actions of these officers and those of Henry Wilson was merely one of degree. Wilson was a blatant gossip who chattered incessantly about the war and its management. Not for him the silent communion of strong, characterful men. Therein lay much of his attraction to civilian politicians, many of whom thrived on his knockabout, apparently well-informed, conversation. Perhaps his mistake lay in being too promiscuous an intriguer (if so he were). Crucially, unlike Haig or Robertson or Rawlinson, he had no very ready access to the royal household, where the discreet lobbying of Lord Stamfordham, Clive Wigram, or the King himself evidently paid handsome dividends.

[125] RA GV/King George V's diary/1915: 27 Oct.

[126] Robertson to Haig, 15 Nov. 1915 (quoted in Blake, *The Private Papers of Douglas Haig*, 113–14).

[127] RA GV/King George V's diary/1915: 24–5 Oct.; Haig TS diary, 17, 23, and 24 Oct., 24 Nov. 1915 (TNA, WO 256/6).

[128] Haig TS diary, 14 Nov. 1915 (TNA, WO 256/6).   [129] Wilson diary, 18 Nov. 1915.

[130] Blake, *The Private Papers of Douglas Haig*, 138.

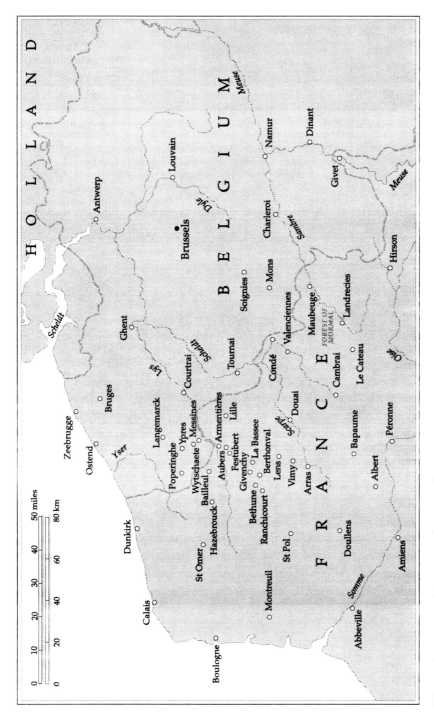

The northern sector of the western front, 1914–18

9

IV Corps

When Wilson returned to France just before Christmas 1915, Haig, after all, gave him IV Corps. 'He was quite nice,' noted Wilson, 'but he is always foreign to me.' Wilson was hurt that his knowledge of the French, lately so valued by Kitchener, was quite ignored: 'Haig never once mentioned the French nor asked my advice & as I was not going to give it unasked the subject was never raised! I feel as though my work with the French for many years has been of absolutely no use at all in Haig's eyes.'[1] The following day, 22 December 1915, Wilson went to IV Corps headquarters at Labuissière, south-west of Béthune, to take over from Rawlinson. It was, he thought, 'a fine Command', including nearly 70,000 men. 'It is so curious', he wrote, 'being in command of 4 Divisions—a force equal to what we started the war with. I have an immense deal to learn about everything.'[2] Sidney Clive thought it would 'be a great rest' for Wilson, 'but he will feel not being in the centre of affairs'.[3]

In his corps Wilson had the 1st, 15th, 47th, and 16th Divisions, which together neatly reflected the different elements making up the British army in the middle of the Great War. The 1st Division was a pre-war regular formation which had been in France since August 1914, the 47th (London) Division were Territorials who had been sent to Franch in March 1915 and had served at Loos that autumn, while the other two, the 15th (Scottish) and 16th (Irish) were Kitchener 'New Army' divisions which had come out to France during the previous six months. The 16th was mainly composed of Irish nationalist volunteers, who had been encouraged to join up by John Redmond. Buoyed up by the passage of the Irish Home Rule Bill (even though the implementation of it had been postponed for the duration of the war) and moved by the fate of gallant, little (and Catholic) Belgium, Redmond had called on Irishmen to enlist 'in defence of the highest principles of religion and morality and right'. Many thousands of Catholic and nationalist Irishmen (more, indeed, than their Protestant and unionist compatriots) had responded to his call.[4] Rawlinson was very amused at the unionist Wilson being in charge of a nationalist formation. 'Henry Wilson has taken over my

---

[1] Wilson diary, 21 Dec. 1915.   [2] Ibid., 22–3 Dec.1915.
[3] Clive diary, 21 Dec. 1915 (Clive papers, II/2).
[4] Jeffery, *Ireland and the Great War*, 10–15.

Corps,' he wrote to Johnnie Du Cane, 'to which is now attached the 16th South Irish Division, so he will have some friends to look after!!?'[5]

The position of corps commander comprised the third level of the high command of the BEF. At the end of 1915, under the new Commander-in-Chief, Haig, there were three British 'armies'. The First Army (which had been Haig's) was entrusted to Sir Charles Monro. Rawlinson, who had hoped to get the job, was given command of a new, Fourth Army in January 1916. The First Army consisted of four corps: III, XI, I, and Wilson's IV Corps. In battle the corps commander's function was to interpret the wishes of his Army superior and co-ordinate the two or more divisions under him. This level of command, moreover, controlled significant field and heavy artillery units. In quiet sectors of the front, however, it seems that the corps commanders were very much left to themselves, as was Wilson's experience for much of 1916.

The fundamental formation in the BEF was the division. In November 1915 Haig told a conference of corps and divisional generals that 'the division is our real battle unit'. Training, therefore, should 'be under the personal guidance of GOCs Divns, so that they may be able to inspire the unit with their own personal energy and fighting spirit'. The main role of corps commanders and the Commander-in-Chief was 'to assist and guide the instruction'.[6] The corps itself was merely a headquarters with staff officers who administered the various divisions deployed under them from time to time by the army commander and GHQ. During Wilson's eleven months at IV Corps, thirteen different divisions passed through his hands; only one, the 47th, remained with him for more than six months. Charles Carrington, who had the perspective of a front-line infantry officer, contrasted the importance of battalion, brigade, and division with the 'remoteness and anonymity' of the corps headquarters. 'While every man in my company knew Brigadier Sladen and General Fanshawe [the divisional commander] by sight I doubt if one in ten of them knew the Corps Commander's name.' Inevitably, he reflected, the corps commander got blamed for anything that went wrong, and 'since battles in France were mostly disastrous, the Corps Commander was rarely popular'.[7]

Having established himself in the corps headquarters, Wilson set about familiarising himself with his new command. The corps was holding about five miles of line between Loos and a point south of Givenchy. On Wilson's right was IX Corps of General d'Urbal's French Tenth Army and on his left was Hubert Gough's I Corps. A high priority was to get to know the divisions. Understandably enough,

[5] Rawlinson to Du Cane, 27 Dec. 1915 (Rawlinson letter-book, NAM 5201/33/18).

[6] Haig TS diary, 7 Nov. 1915 (TNA, WO 256/6).

[7] Carrington, *Soldier from the Wars Returning*, 104. Paddy Griffith, by contrast (albeit with qualifications), asserts that the army corps represented 'a genuinely important level of leadership, and its commander . . . tended to become an important, if not necessarily an overpowering, figure in the consciousness of most officers and senior NCOs who stayed in the corps for any length of time' (Griffith, *Battle Tactics of the Western Front*, 214).

perhaps, Wilson started with his compatriots in the 48th Brigade of the 16th (Irish) Division, whom he visited on Christmas Day 1915. The division was in training behind the line and Wilson was not much impressed with what he saw. They 'appear to be inferior', he wrote. 'Something of the old Militia type both in officers & men. The men are practically <u>all</u> 3rd Class shots & this means everything.' A note of unionist bias joined his long-held prejudice against part-time soldiers. Hickie, the divisional commander, agreed that he had 'a political Divn of riff raff Redmondites'. On 28 December Wilson inspected two more Irish battalions and thought that 'at least 50 p. c. are quite useless, old whiskey sodden militiamen'. A week later he was equally scathing about another 16th Division brigade, the 47th: 'Old officers, old & useless men, <u>very</u> bad musketry, rotten boots, and altogether a poor show.'[8]

Reporting to Monro on 6 January, Wilson said that 'it would not be safe to put this Division into the line as a Division—in any active part of the line—for at least six weeks'. His opinion of the 16th Division seems to have been coloured both by his political beliefs and also his scepticism regarding the Kitchener New Armies. 'It is certainly not a fighting formation at the present moment,' he wrote, 'in spite of the fact that most of the men enlisted and have been training since last September–October year (1914).'[9] Wilson had caustically dismissed the 16th Division men as 'Johnnie Redmond's pets'. But there was worse. Redmond's brother Willie, a veteran Nationalist MP, was serving in the division: 'Willie Redmond (aged 65?) commands a Compy in the Roy. Ir[ish]!'[10] Redmond, in fact, was only 54, although still well over age for front-line duty, but had been much admired for nobly volunteering for service at the front.

The 16th Division was certainly not the strongest in the army, though it performed more than adequately on the Somme in September 1916.[11] But the 15th (Scottish) Division was also a New Army formation, and after Wilson inspected it on 5 January he thought it 'a <u>very</u> fine body of men & if well officered could do anything'. Two days later he saw them march in after three days' exercise, 'looking hard & well. A fine Division.'[12] He was less impressed by the Territorial division, the 47th. He saw one of the division's brigades (the 141st) on 3 January and thought them 'a nice looking lot of men, but very weak', and he was never very keen on the divisional commander, Charles Barter (a southern Irish Protestant). 'I am always uncomfortable with him', he noted at the end of March, and a fortnight later discussed him with Monro: 'We both want to get rid of him but don't know how.'[13]

⁸ Wilson diary, 25, 28, 31 Dec. 1915 and 5 Jan. 1916.
⁹ Wilson to Advanced 1st Army, 6 Jan. 1916 (Wilson papers, HHW 3/10/2).
¹⁰ Wilson diary, 31 Dec. 1915 and 5 Jan. 1916. For Willie Redmond see Denman, *A Lonely Grave*.
¹¹ Denman, *Ireland's Unknown Soldiers*, 79–102.   ¹² Wilson diary, 5 Jan. 1916.
¹³ Ibid., 3 Jan., 31 Mar. and 16 Apr. 1916. Barter survived until September 1916, when he was summarily dismissed after the attack at High Wood during the battle of the Somme, charged, unjustifiably as it turned out, with 'wanton waste of men' (see *The Times*, 24 and 30 Mar. 1931; Travers, *The Killing Ground*, 182).

Wilson had a high opinion of Arthur Holland (another general with an Irish Protestant background), commanding the 1st Division: 'a fine Division', he noted, '& Holland can be proud of it.'[14] A week after taking over the corps he visited the front line with Holland and his staff officer William Dobbie. Although the 'brasshats' of the Great War are celebrated now for staying well behind the lines, this is an instance where the general (as most of them actually did) went to see for himself. It is worth quoting Wilson's diary entry at length to give a glimpse of him as GOC:

Labuissiere: I left here at 5.15 a.m. for Mazingarbe the Hd Qs 1st Div. & Holland & Dobbie ran me out just under the ridge at Loos. From there we walked round Loos & dropped into a Comm[unicatio]n trench which took us up to the front line. As we were walking over the open, in the dark there was a certain amount of rifle fire swishing past us. Up in the front line all was quiet at first, then some shelling. We went right along, & I was pleased with all I saw, & especially with Holland though he talks a great deal. His trenches were good, with many (18) deep shelters 20' under the surface. His second line though not finished was excellent. We got back by Philosophe after 3 hours walk. Was in office at 11 a.m.[15]

The difference in standard of Wilson's four divisions was reflected in the effort each invested in training. At a meeting of the divisional commanders on 13 January Wilson noted that while the 1st Division had a school of 2 months, the 15th had '6 days now increased to 10'. The 47th had 'no school but a sort of class for Officers & men on arrival lasting 8 days', while the 16th was only just 'starting a School of 19 days'.[16] For much of the war the organisation of training in the British army was highly decentralised, and individual commanders, jealous of their military bailiwicks, were opposed to common training schools. With his own background in officer education, however, it is not surprising that Wilson took an interest in the topic, although it was difficult to co-ordinate arrangements between divisions which were moved in and out of his corps in a largely random fashion. He made a point, however, of speaking at the various divisional schools. On 22 February, for example, he 'gave an address to a class of 47th Div. Officers who were just finishing their course', and three days later at the 15th Division school he spoke for three-quarters of an hour 'about Discipline, pride of profession etc'.[17]

He also began to lecture more generally within the corps. Harry Lewin, Lord Roberts's son-in-law, who was serving in the 1st Division, persuaded Wilson to do a lecture and gave Charles Callwell an account of the occasion. 'A distinguished officer of your division', began Wilson,

has told me that I ought to inflict this lecture upon you, because the general view of all young officers is that Corps Commanders are fat, old, pot-bellied blighters, who live far

---

[14] Wilson diary, 7 Feb. 1916.
[15] Ibid., 30 Dec. 1915. There were certainly other occasions when Wilson visited front-line trenches, see e.g. his diary 1, 9, 24 Aug. 1916.   [16] Ibid., 13 Jan. 1916.
[17] Wilson diary, 22 and 25 Feb. 1916.

back in safety in 'chatoos', eat and drink a great deal, and know nothing of the realities of war. This being the case, I felt that if any of you were kind enough to avail yourselves of my invitation to come here this evening, you would at least realize that I am *not pot-bellied*.[18]

In his diary Wilson noted that his lecture 'on the European situation before the war and now...went off quite well'.[19] Reasonably enough, he said that one of the principal purposes of the lecture was 'to meet each other', and he gave the same talk seven times between February and August 1916 to different audiences in the corps.[20]

Ten years after hearing one of Wilson's lectures, R. G. Thompson, a lieutenant in the 1st/23rd battalion, the London Regiment, 47th Division, recalled it starting thus: 'Well, most of you have now been in France a fortnight, and being Englishmen I have no doubt you have in these two weeks mastered the French idiom. Now, I'm going to suggest a good test for your French. Get hold of a Frenchman—a refugee from the occupied area if possible—there are plenty in this town—and explain to them in French exactly what is meant by a conscientious objector.'[21] Writing to his wife in April 1916, Lieutenant Christopher Stone said they had 'all had to go (in a motor-bus) to hear our Army Corps Commander (Sir Charles Wilson [*sic*]) lecture. It was really very interesting, and he's a splendid looking man and was most amusing and sensible.'[22] A fortnight later Captain Beaumont Tansley, a gunner in the 47th Division, noted in his diary a 'lecture on "Days before the War" by Corps Commander—Sir Henry Wilson—extraordinarily funny with many dirty stories!'[23]

Wilson spent quite a bit of time building up his various corps schools. In March he tackled Haig's Chief of Staff, Launcelot Kiggell, 'about giving us proper teachers for our Schools', and in April he set up a new officers' school at Pernes, which, among other things, taught 'trench engineering', Lewis gunnery, and musketry.[24] In July, finding that the head of the 'Cavalry and Cyclists School' did 'not understand the elements of teaching', he devised a scheme himself and spent two days supervising it.[25] In August he heard a rumour that Haig was proposing to abolish

---

[18] Callwell, *Wilson*, i. 275. The first page of Wilson's holograph notes for this lecture reads: 'APOLOGY. Detach oneself. EMERSON. SCOTCH MINISTER. LADY and PURSE' (Wilson papers, HHW 3/10/9).

[19] Wilson diary, 13 Feb. 1916.   [20] Lecture notes (Wilson papers, HHW 3/10/9).

[21] Letter to the editor from R. G. Thompson, *Sunday Times*, 29 May 1927. Another version of this story, from a 2nd Division officer, had Wilson saying: 'Imagine, just imagine yourself trying to explain to a Frenchwoman what a conscientious objector is?' (Christopher Stone to his wife, 1 Apr. 1916, in Sheffield and Inglis (eds.), *From Vimy Ridge to the Rhine*, 48).

[22] Stone to wife, 1 Apr. 1916. Stone's naming of Wilson as 'Sir Charles' rather confirms Charles Carrington's point about the remoteness of corps commanders.

[23] Tansley diary, 17 Apr. 1916 (Tansley papers).

[24] Wilson diary, 15 Mar., 17 Apr. 1916; Lord Charles Cavendish-Bentick ('Daddy') (head of IV Corps School) to Wilson, 16 Dec. 1916 (Wilson papers, HHW 2/84128).

[25] Wilson diary, 18, 20, and 22 July 1916. It has to be said that, at the receiving end, intensified training was not always appreciated. A history of the 63rd Division refers to 'the orgy of instruction' in Wilson's corps from May to September 1916 (Jerrold, *The Royal Naval Division*, 178).

corps schools in favour of divisional ones. 'By Gad he is a stupid man', wrote Wilson, and he lobbied (in vain, as it turned out) to preserve schools at the corps level.[26]

Reflecting in October 1916 on the policy to be adopted over the winter, Wilson thought that from late November the line should be held 'as lightly as we can', with 'a lot of gunning & mortaring'. Then '<u>rest</u> and <u>train</u> our Divisions so that we may start the spring offensive with full Divisions well trained & in good heart. The moment the winter comes we should all turn on to the schools.' But, he added, 'it is curiously <u>stupid</u> how Haig & Kigg. ignore the schools'.[27] Haig was certainly slow to systematise training within the BEF. A dedicated training section was not established at GHQ until January 1917, and a central BEF Training Directorate not until July 1918.[28]

Wilson's year as a corps commander is frequently cited to demonstrate his inadequacies as a fighting soldier. Apart from Burma, right at the start of his army career, and a little regimental soldiering, his career was entirely spent in staff positions. His chief engineer, Edward Kenyon, judged him 'a brilliant Staff officer, but not a great Commander'.[29] Two episodes during 1916, when he was tested as a commander in the field, not only enable his performance to be assessed, but also illuminate some of the wider challenges of command on the western front. The first was in May 1916, when a surprise German attack captured some of his line, and he failed to recover it, nearly losing his command in consequence. The second concerns an offensive at Vimy which he was planning during the autumn.

Early in March the 20-mile front of the French Tenth Army was taken over by the British First and Third Armies. It had been a quiet sector for some time, 'a state approximating to a suspension of arms existed', and 'the enemy, protected as a rule by thick wire, seemed used to a policy of "live and let live" '.[30] The writer J. B. Priestley was among the soldiers who moved into positions formerly held by the French. With the Germans dug into the higher ground, and the whole front astride a grim, industrial region, it was, concluded Priestley, 'a very sinister sector into which we crept'.[31] During the change, Wilson's corps was moved slightly to the south of Givenchy, with positions parallel to the Vimy ridge, and he moved his headquarters to Ranchicourt. His command was also temporarily reduced in size. He lost the 16th Division (which he did not mind) and the 1st and 15th (which he did), and acquired the 2nd and 23rd Divisions, the former a regular formation which had been out in France since the beginning, and the latter a New Army

[26] Wilson diary, 11, 28 Aug., 6 and 7 Sept. 1916. The IV Corps school was closed in December 1916 (Cavendish-Bentick to Wilson, 19 Dec. 1916 (Wilson papers, HHW 2/84/134)).

[27] Wilson diary, 21 Oct. 1916. Richard Butler was Haig's Deputy CGS, and John 'Tavish' Davidson, DMO in the BEF.

[28] Bidwell and Graham, *Fire-Power*, 43; Griffith, 'The Extent of Tactical Reform', 3–4 and 20 n. 14.   [29] Maj.-Gen. E. R. Kenyon, TS memoirs (Kenyon papers, 84/24/1).

[30] Edmonds, *History of the Great War: France and Belgium, 1916*, i. 210.

[31] Priestley, *Margin Released*, 105–6. Priestley was a corporal in the 10th battalion, Duke of Wellington's Regiment, 69th Brigade, 23rd Division.

division, which Wilson thought stronger than the 47th.[32] On 2 April he learned that the 23rd Division was to be moved away, and 'a long list of guns to be taken also'. 'We shall', he wrote, 'be pretty thin if the Boch like to fight us.'[33]

For the moment the enemy remained comparatively quiet, and Kiggell told Monro towards the end of March that 'so far as we are capable of judging, nothing on any considerable scale is threatened on your front'.[34] Haig, meanwhile, instructed that mining operations be mounted and 'the the principle of aggression should be instilled into the troops'.[35] The chalk of the Vimy ridge was especially suited to underground mining. On 3 May troops from the 47th Division blew up three mines (with 42,000 pounds of explosive) and seized a section of the German lines, '& the whole operation only cost 14 casualties & 5 of these were from our own guns'. There was another successful mining operation on 15 May, but there was no particular response from the Germans, other than an immediate heavy bombardment in each case.[36] Writing from an ordinary soldier's perspective (but also with the benefit of hindsight), J. B. Priestley asserted that *because* 'it had been quiet recently around there', the British had 'of course' to 'hot it up for the sake of our morale, to keep our fellas on their toes'. This was 'in spite of the fact, not hard to discover on the map and all too obvious to any staff officer who went to see for himself, that if we did start anything the Germans, higher up, well dug in, and in places not more than twenty yards away, would have the better of it'. So it was to be: 'having asked for it, God knows why, we caught a packet. Outside any plan of campaign, without any battle being fought, any honours being won, we went through the mincer.'[37]

Relying on what turned out to be a false sense of security, further British units were withdrawn from this sector in order to build up reserves to the south along the Somme, in preparations for the planned major offensive. As part of this redeployment, IV Corps took over some line near Berthonval from XVII Corps, commanded by Julian Byng. 'Bungo to lunch,' wrote Wilson on 19 May, '& tells me that the part he hands over tonight to me is a beastly bit, overlooked by craters which he cannot get at.'[38] Apart from this handover being in progress, the situation in the Berthonval sector was potentially complicated by two further factors. First, the corps (and army) boundary, between IV and XVII Corps (First and Third Army), ran through the southern part of the sector. Second, there was some fluidity in the First Army command structure. Sir Charles Monro, the army commander, went on leave on 9 May, leaving Wilson in temporary command. He was expected back on 21 May. Of Wilson's three divisional commanders, William Walker (2nd Division) had been on sick leave (returning 22 May), and Barter

---

[32] Wilson diary, 7 Mar. 1916. In May he got the 63rd (Royal Naval) Division, which was composed of surplus navy reservists, and had served at Gallipoli.   [33] Wilson diary, 2 Apr. 1916.
[34] Kiggell to Monro, 25 Mar. 1916 (TNA, WO 158/46).
[35] Edmonds, *History of the Great War: France and Belgium, 1916*, i. 213. The account of the Vimy fighting below is principally drawn from this work, pp. 210–26.
[36] Ibid. 213–14; Wilson diary, 3–4 May 1916.   [37] Priestly, *Margin Released*, 107.
[38] Wilson diary, 19 May 1916.

(47th Division) had also gone on leave (returning the same day as Walker). Their absence meant that subordinate brigade commands were disrupted by individuals acting up in their absence.

What the British did not know was that the Germans opposite, badly troubled by mining operations, had carefully been planning an attack to capture the British mine-shafts at Berthonval. By a curious irony, the enemy commander, Alexander von Freytag-Loringhoven, was deputy chief of the German General Staff, who had specially requested a temporary posting to gain some experience of front-line service. He might, mused Charles Carrington, 'have been described as Wilson's opposite number in the German Army'.[39] Late in the afternoon of Sunday, 21 May—'another perfect summer's day the fourth in succession'—Wilson noted the start of a 'very heavy' German barrage. Over a four-hour period an estimated 70,000 shells fell into a 1,500-yard stretch of the British front. An assault began at 7.45 p.m., and by the end of the evening the Germans had moved forward up to 800 yards along a front of about a thousand yards. Wilson appears to have done all he could in the confused circumstances. At about 5.00 p.m. he went to Brigadier-General Cuthbert (temporarily commanding the 47th Division) to ask if he could 'help with Inf. or guns but he did not want either', and was moving up '2 or 3' battalions. At 10.00 p.m., 'owing to contradictory but unsatisfactory reports that we had lost trenches etc., I ordered the [99th] Bde. of the 2nd Div. [in reserve about 10 miles from the front] up by 'bus & lorry . . . & I ordered another Bde. of 2nd Div. [the 6th] to stand by'. Before he went to bed at 1.30 a.m., by which time it was clear that ground had been lost, he ordered up artillery reinforcements and 'strong aeroplane support—and arranged in my own mind that I would retake tonight (22nd) if the various local counter attacks were not successful'.[40]

Wilson was up at 5.45 a.m. the next morning (22 May): 'Situation clear enough', he noted. 'By a savage bombardment I have been knocked out of rotten trenches which we only took over on Saturday morning.' At 8.30 he had a meeting with Byng, Cuthbert, and their artillery commanders. It was agreed not to 'wait for some 60 p[ounde]rs & 6' How[itzer]s which the Army is sending in tonight', and, following an all-day bombardment, to attack at 1.30 a.m. next morning 'at rise of moon'. With artillery help from I and XVII Corps, Wilson 'settled we should fire 1 r[oun]d per battery per minute; so with 53 batteries we shall be getting quite a serious force, & may do some good'. Expecting Barter's return that evening, Wilson told Cuthbert that he would keep Barter at headquarters and leave Cuthbert in command of the operation.

At three o'clock in the afternoon Allenby (GOC First Army) came round 'to offer any help he could give'. There matters stood until 5.00 p.m. when Monro, back from leave, arrived and argued firmly that the attack should be postponed. There would, he said, be a large increase in heavy artillery (two batteries of

[39] Carrington, *Soldier from the War Returning*, 106; Edmonds gives 'the German acccount of the Vimy fighting' in *History of the Great War: France and Belgium, 1916*, i. 224–6.
[40] Wilson diary, 21 May 1916.

60-pounders and the howitzers), 'we would have more dark in which to consolidate', and there would be more time 'in which to elaborate our plans, reconnoitre, get up wire etc. & reserves. Against all this I put the consolidation of the Bosh in the delay of a night & a day. However I gave in & made the change.' The attack was postponed until dusk on 23 May. That evening, as Walker and Barter had returned, Wilson put them back in command of their divisions. It had been 'another marvellous day of sunshine'.[41] Haig's opinion, which apparently Monro was conveying, was that 'our counter attack should not be delivered until full preparations have been made', and he was prepared to provide 'all guns and ammunition necessary'.[42]

Next day there was a big meeting at Wilson's headquarters. The two army commanders, Monro and Allenby, were there, along with two officers from GHQ: John Headlam, Haig's artillery commander, and John Davidson, his DMO. They reported Haig's views and suggested that there would be a delay of 'about a fortnight' while the additional guns were brought up. But Allenby (and, it appears, Monro) agreed with Wilson that he ought to go ahead with his 'limited objective'. 'No one can say whether it will be successful,' wrote Wilson in his diary, 'but if beaten back we shall only be where we now are.' In any case, having 'shot some 40,000 rounds in 48 hours…the Boch has had a good doing'. The Germans had been warned about the planned counter-attack by a British deserter on 22 May, and they put down a heavy bombardment just before the attack began at 8.25 p.m. Battalions from three brigades were involved. On the left and right those from 142nd Brigade (47th Division) and 7th Brigade (25th Division in XVII Corps) achieved some initial success, but Wilson learned at 9.15 p.m. that in the centre two battalions from 99th Brigade 'did not start because the Boch barrage was so heavy'. Before going to bed at half-past eleven Wilson ordered 'that if the 99th did not start before 1 a.m. they ought not to go at all unless they could pinch a couple of hundred yards' up to the old trench line. When this order was communicated to Monro at 12.15 a.m. he decided to call a halt to the whole attack.[43]

Although Wilson nursed hopes of another quick counter-attack over the next few days, this was vetoed by Monro, and, apart from recovering some ground which the Germans did not want to occupy, that is where matters rested after the action of 21–3 May. But there were serious recriminations about the affair, and, in turn, battalion, brigade, division, and corps commanders got it in the neck. At the bottom of the command heap were the two 99th Brigade battalion commanding officers: Major A. G. M. Sharpe (1st Royal Berkshire Regiment) and Major R. Rostron (22nd Royal Fusiliers). Both were only temporarily in command. Sharpe was acting for Lieutenant-Colonel Randle Barnett-Baker, who had moved

[41] Wilson diary, 22 May 1916.   [42] Haig TS diary, 22 May 1916 (TNA, WO 256/10).

[43] Wilson diary, 22–3 May 1916. There is a vivid front-line account of the 99th Brigade experience in Christopher Stone to his wife, 29 May 1916 (Sheffield and Inglis (eds.), *From Vimy Ridge to the Rhine*, 53–4).

up to command the brigade, and Rostron's usual CO was away sick. At the next level, Barnett-Baker was acting for Richard Kellett, who was commanding the 2nd Division while Charles Barter was away on leave. On the evening of 23 May, Sharpe, the senior of the two battalion commanders, had cancelled the attack as he believed there was no prospect of success. Wilson thought that Barnett-Baker ought to have been back in command, since Barter and Kellett had resumed their normal duties on 22 May. Barnett-Baker, however, had been kept at brigade head-quarters by Kellett before the attack, but had gone down to the front line at about 10.15 p.m. Barnett-Baker told Wilson afterwards that, having reorganised the troops, 'he would have launched the attack but for Monro's wire. He was absolutely clear that the place could & would have been taken, with even one Battn.' Having heard this, Wilson seems to have decided that Sharpe's decision not to launch the attack was merely due to 'funk': 'My own feeling is to try Sharpe & Rostron by Court Martial.'[44]

Kellett (a Tipperary man) was meanwhile being reported on adversely to Haig. One of Haig's staff officers, a Major Armytage, visited the front on 25 May and returned to GHQ saying that he had found Brigadier General Kellett to have been 'in complete ignorance of the situation'. Haig sharply told Monro that 'the divisional commander should be asked to state how such an incompetent brigadier should have been allowed to retain his command so long, and also that GOC IV Corps should be asked to explain'. He added that IV Corps had been 'the most efficient one in the army when Sir H. Wilson took over the command', but that 'since then it had much decreased in military value'. There was 'no doubt', decided Haig, that Wilson had 'failed as a commander in the field'. Monro was instructed to 'get things put right without delay'.[45] Wully Robertson was over staying with Haig at the time, and one supposes that the two men might have had a bit of a chuckle together at Wilson's predicament.

On Saturday 27 May General Charteris from GHQ called in at Wilson's head-quarters (Wilson was out seeing Walker about 'the Armytage episode') and, over tea in the mess, formed the opinion that IV Corps officers 'were down-hearted'. He reported to Haig that they 'spoke of the British climbing to victory on the backs of the French. That General Wilson spoke of the French troops as being "better fighters than the British", and that the Germans were "better men than ours" '. Haig thought that 'all this seems to spring from General H. Wilson's inexperience as a commander', and 'his infatuation for the French'. When Wilson heard of this the following Tuesday he thought: 'The d—— fool, they were pulling his leg', but spent the whole morning writing a note to Monro

[44] Wilson diary, 24–5 May 1916; Notes on the attack on Vimy Ridge, 23 May 1916 (Wilson papers, HHW 2/83/17). See also Sheffield, 'The Effect of War Service', 70.

[45] Haig TS diary, 27 May 1916 (TNA, WO 256/10). Wilson was enraged by Armytage reporting adversely 'as a result of a short & perfunctory visit to men whom he did not know and about a situation of which he was perforce ignorant' (Wilson to Monro (draft), 28 May 1916 (Wilson papers, HHW 2/83/17)).

about it.[46] He 'found it difficult to state in official language what passed', but said that it all stemmed from some 'absurdly & extravagantly optimistic remarks' which Charteris had made:

Gen. Charteris talked of 'sweeping victories' within 2 mos., the others demurred. Gen. Charteris was inclined to belittle the French, the others gave our Ally unstinted praise. Gen. Charteris thought nothing of the Germans, the others had a high opinion of them. And so it went on, Gen. Charteris being called a 'professional optimist' ... In fact, to put it shortly, it became a game of pulling Gen. Charteris' leg. That he should have been so taken in & that he so misjudged the temper & tone of this Staff as to report that it was in a pessimistic & despondent mood is quite beyond my understanding.[47]

A few days later Haig had another talk with Monro about IV Corps. Monro told him he wanted 'to carry on with the present Staff'. He had spoken to Wilson 'and he hoped things would improve. The Corps had a difficult situation to contend with.'[48] Several months later Arthur Lee told Viscount Duncannon, Wilson's ADC, 'how nearly I was dégommé [*sic*] after May 21st & how I was saved by Charlie Monro putting in a tremendous report in my favour in the face of which Haig was unable to proceed'.[49] The damaging story which reached Lloyd George was that Wilson, having been attacked, 'did not see his way to counter-attack'. Tasked with this by Lloyd George on a visit at the front in September 1916, Harry Lewin had (so he assured Wilson) stoutly stood up for him, telling the Prime Minister that he had counter-attacked, but explaining the difficulties of so doing.[50]

So, for the moment, Wilson stayed put. None of the other generals were removed, and the two battalion commanders were not court-martialled.[51] Kellett, 'universally loved' by his subordinates, never got the division he might have expected. Barnett-Barker was killed in action commanding the 99th Brigade in March 1918.[52] Tim Travers cites Wilson and the unsuccessful Vimy attack of May 1916 as an example 'of an unsuccessful attempt at degumming' (wartime slang for the removal of senior officers, from the French *degommer*, to unstick).[53] It was an instance, he suggests, coloured by personal rivalry and animosity. There was little love lost between Wilson and Haig, who in early June thought Wilson 'seems to acquire a more evil look each time I see him!'[54] Haig's angry reflections on 25 May regarding IV Corps and Wilson appear more extreme than were necessarily

---

[46] Haig TS diary, 28 May 1916 (TNA, WO 256/10); Wilson diary, 30 May 1916.

[47] Draft memo, Wilson to Monro, n.d. [30 May 1916] (Wilson papers, HHW 2/83/21).

[48] Haig TS diary, 2 June 1916 (TNA, WO 256/10).   [49] Wilson diary, 13 Sept. 1916.

[50] Harry Lewin to Wilson, 14 Sept. 1916 (Wilson papers, HHW 2/84/12).

[51] Rostron, however, who had already been afflicted with shell-shock, had a nervous breakdown during the Vimy action, and was sent home on leave by Barnett-Barker (Sheffield and Inglis (eds.), *From Vimy Ridge to the Rhine*, 160 n. 10).

[52] Sheffield, 'The Effect of War Service', 70. Kellett was killed in an accident while riding with the Tipperary Hunt in 1931 (*The Times*, 13 Nov. 1931).   [53] Travers, *The Killing Ground*, 13–15.

[54] Haig TS diary, 23 June 1916 (TNA, WO 256/10). Wilson's comment on the same occasion was 'Haig quite pleasant but I don't understand him' (Wilson diary, 23 June 1916).

justified by a relatively minor setback (though one that cost over 2,000 British lives, which no one at the time, apart from Major Sharpe, seems to have taken into account). As for Wilson's failure 'as a commander in the field', one botched counter-attack seems little enough to go on, especially since it had been launched with the approval of both Monro and Allenby. In his after-action report Wilson blamed the confused command situation for the failure: not only the muddle with officers returning from leave, but also 'interference from behind by men who <u>cannot</u> know the facts', a scarcely veiled criticism of Monro (and by inference Haig) who pulled the plug on the operation early in the morning of 24 May.[55] In 1936 Sir Henry Karslake, a gunner and staff officer during the war, told Liddell Hart that 'there was no scope for generalship in France. Army and Corps commanders were mainly cogs in the machine. Whether they got decorated or degummed largely depended, not on their plans, but on how the enemy on their sector behaved on a particular occasion.'[56] Thus, precisely, it may have been with Henry Wilson.

Wilson had hoped to retake the lost ground on his front as soon as possible, and Haig had promised reinforcements, but this was rescinded in view of the British build-up for a summer offensive. The strategy for 1916 agreed at the Allied conference at Chantilly in December 1915 was for there to be a co-ordinated series of Russian, French, and British offensives. But this planning was upset by the titanic German assault against Verdun which began in late February, sucking in more and more French troops, and the failure of the Russians to take on the Germans in the east. This meant that the British, and in particular Rawlinson's Fourth Army, were left to shoulder the major responsibility on the Somme.[57] Wilson highlighted the allied and European-wide dimension to the 1916 strategy after a conversation with Joffre in April. Joffre had described how he believed Pétain had got Verdun 'well in hand', and how he was building up a large Franco-British army in Salonika 'which would pin down the Bulgar Army & thus bring in Roumania'. Meanwhile Russia was well supplied with all kinds of munitions, apart from heavy guns. He went on to speak 'of our great offensive but gave no date'. Wilson hoped 'so much it won't be attempted before Russia is really ready to move in such weight that she can take 20–30 Boches Divs. off us.' At the end of the month Rawly told Wilson that no date had been set yet for the offensive, though Wilson very much wished it would not be before September, in order to give time for Russia to build up strength for its offensive.[58]

Preparations for the big push continued, but Wilson was concerned about the resources available. This certainly reflected French worries. Foch told him in May that 'until we have <u>far</u> more heavy guns & <u>far</u> more ammun., an attack on a big

[55] Notes on the attack on Vimy Ridge, 23 May 1916 (Wilson papers, HHW 2/83/17).

[56] Talk with Sir H. Karslake, 26 Nov. 1936 (Liddell Hart papers 11/1936/111).

[57] For a lucid analysis of British strategy on the Somme, stressing the extent to which the British were *not* beholden to the French, see Greenhalgh, 'Why the British Were on the Somme in 1916', 147–73.   [58] Wilson diary, 7, 29 Apr. 1916.

scale is suicidal', and the following month the French opposition leader Georges Clemenceau (who had apparently come to Rouen specially to see Wilson) said it would be 'mad' to attack prematurely. 'There was', he said, 'no hope of breaking through unless we had unlimited Ammun. which we have <u>not</u> got & were prepared to face a loss of 25,000 which we aren't.'[59] Wilson took a more optimistic line after staying the night with Rawlinson a week before the offensive was due to start. The statistics were impressive: five corps; 438 heavy guns in a total of 1,550 guns; 'he is going to fire 200,000 rds a day for 3 days bombardment' along a 20,000-yard front, and Wilson thought that 'we run a serious chance of doing something considerable here', an opinion widely shared throughout the BEF.[60] But, as it turned out, even the unprecedentedly heavy barrage laid on the Germans during the days leading up to the battle of the Somme was not enough.[61]

Two days after the battle started Wilson glumly noted British losses 'up to 50,000', which was 'very heavy for what we have accomplished which except for the line Montaudon–Fricourt is practically Nil'.[62] But who was to blame? On 5 July Wilson was inclined to point the finger at Haig who, he wrote, was 'a good stout hearted <u>defensive</u> soldier with <u>no</u> imagination, & very little brains & very little sympathy'. Yet at lunch that day, when Foch (who had declined an invitation from Haig in order to meet Wilson) said that Haig 'is stupid & has no stomach for fighting', Wilson though this 'not quite fair'. What of Rawlinson? Foch said Rawly had told him 'that it was Haig who had planned all this attack. That of course was not so,' noted Wilson. Rawly had told him ten days before that 'he had done it all himself & Haig had been very good to him about giving him a free hand'. The only bright spot was the comparative success of French troops under Foch at the southern end of the battlefield. Foch told Wilson that the reason for British failure (and, conversely, for his success) was 'not nearly sufficient concentration of fire before Inf. attack'.[63] Wilson, too, was critical of artillery deficiencies. On 23 July he noted attacks at High Wood and Guillemont had been 'completely held up by M[achine]. Guns. This is bad Art. work on our side.' On 28 July he had a long talk with Bill Furse, a gunner (and a Staff College teacher under Wilson) who had been commanding the 9th (Scottish) Division at Delville Wood. Furse thought 'we are squandering our men ... partly because of indifferent Art., partly because of indifferent Ammun., partly because of indifferently trained Inf.'[64]

We can see Wilson and his colleagues at IV Corps taking into account some of the 'lessons' of the Somme while they planned a major attack at Vimy. That there was in any case a 'learning curve' was clear from the experience of the 47th Division, parts of which had done so badly in May. Things had improved so much that a one-battalion raid on the night of 27–8 June was 'most successful'. The

---

[59] Wilson diary, 7, 12 May, 11 June 1916.   [60] Ibid., 22 June 1916.
[61] For a critical exploration of the Somme, see Prior and Wilson, *Command on the Western Front*.
[62] Wilson diary, 2 July 1916.   [63] Ibid., 5 July 1916.   [64] Ibid., 23, 28 July 1916.

planning was done over a period of about a week, and Bill Thwaites, commanding officer of 141st Brigade (who had been wounded at Vimy on 23 May) had 'worked it all out in admirable detail'. The raid began with a gas attack, which General Barter told Wilson 'killed between 300–600 Boches, & a good many were bayonetted'. The British suffered only thirteen casualties.[65]

Paddy Griffith has noted that by the end of 1915 preparations for attacks 'had been reduced to a routine that was designed to leave as little as possible to chance'.[66] Over dinner on 14 August 1916, John Shea, who had been on the Somme, told Wilson the main lesson to be learned 'was the absolute necessity for previous practice over a trial & exact imitation course'.[67] Bearing in mind that some extraordinarily detailed planning went into the Somme offensive, this was not necessarily a guarantee of success. But the Vimy planning seems to have been pretty comprehensive. Wilson was fortunate in August 1916 that he had two 'élite' divisions in his corps: the 63rd (Royal Naval), which had been rather weak when he got it in May, but had steadily smartened up since; and Bill Furse's 9th Division, which had been transferred to his corps in July.[68] Furse, too, had some first-class staff officers, notably his artillery commander, Hugh Tudor.[69] The idea began with a proposal by Furse to mount a small-scale gas attack. On 14 August, however, Wilson learned from Richard Haking (temporarily in command of First Army) that Haig 'might call on me to attack the Vimy [ridge] any day at short notice so as to pin down all the Boches & guns now there'. Wilson thought their 'gas attack plan without the gas, but smoke' would 'do as a basis', but was concerned about whether he had enough artillery available. Haking promised to help with guns, and told Wilson 'he was very anxious for my sake that this should be a success'. Wilson, however, resisted pressure from Haig to attack before he was ready: 'I said I could not do it without a moderate chance of success. Of course I could lose 5000–7000 men any day Haig liked but I could not take & keep the Vimy trenches before the 1st September.'[70] Since Haig had specifically allotted the task to IV Corps, this perhaps was Wilson's second (but final) chance.

Much intensive work was done over the last two weeks of August. Dummy Vimy trenches were dug, and units repeatedly taken over them. The pros and cons of using gas were discussed. Furse preferred not, and eventually it was decided to employ 'a short hurricane bombardment'.[71] Wilson, too, was quite open to any technological advances which might assist his troops. His men experimented with

[65] Ibid., 21–8 June 1916. Thwaites had served in the War Office alongside Wilson in 1905–6. In July 1916 he was promoted to be GOC of 46th Division. In September 1918 Wilson brought him into the War Office as DMI. For the successful British 'random gas attack' technique, of which this was an example, see Griffith, *Battle Tactics*, 62.   [66] Griffith, 'The Extent of Tactical Reform', 3–4.
[67] Wilson diary, 14 Aug. 1916. Shea was commanding the 30th Division.
[68] The description 'élite' is from Griffith, *Battle Tactics*, 82. Wilson also had the less-well-regarded 37th Division, whose GOC, Count Gleichen, was degummed in October.
[69] Both men are identified by Griffith as among 'the truly effective individual commanders within the BEF'. Griffith, by contrast, uses the words 'Machiavellian', 'egregious', and 'erratic' about Henry Wilson (ibid. 83, 37, 215).   [70] Wilson diary, 9, 14–15, 17 Aug. 1916.
[71] Ibid., 16–27 Aug. 1916.

a captured German *Flammenwerfer* (flamethrower), but the first time it did 'not come off' and on a second trial 'only went some 20 yds'.[72] At the beginning of April Wilson complained that his aeroplane squadron was equipped only with 'slow and poor power' Vickers fighters, 'not a single really fast up to date machine'. In mid-May he pronounced some experiments in blowing up trenches with hydraulic-driven explosive pipes—a variation of the 'Bangalore torpedo' used for clearing wire—as 'quite good'.[73] He was much more impressed with a 'wonderful' sound-ranging instrument, which was developed for locating enemy guns, and which the artillerymen of the Canadian Corps were to use before their successful assault at Vimy the following year.[74]

At the end of August 1916 Wilson was told that the attack would not be ordered before 10 September, that further big pushes were planned on the Somme, and that Haig, indeed, was 'convinced he will smash the Bosh on the Somme next month!'[75] On 7 September GHQ changed their mind again, announced that there would be no attack before the beginning of October, and that they now wanted 'the whole of Vimy Ridge taken', which would mean a joint action between Wilson's troops and Sir Charles Fergusson's neighbouring XVII Corps. Haking calculated that this would take some four to six divisions. Wilson said it 'would take at least 14 Divs & a great mass of Art.'. Meanwhile, as planning continued for a more restricted three-division attack, GHQ ordered some of Wilson's heavy guns down to the Somme, jeopardising his artillery preparations. Some of the issues common to western-front infantry operations are evident in the planning. Furse wanted to dig a new 'jumping-off' trench in no-man's land as his men had to cross 300 yards of open ground, but Wilson decided not 'for it would undoubtedly give our attack away'. Besides, the attack was predicated on a major advance occurring on the Somme, so there would be 'very few Boches or Boch forces opposite us'. A special effort, too, was put into organising mining operations and co-ordinating artillery and air reconnaissance.[76]

This planning, however, was vitiated by GHQ's decision to move both the 9th and 63rd Divisions down the line to the Somme, and, when Wilson did not get any troops to replace them, his command began to wither away. On 10 October he was told ('a tremendous surprise') his corps was to be transferred to the Somme Reserve Army commanded by Hubert Gough. 'I don't like going under Goughie', he thought, 'but it can't be helped.' Gough's flamboyant and impulsive manner was not universally admired. Douglas Loch told Wilson that 'Goughie is the best hated & most useless & dangerous General we have got'.[77] By 18 October Wilson

[72] Wilson diary, 29 Feb. and 30 Mar. 1916.   [73] Ibid., 1 Apr. and 15 May 1916.
[74] Ibid., 2 Aug. 1916; Rawling, *Surviving Trench Warfare*, 93–4, 111.
[75] Wilson diary, 30–1 Aug. 1916   [76] Ibid., 6, 9–14 Sept. 1916.
[77] Ibid., 15, 20 Aug., 3 Sept., and 10 Oct. 1916. Gough, however, was indulged and supported by Haig, until he sacked him during the German offensive in the spring of 1918 (see Simkins, 'Haig and the Army Commanders', 87–90). For an unconvincing defence of Gough, see Farrar-Hockley, *Goughie*.

had no divisions at all, and was effectively kept cooling his heels to the extent that on 11 November he decided to take a fortnight's leave back home.[78] Though Wilson never got his chance to mount a significant attack, the planning did not go to waste. Even James Edmonds had to concede that the work done by IV Corps staff in 1916 for an operation at Vimy 'formed the basis for the successful one in April 1917'.[79]

As his IV Corps responsibilities shrank, Wilson reflected on the best fighting strategy to adopt on the western front. Like Haig (and nearly everyone else) he remained attracted by the possibilities of 'one big push', which would break the Germans and win the war. But the balance of forces had to be right. When Wilson spoke to Esher in October 1916 of fighting '2 Sommes' (a phrase he repeated to Lord Northcliffe in November), it was not that he wanted to repeat the protracted and costly events of 1916. He agreed with Johnnie Du Cane that the GHQ strategy 'to slog on at one spot' was 'dreadfully lacking in imagination'. What he envisaged was that if Russia, Romania, and Italy (the latter two having come in on the Allied side) would engage the Germans in the spring of 1917, thus drawing off 15 or 20 divisions, and if the BEF divisions were brought up to full strength, totalling 'at least' one-and-a-half million men, an offensive could be mounted which 'would completely smash the Boch line'.[80] But Wilson also favoured a 'bite and hold' approach, in keeping with the more modest ambitions of his planned Vimy attack. In November 1916 he noted with approval that Gough had decided on a staged series of attacks around Beaumont Hamel: 'This is what I have advocated as being the only possible chance of succeeding.'[81]

One unpleasant task which Wilson faced as a corps commander was that of reviewing death sentences passed on soldiers accused of capital crimes, including desertion and cowardice. The procedure was that after a field general court-martial had imposed a death sentence, the papers would pass up the chain of command, so that by the time they reached Wilson the man's battalion commanding officer, brigadier, and divisional general would have recorded their views. From Wilson the papers went to the army commander and, finally, to Sir Douglas Haig himself.[82] Records survive of him reviewing the cases of six soldiers who were executed while serving in his command. Three came before him in February 1916. The first of these was a 20-year-old private in the Black Watch called John Docherty, who had gone absent in December 1915 and had been court-martialled. Although he was given a five-year prison sentence, he was returned to his unit. In January 1916 he went absent again, but had been picked up by the military police in Béthune

---

[78] Wilson diary, 18 Sept., 18 Oct., and 11 Nov. 1916.

[79] Edmonds, *History of the Great War: France and Belgium, 1916*, i. 223.

[80] Wilson diary, 28 Oct., 8 and 16 Nov. 1916. On New Year's Eve 1916 Wilson agreed with Derby that the Somme attack ought to have been stopped at the end of July (ibid., 31 Dec. 1916).

[81] Ibid., 10 Nov. 1916. Beaumont Hamel was captured (by the 51st (Highland) Division, commanded by 'Uncle' Harper) on 13 November, but there was no further advance.

[82] For general treatments of the executions of British soldiers during the First World War, see Putkowski and Sykes, *Shot at Dawn*, and Babington, *For the Sake of Example*.

after only a day's freedom. A medical examination found that he was suffering from 'neurasthenia', the Great War catch-all diagnosis for shaky nerves. But his divisional general, Frederick McCracken, said that desertion in Docherty's battalion was 'too prevalent' and that a deterrent was needed, with which Wilson agreed. Haig confirmed the sentence and Docherty was shot on 15 February. He was the first 'Kitchener man' to be executed.[83]

The next case to come before Wilson was that of Private William Hunter. Hunter had joined up at the age of 16 and had served in France since January 1915. In September, still only 17 years old and having 'lost heart' with soldiering, he deserted, remaining at large in France for two months. He subsequently escaped from custody, and was finally picked up in January 1916. His court-martial, which was told that he was 'of little value as a fighting soldier', sentenced him to death. 'I think this man ought to be shot,' wrote Wilson on 12 February, 'except that he is very young.' Being under 18, Hunter, indeed, should not have been in France at all, and Wilson recommended that the sentence be commuted to (only) five years' penal servitude. Haig disagreed and Hunter was shot on 21 February.[84] The third case was different, as the crime was murder. The accused, Private Arthur Dale, having spent the morning drinking in a French bar, fatally shot Lance-Corporal J. Sneddon (a member of the same platoon) after Sneddon had thrown him out of the bar. Wilson was moved to be lenient. 'Three things—', he wrote, '(1) The man was drunk. (2) There was apparently no motive for the crime. (3) The man has a very good character.' But Wilson's superiors disagreed and Dale was executed on 3 March.[85]

Wilson said nothing in his diary about any of these cases. The day he confirmed his first death sentence was Sunday 6 February. 'To church at 9.30 then Office till lunch', during which, presumably, John Docherty's fate was sealed.[86] The evidence from the cases which came before Wilson suggests that, apart from the morality of the system itself (a matter of considerable subsequent debate), it was not an entirely summary process, and some thought was given to the decisions made.[87]

It is difficult to get very much of an impression of how Wilson regarded the general matter of military casualties in the 'mincing machine' of the western front. There are references in his diary, as we have seen, to the costly nature of successive attacks, and while he obviously accepted the need for casualties, there is no indication of the extent to which (if at all) these losses affected him personally. There

[83] Field General Courts-Martial records (TNA, WO 71/444); Putkowski and Sykes, *Shot at Dawn*, 62–3. I am most grateful to Julian Putkowski for helping me with this.

[84] Minute by Wilson, 12 Feb. 1916 (TNA, WO 71/480); Babington, *For the Sake of Example*, 57–8.

[85] Minute by Wilson, 24 Feb. 1916 (TNA, WO 71/451); Putkowski and Sykes, *Shot at Dawn*, 69.

[86] Wilson diary, 6 Feb. 1916.

[87] See Bowman, *Irish Regiments in the Great War*, for a thoughtful general exploration of discipline and morale; and for the campaign to secure pardons for the executed soldiers, see Corns and Hughes-Wilson, *Blindfold and Alone*, part 3.

were, however, deaths enough among his colleagues and friends to bring home to him the human cost of the war. Over the first year or so of the conflict, indeed, we can see the destruction of the old pre-war professional British army reflected in his diary. On 12 September 1914 he noted the death of George Morris, whom he had appointed an instructor at the Staff College. A month later Wilson was 'greatly distressed' by the death of Hubert Hamilton, killed by shrapnel. 'Hamie', a Staff College contemporary, was commanding the 3rd Division. On 31 October Rupert Ommanney, a key member of the 'W.F.' ('With France') planning team, died when the 2nd Division headquarters was shelled. Another of the 'W.F.' group, 'Fanny' Farquhar (with whom Wilson had toured the Franco-Belgian frontier in October 1911) was killed—'a great loss'—commanding Princess Patricia's Canadian Light Infantry in March 1915. Wilson was hit hard by the death in November 1914 of Hugh Dawnay, an old friend since they had served together on Lord Roberts's staff in South Africa. 'Oh the pity of it', he wrote.[88]

In February 1915 'poor Johnnie Gough' died of wounds. Gough, a real high-flier and a safer bet than his brother Hubert, had been Haig's Chief of Staff. It was, wrote Wilson, 'a great loss, although lately he has not been nice to me or about me'.[89] Wilson felt for those at home, too. 'Poor Nesta', he thought when he heard that her husband, Billy Williams, had been killed in an accident at the Trench Mortar School in August 1915, and he arranged for Williams's grave to be photographed for her.[90] Occasionally, there was a sardonic comment to be made. Early in September he learned from 'Uncle' Harper that Herbert 'Sparrow' Scott had died 'of collapse & diabetes'. Apparently when told 'that he was really bad', Scott had said, 'righto—I have had a very good time. I only wish I had drunk more port.' Scott was a Rifle Brigade colleague, and an Irishman from county Cavan. His death hit Harper particularly hard. 'Write me a line,' he asked Wilson, 'as I find drink even does not produce the exhilarating effect it ought to.'[91]

Christopher Stone's account of a Wilson lecture in April 1916 described him imploring his audience 'to try and make England as a whole come into the war and to take part in it as the French & the Russians & the Germans do'. Stone agreed. 'It's all very true,' he wrote, 'and I don't see how we can finish the war this year unless we can put a stop to strikes & conscientious objectors and party politicians.'[92] Stone's view reflected a continuing widespread dissatisfaction with the government and the way the war effort was being run, which was increasingly personalised on the prime minister, Herbert Asquith. Wilson, along with his right-wing conservative friends, had been pressing Bonar Law to topple Asquith and the government since before Christmas 1915. Law, worried about the passions which

[88] Wilson diary, 12 Sept., 14, 31 Oct., and 7 Nov. 1914, 21 Mar. 1915. On Sunday 23 Jan. 1916, when Wilson was at home in London, George Morris's widow came to visit, 'so pretty & so pathetic'.
[89] Ibid., 22 Feb. 1915; Beckett, *Johnnie Gough*, 195–6.
[90] Wilson diary, 18, 30 Aug. 1915.
[91] Ibid., 4 Sept. 1915; Harper to Wilson, 3 Sept. 1915 (Wilson papers, HHW 2/77/54).
[92] Christopher Stone to his wife, 1 Apr. 1916 (Sheffield and Inglis (eds.), *From Vimy Ridge to the Rhine*, 48).

might be released by the general election he assumed would follow the government's fall, counselled caution. A unionist-dominated coup against Asquith would alienate both Radicals and Irish nationalists, and certainly undermine the national unity he rightly believed was essential for the successful prosecution of the war. Law (unlike Wilson) had both a keen appreciation of public opinion and a ready grasp of the need to stay in step with it.[93] Yet part of the problem, as Winston Churchill saw it, was that the government 'have no opposition'. Writing to Wilson in March 1916 (when Churchill was commanding a battalion of the Royal Scots Fusiliers at Ploegsteert in Belgium), he argued that the only checks on Asquith's administration were 'their own incompetence—& the intelligent Hun'.[94]

Churchill was by no means the only Member of Parliament serving in France. In fact, the First World War was remarkable for the number of MPs who combined military service while retaining a seat in parliament. After taking over IV Corps, Wilson appointed two Unionist MPs as aides-de-camp: Geoffrey Locker-Lampson and Viscount Duncannon, son of the Earl of Bessborough. The well-connected Duncannon, whose family had extensive property in county Kilkenny and were prominent supporters of the Irish Unionist Alliance, was to remain with Wilson for the rest of the war, and he proved to be extremely important in facilitating Wilson's links with Conservative politicians back home.[95]

From February 1916, once he had settled in at IV Corps, Wilson, moreover, who had had the good fortune (with Huguet's help) to secure the services for his mess of the departing Sir John French's very capable French chef, entertained a steady stream of fellow soldiers, MPs, and other visitors to his headquarters.[96] There was much talk about the shortcomings (to put it mildly) of Asquith as a war leader. But the problem was the need to find some credible replacement. After spending ten days at home in January 1916, Wilson concluded 'that so long as we keep Squiff as P.M. we shall never go to war'.[97] In London he dined with Charlie Hunter, Austen Chamberlain, Edward Carson, and Bonar Law ('a nice decent Christian, but lacking in character'). He spent one evening with Arthur Lee, Geoffrey Robinson, and Lloyd George, who had 'not much opinion of Robertson' (no doubt music to Wilson's ears) and was 'very nervous of Labour troubles on Clyde & Tyne'.[98] Since the formation of Asquith's coalition government in May 1915, Lloyd George had headed the newly created Ministry of Munitions, where he had, with some success, toiled to co-ordinate and intensify the domestic, civilian war effort.

[93] Law to Wilson, 26 Dec. 1915, 31 Mar., and 10 Apr. 1916 (Wilson papers, HHW 3/82/78, 90 and 2/77/116); French, *British Strategy and War Aims*, 170.

[94] Churchill to Wilson, 13 Mar. 1916 (Wilson papers, HHW 2/82/59).

[95] Callwell, *Wilson*, i. 274; Buckland, *Irish Unionism, 1885–1923*, 171.

[96] For the acquisition of French's chef, see Callwell, *Wilson*, i. 276–7. In his exhaustive study of French, George H. Cassar says both that meals at GHQ were 'simple and over quickly', and that French enjoyed 'good food' (Cassar, *The Tragedy of Sir John French*, 179, 181).

[97] Wilson diary, 30 Jan. 1916.

[98] Ibid., 24–8 Jan. 1916. Industrial relations were a constant worry during the war. For a fascinating exploration of the state response to labour unrest on Clydeside see Rubin, *War, Law and Labour*.

Wilson's next visit home, during Easter week, was dominated by events in Ireland. On Easter Tuesday, 26 April, he learned that 'a lot of rebels' had 'captured the G.P.O. in Dublin'. His first thought was for the political effect it might have: 'This is good,' he wrote, '& ought to shake Squiff & his brood.' On Wednesday, reflecting the widespread (and understandable) assumption that the Germans were involved in the Dublin events, he thought it 'a marvellous state of affairs, & I should think almost equal to the capture of Verdun from the Boch point of view'. On Thursday he spent an hour with Edward Carson and James Craig, to whom he 'insisted on the vital necessity of getting rid of Squiff or we would certainly lose the war'. Later the same day Bonar Law told him that he and some others had thought Wilson should have been sent to Dublin to take charge (a strikingly crazy idea), but then agreed his 'Ulster record made it impossible'. Wilson, meanwhile, thought that Sir John ('Conky') Maxwell, who had been sent over to Ireland as GOC, should arrest Augustine Birrell (the Chief Secretary for Ireland) 'and try him for his life'.[99]

The 1916 Rising marked a hugely significant, and progressively important, shift away from constitutional nationalist politics, and Ireland was to remain a political and military running sore for the rest of Wilson's professional career. After a couple of months in Dublin, Maxwell had decided of the rebels, 'I don't know that they are pro German, but I do that they are anti-British Government'. He surely confirmed Wilson's evaluation of the Irish situation: 'The people except in town slums are well off & contented & if it were not for political agitation fostered by newspapers, out of work solicitors, some clergy & demagogues all would be well, always remembering that the Irish dearly love a row.'[100] Towards the end of the year, when Maxwell was moved on, Jemmy wrote to his brother from Currygrane to say that 'of course it is to placate that gigantic fraud Redmond'. Still ploughing his lonely unionist furrow in central Ireland, Jemmy complained that 'loyalist people here are so timorous [sic]. I believe we have a grand case & that the Union is still the only possible policy.' But there was little he could actually do (and indeed, for 'timerous' one could read 'realistic'). Like an isolated and gloomy settler in a hostile land (which was not, perhaps, so very far from the truth), he said 'we are holding on here, but, it is a great struggle, &, one sees little daylight ahead'.[101]

Meanwhile, even conservatives were warming to Lloyd George. They were impressed with his vigorous management of the Ministry of Munitions and his increasingly powerful support for some sort of national service, which, beyond purely military conscription (which was eventually adopted in May 1916), could help ensure the most efficient and effective use of the nation's human resources.[102]

---

[99] Wilson diary, 25–7 Apr. 1916. Birrell was not arrested, but he did resign.

[100] Maxwell to Wilson, 4 July 1916 (Wilson papers, HHW 2/83/60). For the wartime Irish context, see Jeffery, *Ireland and the Great War*, 5–68.

[101] James Mackay Wilson to Henry Wilson, 5 Nov. 1916 (Wilson papers, HHW 2/84/90).

[102] Lloyd George's public support for national service, however, was accompanied by private criticism of the waste of manpower on the western front (Grieves, *The Politics of Manpower*, 71). For the background to wartime conscription, see Simkins, *Kitchener's Army*, 138–61.

In April Carson told Wilson that 'L.G. had played a good part' in stiffening Cabinet resolve. Milner and Geoffrey Robinson suggested 'a plan to kick out Squiff by getting L.G. to resign', which Wilson found 'most interesting'.[103] In mid-June Wilson came to London for a week's leave (when he moved back into his beloved 36 Eaton Place), but on arrival found a wire recalling him at once. He still managed to fit in lunch with Austen Chamberlain, a discussion about Ireland with Jemmy, a visit to the War Office to see Robertson and be briefed about the Russian offensive in Galicia, as well as a long talk during the evening with Fred Oliver, Charlie Hunter, and Lord Milner. Milner saw 'no chance of getting rid of Squiff', looked 'on B.L. as absolutely useless, & L.G. as the only chance, but rather a broken reed as he cannot make up his mind to resign'.[104]

On 5 June Lord Kitchener, who had been increasingly sidelined as Secretary for War (not least by Robertson's assertion of a much-expanded role for the CIGS), was drowned off the Orkney Islands, when the cruiser carrying him on a morale-boosting mission to Russia struck a mine. 'What a business,' noted Wilson, 'though in my opinion no loss to the nation.'[105] Lloyd George, who had been due to accompany Kitchener but had been detained at home attempting (in vain) to sort out the government's Irish policy in the wake of the Rising, became War Minister.

No significant policy changes accompanied Lloyd George's five-month stint at the War Office. Unlike the Ministry of Munitions, which was his own creation, Lloyd George now headed a department with a strong ethos of its own, and in which the CIGS, Wully Robertson, was officially established as the government's chief military adviser and effective director of British military strategy. But it soon became clear that the 'Welsh Wizard' was prepared neither to act merely as some sort of figurehead (as Kitchener had latterly been), nor uncritically fall in with the demands of the military as articulated by Robertson in London or Haig in France. In September 1916, on an information-gathering visit to France, he put British military noses badly out of joint by going to see Foch and (as Foch told Wilson) quizzing him about British tactics on the Somme, asking why 'why we took so few prisoners, why we took so little ground, why we had such heavy losses, all these in comparison with the French'. The next day, apparently at Arthur Lee's suggestion, Lloyd George went to see Wilson and asked him the same questions. Both men gave essentially the same answers, defending the British performance and stressing how comparatively inexperienced the new mass British army was. Wilson noted, however, that Lloyd George was 'evidently dissatisfied with the whole thing'.[106] Both Haig and Robertson were annoyed at Lloyd George's actions[107], but Lloyd George's propensity to bypass normal channels of information, and the generals' offended reaction, coloured by military *amour propre* and a clear sense that

---

[103] Wilson diary, 27 Apr. 1916.   [104] Ibid., 14 June 1916.   [105] Ibid., 6 June 1916.
[106] Ibid., 12–13 Sept. 1916. Lee was Lloyd George's 'Military Secretary'.
[107] Haig TS diary, 17 Sept. 1916 (TNA, WO 256/13). For Robertson's view, see Hankey diary quoted in Roskill, *Hankey: Man of Secrets*, i. 300–1.

civilians should not interfere in military matters, set a pattern which was to be repeated for the rest of the war.

On 24 September Cecil Wilson, who had been unwell for some time, was operated on for gallstones, of which 150 were removed, and, for good measure, her appendix too. Wilson got home as soon as he could at the beginning of October, and stayed in London for ten days. He found Cecil 'wonderfully well', and sufficiently recovered to enjoy their silver wedding anniversary on 3 October.[108] Three weeks later Wilson got home for a fortnight. The day he arrived back in London he was summoned to see Lloyd George in his flat in St James's Court, and was bluntly asked 'if I still thought we could beat the Boch. I said I had not a doubt of it <u>if</u> he would give us the men so that we could "mount" two Sommes at once', an opinion which Lloyd George cannot have found very palatable. Yet Wilson was not prepared to commit unlimited resources to the western front. When Lloyd George asked him about the possibility of reinforcing Russia, Wilson 'told him that Haig ought to be told <u>exactly</u> how many men he was going to be given & when, & then he could calculate what fronts he could attack on & from that, how many guns he would require—when these were given to him, then all the other guns should go to Russia'.[109]

Grumbling dissatisfaction with Asquith's war leadership had been growing for some time, and during November 1916 'the triumvirs' Lloyd George, Carson, and Bonar Law (as John Grigg named them) resolved that the higher direction of the war effort should be put in the hands of a small 'war council' headed by Lloyd George. Asquith rejected the scheme early in December, whereupon Lloyd George offered his resignation. Failing to get support from the Conservatives, Asquith in turn resigned and, after a day's high political excitement, on 6 December Lloyd George took over as Prime Minister.[110]

Lloyd George had long been an admirer of Henry Wilson's capabilities, and certainly felt his talents were inadequately employed as a corps commander. It was an opinion shared by many. When, in October 1916, Walter Guinness (a Conservative MP then commanding an infantry battalion) stayed the night at Wilson's headquarters, Wilson struck him 'as a man of great brilliance and width of view and it seems a pity that he should be wasted on the Command of the 4th Army Corps. It is said that those above him are afraid or jealous of his brilliant tongue.'[111] Certainly, any hopes Wilson may have had of promotion in the BEF seemed forlorn. Even though he had temporarily taken charge of the First Army in Monro's absence during May, in August, when Monro left to become Commander-in-Chief in India, Richard Haking, junior to Wilson, was put in

---

[108] Wilson diary, 24 Sept., 1, 3 Oct. 1916.   [109] Ibid., 13 Nov. 1916.

[110] There is an excellent account of these events in Grigg, *Lloyd George: From Peace to War*, 435–74.

[111] Guinness diary, 25 Oct. 1916 (in Bond and Robbins (eds.), *Staff Officer*, 129). Guinness (a member of the brewing family), then Lord Moyne serving as British Resident Minister in the Middle East, was assassinated in Cairo in November 1944.

over him. Monro had recommended Wilson to succeed him, but 'of course Haig would not have [it]. And how pleased Robertson will be.'[112]

Wilson's time at IV Corps had not much (if at all) enhanced his professional reputation, and despite the port-and-cigars suggestions of his political and journalistic dining-companions that he should be promoted to command an army, or be CIGS, or even commander of the BEF itself, there was little likelihood of preferment so long as Haig and Robertson (and Asquith) remained in place. But Lloyd George came to his rescue. Out of the blue while at home in London, on 26 November 1916, Lloyd George (still Secretary for War) told Wilson that he wanted him to go to Russia as part of a high-powered mission. Two days later ('He was immensely flattering'), he said Wilson was to 'represent the British Army in Petrograd as the "greatest strategist we possess" . . . I', he added, 'was at last getting my chance, & that it was ridiculous that I should still be in command of a Corps "reporting to Haig that I had raided the enemy's trenches & taken 2 prisoners"!' Wilson 'need not worry' if his 'Corps was filled up as I would get better things'. Within a week Wilson had travelled back to France, said goodbye to his corps staff (who were 'struck dumb' about the news), handed over the command (by telephone) to 'Wooly' (Sir Charles) Woolcombe, called in on Foch, lunched in Paris with Lord Esher (who did not think 'we can win the war'), and returned to London to begin making arrangements for the trip east.[113]

[112] Wilson diary, 6 Aug. 1916.   [113] Ibid., 26 Nov.–2 Dec. 1916.

1. Cecil, Lady Wilson, at the Chelsea Flower Show, 25 May 1921.

2. Wilson in 'civvies', March 1922, a strikingly unmilitary figure.

3. Lord Roberts, Sir Alfred Milner and some staff officers, Cape Town, December 1900. *From left, standing*: Hereward Wake, Archibald Murray, The Earl of Kerry, F. J. Henley, Henry Cowan, Wilson, Lord Stanley, Sir Henry Rawlinson, Richard Chester-Master, Walter Cowan, Lord Herbert. *Sitting*: John Hanbury-Williams, Sir Alfred Milner, Lord Roberts, Sir Ian Hamilton.

(236-129)   S. Bartholomew.

LESSONS.

Matins—Genesis xxviii. v. 10 to v. 18; 1 Corinthians iv. v. 18 and v.

Evensong—Deuteronomy xviii. v. 15; Matthew xxviii.

4. Wilson's diary for 24 August 1914, on the second day of the retreat from Mons: 'An anxious night followed all day by a retirement to the line Maubeuge—Valenciennes . . .' (Photograph courtesy of the Imperial War Museum, London.)

5. The last days of imperial Russia: members of the Allied Mission at Tsarkoe Selo, 3 February 1917. Emperor Nicholas II is sitting in the middle of the front row, with Wilson just behind his left shoulder. (Photograph courtesy of the Imperial War Museum, London.)

6. Military Section, British Delegation to the peace conference, 29 March 1919. *From left, standing*: C. H. Beadon, J. H. Morgan, Gwilym Lloyd George, T. W. W. Heywood, A. H. Henniker, Charles Webster, J. P. S. Grieg, Stanford, O. E. Wynne, Hon. D. Lindsay, John Marshall-Cornwall, Lord Hartington. *Sitting*: Richard Meinertzhagen, Percy Radcliffe, Wilson, William Thwaites, E. Fitzgerald Dillon. (Photograph courtesy of the Imperial War Museum, London.)

7. Wilson, Sir William Robertson and Winston Churchill during an Army Council visit to the Rhine in August 1919. (Photograph courtesy of the Imperial War Museum, London.)

8. Four of the most powerful men in the British empire, in Paris for a meeting of the Supreme War Council, February 1921. From left: Sir William Thwaites (Director of Military Intelligence), Sir Maurice Hankey (Cabinet Secretary), Wilson, Lord Riddell (Managing Director of the *News of the World*).

9. Wilson and Marshal Foch: good friends, arm in arm, at the San Remo conference, April 1920. Maxime Weygand is behind Foch's right shoulder.

10. Wilson speaking at the unveiling of the war memorial at Liverpool Street station, 22 June 1922. Note the sword.

Metropolitan Police Office.

JUNE 23RD, 1922.

SPECIAL MEMORANDUM.

JAMES CONNOLLY, age 24, height 6ft., complexion fresh, full face, clean shaven, eyes blue, hair dark brown, well built; dress, Scotch fawn sports jacket, blue serge trousers, blue and white striped shirt, light brown trilby hat, no waistcoat, black shoes.—JOHN O'BRIEN, age 24, height 5ft. 7½, complexion fresh, rather thin face, high cheek-bones, high forehead, blue eyes, clean shaven, hair very dark brown, large ears, right wooden leg; dress, black jacket and trousers, no vest, blue striped shirt, brown trilby hat; occupations and addresses refused.

JAMES CONNOLLY.   JOHN O'BRIEN.

The above described two men, whose portraits are herewith, will be charged concerned together with the murder of Sir Henry Wilson, and the attempted murder of Police Constables March and Sayer, and civilian, Alexander Clark, by shooting with revolvers at and in the vicinity of Eaton Place, S.W. Both men have declined to give any information concerning themselves or where they reside. Any information respecting them will be gladly received by Police of New Scotland Yard or Superintendent Bacchus, Walton Street Police Station.

It is also desired to trace driver of taxi-cab who was engaged by Sir Henry Wilson, who left the cab to enter his house, 36, Eaton Place, when he was shot.

11. Metropolitan Police handbill for 'James Connolly' (Reggie Dunne) and 'John O'Brien' (Joseph O'Sullivan). Dunne's faint smile perhaps derives from his choice of *nom de guerre*, while O'Sullivan's face suggests that he had been handled roughly at the time of his arrest.

10

Coalition warfare

The replacement of the rather languid and intellectual Asquith by the markedly more charismatic and demotic Lloyd George in December 1916 was not just a matter of personalities, important though that was, and Lloyd George's conception of a small war council was not merely a device to manoeuvre Asquith out of the premiership, though it succeeded in this aim. It also reflected a continuing domestic political and administrative response to the challenges of the war. Just as the pre-war political norms of an adversarial parliamentary party system had been replaced by a coalition government of more-or-less national unity, so the machinery of government also underwent a process of change and adaptation to meet the novel circumstances of modern, large-scale war.

At the Ministry of Munitions Lloyd George had appointed 'men of first-class business experience' to ginger up the administration of war production and supply. He extended this successful innovation to the War Ministry in 1916, bringing with him Eric Geddes (who had been a railway executive before the war) to be Director-General of Transportation. The progressive (and necessary) integration of the civilian and military war effort produced an unprecedented expansion of government in Britain. Military conscription was accompanied by the regulation of the civilian labour force. The Munitions of War Act in 1915 established compulsory arbitration procedures and effectively made strikes illegal in wartime. Trade unions were drawn into formal consultation arrangements with employers and government. This raised the status of the unions, but it also excluded more radical shop-stewards who demonstrated their power by leading stoppages on 'Red Clydeside' and South Wales (among other places) in 1915 and 1916. State control became ubiquitous across a whole range of activity, regulating eating (food rationing began in 1917), drinking (licensing laws were imposed at the end of August 1914), and even time itself ('Summer Time' was introduced with the Daylight Saving Act of 1916).[1]

After becoming Prime Minister, Lloyd George also overhauled the central machinery of government. The plan for a small 'war council' developed into an inner, 'War Cabinet', headed by Lloyd George, and initially including Bonar Law,

---

[1] There is no satisfactorily comprehensive social history of Britain during the war, but see De Groot, *Blighty*, and Bourne, *Britain and the Great War*; for Geddes, see Cline, 'Eric Geddes'; and, for wartime industrial relations, Middlemas, *Politics in Industrial Society*, 68–119.

Curzon, Milner, and Arthur Henderson, which would decide high-level strategic and policy priorities and generally oversee the conduct of government business. Lloyd George also established a proper Cabinet secretariat, based on the Committee of Imperial Defence organisation and headed by the indispensable Sir Maurice Hankey. Hankey's office serviced the work of the War Cabinet and its proliferation of subcommittees, and, for the first time, provided a proper, systematic record of Cabinet meetings and decisions. While Hankey provided the essential bureaucratic underpinning for the War Cabinet, Lloyd George additionally retained a separate secretariat of policy advisers, who collectively became known as the 'Garden Suburb', as they were housed in a series of huts in the garden of 10 Downing Street. He also habitually sounded out ideas with and sought information from a wider circle of friends and acquaintances, including Henry Wilson from late 1916 onwards.[2] Operating outside the 'usual channels', of course, frequently upset the government's official policy advisers, above all on the military side, who had an especially well developed sense of hierarchy.

The novel experience of 'total war', which had such important domestic ramifications, was accompanied on an international level by a closer wartime alliance than Britain had ever had in the past. Rather like the domestic situation, where the demands of the war stimulated a progressive shift from 'business as usual' (a phrase used by Lloyd George on 4 August 1914 to a meeting of businessmen and bankers),[3] to a much more organised 'system of war socialism',[4] Britain's relationship with its allies, above all France, steadily moved from haphazard improvisation to increasingly formal and permanent arrangements. As David French has observed, 'business as usual' itself was only possible so long as France and Russia were both willing and able 'to fight without significant British military help'.[5] Since this was not the case, Britain had perforce to raise and deploy a Continental-scale mass army to fight alongside its allies. The sustained and intense nature of this Continental commitment, moreover, underpinned the emergence of new inter-Allied structures.

At the top level, Anglo-French co-ordination began with individual visits, such as Kitchener's to Paris in September 1914, and his French counterpart Millerand's to London in January 1915.[6] The first formal conference between the British and French governments did not take place until July 1915 at Calais, nearly a year into the war. It was, wrote Hankey afterwards, 'an important point in the development of the Supreme Command of the Allies'.[7] In November 1915 matters were put on a more systematic basis when an intergovernmental conference in Paris agreed to establish a permanent 'Standing Committee of an advisory character', with an

---

[2] For the impact of the war on the central machinery of government, see Mackintosh, *The British Cabinet*, 345–79.

[3] French, *British Economic and Strategic Planning*, 92 (see also ch. 4 'The Failure of "Business as Usual" ', 98–123).   [4] Taylor, *English History*, 113.

[5] French, *British Way in Warfare*, 169.

[6] The development of systematic co-ordination is usefully summarised in Bell, *France and Britain*, 65–7, 73–7.   [7] Hankey, *The Supreme Command*, i. 348.

'elastic' membership, but including 'the Prime Ministers of any of the Allies and of such other members of Governments and Staffs as were required for discussion of the subjects brought before it'. Although Asquith had proposed that there be a permanent secretariat, Briand objected. Nevertheless, French and British 'Security-Liaison Officers' (Hankey for Britain) were appointed, which ensured, at least, that at future meetings minutes were taken and decisions recorded.[8] Henry Wilson was in attendance at the Paris meeting, and was not impressed: 'these useless irregular mass meetings of Cabinet ministers are useless [*sic*].' Joffre, moreover, agreed with him 'that at meetings of this size no decisions are possible & so it is all waste of time'.[9] Wilson, indeed, had for some time favoured the creation of a small, high-level Anglo-French body to review strategic policy. He urged Bonar Law to get the British and French governments 'to agree never to plunge into... ridiculous ventures like Antwerp, Dardanelles, Asia Minor or Salonica until the problem had been thoroughly discussed at a meeting of 6 men; the two Foreign Ministers, the two War Ministers & the two Cs-in-C'.[10]

On 6–8 December 1915, at Joffre's headquarters in Chantilly, a meeting of military commanders marked the first proper effort to co-ordinate strategy among all the Allies. On the British side were Murray (CIGS), Sir John French (it was his last high-level meeting as CinC of the BEF), Robertson, and Wilson. Joffre, with his Chief of Staff, Pellé, and Huguet represented France, and General Porro, Chief of Staff to the Italian commander Luigi Cadorna, attended. For Russia there was General I. G. Zhilinski, who had been Chief of Staff before the war and was currently the Russian military representative in Paris, along with Count Ignatieff, the Russian military attaché. Serbia and Belgium were also represented, though, judging from Wilson's notes of the conference (he recorded them as 'Serb' and 'Belgian', while everyone else was named), they evidently made little impression.[11] This was the meeting which resolved that Allied efforts in the three principal battle-fronts—the Anglo-French, Russian, and Italian—should be co-ordinated during 1916. Perhaps reflecting the seriousness with which they were taking the proceedings, during the first day of the conference Wilson and his old pal Earl Percy (who had come over from London as Murray's staff officer) exchanged notes like schoolboys in class. 'For some reason which I cannot understand,' wrote Wilson, 'our Govt is against setting up a machinery', adding (a little obscurely, but in line with his known views on big conferences), 'a mass meeting between two vomits is no way to come to a decision'. 'Our Government think that the problem can be solved by closer co-operation between the General Staffs', responded Percy. 'Our Govt is A ASS,' replied Wilson: 'And look where we have got ourselves.'[12]

Co-ordinated action did not quite work out as hoped in 1916. In the spring and early summer there was some inconclusive activity on the Italian front, where

[8] Ibid., ii. 450–2.   [9] Wilson diary, 17 Nov. 1915.
[10] Ibid., 21 Oct. 1915.
[11] Notes of conference at Chantilly, 6 Dec. 1915 (Wilson papers, HHW 2/79/64).
[12] Ibid.

an Austrian offensive launched in mid-May made some progress. During June, as the French defended Verdun and the British were gearing up for the Somme, the Russians achieved unexpected successes against the Austrians in Galicia. Their advance petered out, however, once German reinforcements stiffened Austrian resistance. Romania, encouraged by the initial Russian advances, joined the Allies at the end of August, but collapsed in the face of a German–Bulgarian–Turkish force which occupied most of the country by the end of the year, at which time the overall strategic situation was not much different from what it had been a year earlier.

Despite the lack of any significant progress, the concept of co-ordinated Allied action remained the only sensible way of progressing. For British politicians like Lloyd George who were interested in alternatives to costly western-front slogging-matches, there were considerable attractions in exploring the possibilities of putting pressure on Germany or its allies in other places. The British debate between so-called 'Westerners', who believed that all (or nearly all) resources should be concentrated on the western front, and 'Easterners', who favoured a wider strat-egy, bringing pressure to bear on the eastern front and the Central Powers as a whole in places such as north Italy, Gallipoli, Palestine, Mesopotamia (Iraq), and the Caucasus, arose out of the evident inability, at appalling human cost, of the generals to 'win' the war in the west. There was, moreover, a clear limit (though the actual numbers were a matter of some debate) to the reserves of men Britain could supply to fight in whatever theatre. What, however, Britain could supply (so the argument went) was money and material to bolster up allies, and since Russia had the greatest reservoir of manpower, it made sense to explore the ways in which Britain (and France) could support and encourage its efforts against Germany.

In December 1916 the Allied military leaders, again meeting at Chantilly, came to much the same conclusions they had done a year before, and decided that in 1917 the allies should once more mount co-ordinated attacks on each of the main fronts. A simultaneous political conference in Paris came to the same conclusion, additionally resolving that a special effort should be made to co-ordinate strategy between west and east. 'The only chance of a really great success in 1917', asserted Lloyd George, 'was completely effective co-operation with Russia.'[13] Indeed, a 'legend' propounded afterwards by Lloyd George was 'that Russia, had she received proper help from her western allies, could have contributed decisively to an overthrow of the German Empire quite early in the war'.[14] In September 1916, with the aim of countering pro-German sentiment in Russia and sorting out the supply of munitions, he had first suggested a conference in Petrograd (St Petersburg), telling Asquith that 'a person or persons of high standing and influ-ence in this country' should be sent.[15] The original idea was for Robertson to go,

[13] At an Anglo-French conference, 28 Dec. 1916 (quoted in French, *The Strategy of the Lloyd George Coalition*, 45).   [14] Stone, *The Eastern Front*, 12.
[15] Lloyd George to Asquith, 28 Sept. 1916 (quoted in Neilson, *Strategy and Supply*, 225). For Lloyd George and the Petrograd conference see ibid. 162–3, 225–6.

but he flatly refused (dismissing it as 'the K[itchener] dodge'[16]), even when Lloyd George suggested that he himself might also go. In the end Lord Milner, recently elevated to the War Cabinet, agreed to lead the British delegation. Other members of the party, a banker and two munitions experts, reflected the practical intentions behind the mission.

Wilson had expected that they would leave for Russia almost at once, hence his hurried farewell from IV Corps at the end of November 1916, but the departure was delayed, in part because Lloyd George wanted to sort out Allied policy in the Balkans first. Although Wilson found the delay 'maddening', it did mean he spent a quiet Christmas with Cecil at home in Eaton Square. On Christmas Day his mother came to lunch. They went to the three o'clock service at Westminster Abbey ('beautiful singing'), visited the YMCA 'men's and officers' huts' at Victoria Station, and called in on Austen Chamberlain.[17] The seasonal visit to the YMCA was of a piece with Cecil's war charity work with the Officers' Families Fund, organised by Lady Lansdowne, wife of an Anglo-Irish Tory grandee and herself a Hamilton from county Tyrone, a daughter of the Duke of Abercorn.[18] New Year's Eve, a Sunday, was also spent at home (though in the morning Wilson had spent an hour at the War Office being briefed on the general situation by Robertson). He also had a long conversation with Eddie Derby, who told him that Lloyd George was 'convinced we can't win in the West and so is determined to weaken Haig as much as possible'. Reflecting on the year as a whole, Wilson thought it had been one 'of indecisive fighting, both sides claiming victory, &, on the whole, victory inclining to us and the final decision brought nearer'. Optimistically, he believed that Germany was 'mad keen' to get a peace in 1917, and that 'if we behave like good soldiers for the coming year', he was 'certain we shall knock the Boches over the ropes'.[19]

On New Year's Day 1917 Wilson was summoned to 10 Downing Street to see Lloyd George, who told him he wanted to take him to Italy, where an Allied conference had been hurriedly arranged, but he was 'afraid it may put Robertson's nose out of joint'. He told him Robertson had wanted to take Haig, 'but he (L.G.) could'nt stand "two Scotchmen of that sort" '. Lloyd George added 'that he & I were going to do a lot of work together'.[20] The Prime Minister got his way, and Wilson travelled to Rome, evidently enjoying his new role as a prime-ministerial adviser. There was clearly much potential (if only on a personal level) for friction

---

[16] Hankey diary, 21 Nov. 1916 (quoted in Roskill, *Hankey*, i. 320); 'L.G. suspected of dark plot to get rid of W.R. for a few weeks, & so have free play with the operations' (Clive diary, 8 Nov. 1916, Clive papers II/3). See also Robertson to Haig, 8 Nov. 1916 (in Woodward, *Military Correspondence of Sir William Robertson*, 104).   [17] Wilson diary, 20, 25 Dec. 1916.
[18] Cecil got a CBE for her wartime work as 'Head of the Clothing Branch' (Trench, *The Wrays of Donegal*, 379; *London Gazette*, 8 Jan. 1919 Supplement, p. 451).
[19] Wilson diary, 31 Dec. 1916.
[20] Ibid., 1 Jan. 1917. Robertson was not Scottish at all, but a 'Lincolnshire lad', born in Welbourn, near Leadenham, about 12 miles south of Lincoln (Bonham-Carter, *The Strategy of Victory*, 1–2).

between Robertson and Wilson. Robertson consistently believed both that only professional soldiers were fully qualified to advise the government on military strategy, and also that this advice should properly only be given by the CIGS. He was certainly very conscious of the new Prime Minister's propensity for ignoring established constitutional proprieties, and was no doubt apprehensive about what role Wilson would take in the new political dispensation. On New Year's Eve, indeed, appealing to his loyalties as a fellow soldier, he had explicitly sought Wilson's support. ''Elp all you can', he said, 'because I am carrying a 'eavy load.'[21] Yet in the Easterner–Westerner debate they always broadly agreed that the Allies could only in the end win the war on the western front, and at the Rome conference Wilson approved of Robertson's blocking plans to transfer heavy guns to the Italian front for a major offensive there, or to reinforce the Anglo-French army which had been deployed in Salonika since October 1915 after Bulgaria joined the war on the side of the Central Powers.[22]

The fifty-strong party for Russia (including French and Italian delegations) eventually set off from London on 19 January, taking a special train to Oban on the west coast of Scotland where they joined the *Kildonan Castle* for the five-day voyage around the North Cape to Port Romanov (now Murmansk), which, being ice-free, had been developed in 1915 to receive Allied supplies to Russia. The day before he left Wilson had a long session at the War Office with Robertson, who was gloomy about Russia. All the news, he said, 'tends to forecast a revolution & even the downfall of the Czar'. Going over his briefing papers on the boat, Wilson concluded that the state of affairs in Russia was 'none too reassuring. They seem to be somewhere near a Revolution, & there is great discontent with the Government & even with the Czar. He seems to be as devoid of character & purpose as our poor miserable King.'[23] During the voyage Milner told Wilson that he had 'no hopes of decision in the West'. Wilson, by contrast, had 'enormous hopes if we can get a real move on the Russians'. General de Castelnau, Wilson's French opposite number, unsurprisingly 'insisted on the importance & decisive character of our Western front provided always that Italy & Russia held, at least the forces now opposite to them'.[24] The military men agreed that the overall aim of the mission, apart from the morale-boosting effect it was supposed to have on the Russians, was to assess what further assistance Russia required, and how it might most effectively be provided, in order to ensure that significant German forces were held down on the eastern front. But the problems, even of supply, were formidable, and the inadequacies of the Russian infrastructure were quickly brought home to

---

[21] Wilson diary, 31 Dec, 1916.

[22] Ibid., 5–7, 11 Jan. 1917, 'Notes on conference at Rome' (Wilson papers, HHW 3/11/3); Woodward, *Lloyd George and the Generals*, 140–1. This book is also good on the Lloyd George–Robertson relationship generally.

[23] Wilson diary, 18–20 Jan. 1917. The *Kildonan Castle* had a couple of other brushes with history. In November 1909 M. K. Gandhi travelled out from England to South Africa on it, and in 1915 it had served as a hospital ship off Gallipoli. [24] Wilson diary, 23–4 Jan. 1917.

them. The train journey from Murmansk to Petrograd (albeit with one overnight stop) took four-and-a-half days, at an average speed of only 8 miles an hour.[25]

Wilson's instructions as 'Senior Military Representative with the British Mission' directed him 'to discuss with the Allied General Staffs, as represented at the Conference, the strategic plans for the campaign of 1917', and explore 'the best methods of co-ordinating the Allied efforts'. He was also instructed to assess what could be done to re-equip the Russian army, provided that they could 'make proper and immediate use of anything we may send'.[26] But, as Milner reported afterwards, all the Russians were interested in was presenting 'an exhaustive list' of all their wants (which were very considerable) 'and asking us to foot the bill'.[27] Wilson spent a week in Petrograd, and a 'Military Committee' was formed which agreed unremarkably that 1917 'should be made decisive', 'we must bring off our attacks together', and ' "Side Shows" must be avoided'.[28] Over lunches in the British embassy he heard that there was much talk of revolution, and even that senior Russian officials spoke openly about 'the advisability of murdering the Tsar & the Empress or the Empress alone & so on. An extraordinary state of affairs', he thought.[29]

One day the visitors went to be presented to the emperor at the imperial palace at Tsarkoe Selo (now Pushkin) outside Petrograd, an event captured in a striking photograph, in which Wilson stands behind the seated Nicholas II. The emperor 'was most affable & talked to every single one of us', wrote Wilson. 'We were received in a charming suite of rooms, with Court Officers in quaint uniforms & some servants in marvellous, Catherine [the Great] clothes & feathers in bonnets.' It was, he thought, 'a murderous pity that the Emperor is so weak & so under the Empress' thumb; for according to all the accounts I get he & the Empress are heading straight for ruin'.[30]

On 7 February Wilson left to visit the front with Colonel Alfred Knox, an Ulsterman who had been military attaché in Russia since 1911, had spent long periods of time at the front, and was believed to be especially well-informed about the Russian army.[31] Wilson started in the north, where he visited General Ruzski's headquarters at Pskov, on the line to Riga. Ruzski, he decided, 'asked good clean cut, sensible questions', and had a 'capable, hard, Chief of Staff' in General Danilov (whom Wilson had met at Foch's manoeuvres near Nancy in 1913), and he concluded that the high command was sound.[32] Wilson went on to

---

[25] With no stops, the return train journey averaged 10 miles per hour. The sea voyage out, by contrast, averaged 13 knots (or about 15 miles) per hour.

[26] Instructions for General Sir H. Wilson, by W. R. Robertson, 17 Jan. 1917 (Wilson papers, HHW 3/12/18).

[27] Neilson, *Strategy and Supply*, 236. Ch. 6 (pp. 225–48) of this book contains the best account of the Petrograd conference.   [28] Wilson diary, 1 Feb. 1917.

[29] Ibid., 29–30 Jan. 1917.   [30] Ibid., 31 Jan., 3 Feb. 1917.

[31] Neilson, *Strategy and Supply*, 29–33.

[32] Wilson diary, 8 Feb. 1917. Stone dismisses Ruzski as 'a boneless wonder' (*The Eastern Front*, 226). His tenure in high command appears to have been mainly due to the Emperor's patronage. Less than a month after Wilson visited him he had the task of persuading Nicholas II to abdicate.

the Russian position in front of Riga, where, braving 'a little desultory shelling & one Boche aeroplane', he was 'much more pleased with the front system & organization than I thought I should be. The men', he added, 'are well fed & well clothed.' He liked the optimistic commander here, General Radko-Dmitriev, 'a stout-hearted little fellow', and felt sure 'that the Boches will now never take Riga'.[33] Further south, at Minsk, he was impressed by General Evert (though he thought him 'not sufficiently in touch') and his staff. Discussing the situation with Knox during tedious train journeys, he concluded that the Russians 'are not nearly so hopeless as painted at home'. When he got to Moscow, however, he noticed widespread opposition to the emperor, and painful shortages of bread and coal. 'There will be terrible trouble one day here', he noted.[34] Back in Petrograd for a few days before leaving on 21 February, the political situation seemed less critical and Wilson's spirits rose, buoyed, perhaps, by an agreeable round of supper parties and a visit to the ballet. 'Even if the Tsar & Tsarina are assassinated', he wrote, 'it will not make for a separate peace,' and, 'with luck, the Russians may do great things.'[35]

Although, in effect, he privately anticipated the first Russian revolution of 1917, following which the Kerensky government continued to fight (though they did no 'great things') until it collapsed in the October Bolshevik revolution, his official report on the mission told a very different story. Russia's loyalty, he wrote, was profound and 'may be counted on for the future of the war'. He noted the internal administrative 'chaos' which reigned in Russia, but was 'confident' they would 'solve their difficulties'. He praised the generals and staffs of the Russian army, and bluntly said that the men were 'wonderful' and pronounced their morale as 'good'. Regarding the domestic political situation, he did not think that there would be any 'deadly internal upheavals' during the war.[36]

How could he have got it so wrong? Within a fortnight of completing his report on 3 March, the Tsar had abdicated. Evidently (borrowing Tom Paine on Edmund Burke), while admiring the plumage, Wilson failed to see the dying bird. But even after the fall of the Tsar, the British ambassador in Petrograd was reporting that it would have no 'ill effect on the war'. Indeed, many observers believed that the arrival of a constitutional regime, pledging democratic reform, would actually *strengthen* the Russian effort against the Germans. But, beyond this, Wilson's assessment of the essential 'soundness' of the Russian army was ill-judged, and he must have been badly advised by the highly regarded Knox. Wilson reported that two Russian chiefs of staff had told him 'that Knox knows Russia and the Russian Army better than almost any Russian officer', and Wilson

    [33] Wilson diary, 10 Feb. 1917. The Germans in fact took Riga in September 1917.

    [34] Ibid., 12–16 Feb. 1917.

    [35] Ibid., 18 Feb. 1917. For the social side of the Mission, see Buchanan, *Victorian Gallery*, 28–9, 37–9; Hoare, *The Fourth Seal*, 205–6.

    [36] Allied conference at Petrograd, report by Sir H. Wilson, 3 Mar. 1917 (Wilson papers, HHW 3/12/14; there is also a copy in TNA, CAB 17/197).

himself admitted that he attached 'more weight to Knox's opinion on any matter affecting the Russian Army than I do to the opinion of any other man in Russia'.[37] The best that can be said for Wilson's (and Knox's) assessment of the Russian situation (which was more optimistic than Milner's[38]) is that it was a faithful reflection of what he heard and saw while he was in Russia. That the senior Russian generals he met were so deluded, and the ordinary soldiers he saw were so well fed and cheerful, is not surprising. The former could scarcely contemplate admitting to a foreign visitor the actual parlous state of the entire Russian state, even if, cocooned by their privileged military status, they were aware of it themselves. And the latter, one supposes, were specially selected for the occasion. Not for the first (nor the last) time was Wilson's judgment of a political situation skewed by a narrow military vision, reinforced, moreover, by an element of wish-fulfilment.

When Wilson got back to London he found himself in great demand to resume liaison duties between the British and French armies on the western front, in preparation for a renewed Allied offensive. Much of the pressure for this came from France, where there had been changes in both the government and the military high command. As in Britain, dissatisfaction with the progress of the war raised questions about the competence of the existing political and military leadership.[39] In December 1916 the French Premier, Aristide Briand, reshuffled his government and replaced Joffre as Commander-in-Chief with Robert Nivelle, who had done well under Pétain at Verdun, and was politically more acceptable. Nivelle asserted that he could break the deadlock in the west with a concentrated, massed attack that would 'rupture' the German line in forty-eight hours. At a meeting in London in mid-January, Nivelle (who spoke fluent English, and got on well with politicians) sold his plan to Lloyd George and the War Cabinet.[40] Lloyd George was so impressed with Nivelle, and so attracted by a strategy whereby British forces merely took a supporting role to the French, as well as by an opportunity to assert political control over the military, that he agreed to the establishment of a unified Allied military command, subordinating the British army to the French. As Henry Wilson heard it ('a most amazing story') from Robertson's ADC, Colonel C. C. Lucas, 'Haig was to be put under Nivelle &

---

[37] Ibid. After the revolution, the fiercely anti-Bolshevik Knox headed the British Military Mission in Siberia, and was for a time equally sanguine about the chances of the White Russian forces. He went on to be a Conservative MP for twenty years. For his role in Russia in 1918–20, see Ullman, *Anglo-Soviet Relations*, vols. 1 and 2. Knox was not the only optimistic British soldier in Russia. Archie Wavell, heading the British military mission to the Russian forces in the Caucasus, wrote that, while the political situation was 'chaotic', he had faith in the Russians' 'capacity for muddling through', and believed they would 'carry out all right without any great internal disturbance' (Wavell to Wilson, 7 Feb. 1917, Wilson papers, HHW 3/12/57).

[38] See Neilson, *Strategy and Supply*, 243. Long afterwards, Lloyd George ridiculed Wilson's falling under the 'hypnotism of the established order' (*War Memoirs*, i. 938–43).

[39] To a greater or lesser extent, this phenomenon occurred in all the belligerent powers. See the observations in Gooch, *Armies in Europe*, 145–80.

[40] This account of Nivelle and his offensive draws on Hankey, *The Supreme Command*, ii. 612–31.

[. . .] I was to be British Chief of Staff under Nivelle!' Lucas furthermore hinted 'that Haig & R. thought this was all my doing! Ye Gods', thought Wilson.[41]

Robertson and Haig were appalled by the proposal. Both considered resigning, and Haig used his access to King George V to support his position.[42] Wilson, who told Robertson that all he wanted to do was to return to commanding a corps, told Eddie Derby (whom Lloyd George had appointed Secretary for War in December) he was not at all keen to be a 'liaison for Haig as Haig did'nt like me and Robertson was jealous & afraid of me'.[43] In the end Hankey brokered an arrangement whereby Haig would temporarily come under the 'general direction' of Nivelle for the duration of the offensive, and Wilson would be 'Chief Liaison Officer', based at Nivelle's headquarters at Beauvais but reporting directly to Haig. Wilson remained unhappy about his proposed role, but came under great pressure to agree. Haig rang him up and asked him 'as a favour' to go to Beauvais. Robertson assumed that Wilson would take the position, but was 'staggered' when he insisted on various conditions, including a clear definition of both Haig's and his status; an explicit invitation from Haig, Nivelle, and the War Cabinet offering him the post; and 'power to resign at any moment when I thought it in the interests of the public service to do so'. These, however, were met. Nivelle, indeed, was so keen to have Wilson that he came to 36 Eaton Place to persuade him in person. He told Wilson that he had a low opinion of Haig ('a man of indifferent brain, of narrow vision, of suspicious mind and very difficult to get on with'), and also that Lloyd George would like to get rid of him, and (as Wilson wrote in his diary) 'appealed to me "in the name of God" to accept the post offered as I "was the only man in England who could save a most dangerous situation" '.[44]

On 17 March Wilson, raised to lieutenant-general (a promotion which Robertson had blocked the previous November[45]), was officially appointed 'Chief of British Mission to French Army'. Whatever they thought privately, Robertson and Haig both assured Wilson of their support. Others did not. While the new arrangements were being discussed Hubert Gough wrote a long letter to Clive Wigram (for the King) complaining sharply about Wilson. Although Gough was a man of violently opinionated views, and thus the letter may not be as fully representative of army opinion as he implied, the letter is worth quoting at length as it vividly expresses what might be called the case against Wilson:

I think you ought to know, & so ought His Majesty, what a great many <u>soldiers</u> think of Henry Wilson, for it seems that there is a great misapprehension in the minds of many

[41] Wilson diary, 5 Feb. 1917. That Lucas secretly came to warn Wilson (at home) of the proposal (and came to see him again on 6 February, apparently without Robertson's knowledge) suggests that Lucas was not necessarily so unremittingly 'devoted' and 'faithful' a servant to Robertson as has been asserted (see Robertson, *From Private to Field Marshal*, 339; Bonham-Carter, *The Strategy of Victory*, 398; Woodward, *Military Correspondence of Sir William Robertson*, 339).

[42] Blake, *The Private Papers of Douglas Haig*, 198–212.   [43] Wilson diary, 6–7 Mar. 1917.

[44] Ibid., 13 Mar. 1917.

[45] 'Lloyd George and Bonar Law were at the bottom of it', Robertson to Haig, 30 Nov. 1916 (Haig TS diary, 30 Nov. 1916 (TNA, WO 250/14)).

<u>civilians</u> as to his abilities as a soldier. Henry Wilson was very unfavourably summed up in peace during his term of the Staff College Commandantship by reason of the vague, super- ficial, & unsound tactical theories he enunciated there. In this war he has been tried twice:—once as a prominent member of the G.H.Q. Staff under French, &, then again in command of a Corps. He has distinctly failed in both capacities, & always from the same causes; lack of thoroughness, lack of practical knowledge & practical sense, lack of knowl- edge of how troops should be handled & moved. On Sir John French's Staff he cannot of course be made wholly responsible for the appalling want of Staff work that was evident on the General Staff side at that time, the lack of any orders, co-ordination, or control most frequently, & sometimes also the issue of orders which were totally at variance with the sit- uation & impossible of execution. But as the second senior Staff officer, he cannot be wholly exempt from blame. A really good & able soldier in his position would have been able to put a great many things right.

When he came to command a Corps, he served alongside me, and also under me. I found that, in fact, he did not 'command' the Corps! His influence on work & on opera- tions was nil. His subordinates were neither guided, nor controlled, nor driven—Neither work nor tactical operations were 'caught hold of' or organised. His effort at a counter- attack on the Vimy plateau last June was a hopeless affair, badly planned, organised & exe- cuted.

We soldiers ask with wonder what has he <u>done</u> to establish a reputation?

There is only one answer. He talks—But he can't act. He has neither decision, capacity for organisation, or 'drive'.

As to his private character, he is an active & thorough intriguer & that is well known.

As to his influence with the French, it is due to his capacity for intrigue,—for talk,—& to the French incapacity to form a sound judgment on English soldiers.

Such is my opinion of Henry Wilson, & it is shared by a great many soldiers. So you can see my reasons for considering him a danger in any position of power, & if he was the C.G.S. to a French Chief of the British Army, it would indeed be the handing over, body and soul, of the British Army to the French, & with it the British Empire.[46]

Rather confirming Gough's point about *civilians* favouring Wilson, the King also received a note of a conversation his secretary, Lord Stamfordham, had had with Lord Curzon. Curzon said that 'the P.M. and the French' had selected Wilson to handle liaison, 'but both Haig and Robertson disliked him'. Curzon, however, 'considered Wilson had great ability and was admirably suited for the post'.[47] George V, nevertheless, was so concerned about the apparent placing of British forces under French command that he raised it with Lloyd George, who was wholly unrepentant and said that if there were any 'public expression of feeling' (presumably by the King), he would call a general election. The King, evidently aiming to smooth rather than ruffle feathers, had spoken to Haig and ascertained that, 'although he had no great faith in Sir Henry Wilson he was quite prepared to

[46] Gough to Wigram, 3 Mar. 1917 (Royal Archives, RA PS/GV/Q 832/296). Gough included an equally critical assessment of Wilson in his memoirs, published thirty years after Wilson's death: *Soldiering On*, 171–3.

[47] Memorandum on a conversation between Lord Curzon and Lord Stamfordham, 4 Mar. 1917 (Royal Archives, RA PS/GV/Q 1079/6).

accept the appointment', so long as his duties were clearly defined.[48] Wilson's old patron Lord Esher also put in a word for him. Evidently responding to a recital of Wilson's frailties, he told Stamfordham: 'I agree with all you say about Henry Wilson. As you know I have always liked him and have never ceased rubbing into D.H. and Robertson that he is the ablest soldier in the Army from the points of view of imagination and staff knowledge.' Esher hoped Haig and Wilson would 'get on well together now, if people will stop trying to instil drops of poison'.[49] By this stage the King, taking his proper constitutional cue from Lloyd George, had already interviewed Wilson. He told him that 'he could not save' Haig if he persisted in being anti-French, and assured Wilson that he had his (the King's) 'complete confidence'.[50]

Wilson got to Beauvais on 18 March. He promptly went to see Nivelle, bringing with him 'a very nice letter' Haig had written to the French commander saying Wilson had 'his full confidence' (which was more than Nivelle had for Haig). At first things went quite well. Nivelle consulted Wilson constantly, and Haig gave what help he could, though the atmosphere was always better in the absence of Kiggell (Haig's Chief of Staff), who, as Wilson put it, 'hates the French'.[51] Nivelle aimed to mount his offensive at the Chemin des Dames, along the River Aisne, to the south of the Somme battlefield. But the planning was upset by the revolution in Russia, which undermined any possibility of co-ordinated attacks in east and west, as well as the withdrawal of the Germans along a 50-mile stretch of the front (part of which faced the planned French attack) to the strongly prepared defences of the 'Hindenburg Line'. Nivelle, however, now argued that the offensive must proceed, both to take German pressure off Russia and also to move before the Germans might consolidate their defences in the rest of the attack zone. The British contribution was to attack at Vimy, and draw German troops away from the Aisne.

Wilson had been right to want his duties and status precisely defined, for he was in a very difficult position. That he was the choice of British politicians seeking to assert control over the existing military high command, and French leaders who saw him as an ally in the British camp, was bad enough, but his personal relationships with Robertson and Haig also left much to be desired. At best, he might (as in 1914–15) be able to lubricate relations between the British and French armies, and contribute to an atmosphere of close co-operation and trust between the two. But, if things did not go well, he would inevitably share some of the blame, whether or not it was actually his fault.

It soon became clear, moreover, that his role was not confined just to liaison between Haig and Nivelle, but also between Nivelle and Robertson. Robertson was understandably touchy about his position as principal military adviser to the British government, and after Wilson had been in Beauvais for only just over a

    [48] Memorandum of a meeting between King George V and the Prime Minister, 12 Mar. 1917 (Royal Archives, RA PS/GV/Q 1079/35).   [49] Esher to Stamfordham, 26 Mar. 1917 (ibid. 724/92).
    [50] Wilson diary, 15 Mar. 1917.   [51] Ibid., 18, 22–3 Mar. 1917.

week, he evidently felt he was not being kept sufficiently informed about the situation in France or the decisions being taken there. He came out to France on 27 March and told Wilson that he (Wilson) 'must be in direct comm[unicatio]n with him [Robertson] as well as with Haig'. He laid down that while Wilson remained under Haig's command, he was also to act as a 'ready means of communication' between the CIGS and the French Commander-in-Chief. As Kiggell put it, Wilson had to keep the CIGS 'informed on any questions of fact which he may desire to know but where an opinion is required the matter should be referred to the C.-in-C. [Haig], who alone can be responsible for opinions or advice'.[52] The situation, thus, was that while Wilson was formally answerable to Haig, Robertson wanted to be kept directly informed of everything that was going on (all the 'facts'). Nivelle, moreover, was relying on Wilson to ensure that the British generally fell in with his plan of attack, which was increasingly coming under criticism from French politicians. In mid-March, however, there was a change of government in Paris. Briand was replaced as Premier by Alexandre Ribot, whose new War Minister, Paul Painlevé, had little confidence in either Nivelle or the proposed offensive.

At first the plan went well. In a well-executed operation launched on 9 April the British subsidiary attack—mostly mounted by Canadian troops—captured the Vimy ridge. On 16 April Nivelle's push at the Chemin des Dames also began quite successfully, the French making modest inroads, but the dramatic breakthrough upon which his whole plan depended (and which he had promised) never came. Failing to break through on the first day, Nivelle merely renewed the assault, but at catastrophic cost to the French army: he 'sacrificed 120,000 men in proving himself wrong'.[53] On the first evening of the offensive Wilson found Nivelle 'in wonderfully good spirits on the whole but of course disappointed'. The next day, however, it was 'quite clear' to Wilson that 'so far, the great attack has been a failure', and Foch (who himself had fallen out of favour, and had effectively been sidelined since the fall of his patron Joffre in December 1915) assured him 'that Nivelle was done'. He would be 'dégommé & Pétain put in his place, who will play a waiting game until USA come on the scene say a year hence'.[54] Foch was right. The failure of Nivelle's offensive had a markedly demoralising impact on the French army, especially since he himself had raised such high hopes for its success. Reflecting a wider war-weariness across French society, labour unrest on the home front was matched by a series of military mutinies affecting some sixty-eight divisions.[55] In these circumstances Pétain's cautiously defensive strategy looked much more attractive to Painlevé than Nivelle's apparently groundless (and costly) optimism.

[52] Ibid., 27 Mar. 1917; Robertson to Haig, 29 Mar., and Kiggell to Wilson, 6 Apr. 1917 (Wilson papers, HHW 3/13/1).   [53] Liddell Hart, *Foch*, i. 248.
[54] Wilson diary, 16–17 Apr. 1917. The USA had entered the war on 6 April.
[55] Jean-Jacques Becker calls it 'the crisis of morale (Spring 1917)' (see Becker, *The Great War and the French People*, 205–35).

Wilson was afraid (as he told Haig) that 'L.G. & Painlevé were determined to take a more active command of the major operations of the war', and Nivelle complained to him about 'les cochons [swine] de politiciens'.[56] Wilson, who was seeing the French Commander every day (sometimes more than once), was very sympathetic, and did his best to defend Nivelle to Painlevé. Over dinner on 26 April with the French War Minister, Wilson outlined what he thought were the three possible strategies which could be followed on the western front. The first was 'Somme, i.e. wearing down the Boche', which Wilson favoured. Second was 'Verdun', not in the dogged defence sense, but 'whirlwind attack', which Nivelle had executed with success (though on a comparatively small scale) in counter-attacks during the battle of Verdun, and which, of course, had failed on the Chemin des Dames. The third was 'Pétain, i.e. do nothing!' Wilson thought this last option would be 'disastrous' and that 'a Somme with intelligence is our only chance'. But when he pressed this on Painlevé, the minister 'urged the advantages of Pétain & seemed to think he could hold & use up as many Boches Divisions by making faces as he could by fighting like the devil. We talked and talked, & the more I got him to talk the more hostile he got to Nivelle.' The conclusion Wilson drew from the evening was that 'Nivelle is done'.[57]

So he was, though not until after a fortnight's intense activity. Pétain was appointed Commander-in-Chief on 10 May, with Foch as chief of the French General Staff. Foch's promotion pleased Wilson—'we are more than fortunate in having Foch in Paris', he told Robertson[58]—but Pétain's proved to be more prob-lematic. Early in May Lord Esher told Clive about a 'supposed plot of Leroy Lewis & Repington to use the changes to get rid of H.W., this being effected by telling Painlevé and Pétain that he is a great pro-Nivellite, and against them'.[59] When Pétain, moreover, began to communicate directly with Haig, rather than through Wilson as Nivelle had done, Clive thought that it 'practically cuts out H.W.'s raison d'être'.[60] Wilson also began to feel that Haig no longer valued his opinion, and wrote to him that without his 'entire and absolute confidence' he would resign. There was certainly an air of the prima donna to Wilson's complaint that for three weeks Haig had 'never asked my opinion nor called on me for assistance in any shape or form'. 'Don't be a B.F.', replied Haig, inviting Wilson to dinner, when he smoothed his ruffled feathers. 'He is quite all right again', wrote Wilson in his diary.[61]

Whatever the case with Haig, Wilson's relations with Pétain were never very good. Foch, who had been in London for a conference, told him at the end of May

[56] Wilson diary, 19 Apr., 1917.   [57] Ibid., 22, 24 Apr. 1917.

[58] Wilson to Robertson, 19 May 1917 (Wilson papers, HHW 2/85/65 no. 22).

[59] Clive diary, 2 May 1917 (Clive papers, II/4). Leroy Lewis was the British military attaché in Paris. Repington visited France at the end of April, when he interviewed Painlevé and stayed with Pétain (Morris, *The Letters of Lieut.-Col. Charles à Court Repington*, 266–9).

[60] Clive diary, 26 May 1917 (Clive papers, II/4).

[61] Wilson to Haig, 13 May, and reply 14 May 1917 (Wilson papers, HHW 2/87/18; also in Haig TS diary, 13–14 May 1917 (TNA, WO 256/18)); Wilson diary, 13–14 May 1917.

that Pétain was opposed to Wilson remaining at the French GHQ at Compiègne, and 'that he looked on me as a Nivellite'. Foch 'rather astonished' Wilson by saying he had raised the matter with Robertson, 'who was graciously disposed towards me & said no doubt Haig would fit me out with a Corps, to which Foch had replied "Is that your idea of making use of Wilson?" '[62]

On 1 June Wilson wrote to Haig from Compiègne that he was 'beginning to feel that I am not doing much good here'. 'Doubtless the atmosphere is not very congenial to him, now that Nivelle is in disgrace', noted Haig, who had 'heard privately from London' that Painlevé had told Lloyd George 'that H.W. is not welcome to them!'[63] Wilson consulted Foch again ('and he really is my friend') who bluntly told him that he 'ought to go and ask for a command'.[64] Clearly hesitating before taking an irrevocable step, Wilson went to sound out opinion at home about resigning, but no one tried to dissuade him. He told Robertson, 'I did not think I would take a Corps, but just come home on ½ pay & then ponder what I should do'; he went to see Lloyd George, who merely said he was not surprised about him resigning. Curzon was 'very much shocked' and said that the 'French had found I was too clever for them'; J. C. Smuts (the South African leader who was shortly to join the War Cabinet) approved of Wilson's returning to London, 'as Robertson was good but much too narrow & not adaptable enough'. According to Duncannon, Milner was 'most flattering' about Wilson, '& would not hear of a Corps or of an Army & said I would be employed very soon on most important work'.[65] After Wilson told Eddie Derby (now War Minister) that he planned to resign, Derby wrote to the Prime Minister saying that Wilson 'had very great ability which I think might be made use of. As a Corps Commander not only is he not very good but his particular abilities would be lost to the country.'[66]

At home Wilson also pressed forward his argument that in order to encourage France *not* to 'sit down to a defensive war' for the next year or eighteen months, Britain would have to 'get some notable successes military or diplomatic'. With Russia out of the war a 'striking military success' was impossible, so 'we must get a striking diplomatic success & we must carry Turkey & Bulgaria out of the war'. Lloyd George was so impressed (apparently) with this argument (which certainly echoed his own desire to avoid costly battles on the western front) that he told Wilson 'to go at once & see B.L. & Milner & Curzon & tell each of them individually what I had said, & then come & attend the War Commee tomorrow at 12 noon'.[67] If Sir Sam Fay was right about the attraction of politics to Wilson, this licence from the Prime Minister to brief the War Cabinet both individually and collectively must have been like a dream come true. At the very least it was

---

[62] Wilson diary, 31 May 1917.
[63] Wilson to Haig, 1 June 1917 (Wilson papers, HHW 2/87/18); Haig TS diary, 1 June 1917 (TNA, WO 256/19).   [64] Wilson diary, 2 June 1917.
[65] Ibid., 6–10 June 1917.
[66] Derby to Lloyd George, 8 June 1917 (Lloyd George papers, F/14/4/51).
[67] Wilson diary, 7 June 1917.

immensely flattering, and the apparent high value which Lloyd George placed on Wilson's opinions may well have confirmed his decision not to accept a battlefront command.

Returning to France, Wilson stayed the night with Haig and told him that he would resign 'because the French Minister of War does not get on with him'. While he was at GHQ, news came in that 'Squibbie' Congreve, GOC of XIII Corps, had been wounded, and Haig immediately offered Wilson the command. Haig wrote in his diary: Wilson 'refused on the ground that there are several divisional commanders better qualified than he is. I admire him for having refused because he knows he lacks experience in the practical handling of troops.'[68] Not everyone agreed. Lord Charles ('Daddy') Bentinck, who had served under Wilson in IV Corps, thought Haig 'ought to have <u>ordered</u> you to take a Corps and not allow you the chance of being an ass. How many Divisional Generals do you suppose have half your brains and are we winning this damned war so easily that we can afford to do without brains?'[69] Foch, noted Eric Dillon, Wilson's liaison colleague, was 'horrified at H.W. refusing the command of a Corps'.[70] Before leaving, Wilson took a tour down the French line to the Vosges and the Swiss frontier, calling in on Huguet and de Castelnau on the way. Everywhere he went there were signs of French demoralisation, and even talk of revolution, all confirming his view that France 'wants very careful handling if she is to carry on to next year'.[71]

In Paris, Wilson got an appointment to see Painlevé at five o'clock in the evening. But the minister stood him up: 'as he did'nt send for me by 25 to 6 & as no orderly officer came to see me, or apologize, and as I found myself waiting with a <u>pronounced</u> whore! I walked out & told the messenger I could not wait any longer.' Later he had dinner alone with Foch and his wife in their new flat in the Avenue Saxe. Foch was 'desperately sorry' Wilson was going, and was 'anxious about the outlook'. He was worried that the French government might treat for peace, 'as both the Army & France are tired out', and that Pétain 'will not fight'. He 'likes and admires Milner, thinks L.G. very quick but entirely unreliable & has the lowest opinion of all his own Govt.' The next day Wilson and Duncannon had lunch in the Bois de Boulogne, where there was no sign of demoralisation. It was 'exactly the same as peace with crowds of Tarts & young men, & Millicent Duchess of Sutherland & her second boy were there & we had a long talk. She was far the most beautiful woman there.'[72]

[68] Haig TS diary, 11–12 June 1917. Wilson's own diary account for 12 June substantially confirms Haig's note. On 11 June, however, Wilson wrote that one reason he would not take a corps was 'partly because I could not serve under Gough'. Haig ignored Wilson's recommendation of 'Uncle' Harper for XIII Corps, appointing Frederick McCracken instead.
[69] Bentinck to Wilson, 14 June 1917 (Wilson papers, HHW 2/85/90).
[70] Dillon diary, 16, 17 June 1917 (quoted in Dillon, *Memories of Three Wars*, 89).
[71] Wilson diary, 21 June 1917.
[72] Ibid., 23–4 June 1917. The duchess, who led a flamboyant life, organised a Red Cross ambulance unit during the war, and was nominally based first at Calais and then St-Omer (see Stuart, *Dear Duchess*, 124–43; and Sutherland to Wilson, n.d. (1918) (Wilson papers, HHW 2/67/18)). Sutherland's novella, *That Fool of a Woman*, appears to be semi-autobiographical.

Back up towards the front Wilson went to say farewell to his British colleagues at the French headquarters. Sidney Clive recorded the event in his diary: 'H.W. back; he came to the office; and we lunched with him; then he went for good. Rather pathetic, that he of all people should give up his job because the French were not nice to him. He was depressed at going; & I cannot see what job they will put him in now.'[73]

Wilson then went on to stay with Haig, who, encouraged by the capture of the Messines (Mesen) ridge just south of Ypres (Ieper) by Plumer's Second Army on 7 June, was planning a further offensive in Flanders aimed at breaking out of the Ypres salient and turning the Germans' right flank by driving up the Belgian coast towards Ostend. Haig was keen to secure Wilson's help in persuading the government to approve this, which Wilson, anxious in turn to encourage the French, willingly agreed to do. He was (with, as it turned out, ominous anticipation) 'absolutely convinced that we should attack all we could right up to the time of the mud'. According to Wilson's diary record, Haig was very friendly, begging him 'to do something with my "great brains" ', and assuring him 'that there was always a bed & a welcome at his Hd Qrs'. Wilson told him 'that if no employment was found for me I would probably get into mischief but it would always be mischief of a sort to, & with the object of, beating the Boches, & he said he knew it well, & he trusted me absolutely; that I had been invaluable to him & so on'.[74] Haig's diary entry about the meeting is shorter, and evidently records what *he* thought was important in the conversation: 'I had a long talk with Sir Henry Wilson. He thinks that by the British continuing the offensive is the only way to save France. The French army is in a state of indiscipline not due to losses but to disappointment, H.W. left for London. He said he will "get into mischief if not employed soon"!'[75]

The 'mischief' spoken of was politics. Despite the airy uncertainty about his future which he displayed to his military colleagues, it is evident that once Wilson had decided to give up the liaison job, he had begun to think seriously about his future, and even consider the idea of entering parliament. The previous year, when he had been champing at the bit at IV Corps, the Conservative MP Arthur Steel-Maitland had raised the possibility: he 'wanted to know if I would go into the H. of C. as he would give me a seat anytime'.[76] In June 1917 Esher came down from Paris to see Wilson at Compiègne, where he and Duncannon proposed that he should enter the Commons and 'form a small party of 20–30 men who will work together and force the Govt along the right path'. Esher promised to come over as well '& work under me & work the Press. It is all rather tempting,' mused

---

[73] Clive diary, 26 June 1917 (Clive papers, II/4). It is possible that Clive, who had been supplanted by Wilson as the principal British liaison officer at the French HQ, regarded his departure with not unmixed emotion.　　　　　　　　　　　　　　[74] Wilson diary, 28 June 1917.

[75] Haig TS diary, 28 June 1917 (TNA, WO 256/19). On the whole, Haig's diary entries are, in any case, more laconic than Wilson's.

[76] Wilson diary, 20 Aug. 1916. Steel-Maitland was a party 'fixer', and first Chairman of the Conservative Party Organisation, serving from June 1911 to Dec. 1916.

Wilson, 'but it would mean final parting from soldiering and there is also the great practical difficulty of money.' Wilson calculated that with his private income of £300 a year, and his military half pay of £600 (which, less income tax, totalled £450), he would only have £750 to live on, and he could not keep on his house at Eaton Place for under £1,500 a year.[77] Esher and Duncannon's suggestion to Wilson was part of a wider scheme to form a new 'National' political party, drawing together kindred spirits from across the political spectrum who would together properly address the 'business' of war.[78] Esher, moreover, a long-time admirer, felt strongly that Wilson was 'not allowed by our idiotic government to pull his real weight'.[79]

Wilson then consulted his politically well-connected brother, Jemmy, who counselled caution. 'It is a serious step for you,' he wrote, '&, I half fear if once elected you would never get taken on by W.O. again.'[80]When he got home to 36 Eaton Place on 28 June, he found two further letters from his brother awaiting him. Jemmy reported that two parliamentary vacancies were about to occur in Ulster, and that 'once Ulster realized who you were, & that you were in the Curragh show, you would go in "as round as a hoop". . . How W.R. [Robertson] would hate to see you there!' he added.[81] On Jemmy's advice Wilson went to see Edward Carson, who first rather unenthusiastically said that if Wilson 'decided to stand for the House, he would see about an Ulster seat', and a few days later thought it might be better if Wilson found an English seat. Duncannon mean-while rushed about gathering support—among Conservatives and Liberals—for Wilson and the proposed new party. He found an ally in David Davies, the Liberal MP for Montgomeryshire, who had been one of Lloyd George's private secretaries (and had gone with the Milner Mission to Russia). Duncannon and Davies 'agreed to form a combined meeting of Tories & Rads. to push the claims of the war, the detachment of Turkey & Bulgaria, & the question of Man Power'. Wilson reasonably argued that any new party must adopt some clear policy, and suggested 'the vital necessity of conscription for Ireland'.[82] This policy had some superficial attractions—both relieving the overall manpower problem and also demonstrating 'firm government' over rebellious Ireland—but it would clearly be most attractive to Tories, and it also carried political difficulties which Wilson simply ignored (or assumed did not exist).

Wilson, meanwhile, was invited on 3 July (at very short notice) to brief the War Cabinet on the current situation in France, and he seems to have nursed a private hope that he might be invited permanently to join the 'war committee', perhaps in

---

[77] Wilson diary, 13 June 1917. Wilson's calculations did not take into account the MP's salary of £400.   [78] On this subject, see Wilson, 'National Party Spirits'.

[79] Esher to H. A. Gwynne, 1 June 1917 (quoted in Wilson, *The Rasp of War*, 218).

[80] J. M. to Henry Wilson, 19 June 1917 (Wilson papers, HHW 2/96/33).

[81] Wilson diary, 28 June 1917; J. M. to Henry Wilson, 22 and 27 June 1917 (Wilson papers, HHW 2/96/34–5). The former letter is endorsed, in Cecil Wilson's writing: 'It was in 1917 he first thought of being an "MP". Cecil Wilson.'

[82] Wilson diary, 29 June–10 July 1917. Carson was a notorious hypochondriac and prone to peri-ods of depression. Wilson may have caught him at a bad time.

a position analogous to Smuts, who was not a member of the British legislature. On 7 July he asked Bonar Law about the possibility, but he 'said it was quite impossible', and added (to Wilson's evident chagrin) that he 'could do no possible good' in parliament. Robertson told him 'there was absolutely no way of employing me at home', while Milner said he wanted Wilson to be Commander-in-Chief in the Balkans in place of the French General Sarrail. Wilson dismissed the idea: 'I can't think there is much to be done there.'[83]

While faced with an uncertain future, Wilson managed to enjoy the comforts of being back in England. He spent a weekend (gardening all day Sunday) at Grove End, which he and Cecil had reoccupied, and on 11 July set off for a week in Ireland. At home in Longford—it was eight years since he had been back—he talked politics with Jemmy. Eamon de Valera for Sinn Fein had just won a by-election in East Clare, a seat left vacant by the death of Willie Redmond while serving in the army on the western front. Wilson thought it '<u>very bad</u>', and they both agreed 'that we <u>must</u> accept the Clare challenge & clap on conscription or we shall have to fight for Ireland'. He went to Galway for the night and found it full of Sinn Féin flags, 'green, white, yellow with I.R. [Irish Republic] on the white'. Everyone he spoke to—judges, landowners, a Redmondite local politician, police officers, and 'some natives'—agreed on 'the hopelessness of the outlook & the <u>necessity</u> for conscription'. Then he went to Belfast—'so rich in money, enterprise and organizing capacity and <u>so</u> loyal'—where again everyone was for conscription, and he met some Ulster Unionist leaders who encouraged him to consider a Belfast constituency. Richard Dawson Bates, secretary of the party, said it would be 'no contest'.[84]

Back in London, Wilson told Milner 'how absolutely necessary it was to put on conscription at <u>once</u> & that <u>no</u> reason other than the rank cowardice of the Govt could be produced for not doing so'. Milner agreed (so Wilson noted), but 'said it was quite impossible'. He said Duke (the Chief Secretary for Ireland) was 'no use & that we were moving towards a crash which was inevitable'. With the marvellous assurance of the landed class, Wilson thought 'it was a d—— shame to let the poor ignorant Irish peasants get into this terrible state'.[85] Wilson retained his passionate (which is probably not too strong a word for it) support for conscription in Ireland against all counter-argument. Ireland, of course, was a political blind-spot for him, a fact which some of his English political friends did not fully appreciate.

Wilson had always been in favour of applying conscription to Ireland, just the same as in Great Britain. Discussing the manpower demands of the western front with Lloyd George in November 1916, Wilson asked him 'why he did not clap conscription on Ireland', which would, thought Wilson, produce two to three hundred thousand 'good Irish soldiers'. Wilson's refusal to appreciate the potential political costs of the measure was of a piece with his lifelong unionism, and he dismissed Lloyd George's concerns about the 'moral effect abroad to see the Irish Members carried squealing out of the House; & that there would be serious

[83] Ibid., 3, 7 July 1917   [84] Ibid., 11–18 July 1917.   [85] Ibid., 20 July 1917.

troubles in Ireland'. 'Nobody abroad', maintained Wilson (blithely ignoring Irish-American and Irish-Australian opinion), 'cared a d—— if Johnnie Redmond acted the part of a baby.'[86] Later the same month he had been surprised that the King (with an unusually acute sense of what was politically possible) was opposed to Irish conscription 'until the people agreed!', and he simply refused to accept 'Conky' Maxwell's opinion that 'there would be serious trouble in North & South if conscription were put in'.[87]

For about a month in the summer of 1917 Wilson appears genuinely to have toyed with the idea of going into parliament, if not also taking on the leadership of Duncannon's new party. But the lukewarm attitude of Carson—still the most important Irish unionist leader—and the difficulty which Duncannon had in trying to assemble a quorum of potential members from among his fellow MPs, took the steam out of the whole exercise. For Wilson, in any case, the possibilities of a military job improved. Johnnie French, who was Commander-in-Chief of home forces, was very encouraging, and on 24 July told him that Lloyd George was 'determined to get rid of Robertson' whom he thought 'has only the brains of a "superior clerk" '.[88] On 14 August Lucas told him that Lloyd George was trying to get rid of *both* Robertson and Haig. Wilson thought this 'very unwise, certainly as regards Haig who is the best we can produce for monotonous siege work'. The same day Robertson himself asked Wilson about taking on a home command, and a week later Derby officially offered him the Eastern Command, an attractive proposition since the headquarters was at 50 Pall Mall in London, the duties were not overly heavy, and (not an unimportant consideration) he returned to full pay. Wilson accepted the offer and took over the command on 1 September.[89] For the moment, at least, parliamentary ambitions were put on hold.

There are two interpretations of Wilson's political activities in the summer of 1917. Keith Wilson argues that 'for Wilson the formation of the National Party was essentially a *divertissement*. It filled in the time whilst he was kicking his heels whilst angling for an acceptable military appointment.'[90] By contrast, but much more speculatively, Brock Millman asserts that Wilson's 'mischief' was a plot, or conspiracy, by which Wilson effectively blackmailed Lloyd George into facilitating his (Wilson's) 'rise to power'. Wilson, he argues, 'would not have come to the attention of the prime minister without resorting to intrigue'.[91] This is nonsense.

---

[86] Wilson diary, 13 Nov. 1916.

[87] Ibid., 21, 23 Nov. 1916.

[88] Ibid., 24 July 1917. Robertson, for his part, did not think much of Lloyd George: 'an under-bred swine' (Robertson to Kiggell, 9 Aug. 1917, in Woodward, *Military Correspondence of Sir William Robertson*, 213).

[89] Wilson diary, 14, 21 Aug. 1917. Judging from Wilson's diary, apart from intermittent office work the Eastern Command responsibilities mostly seem to have taken up just one day a week, visiting coastal defences and some other barracks.

[90] Wilson, 'National Party Spirits', 218; see also id., 'Over the Top?', 77–82.

[91] Millman, 'Henry Wilson's Mischief'.

Wilson as a politician—even if Lloyd George ever contemplated the possibility—was no threat to the Prime Minister, who could easily see off a neophyte parliamentarian supported by a motley band of dissidents, few of whom were actually in the House of Commons.[92] Wilson as a soldier (with whom Lloyd George had been well acquainted for some years) could, however, serve as an extremely useful source of military advice who was *not* Sir William Robertson.

In the early summer of 1917 Lloyd George had endeavoured to improve the process of British strategic decision-making by establishing a 'War Policy Committee', consisting of himself, Curzon, Milner, and Smuts (with Hankey as secretary), to review policy as a whole.[93] Following the failure of the Nivelle offensive, it was conceded that a 'war of attrition' was the only realistic policy on the western front. With the collapse of Russia (though sporadic fighting against the Germans continued until the autumn), Lloyd George favoured reinforcing Italy to bring pressure on Austria, which might in turn enable the Allies to knock out Bulgaria and Turkey. But Robertson and Haig were against moving any resources to Italy, and favoured the plan for an offensive in Flanders. Aware of the need to offer support to the French in the west (and secure some morale-boosting success), the committee grudgingly assented to Haig's plan, 'but not to allow it to degenerate into a drawn out, indecisive battle of the "Somme" type. If this happened, it was to be stopped and the plan for an attack on the Italian front would be tried.'[94]

Haig's offensive, which became known as the third battle of Ypres, began on 31 July 1917, as did a month of rain, which turned the marshy Belgian land into a quagmire. 'The weather has been damnable & the mud awful', noted Wilson on 17 August.[95] Although the weather cleared up for a spell in September, and some limited success was gained, the rains, and the mud, returned in October, and the advance, such as it was, ground to an inconclusive halt at the tiny village of Passchendaele (Passendale). It is against the background of this nightmarish battle that Lloyd George and his colleagues began to contemplate significant changes in both the British and the inter-Allied military decision-making machinery.

In Britain the Prime Minister sought some alternative to Robertson (if not also Haig). John French was a willing accomplice. On 14 August French told Sir George Riddell, confidante of the Prime Minister and managing director of the *News of the World*, that Robertson was 'anxious to get the whole of the military power into his own hands, that he is a capable organiser but not a great soldier, and we are suffering from a lack of military genius'. Henry Wilson, on the other

---

[92] Apart from Duncannon, Davies, Sir Henry Page Croft (who took on the leadership of the party), and a few other MPs, most of the support came from journalists: H. A. Gwynne and Ian Colvin of the *Morning Post*, Leo Maxse of the *National Review*, and F. S. Oliver. There was also Lord Esher, who represented no one but himself.

[93] Hankey, *Supreme Command*, ii. 670–86; French, *The Strategy of the Lloyd George Coalition*, 94–123.   [94] Hankey diary, 16 July 1917 (quoted in Hankey, *Supreme Command*, ii. 683).

[95] Wilson diary, 17 Aug. 1917.

hand, 'one of the best brains in the Army', was 'without a job, and no steps are being taken to ascertain the views of our leading soldiers'. Riddell, as no doubt French had hoped, passed this on to Lloyd George.[96] On 16 August Brinsley Fitzgerald (French's private secretary) told Wilson that, 'with the idea of clipping Robertson's wings', Lloyd George and French had had the idea that all Robertson's proposals should be submitted to a committee of three soldiers, French, Wilson, and one other. Wilson thought it 'a ridiculous & unworkable proposal'. A week later he and French had lunch with Lloyd George at Riddell's house Great Walstead in Sussex. French 'was quite good about Haig who he said was right in fighting & asking for all he could get. He was not so good about Robertson.' According to his diary, Wilson told Lloyd George that his plan for a committee of three 'to overhaul Robertson's work was [a] bad plan & unworkable & not fair on Robertson', and suggested instead an inter-Allied body 'of 3 PMs & 3 soldiers to be over all C.I.G.S.s & to draw up plans for the whole theatre from Nieuport to Baghdad'. He claimed he 'had had this plan for 2½ years', and it was the only plan 'which would allow us to really draw up a combined plan of operations'.[97]

'Two and a half years', which went back to early 1915, was perhaps stretching it a bit. Wilson nevertheless had, as we have seen, from at least October been suggesting to Bonar Law the idea of a small, powerful body to co-ordinate Franco-British policy-making. Bonar Law appeared to think this was 'an excellent idea', but took no action.[98] In December Wilson wrote to him asking him, again to press for his proposed

small mixed Committee . . . to deal with these problems and to obviate useless and mischievous 'mass meetings'; visits of high officials bent on saving reputations, and not on winning the war; occasional and irregular correspondence; passage of irresponsible and ignorant liaison officers, and indeed all the makeshifts and subterfuges which come from not facing the problems and the position fairly and squarely and not meeting our friends face to face and speaking out like men and gentlemen.[99]

This was an admirable objective, but also a counsel of perfection, revealing a degree of political naivety. If it were to be any use, his proposed committee would have to have some executive power, and it would inevitably trespass on existing political and military vested interests. At the inter-Allied level, too, the added problem of national sovereignty, and the jealous protection of independent command, were considerable obstacles.

By 1917, however, the erosion of military vested interests was exactly what Lloyd George wanted. At the Great Walstead lunch the Prime Minister asserted that he was 'satisfied with Haig but profoundly dis-satisfied with Robertson, who he said thought himself the greatest soldier & strategist that ever lived'. He 'was

[96] Riddell diary, 14 Aug. 1917 (quoted in McEwan, *The Riddell Diaries*, 195).
[97] Wilson diary, 16, 23 Aug, 1917.   [98] Ibid., 21 Oct. 1915.
[99] Wilson to Bonar Law, 3 Dec. 1915; he also sent a copy to Carson (Wilson papers, HHW 2/77/91, 92).

quite clear' that 'we were not winning the war by our present plans ... but that he did not know how or what we should do and he had no means of checking or altering Robertson's & Haig's plans though he knew they were too parochial'. Impressed by the 'committee of six' plan (and saying that Wilson should be the 'English' representative), he sent Wilson off to sell the idea to the rest of the War Cabinet.[100]

Although Lloyd George spoke to Hankey about 'a new, and not very well-thought-out scheme for an Allied Council and General Staff in Paris to direct the war', over the next few weeks nothing much happened about Wilson's proposal for a 'Superior War Council'.[101] At Great Walstead, Wilson had observed that while nothing much was possible on the western front or in Italy during the winter months of 'mud & snow', 'the weather a little further down the line in Asia Minor & Egypt is perfect'. Lloyd George was strongly attracted to the possibility of knocking out Turkey with victories in Palestine, where Allenby had been in command since June, if not also further east where Sir Stanley Maude's 'Mesopotamian Expeditionary Force' had taken Baghdad earlier in the year. Late one Friday night (it was after 10.00 p.m.) in early October, he summoned Wilson to Riddell's London house where he quizzed him again about the possibilities of doing something in the Middle East. Wilson assured him 'that if a really good scheme was thoroughly well worked out, we could clear the Turks out of Palestine & very likely knock them completely out <u>during the mud months</u>, without in any way interfering with Haig's operations next Spring & Summer'. When Wilson raised the matter of a 'superior organization', Lloyd George said it 'was the best plan but the French (& Italian) Govts were absolutely <u>rotten</u>', and 'so it was impossible to get such an organization started'.[102] Meanwhile, faced with Robertson and Haig's continued opposition to any 'eastern' adventures, or the transfer of resources from the western front, Lloyd George revived a version of his original scheme for 'clipping Robertson's wings' by getting the War Cabinet on 11 October to invite French and Wilson each to consider the broad strategic position and submit proposals as to future military policy.[103]

Although Henry Wilson did not become Chief of the Imperial General Staff—professional head of the British army and principal military adviser to the British Government—until February 1918, it was inevitable (or nearly so) that he would do so from this moment in October 1917 when Lloyd George explicitly and formally sought his and John French's advice as to the future direction of British strategy. The invitation, put through the War Cabinet, was of a different order to

[100] Wilson diary, 23 Aug. 1917. Over the next few days Milner, Bonar Law, and Carson all welcomed the scheme (ibid., 23–7 Aug.).

[101] Hankey diary, 30 Aug. 1917 (quoted in Hankey, *Supreme Command*, ii. 695); Wilson diary, 4 Sept. 1917.

[102] Wilson diary, 5 Oct. 1917; Riddell, *Lord Riddell's War Diary*, 281. Riddell's house, which Lloyd George often used for confidential meetings, was at 20 Queen Anne's Gate.

[103] Woodward, *Lloyd George and the Generals*, 209–10.

the occasional, informal soundings he had taken from Wilson (and others) up to then. The Prime Minister's neat medical analogy, moreover, 'that the patient after a 3 years course of treatment not being yet cured, he [Lloyd George] thinks it advisable to call in another couple of specialists',[104] scarcely concealed the fact that Robertson's advice was not just being tested, but clearly rejected, and his position fundamentally undermined. And while Robertson was on the way out, Wilson was on the way in.

[104] Wilson diary, 9 Oct. 1917; Robertson, *Soldiers and Statesmen*, ii. 257.

11

Winning the war

By October 1917 it was perfectly clear to anyone close to Lloyd George that he wanted to get rid of both Robertson and Haig, and the device of asking Wilson and French's advice was specifically designed to undermine, if not actually drive out, the other two men. The night before the War Cabinet meeting of 11 October, Lloyd George dined with Wilson and French (this time at French's house) to prepare them for it. He asserted that Robertson was 'afraid of Haig, & that both of them are pigheaded, stupid & narrow visioned'. Haig had 'submitted what LG called a "preposterous" paper' which set out 'to prove that the West front is the only front', but 'LG says that, in fact, on Haig's own showing the Western front is a hopeless front', yet Haig still claimed that he could defeat the Germans. Above all was the tremendous importance of the next day's meeting. 'It was', said the Prime Minister, with typical hyperbole, 'going to be the turning point of the war.'[1]

At the Cabinet, Lloyd George outlined what he regarded as the four 'alternative policies'. First was 'concentration of the whole of our forces on the Western Front' (which was, noted Wilson, 'Haig's policy'); second was 'concentrate mainly on the Western Front', but 'utilise the forces now in the various overseas theatres', such as Palestine and Mesopotamia, 'as actively as possible'. The third option was essentially a holding operation (as favoured by Pétain), 'until Russia recovered' and the United States was supplying enough troops to ensure superiority; and the final one consisted of 'knocking the props from under Germany' by 'military and diplomatic' operations against enemy allies such as Turkey and Bulgaria. The Prime Minister's preference was for some combination of the second and last options, by which success might be achieved at reasonable human cost. With this in mind, French and Wilson were to report on 'the present state of the war and the future prospects and future action to be taken'.[2]

Over the next week Wilson worked at his 'state paper', consulting Macdonogh (Director of Military Intelligence), who 'did not believe in breaking the German Army', but did think 'perhaps in the next 12 mos—in breaking the heart of the German people', and Macready (Adjutant-General), who gave a very pessimistic

---

[1] Wilson diary, 10 Oct. 1917. For an analysis of Haig's paper, which claimed that he could gain 'decisive results' in 1917 or 1918, see Woodward, *Lloyd George and the Generals*, 208–9.

[2] Wilson diary, 11 Oct. 1917; memo by Wilson, Oct. 1917 (Wilson papers, HHW 3/13/25); War Cabinet meeting, 11 Oct. 1917 (TNA, CAB 23/13/247(b)).

forecast of manpower, suggesting a shortfall of up to 300,000 men 'a year hence'.[3] On 17 October Lloyd George had another private meeting with Wilson and French to go over their draft papers. He heartily agreed with Wilson proposing 'a Superior Direction over all the CGSs & CinCs', but, evidently fearing Robertson and Haig's reaction, wanted him to modify the paper to remove 'all semblance of dictation' by the proposed new body.[4]

Among the documents Wilson was given to examine while writing his paper were appreciations by both Haig and Robertson. His own, annotated, copies of two of these illuminate some of the strategic issues under consideration. A Haig memorandum of 8 October examined the 'role of British forces in the event of Russia being unable to maintain an active part in the war, and having regard to the weakened state of France and Italy'. Emphasising his commitment to a 'western' strategy, Haig stated 'that success on the western front is the only real alternative to an unsatisfactory peace', to which Wilson commented: 'This is true, but what is under consideration is whether such a success would not be made easier if Turkey (& Bulgaria) were knocked.' Wilson, on the other hand, agreed with Haig's assertion that 'it is beyond question that our offensive must be pressed as long as possible'. Although the main weight of this would clearly be in the west, Wilson was not so sure about its timing. Haig wrote that 'decisive success is expected next year'—this was the sort of optimistic prediction (in the light of persistent failure) which so alienated Lloyd George—'if we use the full power of the Empire's strength and if the Russians can keep the present number of German Divisions facing her'. But Wilson had his doubts. 'The assumption about Russia', he wrote (with considerable understatement), 'is a large one.' From a paper by Robertson on 'Future military policy', Wilson extracted a statement that 'the first rule in all wars is to concentrate in the main theatre all forces that can be employed. Any departure from this rule has invariably proved disastrous.' Against this he wrote: 'I don't think this is quite a fair assertion. Napoleon frequently carried on several campaigns at once.'[5] While this further confirms the attractions to Wilson of operations beyond the western theatre, the reference to Napoleon was perhaps unfortunate, since what Paul Kennedy has identified as 'imperial overstretch', with overcommitment on more than one front, certainly contributed to French defeats from 1813 onwards.[6]

French's and Wilson's papers criticised the British high command, both at home and on the Continent. In his memorandum, Wilson affirmed that he had 'always been' and would 'always remain an ardent "Westerner" for the simple reason that it is along the west front that the bulk of the forces of our principal enemy is disposed and the death-grapple must always be with those forces'. He argued, nevertheless, that the 'death-grapple must be engaged in at the time and

---

[3] Wilson diary, 12, 16 Oct. 1917.   [4] Ibid., 17 Oct. 1917.

[5] Notes on Sir D. Haig's memo of 8 Oct. 1917, and on 'Future military policy' by Sir W. Robertson (Wilson papers, HHW 3/13/16, 17).

[6] Kennedy, *The Rise and Fall of the Great Powers*, 173–7.

place and in the manner best suited to our cause'. It was, he argued, 'no use throwing "decisive numbers at the decisive time at the decisive place" ' if 'the decisive numbers do not exist, if the decisive hour has not struck and if the decisive place is ill chosen', music, no doubt, to Lloyd George's ears. Central to both reports was the recommendation that some high-level inter-Allied council be formed. 'The superior direction of this war has, in my opinion,' wrote Wilson, 'been gravely at fault from the very commencement—in fact, it is inside the truth to say that, there has never been any superior direction at all.' The 'net result', he concluded, 'seems to me to be that we take short views instead of long views, we look for decisions to-day instead of laying our plans for to-morrow, and as sequence we have constant change of plans'. This being the case, there was a need for 'an intelligent, effective and powerful superior direction. And by this I mean a small War Cabinet of the Allies, so well informed and above all intrusted [*sic*] with such power that their decision and orders are instantly obeyed.' He admitted the difficulties of creating such a body, but denied 'the impossibilities'. 'Every other conceivable variant' had been tried, 'and always with the same miserable result.' Without deciding firmly to 'really direct and command the main issues of this war', he asserted that the government was 'gambling with the future in a manner we have no right to', and 'running a very serious chance of losing the war by stalemate'.[7]

In Stephen Roskill's opinion, Wilson's 'superbly argued case' lent support to Churchill's view that 'in Sir Henry Wilson the War Cabinet found for the first time an expert adviser of superior intellect, who could explain lucidly and forcefully the whole situation and give reasons for the adoption or rejection of any course'.[8] As Hankey also appears to have come round to this view, it confirms the importance of the paper for both Wilson himself and the higher direction of the war. It was, moreover, a moment when Wilson could have dished himself by writing something more personally opinionated than he did. French's paper was explicitly critical of Haig and Robertson, and indeed, French bluntly told Hankey (with, as Hankey noted, 'envy, hatred and malice in the old boy's heart') that his aim was to 'break down the Haig–Robertson ring'.[9] By contrast, Wilson's paper was much less *ad hominem*, and while it criticised the fruitless slogging-match strategy which Haig appeared to have adopted, and argued the possibilities for so-called 'side-shows', it did not dispute the primacy of the western front as the single most important theatre of operations. Above all, it did not read, as French's did, like the work of an embittered and revengeful rival. If it had, Wilson might not have got any further up the military greasy pole, for it would have confirmed for potentially unsympathetic observers his reputation as a self-serving 'intriguer', and made it exceptionally difficult for Lloyd George to advance him.

[7] 'The present state of the War and the future prospects and future action to be taken', memo by Wilson, 20 Oct. 1917 (TNA, CAB 27/8 W.P.61; copy in Wilson papers, HHW 3/13/25). French's paper, with the same title, is in TNA, CAB 27/8 W.P.60.

[8] Roskill, *Man of Secrets*, i. 444; Churchill, *The Great War*, iii. 1105.

[9] Hankey diary, 24 Oct. 1917 (quoted in Roskill, *Man of Secrets*, i. 446); see also Holmes, *The Little Field-Marshal*, 331–2. French was 65 years old in Oct. 1917; Hankey was 40.

Wilson delivered copies of the two papers to Maurice Hankey on 20 October. Hankey was appalled by their contents. 'The Reports', he wrote, 'confirmed my worst anticipation.' The proposal to set up 'a central council, including a staff of generals in Paris, to be independent of the national General Staffs', was alone 'enough to drive Robertson into resignation'.[10] Four days later Wilson breakfasted with Lord Derby and learned that he had not yet summoned up the nerve to show the papers to Robertson or Haig. French's, he said, was 'too personal', and Wilson's 'too unanswerable'. If they were shown to the two generals, 'there would be a hell of a row which might mean resignation of Haig, R. & himself!' Lloyd George ordered French to tone down his comments about Robertson before the paper could be circulated, which, with Wilson and Hankey's help (and some ill grace), he did, and on 26 October both papers were finally sent to the CIGS.[11] By this stage, however, matters had been overtaken by disaster on the Italian front.

On 24 October a German–Austrian offensive began in what became known as the battle of Caporetto. In two weeks they drove the Italians up to 90 miles back, until the line stabilised along the line of the River Piave in mid-November. But for a while things looked very black indeed. On 28 October Wilson noted in his diary that 100,000 Italian troops had been taken prisoner, and they had lost 700 guns. 'This is the devil!', he wrote, 'Pigs of organ grinders. This will probably be followed by internal Revolution.'[12] Having got the War Cabinet to agree to the proposal for a 'Supreme War Council', Lloyd George sold the idea to the French (who saw it as a means to get the British to take over more of the front line in France), and on 2 November told Wilson 'that France & England had agreed to my proposed Superior Direction & the Cabinet had selected me as the Mil. Representative'. Knowing all too well how to flatter and manipulate people, the Prime Minister then told Wilson that 'the whole future of the war rests on your shoulders, you must get us out of the awful rut we are in; I don't like your politics but I do like & admire you as a man & a soldier'. The next day Wilson was on his way to Italy with Lloyd George, Smuts, and Hankey for a morale-boosting conference at Rapallo.[13]

Lloyd George, for all his seductive talk, was not the only politician displaying faith in Wilson. As he was leaving London, Milner wrote him a note: 'Good-bye and good luck. Our hopes are now centred on you—at this eleventh hour.'[14] The British party reached Rapallo on 5 November, where Robertson, who had gone out ahead to oversee the deployment of British reinforcements on the Italian front, told Wilson he was opposed to the council and did not see how it could work 'without responsibility'. Wilson asked him 'if, looking back over 2 years, he was satisfied with the conduct of the war & whether he would act in the same way again'. Robertson apparently 'replied in the affirmative. What a curious frame of

[10] Hankey diary, 20 Oct. 1917 (quoted in Hankey, *The Supreme Command*, ii. 715).
[11] Wilson diary, 20, 24, 26 Oct. 1917.   [12] Ibid., 28 Oct. 1917.
[13] Ibid., 2–3 Nov. 1917; see also Hankey's account in *The Supreme Command*, ii. 716–19.
[14] Milner to Wilson, 3 Nov. 1917 (Milner papers, dep. 354, fo. 234).

mind!' wrote Wilson. 'Since he has been C.I.G.S. we have lost Roumania, Russia & Italy & have gained Bullecourt, Messines & Paschendal!' The next day a Franco-Italian-British conference decided to proceed with the Supreme War Council (SWC), which was formally established on 7 November. It was originally constituted 'with a view to the better co-ordination of action on the Western Front' (meaning the battle theatre which ran from the English Channel to the Adriatic). The council was 'composed of the Prime Minister and a Member of the Government of each of the Great Powers whose armies are fighting on that front', a formulation which facilitated the practical exclusion of Russia. The council's function was 'to watch over the general conduct of the war', and meetings were to be held at least once a month. 'Permanent Military Representatives' were to be appointed by each power, who would act in an expert advisory capacity, and to whom the military authorities of each country would submit 'all the proposals, information and documents relating to the conduct of the war'. Wilson was appointed the British representative, Foch the French, and Cadorna the Italian.[15] Wishing Wilson and Foch success, Lloyd George told them that 'the fate of Europe depends upon what you are able to do now'.[16]

Reflecting on the appointment of Wilson, Maurice Hankey, the indispensable bureaucrat, now gave his whole-hearted support. Hankey's backing for Wilson confirms that his rise was not merely a function of Lloyd George's political machinations. Hankey's opinion, moreover, is significant, for he had not always been an admirer of Wilson, and had a more detached perspective than the Prime Minister, being less engaged in the effort to supersede Robertson and Haig. In a note for Lloyd George, Hankey asserted that it would 'be difficult to find any Officer in the British Army more peculiarly suited to the post for which he is designated than General Sir Henry Wilson'. The most telling recommendation was the role Wilson could play in inter-Allied relations. 'Very few British Officers of any rank have the same intimate knowledge of and sympathy with the French Army', he wrote, noting also Wilson's 'close personal friendship with General Foch'.[17]

Robertson was not pleased, and even contemplated resignation over the issue (as he also had done when French and Wilson were invited to write their 'state papers'). 'His general sulkiness was apparent to all', wrote Lloyd George in his memoirs, and his 'whole attitude' during the conference 'was sullen and unhelpful'.[18] 'Robertson's hostility increases', wrote Wilson in his diary, 'as he sees me getting more power.'[19]

[15] Wilson diary, 5–7 Nov. 1917; Hankey, *The Supreme Command*, ii. 719–23; French, *Strategy of the Lloyd George Coalition*, 164.

[16] Frances Stevenson diary, 9 Nov. 1917 (in Taylor, *Lloyd George: A Diary by Frances Stevenson*, 167).

[17] Note in regard to General Sir Henry Wilson, 16 Nov. 1917 (quoted in Roskill, *Hankey: Man of Secrets*, i. 459–60).

[18] Hankey, *The Supreme Command*, ii. 720–1; Woodward, *Lloyd George and the Generals*, 209; Lloyd George, *War Memoirs*, ii. 1440–1.   [19] Wilson diary, 6 Nov. 1917.

But Robertson was right to be angry. Although he claimed afterwards that at a political level the SWC 'filled a much-felt want', and enabled the proper co-ordination of Allied policies, he argued that the military arrangements 'did nothing to improve the system of *military* command', as the appointment of independent advisers could only 'produce divided responsibility, delay, friction, and confusion'.[20] He was also quite right to assume that Lloyd George saw the SWC as (among other things) a device to get rid of him. Each ally, indeed, while paying lip-service to the fine aim of improved co-operation, wanted and expected rather different things from the council. The French saw it as a mechanism for securing overall control of the Allied armies in the west, and Painlevé (who had become French Premier in September) had originally proposed that Foch should be *both* chief of the French staff *and* permanent military representative, which would have completely obviated Lloyd George's plan for the SWC to provide independent military advice. Italian support for the new body was much more straightforward. In the aftermath of Caporetto, they were happy to agree to the council simply in order to copper-fasten Franco-British support on their front.

In the short term only the Italians got what they wanted. Wilson and Foch's first instructions as military representatives were to inspect the Italian front and assess what assistance was required. Although things still looked bad (at one point Wilson, having interviewed a number of pessimistic Italian commanders, feared that Venice would fall, which would mean 'the loss of the Adriatic & a serious threat therefore to Salonica & Egypt'[21]), the Italians held the line of the River Piave and Venice was saved. The younger and more dynamic Armando Diaz replaced Cadorna as the Italian Commander, and Allied reinforcements—six French and five British divisions, the latter commanded by Herbert Plumer—were in place by early December. Reflecting the reality that the Italians were very much junior partners in the alliance, Wilson at times operated as if he had executive command of Italian forces. For example, he instructed Diaz to prepare defensive positions along the River Brenta, 20 miles beyond the Piave. Diaz said he would see to them 'at once'.[22]

Lloyd George's promotion of the SWC carried with it some risks. In the late autumn of 1917 he could not be absolutely sure of winning an open contest against Robertson and Haig, for both men had considerable political and popular support, especially among right-wing conservatives, whose 'house journal', the *Morning Post* (briefed, among others, by Robertson), consistently took the line that military decisions ought to remain in the hands of soldiers rather than politicians.[23] There was also the risk of Asquith and his Liberal friends exploiting any perceived chink in Lloyd George's armour. For his part, the Prime Minister mobilised his own press campaign, and aimed to see off his critics with a hard-hitting speech

[20] Robertson, *From Private to Field-Marshal*, 328.   [21] Wilson diary, 9 Nov. 1917.

[22] Ibid., 10 Nov. 1917.

[23] See, e.g. Robertson to H. A. Gwynne, 1 Sept. 1917 (in Wilson, *The Rasp of War*, 232).

on 12 November, at a lunch in Paris at which Painlevé publicly announced the establishment of the SWC. Lloyd George emphasised the continued incoherence of Allied policy-making, and pointedly reflected on the human costs of the alleged victories which had been won in France and Flanders. 'When I look at the appalling casualty lists,' he said, 'I sometimes wish it had not been necessary to win so many', and he unfavourably compared the small advances achieved on the western front with the Austro-German advance at Caporetto.[24] There was a stormy reaction to this at home, and Robertson went so far as to brief Asquith about the government's proposals. Lloyd George, however, who always thrived in the parliamentary arena, carried the Commons in a full-dress debate on 19 November, disingenuously telling MPs that the primary aim of the SWC was the 'co-ordination' of Allied policy-making.[25]

On the same day as the Commons debate, Wilson returned to Paris to begin sorting out arrangements for the SWC, assisted by his old friends Charles Sackville-West ('Tit Willow') and Leo Amery. Tit Willow, 'an accomplished staff officer, a good linguist and a diplomat by nature',[26] had been a favourite since he had been teaching at the Staff College during Wilson's time as Commandant. Wilson had tried (and failed) to get Haig to give him a division, and he had been languishing at home running an officers' school at Aldershot.[27] Amery, still a Conservative MP, had been on Hankey's staff since March 1917, serving in a quasi-bureaucratic, quasi-political role, which was helpful to Hankey (as he later affirmed), while giving Amery considerable licence to reflect broadly on Allied and imperial strategy.[28] Amery's job was to liase between the War Cabinet secretariat and the SWC, and he was certainly alert to the politics of the new arrangements. After attending a Cabinet meeting on 12 November, he recorded 'the general feeling a good deal that L.G. had carried them farther than they were quite willing to go. Derby and the CIGS both in rather a touchy and contentious state of mind.'[29]

Derby, an amiable man who owed his position in the Cabinet mainly to his Lancashire power-base and high Tory connexions, tended to side with Robertson rather than Lloyd George, though not in any decisive fashion.[30] As the trial of strength between Lloyd George and Robertson intensified, Derby (with whom Henry Wilson remained on friendly terms throughout) constantly agonised about whether he should resign, but invariably found himself unable to do so. Reflecting

[24] Woodward, *Lloyd George and the Generals*, 224–5.
[25] *Hansard*, 19 Nov. 1917, H. C. deb 5s, vol. 99, col. 893–906.
[26] Macready, *In the Wake of the Great*, 28. Gordon Macready served under Sackville-West at Versailles in 1918.
[27] Wilson diary, 15 May, 17, 19, Sept. 26 Oct. 1917. On 15 Oct., moreover, Wilson had gone over his draft paper on future military policy with Sackville-West.
[28] Hankey, *The Supreme Command*, ii. 658; Amery, *The Leo Amery Diaries*, 144–79.
[29] Amery diary, 12 Nov. 1917 (in Amery, *The Leo Amery Diaries*, 179).
[30] See C. P. Scott diary, 12–13 Nov. 1917 (in Wilson, *The Political Diaries of C. P. Scott*, 312); and Riddell, *Lord Riddell's War Diary*, 293–4.

longstanding Tory suspicions of Lloyd George, and representing a significant strand of opinion in the Conservative party, Derby's position nevertheless demonstrated how delicately the Prime Minister had to tread in the quest for clear civilian control of the military, while not jeopardising parliamentary support for his coalition government.

When Henry Wilson reached Paris on 19 November, Tit Willow told him 'of the way the W.O. is blocking things, Edie [*sic*] Derby terrified, Wully sulky, Maurice [the DMO] hostile. All this', wrote Wilson with considerable understatement, 'will have to be straightened out.' In the meantime he went to see Georges Clemenceau, 'the Tiger', who had succeeded Painlevé as French Premier the previous week. With his radical and populist sympathies, and his unwavering determination to secure final victory, he had much in common with Lloyd George. Wilson, however, found Clemenceau 'not much interested in the Supreme Council', though the following evening when Wilson called at nine o'clock (the Frenchman was going to bed, but stayed up to see him) he appeared more enthusiastic and told Wilson he wanted the council 'to have much more power than it now has'.[31] Wilson's ready access to the most senior French politicians—President Poincaré also saw him—not only reflected the regard with which he was held in France, but also his perceived closeness to Lloyd George. Clemenceau, who was 'charming' to Wilson, certainly seems to have assumed that Wilson would convey his views directly to the British Prime Minister (which he did over lunch at 10 Downing Street on 22 November).[32]

Although Lloyd George had established Wilson as the British military representative on the new SWC, Wilson's precise status was far from clear. Lloyd George persuaded the Cabinet to agree that while Wilson was 'subject to the authority of the Army Council', it was 'understood' that he would 'have unfettered discretion' as to the advice he gave. Robertson (and Derby) were unhappy with this and Derby got the Prime Minister to agree that Robertson should accompany Wilson to all SWC meetings, thus neutralising Wilson's opportunities to act independently. At the same time, Lloyd George arranged with Wilson that 'I should send my reports to him & not to anyone else'.[33] This was typical Lloyd George sleight of hand. A few days later, on the way to Paris for the first formal meeting of the SWC, Wilson had 'long talks in the train with Milner & L.G.', mostly about Derby's obstructive attitude. 'It is quite clear to me that Robertson & his gang mean to obstruct all they can', wrote Wilson. 'Well we shall have a fight.'[34] In Paris there was a panic when the British party heard that Clemenceau,

---

[31] Wilson diary, 19, 20 Nov. 1917. Sir Frederick Maurice was DMO Dec. 1915–Apr. 1918. Describing William Robertson as a 'soldier shipwrecked on the desert island of politics', Sir Edward Spears said that Maurice was 'his Man Friday' (Maurice, *The Maurice Case*, 3).

[32] Wilson diary, 22 Nov. 1917. Later that month Clemenceau told Wilson 'to come to him whenever I wanted without appointment & without ceremony' (ibid., 30 Nov. 1917).

[33] War Cabinet meeting, 16 Nov. 1917 (TNA, CAB 23/4 W.C. 276); Woodward, *Lloyd George and the Generals*, 226–8; Wilson diary, 22 Nov. 1917.   [34] Wilson diary, 27 Nov. 1917.

too, wanted to make Foch both Chief of Staff and permanent military representative. In the end Maxime Weygand was appointed, though, as Foch's man, there was still a question-mark over how independent his advice might be. But the matter of French representation demonstrated that discussion of the crucial issue of SWC membership and its relationship with the existing military command structure was not confined to the United Kingdom. Wilson thought that Clemenceau's legerdemain in getting Weygand was 'just the sort of little trick that would appeal to a Frenchman', and he correctly assumed that the French Premier's underlying aim was to install Foch as an Allied generalissimo, at least on the western front.[35]

The first official meeting of the Supreme War Council was held in the Hotel Trianon at Versailles on 1 December 1917. Clemenceau took the chair. Along with Lloyd George, Vittorio Orlando (the Italian Premier) attended, and Colonel Edward M. House represented President Wilson of the United States. Milner was there, and the full complement of military representatives: Wilson, Weygand, Cadorna, and Tasker H. Bliss, who had just retired as the American Chief of Staff. Robertson had come over from London, and Foch was present too. The formalities went very well. Clemenceau's opening speech had been drafted by Maurice Hankey, as had the resolutions, and, bearing in mind 'the need for framing our policy for 1918', the military advisers were charged with exploring 'the nature of the campaigns to be undertaken in 1918, and to prepare recommendations'. They were also specifically asked 'to weigh carefully' whether 'the final objective' (which was 'the overthrow of Prussian militarism') might not 'be brought nearer final achievement by the overthrow, first of all, of Germany's allies'.[36]

Lloyd George had good cause to be pleased. Although Henry Wilson was, in fact, the only really independent military representative, that was good enough for the British Prime Minister, who could reasonably hope that through Wilson he could curb, if not neutralise, Robertson and Haig. Developments in both Palestine and on the western front also strengthened his hand. At the end of October the Egyptian Expeditionary Force under Allenby began the 'third battle of Gaza', pushing back the Turks, capturing Gaza on 7 November, Jaffa on the 17th, and Jerusalem on 9 December, an achievement, as Lloyd George wrote afterwards, 'of immense importance, alike on military and sentimental grounds'.[37] Not only did it demonstrate the possibilities of a 'side-show', but it provided a much-needed boost to British morale, at a time when the news from France was as gloomy as ever. Haig had launched an attack at Cambrai on 20 November, which at first went extremely well, but by the end of the month had achieved nothing. The final collapse of Russia also threatened to release German troops from the east. On 16 December the new Bolshevik government signed an armistice at Brest-Litovsk. Against this, there were high hopes that American

[35] Ibid., 3 Dec, 1917.
[36] Hankey, *The Supreme Command*, ii. 729–33; Lloyd George, *War Memoirs*, ii. 1650–2.
[37] Lloyd George, *War Memoirs*, ii. 1091.

troops would (at the very least) cancel out any enemy advantage from an eastern peace. Yet the build-up of American forces was frustratingly slow. By the end of 1917, nine months after entering the war, there were only four divisions ready to fight in France.[38]

For the Allies the questions remained open as to how long a defensive stance might be held, and, while it was maintained, what operations might be sanctioned on other fronts. These were precisely the sort of issues the SWC was supposed to address. And so it did. Egged on by Wilson, the military representatives began with a general review of the situation, and by 13 December had completed their first joint note. It recommended that 'a co-ordinated system of defence from the North Sea to the Adriatic must be adopted by the Allies', and that behind the front line (as Wilson put it in his diary) there should be 'utmost development of defence, of Reserves & of mobility', so that when the time came for an offensive the troops would be sufficiently rested and prepared, and communications along the whole front improved and integrated.[39]

Wilson meanwhile found himself in the perhaps unexpected position of defending Haig. Arthur Capel, a well-connected wealthy English businessman long resident in Paris, who spent the war in a number of more-or-less formal liaison jobs,[40] told Wilson that Clemenceau was 'furious' with Haig and wanted to replace him with Allenby. Wilson thought there was 'no cry for this', and told Capel 'that in my opinion Haig would be the best man when bad times came & they were assuredly coming'. Wilson and Capel went to see Clemenceau, who gave them a lecture on the deficiencies of 'the English' and demanded that they take over some of the French line. Wilson persuaded him to submit his case to the SWC. Later, at dinner with Foch, there was more criticism of the British high command. Foch, who favoured Plumer as the British Commander-in-Chief, thought Haig would 'have to go owing to colossal losses & no gains'. Wilson told him he blamed Robertson 'much the most'.[41] Wilson, with his star clearly in the ascendant, could now afford to be dismissive of Robertson. On 23 December Milner told him that 'he thought L.G. was going to kick out Robertson & put me in his place', as 'he had great confidence in me & none in Robertson'. Evidently enjoying his new role, however, Wilson thought he 'would rather stay here provided always that I am given more & more power'. A week later, when Milner repeated his opinion, Wilson was more explicit. While opposed to taking Robertson's place, he was 'all in favour of L.G. giving me more power at Versailles & reducing R. from the position of a Master to that of a servant'.[42]

Between 8 December and Christmas the military representatives signed six joint notes on a variety of topics, including the reorganisation of the Belgian army,

[38] Smythe, *Pershing*, 61, 69.

[39] Joint Note no. 1, 13 Dec. 1917 (TNA, CAB 27/8 W.P. 69); Wilson diary, 13 Dec. 1917.

[40] On the subject of liaison, Capel was also for a time the lover of Coco Chanel (see Madsen, *Coco Chanel*, 49–55).   [41] Wilson diary, 13 Dec. 1917.

[42] Ibid., 23, 30 Dec. 1917.

reinforcements for Italy, and the situation in Salonika. There was scarcely a break, even on Christmas Day when Wilson 'worked all afternoon at the problem of taking over line from French'.[43] Wilson had gathered round him some familiar faces, congratulating himself on having created a 'very good' staff, 'all of whom have been for years in the line & all of whom know their business'.[44]

Under Sackville-West, the Chief of Staff, Wilson formed three main sections: 'Allied', under Herbert Studd; 'Enemy', under Hereward Wake; and 'Material and Manpower', under Frederick Sykes. Studd and Sykes had both served in the Directorate of Military Operations before the war, while Wake had been Lord Roberts's ADC in South Africa and a student at the Staff College when Wilson was Commandant. There was also a 'Political' branch under Leo Amery, which shared their premises, but formally reported to Hankey in London. Studd and Wake respectively had to keep up the Allied and enemy situation 'from the Operations and Intelligence point of view', while Sykes 'dealt with Allied and enemy man-power problems, aircraft, munitions and transport'. Sykes recalled it as being a cheerful place, with Wilson 'always original, versatile, and resourceful, and never despondent'.[45] Another member of the Versailles staff told Charles Callwell that Wilson 'did love talking and having others round him to talk to and to argue with—especially the latter', and he remembered Wilson 'saying once, "Oh, we can't have So and So living in our mess—he never talks, and if people don't talk and argue there is no means of sharpening one's wits." '[46]

At the end of December Wilson was summoned to London to give Lloyd George his opinion as to the prospects for the coming year. It was, too, an opportunity to spend New Year's Eve at home with Cecil.[47] The 'campaign of 1918' paper eventually emerged as the famous 'Note 12', which Lloyd George described as a 'remarkable' memorandum, embodying 'a comprehensive but compendious review of the whole position'.[48] Wilson based his conclusions on a 'war game'—a favourite device of his since Staff College days—which he began just after Christmas between the 'Allied' and 'Enemy' branches of his staff. The exercise became a bit of a party-piece for visitors to Versailles. He showed it to Robertson on 10 January, Pershing on the 12th, and Smuts on the 15th, and was especially pleased when Herbert Lawrence, who had replaced Kiggell as Haig's Chief of Staff, asked to come to see it. 'Just imagine!', wrote Wilson. 'And G.H.Q. has never played one!'[49] 'War games' were not to Haig's taste (especially when they

[43] Ibid., 24–5 Dec. 1917.

[44] Ibid., 10 Jan. 1918. Rawly, however, thought Wilson's staff were 'not of the calibre to carry much weight with the Army either in France or at home' (Rawlinson to Clive Wigram, 9 Feb. 1918 (Royal Archives, RA GV Q2522/2/116)).

[45] Sykes, *From Many Angles*, 207. By contrast, Archie Wavell, who served at Versailles for a few weeks in early 1918, said the SWC was 'the only place I was at during the whole war which had a pessimistic attitude towards winning it' (Connell, *Wavell*, 135).　　　　[46] Callwell, *Wilson*, ii. 43.

[47] Wilson diary, 28, 31 Dec. 1917.　　　　[48] Lloyd George, *War Memoirs*, ii. 1631.

[49] Wilson diary, 10, 12, 15 Jan. 1918. According to 'Boney' Fuller, GHQ nicknamed Versailles the 'Supreme "W.C." ' (Fuller, *Memoirs*, 233).

supported unpalatable policy advice). In mid-January he learned that Wilson and the military members of the SWC were recommending that he take over some line from the French. Haig (with reason) was also concerned about the status of the Versailles advice. 'The Government now have two advisers!', he wrote. 'Will they accept the advice of the Versailles gentlemen (who have no responsibility) or will they take my advice?' Wilson, he added, had 'arrived at his conclusion (so he writes) as "the result of a War Game" and on "mathematical calculations". The whole position', thought Haig, 'would be laughable but for the seriousness of it.'[50]

Beyond the separate issue of multiple sources of government advice, Wilson's efforts (derided by Haig) to put policy analysis on a more systematic and scientific basis than hitherto seem wholly admirable.[51] Haig, certainly, had been ill-served by his own staff, especially his Intelligence chief from December 1915 to December 1917, John Charteris, whose briefings, according to one colleague, 'seemed intended to bolster up our own morale rather than to paint a true picture of the enemy's strength and fighting qualities'.[52] Desmond Morton, one of Haig's ADCs from September 1917 to April 1919, told Liddell Hart that Haig 'hated being told any new information, however irrefutable, which militated against his preconceived ideas or beliefs', a consequence of which was 'his support for the desperate John Charteris', who was 'incredibly bad' as head of GHQ Intelligence, and 'always concealed bad news, or put it in an agreeable light'.[53]

Joint Note 12 contained 'advice on the military action to be undertaken during 1918'. Among the assumptions made by the 'Versailles gentlemen' was that 'the safety of France' could be 'assured', even in view of an anticipated enemy attack, given that the French and British forces were 'maintained at their present total aggregate strength', and that they would continue to be reinforced by at least two American divisions per month. They also recommended substantial increases in guns, machine guns, planes, and tanks, as well as improvements in defences and rail transportation. Very significantly (as it would turn out) they argued that 'the whole Allied front in France be treated as a single strategic field of action, and that the disposition of the reserves . . . and all other arrangements should be dominated by this consideration'. Allowing that Italy was also safe, the soldiers maintained that the enemy could not in 1918 'gain a definite military decision in the main

---

[50] Haig TS diary, 14 January 1918. On 30 January Haig dismissed another Versailles war game as 'rather a waste of time' (TNA, WO 256/27), and Wilson noted that while the exercise was being demonstrated, Haig 'was frankly bored & read some memorandum he had in his hand' (Wilson diary, 30 Jan. 1918).

[51] The 'war game' technique is well proven, and accords neatly with Thomas Schelling's definition of strategic analysis: 'the art of looking at the problem from the other person's point of view, identifying his opportunities and his interests' (Schelling, *Choice and Consequence*, 200).

[52] James Marshall-Cornwall, unpublished memoirs (quoted in Andrew, *Secret Service*, 166).

[53] Morton to Liddell Hart, 17 July 1961 (ibid. 168). Wilson himself was not always completely open to negative intelligence reports, as it appears had been the case in October 1914, when he and Sir John French's Operations branch had been inclined to dismiss pessimistic intelligence reports from George Macdonogh (Gardner, *Trial by Fire*, 153–7).

theatres'. The situation was effectively the same for the Allies. 'Apart from such measure of success as is implied in the failure of the enemy's [anticipated] offensive', and 'leaving out of account such improbable and unforeseen contingencies as the internal collapse of the Enemy Powers, or the revival of Russia as a serious military factor', no Allied victory in the west could be predicted for 1918. This left the Turkish theatre. Here the soldiers believed a 'decisive result' might be possible, bearing in mind that 'the present condition of Turkey is one of almost complete material and moral exhaustion'. At French insistence, the paper categorically ruled out moving any troops from the west, asserting that the existing forces in the Middle East, with enhanced mobility and technical support, and extra air power, should be sufficient to bring about 'the final collapse of Turkey'. If the Allies acted quickly, moreover, they might be able to help 'such elements of resistance to German domination as may still exist in Roumania and Southern Russia'. And even if Turkey were not overwhelmed, 'a lesser measure of success', such as liberating the Arab regions of the Ottoman empire, would 'compel the Germans to divert considerable forces to the East in order to save Turkey from destruction'.[54] Either way, it appeared to be a good bet.

Clearly recognising the primary importance of the western front, this note was no simple 'Eastern' manifesto. Yet it certainly embodied Lloyd George's policy preferences, and, presumably, vindicated his support for Wilson and the SWC. 'Wilson is playing the tune called by Lloyd George', wrote Haig in his diary. Robertson thought the paper was 'd——d rot in general. It simply advocates doing all sorts of wonderful things in Palestine, and a great offensive in the west, regardless of means' (which it did not). He assured Haig he had 'told the war Cabinet they cannot take on Palestine & I shall stick to my guns and clear out if I am overruled'.[55]

Joint Note 12, along with Note 14, proposing the creation of a 'General Reserve', was considered at the second formal session of the full SWC, from 30 January to 2 February. Lloyd George, Milner, and Hankey came over to Versailles and stayed with Wilson. 'The great fight', wrote Wilson in his diary, 'was about our 1918 Note & the Reserve note. Robertson fought both but was over-ruled on the 1918 Note & L.G. was angry with him & said afterwards to me that he would have to get rid of him.' There was a further argument about the command of the proposed central reserve which was again decided in line with Lloyd George's wishes. An 'executive board' was created for this, comprising all the military representatives except Weygand, who was replaced by Foch for this purpose, a decision which ensured Clemenceau's agreement. Robertson pressed to be on the board, but in vain; '& so', recorded Wilson, 'the long duel between me and Robertson has ended in his complete defeat. . . . I wonder will he resign.'[56]

[54] '1918 campaign', 19 Jan. 1918 (Wilson papers, HHW 3/14/1).
[55] Haig TS diary, 26 Jan. 1918 (TNA, WO 256/27); Robertson to Haig, 24 Jan. 1918 (in Woodward, *Military Correspondence of Sir William Robertson*, 274).
[56] Wilson diary, 1–2 Feb. 1918.

This diary entry (for 2 February) is noteworthy for the fact that Wilson for the first time explicitly characterised the military policy debates as a personal contest between himself and Robertson. Up to this point, while recognising Lloyd George's increasing desire to be rid of Robertson (if not also Haig), Wilson had tended to write about the discussions as if they were merely abstract policy issues. In this there may have been an element of self-deception, for in Versailles, Paris, and London the debate was widely regarded (and has been described since by historians) as a highly personal contest between able and powerful men—'Lloyd George and the generals', 'Easterners versus Westerners', 'Robertson versus Wilson', and so on. But this 'personalisation' of the debate, which coloured (and colours) attitudes and responses to it, also tended to impede any dispassionate evaluation of the SWC machinery in general, and the proposals of the military representatives, as contained in the '1918 campaign' paper or concerning the general reserve.

The creation of the SWC was an extremely important advance in the co-ordination of Allied policy- and decision-making. The permanent military representatives comprised an embryonic inter-Allied staff, for the first time regularly and systematically working together with the aim of harmonising coalition arrangements on all sorts of subjects, including prosaic but important topics such as railways or tank production, as well as high-level policy formulation. The new machinery offered, for the first time, the possibility of 'joined-up' coalition staff work. The council itself, with provision for regular meetings and a proper secretariat, was an extraordinary advance on the haphazard, hand-to-mouth arrangements which had hitherto existed. For the British government (at least) the creation of an independent 'think-tank' staffed by experts, with a wide-ranging brief to explore military policy issues, raised the possibility that decision-making might be improved by being better informed.

As for specific policy advice, the '1918' proposals, if taken at face value, did offer a reasonable case for both the British and French to take the opportunity of a defensive 'breathing space' through 1918, when they could gather strength until, with powerful American support, they could deliver a 'knock-out blow' to the enemy in the west. In the meantime comparatively cheap victories in the Middle East (along the lines of Allenby's successes in late 1917) had the potential to deliver considerable collateral benefits. And the general reserve idea was sound, embodying as it did a conception of the zone from the Channel to the Adriatic as one front, behind which would be organised a coalition central reserve held ready to be moved wherever it was needed, in sharp contrast, for example, to the higgledy-piggledy despatch of French and British divisions to Italy after Caporetto. Sidney Clive thought that if the 'Versailles committee' had existed 'two to three years ago' when divisions were being sent to Salonika and the Middle East, 'when we might have sent Divns to Italy, they would have been of the utmost value'.[57]

---

[57] Clive diary, 24 Feb. 1918 (Clive papers II/4).

But these issues also inevitably involved personal ambitions and animosities, entrenched institutional positions, and professional *amour propre*. In the end it was the 'executive war board', established to take control of the general reserve, which proved the breaking-point for Robertson. He regarded Foch's appointment as chairman of what he called 'the Versailles Soviet' as effectively creating an Allied 'generalissimo'. The granting of executive control over the reserves, moreover, meant that Haig would be subject to two authorities. The 'ridiculous system of setting up, practically, two CIGSs', he wrote to Lord Stamfordham, 'must result in failure and destruction of confidence amongst the troops as to who really is their Commander'. At the same time, aiming to see that his case was defended in the press, Robertson wrote to H. A. Gwynne, acknowledging that 'the little man' (Lloyd George) was 'all out for my blood'. In writing to Gwynne, all Robertson was trying to do, he claimed, was 'to see that the fine British Army is not placed at the mercy of irresponsible people—& some of them foreigners at that'.[58]

On 10 February Milner (who was being spoken of as Secretary for War in place of Derby) told Wilson that Lloyd George had decided to send Robertson to Versailles and install Wilson as CIGS. Judging by his diary, Wilson did not particularly welcome the news. Having, with congenial colleagues, successfully set up the new organisation in France, where he had high status and, apparently, real influence, the idea of moving to London did not seem so attractive. Talking to Milner, indeed, Wilson was evidently anxious to keep control of the SWC. If Robertson refused the job, they 'agreed that we would put in someone junior to me & let me have a directing voice in Versailles if I was C.I.G.S.'. When he saw Derby the next day, Wilson learned that, under Lloyd George's proposal for Wilson to be CIGS, 'Robertson at Versailles is distinctly put under me'. Wilson thought Robertson would refuse. In that case, said Derby, 'Robertson was OUT'.[59]

So it was to be, but not before another week's excitement and political uncertainty. Derby inevitably vacillated, Asquith in parliament scented political advantage, and there was even talk of the government falling.[60] Rawlinson thought the 'solution' was 'to put Wullie at Versailles with creative authority and move H.W. to London where he will not be able to do so much mischief— especially if Squiff replaced L.G. as P.M.'.[61] Spotting what seemed to be a neat way of getting rid of Robertson, Lloyd George raised the possibility of him and Plumer (then commanding the British forces in Italy) changing places, but Plumer refused point blank.[62]

Robertson did not go without a struggle. He was in a terribly difficult position, and it is hard not to have sympathy for his predicament. He had done nothing *wrong*, and yet was possibly faced with the premature end of his professional

---

[58] Robertson to Lord Stamfordham, 4, 11 Feb.; to Gwynne, 7 Feb. 1918 (in Woodward, *Military Correspondence of Sir William Robertson*, 284–9).   [59] Wilson diary, 10–11 Feb. 1918.
[60] There is a good, detailed account of the crisis in Woodward, *Lloyd George and the Generals*, 262–78.   [61] Rawlinson to H. A. Gwynne, 14 Feb. 1918 (Gwynne papers).
[62] Powell, *Plumer*, 249–52.

career at a moment when the war was far from won. He had, too, friends in high places, including the King himself, who thought it would be 'a national calamity' if Robertson were dismissed.[63] The King had Stamfordham tell Lloyd George that he 'strongly deprecated the idea of Robertson being removed', to which the Prime Minister responded that 'he did not share the King's extremely favourable opinion' of Robertson, 'who had never fought at the Front, had hardly ever visited the trenches, and was not known by the rank and file'. Robertson stood firm on the constitutional issue, that 'one man only could give orders to the Army, and that was the C.I.G.S.', with which some ministers (including Curzon and Balfour) sympathised. But he lost their support by showing his personal feelings at a Cabinet meeting on 14 February when, as Balfour told Stamfordham, 'he revealed an evident personal dislike of Sir H. Wilson'. Robertson himself told Stamfordham that he would serve at Versailles under Plumer, 'but certainly not if Sir H. Wilson his Junior was to become C.I.G.S.'. Lloyd George, for his part, dismissed the royal intervention, asserting that the government would resign if the King insisted on Robertson remaining in office 'on the terms [Robertson] laid down'.[64]

On 18 February 1918 Derby appointed Wilson Chief of the Imperial General Staff (he was formally gazetted to the post the following day), and Robertson, who refused to 'resign', was transferred to the Eastern Command. Perhaps aware that Robertson was utterly dependent on his army pay, Lloyd George had asked Haig if he might be put in to command Rawlinson's army, Rawly being earmarked to succeed Wilson at Versailles, but Haig (as Lloyd George told Wilson) said Robertson 'was quite unfitted to command troops'. Haig, in fact, though frequently bracketed with Robertson by Lloyd George, rather distanced himself from his military colleague during the February 1918 crisis, and told Lloyd George that while 'he did not quite like H.W. coming here [London], and thought the Army might be very shocked', conceded 'that it was a matter for the Government' and that 'he was prepared to accept whatever was decided by the War Cabinet'. In the end Robertson had to accept the government's decision as well, though he did so with understandable ill-grace. The day he took over from him, Wilson ran into Robertson at the War Office. 'He was both grumpy and ungracious & said he had nothing to say—and indeed said nothing', noted Wilson. 'And this', he added gratuitously (demonstrating, moreover, that he could be grumpy too), 'was how the great C.I.G.S. helped his successor in handing over at a critical period in the greatest war of the world.'[65]

[63] RA GV/King George V's diary/1918: 12 Feb.

[64] Memo by Stamfordham, *c.*18 Feb. 1918 (Royal Archives, RA PS/GV/F 1259/32). Two months later, when Stamfordham, on the King's behalf, complained about the removal of Trenchard as Chief of the Air Staff, Lloyd George sharply told him that 'we owed our present disaster' to soldiers like Haig and Robertson who 'were backed by the Court & that this sort of thing was intolerable' (Wilson diary, 13 Apr. 1918).

[65] Wilson diary, 17–18 Feb. 1918; Lloyd George to Milner, 9 Feb. 1918 (Milner papers, MS Milner dep. 355 fo. 23).

A letter from Ferdinand Foch clearly illustrates the welcome with which many French leaders greeted the appointment. Foch wrote of his 'great satisfaction', and referred to their own mutual understanding ('notre entente'), particularly in difficult times, hoping this would continue in the future.[66] One of the matters which Foch appears to have had in mind was that of the general reserve, which Wilson still saw as essential. As CIGS, however, he took a slightly different view of the London–Versailles relationship than before. Now that Wilson 'has become C.I.G.S. in London,' Haig noted mordantly in his diary, 'he did not appear so anxious to make the Versailles Staff under Rawlinson very strong'.[67] Rawlinson, in any case, had his own ideas about the reserve, which were closer to Haig's than Wilson's, as became apparent when Wilson and Rawlinson visited Haig's headquarters during the last week of February. Haig, wrote Wilson, 'flatly refuses' to release any of his divisions in France to the reserve. Rawly thought Haig's arguments were 'unanswerable', as only he could judge 'how many divisions he needs to hold his front and he naturally does not place any reliance on a committee acting promptly'.[68] Sackville-West wrote privately to Wilson that as Rawlinson 'backs D.H. the situation is getting just the same as when Wully always said yes to D.H. Versailles is to become an appanage or buffer between L.G. & D.H. & you are left out.' Rawly, indeed, was 'so lié with D.H.' that he was in no position 'to give any independent advice'.[69]

Despite Wilson (and Foch) urging Rawlinson to press ahead with the general reserve and executive board, nothing was possible without Haig's agreement, and although the French had initially committed eight divisions, Pétain (as suspicious of Foch as Haig was of Wilson) was none too keen to co-operate either. He and Haig countered the general reserve scheme with a mutual understanding to assist each other with reinforcements as necessary. Wilson raised Haig's intransigence with Lloyd George, but the Prime Minister, presumably not wanting to risk another political storm, refused to act. Haig's attitude, he said, 'was very stupid & short sighted but agreed we could not force Haig at this moment'.[70] Wilson, in fact, defended Haig's position to the Cabinet. He 'was faced with a possibility of an immediate attack; and he did not like to risk the dislocation of his arrangements [with Pétain] at this particular juncture by allocating a portion of his Reserves to the Inter-Allied General Reserve'.[71] Wilson was inclined to blame the French for the failure of his scheme. 'D.H., Petain, Clemenceau & Rawly make a "combine",' he told Tit Willow, 'the principals being Clemenceau & Petain & the tools being D.H. & Rawly.' But in any case (he wrote in his diary), 'it is clear if we have to choose between a Gen. Res. & Haig we must choose Haig wrong as I

[66] Foch to Wilson, 20 Feb. 1918 (Wilson papers, HHW 2/24A/1).
[67] Haig TS diary, 25 Feb. 1918 (TNA, WO 256/27).
[68] Wilson diary, 25 Feb. 1918; Rawlinson journal, 25 Feb. 1918 (quoted in Maurice, *Rawlinson of Trent*, 210).
[69] Sackville-West to Wilson, 5 Mar. 1918 (2 letters) (Wilson papers, HHW 2/12B/4, 5).
[70] Wilson diary, 27 Feb., 4 Mar. 1918.
[71] War Cabinet meeting, 6 Mar. 1918 (TNA, CAB 23/13/360A).

believe him to be'. At a meeting of the SWC held in London on 14–15 March, Foch, under protest, acquiesced in the abandonment of the reserve.[72] 'The Executive war board is dead, dead as a doornail,' lamented Tit Willow on 21 March, '& as you are not here—a jolly good job too.'[73]

The very same day the storm broke on the western front, when the Germans launched their great spring offensive. Although some sort of enemy push had been anticipated, the sheer strength and size, and the precise location, of the attack caught the Allies by surprise. In the British sector along the Somme the Fifth Army under Hubert Gough took the main weight of the German advance, and were driven back towards the vital railway junction of Amiens. In his diary Wilson recorded 23 March as 'an anxious day'. Walter Kirke, the deputy DMO, flew over to GHQ and back again, and reported his impression 'that the 5th Army is pretty broken'. The Cabinet sought to obtain reinforcements wherever they could be found, and 'decided to send out the 50,000 boys (trained) of 18½ years & up to 19, and some other lots which will make 82,000 which with the 88,000 returning from leave will mean 170,000 in the next 17 days'. A division was summoned from Italy, and Allenby was instructed to hold one ready. Wilson even cabled Lord Reading (British ambassador in Washington) 'asking him to press on Pres. Wilson the vital importance of sending over Inf[antry]'. It was, wrote Wilson, 'a marvellous fine day but with fog in Channel & haze in France but not an inch of mud. "Le bon Dieu est Boch".'[74]

On 24 March the apparently relentless German advance continued. Foch telephoned Wilson 'asking what I thought of situation & we are of one mind that someone must catch a hold or we shall be beaten'. Wilson, who told Foch he would come over to see him, thought the perilous situation exposed 'the entirely inadequate measures taken by Haig & Petain in their mutual plans for assistance'. Haig himself was extremely concerned that Pétain, aiming to 'cover Paris at all costs', would not stick by the British right flank. This would lead to disaster. 'Our army's existence in France', wrote Haig, 'depends on keeping the British and French armies united.' With Pétain beginning to appear defeatist, Haig called for Wilson and Milner 'to come to France at once in order to arrange that General Foch or some other determined general, who would fight, should be given supreme control of the operations in France'. Wilson got to Haig's headquarters at Montreuil at 11.30 a.m. on Monday 25 March (having left London at 6.50 a.m.). There he indulged in a bit of 'I told you so': 'I could not help reminding him that it was he (D.H.) who with Clemenceau's assistance killed my plan of the Gen. Res.'[75] Wilson's unattractive (and unnecessary) sneer perhaps reflected the tension and anxiety of the moment as much as anything else. But it also has to be said that

---

[72] Wilson to Sackville-West, 9 Mar. 1918 (Wilson papers, HHW 2/12B/7); Wilson diary, 13–15 Mar. 1918.`   [73] Sackville-West to Wilson, 21 Mar. 1918 (Wilson papers, HHW 2/12B/11).
[74] 23 Mar. 1918, Wilson diary, and War Cabinet meeting (TNA, CAB 23/5/371).
[75] 24–5 Mar. 1918, Wilson diary, and Haig TS diary (TNA, WO 256/28).

the existence of the general reserve might not have made much difference. For all his pessimism, along with the compulsion to protect Paris, Pétain did give Haig very substantial help. He immediately ordered twelve French divisions to reinforce the British, and it is not at all clear that an inter-Allied 'executive board' could or would have done as well, or done it as rapidly.

Pétain, nevertheless, had lost Haig's confidence and, more crucially, that of Clemenceau too. A full-dress meeting at Doullens on 26 March—Poincaré, Clemenceau, Foch, Pétain, Milner, Haig, and Wilson—agreed to appoint Foch (in Haig's words) 'to co-ordinate the action of all the Allied Armies on the Western front'.[76] What this actually meant in practice was not very clear, but his position was further defined over the next three weeks. On 3 April a conference at Beauvais (this time including Lloyd George and the American commander, Pershing) entrusted Foch with co-ordinating 'the action of the British, French, and American Armies on the Western Front', as well as 'the strategic direction of military operations', and on 14 April he was given the title of 'Commander-in-Chief of the Allied Armies in France'.[77] Together with the creation of the Supreme War Council, Foch's appointment as Allied 'generalissimo' marked the apotheosis of the Anglo-French alliance in particular, and the coalition war effort in general. Although in 1914–18 there was nothing to match the integration of Allied staffs which occurred in the Second World War, nor was Foch's position equivalent to Eisenhower's as 'Supreme Allied Commander', the formal relationships between the Allied powers in 1918 were light years beyond anything which could have been anticipated in 1914. 'From the point of view of relations between France and Britain', indeed, it was 'not the specific achievements' of the SWC and the Allied Commander-in-Chief which mattered, 'but their very existence'.[78]

The German attack at the Somme in March 1918 was the first of a series of pushes between March and May—along the River Lys south of Ypres/Ieper against British (and Portuguese) divisions in April, and in the Chemin des Dames towards the Marne against the French in May—in which alarming initial advances slowed down as the Allied forces regrouped and the Germans ran out of steam. The initial German successes, however, provoked 'the worst military manpower crisis since the outbreak of the war'.[79] One reason for the decision to 'tread water' in the west during 1918 had been so as not to fritter away precious manpower in costly attritional engagements, leaving the British weakened vis-à-vis the Americans, and to build up resources for a 1919 offensive. But the spring crisis in 1918 compelled the government ruthlessly to exploit domestic manpower reserves just to 'hold the line'. Apart from despatching 'boys' and 'combing out'

---

[76] Haig TS diary, 26 Mar. 1918 (TNA, WO 256/28).

[77] Liddell Hart, *Foch*, ii. 308, 314–15.

[78] Bell, *France and Britain*, 77. David French has argued that the 'major role' of the SWC after Foch became CinC was that it provided a mechanism whereby the European allies could exert influence on United States policy (French, *Strategy of the Lloyd George Coalition*, 227).

[79] Grieves, *The Politics of Manpower*, 187.

men in industrial occupations, a prime source of manpower was Ireland, or so
Henry Wilson and his unionist pals thought. Not for the first (or last) time,
however, Wilson's judgment on an Irish issue was badly skewed by the strength of
his Irish political beliefs.

Wilson's southern Irish unionist opinions were challenged by the sharp growth
of militant nationalism following the suppression of the 1916 Rising. In 1917–18
the government set up an 'Irish Convention' to explore what sort of political settlement could be reached which could accommodate the continued intransigence
of unionists, especially in Ulster, with the growing separatism of nationalists. This
was a very tall order, even in the absence of the main republican party, Sinn Féin,
which refused to take part, and the convention was wound up in April without
coming to any useful conclusion. Wilson, meanwhile, was certain that Ireland
should bear its share of the war effort, and that conscription might produce an extra
150,000 men. Besides the military benefits, compulsory national service would also
bring the 'smack of firm government' to Ireland, and usefully round up not just
malingerers but political malcontents as well. At the end of January, however, Lloyd
George told Wilson that he was against conscripting Ireland, on the grounds that
the costs outweighed the benefits. It would, he thought, provoke trouble not only in
Ireland but also 'with the English Unions, with the Colonies [the powerful Irish-
Australian community took a keen interest in Irish affairs] & with America'.[80]

Lloyd George's sensible position on Irish conscription was shared by the Irish
administration itself which consistently warned that bloodshed would inevitably
accompany its introduction, and predicted that it would destroy John Redmond's
constitutional nationalist party.[81] But the reservations about Irish conscription
were swept away by the spring offensive, following which the pressure to impose
the measure became irresistible. On 24 March Wilson noted that Milner 'was
nearly as strong as I was for the necessity of levée en masse in England & Ireland',
and the following day, despite continued warnings from some ministers (as well as
the head of the Royal Irish Constabulary), with Lloyd George's support the Cabinet
agreed to conscript Ireland.[82] The decision was not taken in a policy vacuum. In
Britain the government wanted to extend conscription into the essential war indus-
tries and needed the co-operation of labour, which it was thought would be with-
held if conscription were *not* imposed on Ireland. The Prime Minister, moreover,
hoped to kill two troublesome Irish birds at once by linking Irish conscription with
home rule. When he introduced a new Military Service Bill, including Irish
conscription, in parliament on 9 April, he added that the government also
intended 'to pass a measure of self-government in Ireland'. To meet unionist
concerns, Ulster would be provided with some as yet undefined safeguards.[83]

---

[80] Wilson diary, 31 Jan. 1918.
[81] For the issue as a whole, see Ward, 'Lloyd George and Irish Conscription'; and Gregory, ' "You
might as well recruit Germans" '.
[82] Wilson diary, 24 Mar. 1918; War Cabinet meeting, 25 Mar. 1918 (TNA, CAB 23/5/370).
[83] Ward, 'Lloyd George and Irish Conscription', 113–14.

This satisfied nobody, and stimulated an extraordinary response in Ireland. A pan-nationalist coalition of Redmondite constitutionalists, labour, Sinn Féin, and the Catholic Church mobilised mass opposition to the measure, radicalising Irish political attitudes at a time when it was by no means certain Sinn Féin could become the majority nationalist Irish political party, and, in fact, laying the basis for the Sinn Féin triumph in the general election of December 1918. Ironically, conscription was never imposed on Ireland. Once the crisis on the western front had eased, its implementation was first postponed then quietly forgotten. But the *threat* was enough to galvanise and alienate nationalist Ireland. It is, indeed, not too much to say that the ramifications of a British military retreat from the Somme and the Lys in 1918, made inevitable a political retreat from the Liffey and the Lee in 1921.

Wilson, blithely impervious to the opinions of the majority of the Irish population, continued to favour Irish conscription through the spring and early summer of 1918. The linking of conscription with home rule did not much trouble him, reckoning that the nationalists would reject any measure which protected Ulster and partitioned the island. Like many Ulster unionists, Wilson seems to have regarded partition (for all nine Ulster counties, or, as was increasingly suggested, the six most unionist counties) as no more than 'a tactical ploy devised by their leaders to crush Home Rule'.[84] Talking to John French the day before French was appointed 'Viceroy and Commander-in-Chief' in Ireland—a strong man (and one with an Anglo-Irish background) put in to maintain order and enforce conscription—Wilson asked him about the Home Rule Bill. French told him that Lloyd George had promised 'an absolute veto by Ulster on matters affecting Ulster'. This, wrote Wilson, was 'good enough for me as Ulster is safe-guarded & the Rebels cannot accept'.[85]

From the moment he became CIGS, Henry Wilson (as had Robertson before him) attended War Cabinet meetings on a very regular—sometimes daily—basis. His position as the government's chief military adviser was further consolidated by being included in a small committee which Lloyd George formed in May 1918 as a sort of 'inner' War Cabinet to deal with military and naval matters. In April Eddie Derby was packed off to Paris to be ambassador, and Milner became Secretary for War. With departmental responsibility, he lost his place on the War Cabinet but remained within the Prime Minister's inner circle as one of 'the little triumvirate of Lloyd George, Milner, and Henry Wilson, known as the X Committee, which', asserted Amery afterwards, 'really ran the war during the critical spring and summer months of the German offensive'.[86] Hankey was dismayed when he heard about the new body. The Prime Minister, he wrote, 'has invented a new and most tiresome method of doing business. He puts the War Cabinet at noon and has a private meeting of his own with Lord Milner and C.I.G.S. at 11 a.m., when I have to attend and am expected to keep a

---

[84] Jackson, *Sir Edward Carson*, 54.   [85] Wilson diary, 5 May 1918.
[86] Amery, *My Political Life*, ii. 157.

record.'[87] Hankey brought Leo Amery in to help. After the first meeting Amery noted that it had been 'a very interesting and free and easy gathering, which may very possibly develop into the real War Cabinet. Anyway, I live in hopes that it may.' Later he qualified this diary entry by adding: 'But it didn't.'[88]

Amery, who claimed 'we met almost daily, sometimes twice a day', overstated the significance of the X Committee in his memoirs.[89] David French's observation that from May 1918 the group henceforth 'conducted much of the purely military and naval business which had hitherto fallen to the war Cabinet or its ad hoc sub-committees' also seems a bit of an exaggeration.[90] The committee only officially met thirty-two times between 15 May and 25 November 1918.[91] Two-thirds of these meetings, however, were between May and July, when the committee did play an important role, especially in late May and early June when unsettling news of Allied reverses in France came pouring in all too frequently, and even Wilson feared that the French might be 'done'.[92] The pre-Cabinet 'conversations' (as Wilson described them in his diary) enabled him to brief the Prime Minister on the latest situation, and allowed Lloyd George freely to discuss and anticipate the issues which would arise in Cabinet. Once the German tide had been stemmed in the west, however, and the situation had become less strained, Lloyd George seems to have had less use for these private chats. Wilson's importance as a source of the latest news obviously declined when the news itself was less urgent, and perhaps too his value as a policy sounding-board had fewer attractions for Lloyd George now that Robertson was out of the picture.

Where Wilson did help in mid-1918 was in his old role of Franco-British liaison. In April he travelled over to France four times. On each occasion he saw both Foch and Haig (and, in three out of four, Clemenceau as well). On 10 April, when Dunkirk was threatened and it seemed as if the two armies might split apart, the British moving to cover the Channel ports and the French to protect Paris, he got Foch to recognise the need for the French to remain in contact with the right flank of the British, and agree to 'the vital necessity of covering the Ports', this 'most important of all points'. On 15 April Milner, who had been sent to Versailles to steady the French, wired for Wilson, 'as I alone can bridge the gulf'.[93] A week later, having been reassured by the Admiralty that 'the loss of the Channel Ports did not mean the loss of the Channel', Wilson decided that, if necessary, 'we ought to fall back with the French & give up Calais & Boulogne'. This was agreed at a meeting at Abbeville, held during a session of the SWC on 2 May, but, fortunately, the decision never had to be implemented.[94]

[87] Hankey diary, 16 May 1918 (in *Roskill, Hankey: Man of Secrets*, 553).

[88] Amery, *The Leo Amery Diaries*, 220–1.

[89] Amery, *My Political Life*, ii. 157. Milner's biographer ('It became their custom to meet each morning') also exaggerates the importance of the committee (Gollin, *Proconsul in Politics*, 510).

[90] French, *Strategy of the Lloyd George Coalition*, 232–3.

[91] The 'X Committee' minutes are in TNA, CAB 23/17.   [92] Wilson diary, 31 May 1918.

[93] Ibid., 10, 15 Apr. 1918.

[94] Ibid., 24 Apr. 1918; Haig TS diary, 2 May 1918 (TNA, WO 256/31).

For all his Francophilia, however, Wilson worried that the French had ambitions 'to take us over militarily & economically'.[95] Despite the views of some critics, he was never unquestioningly in thrall to the French, and even Foch came in for some sharp criticism in early June when the French situation seemed especially perilous and they were falling back towards the Marne.[96] Although Foch was an old friend, and the Anglo-French alliance had been close to his heart for years, even Wilson was not prepared to allow the French free rein in terms of command, nor did he accept the criticisms which Foch, among others, from time to time levelled at the British that they were not pulling their full weight on the western front. In August Wilson was hurt by Foch's assertion that 'England [*sic*] was not playing the game of a good & loyal comrade'. Wilson assured him that this was emphatically *not* the case, adding a revealingly patriotic *apologia pro vita sua*.

For 27 years [he wrote to Foch] I have worked for one object & one object only & that was, & is, the safety & greatness of my country. If then I have to say, & to do, things which are distasteful to my friends I hope they will credit me with the fact that these things are <u>at least</u> as distasteful to me as they are to my friends. I know you will understand the spirit in which I pen these few lines to the oldest & the greatest friend I have in the French Army.[97]

Foch's admiration for Wilson also had its limitations. In October 1918 he told Lord Derby that he thought Robertson 'was a far sounder man than Wilson', and that he had more faith in Robertson's attention to strategic detail than Wilson's. On the other hand, he fully recognised Robertson's significant failure to take into account the views of 'the government of the Country, who represented the people'.[98]

Having visited the Italian front towards the end of June, and been encouraged by what he saw there, Wilson began to think about the longer-term future. 'When we are safe on our front', he wrote, 'I most certainly intend to exploit all the outside theatres capable of exploitation.'[99] This propensity to take a wider view, which was one of the things which had attracted Lloyd George's attention, was most fully expressed by Wilson in a long paper prepared for the Cabinet in July 1918 on 'British military policy, 1918–19'.[100] It restated the view that the best which could be hoped for in 1918 was to hold the line in the west. It recommended some limited attacks in 1918 to secure a tactical advantage in preparation for a major offensive the following summer. Then the Allies would have a slight superiority in numbers, but, argued Wilson (picking up on a point made in Note 12 at the beginning of the year), a major edge in terms of machine guns, tanks, aircraft, and artillery. Placing faith in the latest technical advances, but not being over-optimistic, Wilson argued that 'properly supported by the fullest equipment

95 Wilson diary, 11 May 1918.   96 Ibid., 2, 6 June 1918.
97 Wilson to Foch, 12 Aug. 1918 (Wilson papers, HHW 2/24B/2).
98 Derby diary, 11 Oct. 1918 (Dutton, *Paris 1918*, 256–7).
99 Wilson diary, 25 June 1918.
100 Wilson, 'British Military Policy, 1918–19', 25 July 1918 (TNA, CAB 27/8 W.P. 70).

of every mechanical auxiliary, and efficiently directed under one supreme command', there would be 'a fair chance of achieving substantial military success'. Assessing Wilson's 'very able paper', Paul Guinn observed that 'no other practical general plan of action was suggested', and that 'in its emphasis on mechanical warfare' the paper 'undoubtedly indicated the right road'.[101]

While Wilson opposed reducing the numbers of British troops in the west, he noted the dangers to the British position in Mesopotamia and Persia (Iran), perhaps even India, posed by the Germans and Turks exploiting the collapse of the Russian empire and thrusting into the Caucasus and Central Asia. He therefore recommended the reinforcement of the British presence in the region. Surveying the security of the British empire in the Middle East and in India, Wilson even essayed a prediction about the 'next war'. Then, he asserted, 'we may be fighting Germany alone and unaided while she will have Turkey and perhaps part of Russia, if not on her side, at least under her thumb'. In these circumstances Germany, 'with no preoccupations in Europe, could concentrate great armies against Egypt or India by her overland routes, which are beyond the reach of our sea power'.

But at the core of the study was an understanding that ultimately the war could only be won in the west. It was 'Wully redivivus', Lloyd George grumbled to Hankey.[102] Twenty years later he singled the study out in his memoirs for particular excoriation. He noted that since Wilson had consulted both Haig and Pétain, and had been able to draw on all the great resources of the General Staff at home, the paper was not the 'mere personal opinion of a very clever but somewhat erratic officer', but represented the sum of British 'military wisdom' in general. Yet, 'alike in fact and forecast', he wrote, 'it was wrong, grotesquely wrong'. The best Wilson had been able to predict was that 'the German offensive may be fought to a standstill before any strategical decision has been obtained'. Lloyd George, with the undeniable benefit of hindsight, scornfully observed that 'an Allied advance' did 'not figure at all'.[103]

But few people (and certainly not Lloyd George) *did* forecast the Allied advance in the 'hundred days' which began with the battle of Amiens on 8 August 1918. These successes stemmed in part from much improved British battle tactics and the unprecedentedly close co-ordination of infantry and artillery, towards which Wilson and his colleagues had been groping in 1916.[104] SWC Note 12 had dismissed 'such improbable and unforeseen contingencies as the internal collapse of the Enemy Powers'. But this in effect was what happened in the late autumn of 1918, and, as if to vindicate the case for 'side-shows', Bulgaria sued for peace in

---

[101] Guinn, *British Strategy and Politics*, 314.

[102] Hankey diary, 30 July 1918 (in Hankey, *The Supreme Command*, ii. 830). Amery, for his part, complained to Wilson about 'his under-valuation of the Palestine–Mesopotamia area' (Amery diary, 1 Aug. 1918, in Amery, *The Leo Amery Diaries*, 230).

[103] Lloyd George, *War Memoirs*, ii. 1857–66.

[104] For a stimulating discussion of the 1918 victories, see Sheffield, *Forgotten Victory*, 237–63.

September, Turkey in October, and Austria-Hungary at the beginning of November. The Germans, defeated in battle and falling back towards their frontier, were finally left isolated at a time when the government, indeed the whole political system, was beginning to buckle under the prolonged strains of fighting a total war. 'I never thought we could bring down the Boche Empire so quickly', wrote Rawly to Wilson on the day the war ended, 'when I began hammering on Aug. 8th. It is really wonderful—We have now secured for the Empire a really firm foundation on which to build.'[105] At the moment of victory it was an understandably optimistic conclusion, but one which was not to be borne out by the imperial crisis-ridden years which followed.

Thirty-five years after the end of the Great War, Leo Amery in his memoirs recalled a dinner party comprising himself, Austen Chamberlain, Frederick Oliver, and Geoffrey Dawson, at which they all agreed separately to write down, in order of importance, the four men 'who had made the most difference to winning the war by being where he was'. All four lists turned out to be identical: 'It was Lloyd George, Milner, Henry Wilson and Hankey'. These four, wrote Amery, 'were the men whom no one could have effectively replaced in the particular part each had to play'. Lloyd George and Milner were obvious choices, and Hankey, 'in his quiet, unobtrusive way', had 'in effect, both devised and continually oiled the machine which won it'. As for Wilson, Amery noted that he had 'often been freely disparaged as a talker and intriguer. But, apart from the creation of the Supreme War Council, no one could have more successfully overcome Lloyd George's suspicion of the Army and worked hand in glove with him.'[106] It was, perhaps, no coincidence that the four men on Amery's list comprised the X Committee, with which he, too, could be associated, but did Wilson actually deserve to be included in this select company?

That he presided as the government's chief military adviser for the last ten months of a victorious war might be reason enough, although it could be argued (albeit with some violence to the facts) that he owed his position merely to the fact that he was Lloyd George's creature. That his military and strategic judgment was flawed is uncontestable, though it was not so dire as Lloyd George afterwards asserted, nor was it so wildly out of kilter either with the underlying thrust of British strategy generally or the widely held assumptions of many of his military colleagues. But he turned out to be the most successful CIGS of the war. Indeed, no other high-ranking soldier in the British army could have made such a significant contribution both at home and to the maintenance of Britain's principal foreign alliance as did Henry Wilson. The predictions of disaster made by his critics should he replace Robertson were not fulfilled, even in the western front crises of March–June 1918. Wilson did not make matters worse; rather the contrary, in fact. His appointment as CIGS took much of the friction out of British civil–military

[105] Rawlinson to Wilson, 11 Nov. 1918 (Wilson papers, HHW 2/13B/6).
[106] Amery, *My Political Life*, ii. 172.

relations, and he provided a necessary buffer between Lloyd George and the rest of the British military hierarchy which his predecessor had failed to do, so much so that even Haig, at a dinner after the war, 'paid tribute to Henry Wilson's work, but said nothing about Robertson who had backed him so blindly'.[107] With his unequalled reputation in France, and close personal friendship with Foch, Wilson was also uniquely well qualified to oil the wheels of the Franco-British alliance. All this being so, Amery's assertion that no one could have effectively replaced him in the particular part he had to play appears to be incontestable. Perhaps, indeed, Henry Wilson was 'one of the men who won the war'.

[107] 'Talk with Maurice Hankey', 8 Nov. 1932 (Liddell Hart papers, 11/1932/43). Robertson was present at the dinner, and on leaving remarked 'I'll never go farting with 'aig again!'

12

Defending the empire

In the immediate aftermath of the war, both as a confidante of the Prime Minister and as professional head of the army, Henry Wilson continued to play a central role in the policy-making process. As the whistle was about to blow on the western front he began to worry about future military commitments. The internal political turmoil which had steadily undermined the German war effort now threatened to engulf the whole state. 'Our real danger now', he wrote in his diary on 10 November, 'is not the Boch but Bolshevism.' That evening, as he waited at 10 Downing Street for confirmation from Paris that an armistice had been signed, he thought it 'certain that Bolshevism will sweep over Germany'.[1] With the end of hostilities, moreover, came the need for the military to supply post-war garrisons across the empire, as well as armies of occupation. Understandably, perhaps, in the euphoria of the moment, Wilson was unable to get the politicians to concentrate on these matters. On 13 November he noted the 'most useless War Cabinet I have ever attended. I brought up the question of a Post Bellum Army but entirely failed to get up any interest in the subject by anyone. It was d——— as we shall have chaos.'[2]

Although Wilson foresaw the establishment of a long-service voluntary army on the pre-war model, he also pressed for the continuance of conscription, not merely to supply the occupation forces, but also as a general good. He told Lord Cavan that it was 'the only <u>fair</u> way of solving the problem'; that 'even if there was never going to be another war it ought to be enforced as a part of necessary moral and physical training; and that it was 'truly democratic'.[3] But there was strong opposition to the extension of compulsion, or indeed any delay in demobilisation. 'Send the boys home,' demanded the *Daily Herald* on 7 December. 'Why in the world the delay? The war is not officially "over", but everybody knows in fact it is over.'[4] Against this, Wilson bluntly told the Cabinet that substantial numbers of troops were needed for the immediate future. Early in December he circulated a paper summarising the 'military commitments remaining after peace has been signed', in which he estimated that between 350,000 and 500,000 soldiers would be required to serve in armies of occupation, in the Middle East as well as Europe,

[1] Wilson diary, 10 Nov. 1918.　　[2] Ibid., 13 Nov. 1918.
[3] Wilson to Cavan, 18 Dec. 1918 (Wilson papers, HHW 2/28B/10).
[4] Quoted in Graubard, 'Military Demobilisation', 300.

'for an unknown period after Peace has been signed. No machinery as yet exists for their provision,' he concluded, 'since it would be unsafe to assume that they will be obtainable on a voluntary basis.'[5]

Two factors exacerbated the demobilisation crisis: the general election which Lloyd George called for December 1918, and the attitude of the servicemen themselves. During the election campaign the Prime Minister promised that demobilisation would be speeded up. But it also became clear that Milner was not the best man to grapple with the problems of the War Office. Lloyd George, who needed someone more dynamic for the job, bullied him into resignation, to be replaced with Churchill. 'Whew!' wrote Wilson in his diary when he first learned of the possible change.[6] The election was a triumph for Lloyd George and the coalition, which emerged with a working parliamentary majority of over 300 MPs.[7] Although the result left the Prime Minister in an extremely strong political position, from which he could press forward with plans for domestic 'reconstruction', the balance of power within the coalition threatened to limit his freedom of action. Ultimately his government depended for survival on Conservative and Unionist backbenchers, for the most part wedded to financial orthodoxy, anxious to reduce taxation and state interference from their high wartime levels, and heartily suspicious of 'progressive' social policy.

While voters were clearly inspired by the longer-term assurances of improved social conditions at home offered by coalition candidates in the election, over the turn of the year 1918–19 demands for definite and immediate demobilisation began to escalate alarmingly among servicemen. There was a particularly serious incident at Folkestone on 3 January, when 10,000 soldiers returning from Christmas home leave refused to embark for France. The next day at Dover there was a similar demonstration, involving 2,000 men, and a wave of protests followed at other army camps at home and abroad.[8] Acutely aware that revolution in Russia and Germany (among other places) had been spearheaded by mutinous servicemen, Wilson and his military colleagues pressed the government to take a hard line. The Prime Minister, thought Wilson 'must make it clear to the country that the war is not over, that we are demobilizing quite fast enough'. If he did not do this, 'the whole Army will turn into a rabble'. All the trouble, he concluded, was 'due to Lloyd George & his cursed campaign at election for vote-catching'.[9]

With typical energy, Churchill began to sort out the mess after he took over as Secretary for War in January 1919. He abandoned the old scheme and replaced it with what was in effect a 'first in, first out' system, which took the steam out of the soldiers' protests. At the same time, with Wilson's backing, he persuaded the Cabinet to extend compulsory military service (for the most recently conscripted men) until April 1920, so as to 'tide over the period until we could raise a voluntary

---

[5] Memo by CIGS, 5 Dec. 1918 (TNA, CAB 24/71, GT6434).
[6] Wilson diary, 16 Dec, 1918. Churchill did not take over as Secretary for War until 10 Jan. 1919.
[7] Coalition MPs, 478; others, 229 (including 73 abstentionist Irish members).
[8] Rothstein, *The Soldiers' Strikes*, 37–85.   [9] Wilson diary, 6 Jan. 1919.

army of sufficient size to meet our requirements'.[10] Even with this measure, there was a dramatic fall in the size of the army, from 3.8 million men in November 1918 to 890,000 a year later, and 430,000 in November 1920.[11]

Another domestic worry was labour unrest, which had begun to increase in the summer of 1918. In August even the London police had gone on strike, demanding more money and the right to form a trade union, and Wilson's old friend Nevil Macready had been drafted in as Metropolitan Police Commissioner to sort the situation out. Approving the deployment of troops as strike-breakers in September 1918, Wilson observed that a railway strike was 'really a challenge to the Govt of the country', and throughout the post-war years underlying apprehensions about the 'revolutionary' potential of strikes powerfully informed official responses to labour unrest.[12] Whether there was any real likelihood of revolution or not, the apprehension of many British leaders was real enough, fuelled especially by the re-emergence in 1919 of the 'Triple Alliance', a loose combination of miners, railwaymen, and transport workers, pledged to co-ordinate industrial action on issues of common interest. Wilson, while on the whole doubting that Great Britain was really in a 'revolutionary condition', certainly believed that employers and government should take a firm line with strikers. But in this he was repeatedly to be disappointed, as politicians (and above all Lloyd George) dismayingly demonstrated a 'genius for giving in'. When the Cabinet settled a railway stoppage in December 1918 by making concessions to the workers, Wilson bluntly observed that 'this giving in to all demands means ruin for the country'.[13] It was, indeed, to be a sort of leitmotif of Wilson's three peacetime years as CIGS.

As if there was not enough to do at home, in the wider world there was much unfinished wartime business, continuing problems of imperial defence, along with some new nationalist challenges to be met, and of course, the small matter of negotiating and imposing a peace settlement. The most urgent post-war military commitment concerned Russia where, following the revolution, British troops had been deployed to bolster up anti-Bolshevik forces which remained committed to war against the Central Powers. After November 1918, however, British (and other Allied) formations found themselves increasingly being drawn into active support for the counter-revolutionary side in the Russian Civil War. Not everyone thought this was a bad thing. Winston Churchill powerfully argued that not only did Bolshevik Russia represent as great a threat to the British empire as imperial Russia historically had done, but that the revolutionaries themselves should be crushed before they fatally infected the whole world with their poisonous communist ideology.

In Russia at the end of 1918 there were British forces in the far north, based on Murmansk and Archangel, and in the south, mostly in the Caucasus region. Two

---

[10] Ibid., 16 Jan. 1919; memo by Churchill, 27 Jan. 1919 (TNA, CAB 24/73, GT6673).

[11] Jeffery, 'The Post-war Army', 214.

[12] Wilson diary, 24 Sept. 1918. Labour unrest, and the government response, in the post-war period are exhaustively covered in Jeffery and Hennessy, *States of Emergency*, 10–68.

[13] Wilson diary, 6 Oct. 1919 and 6 Dec. 1918.

days after the armistice Wilson laid out three policy options for the Cabinet: withdraw all British forces and build up a 'cordon sanitaire' of independent states around Russia; embark on active military measures against the Bolsheviks; or (his preferred option) to 'do all we can in the way of material to give our friends a fair start, and then to withdraw'.[14] Although at the end of December the Cabinet agreed in principle against intervention, shortly after he arrived at the War Office Churchill instructed the General Staff to work on a 'concerted scheme for waging war against the Bolsheviks'. Lloyd George was horrified. 'An expensive war of aggression against Russia', he wrote, 'is a way to strengthen Bolshevism in Russia and create it at home.' Wilson, for his part, dryly commented that 'the invasion and occupation of Russia at the present time is not considered to be a practical military proposition'. He was not against some limited involvement, but what was necessary was 'to frame a policy for military operations which is within our powers'.[15]

In the face of this political and military opposition, Churchill had to abandon his ambitions for active military operations. In August 1919 Henry Rawlinson was sent out to superintend the British withdrawal from north Russia. Rawly was sympathetic to the plight of the 'White' anti-Bolsheviks, but he found them 'a curious crew to deal with—Of course they are in a tight place here and I am sorry for them but they seem to be quite helpless and want us to do everything for them'. Some of his own soldiers, moreover, were openly complaining that 'we are deserting our friends'. Yet the 'Whites' were uncertain allies at best, and Rawlinson told Wilson he would 'be thankful if we can only get away without having to open fire on them'. Wilson complained to Churchill that 'one cannot help getting tired of constantly nursing children who resolutely refuse to grow up'.[16] By the end of September the last British troops had embarked at Archangel, reflecting a process, which was to become all too familiar in this period of 'imperial crisis', of scaling-down or even liquidating British military responsibilities, and bringing expensive commitments into line with limited peacetime resources.[17]

Perhaps more than anywhere else in the post-war years, this was best illustrated by British commitments in south Russia and the Middle East. These proved to be especially intractable, since they impinged on the defence of India and its communications—the keystone of the British imperial strategic system. During

[14] 'Present and future military policy in Russia', memo by CIGS, 13 Nov. 1918 (TNA, CAB 24/70, GT6311).

[15] Churchill to Lloyd George and vice versa, 13 and 16 Feb. 1919 (Lloyd George papers, F/8/3/14 and 18); 'Future military operations in Russia', memo by CIGS, 24 Feb. 1919 (TNA, CAB 24/75, GT6885).

[16] Rawlinson to Wilson, 16 and 27 Aug.; Wilson to Churchill, 1 Sept. 1919 (Wilson papers, HHW 2/13B/15 and 16; 2/18A/45).

[17] See also Gallagher, *The Decline, Revival and Fall of the British Empire*, 86–99. The notion of an 'imperial crisis', brilliantly expounded in Gallagher, 'Nationalisms and the Crisis of Empire', underpins Jeffery, *The British Army and the Crisis of Empire*, on which I have drawn heavily for this and the following chapter.

the last year of the war a motley selection of British forces had begun to push northwards and eastwards from Mesopotamia (Iraq) into Persia (Iran) and the fringes of the disintegrating Russian empire. Early in 1918 'Dunsterforce', commanded by Lionel Dunsterville (the original for Kipling's 'Stalky'), was sent out from Baghdad to help secure the Caucasus front the Russians had held against the Turks. Dunsterville reached Baku on the Caspian Sea, but was pushed back to Kasvin in north Persia, where he was dismissed (as 'too much of a Don Quixote') and the expedition reorganised as 'Norperforce'.[18]

After the Turkish armistice Norperforce sent troops once more to Baku, where they supported one of the oddest 'sideshows' of the time, the Royal Navy Caspian Squadron, comprising armed merchant ships, wooden torpedo-boats, and two aeroplanes. Across the Causcasus from Baku, beginning on 22 December 1918, a full division began deploying at Batum and along the railway line to Tiflis. There were British troops, too, on the eastern side of the Caspian, where by December troops from General Wilfrid Malleson's intelligence mission ('Malmiss'), based at Meshed in north-eastern Persia, had been deployed along the railway from the Caspian port of Krasnovodsk to Askabad and Merv. British forces were also deployed across Persia: the 'East Persia Cordon' along the Afghan frontier; the 'South Persian Rifles', a mixed British, Indian, and Arab force securing the Anglo-Persian Oil Company's installations around Abadan; and the 10,000-strong 'Bushire Expedition'.[19]

These scattered forces were merely outliers for the main concentrations of British strength in the region: in Mesopotamia itself, where the British had reached as far north as Mosul; along the south-eastern shores of the Mediterranean, from Egypt through Palestine and up to the 'Greater Syria'; and, after December 1918, Sir George Milne's 'Army of the Black Sea' (part of the Allied occupation force in Turkey), with its headquarters at Constantinople. 'From the left bank of the Don to India is our interest & preserve', Henry Wilson had written shortly after the armistice with Turkey.[20] Together, this widely spread military presence confirmed Britain's position as the leading power in the region, and underpinned its forty-year 'moment in the Middle East'.[21] It also sustained the visions of ardent British imperialists. For Leo Amery it was part of 'that Southern British World which runs from Cape Town through Cairo, Baghdad and Calcutta to Sydney and Wellington'.[22] For Curzon (who was a member of the War Cabinet) it was an opportunity firmly to secure Britain's most important imperial possession and protect India from any future Russia threat. In December 1918 he asserted the 'supreme importance' of the Caucasus, over which it was

[18] Dunsterville, *Stalky's Reminiscences*, 271–86; Gen. W. R. Marshall (GOC Mesopotamia) to Wilson, 21 Sept. 1918 (Wilson papers, HHW 2/21/4).

[19] Jeffery, *The British Army and the Crisis of Empire*, 133–4.   [20] Wilson diary, 5 Nov. 1918.

[21] See Monroe, *Britain's Moment in the Middle East, 1914–56*. The 1981 revised edition of this work unconvincingly extends the 'moment' to 1971.

[22] 'British war aims', memo by Amery, 8 June 1918 (Lloyd George papers, F/2/1/24).

'essential, in the interest of India and our Empire, that we should exercise some measure of political control'.[23] Following the collapse of the Russian empire, new independent national republics—Georgia, Armenia, and Azerbaijan—had sprung up in the region. With British support, so the argument went, a *cordon sanitaire* could be constructed around the Bolsheviks, and a new British sphere of influence be established to protect the vital arc of empire from Egypt to India.

Curzon also hoped to establish Persia as a British client state, both to reinforce the defence of India and to safeguard the British-controlled oil-fields near the Gulf. By the summer of 1919 he seemed to have achieved his aim with a painstakingly negotiated Anglo-Persian agreement. But the agreement was never ratified. As in other cases, local nationalism provided a counterweight to great-power imperialism. In any case, the visionary and expansive plans for imperial defence in the Middle East had been born of a 'war imperialism' in which money and effort were prodigally committed to virtually any plan which might contribute towards winning the war. But in the hard light of the post-war world, and vividly illustrating the consequences of imperial overstretch, overseas vision had to be tempered with domestic economy. Opposition at home (and abroad) grew up to what Henry Wilson termed Britain's 'interference' in everyone else's affairs. Quoting his deputy CIGS in August 1921, Wilson wrote that 'the habit of interfering with other people's business, and of making what is euphoniously called "peace" is like "buggery": once you take to it you cannot stop.'[24] Whatever the truth of this remarkable assertion, the Treasury had not the money and the War Office not the men to support a massive extension of empire in the Middle East, even in the high cause of defending India.

Apart from the difficulties posed by the over-extension of imperial commitments, there were urgent defence problems *within* the empire, which stemmed from increasingly militant nationalist challenges. In part these were a response to common experience during the war, when 'normal' political debate had been suspended, when such challenges as had emerged had been sharply repressed (as in Ireland from 1916), and when national aspirations had been encouraged by the rhetoric of Allied war aims, especially as articulated following the entry of the United States into the war in 1917. The 'primary and original cause of our troubles in the East from Egypt, though Palestine, Mesopotamia, and Persia to India,' decided Maurice Hankey at the beginning of 1921, was 'President Wilson and his fourteen points, and his impossible doctrine of self determination'. The 'adoption of this principle at the peace conference', he argued, had 'struck at the very roots of the British Empire all over the world from Ireland to Hong Kong', and had 'got us into a hideous mess'.[25] So it had, although the British policy-makers'

[23] Cabinet eastern committee 40th meeting, 2 Dec. 1918 (TNA, CAB 27/24).

[24] In the original, 'hinder' (crossed out) appears before 'buggery'; a supererogatory qualification (Wilson to Sackville-West (military attaché in Paris), 11 Aug. 1921 (Wilson papers, HHW 2/12G/50)).   [25] Hankey diary, 3 Jan. 1921 (Hankey papers, HNKY 1/5).

own inability to concede the legitimacy of nationalist aspirations was an additional factor exacerbating the situation.

Wilson's identification of 'peacemaking', and Hankey's of the peace conference, reflect the centrality of the post-war efforts to secure a satisfactory peace settlement. For much of the first half of 1919, indeed, led by Lloyd George, a large part of the British decision-making elite decamped to Paris. Wilson, for example, spent the equivalent of four months in Paris between New Year and the end of June.[26] He was officially head of the 'military section' of the British delegation, which also included the DMO, Percy Radcliffe, and the DMI, Bill Thwaites, and officers from their two directorates. The maverick adventurer Richard Meinertzhagen, who hated the 'democratic slowness' of the conference, came from military operations.[27] From military intelligence was James Marshall Cornwall, who had done well as an intelligence officer on the western front, before taking over the foreign intelligence section M.I.3, and C. K. Webster, an extremely able international historian, who had been drafted into the War Office in 1917 and was secretary to the military section. Much later, as Professor Sir Charles Webster, he would reminisce about his days at the peace conference. Uncomfortable in his major's uniform, and looking a shambles, Webster recalled meeting Sir Henry Wilson on a station platform in Paris. 'Webster,' said Wilson, 'I had not intended to come to this conference, but the sight of you has made it all worth while.'[28] There were also a couple of political appointments to the section: Lord Hartington, heir to the Duke of Devonshire, and later a Conservative MP, and (Wilson was no fool) Lloyd George's younger son, Gwilym.

Much of the work of the section was spent advising on the military clauses of the proposed treaty. What sort of army, for example, should Germany be permitted, and what security should the French be allowed to have along their frontier with Germany? On both issues Wilson and his colleagues were inclined to be less stringent than the French. There was a debate about the future German army, Wilson favouring a voluntary, long-service force (following the traditional British model), while the French preferred a conscript army. The eventual decision combined Wilson's voluntary principle with a limit of 100,000 men, which the French proposed. Regarding security along the Franco-German frontier, Foch wanted France permanently to occupy territory up to the River Rhine. Wilson sympathised with this 'from a purely military point of view', but felt it was impossible politically. Here the compromise led to the Rhineland being demilitarised, together with an Allied occupation for up to fifteen years.[29]

---

[26] 117 out of 181 days.   [27] Cocker, *Richard Meinertzhagen*, 109.

[28] An anecdote recounted by Webster's executor, Fred Parsons (letter to author, Nov. 1996). I am grateful to Alan Sharp for his help with this.

[29] Wilson diary, 19 Feb., 1 and 7 Mar. 1919. The details of the negotiations can be followed in the best single account of the peacemaking: Sharp, *The Versailles Settlement*. See also MacMillan, *The Peacemakers*.

Throughout early 1919 Wilson remained an important member of Lloyd George's 'inner circle'. The warm companionability between the two men is reflected in an exchange of letters in February 1919. As his diaries testify, Wilson was a great recorder of anniversaries, each new year assiduously entering an engaging mix of significant private and more public events. On 20 May, for example, we find: 'Little Trench [Cecil's niece] got diptheria 1904'; 21 July 'K. Edward gave me DSO 1908'; 14 October 'Hamie killed 1914'; 6 December: 'Asquith resigned 1916.' Two events were noted at the head of his diary page for 16 February 1919: 'Won Ski Test Medal Adelboden 1906', and 'Appointed C.I.G.S. 1918'. On 19 February, the first anniversary of being officially 'gazetted' CIGS, Wilson wrote to Lloyd George noting the anniversary, the 'many anxious and difficult times' they had been through together, and thanking him for his 'constant support and most courteous treatment'. This provoked a gratifying response from the Prime Minister, who offered 'felicitations' on his 'first birthday as C.I.G.S.'. Wilson had 'turned out a fine infant and in every way fulfilled the highest expectations of the anxious parent. What a time we have been through!' continued Lloyd George. 'Your foresight, resource, courage and good cheer contributed materially to ultimate triumph.'[30]

Concerned about the general progress of the conference and keen to review British peace aims, at the end of March 1919 Lloyd George took a party of close advisers away to a hotel in Fontainebleau south-west of Paris. 'I am going to Fontainebleau for the week-end,' he told Lord Riddell, 'and mean to put in the hardest forty-eight hours' thinking I have ever done. The Conference is not going well, and I must try to pull things together.'[31] Along with his private secretary, Philip Kerr (later Lord Lothian), the Prime Minister took Maurice Hankey, Henry Wilson, and Edwin Montagu. In his memoir of the peace conference (published 20 years later), Lloyd George erroneously said that Smuts was among the group at Fontainebleau, an assertion repeated by Hankey (among others).[32] Montagu was there for his financial expertise. Although currently Secretary of State for India, he had previously been Financial Secretary to the Treasury, and in Paris served as 'British Minister for Finance at the Peace Conference'.

The inspiration for the 'away week-end', which ran from Saturday evening to Monday morning, seems to have come from a lecture Wilson gave to Maurice Hankey and his wife after dinner on 18 March, and which Hankey wanted Lloyd George 'to hear at first hand'. Wilson expressed a worry (shared by Philip Kerr) that the proposed harsh peace terms might 'put Germany in an utterly impossible situation', and he was deeply concerned (as he had been since the armistice) about the threat of anarchy spreading from the east across Europe. 'England,

---

[30] Wilson to Lloyd George, and reply, 19 and 21 Feb. 1919 (Wilson papers, HHW 2/17B/4 and 2/90/6).   [31] Riddell diary, 21 Mar. 1919 (quoted in Riddell, *Intimate Diary*, 36).
[32] Lloyd George, *The Truth about the Peace Treaties*, i. 403; Hankey, *The Supreme Control*, 100. Roskill repeats the error (*Hankey*, ii. 70). For Smuts's actual movements, see Hancock, *Smuts*, 514–15.

France & Germany', argued Wilson (as recorded in his diary), 'ought to combine ag[ains]t Bolshevism, otherwise the Boches will join the Bolshevists & presently ally herself with Russia & Japan.'[33]

At Fontainbleau, Lloyd George adopted Wilson's well-tried 'war game' technique, with different individuals taking on 'national' (or equivalent) roles. Wilson was separately to represent Germany and France, 'Montagu was to be an inhabitant of Mars on a visit, & Hankey was to be purely insular Briton'. After tea on the Saturday afternoon Wilson led off with a brief critique of a familiar *bête noir*. 'To build on the League of Nations', he asserted, 'was to build on shifting sands.' It was 'in truth a machinery set up to interfere in everybody's business & this by 3rd or 4th rate men & by 10th rate powers'. Then he 'became a Boche'. 'I remember well', wrote Hankey over forty years later, 'that he wore his military cap back to front', which 'gave him the appearance of a German officer!' Wilson argued that, although, as a German, he wished 'to come to an agreement with England & France', the 'crushing terms' being imposed would drive him into an alliance with Russia. After dinner Montagu and Hankey played their parts, the former advocated cancelling all war debts, the latter 'very nervous & little use. He thought we must remain in the League of Nations.'

On Sunday the British representatives on the Reparations Commission, Lords Sumner and Cunliffe came for lunch.[34] Nicknamed 'the Heavenly Twins' by John Maynard Keynes (a fellow member of the British delegation), they tended to take a hard line—in sharp contrast to Edwin Montagu's more liberal approach—on Germany's ability to pay compensation.[35] After lunch Wilson took on the role of a French *woman*, insisting that 'the unenfranchised French women were the real source of French public opinion'. Skilfully blending 'pathos and humour' (as Hankey recalled), Wilson stressed the terrible losses France had suffered, and explained its 'overwhelming insistence on restitution and full reparation by the enemy above everything else'. Lloyd George then summed up 'his views of Peace terms', among which (as Wilson noted in his diary) were: 'Refuse to put too crushing terms on Germany either in money or in cessation of territory or other ways'; 'Put her in a position to stop Bolshevism spreading into her country'; retain for the British Empire former German territories in Africa and Turkish in the Middle East (including Palestine, Mosul and Mesopotamia); and 'Draw the Empire closer by every possible means'. In order to reassure the French, Lloyd George resolved that Britain and America should 'promise immediate support if Germany attempts to invade France' and, even, 'Build Channel Tunnel to help in this guarantee'.[36]

[33] The two sources on which I have drawn for the background and course of the Fontainbleau conference (as described in the ensuing paragraphs) are Hankey, *The Supreme Control*, 97–102, and Wilson diary, 18–23 Mar. 1919.
[34] Sumner was a judge and Cunliffe had been governor of the Bank of England.
[35] Lentin, *Lloyd George and the Lost Peace*, 23–4.
[36] For a discussion of the French guarantee, see ibid. 52–6; and, for the Channel tunnel, Sharp, 'Britain and the Channel Tunnel'.

Wilson was 'delighted' with Lloyd George's conclusions. The Welshman's trenchant support for an Anglo-French alliance, indeed, was as firm as anything which Wilson had advocated in the years before 1914. Based on the weekend discussions, Hankey and Philip Kerr drafted the 'Fontainbleau memorandum', which 'became the basis of Lloyd George's perception of a post-war settlement'.[37] The memorandum outlined 'the kind of Treaty of Peace' which Britain was prepared to sign, and emphasised the need to temper severity with justice. Echoes of Wilson's two presentations came through in the final text. Lloyd George raised the danger 'that Germany may throw in her lot with Bolshevism', and presciently observed that the establishment of small independent national states on its borders might have unfortunate consequences. He could 'not imagine any greater cause for future war' than that Germany 'should be surrounded by a number of small States . . . each containing large masses of Germans clamouring for reunion with their native land'. As for reparations, he argued that 'we cannot both cripple' Germany and 'expect her to pay'. Nevertheless (and reflecting Sumner and Cunliffe's contribution to the weekend's discussions), he also acknowledged the need to exact 'as large an indemnity out of Germany as possible'.[38] The Fontainbleau memorandum, however, also explicitly challenged French policy, denouncing, for example, aspirations for a French military frontier on the Rhine. Clemenceau grumbled that while British policy expected France to make strategic sacrifices in Europe, it was reinforcing the security of the British empire, notably with the acquisition of territory in the Middle East.[39]

Lloyd George's memorandum, which contained much good sense, alarmed the French, but their concerns were substantially defused by the decision to impose an Allied occupation of the Rhineland for at least fifteen years as well as the assurance of an alliance. On 28 June 1919 Lloyd George and President Wilson signed British and American treaties of guarantee in the event of future 'unprovoked aggression by Germany'. That both treaties were stillborn due to the subsequent failure of the United States to ratify theirs was to be a source of much disappointment and complaint on the part of the French, but the promise of an Anglo-American guarantee was enough to let Clemenceau sign the Treaty of Versailles later the same day.[40]

Between March and June 1919 the apparently interminable slowness of the peace negotiations irritated and frustrated Henry Wilson. 'I think the Frocks have gone mad,' he wrote on 28 March. 'They sit and talk all day.' He was also keen to keep British involvement on the Continent as limited as possible, and was 'sure we ought to clear out of Europe except the Rhine. I don't want to get mixed up in the mess the French Frocks are making.' 'Every day,' he noted on 3 May, 'instance

[37] Morgan, *Consensus and Disunity*, 133. Morgan says the memorandum was 'drafted it would appear largely by Kerr and Hankey with the assistance of Smuts [*sic*] and some advice from Montagu'. Wilson's role is omitted.   [38] Lloyd George, *The Truth about the Peace Treaties*, i. 404–9.

[39] Dockrill and Gould, *Peace without Promise*, 29.

[40] Lentin, 'Lloyd George, Clemenceau and the Elusive Anglo-French Guarantee Treaty'.

after instance crops up of the shifting base on which we are building', and added a long catalogue of how new states in central and eastern Europe were adding to the prevailing turmoil. The 'Esthonians—a small State—threaten to make a separate peace with the Bolsheviks'; the Finns were 'marching on Petrograd'; the 'Yugos are attacking the Austrians'; the Romanians 'throwing the Hungarians over the [River] Theiss'; the Bulgars 'are becoming truculent & have imprisoned some Greeks—and so on ad infinitum'. 'Paris', he concluded, 'remains paralytic & impotent, owing entirely to her own action of building on small states, and on Leagues of Nations without power to enforce decisions.'[41]

One of the reasons why Lloyd George kept Wilson in Paris was the possibility that the Germans might have to be compelled to agree the terms presented to them. On 16 June Wilson assured the Prime Minister that the thirty-nine-division Allied force earmarked by Foch would be sufficient to 'march into Germany' and occupy Berlin. Wisely, however, he warned that if this action did 'not immediately bring us the desired result the straggling occupation of an enormous country where our troops can nowhere be strong, and in which we shall probably have to rule by martial law fills me with apprehension.'[42] Wilson's increasingly plangent assertions of the *limits* of British military power in the post-war period was to be repeated again and again during his time as CIGS. Across Europe and even within the British empire, his gut reaction to disorder or challenge was simply to 'govern or get out'. Where essential British interests were not directly affected, as in the Balkans or Russia, or along the more remote frontiers of the Middle East, withdrawal was the best option. British power had to be husbanded and, as he was increasingly to stress, concentrated only on those places 'vital' to the existence of the empire.

Happily (for the Allies) the Germans, after a short delay, agreed unconditionally to sign the treaty. Wilson, en route for London, heard the news in Le Havre on 22 June. 'P. T. [his private secretary Major W. W. Pitt Taylor] & I went for a walk in the town,' wrote Wilson in his diary: 'Great crowds but on the whole very quiet & orderly. We went into a Chapel which was lit up, crowds passing in & out and looking at a figure (lit up) of the Virgin Mary. So after nearly 5 years of war here comes Peace at last, & yet I am as certain as I can be that the Boches have no intention of carrying out our Peace Terms, & in my judgment this ending is a disaster.'[43]

The actual signing of the Versailles treaty took place a week later, on the fifth anniversary of the Sarajevo assassinations. Coloured perhaps by his disenchantment with the work of the 'Frocks', Wilson had nothing good to say about the occasion. Some thousand people, he reckoned, had crowded into the Hall of Mirrors, including '150 ladies which I thought all wrong'. The two German representatives, Herman Müller and Johannes Bell, 'were a villainous looking couple'

[41] Wilson diary, 28 Mar., 26 Apr., 3 May 1919.
[42] Wilson to Lloyd George, 16 June 1919 (Wilson papers, HHW 2/90/21).
[43] Wilson diary, 22 June 1919.

with 'low typed faces & a sort of 3rd Class School master demeanour & carriage'. The Germans were followed by a long succession of Allied signatories. 'I have never seen a less impressive ceremony', wrote Wilson. There was 'a constant buzz of conversation', and the whole thing was 'unreal, shoddy, poor to a degree. The fountains played & some guns fired & we went away. Considerable but very undemonstrative crowds & the thing was over. It only took 45 minutes from 3.10 pm to 3.55 O'c.'[44]

It was not all work in Paris. Wilson evidently enjoyed the conference socialising, and his cheerful gregariousness made him a welcome guest at lunch or dinner. Frances Stevenson, Lloyd George's secretary and mistress, noted a 'merry lunch' with Wilson on a crossing from London to Paris in March 1919. A couple of months later: 'Dined at the Pré Catelan. Evelyn Fitzgerald being the host. D. ['David'—Lloyd George] & Churchill & C.I.G.S. & others there also, & we had a very merry time.'[45] Wilson enjoyed female company. From the summer of 1918 and throughout 1919 he regularly saw Beatrice, wife of the Earl of Pembroke, though apparently without any (or much) impropriety. He nicknamed her 'Prisoner' in his diary, and noted six meetings between 13 August and 19 September 1918.[46] She was a friend of Lord Derby's daughter, Victoria, and came with her to stay at the embassy in Paris, where Wilson took them both out for drives in his car.[47] Wilson continued to see her in 1919, both in London and again in Paris, occasionally accompanied by Cecil.[48] A good social 'catch', Wilson also appears to have been pursued by various hostesses. One Friday night in April, Wilson and Lady Johnstone, the American wife of Sir Alan Johnstone, who was British minister at The Hague, 1910–17, dined with Lloyd George and Frances Stevenson. 'Lady Johnstone', the latter recorded, 'is one of these rather vain women, who have been very beautiful & still expect a lot of attention. She made a great fuss of C.I.G.S., trying to give the impression that he was fond of her—as he may be— but was very annoyed when he refused her invitation to spend Sunday with him. He turned to me & said under his breath: "You see, I like to start the week fresh." '[49]

While at the peace conference Wilson also had his portrait painted by a fellow Irishman (and family acquaintance) Sir William Orpen, a British official war artist

[44] Wilson diary, 28 June 1919. Margaret MacMillan reports a 'huge and enthusiastic crowd' (*Peacemakers*, 487).

[45] Frances Stevenson diary, 5 Mar., 17 May 1919 (Stevenson papers, FLS/4/11). Capt. Evelyn Fitzgerald, a stockbroker by profession, was private secretary to Gen. Sir John Cowans, Dec. 1914–Mar. 1919.

[46] She also appears as 'P.' and 'B.P.' (Wilson diary, 13, 28 Aug., 4, 5, 19, 20 Sept. 1918). In two of these entries (13 Aug. and 19 Sept.) 'Lady Pembroke' has been written next to 'Prisoner' in what looks very like Cecil Wilson's handwriting.

[47] Ibid., 5–8, 27–9 Oct. 1918. See also mentions of 'Lady B.' (Beatrice) in Lord Derby's diary, Oct.–Nov. 1918, quoted in Dutton, *Paris 1918*, 246–334.

[48] See, e.g. Wilson diary, 8, 16, 18, 30 Jan., 7, 21, 24, 26 Feb., and 15, 21, 24, 29 Mar. 1919.

[49] Frances Stevenson diary, 4 Apr. 1919 (Stevenson papers, FLS/4/11). Asked about Henry Wilson's relations with women, his niece, Bridget, Lady Blackburne, said that he 'liked good looking women', and that, while Lady Pembroke was a 'great girl friend', it 'didn't mean they slept together' (in conversation with the author, 8 May 1985).

who had been kept on in France to record the proceedings. Wilson left an account of the experience in his diary: 2 March 1919: 'I gave Orpen an hour's sitting for my portrait. Result clever but appalling!'; 7 March: 'I gave Orpen another hour's sitting. His picture is very clever but it makes me look an <u>awful</u> blackguard'; 9 March: 'I gave Orpen a third sitting. The picture is slightly less repulsive.' Orpen recalled Wilson giving 'his views on the brains and merits of many of the delegates, views full of wit and brilliant criticism'. Apparently stung by the portrait, Wilson called Orpen 'a nasty little wasp', and informed him that 'he kept a "black book" for any of his lady friends who said the sketch was like him.'[50] Wilson told Frances Stevenson that Orpen's portrait was 'going to fetch the biggest price any portrait ever fetched. There are going to be two bidders—one is Scotland Yard; the other is Madame Tussaud's.' Stevenson herself sat for Orpen, whom she described as ' a charming little man'. The Wilson portrait she thought was 'wonderfully good'.[51]

Having his picture painted by one of the most fashionable society portrait-painters of the day reflected the extent to which Wilson was now established in the highest levels of the British military hierarchy. As one of 'the men who had won the war', moreover, he was due for numerous public rewards. In June 1919 Churchill offered him 'a Peerage and a Grant' or promotion to Field Marshal. 'So of course I accepted the Field Marshal.'[52] For a career soldier, promotion to the highest rank of all was the greatest possible military reward. Recommending the promotion to the Prime Minister, Churchill argued that Wilson's great services constituted 'an ample case for a Field-Marshal's baton', even though he had 'not held a great command in the field'. During the war the responsibilities of the CIGS, he asserted, had been 'very similar to those of a Commander-in-Chief in the field'.[53]

The public announcement of Wilson's promotion was made by Lloyd George on 24 July at a dinner given for Wilson in the House of Commons, and attended by over 200 MPs.[54] Lloyd George, generous and fulsome, said that Wilson had 'rendered three very distinguished services' to his country: the organisation before August 1914 of the expeditionary force, 'the work he did in smoothing difficulties between Allies', and 'the part he took in co-ordinating the strategy of the Allies and getting something like unity of command'. Wilson replied with one of those whimsical offerings which his admirers loved and his critics deplored. He told the

---

[50] Orpen, *An Onlooker in France*, 105.

[51] Frances Stevenson diary, 3, 4 Apr. 1919 (Stevenson papers, FLS/4/11). The painting of Wilson is now in the National Portrait Gallery, London.

[52] Wilson diary, 22 June 1919.

[53] Churchill to Lloyd George, 23 June 1919 (Gilbert, *Winston S. Churchill*, iv. Companion Part 1, 710). On his recommendation, Plumer and Allenby were also promoted to field marshal.

[54] The dinner was remarkable in that, although both lamb and chicken were on the menu, the only red wine served was port, Dow 1904, which (albeit a light vintage) seems very young. The other wines were (in order): 'Old Golden' sherry, Loudenne Blanc (a Bordeaux), and champagne (Melnotte extra sec 1906, a very good year) (menu in Wilson papers, HHW 2/90/28).

story (an old favourite) of how, when a young lieutenant stationed in Belfast in 1891, a messenger charged with delivering a telegram to 'the ugliest man in the British Army' had unerringly found him. He paid particular tribute to two French generals (Huguet and Foch), three British officers (French, Haig, and Maurice Hankey, whom he described as 'Hanky panky'), and three 'Frocks' (which he explained meant 'Statesmen—terms of endearment'): his successive chiefs as War Minister, Derby, Milner, and Churchill. Finally, Wilson praised the Prime Minister, who had invariably been 'kind, considerate, and helpful'.[55] Wilson was officially gazetted with the promotion on 31 July, and, at the age of 55, became the second-youngest non-royal Field Marshal (after Wellington) in the history of the British army.[56] A week later, along with other rewards for war service, Lloyd George told parliament that Wilson was to be made a baronet (a hereditary knighthood) and receive a grant of £10,000.[57] There were also honorary degrees from Cambridge, Trinity College Dublin, Oxford (in 1921), and Queen's University, Belfast (1922). In 1920 he was given the freedom of the city of Belfast, the 'only town', he told the assembled civic dignitaries, he 'wanted to be freeman of'.[58]

Wilson's promotion (his pay as a field marshal was £3,600 a year) and the £10,000 grant improved his financial situation, which was just as well, since Jemmy was clearly having difficulty extracting income from the old family estate at Currygrane. In June he resolved to help his elder brother by paying for his niece Bridget's schooling.[59] In the autumn of 1919 Henry and Cecil began some leisurely house-hunting, looking at various properties on the south coast and in the home counties, but nothing came of this. They still had Grove End, where Wilson loved to escape for a spot of intensive gardening. On Palm Sunday 1920, for example: 'A whole day in garden. No bag nor telephone from W.O. Such peace.'[60] The Wilson's housekeeper in 1919 fondly described their stays at Grove End as a kind of 'idyll' of 'ripe middle age, when they came down for week ends'. The Wilsons 'were like a pair of happy children, Sir Henry threw off his London clothes, [and] put on his old garden ones'. Lady Wilson 'had a skirt about 27 years of age, both ran out to the garden, digging, planting, raking, enjoying every minute of the day'. When Cecil came down ahead of her husband, 'she & I had a busy time polishing the table, doing the flowers, everything to "Make it nice for Henry". No wife could have been more devoted, no husband more appreciative of what she did.'[61]

In the spring of 1920 he bought a yacht from Lord Dundonald. It was a 40-ton cutter, *White Heather*, which cost him £850. Wilson kept the boat on the Solent,

---

[55] *The Times*, 25 July 1919. 'What a speech for the chief soldier of the Empire at the end of the greatest war', reflected Robertson (Robertson to H. A. Gwynne, 26 July 1919 (Gwynne papers)).

[56] Since Wilson, only Harold Alexander, in 1944, has become a field marshal at a younger age.

[57] Robertson was also awarded a baronetcy and £10,000; Haig got an earldom and £100,000 (*Hansard*, 6 Aug. 1919 (119 H.C. Deb. 5s, col. 415–21)). The money was held in trust and only the income could be used (see Bonham-Carter, *The Strategy of Victory*, 377).

[58] *The Times*, 8 Apr. 1920.   [59] Wilson diary, 3 June 1919.   [60] Ibid., 28 Mar. 1920.

[61] First World War memoirs of Mrs Rose Bingham, p. 16 (Bingham papers, PP/MCR/326).

and was to get huge pleasure out of her. Nevertheless, and perhaps because of this new expenditure, money seems to have remained tight, and for £325 Wilson let 36 Eaton Place for seven weeks in the middle of 1920, while he moved into a small flat in Knightsbridge and Cecil stayed at Grove End.[62] A year later he replaced *White Heather* with a 50-ton yawl, *Pleiad*, which he bought for £1,850.[63] Although his finances had apparently improved, this was a considerable extravagance, especially when put in the context of his money as a whole. His estate in 1922 amounted to just £10,678 10*s*. 11*d*., which presumably included the value of the yacht.

After the signing of the Versailles treaty Lloyd George turned from foreign to domestic affairs. The prospect he had offered in the 1918 election campaign of domestic reconstruction and reform was underpinned by a fundamental democratisation of the British political system, In 1918, for the first time, all adult males had the vote, which had also been extended to most adult females, resulting in a threefold expansion of the electorate. This, in turn, underscored the increasing importance of public opinion to policy-making. Lloyd George, a populist politician par excellence, and, unusually, a Prime Minister with no secure party base, set very great store by the 'touchstone' of opinion. During the post-war years, moreover, there was evidently not much political mileage in 'defence', and behind the Whitehall and Westminster policy debates there was, as Michael Howard put it, 'the heavy and ominous breathing of a parsimonious and pacific electorate'.[64]

This was the context of the wide-ranging review of government policy which Lloyd George embarked upon on his return from Paris. On 5 August he told the Cabinet that scarce resources had to be directed away from the armed forces and towards social and industrial reconstruction. He warned his colleagues about the effect on public opinion of continuing high military spending. British arms, he observed, 'had destroyed the only enemy we had in Europe', and if the country now 'maintained a larger Army and Navy and Air Force than we had before we entered the War, people would say, either that the War had been a failure, or that we were making provision to fight an imaginary foe'. While external threats had been eliminated, there were now dangers on the domestic front. The government 'could not take risks with labour. If we did,' he continued, 'we should at once create an enemy within our own borders, and one which would be better provided with dangerous weapons than Germany.' The first priority, therefore, was to provide for 'the health and labour of the people and to lay at once the sure foundations of national health and industrial prosperity'. The inexorable logic of this meant serious spending cuts for the service ministries. Churchill, as secretary for both war and air, hazarded that the army, 2 million strong at the beginning of

---

[62] Wilson diary, 19–20 May 1920. Eaton Place was let for 48 guineas a week; Wilson rented the flat for £8 a week.   [63] Ibid., 20 Oct. 1921, 14 Mar. 1922.

[64] Howard, *Continental Commitment*, 79. The Treasury was equally parsimonious, if not also pacific (see O'Halpin, *Head of the Civil Service*, 112–23). For Lloyd George's attitude, see Morgan, *Consensus and Disunity*, 148.

1919, could be reduced to about 320,000 men by the following spring. This compared to a pre-war figure of about 255,000. When Lloyd George asked why so much larger a force was required than in 1914, Churchill remarked that 'our responsibilities during the War had considerably increased, especially in regard to Ireland and the East'.[65]

Arising from this discussion came the definition of the famous 'ten year rule' at a Cabinet meeting ten days later. The rule instructed the service ministries, when framing their estimates, to assume that 'the British Empire will not be engaged in any great war during the next ten years, and that no Expeditionary Force is required for this purpose'. It was affirmed that the 'principal function' of the army and air force was 'to provide garrisons for India, Egypt, the new mandated territory ... under British control, as well as to provide the necessary support to the civil power at home'. With this in mind, it was finally agreed that the navy should aim at a maximum estimate of £60 million, and the army and air force should aim at a *joint* estimate of £75 million. This compared to total defence expenditure for 1919–20 of £766 million.[66] Wilson accepted the Cabinet's primary assumptions, as he put it, 'that no great European War was likely for some years, that no invasion was possible & that we were terribly impoverished', and concluded that savings should be made on home defence. Yet outside Britain, like Churchill, he thought that 'our own dangers' were 'much greater than in 1914'. The only sensible way to proceed was with an assessment 'of what troops we require to keep our four storm centres quiet—Ireland, Egypt, Mesopotamia & India. From these requirements we can build & not from the allotment of an arbitrary sum.'[67]

Concerns about domestic security, which had been sharpened by labour unrest at the end of 1918, were revived by another railway strike in September 1919. Troops were deployed to keep the trains running, but Wilson worried about the available manpower in any future strike. Instead of the 100,000 men then available, following the completion of demobilisation, he would be left with only 40,000 infantry, made up of 12,000 temporarily retained conscripts and 28,000 regulars 'mostly recruits with young and inexperienced non-commissioned officers, and weak in training and discipline'. It was 'of paramount importance', he told the Cabinet, that the army 'should not be used, except as a last resort, in any future industrial disturbances, but be allowed to prepare itself for its legitimate duties in the defence of the Empire'.[68]

All the same, there were persistent anxieties concerning the possibilities of disorder fuelled by labour unrest. On 15 January 1920 Wilson went to a meeting

---

[65] War Cabinet meeting, 5 Aug. 1919 (TNA, CAB 23/15/606A). See also Ferris, *The Evolution of British Strategic Policy*, for a useful and provocative account.

[66] War Cabinet meeting, 15 Aug. 1919 (TNA, CAB 23/15/616A).

[67] Wilson diary, 7 and 15 Aug. 1919. These views were embodied in a Cabinet memo, 'The Future of the army', circulated by Churchill, 20 Aug. 1919 (TNA, CAB 24/87, GT8039).

[68] 'The employment of troops in industrial disturbances', 12 Nov. 1919 (TNA, CAB 24/93, CP111).

of the Cabinet 'supply and transport' committee which had been set up specifically to make plans for coping with serious strikes. 'An amazing meeting', he noted. 'One after another got up & said that we were going to have the triple Red revolution strike. One after another said there was nothing to be done... not one of them except Walter [Long, First Lord of the Admiralty] & Winston [Churchill] were [*sic*] prepared to put up a fight.'[69] Wilson, Churchill, and Long had been summoned to Paris by Lloyd George for a meeting of the Supreme War Council (which continued to deal with peace-settlement business), and they travelled over that same Thursday evening. Over the weekend they retailed the alarmist opinions circulating in London, but to a rather sceptical audience. At nine o'clock on Monday morning Bonar Law, still in bed, was treated to a long harangue from Wilson about the perilous state of England, but 'Bonar said he did not believe in a Revolution'.[70] Hankey thought Wilson and the others simply had the 'wind up', and told Lloyd George it 'was difficult to understand the reason for the very obvious preoccupation of the First Lord and the C.I.G.S. as to the future'. So far as he could judge, 'although there were many clouds on the horizon, the sky seemed to be getting clearer'.[71] Lloyd George, in any case, was more concerned with treating the causes of domestic discontent than merely addressing the symptoms. As Tom Jones, Assistant Cabinet Secretary, put it: 'What Churchill and co. forget is that there are other means of averting discontent than with civil guards and the military.'[72]

Back in London, however, Wilson had the General Staff work on plans for 'mutiny & Revolution' in Great Britain, and early in February he outlined to a meeting of home army commanders his 'proposals of 18 Battns (of which 10 are Guard) to safeguard London', and his general policy of concentrating troops in the south of England, but 'near the salt water' in case (with a railway strike) they had to be moved by sea.[73] During the spring and early summer of 1920 the position at home seemed to improve, despite a deteriorating economic situation producing inflation, pay-cuts, and rising unemployment. But in September came the prospect of a national coal strike, accompanied by reports of unrest among unemployed ex-servicemen. 'It must be remembered', reported the police Special Branch ominously, 'that in the event of rioting, for the first time in history the rioters will be better trained than the troops.'[74] The army's plans were dusted off in October when the miners came out and it seemed that the railwaymen and transport workers might join them. Wilson feverishly made arrangements to move tanks, which he had concentrated at Woolwich, to 'Scotland, York,

---

[69] Wilson diary, 15 Jan. 1920.   [70] Ibid., 19 Jan. 1920.
[71] Hankey to Lloyd George, 17 Jan. 1920 (Lloyd George papers, F/24/2/3).
[72] Jones to Hankey, 19 Jan. 1920 (quoted in Jones, *Whitehall Diary*, i. 98).
[73] Wilson diary, 15, 22, 28 Jan., 2, 6 Feb. 1920. For the wider context, see Jeffery, 'The British Army and Internal Security'.
[74] Home Office Directorate of Intelligence weekly 'Report on revolutionary organisations in the U.K.', 2 Sept. 1920 (TNA, CAB 24/111, CP1830).

Worcester & Aldershot'.[75] This time even Hankey was rattled. 'I cannot see my way through these strikes,' he wrote, 'I think that economic causes will break them in time, but there are extremists at work and serious trouble may come.'[76] But the government, which had taken national control of the mines during the war, temporarily settled the strike on the miners' terms, leaving a more permanent arrangement to be made after the pits were handed back to their private owners, which was scheduled to happen at the end of March 1921.

Throughout his time as CIGS, one of Wilson's most persistent concerns was the problem of simultaneously having to meet demands for military manpower at home and abroad. In the autumn of 1920, for example, the domestic industrial crisis coincided with a rebellion in Mesopotamia and fears that troops might be required in Egypt, where there was an upsurge of nationalist feeling. In February 1921, on holiday in Madrid (though regularly receiving War Office papers), he pondered on whether 'we shall want troops in England', while 'we certainly should in Ireland', in Constantinople, and in India.[77] One commitment which particularly irritated him was for troops to supervise a League of Nations plebiscite in Silesia, which was being partitioned between Germany and Poland under the terms of the peace treaty. On his return to London, Wilson learnt that a coal strike was in the offing, and that the 'Triple Alliance' as a whole might come out. 'This is nice,' he thought, 'seeing we have only 10 Guard & 18 Line Battns (of which 7 are Irish) in the U.K. & we are just sending 4 Battns from the Rhine to Silesia.'[78]

On 1 April the mine-owners, having failed to come to any agreement with the union leaders, began a lock-out. The next day Wilson went down to Chequers to see Lloyd George and urged on him 'the necessity for bringing back the 4 Battns from Silesia'. He argued that even if the Triple Alliance did not strike, 'we would still want them for Ireland', and told the Prime Minister that unless he could bring back not only the Silesian battalions, but also three from Malta, one from Egypt and, if possible, two from Constantinople and three more from the Rhine command, he 'would only be able to hold England at the cost of losing Ireland ... I asked L.G. if he wanted to be PM of England or of Silesia.' On 4 April the Cabinet, 'notwithstanding the political objections to a withdrawal of troops from Upper Silesia', agreed that 'the risk at home from Sinn Feiners, Communists, and other dangerous elements, was sufficiently great to necessitate their return'.[79] Wilson scraped up what forces he could, ordering battalions home from Malta and Egypt, mobilising the Reserves, and borrowing sailors from the Admiralty. It was also decided to raise a special paramilitary 'Defence Force', which eventually numbered some 80,000 men.[80]

[75] Wilson diary, 21 Oct. 1920.
[76] Hankey diary, 22 Oct. 1920 (Hankey papers, HNKY 1/5).
[77] Wilson diary, 20 Feb. 1921.   [78] Ibid., 28 Feb. 1921.
[79] Ibid., 2 Apr. 1921; Cabinet meeting, 4 Apr. 1921 (TNA, CAB 23/25/17(21)).
[80] Jeffery and Hennessy, *States of Emergency*, 58–64.

In the end the crisis abated. On 15 April—'Black Friday'—the Triple Alliance failed to strike and the miners had to struggle on alone until they returned to work, defeated, on the owners' terms at the start of July. Economic depression and mass unemployment took the steam out of labour militancy, and the threat (real or perceived) of a British revolution passed. But in Henry Rawlinson's view the emergency had had its advantages for Wilson. 'The crisis', he wrote, 'will have been useful to you in gaining your ends. It will, at any rate, have frightened the "frocks" into withdrawing some of their more distant commitments, and make you stronger at home in the event of any serious trouble.'[81]

Be that as it may, 'more distant commitments' were trouble enough, and Wilson laboured mightily between 1919 and 1922 to reduce these to manageable levels. Frequently he had the support of generals on the spot, if not also of politicians at home. The Caucasus was a case in point. The British presence there was regarded as vital by Lord Curzon, who succeeded Balfour as Foreign Secretary in October 1919. The troops who had to implement this policy took a different view. George Milne went on a tour of inspection at the start of 1919. 'The country and the inhabitants', he wrote to Wilson while travelling between Tiflis and Baku, 'are equally loathesome and we seem to be accepting an enormous responsibility for no very good reason.' Milne accepted that a British withdrawal 'would probably lead to anarchy', but he could not see 'that the world would lose much if the whole of the country cut each other's throats. They are certainly not worth the life of a single British soldier.'[82] Wilson agreed. In an important paper on 'the military situation throughout the British empire, with special reference to the inadequacy of the numbers of troops available', which Churchill circulated to the Cabinet on 3 May 1919, Wilson reaffirmed that he had 'for a long time past consistently urged that all military commitments not vital to the British Empire should be cut down with a view to concentrating all available troops at the essential points'. A British division had been deployed in the Caucasus to oversee the evacuation of Turks and Germans. This had now been accomplished, 'and nothing is to be gained by delaying the withdrawal of our troops. On the contrary, every day that we stay there sees us more deeply committed and makes it more difficult to disentangle ourselves.' Hopes had been raised that the Italians might send troops, but their 'alleged intention' to 'take over this hornet's [*sic*] nest is hardly a sufficient reason for further delay'.[83]

While the Italians (wisely) never got involved in the Caucasus, the continuing pressure of demobilisation and calls for British troops in other places, forced withdrawals from the region. At the end of August, Baku and the Caspian naval personnel were evacuated. By about mid-October 1919 the only troops remaining in the Caucasus were three infantry battalions at Batum. This was still too much for Wilson. In January 1920 he told a ministerial conference that 'the real question'

[81] Rawlinson to Wilson, 27 Apr. 1921 (Wilson papers, HHW 2/13D/16).
[82] Milne to Wilson, 22 Jan. 1919 (ibid. 2/37/5).
[83] Memo by CIGS, 26 Apr. 1919 (TNA, CAB 24/78, GT7182).

was the defence of India and Mesopotamia, and that 'the command of the Caspian did not affect the defence of India unless we were prepared to hold the line Batoum—Baku—Krasnovodsk—Merv', which would entail retaining troops indefinitely in the Caucasus, with an enormous expense of men and money. Although Lloyd George agreed with Wilson, Curzon dug in his heels and the troops stayed.[84] Wilson then adopted underhand tactics. Early in February he took advantage of Curzon's absence in France on holiday to persuade the Cabinet to sanction evacuation, but on his return Curzon got the decision reversed.[85] With Bolshevik forces advancing down the eastern coast of the Black Sea, Wilson then unilaterally gave Milne complete authority to withdraw from Batum at any moment, if he thought the position was untenable. Curzon, furious, complained to Bonar Law about Wilson's 'unpardonable abuse of authority'.[86] But Wilson was not to be put off. 'Batoum is getting into a mess,' he wrote in his diary on 12 April, '& I have written F.O. for the 100th time saying I want to get out of it. . . . Our interference in everybody's business is madness.' On 5 May the Cabinet discussed Batum, '& to my disgust Curzon by a long winded jaw persuaded the Cabinet to allow our 2 Battns to remain on for the present. Winston did not fight. I did but was overruled. I am very disgusted as we shall now be kicked out, a most undignified proceeding.'[87]

The 'kicking out', in fact, happened not at Batum but from Enzeli on the Caspian Sea coast in north-west Persia. On 19 May Wilson received a wire from Teheran 'to say our garrison at Enzeli . . . had been surrounded by Bolsheviks and made prisoners! A nice state of affairs which will have a <u>bad</u> effect in the East. For months I have been begging the Cabinet to allow me to withdraw from Persia & from the Caucasus. Now perhaps they will.'[88] The next day Churchill urged Curzon to allow an immediate British withdrawal from the Caucasus, Transcaspia, and Persia. 'If we are not able to resist the Bolsheviks in these areas,' he wrote, 'it is much better by timely withdrawals to keep out of harm's way and avoid disaster and shameful incidents such as that which has just occurred.' On 4 June Lloyd George gave his permission to evacuate Batum. Five days later the operation was completed.[89]

As Churchill had observed, the remaining British forces in Persia were also exposed to the Bolshevik threat. Curzon insisted on their retention, supported by Milner, the Colonial Secretary, who marshalled a series of classic imperial arguments. He had his own 'domino theory' for the region. If Persia were lost, he asserted, 'we should lose Mesopotamia & then India was in danger'. Colleagues,

---

[84] Conference of ministers, 18 Jan. 1920 (TNA, CAB 23/25, S11).

[85] Conference of ministers, 3 Feb., and Cabinet meeting, 18 Feb. 1920 (TNA, CAB 23/20/10(20), appendix II and 23/20/11(20)).

[86] Curzon to Bonar Law, 4 Mar. 1920 (Davidson papers).

[87] Wilson diary, 12 Apr. and 5 May 1920.   [88] Ibid., 19 May 1920.

[89] Churchill to Curzon, 20 May 1920 (Curzon papers, F.112/275); Wilson diary, 4 June 1920; Nicol, *Uncle George*, 214.

he told the Cabinet, were, moreover, confusing the *actual* high cost of maintaining troops in the region, while 'the whole of the Near East' was 'in a state of raging chaos', with the *probable* future costs, when, for example, some agreement had been reached with Russia. To this he added the self-justifying argument that with-drawal would mean that all the money already committed would simply have been wasted; a neat argument indeed. 'It is evident', he wrote, 'that if we have no policy at all but that of gradual withdrawal', the Persians were 'bound to lose all faith' in Britain: 'a Bolshevik Revolution in Persia would involve consequences for the British Empire which it would be worth our while to spend not one, but many millions to avert.' A final argument concerned Britain's 'vital' strategic and economic interest in the oil resources, actual in Persia and potential in Iraq.[90]

Little of this washed with Churchill or Wilson. 'Fancy spending the whole cost of a British Territorial Army on a weak and futile interference in the affairs of Persia!' wrote Churchill in February 1920, and he did not 'consider that the military resources of the British Empire on the voluntary system' would allow 'effective resistance to a Bolshevik advance short of the main frontiers of India'.[91] Through the summer of 1920 the two men repeatedly pressed for evacuation. In August, for example, they 'went over all the military reasons for coming out of Persia', and again 'all the old arguments were produced by Curzon and Milner to remain'.[92] The decision to withdraw was not finally made until late in 1920, when financial considerations forced the issue. 'The cry for retrenchment in this country', wrote Wilson in December, meant 'that the Government will be forced to come away from Persia.' So it was, and the evacuation began in the spring of 1921.[93]

Many of the arguments advanced for and against the British presence in Persia applied with equal force to Mesopotamia. Late in 1919 the General Staff had observed that, 'with Palestine, Arabia and Persia, Mesopotamia forms an impor-tant link in a chain of contiguous areas under British influence, extending from Egypt to India'.[94] Within a few months, however, they were beginning to worry about the costs of staying in the country. The main purpose of the wartime campaign had been to secure the southern Persian oilfields, which did not actually require the occupation of the whole 'vast territory'. But 'any attempted with-drawal' from it 'at the present moment may lead us into difficulties that would not have arisen had our advance in the first instance been limited'. Involvement in a predominantly Muslim country was a further consideration, and Wilson and his colleagues worried about the effect of the continuing delays in securing a satisfac-tory peace settlement with the Turks (which was not to be concluded until 1923).

[90] Wilson diary, 21 May 1920 (reporting Milner in Cabinet); memo by Milner, 24 May 1920 (TNA, CAB 24/106, CP1337).
[91] 'Note on the army estimates 1920–21', 7 Feb. 1920 (TNA, CAB 24/97, CP586).
[92] Wilson diary, 12 Aug. 1920.
[93] Wilson to Sir Aylmer Haldane (GOC Mesopotamia), 28 Dec. 1920 (Wilson papers, HHW 2/55/5); Cabinet meetings, 8 Dec. 1920 and 4 Jan. 1921 (TNA, CAB 23/23/67(20) and 23/24/1(21)).
[94] 'The situation in Mesopotamia', Nov. 1919 (TNA, CAB 24/93, CP120, appendix I).

The General Staff had, 'for many months, repeatedly pointed out that the policy of antagonizing the Turks, and thereby embittering the whole Mussulman world, was involving us in unnecessary expense at the present time and laying up for us untold liabilities in the future'.[95]

In May 1920 a joint paper from Churchill, Wilson, and Sir Hugh Trenchard (Chief of the Air Staff) highlighted 'the waste of money' entailed by the occupation of Mesopotamia. Churchill complained that there was an immense army (of about 10,000 British and 50,000 Indian troops) in the country, covering an enormous area at a vast cost. Warming to his theme in devastating Churchillian prose, the Secretary of State observed that:

a score of mud villages [this included the cities of Baghdad, Basra, and Mosul], sandwiched in between a swampy river and a blistering desert, inhabited by a few hundred half naked families [the population of Iraq was about 2.8 million], usually starving, are now occupied, have been occupied for many months, and are likely to remain so occupied in the future unless policy is changed, by Anglo-Indian garrisons on a scale which in India would maintain order in wealthy provinces of millions of people.

Wilson was less extravagant, merely describing the situation as 'very unsatisfactory'. Trenchard, however, offered a ray of hope for saving money with a 'preliminary scheme for the military control of Mesopotamia by the Royal Air Force'.[96]

Matters were brought to a head by a rebellion which broke out at the end of June 1920. The army commander in Baghdad, Sir Aylmer Haldane, soon began calling for reinforcements. On 15 July Wilson told Lloyd George that this was just what he had been prophesying, and that what was essential was 'concentration of forces'. He asked if he might withdraw from Persia, but the Prime Minister said 'Curzon would not stand it'.[97] On 18 August Wilson, who was worried by the worsening industrial situation at home and was being pressed to send more troops to Ireland, told Curzon that though 'our military resources are practically exhausted', the General Staff would 'carry out the Government policy to the best of our ability'.[98] Churchill similarly gave his reluctant support, telling Lloyd George he had 'told Henry Wilson that, now the Cabinet have definitely decided that we are to plough through in that dismal country, every effort must be made to procure vigorous action and decisive results'.[99] Although Haldane managed get the country back under control by October, the War Office felt that the events of the summer and autumn had demonstrated 'we ran things too fine and that a great disaster was only narrowly avoided'.[100]

---

[95] 'Possibility of reducing the garrison of Mesopotamia', 20 Feb. 1920 (TNA, CAB 24/99, CP707).   [96] 'Mesopotamia', 1 May 1920 (TNA, CAB 24/106, CP1320).
[97] Wilson diary, 15 July 1920.
[98] Wilson to Curzon, 18 Aug. 1920 (Wilson papers, HHW 2/20B/6).
[99] Churchill to Lloyd George, 26 Aug. 1920 (Lloyd George papers, F/9/2/41).
[100] 'The situation in Mesopotamia', memo by DMO, 'concurred in by CIGS', 10 Dec. 1920 (TNA, CAB 24/116, CP2275).

With the pressure for withdrawal intensifying, modern technology came to the rescue, and the Cabinet seized on Trenchard's 'air policing' scheme as a marvellous way of having their cake and eating it. Not only could they secure Iraq, but they would also save money, and Churchill, now Colonial Secretary, announced the scheme for air defence, supported by local Arab levies, as part of a wider, Middle Eastern settlement at the Cairo conference in June 1921, securing final Cabinet approval the following month.[101] Wilson, while glad that the army would be rid of responsibility for Iraq, did not think the country could be run by 'Hot Air, Aeroplanes & Arabs'.[102] 'Nor can Winston call on me any longer to pull him out of a mess,' he acidly wrote to Rawlinson (who had become Commander-in-Chief in India), 'nor can he call on you, and so having got into a mess, whenever that day comes, he can only hop into an aeroplane and fly away, shouting Ta-ta to any poor bloody native who is stupid enough to back us.'[103]

Wilson's objections to the retention of scattered garrisons across the Near and Middle East were primarily based on his perception of long-term British imperial interests, a realistic evaluation of the available resources, and the actual military situation on the ground. Many of the problems in the region, moreover, stemmed from the impact of 'war imperialism',[104] by which high levels of manpower and military spending, acceptable in wartime, continued largely unchecked in the immediate post-war period. Rather than any carefully planned and phased scaling-down of commitments, British politicians and service chiefs responded slowly and haphazardly as the costs of imperial over-extension became increasingly hard to bear. From a military perspective, however, Wilson endeavoured to systematise the challenges by ranking the problems of imperial defence in order of priority. In July 1920 he noted in his diary: 'What is essential is <u>concentration</u> of forces in theatres <u>vital</u> to us viz:—England, Ireland, Egypt, India, Mesopot. In that order.'[105] A few weeks later, in a paper for the Cabinet finance committee, he asserted that 'ever since January 1920' the General Staff had 'consistently and repeatedly advocated the urgent necessity of concentrating our forces in those areas which are vital to us'. The highest priority, he said, should be given to the defence of the 'main bases' of the empire: Great Britain and Ireland in the west, and India in the east. 'On their stability', he continued, 'depends the whole political, economic and military structure of the Empire.' Next in importance was Egypt, 'the "Clapham Junction" of Imperial communications, and the chief connecting link

[101] Cabinet meeting, 18 Aug. 1921 (TNA, CAB 23/26/70(21)). For Churchill's wider Middle East settlement, see Darwin, *Britain, Egypt and the Middle East*, 208–42 (this is an especially good treatment of post-war imperial policy in the region); and Klieman, *Foundations of British Policy*.

[102] Wilson diary, 2 Dec. 1921.

[103] Wilson to Rawlinson, 5 Oct. 1921 (Wilson papers, HHW 2/13E/29). 'Air policing' actually had some modest success, though the establishment in Iraq of stable government under British hegemony was as much due to wider political factors as the specific efficacy of the RAF (see Omissi, *Air Power and Colonial Control*, for a useful critical discussion of the technique).

[104] A concept usefully illuminated in Darwin, *Britain, Egypt and the Middle East*, e.g. 208.

[105] Wilson diary, 15 July 1920.

between the two main bases'. Then there followed (in rank order) 'areas of only secondary importance': the Rhine ('an outpost to Great Britain'), Mesopotamia ('oil fuel'), Palestine, Persia, and the Black Sea.[106]

Despite Wilson's success in securing the evacuation from the Caucasus, he failed in his efforts to bring home the remaining occupation forces in Turkey. Lloyd George was untypically inflexible regarding the Turkish peace settlement. He was 'persuaded that the Greeks are the coming power in the Mediterranean',[107] and his adamant philo-Hellenism was embedded in the Treaty of Sèvres, signed in August 1920 with the Turks, which (among other things) transferred territory in Asia Minor to both Italy and Greece. Lloyd George was prepared to support Greek territorial ambitions, as a reward for siding with the Allies in the war and in the hope that a strong Greece, backed by Britain, could help secure British strategic interests in the region.[108] Although the Greeks briefly succeeded in pushing back Turkish forces in both Thrace and Anatolia in the summer of 1920, Wilson (rightly as it turned out) had no confidence in their long-term ability to become the predominant power in the Near East. In the autumn of 1919, worried about the dangers of alienating Muslim opinion by imposing a harsh treaty on the Turks, he had argued that Britain ought to 'make love to the Turk'.[109]

During 1920 and 1921 Wilson pressed for a British withdrawal from Constantinople, particularly in the face of resurgent Turkish power under the nationalist leader Kemal Atatürk (as he was to become). Wilson told a Cabinet committee in June 1921 that the situations in Turkey and Ireland 'were substantially the same & the choice of solutions the same i.e. either knock the gentlemen on the head or come out'. In Ireland, he argued, 'we must knock the gentlemen on the head so we can't come out. In Turkey we can't knock the gentlemen on the head & so we must come out, but come out & make love to Kemal.'[110] In December he wrote to his old friend Tim Harington, by this time commanding the remaining British occupation forces in Turkey: 'We will never do any good until we clear out of Constantinople altogether, and we will certainly never do any good until we make friends with the Turks.'[111] But it was not to be, at least during Wilson's lifetime. Lloyd George's continued tough line towards the Turks led to the 'Chanak crisis' of September–October 1922, when war with Turkey was threatened, and which precipitated the fall of his government. Not until a new peace treaty, that of Lausanne, replaced Sèvres in 1923, were Anglo-Turkish relations established on a more secure basis.

The British retention of Palestine, which was taken on as a 'mandate' from the League of Nations, was another failure for Wilson. After a meeting with Chaim

[106] Memo by CIGS, 5 Aug. 1920, Cabinet finance committee FC49 (Philby papers, box 6, file 3).
[107] Wilson diary, 15 June 1920.
[108] For the general context of the Turkish peace settlement, see Dockrill and Gould, *Peace without Promise*, 181–252.
[109] Wilson to Sackville-West, 11 Oct. 1919 (Wilson papers, HHW 2/12E/7).
[110] Wilson diary, 1 June 1921
[111] Wilson to Harington, 14 Dec. 1921 (Wilson papers, HHW 2/46B/42).

Weizmann (the Zionist leader and later first President of Israel) in May 1919, Wilson professed himself 'all in favour of the Zionist movement', apparently on the grounds that Jews, rather than British troops, could take over responsibility for the territory.[112] Palestine, he thought, was one of 'those countries which do not belong to us', and from which Britain should withdraw. He told 'Squibbie' Congreve (the British Commander in Cairo) that 'the problem of Palestine' was 'exactly the same... as the problem of Ireland, namely two peoples living in a small country hating each other like hell for the love of God'. The only answer, he thought, was 'to have an over-riding authority so strong that it can enforce its will on both opposing parties'. In Palestine, however, Britain could not do that, 'for the simple reason that we have not got the troops'. In Ireland, by contrast, and echoing his observations regarding Turkey, he said 'we <u>must</u> be that over-riding authority for the simple reason that we cannot lose the country'.[113]

Unlike Palestine, Egypt was one of the places Wilson thought 'belonged' to Britain. It, too, was compared with Ireland. Both were increasingly recalcitrant imperial territories during the post-war years. A quickly suppressed nationalist rising in the spring of 1919 prompted Lloyd George to appoint Milner to head an inquiry into the future government of the country. When, in the summer of 1920, Milner proposed to give the Egyptians at least some degree of autonomy, Lord Allenby, High Commissioner in Cairo, felt sure it would make 'another Ireland' out of Egypt.[114] What he failed to see, in fact, was that Egypt was already 'another Ireland', since, following the Egyptian rising, the British had been 'reduced to negotiating with men whom before 1914 they were accustomed to manage'.[115] The analogy with Ireland, however, was apt enough, and illustrates the interconnectedness of imperial strategic and defence policy: committing troops to one place produced strains in another; making concessions to nationalists in one part of the empire could encourage activists elsewhere. In August 1920 Churchill told the Cabinet that Milner's proposal to give Egypt a sovereign status outside the empire provided a distressing example both for Ireland and India. Wilson added that the restriction of the British garrison to the Suez Canal area, dependent merely on a proposed treaty with the newly independent Egypt (as Milner recommended), 'must have a far-reaching effect on the military situation of the British Empire'. It would, he confided to his diary, be 'a long step towards the ruin of our Empire'.[116] When the gist of Milner's proposals was contained in the 'Allenby Declaration' of February 1922, which conceded formal independence to Egypt while reserving Britain's 'special interests' in the country, Wilson thought 'the white flag is once more up over 10 Downing Street'.[117]

---

[112] Wilson diary, 16 May 1919.
[113] Wilson to Aylmer Haldane, 28 Dec. 1920; and to Walter Congreve, 12 July 1921 (Wilson papers, HHW 2/55/5 and 2/52B/20).   [114] Wilson diary, 8 Sept. 1920.
[115] Kedourie, 'Sa'ad Zaghlul and the British', 152.
[116] Cabinet memo, 'The Egyptian proposals', 25 Aug. 1920 (TNA, CAB 24/111, CP1803); Wilson diary, 24 Aug. 1920.   [117] Wilson diary, 17 Feb. 1922.

But he was wrong, at least in the short term. Negotiation, compromise, and concession (Lloyd George's 'genius for giving in') supplied in Egypt what pure military force, even if available, was unable to do. From 1922 moderate Egyptian nationalist politicians were found who were prepared to work the system more or less within the British guidelines for the next generation or so, securing British strategic interests in the region, and, with local security subcontracted to local politicians, doing so at comparatively low cost (politically as well as financially). In this respect the parallel with Ireland, in fact, is extremely close, a point which Henry Wilson could not, or *would* not, ever accept.

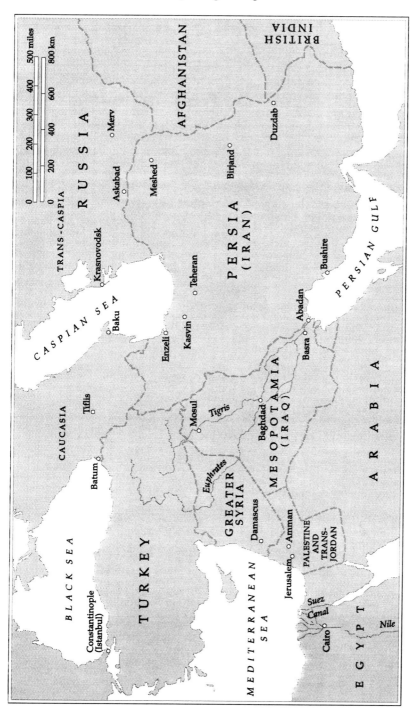

The Middle East, 1918–22

13

Losing Ireland and saving Ulster

A fortnight before the Versailles treaty was signed, in one of a number of long, chatty letters to Wully Robertson (then commanding the occupation army on the Rhine), Wilson remarked that 'Ireland goes from bad to worse and it seems to me that we cannot get out of it, and ought not to get out of it now, without a little blood letting'.[1] What level of violence Wilson meant by 'a little blood letting' is unclear. There is no indication that he anticipated a revival of anything like the organised military conflict of Easter 1916. That he felt there *ought* to be 'a little blood letting', however, clearly stemmed from his belief in the robust and exemplary enforcement of 'law and order'. *Any* violent challenge to what he saw as the properly constituted government of Ireland *must* firmly be resisted. There was nothing much out of the ordinary about this opinion; few people outside extremist political circles were prepared to condone political violence in Ireland. But what particularly distinguished Wilson's position was its unswerving consistency over the years 1919–21. Indeed, his obdurate refusal to contemplate any accommodation with militant Irish separatists was to have serious consequences, both professionally and personally. As elsewhere in the empire, in Ireland it was simply 'govern' or 'get out'. But, unlike other places, he did not regard 'getting out' of Ireland as an acceptable option. As had been demonstrated during the pre-war 'home rule crisis' and with Irish conscription, the one area in which the allegedly supple and pliable Wilson proved utterly inflexible was his homeland.

What has become known as the 'Irish war of independence'[2] is conventionally regarded as having begun on 21 January 1919, when two policemen guarding a consignment of quarry explosive were killed at Soloheadbeg, county Tipperary, by an ambushing party of Irish Volunteers.[3] But for all of 1919 and on into 1920 it

---

[1] Wilson to Robertson, 13 June 1919 (Wilson papers, HHW 2/1A/20).

[2] For a brief consideration of the problematic nomenclature of the conflict, see Jeffery, 'British Security Policy', 163–4.

[3] The authoritative *New History of Ireland Chronology of Irish History* (ed. Moody *et al.*), 396, says the date was 'afterwards regarded as beginning of war of independence'. Nicholas Mansergh wrote: 'Even though it was not immediately apparent, that event signalled the opening of the guerrilla fighting, retrospectively known as the Anglo-Irish war or the War of Independence' (Mansergh, *The Unresolved Question*, 3). Others are less circumspect. Alvin Jackson, for example, says Soloheadbeg marked 'the opening shots of the conflict' (Jackson, *Ireland*, 246). See also Jeffery, 'British Security Policy', 165.

was a funny sort of 'war', marked, to be sure, by a gradually rising tempo of violence, but one which was sporadic and for the most part highly localised.[4] Although early in 1919 Wilson noted that Johnnie French (the Lord-Lieutenant) and Sir Frederick Shaw (the army commander) were worried about 'the serious situation in Ireland', there was not much from a purely 'law and order' perspective to suggest that any part of the country was becoming ungovernable. Assuming, as many did, that violence was endemic in Ireland, it was possible in 1919 to dismiss attacks on policemen and police barracks as just one more of the periodic bursts of 'outrages' (the Ardnamona dynamiters, for example, or land-agitation violence in the early 1880s) which Ireland seemed fated to suffer. That being the case, a firm security policy (such as Wilson favoured) might be all that was required. But the confident assumption that simply 'a little blood letting' would be enough to sta-bilise the situation did not take into account the sharp shift in Irish nationalist political opinion, demonstrated by the dramatic eclipse of the Redmondite Irish Parliamentary party by Sinn Féin in the 1918 general election, the establishment of a separatist Irish assembly—the 'Dáil' (which coincidentally first met on the same day as the Soloheadbeg ambush)—and the emergence of a physical-force organisation (which became known as the Irish Republican Army), many of whose volunteers had been blooded in 1916, and which was set to pose an armed challenge to the British administration in Ireland more serious and more sus-tained than ever before.[5]

In 1919, however, Ireland was not at 'war', a fact amply demonstrated during a brief visit Wilson made in early July, when he found the situation to be serious but by no means catastrophic. He, Cecil, and his mother travelled over on the ferry from Holyhead to 'Kingstown' (Dun Laoghaire), where Johnnie French had arranged a guard of honour to meet him. On 3 July the Wilsons stayed with French at the Viceregal Lodge in Phoenix Park (now Áras an Uachtaráin, the residence of the President of Ireland). French, noted Wilson, 'does not think there will be a Rebellion but he is afraid of much more shooting'. Various dinner guests, including the Protestant Archbishop of Dublin, Dr Bernard, and Sir Charles Barrington, a prominent member of the Irish Unionist Alliance, with a big house at Glenstal, county Limerick,[6] told him the country was 'in a very bad state'. The following day French and Wilson were awarded honorary degrees at Trinity College, and in the afternoon went to Alexandra College, a Protestant girls' school in Earlsfort Terrace, just across the road from University College Dublin: 'Coming away in the motor Johnnie got boohed & hissed by students in the

---

[4] The variable intensity of the violence across Ireland is analysed in Hart, 'The Geography of Revolution in Ireland'.

[5] For the balance between British security and political policies towards Ireland, see the lucid dis-cussion in Townshend, *Political Violence in Ireland*, ch. 7. A good guide to the general political con-text is O'Halpin, *The Decline of the Union*, chs. 6–7.

[6] In May 1921 Barrington's 24-year-old daughter Winifred was killed in an IRA ambush near Glenstal, returning from a fishing party with an officer of the RIC Auxiliary Division (Buckland, *Irish Unionism 1*, 204).

National College opposite, a most disgraceful thing!' The next day, a Saturday, Wilson, wearing his uniform and in an open car, drove his mother to Currygrane, stopping to pick up niece Bridget at Knockdrin Castle near Mullingar where she was at school. 'We got down midday & I found the old place looking so pretty & Jemmy certainly better.' After lunch he drove back to Dublin, completing a 150-mile round trip, across country which outwardly at least would have seemed quite unaffected by any Irish political turmoil. That evening he and Cecil dined with Eddie Saunderson (French's private secretary) at the Royal St George Yacht Club, before catching the night ferry. 'A lovely night, & we have had a very pleasant visit'; it was quite like old times.[7] As it happened, however—and this was a reflection of the new times—he was never to visit Currygrane again.

A month later Wilson was again on the Holyhead ferry, this time travelling through Dublin en route to Belfast, where French took the salute at an official 'Peace Day' celebration. Wilson estimated that 'some 36,000 demobilized Ulstermen marched past in perfect order, all closed up and I never saw a finer more independent well dressed lot of men...the whole of them volunteers'. While in the north he took the opportunity to motor out to the old family homestead at Rashee. 'The Farm', he wrote, 'is only 35 acres & the house'—perhaps he was toying with the idea of getting a base in Ulster—'would never do for a residence.'[8] Wilson was certainly very conscious of his Ulster heritage. When, as a 'Knight Grand Cross of the Order of the Bath' (GCB), he acquired his own supporters to the existing Wilson family coat of arms, he chose a private of the Rifle Brigade and 'a female figure representing Ulster'. Yet, in his pedigree, he was styled 'of Currygrane, co. Longford', and, to the end, Currygrane was the first address he listed in his *Who's Who* entry, thus keeping a foot, as it were, in both southern and northern unionist camps.[9]

There was an intensification of the IRA campaign through 1919, marked by the first military casualties, on Sunday 7 September, when a party of troops about to enter the Methodist church in Fermoy, county Cork, for morning service were attacked, leaving one soldier dead and several wounded.[10] The brunt of the campaign, however, was borne by the police, fifteen of whom were killed in 1919.[11] The Royal Irish Constabulary (RIC) was an armed, semi-military force, some 9,000 strong, and although both Shaw in Dublin and Wilson in London contemplated the possibility of what Shaw (echoing Wilson's 'blood letting' remark) in April 1919 called 'active military operations of a serious nature',[12] their

---

[7] Wilson diary, 3–5 July 1919. Bridget recalled Wilson being in uniform, and the thrill of being taken home for the day 'in a Rolls' (in conversation with the author, 8 May 1985).

[8] Wilson diary, 9–10 Aug. 1919.

[9] See *Burke's Peerage and Baronetage* (1921), 2301–2; letter to the author from Timothy H. S. Duke, Chester Herald, 24 Oct. 1997.   [10] Lee Cole, *History of Methodism in Ireland*, 94.

[11] This includes four men of the Dublin Metropolitan Police (Hopkinson, *The Irish War of Independence*, 71).

[12] 'The military situation throughout the British empire', memo by CIGS, 26 Apr. 1919 (TNA, CAB 24/78 GT7182).

political masters hesitated to commit themselves to an unequivocally military policy. Indeed, throughout the British campaign in Ireland there was a fatal (sometimes literally so) muddle between a civilian security strategy and a military one.[13]

Neither the Cabinet in London nor the administration in Dublin were quite sure exactly how to respond to the Irish situation. As it developed from late 1919, the challenge became increasingly military, but there were quite sound political reasons for the policy-makers not to meet it with military measures. If London formally accepted that the struggle in Ireland was a 'war', and that they were fighting a real 'army', then this would bestow legitimacy upon the IRA and the nationalist cause, thus conceding part of the political battle.[14] What Sinn Féin wanted to establish was that they were fighting a legitimate war for national liberation; that one army was fighting another army. By contrast, the line initially taken by the authorities was that they were effectively dealing with a criminal conspiracy for which the use of the police, rather than the military, was more appropriate. Events on the ground in Ireland progressively undermined this view.

As well as security considerations, there was also the matter of what political settlement was possible. Despite what diehard unionists like Henry Wilson might think, some measure of 'home rule' was inevitable, and was accepted as such by the majority of both conservatives (if grudgingly) and liberals in Britain. But for nationalist Ireland, mere local autonomy within the United Kingdom was no longer going to be enough. And there was still the problem posed by the unionist majority in the north-east, for whom even internal devolution was a step further than they desired. By 1919 it was becoming clear (though not perhaps to nationalists) that some sort of partition was also inevitable. What exactly this would mean, and whether it would be temporary or permanent, had yet to be established. From late 1919 onwards a Cabinet committee struggled with these issues. After much discussion, an arrangement involving the creation of two Irish parliaments was embodied in the Government of Ireland Act, which became law in December 1920. This provided for separate legislatures—still to be subordinate to Westminster—in Dublin and Belfast, the latter being responsible for the six most Protestant counties of Ulster. The two governments were to be linked through a quasi-federal 'Council of Ireland', intended to administer matters of common interest.[15]

Another consideration to be borne in mind about the immediate post-war period (as frequently since) is that Ireland was very low down on the British political agenda. Because the violence of these years so obsessed people and politicians (and the security forces) in Ireland, it is sometimes assumed that the policy-makers in

---

[13] The best guide to the British campaign is the indispensable Townshend, *The British Campaign in Ireland*, on which I have relied heavily in the following account.

[14] See the discussion in Hancock, *Survey of British Commonwealth Affairs*, 119–24.

[15] The best account of these political developments is to be found in Mansergh, *The Unresolved Question*.

London were similarly affected. In fact they were not. As with other British domestic and imperial problems, any sustained appraisal of Irish policy had to take second (at least) place to peacemaking and Lloyd George's settling of world affairs. The combination in 1919 of this factor, together with the Irish situation appearing to be comparatively 'normal', explains, for example, the astounding fact that Sir William Robertson was considered as a possible army Commander in Dublin.

In the happy days before the First World War the Irish command was often used as a suitable last posting for distinguished senior generals approaching retirement. So, it seemed, might be the case in July 1919, when Churchill offered the position to Robertson.[16] Robertson's suitability for the job seems mainly to have depended on the time-honoured army tradition of 'Buggins's turn'. With the Rhine being reduced to a lieutenant-general's command, Churchill told Lloyd George in October that he could not 'leave Robertson without any appointment, and Ireland is the only one open'. In Churchill's opinion, Robertson 'was unquestioningly the best man', an assertion which demonstrated how little he had actually thought about the position. Astonishingly, in February 1920 he assured the Prime Minister that 'long, renewed and careful reflection' had confirmed him in his view of Robertson's suitability.[17] Robertson was undoubtedly an able soldier, but hardly the 'best man' for a job which required subtlety, flexibility, and, above all, some political nous.

Wilson was less certain about the possibilities. In October 1919, 'in view of the fact that we are—apparently—going to have some sort of Home Rule Bill this autumn which, if I know my country, will lead to serious trouble this winter', he suggested that Churchill ought to consult the Prime Minister 'before finally settling' the matter.[18] Bearing in mind Lloyd George's low opinion of Robertson, this advice might not have been calculated to advance the latter's claims. Having seen Lloyd George, Churchill told Wilson the Prime Minister was against Robertson going to Ireland and he wanted Nevil Macready for the job. Lloyd George 'suggested Robertson for India [to be Commander-in-Chief], but I want to send Rawly there'.[19] Macready was in many respects the ideal candidate. He had experience of commanding troops 'in aid of the civil power', in south Wales during a coal strike in 1910, and had been nominated to be 'military governor' in Belfast had the army been deployed there in 1914. Since August 1918 he had been Commissioner of the Metropolitan Police in London. He was, in Asquith's words, a man of 'cool head' and 'good judgment',[20] and Lloyd George was evidently attracted by his liberal sympathies, which set him apart from the general tendency of the British officer corps.

[16] Churchill to Robertson, 21 July 1919 (Robertson papers, I/31/2).

[17] Churchill to Lloyd George, 11 Oct. 1919 and 29 Feb. 1920 (Lloyd George papers, F/9/1/36 and F/9/2/10).   [18] Wilson to Churchill, 12 Oct. 1918 (Wilson papers, HHW 2/18B/21).

[19] Wilson diary, 16 Oct. 1919.

[20] Asquith to Lloyd George, 6 July 1916 (Lloyd George papers, E/2/23/2).

The problem was that Macready did not want the job. He professed to 'loathe' Ireland 'and its people with a depth deeper than the sea and more violent than that which I feel against the Boche'.[21] In his memoirs, Macready claimed that it was only a sense of loyalty to his 'old Chief', Lord French, that persuaded him to take up the appointment.[22] Knowing he was the Prime Minister's preferred candidate, he deftly struck a hard bargain, securing an enhanced pension provision, substantially higher 'table money' (entertaining expenses) than Shaw had been getting, and £5,000 (no less) 'disturbance allowance'.[23] Churchill told Wilson that Macready's appointment had been made 'virtually over my head', and recommended Robertson for promotion to Field Marshal 'as a consolation prize', explaining to him that, 'owing to the repeated murderous outrages in Ireland, the Government decided that it was necessary to appoint an officer with special police experience'.[24] Whatever the circumstances, Robertson's promotion gave him the notable distinction of being the only man ever to rise from the lowest to the highest rank in the British army.

When he was being pressed to accept the Irish command, Macready was also offered an overall role in charge of both police and army. But this he turned down, a decision, however wise it might have been for the sake of his own reputation, that fatally compromised any possibility of a properly co-ordinated security effort being established in Ireland.[25] His appointment in April 1920, nevertheless, and that of a new Chief Secretary, Sir Hamar Greenwood, marked the beginning of a reassessment of Irish policy. Macready was not at all happy with what he found on his arrival in Dublin. 'Before I had been here three hours,' he wrote to Walter Long, 'I was honestly flabbergasted at the administrative chaos that seems to reign here.' He was also 'a little nervous, owing to the disorganisation of the R.I.C., not so much perhaps on account of their morale, as in that crass stupidity which is so often found among police officers who have not been carefully selected'.[26] One of his first proposals was to replace the Inspector-General (chief officer) of the police. General Hugh Tudor, a friend of Churchill with a distinguished war record as an

---

[21] Macready to Ian Macpherson (who had just been appointed Chief Secretary for Ireland), 11 Jan. 1919 (quoted in Townshend, *The British Campaign in Ireland*, 20). This is despite (or perhaps because of) the fact that he had Irish forebears, and his wife was from a Co. Cork family.

[22] Macready, *Annals of an Active Life*, ii. 425.

[23] The increase in table money was from £500 to £1,400. Note enclosed with Churchill to Wilson, 4 Apr. 1920 (Wilson papers, HHW 2/18B/33); file on financial arrangements of Macready's appointment (TNA, WO 32/4815).

[24] Churchill to Wilson, 4 Apr. 1920 (Wilson papers, HHW 2/18B/33); to Clementine Churchill (wife), 27 Mar. 1920 (Gilbert, *Churchill*, companion vol. iv, part 2, 1059); to Robertson, 1 Apr. 1920 (Robertson papers, 7/11/6). Robertson, by coincidence was in Ireland at the beginning of April, staying at the house in Belfast of Lord Pirrie (Chairman of the shipbuilders Harland & Wolff). Robertson had got to know him during the war when he was Controller-General of Merchant Shipbuilding, and he regularly 'week-ended' at Pirrie's English country estate (Robertson, *From Private to Field-Marshal*, 339).

[25] For the desirability of joint army–police command in counter-insurgency operations (such as Malaya, 1948–60), see Townshend, *Britain's Civil Wars*.

[26] Macready to Long, 23 Apr. 1920 (copy in Lloyd George papers, F34/1/19).

artilleryman, but no police experience whatsoever, was persuaded to take the job on. In May 1920 he was appointed 'Police Adviser' in Ireland, and became 'Chief of Police' in November when the existing Inspector-General, T. J. Smith, retired.

In the voluminous correspondence which survives from Wilson's four years as CIGS, that with Macready, containing over 400 letters, is the second-most extensive, after that with Rawlinson, who became Commander-in-Chief in India in November 1920. Only ten of the Macready–Wilson letters antedate Macready's appointment to the Irish command, and the correspondence provides, from the perspective of the two most senior army officers concerned, an extraordinarily vivid and important narrative of the Irish situation as it developed from the spring of 1920.[27] When he learned of Macready's appointment to Ireland, Wilson wrote: 'My Dear, you are an old friend and I am sorry for you and I think you are unwise to take this job but however there it is and you will find nothing but friends in the G.S. [General Staff] and all the help we can give you we will.'[28]

But the relationship between the two men was not as close as this letter might suggest, and Wilson took some offence when Macready effectively ignored his offer of help. Just under a month after he had officially taken up his duties in Dublin, Macready came to London to present a blunt demand for immediate reinforcements, including eight battalions of infantry, a large number of technical and intelligence personnel, and 234 motor vehicles. Wilson only learned of this request the evening before it was to be put before the Cabinet. Macready, he grumbled in his diary, had prepared his paper 'without coming to see me or without any warning or communication'. He thought that 'a vain ass like Macready goes over to Ireland and in a week thinks he can solve the Irish problem'.[29] The Cabinet, who were glad to get some apparently decisive guidance, agreed to supply the mechanical transport and, so far as was possible, the technical personnel. With regard to the additional infantry Macready wanted, however, Wilson raised the problem of the empire-wide shortage of troops. 'If 8 battns were sent to Ireland', he stated, 'we should have very little for our own internal troubles & nothing for India, Egypt, C-ople [Constantinople], etc.' The Cabinet, therefore, decided simply to hold the battalions Macready had requested 'in readiness', should they be required in an emergency.[30]

In order to ease the manpower problem, Churchill proposed that a 'special force of 8,000 old soldiers be raised at once to reinforce the R.I.C.', a suggestion

[27] This is especially so for the insight it provides regarding Macready's private opinions about Ireland, as he destroyed his own diaries and private papers after he had completed his published memoirs (letter to the author from his grandson, Sir Nevil Macready, 4 Nov. 1975).

[28] Wilson to Macready, 30 Mar. 1920 (Wilson papers, HHW 2/2A/8). Wilson habitually addressed his colleague as 'Make-Ready' (echoing Macready's preferred pronunciation of his surname). In return it was 'Dear Henri'. In his memoirs Macready wrote warmly of the clear and unbiased advice, and constant support, he received from Wilson (*Annals of an Active Life*, ii. 428–9).

[29] Wilson diary, 10 May 1920. Macready claimed afterwards that he had come to London 'to consult with Henry Wilson' (*Annals of an Active Life*, ii. 459).

[30] Wilson diary, 11 May 1920; Cabinet meeting, 11 May 1920 (TNA, CAB 23/21/29(20) appendix A).

which bothered Wilson, who favoured a more purely military strategy against the wider nationalist and communist challenge he perceived in Ireland. Macready, he wrote in his diary, 'in reality... is fighting New York & Cairo & Calcutta & Moscow who are only using Ireland as a tool & lever against England, & nothing but determined <u>shooting</u> on our part is of any use'.[31] While Wilson's favoured strategy in Ireland of a firm and robust military campaign was politically quite unpalatable to the Cabinet, his own apprehensions about this 'panic measure of raising 8000 scallywags'[32] were remarkably prescient, and are worth quoting *in extenso*:

I can't imagine what sort of officers and NCOs we can get. I can't imagine what sort the men will be, no-one will know anybody, no discipline, no esprit de corps, no cohesion, no training, no musketry, no mess, no NOTHING. I don't like the idea.... Then to make matters worse Macready proposes to draft these mobs over to Ireland at once & split them up into lots of 25 to 50 men over the country so there would be no hope of forming & disciplining this crowd of unknown men. It is truly a desperate & hopeless expedient bound to fail.[33]

How right he was.

The War Office objected strongly to the creation of 'a Corps of Gendarmerie', and proposed instead the raising of eight 'garrison battalions', a military formation under the Army Act, restricted to service within the United Kingdom. But the Cabinet objected to such an overtly 'military' force and instead decided to enlist ex-servicemen into an 'Auxiliary Division' of the RIC. This was little more than an extension of previous policy, as since November 1919 non-Irish ex-soldiers (who became known as the 'Black and Tans') had been recruited into the Irish police.[34]

Unlike Wilson, who perceived the Irish problem as primarily just a 'law and order' matter, Macready appreciated the underlying political dimension. 'I feel very strongly', he told Wilson in May 1920, 'that your country suffers from a cancer, a disease that is rarely eradicated, and though you may operate severely upon it, it grows again in a worse form later.' While conceding that 'drastic measures would very soon wheel these people into line and outward submission, it would also leave a fresh wound on the already scarred body of this blooming Island of yours'. In the meantime, however, he assured Wilson, 'we will do what we can'. Not unexpectedly, Wilson disagreed with Macready's analysis 'as regards my unfortunate country suffering from cancer. She suffers from nothing at all except a plague of agitators who at any time can be put in their proper place.' But, although he was mistaken about the *causes* of the 'Irish problem', failing to see that the violent republican challenge was sustained by significant underlying political

[31] Wilson diary, 11 May 1920.   [32] Ibid., 13 May 1920.   [33] Ibid., 12 May 1920.
[34] 'Formation of a special force for service in Ireland', 19 May 1920 (TNA, CAB 24/106, CP1317); Townshend, *The British Campaign in Ireland*, 46, 110–11. The 'Black and Tans' were so nicknamed because of the mixture of army khaki and RIC dark bottle-green uniforms they wore.

change, his prediction as to what would happen should the government fail properly to deal with the *symptoms* was not so far wrong. 'If the British Government', he wrote, 'keeps on showing that she is totally incapable of either protecting the lives of loyal subjects or of enforcing law and order, or of driving out these blackguard traitors and murderers, England will undoubtedly presently lose the country.'[35]

The curious combination of 'normality' and insurrection which existed in Ireland, even in the early summer of 1920, is illustrated by the case of General Cuthbert, commander of the army brigade in Fermoy, county Cork, who, together with two staff colonels, was kidnapped by the IRA on 26 June. They had been on a fishing trip, staying in a country cottage, apparently taking no special security precautions. That night soldiers from the Fermoy garrison smashed up the town; 'that is the last thing we want,' thought Wilson, 'although it does their hearts more honour than their heads.' Macready had proposed arresting six leading local IRA men, and holding them until Lucas was released. Wilson rather agreed: 'arrest Sinn Feiners and deal with them as prisoners of war—the Sinn Fein Organization being as much an enemy to England as were the Boches.'[36] While Wilson did not distinguish between Sinn Féin, the political party, and the IRA, Macready did, reflecting his more nuanced appreciation of the situation. Sinn Féin, he argued, 'is merely the name of a political organisation of which many people are what you may call law-abiding citizens, while the people to be dealt with are the I.R.A., etc., who are no doubt also Sinn Feiners by politics'.[37]

The army indiscipline in Fermoy in part reflected the problems faced by largely young and inexperienced post-war recruits, beginning to show signs of strain under the peculiar difficulties of service in Ireland. 'Don't lean too hard on the Army', Macready warned a Cabinet conference on 23 July.[38] The army, moreover, was stretched very thin in the summer of 1920. In July the Iraq rebellion required the despatch of two extra divisions, and in September Wilson had to find troops against the threat of a national coal strike at home. On 6 September he told Macready that he proposed to withdraw ten battalions from Ireland. Macready was appalled, and brusquely replied that if this were done, 'the whole RIC would go & he would have to "put up his shutters"'. A week later Wilson explained his position to the Cabinet, who, he said, had to understand the consequences of the planned withdrawal of troops from Ireland to strengthen the resources available in Britain. Macready, he said, had stated that without these troops it would 'be impossible to maintain even the present semblance of Government control, and a large proportion of the country must be abandoned to the undisputed possession

---

[35] Macready to Wilson, and reply, 21, 25 May 1920 (Wilson papers, HHW 2/2A/12, 13).
[36] Ibid., 28, 29 June (ibid. 2/2A/30, 31). Lucas managed to escape after about a month. He was well treated during his incarceration, and, according to Mark Sturgis's diary, even enjoyed 'some fishing and night poaching' with his captors (Hopkinson, *The Last Days of Dublin Castle*, 21–2).
[37] Macready to Wilson, 30 June 1920 (Wilson papers, HHW 2/2A/33).
[38] Jones, *Whitehall Diary*, iii. 27.

of the revolutionaries'. To this must be added 'the possible defection and resignation of a great proportion of the Royal Irish Constabulary', and the 'moral encouragement' which would be given to Sinn Féin. The 'reduced garrison', he claimed, would 'be practically impotent as an instrument for the maintenance of law and order', unless it could 'be employed for operations of a more military nature, which would only be possible if the Sinn Fein movement were proclaimed as a rebellion'. He also emphasised the 'difficult and unwelcome' duties which the troops had to perform. 'There is a danger', he concluded ominously, 'of approaching the limit beyond which cheerful and willing service is no longer to be obtained.'[39]

Part of the government's response to this was to press ahead with recruitment for the RIC Auxiliary Division, which reached a peak of 1,500 men in July 1921.[40] This influx of inadequately trained ex-servicemen, however, did little to improve policing or co-operation with the military. Tudor, it turned out, was not the man for the job of Chief of Police. At first Macready thought otherwise. Tudor, he told Wilson, 'is going to be a great success', and in June he reported that Tudor was 'doing very well indeed, and getting rid of the incompetent idiots who were in responsible positions'.[41] But the good impression did not last very long, as it became clear that Tudor (with Lloyd George's backing) was happy to condone, or at least turn a blind eye to, police reprisals against presumed Sinn Féiners. Lord Riddell met Tudor over dinner with Lloyd George in June 1920. Following Tudor's graphic description of the difficulties of police-work in Ireland, the Prime Minister 'was very emphatic upon the necessity for strong measures. He said, "When caught *flagrante delicto* you must shoot the rebels down. That is the only way." '[42]

By the beginning of July Wilson had got wind of Tudor's 'shoot to kill' policy, but he could scarcely believe what he had heard. Lloyd George, he wrote in his diary, 'is under the ridiculous belief that Tudor has organised a counter-murder society'. A week later, when Lloyd George himself 'reverted to his amazing theory that Tudor, or someone, was murdering 2 S.F.s to every loyalist the S.F.s murdered', Wilson 'told him that this was absolutely not so. But he seemed to be satisfied that a counter-murder Association was the best answer to the S.F.'s murders.' Wilson's suspicions were further confirmed when Lloyd George, pressed by Lord Derby for more information, meaningfully told him, 'you must not ask me any questions but the thing is in operation already'.[43] Macready was also concerned. 'The action of these "Black and Tans" of Tudor's', he wrote to Wilson in August, 'makes me every day increasingly anxious', and he worried that his troops might have to intervene, 'if they are brought face to face with some of the wild acts of

---

[39] 'The internal situation and military precautions', memo by CIGS, 13 Sept. 1920 (TNA, CAB 24/111, CP1853).
[40] 1,526. The strength of the RIC proper was 14,212, along with 1,126 in the unarmed Dublin Metropolitan Police ('Weekly survey of the state of Ireland for the week ended 27 June 1921 (TNA, CAB 24/125, CP3087)).
[41] Macready to Wilson, 21 May, 11 June 1920 (Wilson papers, HHW 2/2A/12, 26)
[42] 6 June 1920 (McEwan, *The Riddell Diaries*, 314).   [43] Wilson diary, 1, 7, 10 July 1920.

retaliation which these men are carrying out'. He feared further breakdowns in military discipline, and felt there were 'only two things to be done, either for the Government to declare a state of war, or for the Military to disassociate themselves entirely from the Police. After all, the discipline and good name of the Army is worth half a dozen Irelands.'[44] The army, nevertheless, had their own unorthodox methods. When Wilson passed on to Macready Churchill's suggestion, 'whether it would not be possible to lay some more traps for the Sinn Feins in the shape of derelict lorries, aeroplanes, etc.', Macready assured him that 'constant traps have been laid', and 'in many cases have been successful, but naturally we keep this to ourselves, as we have no wish for these "accidents" to be talked and joked about after dinner by Cabinet Ministers'.[45]

In September Wilson and Churchill had a long talk with a Captain Shore from Tudor's staff. 'Shore talks in the calmest way of murdering the S.F.s. He told us he had certain S.F.s marked down and at the slightest show of resistance they will be shot. Many amazing stories', noted Wilson in his diary. Churchill told him that Lloyd George had given Tudor his full support, and 'that he (Tudor) could rely on LG to back him'. Wilson did not like it at all. He felt that 'these "Black and Tans" of Tudors will play the devil in Ireland & in the end we soldiers will have to fall foul of them'.[46] The truth of the matter was, with public opinion in Britain becoming increasingly critical of Irish policy, Lloyd George was prepared to go to almost any lengths to avoid a complete militarisation of the Irish campaign.[47] In April 1920 he had declared firmly that 'you do not declare war against rebels',[48] and he resisted the more overtly draconian proposals of his advisers and colleagues. Wilson, for example, wanted lists of known Sinn Féiners in each district of Ireland to be posted 'on the church doors all over the country; and, whenever a policeman is murdered, pick five by lot and shoot them!'[49] Lord Curzon, who regarded Ireland as being 'in a state of open war', suggested in May 1920 that 'Indian' measures might be applied: troublesome towns and villages could be punished with collective fines and even whole districts blockaded by the British forces.[50]

The parallel with India further confirms the wider imperial context within which Irish policy must be placed. Indeed, events in India already cast a shadow across British military operations in support of the civil power. In April 1919 the British General Dyer's harsh suppression of civil unrest in the Punjab had resulted in the 'Amritsar massacre', in which over 370 Indians had died, and which had inflamed racial tensions, intensified nationalist agitation in India, and provoked a

[44] Macready to Wilson, 28 Aug. 1920 (Wilson papers, HHW 2/2A/44).

[45] Wilson to Macready and reply, 31 Aug., 1 Sept. 1920 (ibid. 2/2A/46, 49).

[46] Wilson diary, 24–5 Sept. 1920.

[47] A powerful argument for the importance of public opinion will be found in Boyce, *Englishmen and Irish Troubles*.   [48] 'Note of conversation', 30 Apr. 1920 (TNA, CAB 23/21/23(20)A).

[49] Hankey diary, 23 May 1920 (Hankey papers, HNKY 1/5). Wilson expressed a similar view in a letter to Macready, 21 Sept. 1920 (Wilson papers, HHW 2/2B/6).

[50] Jones, *Whitehall Diary*, iii. 19–20.

political storm at home.[51] In July 1920, when Churchill and Hamar Greenwood were proposing increased coercion in Ireland, 'trusting to force the Sinn Feiners into a frame of mind favourable to settlement', ministers' enthusiasm for sterner measures was tempered by the acrimonious debates on Amritsar then proceeding in parliament. As Balfour put it: 'the Dyer debate has not helped us to govern by soldiers.'[52]

But 'governing by soldiers', in effect, was what Wilson had in mind when he recommended to the Cabinet in September 1920 'operations of a more military nature' and the imposition in Ireland of martial law. Macready was initially against martial law on the grounds that the kind of stringent regime he thought necessary would not be politically acceptable in England, But with both army and police discipline threatening to break down completely, he began to change his mind.[53] Wilson, who was 'extremely anxious' about the activities of the Black and Tans, continued to press for 'Martial Law and shoot by roster, seeing that we cannot get evidence', and argued that simply 'to have indiscriminate reprisals is a complete confession of the paralysis of government and can only lead to chaos and ruin'.[54] And even Wilson was not wholly blind to the wider political context, at least so far as Britain was concerned. Government in Ireland, he asserted, had to be taken 'out of the hands of the "Black and Tans"'. He thought it 'quite clear' that 'this irregular system of reprisals will neither stop the murders, on the one hand, nor solve the Irish problem on the other. Nothing short of Government action, taken in broad daylight, with the full approval and backing of the English people, will ever bring matters to a satisfactory issue in my unfortunate country.'[55] The key requirement here was the 'full approval and backing of the English people', which was evidently not forthcoming. In November Churchill, reluctant to go as far as martial law, proposed to a 'very "hush-hush"' conference of ministers 'the substitution of regular, authorised and legalised reprisals for the unauthorised reprisals by the police and soldiers which are winked at and really encouraged by the Government'. But this was rejected, his colleagues feeling that 'the moment was not opportune'.[56]

Events in Ireland soon persuaded them otherwise. On 21 November 1920, 'Bloody Sunday', a dozen British officers were shot dead in Dublin, in a co-ordinated attack directed by Michael Collins. The following day Wilson 'urged Winston "for the hundredth time" that the Government should govern, proclaim their fidelity to the Union and declare Martial Law'. He told Macready (who was on holiday in France) that his urgings had 'had no effect whatever'. The Cabinet

---

[51] See Townshend, *Britain's Civil Wars*, 136–9, for a discussion of Amritsar.
[52] Jones, *Whitehall Diary*, iii. 28, 33.
[53] Macready to Wilson, 24, 25 Sept.; and to Chief Secretary, 27 Sept. 1920 (Wilson papers, HHW 2/2B/9A, 9, 10(a)).   [54] Wilson to Macready, 29 Sept. 1920 (ibid. HHW 2/2B/13).
[55] Ibid., 2 Nov. 1920 (ibid. 2/2B/39).
[56] Hankey diary, 13 Nov. 1920 (Hankey papers, HNKY 1/5); Cabinet conference, 10 Nov. 1920 (TNA, CAB 23/23/59(20)A).

'seem to think that it is quite normal for ten or twelve officers to be murdered before breakfast'.[57] A week after Bloody Sunday a police patrol was ambushed at Kilmichael, near Macroom in county Cork, and sixteen Black and Tans were killed, an event which finally led the government to impose martial law in part of Ireland.

On 30 November Wilson met with Churchill and Hamar Greenwood to discuss martial law. 'Greenwood inferred that he had always been in favour of it & so did Winston, their only doubt being whether we had enough troops! What amazing liars', wrote Wilson in his diary. The two ministers wanted to restrict the measure to the Cork area, but Wilson thought it would be no use unless it covered the whole of the island, apart, perhaps, from Ulster.[58] Next day it was discussed by the Cabinet. Lloyd George had been particularly affected by the Macroom killings, which, he thought, 'seemed to partake of a different character from the preceding operations'. While the others had been 'assassinations', this last 'was a military operation and there was a good deal to be said for declaring a state of siege or promulgating martial law in that corner of Ireland'. So, a primarily civil secu-rity effort having failed, along with both covert and overt use of counter-terror, the Prime Minister now turned to the army. But he stopped short of giving them an entirely free rein, and the Cabinet decided only on an 'experiment' of martial law, limited to the south-west of the country.[59]

Martial law was proclaimed on 10 December 1920 over the four Munster counties of Cork, Tipperary, Kerry, and Limerick. On 23 December the Government of Ireland Act became law. It was hoped that a special effort would be made to restore order so that elections could be held as soon as possible, and a top-level conference was held on 29 December to review the situation. Macready and Tudor were brought over from Ireland, as well as General Sir Edward Strickland (commander of the 6th Division, in Cork) and General Gerald Boyd (comman-der, Dublin District). Sir John Anderson, who had been seconded from London to oversee the civil bureaucracy in Dublin, and Henry Wilson also attended. Lloyd George asked if a truce might be feasible over the election period, but Macready, Tudor, and Anderson were unanimously opposed. The Prime Minister than asked 'how long they thought it would be before the extremist gang of the Sinn Feiners was entirely broken?' Macready thought this would be possible only if martial law were 'spread all over the country'. Tudor, Strickland, and Boyd, however, asserted that even without extending martial law the country could be controlled in four months. Macready offered 'possibly in four months'. Wilson, who said any kind of truce would be 'absolutely fatal', thought that 'perhaps in six months' time, if military law was applied to the whole of Ireland, 80 or 90 per cent

---

[57] Wilson diary, 22 Nov.; Wilson to Macready, 24 Nov. 1920 (Wilson papers, HHW 2/2C/5).
[58] Wilson diary, 30 Nov. 1920.
[59] Jones, *Whitehall Diary*, iii. 41; Cabinet meeting, 1 Dec. 1920 (TNA, CAB 23/23/65(20)A). For a superb, forensic investigation of Kilmichael, see Hart, *The I.R.A. and Its Enemies*, 21–38.

of the people would be on the side of the Government'.[60] Depending on the more optimistic of this mixed advice, the Cabinet decided to set the Irish elections for May 1921.

As a concession to Wilson's and Macready's views, martial law was extended over the rest of Munster (counties Waterford and Clare), as well as Kilkenny and Wexford in Leinster. Although Wilson thought this 'a good job', neither he nor Macready thought it was really sufficient. 'With you', wrote Macready, 'I wish to goodness we had Martial Law all over the country.'[61] They were not the only people who complained about this haphazard approach. Sir Warren Fisher, Britain's most senior civil servant, who reported on the Irish administration in February 1921, bluntly remarked that 'Martial Law everywhere is an intelligible policy, or Martial Law nowhere'.[62] But the incoherence of security policy in Ireland simply reflected the political difficulties in settling on *any* policy which might satisfy police and military 'hawks' without alienating the great mass of the Irish nationalist community, or the Liberal and Labour 'doves' in parliament and elsewhere.

Wilson had a break from his duties in London at the start of 1921. Following ten days visiting the British and Allied occupation troops in the Rhineland, and a further week-and-a-half in Paris for a meeting of the Supreme War Council to review the progress of the peace settlement, he and Cecil spent three weeks in Biarritz. In late November 1920 Cecil had undergone major surgery, apparently for cancer of the right breast. It had come as a great shock to Wilson, but Cecil's 'pluck' was 'really wonderful', 'not one word of fear or complaint, braver infinitely than I am'.[63] She recovered steadily and the holiday was part of her convalescence. She thought she would like to have a villa in the resort, and they looked at several properties, but were put off by 'prohibitive prices'. Since King Edward VII's days Biarritz had been greatly favoured by the English, and Wilson found several friends and acquaintances there. He played lots of tennis with David Beatty (Wilson invariably winning), and socialised with Eddie Derby, who as usual was full of gossip. Derby reported a story of Lloyd George's, that before Wilson became CIGS, Robertson 'had repeatedly been to L.G. to get him to remove Edie [*sic*] from being War Minister'. Wilson was 'inclined to think this is not true but in any case it has done for "Wully" in Edie's eyes!'[64]

---

[60] 29 Dec. 1920: Cabinet meeting (TNA, CAB 23/23/79(20)A); Fisher diary (Fisher papers, MS Fisher 16); Hankey diary (Hankey papers, HNKY 1/5). Macready's prediction is according to his letter to Wilson, 10 Feb. 1921 (Wilson papers, HHW 2/2C/35).

[61] Wilson to Macready, and reply, 5 and 6 Jan. 1921 (Wilson papers, HHW 2/2C/28 and 30).

[62] Report by Sir Warren Fisher (Head of the UK Civil Service), 11 Feb. 1921 (Lloyd George papers, F/17/1/9).

[63] Wilson diary, 24–9 Nov. 1920. References to Cecil's health in the diary have partially been obliterated, presumably by Cecil herself after Wilson's death. There was a recurrence of the problem, on her left side, in the spring of 1921 and she had another, apparently less radical (though entirely successful), operation at the end of March (Wilson diary, 8–9, 16, 30–1 Mar. 1921). Cecil survived until 14 Apr. 1930, when she 'died suddenly' of heart failure, having had previous heart attacks (*The Times*, 15 Apr. 1930).   [64] Wilson diary, 31 Jan., 3, 10–11, 15 Feb. 1921.

Having spent an enjoyable few days in Madrid, Wilson got back to London on 26 February. He had a new political master, Sir Laming Worthington-Evans, who had succeeded Churchill on 13 February. 'Worthy', according to Lord Riddell, was 'sensible and painstaking without imagination "the very antithesis of Winston" ',[65] but he made a good initial impression in the War Office, 'with his desire to hear every point of view & not to dictate on subjects he does not know much about' (another contrast with his predecessor).[66] Initially at least, and no doubt feeling the full force of Wilson's personality, he was prepared to support the CIGS's desire for a stricter security policy in Ireland.

Macready was less sure. Writing to Wilson while the latter was in Biarritz, he had remarked on the 'one point on which, I am afraid, you and I do not see eye to eye'. Macready, unlike Wilson, did not believe 'that any amount of repression is likely to solve the difficulty' in Ireland, 'nor do I believe that the killing off of Michael Collins and say fifty of his next best men will improve matters to any appreciable degree'. He asserted that 'practically the whole manhood under the age of about twenty-five of the country, except Ulster, are, so to speak, fanatically patriotic according to their lights', and 'unless you can kill the whole blooming lot, I do not myself believe that any amount of Martial Law will bring an improvement in the state of affairs'. He was no longer prepared to stand by his prediction of December that order might be restored within four months, and now felt that it was 'impossible to enforce real Martial Law at all', as the police were wholly unreliable. Tudor was 'perfectly useless in enforcing discipline', and the higher police officials were not 'equal to the strain and work put upon them'. The underlying argument of Macready's 'lugubrious epistle' (his words) was that only a political settlement would 'solve' the problem.[67] Macready made the same points when he came to see Wilson on his return from holiday. 'He agrees with me that many of the Black & Tans ought to be disbanded, &, of course, that all Ireland should be placed under Martial Law', but 'even so he sees no way of getting permanent peace.'[68]

Wilson hoped that the 'logic of events' in Ireland would compel the Cabinet to extend martial law across the whole island,[69] and the rising tempo of violence certainly presented an increasingly military challenge to the government. Over the second half of 1920 (June–December) 122 police, 49 military, and 27 civilians were killed in Ireland. Over the next *three* months, January–March 1921, these fatalities rose to 87, 44, and 49; and between April and June they were 117, 41, and 81 respectively.[70] The hoped-for extension of martial law also implied the establishment of a unified command, a point which Wilson was keener on than either Macready or the Cabinet, the former for professional, the latter for political

---

65 Wilson diary, 29 Jan. 1921.
66 Philip Chetwode (Deputy CIGS) to Wilson, 21 Feb. 1921 (Wilson papers, HHW 2/58A/30).
67 Macready to Wilson, 10 Feb. 1921 (ibid. 2/2C/35).   68 Wilson diary, 28 Feb. 1921.
69 Wilson to Rawlinson, 5 Jan. 1921 (Wilson papers, HHW 2/13C/6).
70 Townshend, *The British Campaign in Ireland*, app. v, 214.

reasons. Towards the end of March Wilson had a long talk with the King about Ireland. George V wanted 'to abolish <u>all</u> Black & Tans', and asked who had appointed Tudor. Sir William Robertson, he added, had a poor opinion of the Irish police chief, who had served under him on the Rhine. Wilson told the King that Tudor 'was a gallant fellow on service, but a man of no balance, knowledge or judgment & therefore a deplorable selection for his present post'. The King also thought that Macready was not doing well, but Wilson rose to his defence: 'to this I could not agree & I said he was constantly being interfered with by LG and Hamar Greenwood, & that unity of control was essential & to this the Frocks would not agree.' Again the wider, international context bothered Wilson, who told the King that he hated the 'dispersal of our little Army in Silesia, C[onstantin]ople, Persia, Mesopot[ami]a, etc when every available man was wanted in Ireland'.[71]

Troops were also required in Great Britain in the spring of 1921 to meet possible disorder arising from the threatened Triple Alliance strike. Although Worthington-Evans told the Cabinet on 4 April that 'it was not considered desirable' to withdraw any of Macready's fifty-one infantry battalions, it was subsequently decided that first three battalions, and then a fourth, could safely be removed.[72] On 6 April Wilson told Macready that he was 'still busily working under the supposition, or hallucination, that there is going to be a "Red" revolution'. Personally, he did not believe it, 'but as the Cabinet are in a gale of wind, inside and out, I have to act on what they think is likely to happen'.[73] Wilson, meanwhile, began working out 'a scheme by which if this Triple Strike blows over—I can reinforce Macready by 30 Batt[alion]s . . . This with a little more Cav[alry] & Tanks & Armoured cars & Aeroplanes might constitute a "knock out" this summer.'[74] Even Macready, though he still sensibly maintained that 'the final lasting settlement of Ireland, if such is possible, must be found through political and not Military channels', agreed with Wilson that, under pressure, 'the enemy here may suddenly go crack'. Once the elections had been held, he wrote, 'we can begin really active operations and push them on uninterruptedly during June, July, August and September', which would have, he thought (if a little unspecifically), 'all the effect we can hope for'.[75]

The elections for both Irish parliaments went ahead during May 1921. In Northern Ireland the Unionist Party secured an overwhelming majority; in the south, 128 Sinn Féin candidates were elected unopposed to the 132-seat assembly.[76] While the unionists agreed to operate local home rule in the north,

[71] Wilson diary, 28 Mar. 1921.
[72] Cabinet meeting, 4 Apr.; and conferences of ministers, 8 and 9 Apr. 1921 (TNA, CAB 23/25/17(21); and 23/25 22(21), apps. v and viii).
[73] Wilson to Macready, 6 Apr. 1921 (Wilson papers, HHW 2/2D/8A).
[74] Wilson diary, 13 Apr. 1921.
[75] Macready to Wilson (2 letters), 14 Apr. 1921 (Wilson papers, HHW 2/2D/20 and 21).
[76] Northern Ireland House of Commons: 30 Unionists; 6 Nationalists; 6 Sinn Féin; the four remaining members of the Southern Ireland House of Commons were independents, returned for Dublin University (Walker, *Parliamentary Election Results in Ireland, 1918–92*, 45–6, 101–3).

there was no possibility that the southern legislature would function at all. Indeed, the Sinn Féin MPs promptly constituted themselves into the second 'Dáil Éireann'.[77] The Cabinet therefore were faced with the unpalatable alternatives of offering the more moderate Irish nationalists some qualified measure of independence, or imposing direct 'crown colony' rule and full martial law on the twenty-six counties of southern Ireland.

At first more belligerent counsels prevailed. Clearly influenced by Wilson, on 24 May Worthington-Evans proposed to the Cabinet that the Irish garrison be reinforced 'with everything not actually required elsewhere, so that an endeavour should be made to break the back of the rebellion during the three months, July, August and September'. In a supporting paper, Wilson and Macready outlined the action which would be taken 'were it decided by the Cabinet to make a supreme effort in Ireland this summer to re-establish law and order'. In contrast to the optimistic forecasts of the previous December, neither man was prepared to 'promise any definite result'. All they had to offer was a heavily qualified conjecture that a full-blooded military approach *might* work. Apart from the imposition of a thoroughgoing martial-law regime, under a unified command, Wilson, unusually sensitive to the political dimension of the matter, argued that the British and Irish public would have to be bombarded with 'active and intense propaganda' and marshalled behind the government for the policy to have any chance of success. 'I have always said', he told Rawlinson, 'that it is impossible to knock out the Sinn Feins unless we have England on our side.' 'Macready warned about the morale of his troops, for whom service in Ireland inflicted strains 'incomparably greater' than 'in time of actual war'. The 'present state of affairs in Ireland', he asserted, 'must be brought to a conclusion by October, or steps must be taken to relieve practically the whole of the troops together with the great majority of the commanders and their staffs'. This was in effect an ultimatum to the government, since he was 'quite aware that troops do not exist to do this'.[78]

But, to Wilson's delight, the Cabinet agreed to the proposed intensification of coercion in Ireland, 'in the event of a refusal on the part of Southern Ireland to put into operation the Government of Ireland Act'.[79] 'The "Frocks" ', he wrote to Tit Willow in Paris, 'are, I verily believe, going to allow me to send over all the troops I have got in England to Ireland.'[80] Between 14 June and 7 July Ireland was reinforced by seventeen infantry battalions, bringing the command to its peak strength of about 60,000 troops, but the Cabinet, in the end, drew back from the brink. It seems that both the British government and the Irish republicans were

[77] The first Dáil comprised the Sinn Féin MPs returned in the 1918 UK general election.

[78] 'Ireland and the general military situation', memo by Worthington-Evans; 'Ireland', memo by Wilson and Macready, 24 May 1921 (TNA, CAB 24/123, CP2964–5); Wilson to Rawlinson, 23 June 1921 (Wilson papers, HHW 2/13D/25).

[79] Cabinet meeting, 24 May 1921 (TNA, CAB 23/25/41(21)).

[80] Wilson to Sackville-West (British military attaché in Paris), 28 May 1921 (Wilson papers, HHW 2/12G/38).

materially influenced by the sombre prospect of a final military 'push', and that this acted as a catalyst towards a truce pending talks between the British and Sinn Féin. On 24 June the Cabinet decided to invite both Eamon de Valera (the republican leader, charmingly described by Macready to Wilson as 'your Cuban Jew compatriot'[81]), and Sir James Craig, the newly installed first Prime Minister of Northern Ireland. Following some preliminary talks, the truce came into effect on 11 July 1921.

Wilson, who thought the truce was the product of 'rank, filthy cowardice',[82] nursed hopes that the Anglo-Irish negotiations would break down and there might yet be a final 'push' in Ireland. In August de Valera was demanding so large a degree of independence that even Macready thought 'we should go straight back to operations', and Wilson began to discuss the possibility of raising 20,000 to 30,000 men to bring the Irish garrison up to strength. Worthington-Evans asserted that, if de Valera refused Lloyd George's offer of 'dominion home rule' (along the lines of Canada or Australia), parliament would be recalled and a call for recruits 'up to 80,000 to 100,000 would be made'.[83] Early in August Lloyd George proposed what Wilson called 'a monstrous plan of withdrawal & blockade', whereby the army and police would withdraw from the interior of southern Ireland, and hold only the main towns and cities on the coast. Wilson thought the scheme 'as ridiculous as it was impossible', but Macready jocularly suggested that if the Dáil were in session in Dublin, 'Boyd could round up the whole bally lot, who might be shot by mistake while being rounded up'.[84] The Cabinet Irish Committee began to contemplate an even more draconian policy, somewhat along the lines of that employed in South Africa in 1901–2, and asked the War Office to examine the practicability of dividing southern Ireland 'into sections by means of blockhouses and barbed wire'. Lloyd George told Macready that 'entirely new methods' would have to be employed, 'such as devastating and denuding tracks of country, removing all inhabitants'. The Prime Minister was unhappy with the military in Ireland and, amazingly, declared 'that Tudor's methods were far more effective'.[85]

Despite, and perhaps because of, this sabre-rattling, in September the Cabinet agreed to open formal negotiations with Irish nationalist representatives, and by October a full-scale conference in London had been arranged. The threat of renewed hostilities hung over the talks to the end, and, whether bluff or not, it was this threat Lloyd George finally used to bring the Irish delegates to sign a treaty on 6 December 1921, which provided for southern Ireland to become

---

[81] Macready to Wilson, 8 July 1921 (ibid. 2/2E/35). De Valera was born in New York, of an Irish mother and a Spanish father.   [82] Wilson diary, 11 July 1921.

[83] Ibid., 13 and 18 Aug. 1921.

[84] Ibid., 5 Aug. 1921; Wilson to Macready and reply, 11 and 14 Aug. 1921 (Wilson papers, HHW 2/2E/58 and 60).

[85] Cabinet committee of Ireland, conclusions of meetings, 17 and 18 Aug. 1921 (TNA, CAB 27/130, CIP2); extract from Macready diary, 3 Sept. 1921, enclosed with Macready to Wilson, 6 Sept. 1921 (Wilson papers, HHW 2/2F/4).

independent (as the 'Irish Free State'), while remaining formally within the British empire.[86]

Henry Wilson waxed lyrical on this 'shameful & cowardly surrender to the pistol'. 'What is going to happen in Ireland', he wrote to Rawly, 'goodness knows. It will be great fun if they start pistoling each other instead of pistoling us. But if they do start a form of murder government I am most anxious that we should get all our troops out before one set of murderers call on the British troops "in aid of the Civil power" to shoot another set of murderers.'[87] It is clear that Wilson let his obsession with Ireland cloud his professional military judgment. In June 1921 Lloyd George complained that the CIGS 'feels intensely on Ireland and I can never get a sane discussion with him'. The following month, when the Prime Minister told Wilson that de Valera was coming over to London and he would have a chance of 'talking with him', Wilson replied that he 'did not speak to murderers', and bluntly declared that he would hand de Valera over to the police if he met him'.[88] Lloyd George's response to Wilson challenging him over parlaying with 'murderers'—'Oh nonsense. In public life we must do these things'—demonstrated, as Andrew Gailey has observed, the imperatives of a democratic political system 'which bound its leaders to public opinion rather than principle' (an inclination which applied with especial force in the case of Lloyd George).[89]

Relations between the Prime Minister and his CIGS had become increasingly strained since the war, not only over the question of Ireland, and this incident seems to have been the final break between the two men, for they did not apparently meet again until 10 February 1922. Up till that time, when military information or advice was required at a Cabinet meeting Wilson himself refused to attend, and sent another member of the Army Council in his stead. In October Lloyd George told Lord Riddell that Wilson was 'very difficult', and was not sorry his time was CIGS was up in January.[90] Naturally this also made life awkward for Worthington-Evans, who taxed Wilson with the matter in November 1921. The CIGS told him that he was 'sorry to put him personally to inconvenience', but that he had no intention of changing his 'opinion about the meetings with the murder gangs'.[91] In late December 1921 Eddie Derby noted that Wilson had been 'quite mad on the subject of Ireland', and had allowed this 'to taint all his work'. 'I cannot help feeling', he observed towards the end of Wilson's term as CIGS, 'that as long as he was a soldier he ought not to have allowed his political feelings to get the better of military discipline.'[92] Despite his political loathing for Lloyd George, however, Wilson typically wrote a warm, personal note to the Prime Minister on 18 February 1922. 'My last day as C.I.G.S. brings you very

[86] The most atmospheric account of this is Pakenham, *Peace by Ordeal*.
[87] Wilson diary, 7 Dec.; Wilson to Rawlinson, 10 Dec. 1921 (Wilson papers, HHW 2/13F/20).
[88] Jones, *Whitehall Diary*, iii. 73; Wilson diary, 5 July 1921.   [89] Gailey, 'King Carson', 84.
[90] Riddell diary, 16 Oct. 1921 (quoted in McEwan, *The Riddell Diaries*, 354).
[91] Wilson diary, 3 Nov. 1921.
[92] Derby to Rawlinson, 31 Dec. 1921 and 11 Feb. 1922 (Derby papers, Mss Eur. D.605/15–16).

much to my mind and those glorious days when, together, in rough and boisterous times we fought for our country. I cannot therefore let the day die out', he continued (though with a significant use of the past tense), 'without a word of admiration for the part you then played and for the many kindnesses I then received from you.'[93]

But Ireland, as Macready was wont to remark, was Wilson's own 'beastly country', and it is scarcely surprising that he felt strongly about it. From time to time, indeed, he was touched personally by the Irish 'Troubles'. In September 1920 he heard that '4 men' had gone to Currygrane 'and demanded guns from Jemmy. He had only one old gun & they took that & the Steward's. What a shameful thing.' He thought it would have been 'a great shock' to Jemmy, Alice, and Bridget. 'And all this because a Cabinet of Cowards reigns in Downing St.'[94] In June 1921 Jemmy (who had moved to England) wrote to Henry telling him that Currygrane was 'full of Auxiliaries'. Wilson had told him that it was 'quite impossible to have exceptional treatment in our case', but nevertheless asked Macready if he 'could get Tudor to tell the Officer in Charge to treat the house as kindly as he can'.[95]

In June 1921 Wilson was petitioned about the fate of Seán MacEoin, the 'Blacksmith of Ballinalee', whose family had for many years operated the local smithy which the Wilsons used. MacEoin was commander of the north Longford IRA flying column, which enjoyed considerable success against RIC and Auxiliaries, until he was captured in March 1921, tried and convicted for the murder of a policeman, and sentenced to death.[96] In June MacEoin's mother wrote to Wilson, appealing to him to seek clemency for her son 'John', whom she admitted was 'in the movement' but was 'not altogether bad'. Wilson promised to forward the letter to General Macready (which he did), but told her there was 'nothing else' he could do.[97] Macready thought MacEoin would 'hang to a certainty and is a very bad egg, although he made a very good appearance at the Court and claimed to be a gallant soldier. He may be, but he has committed a good few murders.'[98] The 'Ballinalee connection' was not yet exhausted, however. On 21 June the local Church of Ireland vicar, the Revd Henry Johnson, wrote to Wilson. MacEoin, he argued, was 'an honest misguided man', acting 'very wrongly of course', from 'high patriotic motives'. More striking was a letter from Wilson's brother Jemmy. Writing from Rye in Sussex, he said: 'Had I been at home I feel I would have acted on the same lines' as Johnson. Wilson thought these

---

[93] Wilson to Lloyd George, 18 Feb. 1922 (Wilson papers, HHW 2/10B/13). Lloyd George apparently did not reply.   [94] Wilson diary, 1 Sept. 1920.
[95] Ibid., 6 June; Wilson to Macready, 7 June 1921 (Wilson papers, HHW 2/2E/15). The house in fact survived intact until it was burnt in 1922.
[96] The most reliable source for Longford during the period, and Seán MacEoin, is Coleman, *County Longford and the Irish Revolution*, part ii, 'War'.
[97] Wilson to Macready, 17 June, enclosing Mrs Kate McKeon [*sic*] to Wilson and reply, 14 and 17 June 1921 (Wilson papers, HHW 2/2E/22). Following a fight in February 1921 near Ballinalee, MacEoin had dealt quite chivalrously with the defeated Auxiliaries, so much so that three Auxiliaries gave character evidence on his behalf at his court-martial (Coleman, *County Longford and the Irish Revolution*, 126–7).   [98] Macready to Wilson, 18 June 1921 (Wilson papers, HHW 2/2E/25).

letters should carry some weight. Johnson was 'a real stout, loyal man', and his brother was 'as fearless and loyal a man as walks'.[99]

Macready was not very sympathetic and said he would confirm the death sentence. MacEoin was 'nothing more than a murderer', and 'without doubt responsible for many other atrocities'.[100] In his memoirs, Macready recalled meeting MacEoin while he was in custody, and found him a great contrast to most of the 'rebels' he met, who were 'of a fanatical, bitter cast of countenance'. MacEoin struck Macready 'as a more cheery individual than most of his fellows, and the possessor of a sense of humour of which all those I came across, with the exception of Michael Collins, had not an apparent spark'.[101] After the truce MacEoin, a member of the Dáil, was released, along with all other members of 'Valera's House of Commons'. As Henry Wilson sardonically remarked: 'there was no case for keeping McKeown [*sic*]. He was only a murderer.'[102] In a curious parallel with Wilson's career, MacEoin served as Chief of Staff of the Irish army in the late 1920s, and then went into politics, becoming a Fine Gael member of the Dáil, and a Cabinet minister in the 1940s and 1950s.[103]

During the summer of 1921 Wilson got in lots of sailing on his new yacht, frequently based at Cowes, where he had been elected a member of the exclusive Royal Yacht Squadron the previous year.[104] Apart from ten days' holiday shooting in Scotland in late August, he sailed every weekend from the end of June to mid-September, when he laid the yacht up for the winter. His constant sailing companion was Cecil's niece, Leonora Coote, 'Little Trench', who was renting a house near Gosport in Hampshire. 'L.T.' was obviously an important companion. 'I told her all my gossip,' wrote Wilson, '& she is so wonderfully intelligent & receptive.'[105] He was an adventurous sailor. In September he noted a 60-mile run from Weymouth to the Solent in under ten hours. 'We made a good passage in rather rough weather (LT and Jack both silent!) . . . the yacht sailing well.'[106]

On 3 August he had a close shave when he was knocked overboard by the main sheet, and was in the water for twenty minutes before being dragged out by Pope (his crewman) and another yachtsman. 'I was rather tired but luckily had not swallowed any water although at the end I was only just above water & the sea slapping me hard.' Dudley Ward, the sailor who came to help, recalled that when Wilson was hoisted out of the water, 'he was violently sick, opened his eyes and looked up and said "We do meet in some funny places, Dudley" '.[107] Typically, Wilson turned the event into an amusing anecdote. Little Trench and her two daughters were on board. 'The children saw me disappearing over the side,' he

[99] Wilson to Macready, 24 June, enclosing H. J. Johnson and J. Mackay Wilson to Wilson, 21 and 22 June 1921 (ibid. 2/2E/30). [100] Macready to Wilson, 25 June 1921 (ibid. 2/2E/31).
[101] Macready, *Annals of an Active Life*, ii. 585.
[102] Macready to Wilson and reply, 9 and 11 Aug. 1921 (Wilson papers, HHW 2/2E/57 and 58).
[103] O'Farrell, *The Seán MacEoin Story*. [104] *The Times*, 3 Aug. 1920.
[105] Wilson diary, 8 July 1921. [106] Ibid., 10 Sept. 1921. Jack Coote was Little Trench's husband.
[107] Ward (Lord Dorchester) to Frederick Sykes, 8 Aug. 1944 (Sykes papers).

wrote to 'Squibbie' Congreve, 'and set up the most terrific howling "Oh the poor darling". Little Trench, who did not see what had happened could not get either of the children to tell her what was the matter, they simply went on shrieking "Oh the poor darling" "Oh the poor darling".'[108] Macready urged Wilson 'for the Lord's sake do not go and drown yourself, as it would certainly be looked upon as a dispensation of Providence by the Catholic Church and their adherents'.[109]

Wilson also had his beloved gardening. He complained to Rawly about the dry spring and early summer of 1921. 'We have had about 13 or 14 years [*sic*] now of no rain', and his potatoes were 'about the size of marbles. I pass easily from a world problem . . . to potatoes which are a much more important topic at the moment.' Writing to Congreve a few days later, just after the Irish truce ('Valera having committed a certain number of murders has been invited to a Conference'), he blamed the hot weather for the fact 'that nothing is growing in my garden and when my time is up on the 19th February next I will apparently have to live on bugs'. He had 'hoped to stock a nice lot of potatoes, beetroot, turnips, carrots, parsnips to carry me on over the lean year; this hope, like many others, has now been shattered'.[110]

The end of 1921 was an intensely gloomy time for Wilson. Apart from the Irish treaty, a government 'committee on national expenditure', chaired by Sir Eric Geddes, issued a report recommending further army cuts: a reduction of 50,000 men (from 210,000), and £20 million off the £75 million army estimate.[111] This, thought Wilson, was 'frankly terrifying', and represented 'in short the kiss [of death] of the Empire'.[112] His 'swan song' at the War Office was a trenchantly argued paper rebutting the Geddes argument that Britain was militarily over-secured by comparison to the pre-war position. The paper contained a dismal list of commitments— India, Iraq, Palestine, Egypt, Constantinople. 'The situation at home', it asserted, 'has changed for the worse since 1914. Before the war the question of internal security in Great Britain hardly existed as a military pre-occupation.' Although in the current year 'the revolutionary forces' had 'received a decided check . . . the snake is only scotched and not killed'. As regards Ireland, Geddes had allowed nothing beyond four battalions for Ulster, which was thought to be a 'bold assumption'. Summarising the position, the paper concluded by declaring that 'we have definite evidence of a world-wide conspiracy fomented by all the elements most hostile to British interests—Sinn Feiners and Socialists at our own doors, Russian Bolsheviks, Turkish and Egyptian Nationalists and Indian

[108] Ibid., 3 Aug. 1921; Wilson to Walter Congreve, 16 Aug. 1921 (Wilson papers, HHW 2/52B/25); Oranmore diary, 30 Oct. 1921 (Oranmore papers). The *Daily Telegraph* (4 Aug. 1921) reported that Wilson had been sailing 'with his daughter and two grandchildren'.

[109] Macready to Wilson, 4 Aug. 1921 (Wilson papers, HHW 2/2E/55).

[110] Wilson to Rawlinson, 6 July; and to Sir Walter Congreve (GOC Egypt and Palestine), 12 July 1921 (ibid. 2/13D/30 and 2/52B/20).

[111] 'Interim report of committee on national expenditure', 14 Dec. 1921 (TNA, CAB 24/131, CP3570).

[112] Wilson to Sackville-West (Wilson papers, HHW 2/12G/70), and Wilson diary, 22 Dec. 1921.

Seditionists'. Thus no reduction at all was possible.[113] The paper had some effect, and a subsequent review headed by Churchill contrived to limit some of the army cuts, but it is no wonder that on 21 December, when Wilson gave a 'farewell address' at the Staff College, he entitled his lecture 'The Passing of the Empire'. He told his nominated successor, Lord Cavan, a steady, nice, but rather dull man, chosen no doubt as being the antithesis of Wilson, that 'before his 4 years were out he would have withdrawn our troops from India & from Egypt'.[114]

Over the turn of the year 1921–2 Wilson increasingly looked forward to the day when he could slough off the cares and frustrations of his job. All he could think for Cavan was that he had 'a horrid job in front of him' and 'the thankless task of carrying out the Geddes Comm[itt]ee'.[115] Wilson focused his frustrations onto the person of the Prime Minister. 'If', he wrote to 'Morlando' (Sir Thomas Morland), 'the highest art and form of statesmanship is to reduce an absolutely peaceful, quiet, thriving country into a hell then Lloyd George is a master.' Egypt would follow Ireland, and India Egypt, leaving Silesia, Constantinople, 'Jewland', and Mesopotamia. 'These would follow in succession' to leave England, which would also go, 'and then we shall be left with Ulster, and from there we shall have to start again and build an empire. Don't laugh, because bear in mind that Portugal once had an empire, and even Venice.'[116]

As the end of his time as CIGS approached, Wilson once more began to think about standing for parliament. In his journal in 1919 C. B. Thomson, the left-leaning officer who had been a Staff College student under Wilson, and whom he had employed both in the Directorate of Military Operations before the war and at the Supreme War Council in 1918, shrewdly predicted Wilson's political future. Thomson had gone to Wilson to tell him he was 'leaving the Army for politics', in part to escape the 'jealousy and intrigue' of army life. Thomson was off to join Labour. 'I did not tell the Field-Marshal which Party I was going to join,' he wrote, 'he would have had a fit.' Thomson, however, was 'pretty sure' Wilson, too, would 'be in politics before he is much older. I like this charming, brilliant Irishman, he has always been good to me. The Conservatives will make a fuss of him, but he, though with them, will never quite be of them.'[117]

Wilson was offered a seat in the Northern Ireland parliament, and Lord Dufferin told him 'they would make me a minister'.[118] There was talk of him fighting an English constituency, but a better offer came up when the Westminster seat of North Down fell vacant on the sitting member becoming a judge. Pressed by Craig, Wilson agreed to stand, so long (he told Rawlinson) as it

[113] Wilson to Rawlinson, 11 Jan. 1922 (Wilson papers, HHW 2/13F/29); 'Interim report of committee on national expenditure', paper by General Staff, 20 Jan. 1922 (TNA, CAB 24/132, CP3619).   [114] Wilson diary, 21 Dec. 1921 and 11 Jan. 1922.
[115] Ibid., 23 Dec. 1921 and 1 Jan. 1922.
[116] Wilson to Morland (GOC, Rhine Command), 13 Dec. 1921 (Wilson papers, HHW 2/57/59).   [117] Journal entry, 25 July 1919 (quoted in Thomson, *Smaranda*, 118).
[118] Wilson diary, 28 Dec. 1921. Dufferin was Speaker of the Northern Ireland Senate.

should only be until the next general election, he was unopposed, and 'that it would only cost me from one hundred to two hundred pounds'.[119] Little Trench had urged him 'to accept North Down', and his cousin, Percy Creed, told him that Wilson's marketability for company directorships would be greatly enhanced as an MP.[120] In due course, on 21 February, three days after he retired as CIGS, Wilson was elected unopposed for the constituency. 'I wonder where all this will lead?', he wrote in his diary. 'It is certain that I am not becoming an M.P. at 58 with a view to a career or with any personal axe to grind.'[121] Maybe so, but he was surely determined to take on Lloyd George. Although Macready had hoped that Wilson would not find himself 'inside the monkey-house at Westminster', once Wilson had become an MP, he had 'no doubt that you will be a thorn in the flesh of our Lloyd before you have finished with him', and he began to feed him titbits of inside information with which he could embarrass the government.[122] Writing to Tim Harington in June 1922, Wilson expressed the strong wish that Lloyd George could be ejected from power. 'All my energies public & private', he wrote, 'are devoted to getting rid of that pack of Cowards the present Cabinet.'[123]

After his death, *Punch* said that Wilson had displayed a 'striking aptitude for Parliamentary life',[124] but it is difficult to substantiate this. He spoke, with commendable brevity, on only seven occasions: twice on the service estimates (rehearsing his opinion that British commitments had increased since before 1914), and the other times on Irish matters.[125] Austen Chamberlain reported that Wilson, 'as always, was incisive, dangerous and mischievous'.[126] Maurice Cowling judges that Wilson represented 'a formidable accession of strength to the Die Hards', the extreme Conservatives in the Commons, who even contemplated him leading their group.[127] On 11 May Carson told Wilson that he 'had made an amazing impression in & out of the House & he begged me to think over taking the Leadership of the Conservative Party! What nonsense.'[128]

In March 1922 Sir James Craig invited Wilson to advise the new Northern Ireland government on security. On St Patrick's Day he presented his plans at a conference at the Ministry of Home Affairs in Belfast. He called for an increase in the number of Special Constables, but counselled against the 'Specials' being an exclusively Protestant body. The police should comprise citizens 'irrespective of class or creed', and 'encouragement should be given to Catholics to join equally with the other religions'. This would allow 'those who were loyal and wished to see

---

[119] Wilson to Rawlinson, 13 Feb. 1922 (Wilson papers, HHW 2/13F/40). Despite his claim that he only wanted the seat until the next election, the parliamentary stipend of £400 a year may have been a factor.   [120] Wilson diary, 4 Feb. 1922.

[121] Ibid., 21 Feb. 1922.

[122] Macready to Wilson, 14 and 23 Feb. 1922 (Wilson papers, HHW 2/2G/60 and 2/2H/1). For copies of letters and other confidential official information sent by Macready to Wilson, see letters of 27 Feb., 8, 20 Mar. 1922 (ibid. 2/2H/4, 7, 11).

[123] Wilson to Harington, 11 June 1922 (Harington papers, box 12).

[124] *Punch*, 28 June 1922, 524.   [125] 15, 21, 22 Mar., 12 Apr., 10, 30, 31 May 1922.

[126] Chamberlain to Winston Churchill, 11 May 1922 (Chamberlain papers, AC 35/1/11).

[127] Cowling, *The Impact of Labour*, 186.   [128] Wilson diary, 11 May 1922.

settled conditions in the Six Counties' to be 'given the opportunity of declaring their willingness to assist in stamping out crime'. Wilson also emphasised the need to keep public opinion on the side of law and order, and said 'it was essential to secure the confidence of all law-abiding people in the ability of the Government to govern'. With the unhappy example of the Black and Tans clearly in mind, Wilson proposed that a senior army officer be appointed as military adviser and to command all the police in Northern Ireland.[129] As Macready commented: 'everything will depend on your getting a really good man', and 'his getting really good officers... not the riffraff that became so-called officers of the Black and Tans'.[130] When Craig reported Wilson's proposals to his Cabinet he said that they were 'merely a strengthening of the existing organization and forces'. Nothing was said about the religious composition of the Specials.[131]

While Craig publicly celebrated the engagement of 'so distinguished a soldier' to advise on security,[132] Wilson, for his part, was not much taken with the Ulstermen. Craig, he thought, was 'a very second rate man, self satisfied, lazy & bad judge of men & events', 'well pleased with himself & full of stories of his passed [*sic*] clevernesses & present greatness'. Richard Dawson Bates (the Minister of Home Affairs) was 'a small man in every way & thought'. Colonel Charles Wickham, head of what became the Royal Ulster Constabulary, was no more than 'a Major of average ability'.[133] Wilson's worries about the Northern Ireland administration evidently fuelled his anxiety to see that firm military discipline was imposed on the police, an attitude further reinforced by the communal sectarian violence which afflicted Northern Ireland in 1922, and in which elements of the Ulster Special Constabulary were implicated. But whatever Wilson's private opinions about Northern Ireland, his high public profile in support of the new Ulster Unionist regime associated him in the eyes of Irish republicans with whatever oppressive and violent action militant loyalists might take in the province. In March 1922, for example, Michael Collins categorised Wilson as 'a violent Orange partisan', and the republican Ernie O'Malley, in one of his books of memoirs, simply blamed Wilson for the Ulster Special Constabulary.[134] Opinions such as this were quite enough to put Wilson's own life at risk.

[129] Secret minutes of a conference at Ministry of Home Affairs, 17 Mar. 1922 (PRONI, HA/20/A/1/8). For the Northern Ireland security situation generally, see Follis, *A State Under Siege*, 82–115, and, for an account markedly less sympathetic to the Unionist administration, Farrell, *Arming the Protestants*.

[130] Macready to Wilson, 20 Mar. 1922 (Wilson papers, HHW 2/2H/11).

[131] Cabinet final conclusions, 27 Mar. 1922 (PRONI, CAB 4/37/13).

[132] As, for example, in the Northern Ireland House of Commons, 14 Mar. 1922 (*Hansard N.I. (Commons)*, ii, cols. 13–14).   [133] Wilson diary, 27 and 17 Mar. 1922.

[134] *The Times*, 24 Mar. 1922; O'Malley, *The Singing Flame*, 85.

14

Death and reputation

Henry Wilson died on Thursday 22 June 1922.[1] He had been invited by the chairman of the Great Eastern Railway to unveil the company's war memorial at Liverpool Street Station in London. At about one o'clock, following an early lunch with the directors of the railway, Wilson made a brief speech and unveiled the memorial, which commemorates the 1,200 railwaymen who lost their lives in the war. As was his wont, Wilson spoke only briefly. 'We soldiers', he said, 'count as our gains our losses. In doing what these men thought was right they paid the penalty', words with which the subsequent press reports made much play. At the end of the ceremony Wilson, accompanied by Lieutenant-Colonel Harold Charley,[2] took an underground train to Charing Cross Station. Wilson's use of public transport was certainly of a piece with his general lack of *amour propre*, and perhaps also a money-saving exercise, though he presumably travelled on the first-class accommodation then provided by the District and Metropolitan Railways. The spectacle of a field marshal in uniform (complete with sword), moreover, is not quite as extraordinary as it might seem. Fellow passengers on the District Line, for example, were accustomed to seeing uniformed Guardsmen travelling from Chelsea Barracks to mount the Bank of England guard.[3]

Wilson and Charley parted at Charing Cross, where Wilson got a taxi. On the way home to Eaton Place he paused at the Travellers' Club in Pall Mall, of which he had been a member for several years, and where he liked to check up on the latest news coming over the agency telegraph machine. At about twenty-past two he reached home, where, at his front door, he was attacked by two men, Reginald Dunne and Joseph O'Sullivan, who shot him dead. Dunne, who was commander of the IRA in London, smuggled a report of the shooting out of prison, which has

---

[1] The following narrative has been assembled from the press reports in *The Times*, *Daily News*, *Daily Herald*, *Daily Mirror*, and *Morning Post*. Rex Taylor, *Assassination*, is devoted to the circumstances of Wilson's death. An essential source is Peter Hart's fine essay, 'Michael Collins and the Assassination of Sir Henry Wilson'.

[2] Charley commanded the first battalion Royal Ulster Rifles, of which Wilson had been honorary colonel since 1916.

[3] The officers travelled first class; the other ranks third. I am indebted to Dr D. B. McNeill for this information.

an authentic air and fits the evidence of witnesses at the inquest and that provided by the post-mortem examination:

Joe [wrote Dunne] went in a straight line while I determined to intercept him (W.) from entering the door. Joe deliberately levelled his weapon at four yards range and fired twice. Wilson made for the door as best he could and actually reached the doorstep when I encountered him at a range of 7 or 8 feet. I fired three shots rapidly, the last one from the hip, as I took a step forward. Wilson was now uttering short cries and in a doubled up position staggered towards the edge of the pavement. At this point Joe fired once again and the last I saw of him he (W.) had collapsed.[4]

At the inquest on 26 June, the taxi-driver recounted seeing only one gunman, who, from a range of about three yards, fired three shots at Wilson. A road-mender, one of two working in the street outside 36 Eaton Place, gave a clearer statement. He

said he saw Sir Henry Wilson get out of a taxi-cab. Sir Henry took a pace across the pavement when witness heard a report. Sir Henry completed the distance across the pavement and had just got his foot on the first step when there was another shot. Sir Henry attempted to put the key in the door when there was more firing. Sir Henry bent down as though to avoid more shots. There was more firing, and witness saw the Field-Marshal fall across the pavement, his head on the kerb. Witness saw a big man with a revolver standing on the kerb about three yards from the General.

Witness said he saw that man actually fire once. He saw a smaller man also with a revolver directly behind the taxi-cab. He would be about four yards from Sir Henry.

The Coroner—So that actually there was one man on each side of the Field-Marshal, about three or four yards from him?—Yes.

Witness said he saw both men fire several shots.[5]

The 'big man' was Dunne, who was six feet tall and 'well built'; O'Sullivan was a few inches shorter.[6]

In the immediate aftermath of the killing, one of the workmen had given the *Daily Mail* a rather more dramatic account, with vivid detail which might owe more to the imaginative powers of the reporter than the recollections of the eyewitness. 'The General', he said:

walked quietly up the steps to the front door, and after taking the key from his pocket fitted it in the lock. Then I heard a shot. My mate shouted, 'Look out, sir,' and the General ducked his head.

I looked quickly at the two men, one of whom was standing on the pavement, while the other was about six paces to the right of him and standing in the road. Both had revolvers and were taking deliberate aim at the General.

One shot hit the General in the right arm just above the wrist, and, dropping the key, the General still ducking, swung round, darted down the steps, shouting to the men.

---

[4] Published in the *Sunday Press*, 14 Aug. 1955.   [5] *Morning Post*, 27 June 1922.
[6] Descriptions of the two men in police notice published on 23 June (copy in IWM Department of Documents).

'You cowardly swine!' he cried, and then another shot hit him in the side, and as he fell another hit him in the leg.

About eleven shots were fired at the General altogether.[7]

At the trial of the two men, the pathologist, Dr Bernard Spillsbury, gave details of the gunshot wounds. Wilson, he said, had wounds from six bullets. He had been fatally injured in the chest by two shots, one from each side. There was also a flesh wound to his right shoulder, one just below his right knee, a shot had passed through his right wrist, and the sixth bullet had grazed the skin on the inside of his left arm.[8] Spillsbury's evidence confirmed that each man had fired a potentially fatal shot.

According to Dunne's own report, he and O'Sullivan had only decided to mount some sort of demonstration on the previous evening, when they had learned of Wilson's scheduled unveiling of the memorial. He said that they had immediately gone to reconnoitre Liverpool Street Station. There they discovered that the booking hall, where the memorial was situated, 'would be closed to the general public'. Since 'there seemed no possibility of a successful operation in the vicinity of the station', they then decided to go to Wilson's house and wait for him there.[9] In his dramatised (and only haphazardly sourced) account of the events, Rex Taylor says that Dunne told both J. H. MacDonnell (his lawyer) and Denis Kelleher (adjutant of the London IRA) that they had not planned to kill Wilson, and the shooting had happened in the heat of the moment.[10] True or not, both men were certainly prepared to kill. They each carried British service-issue Webley revolvers, and O'Sullivan had taken part in a previous IRA killing in April 1921.[11] On the other hand, very little thought had evidently been given to the scheme, whatever it was. There was no escape plan, and the fact that O'Sullivan, who was employed as a messenger in the Ministry of Labour, had been 'at work at his duty up to one o'clock on the day of the murder',[12] adds weight to the claims of spontaneity.

Following the attack, Dunne and O'Sullivan attempted in vain to commandeer a taxi, and after a 'hue and cry' of about three-quarters of a mile through Belgravia, during which they shot and wounded two policemen and a civilian, they were arrested in Ebury Street. Once their true identities had been established, it emerged that both men had served in the British army. O'Sullivan, from Bantry, county Cork, had enlisted in the Royal Munster Fusiliers in January 1915, and as a result of war injury had lost his right leg below the knee, a handicap indeed as he tried to escape on 22 June. Dunne, an expatriate from a British army family, had

---

[7] *Daily Mail* report, quoted in *Belfast News-Letter*, 24 June 1922.

[8] *Rex* v. *Reginald Dunne & Joseph O'Sullivan*, 18 July 1922, transcript of shorthand notes (TNA, HO 144/3689).

[9] Dunne report (*Sunday Press*, 14 Aug. 1955). The memorial has since been placed at the mezzanine approach to the station.   [10] Taylor, *Assassination*, 181–3.

[11] Hart, 'Michael Collins and the Assassination of Sir Henry Wilson', 198.

[12] Note by Commissioner of the Metropolitan Police, 22 June 1922 (TNA, HO 144/3689).

joined the Irish Guards in June 1916. At their trial Dunne linked his war service
with his later actions as an IRA man. Addressing the jury, he said he had 'no
doubt' that several of them had done their 'best in the recent great European War.
I also took my share in that war,' he continued, 'fighting for the principles for
which this country stood. Those principles I found as an Irishman were not
applied to my own country and I have endeavoured to strike a blow for it.' In a
longer statement, which he was not allowed to read out in court, Dunne went into
greater detail about his motivation. Wilson, he said, was 'the man behind what is
known in Ireland as the Orange Terror'. As 'Military Adviser' to the Belfast
government, 'he raised and organised a body of men known as the Ulster Special
Constables, who are the principal agents in his campaign of terrorism'. 'What we
have done', he concluded, 'was necessary to preserve the lives, the homes, and the
happiness of our countrymen in Ireland.'[13]

None of this patriotic, political justification washed with the trial jury, who
took just three minutes to decide on the men's guilt. For Irish republicans,
however, their 'guilt' was a glorious thing. 'It was a good day for Ireland', wrote
O'Sullivan's cousin, 'that day yourself and your hero of a companion went out and
layed [*sic*] the second Cromwell dead at your feet.'[14] Reggie Dunne and Joe
O'Sullivan were sentenced to death and, after an appeal had been rejected, hanged
at Wandsworth Prison on 10 August 1922.[15] Apparently as a reprisal for their execution, later that day the Wilson family home of Currygrane was burnt down.[16]

There is no longer any mystery about the question of 'who gave the order' for
Henry Wilson's shooting. Peter Hart's fastidious, forensic investigation of the
matter, first published in 1993, convincingly concludes that 'there is no solid
evidence to support a conspiracy theory linking Michael Collins or anyone else to
the murder', and that 'we must accept the assertions of the murderers that they
acted alone, in the (grossly mistaken) belief that Wilson was responsible for
Catholic deaths in Belfast'.[17]

Nevertheless, at the time of Wilson's death wild rumours and conjecture swept
through London about who was ultimately responsible for the killing. That the
two gunmen were Irish republicans was evident from the start. Although at the
time of their arrest both men gave false names, Dunne's *nom de guerre* of James
Connolly (one of the executed leaders of the 1916 Rising) was a clear sign of
political allegiance. But was there a wider conspiracy, involving the republican

[13] *Rex* v. *Reginald Dunne & Joseph O'Sullivan*, 18 July 1922, transcript of shorthand notes; TS
copy of Dunne's statement, 17 July 1922 (TNA, HO 144/3689).
[14] 'Bob' to O'Sullivan, 25 July 1922 (intercepted letter) (TNA, PCOM 8/367).
[15] Papers relating to their execution are in TNA, PCOM 8/367 and 368.
[16] But see the comments in Coleman, *County Longford and the Irish Revolution*, 145, which suggest that local agrarian agitation may have been a factor.
[17] Hart, 'Michael Collins and the Assassination of Sir Henry Wilson', 170. The allegation that
Collins was involved is, however, remarkably persistent. In 2004 Nicholas Canny wrote that Wilson
'was assassinated . . . by two agents of Michael Collins' ('Foreword', in Kenny (ed.), *Ireland and the
British Empire*, p. xii).

movement in Ireland? Early in January the Dáil in Dublin had approved the Anglo-Irish treaty by a small majority, and a pro-treaty 'provisional government' led by Arthur Griffith and Michael Collins had been formed. The anti-treaty wing of Sinn Féin and the IRA, however, still firmly committed to the aim of a fully independent Irish republic, broke away. And at the time of Wilson's death there was an armed stand-off in Ireland between the two groups, with anti-treaty forces under Rory O'Connor having occupied the Four Courts in Dublin.

For a hastily convened conference in 10 Downing Street at five o'clock on the afternoon of the killing, suspicion pointed to the 'extreme section of the I.R.A.', especially those in the Four Courts, 'from which are believed to emanate the principal plots'. Ministers agreed that the challenge represented by O'Connor's defiant stand was intolerable, and that the provisional government in Dublin 'should be pressed to deal with the matter'.[18] Macready was summoned to London, where (as he recalled in his memoirs) he found 'the Prime Minister and certain members of the Government in a state of suppressed agitation on which considerations of personal safety seemed to contend with the desire to do something dramatic as a set-off against the assassination of Henry Wilson'. He was asked if the Four Courts 'could be captured at once' by British troops. He was sure that it could, but, aware that this would undoubtedly plunge Ireland into a grave crisis, and do much to reunite the pro- and anti-treaty factions, on his return to Dublin he deliberately delayed taking military action.[19] O'Connor, in fact, was not responsible for Wilson's killing, but the *suspicion* of his complicity, and the consequent British pressure on Dublin, were very important factors (though not the only ones) in the Irish government's eventual decision to attack the Four Courts which, in turn, helped precipitate the Irish Civil War of 1922–3.[20]

Henry Wilson's death became him as much as any other event during his lifetime, and it rapidly achieved a mythic quality. The *Belfast News-Letter* called him the 'martyred Field Marshal'.[21] Much turned on the question of his sword: did he or did he not use it when he was attacked? Lord Arthur Hill, a veteran Unionist MP, who called at the house during the evening after the killing, told the *Morning Post*: 'it was fairly evident that Sir Henry had had recourse to the only weapon about him—his sword. It was plain that he drew the sword; when he was discovered the weapon was found out of its scabbard.' Asked if the sword 'might have been dislodged in the fall', Lord Arthur said that was 'impossible', as 'there was a clip which rendered it necessary to use very material effort to draw the sword from its scabbard'.[22] One witness told the *Daily News* that when Wilson 'reached the top of the steps he hesitated before trying to open his door and drew his sword and prepared to defend his life, but the sword was no match against the revolvers'.[23]

18 Conclusions of a conference of ministers, 22 June 1922 (TNA, CAB 21/255).
19 Macready, *Annals of an Active Life*, ii. 652–4.
20 See Hopkinson, *Green Against Green*, 112–22.   21 *Belfast News-Letter*, 24 June 1922.
22 *Morning Post*, 23 June 1922.   23 *Daily News*, 23 June 1922.

At the inquest on 26 June, Amy Cornabie, a maid in the Wilson household, who rushed out of the house after the shooting to find Wilson lying on his back on the pavement, was specifically asked by the coroner: 'was his sword drawn?' 'Yes, sir', she replied, it was lying by his side. 'Had he got his hand on it?—No, sir.'[24] Reporting the scene outside 36 Eaton Place before Wilson's funeral on 26 June, *The Times*'s reporter described that, when the front door was opened, it was possible to see the sword 'still standing in the hall where it had been placed after he had drawn it for the last time in an attempt to thwart his assassins'.[25] 'A soldier's duty he did', wrote 'one who knew him' in a memoir for the *Daily Mirror*, and he 'met a soldier's death.'[26]

By the time Charles Callwell came to write his official biography five years later, the story of the sword had become fixed. Wilson was approaching his front door when 'one of the two young men who had been loitering at the street corner' shot at him 'but apparently missed. The Field-Marshal turned and drew his sword. Both men at once opened fire and their victim fell, mortally wounded.'[27] In the hands of one of his most astringent critics, the action became emblematic of Wilson's flaws. 'He turned and drew his sword,' wrote Sir Andrew MacPhail. 'It was a courageous but fatal gesture. He had not engrained into his nature that swords are obsolete, that flesh and blood will not endure fire.' Warming to his theme, MacPhail added that, had Wilson been 'a man of intellectual quickness, he would have observed that his assailants were thirty feet away, and remembered that they were under a nervous strain that would render their aim uncertain'. Had be been 'a man of humour and sympathy, he might have left his sword alone, and if he turned at all, addressed to the two men a few firm kind words. They might have changed their minds and gone away.'[28]

The public reaction to Wilson's killing reinforces how extraordinarily shocking it was. It was a profoundly un-British event; the sort of thing which might (and did) happen on the Continent, but not in England. Some, however, saw a wider, European context. The National Socialist Austrian novelist, Bruno von Brehm, for example, made Wilson's assassination 'symbolic of the tragic confrontation of hero and submen'.[29] At home, condemnation was complete. 'The peculiarly British horror of political assassination, which would make the ordinary Englishman shudder equally at the murder of a Die-Hard leader or a Communist leader, is', asserted the Liberal weekly the *Nation*, 'one of the soundest instincts in our nature.'[30] It was the first assassination of a Member of Parliament in London since Spencer Perceval was shot dead in the lobby of the House of Commons in 1812. (The next was on 30 March 1979, when a bomb planted by the Irish National Liberation Army blew up the Conservative MP Airey Neave in his car at Westminster.) The 'Irish dimension' of the affair was widely remarked, and

---

[24] *Daily News*, 27 June 1922. She repeated this assertion at Dunne and O'Sullivan's trial.
[25] *The Times*, 27 June 1922.   [26] *Daily Mirror*, 23 June 1922.
[27] Callwell, *Wilson*, ii. 346   [28] MacPhail, *Three Persons*, 150–1.
[29] See the brief discussion in O'Brien, *Passion and Cunning*, 53.   [30] *Nation*, 1 July 1922, 463.

parallels were drawn with the Phoenix Park murders of May 1882, when the Chief Secretary, Lord Frederick Cavendish, and the Under-secretary, Thomas Henry Burke, were killed. 'Great as is our loss,' pronounced the *Daily Express*, 'Ireland's is the greater. Ireland's good name, her status as a civilised country, her whole future are imperilled by this dastardly political murder.' In England, 'no such crime has been perpetrated for a century. The Phoenix Park outrage, never forgotten here, long cost Ireland Home Rule. Will the murder in Eaton-place rob her of more than Home Rule?'[31] Stephen Gwynn, a prominent Irish writer and former nationalist MP, said Wilson's murder had been 'a crime against Ireland', and added that the blame for it would be 'placed on Ireland'.[32]

Cecil Wilson, however, bitterly blamed Lloyd George and his government. When Austen Chamberlain, the Lord Privy Seal and leader of the Conservative party, went to Eaton Place to offer his condolences, Lady Wilson is reported to have greeted him with the one word, 'murderer'.[33] As recounted in the *Morning Post*, the incident was less dramatic, though similar in tone. When Chamberlain called on the evening of the tragedy, he was received by 'a niece of Lady Wilson's' (possibly Leonora 'Little' Trench). On ascertaining who he was she said: 'You are the last man who should be in this house to-day', and he had to leave 'without accomplishing his mission'.[34] The day after the killing, Cecil Wilson asked Ronald McNeill, the Ulster-born Diehard MP for Canterbury, to inform Chamberlain of her 'wish that no member of the Government should attend the funeral'. 'No one', wrote McNeill, 'can feel any surprise at her desire who has any knowledge of the sentiments of the late Field Marshal towards the Government since they entered upon friendly intercourse with the criminal conspiracy in Ireland to which he has now fallen a victim.' Lady Wilson at once came under terrific pressure to change her mind. Chamberlain conceded that, while the government would have 'no choice but to obey' her wishes, 'such a course' would be 'deeply distressing to us personally who were so closely associated with him in the greatest task of his life'. Not only that, it would be monumentally insulting to Lloyd George and his colleagues. Both *raison d'état* and political *amour propre* demanded that the government be represented. Lady Wilson was told 'that the absence of Members of the Government' from the funeral 'would be regarded as want of respect to His Majesty', and on those grounds she agreed 'to waive her own feelings in the matter'. McNeill thought this was a specious argument, 'since His Majesty would be personally represented by others than his political advisers'. But even he recognised the public necessity of the political establishment closing ranks on this occasion, and 'did not consider it any part of my duty to tell Lady Wilson that such a use of the King's name was wholly unwarranted'.[35]

---

[31] *Daily Express*, 23 June 1922.
[32] *Observer*, 25 June 1922. Gwynn was MP for Galway, 1906–18.
[33] Dutton, *Austen Chamberlain*, 172. [34] *Morning Post*, 24 June 1922.
[35] MacNeill to Chamberlain (2 letters), and reply, 23 June 1922 (Chamberlain papers, AC 24/4/19–21).

According to Frances Stevenson, Lloyd George was 'very upset, as we all are'. Whatever Wilson had 'done lately,' she wrote in her diary, 'he was a most loveable person, & we were very near to him during the war'.[36] Public effusions of closeness, however, were another thing. In a noisy debate in the House of Commons on the day of the funeral, Lloyd George said that he 'was proud of Sir Henry Wilson's friendship' and that 'he had evidence quite recently, that, that friendship continued on his part after disagreements'. Although the Prime Minster was presumably referring to Wilson's February 1922 'farewell' letter as CIGS, this statement was too much for Wilson's mother, Grace. She wrote to Bonar Law to say that Lloyd George's statement was 'absolutely false', 'sadly a contradiction to my son's feelings', and 'most hurtful to the family'. She asked if he 'would tell the Prime Minister and the Cabinet how very much we feel these mis-statements and that perhaps they will abstain in future from making them'.[37]

The funeral was a solemn and impressive state occasion. *The Times* reported that 'hundreds of thousands' of Wilson's 'fellow-countrymen stood bareheaded and motionless in an unbroken avenue that stretched, often ten and sometimes twenty deep, all the way from Eaton-place to St. Paul's Cathedral'.[38] As with the politicians, the military also closed ranks. Among the pall-bearers, 'who represented all that was most noble and most glorious in modern England', were not only French and Macready, but also Haig and Robertson, 'the victors of the Great War', 'paying the last honours to one who had shared with them the glory and the victory'. Lloyd George and the Cabinet attended, as did Foch, Nivelle, and Weygand from France. 'Among the relatives and intimate friends of the Field-Marshal', reported the *Morning Post*, 'were some twenty loyalist refugees from Ireland, for whom accommodation had been given at the special request of Lady Wilson.' The Irish link, too, was emphasised at the very end. Describing Wilson as 'a warrior Irishman', *The Times* noted that he 'was put to rest' in the cathedral crypt 'between two gallant Irishmen, Lord Roberts and Lord Wolseley'.[39]

Wilson's Irishness was stressed in many of the reports and obituaries accompanying his passing. The *Morning Post*, the English champion of the abandoned southern Irish unionists, and Wilson's favoured newspaper, was especially eloquent on the topic. Wilson, it said, 'died for his country. He was an Irishman—a great Irishman; he was a soldier—a great soldier; and he was a loyal subject of the King.' Readers were reminded that Wilson had been killed on the first anniversary of King George V's speech in Belfast 'which was used as the signal or the pretext for the surrender. In a single year', it continued, 'it is come to this—such is the success of the policy—that the remnant of the Irish Loyalists in the North are

[36] Frances Stevenson diary, 22 June 1922 (Stevenson papers, FLS/4/11).
[37] Grace Wilson to Bonar Law, 29 June 1922 (Bonar Law papers, 107/2/53).
[38] Descriptions of the funeral extracted from *The Times* and the *Morning Post*, 27 June 1922. There is a Pathé newsreel of the event: 'Funeral of Sir H Wilson', <http://www.britishpathe.com> (Film ID: 272.12), accessed 24 May 2005.
[39] According to the *Morning Post*, Wilson's grave 'had been destined for Lord Kitchener'.

fighting desperately for bare life in Ireland, and in London a most illustrious leader can be shot dead at his own door'.[40]

But there were other ways of linking Wilson's death with Ireland. The Liberal-leaning *Daily News*, while calling the killing a 'disgusting outrage', also asserted that Wilson's 'political influence' was 'an almost unmixed danger to Ireland, to this country, and to the world'. The deed, moreover, took 'its place as merely the latest instance of the orgy of murder which has been raging for weeks past in Belfast'. Wilson, furthermore, was not himself blameless: 'A man is responsible for the spirits which he raises; he cannot disavow if he will all connection with their activities, remote as they may be from his own temper and aims.'[41] The *New Statesman* was equally critical. Wilson, 'with his fanatical Orangeism, his remarkable abilities, his great military prestige, and his powerful and inflammatory speeches, did more, perhaps, than any other man' to create the current situation in Northern Ireland, 'and to promote that spirit of ruthless and stupid retaliation which has led to his own death'. In Irish politics, 'Sir Henry Wilson was the counterpart of Mr. Cathal Brugha. Both believed in force and force alone.' Such policies, concluded the commentator, 'do not lead to the establishment either of Republics or of Empires. Their logical outcome is chaos—and the tragedy of Eaton place.'[42]

An obituary in the *Daily Mail* conceded that Wilson 'made enemies, as anyone with his deadly analytical brain and unsparing tongue must do. But not in the Army. Only in the world of politics.' Lord Milner, writing in the *Observer*, dismissed Wilson's alleged 'Prussianism': 'Anything more unlike the typical "Prussian militarist" than this genial, warm-hearted humorous and irrepressibly boyish Irishman cannot possibly be imagined.' He was, moreover, 'one of the noblest members of our race'.[43] In the *Daily Telegraph* T. P. O'Connor, veteran Irish Nationalist MP and journalist, described Wilson 'as typically Irish in many of his qualities: in accent, in the Irish hatred of compromise—one of their chief and greatest weaknesses. Above all he was Irish in the curious combination of violent opinion and personal good nature.' For the *Daily Express* Wilson was 'no halfway man. Even those who could not agree with him admired his undeviating strength of purpose, his marvellous gift of quick and definite decision, and his personality which marked him out as one of the "big" men of the age.'[44]

Of all the obituarists, perhaps the most intriguing was his old foe, Charles à Court Repington, who wrote about him in the *Daily Telegraph*. Wilson, he declared, was one of the army's 'most brilliant and arresting figures'. Repington, in fact, was quite generous-spirited, remarking on Wilson's 'strong and cheerful personality which impressed itself on all who knew him'. His 'chief title to fame was his early realisation of the probability of a war with Germany and his ardent

[40] *Morning Post*, 23 June 1922.   [41] *Daily News*, 23 June 1922.
[42] *New Statesman*, 39/480 (24 June 1922). Brugha was one of the most militant anti-treaty republicans. He died on 7 July 1922 from wounds received during the early fighting of the Irish Civil War.
[43] *Daily Mail*, 23 June 1922; *Observer*, 25 June 1922.
[44] *Daily Telegraph*, *Daily Express*, 23 June 1922.

co-operation with the French in preparation for that contingency and the subsequent prosecution of the war'. Perhaps thinking of how his own military career had ended, Repington noted that Wilson 'was quick to see and seize an advantage', and there was perhaps some ambiguity to his observation that Wilson 'brought rare ability and great flexibility of mind to bear on the conduct of many different negotiations'. He shrewdly assessed the contemporary relationship of soldier and politician. 'It is with democratic politics', he wrote, 'that the modern soldier, who is the chief adviser of the Government at home, has to work and it is essential that he should be able to work efficiently and in harmony with the Cabinet.' Although this was 'easier said than done . . . by mutual concessions it can be done', and he reckoned it possible 'that Sir Henry Wilson may be the precursor of a new type'.[45]

Much sympathy was expressed for Cecil Wilson. An article on her in the strongly right-wing weekly the *Democrat* asserted that 'no man was ever more fortunate in the partner of his joys and sorrows'. The unnamed writer further argued that 'the predominant influence' in Wilson's decision to enter parliament had been 'the firm conviction of Lady Wilson that his country needed him'.[46] According to her family history, Cecil Wilson 'never recovered' from the 'horrifying shock and tragedy of her husband's death'.[47] But she clearly resolved to secure Sir Henry's reputation in every way she could. Late in 1922 she agreed to the setting-up of a 'Field Marshal Sir Henry Wilson Memorial Fund', for 'the benefit of any poor widows and/or the poor children or child of any officer or officers of the Army, British or Colonial'.[48] Although money was raised in 1922, the fund did not become active until after Cecil Wilson died on 14 April 1930. In her will, from an estate totalling £13,400, she left £1,000 to the fund.[49] In the 1960s, along with a number of similar small charities, it was subsumed within the 'Officers' Families Fund'.

Cecil Wilson also began to look for someone to write an 'official biography'. There is some evidence that Wilson had it in mind to write his memoirs. Wilson knew full well that his diaries would make the basis of a sensational publication, and he used to tease friends with quotations from them.[50] He systematically collected all his personal letters as CIGS and had them put to one side for his 'private papers'.[51] When he left office he took with him 130 numbered files containing correspondence with some 65 individuals, apparently comprising virtually all his official and semi-official correspondence from the time he became British military representative on the Supreme War Council in November 1917

[45] 'Dead Field-Marshal: an appreciation', and 'Sir Henry Wilson: some reflections' (*Daily Telegraph*, 23 and 24 June 1922).   [46] *Democrat*, 1 July 1922, 7.
[47] Trench, *The Wrays of Donegal*, 379. The writer was a niece of Cecil's.
[48] The Trust deed is dated 8 December 1922.
[49] *The Times*, 15 Apr., 12 Aug. 1930; will of Cecil Mary Wilson (proved 6 June 1930).
[50] Harry Lewin (Lord Roberts's son-in-law) to Frederick Sykes, 19 Sept. 1944 (Sykes papers).
[51] See e.g. 'H.W.' notes, 4 Jan. and 21 Feb. 1922, with correspondence in Wilson papers, HHW 2/46B/46, 2/2G/68.

until his retirement in February 1922.[52] There was also money to be made. In September 1921 Wilson was told that Wully Robertson had been paid £14,000 for his memoirs.[53] And the strong public demand for memoirs was demonstrated by the sales in 1919 and 1920 of Lord French's book *1914* and Repington's *The First World War*, though James Edmonds thought Repington had lost his 'social position' through basing the latter on his gossip-filled diary.[54]

Lady Wilson asked F. S. Oliver if he would write a biography, but he declined for fear 'of being tied by the leg by the widow'.[55] She then persuaded Sir Charles Callwell, an Irishman and a long-time friend and colleague of Wilson's, to take on the task. Callwell had himself been DMO in 1914–15, was a prolific writer on military matters, and seemed ideally suited for the task. He thought the diaries were 'of rare historical interest, and very illuminating on many matters', but he was also quite alive to their sensitivity. 'They are', he wrote, 'extremely outspoken, and very critical of most soldiers on the British side during the War.' Wilson, he thought, was 'also extremely critical of all politicians, British and French alike; but, as far as I am concerned, the politicians must take their chance'. So far as the soldiers were concerned, however, Callwell wanted to present their position 'reasonably impartially and not to accept all that H.W. says without comment'.[56]

Whatever Callwell's feelings regarding the differential treatment of politicians and soldiers in the biography, from the beginning he seems to have fallen in with Cecil Wilson's desire to press on quickly with publication and to quote extensively from the diaries. Interviewed after the book came out, Callwell was reported as having said he thought it was 'a pity, perhaps, that the diary should be published so early, but that matter did not rest with me'.[57] Cecil Wilson, moreover, had a clear political agenda. Approached in the 1940s by Sir Frederick Sykes (who had been asked by Wilson's sister, Eileen Price-Davies, to explore the possibility of a new memoir), Bill Thwaites said 'Callwell's book' was 'instigated by Henry's widow as a fling at the politicians of the day', in particular Lloyd George.[58] Bill Furse told Sykes that he had 'implored' Callwell not to undertake publication of the diary. 'Lady Wilson', he added, 'was most ill-advised to insist on its publication.' William Bartholomew claimed that 'I for one did my best to stop it [publication of the diaries] but Lady Wilson would have it'.[59] Eileen Price-Davies thought the fault was Callwell's. 'Charlie Caldwell [*sic*]', she wrote, 'had I believe no sense of humour, a serious handicap for anyone attempting to write Henry's life!'[60]

[52] See Jeffery, 'An Introduction to the Papers of Field Marshal Sir Henry Wilson'.
[53] Wilson diary, 19 Sept. 1921. Robertson's book, *From Private to Field Marshal*, was published in 1921.   [54] See Ian Beckett's fascinating study of inter-war memoirs, 'Frocks and Brasshats'.
[55] Ibid., 105.
[56] Callwell to Lieut.-Col. J. H. Boraston, 24 Apr. 1926 (Boraston papers, 71/13/2 folder A).
[57] *Daily Telegraph*, 10 Oct. 1927.
[58] Thwaites to Frederick Sykes, 22 Aug. 1944 (Sykes papers). Sykes was Bonar Law's son-in-law, had been at the Staff College and the Supreme War Council under Wilson, Chief of the Air Staff, 1918–19, and was a Conservative MP in the 1920s.
[59] Furse to Sykes, 24 Aug. 1944, and Bartholomew to Sykes, 22 Aug. 1944 (ibid.).
[60] Price-Davies to Sykes, 1 Sept. 1944 (ibid.).

To be sure, none of Wilson's friends were very amused when Callwell's two-volume *Field-Marshal Sir Henry Wilson: His Life and Diaries* was published in 1927. The book's impact (and its profitability) was heightened by the publication of extracts over a period of thirteen weeks in the *Sunday Times*.[61] 'One by one', wrote an American journalist in England, 'the reputations of prominent figures in the World War are being destroyed by their own apologists or the shortsighted zeal of their injudicious friends. The latest to suffer', he continued, 'is that of Sir Henry Wilson', whose 'letters and diaries' is 'one of the most sensational self-exposures in all literature'.[62] The *Empire Review*, a journal sympathetic to Wilson's politics, warmly deplored the publication. After Wilson's assassination, it argued, 'his fame as a great soldier and a great personality seemed secure. So, indeed, it would have been, but for the most unhappy indiscretion of publishing these two volumes.' It would have been 'better, far better, for Wilson's fame that his Diaries had been buried deep in his grave'.[63] For the *New Statesman*, which did not share Wilson's politics, the diaries revealed that Wilson, 'with all his obvious ability', was 'the typically stupid militarist—almost the only genuine militarist we have had in Great Britain'. While he 'was fundamentally a fool', the journal did 'not think he was so great a fool as ever to have consented, had he lived, to the publication of these diaries'. Though 'extremely interesting, they damn his reputation as a soldier beyond remedy'.[64]

Callwell's book was certainly a disappointment to Wilson's sister Eileen. 'How he could have written it', she wrote, 'is beyond my comprehension.'[65] Although her attempt to commission a new memoir which would 'counteract the bad effect of Charlie Caldwell's [*sic*] book'[66] came to nothing, the effort elicited some interesting recollections of her brother from old colleagues, including an especially perceptive one from Sir Charles Deedes, who had been a student at the Staff College under him, and three times thereafter served on his staff. Deedes maintained that 'H.W.'s claim to greatness depended on his vivid personality. His whimsical methods in studying a problem; his gesticulations; his use of the English language,' he continued, 'were all part of a make up which had a compelling effect on his hearers, but seem to fall rather flat when endeavour is made to portray them in print.' He thought Callwell's book 'fails entirely to give a true picture of the man', and 'the reader is left with the impression of an ambitious, volatile and even fatuous character, an intriguer concerned mainly with his own career', which Deedes thought 'far from the truth'. Deedes, however, although a tremendous admirer, was not blind to Wilson's faults. Assessing his time in command of IV Corps, Deedes said that Wilson's 'easy ability to see both sides of a question

61 *Sunday Times*, 22 May–14 Aug. 1927.
62 'Column from London by Herbert W. Horwill', *New York Times*, 30 Oct. 1927.
63 'The Wilson diaries: part III', by 'Scrutator', *Empire Review*, 47/325 (Feb. 1928), 94, 98.
64 Review by 'C.S.', *New Statesman*, 30/757, 29 Oct. 1027.
65 Eileen Price-Davies to Frederick Sykes, 1 Dec. 1944 (Sykes papers).
66 Ibid., 1 Sept. 1944 (ibid.).

became a weakness, when he found himself in command.... His versatile mind was not suited to making a decision and sticking to it, when he saw so many difficulties in doing so.' On the other hand, 'as an adviser, he was unrivalled, patient, lucid and fair'.[67]

Lloyd George made much the same point in his memoirs, published in the late 1930s, though he also took the opportunity to exact some revenge for many dismissive remarks Callwell had quoted in his biography. 'It was a delight', wrote Lloyd George, to hear Wilson 'unravel and expound a military problem. For that reason he was specially helpful in a council of civilians. But he had no power of decision. That is why he failed in the field.'[68] Churchill was more generous in his war memoirs. Wilson was, he wrote, 'the most comprehending military mind of our day in Britain', and 'a soldier who, although he commanded no armies, exerted on occasion a profound and fortunate influence over the greatest events'.[69]

The apparent facility with which Wilson straddled the military and political sectors suggested that Repington was correct to see him as a type of soldier more suited for the modern, democratic age than many of his contemporaries. It was the Wilson, rather than the Robertson, model which was to be most effective in the future, and the ability to engage effectively with politicians was surely to be part of the 'job specification' of successful Chiefs of Staff in the future. In 1941, looking at a portrait of Wilson which hung in his office, the then CIGS, Sir John Dill (another Irishman), fresh from a testing encounter with the Prime Minister (Churchill), remarked: 'One cannot condemn Henry Wilson so heartily as one used to, now that one has had first-hand experience of politicians.'[70] In the mid-1930s Archibald Wavell, who had been a student at the Staff College under Wilson (and was to know well the vagaries of politicians), recognised the importance of the political dimension. When his new ADC, Bernard Fergusson, 'made some jejune remark about Henry Wilson having been "a political general"; he took me up on this cliché, and listened to my flounderings as he made me define exactly what I meant'. Wavell, who had no particular brief for Wilson, 'did at least impress on me that it was part of a soldier's training to understand the ways of politics without becoming involved in them'.[71]

In the 1960s Wilson was the subject of two biographies, the first of which, *Brasshat* (1961), by Basil Collier, attempted the rehabilitation which Eileen Price-Davies had so desired. Wilson, wrote Collier, had 'the distinction of having been more thoroughly maligned than possibly any public figure of the last half-century'.[72] Collier had (according to the blurb on the dust-jacket) begun by sharing the view that Wilson was a 'political general' and a 'ruthless wire-puller', but 'two years of research' had convinced him 'that Wilson was not only one of the most selfless of public men but by far the ablest British soldier of his day'. From his

---

[67] Note on Henry Wilson, enclosed with Deedes to Price-Davies, 25 Aug. 1944 (ibid.).
[68] Lloyd George, *War Memoirs*, ii. 1688.   [69] Churchill, *The Great War*, iii. 1106.
[70] Kennedy, *The Business of War*, 143.   [71] Fergusson, *Wavell*, 95.
[72] Collier, *Brasshat*, 13.

partisan position, Collier went too far—*The Times*'s reviewer said 'protests too much'[73]—and the figure he described was literally too good to be true. In the same year *Assassination: The Death of Sir Henry Wilson and the Tragedy of Ireland*, by Rex Taylor, was published. Taylor, was an English writer sympathetic to Irish nationalism (though not to the extreme republican wing), who had written a well-received biography of Michael Collins. His book, though concentrated on Dunne and O'Sullivan, and the circumstances of the killing, portrayed Wilson as honourable and brave, and acquitted him of being simply a bigoted Ulster 'Orange Imperialist'. Wilson, moreover, had 'been done to death' on 'the basis of blind hatred and supposition'.[74]

The 1960s were not good years for rehabilitating First World War generals. It was a decade, as Brian Bond has observed, when opinions about 1914–18 were dominated by 'donkeys and Flanders mud'. The notion that the British army in France had been 'lions led by donkeys' perfectly suited the irreverent tone of the decade. Above all, Joan Littlewood's Theatre Workshop production, *Oh What a Lovely War* (and Richard Attenborough's 1969 film adaptation), hit the *Zeitgeist*, and has dominated much of the subsequent cultural understanding of the war.[75] 'Field-Marshal Sir Henry Wilson' features in two of the play's scenes. Ironically, in both cases—and unlike other generals—he is portrayed quite sympathetically. In the first scene, travelling with John French to their first conference with the French high command in August 1914, Wilson is the competent professional, brushed off by his blockhead superior. 'Do you think I ought to organise an interpreter', he asks. 'Don't be ridiculous, Wilson;' replies French, 'the essential problem at the moment is we must have the utmost secrecy.' Wilson tries to interest French in his arrangements for the movement of the army—'No, not just now, thank you'—and also the terrain—'Yes, we know all about your bicycle trips round France', interrupts French. When they meet the French generals, Wilson has to translate the 'French gibberish'. 'Damn it all, Wilson, this is no way to conduct a conference!' exclaims French. In the second scene, a year into the war, generals and society ladies dance and discuss 'intrigue upon intrigue' together. John French is the arch-intriguer, who strings Wilson along, but gives his coveted staff posting to Robertson, telling Wilson it was his own fault: 'You're such a brute. You'll never be nice to people you don't like.'[76]

These cameo appearances did nothing to rescue Wilson's reputation, and per-haps, as A. J. P. Taylor sharply observed in a review of *Brasshat*, 'at least Wilson was too absurd to be a donkey'.[77] Another biography appeared in 1968: *The Lost Dictator*, by Bernard Ash. While not unsympathetic, this was much less favourable to Wilson than *Brasshat*. In his preface, Ash warmly thanked Eileen Price-Davies and Wilson's nephew, Major Cyril Wilson, for the help they had

---

[73] *The Times*, 27 July 1961.   [74] Taylor, *Assassination*, 113–24, 65.

[75] Bond, *The Unquiet Western Front*, 51–73.

[76] Theatre Workshop, *Oh What a Lovely War*, 35–8, 68–73.

[77] Quoted in *The Times*, 10 Aug. 1961.

given. But he also hoped they would forgive him 'for having come to the conclusion that, although he [Wilson] meant the best, he sometimes did the worst and that in the end he was bent on a course which could only have brought disastrous consequences to the country he was so anxious to serve well'.[78] Ash's contention was that, had Wilson lived, 'of course he would have assumed leadership' of the Diehard extremists in parliament, and that 'under his vivid and reckless leadership the extremists would quickly have gained control of the Conservative Party and the Conservative leadership—on which without doubt his sights were already set—would in due course have fallen to him as well'. After the short premiership of Bonar Law, the 'indolent Baldwin' would have been 'no match for the vigour and determination of Henry Wilson'. Ash then sketched out a nightmare scenario of military confrontation and a possible 'blood-bath of civil commotion' into which Britain would be plunged as a consequence of Wilson taking political power.[79]

Ash's fanciful prediction that Wilson might have become some sort of quasi-fascist leader, while it may well have been a useful device to sell his biography, is absurd. What actually happened after Bonar Law (who formed a Conservative administration, and won a general election, following the fall of Lloyd George's government in October 1922) retired in 1923, and Stanley Baldwin beat Lord Curzon to the premiership, is itself instructive. What Baldwin had and Curzon had not, apart from a seat in the Commons, was the capacity to mobilise broad support within the parliamentary party. That the Diehards, numbering no more than 50 out of over 300 Conservative MPs, even with Henry Wilson, could have had a decisive influence is implausible. In any case, there was no election; the selection of the new Prime Minister lay in the hands of the King (who himself had been no great admirer of Wilson). Baldwin's famously understated persona—not so very different from Bonar Law's—was also evidently preferable to Curzon's air of clever over-achievement. Wilson, moreover, had an insufficient capacity for dullness to rise really high in the Conservative Party. Churchill, a not dissimilar character, though politically sharper and more eloquent, only got to the top in the special circumstances of the Second World War. Harold Macmillan had to disguise his youthful, precocious cleverness so as not to alarm the steadier spirits on the Tory backbenches. Wilson, moreover, had perhaps too little patience (and no capacity at all for suffering fools, gladly or otherwise) to endure the humdrum tearoom and constituency-office routine of the modern democratic British politician.

Yet Wilson was a formidable 'catch' for the Ulster Unionists, though how continuingly useful he would have been is difficult to say. Like Enoch Powell, the Tory ex-Cabinet minister who was MP for South Down between 1974 and 1987, the presence of an extremely clever, though maverick, Conservative with a metropolitan reputation among the Ulster Unionist representation at Westminster was

---

[78] Ash, *The Lost Dictator*, pp. vi–vii.   [79] Ibid. 278–9.

both an asset and a liability. On the one hand the Ulster profile in London might be raised; on the other, the fact that the individual concerned could, apparently, only get into the Commons through a Northern Ireland seat might simply confirm for other MPs that Ireland, as it ever had been, was a graveyard for anyone with British political ambitions. The progressive marginalisation after 1922 of Irish and Northern Irish matters at Westminster (a process accepted with relief by British politicians), and the increasing extent, furthermore, to which Unionist political energies were concentrated within Northern Ireland itself, left the ten or so Unionist MPs from the province with little or no effective role to play.

In death, Henry Wilson remained a kind of founding martyr for the Northern Ireland state. For many years a copy of a portrait of him (by Sir Oswald Birley) hung in what was known as the 'Prime Minister's room' in the Parliament Buildings at Stormont in Belfast.[80] Underneath was a framed set of Wilson's medal ribbons, which Cecil Wilson left to Sir James Craig in her will. There is not much else in modern Northern Ireland to commemorate Wilson. A 'Field-Marshal Sir Henry Wilson Memorial Women's Loyal Orange Lodge' was formed in 1930.[81] There is a 'Royal Black Institution' (a senior branch of the Orange Order) memorial lodge in Bangor, county Down, and a 'Sir Henry Wilson Memorial Orange Hall' at Loughbrickland, each, in turn, embedding Wilson in the Orange institution of which he was never a member.

Whether or not he would have become a significant part of the Northern Ireland political establishment, we know that his Irish roots remained important to him and that he bitterly regretted partition and the breaking of the union between Great Britain and Ireland. His last visit to southern Ireland was in January 1922, when he spent twenty-four hours in Dublin en route to Belfast. As in the old days, he crossed over on the night ferry from Holyhead to Kingstown (Dun Laoghaire), though unlike the old days Macready advised him not to use his own name when booking his tickets. 'I rarely do', he wrote. 'You might try Colonel Greenwood, or Valera, or Sharman Crawford.'[82] On his way to have breakfast with Macready at his residence in the Royal Hospital, he found that the drive up, passing old family haunts such as Frascati, 'all now in a foreign & hostile Free State', was 'to me rather eerie'. He told the Lord-Lieutenant, Lord Fitzalan, 'how in the world any sane man' could 'imagine that Collins & Co. none of whom have ever administered 2 Typewriters can be expected to keep law & order over a population of 3 millions of people who have no sense of either and this without either an Army or a Police simply passes my comprehension'.[83]

The Free State government, in fact, managed very well, defeating the republican extremists in the Civil War, creating a successful, unarmed police service, and

---

[80] The original of the Birley portrait, which was painted in the spring of 1922, hangs in Marlborough College.   [81] *Weekly Northern Whig*, 8 Feb. 1930.
[82] Macready to Wilson, 12 Jan. 1922 (Wilson papers, HHW 2/2G/41). Col. Robert Sharman-Crawford was a prominent Ulster unionist.
[83] Wilson diary, 17 Jan. 1922. Fitzalan had succeeded French as Lord-Lieutenant in April 1921.

establishing a resolutely constitutional and conservative new state.[84] The irony of the matter was, that victory in the Civil War was secured in part through employing precisely the kinds of draconian policies—summary executions and all—that Wilson had been pressing for during the war of independence. The crucial difference (which Wilson's blindness to Irish political realities would probably have prevented him from seeing) was that these policies were implemented by a government perceived to be legitimate and which enjoyed widespread popular support. A further irony is that, beyond southern Ireland, Wilson was well aware of the need to secure widely based, democratic political support for any robust policy. We can see this in his insistence in the summer of 1921 that the British government had to 'have England on our side' before launching a renewed offensive in Ireland. Along with his recommendations for Northern Ireland security in March 1922, he urged Sir James Craig to 'get Great Britain warmly on your side'. 'With Great Britain with you,' he wrote, 'there is nothing which can't be done—as witness the last Great War—whilst on the other hand, with Great Britain indifferent, luke-warm or hostile, there is but little that can be done.'[85]

In one of his last letters, written in June 1922 while sailing up Southampton Water after eleven days at sea—'the best holiday I have had for 15 years'—Wilson reflected on the Irish situation. He thought it highly probable that Lloyd George's 'conversations' with the Dublin government would end 'in abject surrender—this time to a Republic'. But, so far as he was concerned, there was 'only one solution to the Irish question & that is the Union, & in the whole Statute Book of these stupid English there is no Act which was such a marvellous success as the Union'. He argued that 'for 107 years from 1800 to 1907 (when Birrell arrived on the scene) it had turned an Ireland of chaos & murder into a prosperous, peaceful & contented country'.[86]

This idyllic, imagined Ireland no longer existed, if indeed it ever had. Yet it was the Ireland of the Longford Wilsons, and of Protestant unionist people like them, middling landowners, believing themselves to be fully Irish, and as emotionally attached to the country as anyone. During the Great War, Wilson's brother Jemmy, based at Currygrane but touring the country to assess public opinion for the Irish Unionist Alliance, pondered on the situation in Ireland. Sometime in 1917 he drafted what was in effect an eloquent epitaph for his—and his brother's—Ireland:

No greater disaster, could in my opinion, overtake a country such as Ireland, than the total elimination of its resident gentry—a process which, alas, is already far advanced. As one travels through the country one is astonished to see so many derelict houses, & neglected demesnes, the houses formerly in many cases of an independent and virile section of the

---

[84] The definitive account of this process will be found in O'Halpin, *Defending Ireland*, chs. 1–2.
[85] Wilson to Craig, 17 Mar. 1922 (PRONI, HA/32/1/319).
[86] Wilson to Tim Harington, 11 June 1922 (Harington papers, box 12). Birrell was the Liberal Chief Secretary who spearheaded the home rule legislation.

body politic, not free from faults indeed—as what section is?—but, taken as a whole, forming, I venture to assert, oases of culture, of uprightness and of fair dealing, in what will otherwise be a desert of dead uniformity where the poor will have no one to appeal to except the Priest or the local shopkeeper (rapidly becoming a local magnate)—whence the rich will fly, & where lofty ideals, whether of social or Imperial interest, will be smothered in an atmosphere of superstition, greed, & chicanery. As in local, so in Nat[ional]. admin- istration there can be no more hope for a country from which the cultured element has been divorced, & the helpful friend of the poor & the protector of the weak driven to seek new surroundings & new occupations. It is surely the duty wherever possible, of the so called English garrison in Ireland to retain its hold, to leaven society with its hopes & aspi- rations that their common country may never become the plaything of a base political clique, whose ambition would be—in spite of all their protests—to see Ireland in the grip of a Tamany [*sic*] Hall administration, where mendacity w[oul]d. flourish, corruption would be rampant & industry w[oul]d. decay. I believe in my heart that even in these days of dreadful crisis with the enemy at our very gates if a perfectly secret plebiscite could be taken, a large majority would be cast in favour of retaining those members of the Landlord class in Ireland, a class whose blood is so freely shed for the Empire, who for years have done their best to discharge their onerous & often thankless duties by their humble neighbours all over Ireland.[87]

This paean of paternalistic conservatism, embodying a romanticised and solipsistic conception of the nineteenth-century social hierarchy, implicitly rejected any Irish democratic imperative and was itself out of touch with the 'real' Ireland. But its combination of local, national, and imperial service aptly exemplified the Wilsons' world view, and what they conceived their duty to be.

By the time Henry Wilson died, all four Wilson brothers had left Longford never to return. In the summer of 1921 Wilson noted that Jemmy had 'been hunted out of Ireland and is living in small lodgings, finding it difficult to pay for his very simple meals'. As for Currygrane, 'he has not been able to get any of the papers out of the safes, any of the pictures, the silver, and even the smaller ornaments. Every day he and I both expect to hear that the place has been burnt to the ground, with everything that we have got in the world that ties us to the past.'[88] So it was to be. Tied to the past in more senses than one, Henry Wilson, the reformist, up-to-the-minute soldier, and his less progressive kind back home, were swept away by the apparently irresistible forces of modern Ireland. If Henry Wilson's life was a tragedy, it was an Irish tragedy.

[87] Draft 'Reflection' by James Mackay Wilson, *c.*1917 (PRONI, D989/A/11/11/1)
[88] Wilson to Walter Congreve, 26 July 1921 (Wilson papers, HHW 2/52B/22).

Bibliography

Public Archives

National Archives of the United Kingdom, London, coded as follows:
  ADM: Admiralty
  CAB: Cabinet
  HO: Home Office
  KV: Security Service
  WO: War Office
Public Record Office of Northern Ireland, Belfast (PRONI), coded as follows:
  CAB: Cabinet
  HA: Ministry of Home Affairs
  D989: Irish Unionist Alliance papers

Private papers, etc.

Asquith–Venetia Stanley letters (Bodleian Library, Oxford)
Bingham papers (Imperial War Museum, London)
Bonar Law papers (House of Lords Record Office)
Boraston papers (Imperial War Museum, London)
Chamberlain papers (Birmingham University Library)
Clive papers (Liddell Hart Centre for Military Archives, King's College, London)
Curzon papers (Oriental and India Office Collections, British Library, London)
Davidson papers (House of Lords Record Office)
Davies papers (Sterling Memorial Library, Yale University)
Derby papers (Oriental and India Office Collections, British Library, London)
Esher papers (Churchill College Cambridge Archives Centre)
Fisher papers (Bodleian Library, Oxford)
Gilbert papers (Bodleian Library, Oxford)
Godley papers (Liddell Hart Centre for Military Archives, King's College, London, and Imperial War Museum, London)
Haig typescript diary (TNA, WO 256/6)
Hankey papers (Churchill College Cambridge Archives Centre)
Harington papers (King's Liverpool Regiment Collection, Merseyside County Museums, Liverpool)
Isaac, W. V. R., 'History of the Directorate of Military Intelligence, 1855–1939' (Ministry of Defence (Central and Army) Library, London)
Kenyon papers (Imperial War Museum, London)
Kiggell papers (Liddell Hart Centre for Military Archives, King's College, London)
Kirke papers (Intelligence Corps Museum, Chicksands, Bedfordshire)
Lloyd George papers (House of Lords Record Office)
Loch papers (Imperial War Museum, London)
Maxse papers (West Sussex Record Office, Chichester)
Milner papers (Bodleian Library, Oxford).

O'Malley papers (University College Dublin Department of Archives)
Oranmore papers (in private hands)
Philby papers (St Antony's College, Oxford)
Rawlinson papers (National Army Museum, London), including South African War Journal (NAM 5201/33/7)
Roberts papers (National Army Museum, London and TNA, WO 105/45)
Robertson papers (Liddell Hart Centre for Military Archives, King's College, London)
Royal Archives (Windsor Castle)
Snow papers (Imperial War Museum, London)
Staff College Roll 1858–1921 (Staff College Library, Camberley)
Stevenson papers (House of Lords Record Office)
Sykes papers (Imperial War Museum, London)
Tansley papers (Imperial War Museum, London)
Vincent papers (Muckross House Library, Killarney, Co. Kerry; transcripts provided by Professor Eunan O'Halpin)
Wilson papers, including Wilson diary, 1893–1922 (Imperial War Museum, London)
Wilson, James Mackay, papers (Public Record Office of Northern Ireland, Belfast, D.989A/8/7)
Woodroffe papers (Imperial War Museum, London)

Published works and theses

ADAMS, R. J. Q., *Bonar Law* (London, 1999).
—— 'The National Service League and Mandatory Service in Edwardian Britain', *Armed Forces & Society*, 12/1 (Fall 1985), 53–74.
ADYE, Sir JOHN, *Soldiers and Others I Have Known* (London, 1925).
AMERY, L. S., *The Leo Amery Diaries*, i, *1896–1929*, ed. John Barnes and David Nicholson (London, 1980).
—— *My Political Life*, 2 vols. (London, 1953).
ANDREW, CHRISTOPHER, 'Churchill and Intelligence', *Intelligence and National Security*, 3/3 (July 1988), 181–93.
—— *Secret Service: The Making of the British Intelligence Community* (London, 1985).
'ARMINIUS', *From Sarajevo to the Rhine* (London, 1933).
ASH, BERNARD, *The Lost Dictator: A Biography of Field-Marshal Sir Henry Wilson* (London, 1968).
ASTON, Sir GEORGE, *Memories of a Marine: An Amphibiography* (London, 1919).
AUSTIN, H. H., *Some Rambles of a Sapper* (London, 1928).
BABINGTON, ANTHONY, *For the Sake of Example* (London, 1983).
BAKER-CARR, C. D., *From Chauffeur to Brigadier* (London, 1930).
BARROW, Sir GEORGE DE S., *The Fire of Life* (London, n.d. [1942]).
BEAN, C. E. W., *Two Men I Knew* (Sydney, 1957).
BEAVERBROOK, LORD, *Politicians and the War, 1914–1916*, 2 vols. (London, 1928).
BECKER, JEAN-JACQUES, *The Great War and the French People* (Leamington Spa, 1985).
BECKETT, IAN F. W., 'Frocks and Brasshats', in Brian Bond (ed.), *The First World War and British Military History* (Oxford, 1991), 89–112.
—— *Johnnie Gough V.C.: A Biography of Brigadier-General Sir John Edmond Gough, V.C., K.C.B.* (London, 1989).

—— 'King George V and His Generals', in Matthew Hughes and Matthew Seligmann (eds.), *Leadership in Conflict, 1914–1918* (London, 2000).

—— (ed.), *The Army and the Curragh Incident, 1914*, Army Records Society, vol. 2 (London, 1986).

—— and JEFFERY, KEITH, 'The Royal Navy and the Curragh Incident 1914', *Historical Research*, 62/147 (1989), 54–69.

BECKETT, J. C., *The Anglo-Irish Tradition* (London, 1976).

BELL, P. M. H., *France and Britain 1900–1940: Entente and Estrangement* (London, 1996).

BENCE-JONES, MARK, *Burke's Guide to Country Houses*, i, *Ireland* (London, 1978).

BENNETT, EDWARD W., 'Intelligence and History from the Other Side of the Hill', *Journal of Modern History*, 60 (June 1988), 312–37.

BENSON, E. F., *Our Family Affairs 1867–1896* (London, 1920).

BERTIE, Lord, *The Diary of Lord Bertie of Thame, 1914–1918*, ed. Lady Algernon Gordon Lennox, 2 vols. (London, 1924).

BEST, GEOFFREY, 'Militarism and the Victorian Public School', in Simon and Bradley, *The Victorian Public School*, 129–46.

BIDWELL, SHELFORD, and GRAHAM, DOMINICK, *Fire-Power: British Army Weapons and Theories of War, 1904–1945* (London, 1982).

BLAKE, ROBERT, *The Unknown Prime Minister: The Life and Times of Andrew Bonar Law, 1858–1923* (London, 1955).

—— (ed.), *The Private Papers of Douglas Haig 1914–1919* (London, 1952).

BOND, BRIAN, *British Military Policy Between the Two World Wars* (Oxford, 1980).

—— *The Unquiet Western Front: Britain's Role in Literature and History* (Cambridge, 2002).

—— *The Victorian Army and the Staff College 1854–1914* (London, 1972).

—— and CAVE, NIGEL, *Haig: A Reappraisal 70 Years On* (Barnsley, 1999).

—— and ROBBINS, SIMON (eds.), *Staff Officer: The Diaries of Walter Guinness (First Lord Moyne), 1914–1918* (London, 1987).

BONHAM-CARTER, VICTOR, *The Strategy of Victory, 1914–1918: The Life and Times of the Master Strategist of World War I: Field-Marshal Sir William Robertson* (New York, 1964); published in UK under the title *Soldier True* (London, 1963).

BOURNE, J. M., *Britain and the Great War, 1914–1918* (London, 1989).

BOWMAN, TIMOTHY, *Irish Regiments in the Great War: Discipline and Morale* (Manchester, 2003).

BOYCE, D. G., *Englishmen and Irish Troubles: British Public Opinion and the Making of Irish Policy, 1918–22* (London, 1972).

BUCHANAN, MERIEL, *Victorian Gallery* (London, 1956).

BUCKLAND, PATRICK, *Irish Unionism 1: The Anglo-Irish and the New Ireland, 1885 to 1922* (Dublin, 1972).

—— *Irish Unionism, 1885–1923: A Documentary History* (Belfast, 1973).

CALWELL, C. E., *Field Marshal Sir Henry Wilson: His Life and Diaries*, 2 vols. (London, 1927).

CANNADINE, DAVID, *The Decline and Fall of the British Aristocracy* (New Haven, 1990).

—— *Ornamentalism: How The British Saw Their Empire*, Penguin edn. (London, 2002).

CARRINGTON, CHARLES, *Soldier From the Wars Returning* (London, 1965).

CASSAR, GEORGE H., *The Tragedy of Sir John French* (London, 1985).

CHAPMAN-HUSTON, DESMOND, and RUTTER, OWEN, *General Sir John Cowans: The Quartermaster-General of the Great War*, 2 vols. (London, 1924).

CHARTERIS, JOHN, *At G.H.Q.* (London, 1931).

CHURCHILL, WINSTON S., *The Great War*, 3 vols. George Newnes edn. (London, n.d. [1933]).

—— *The World Crisis 1911–1914* (London, 1923).

CLINE, PETER K., 'Eric Geddes and the "Experiment" with Businessmen in Government, 1915–22', in K. D. Brown, *Essays in Anti-Labour History* (London, 1974), 74–104.

COCKER, MARK, *Richard Meinertzhagen: Soldier, Scientist and Spy*, pbk edn. (London, 1990).

COLEMAN, MARIE, *County Longford and the Irish Revolution 1910–1923* (Dublin, 2003).

COLLIER, BASIL, *Brasshat: A Biography of Field Marshal Sir Henry Wilson* (London, 1961).

COLSON, PERCY, *White's 1693–1950* (London, 1951).

CONGREVE, BILLY (ed. Terry Norman), *Armageddon Road: A VC's Diary, 1914–16* (London, 1982).

CONNELL, JOHN, *Wavell: Scholar and Soldier: To June 1941* (London, 1964).

COOGAN, JOHN W., and COOGAN, PETER F., 'The British Cabinet and the Anglo-French Staff Talks, 1905–14', *Journal of British Studies*, 24/1 (1985), 110–31.

CORBETT-SMITH, ARTHUR, *The Retreat from Mons* (London, 1916).

CORNS, CATHRYN, and HUGHES-WILSON, JOHN, *Blindfold and Alone: British Military Executions in the Great War* (London, 2001).

COWLING, MAURICE, *The Impact of Labour 1920–1924: The Beginning of Modern British Politics* (Cambridge, 1971).

DALY, GABRIEL, 'Church Renewal: 1869–1877', in Michael Hurley (ed.), *Irish Anglicanism 1869–1969* (Dublin, 1970), 23–38.

DARWIN, JOHN, *Britain, Egypt and the Middle East: Imperial Policy in the Aftermath of War, 1918–1922* (London, 1981).

DAWSON, LIONEL, *Sound of the Guns: Being an Account of the Wars and Service of Admiral Sir Walter Cowan* (Oxford, 1949).

DE GROOT, GERALD J., *Blighty: British Society in the Era of the Great War* (London, 1996).

—— *Douglas Haig, 1861–1928* (London, 1988).

DENMAN, TERENCE, *Ireland's Unknown Soldiers: The 16th (Irish) Division in the Great War* (Dublin, 1992).

—— *A Lonely Grave: The Life and Death of William Redmond* (Dublin, 1995).

DILLON, VISCOUNT, *Memories of Three Wars* (London, 1951).

DOCKRILL, MICHAEL L., and GOULD, J. DOUGLAS, *Peace Without Promise: Britain and the Peace Conferences, 1919–23* (London, 1981).

D'OMBRAIN, NICHOLAS, *War Machinery and High Policy: Defence Administration in Peacetime Britain, 1902–1914* (London, 1973).

DOOLEY, THOMAS P., *Irishmen or English Soldiers?* (Liverpool, 1995).

DUNSTERVILLE, L. C., *Stalky's Reminiscences* (London, 1928).

DUTTON, DAVID, *Austen Chamberlain: Gentleman in Politics* (Bolton, 1985).

—— (ed.), *Paris 1918: The War Diary of the 17th Earl of Derby* (Liverpool, 2001).

EDMONDS, Sir JAMES, *History of the Great War Based on Official Documents: Military Operations, France and Belgium, 1914*, vol. 1 (London, 1922).

—— *History of the Great War Based on Official Documents: Military Operations, France and Belgium, 1916*, vol. 1 (London, 1932).

ESHER, REGINALD Viscount, *The Tragedy of Lord Kitchener* (London, 1921).

FALLS, CYRIL, *The First World War* (London, 1960).

FARRAR-HOCKLEY, ANTHONY, *Goughie: The Life of Sir Hubert Gough* (London, 1975).

FARRELL, MICHAEL, *Arming the Protestants: The Formation of the Ulster Special Constabulary and the Royal Ulster Constabulary 1920–27* (Cork, 1983).

FAY, Sir SAM, *The War Office at War* (London, 1937).

FERGUSON, NIALL, *The Pity of War* (London, 1998).

FERGUSSON, BERNARD, *Wavell: Portrait of a Soldier* (London, 1961).

FERGUSSON, Sir JAMES, *The Curragh Incident* (London, 1964).

FERGUSSON, THOMAS G., *British Military Intelligence, 1870–1914: The Development of a Modern Intelligence Organization* (London, 1984).

FERRIS, JOHN, *The Evolution of British Strategic Policy, 1919–26* (London, 1989).

FITZPATRICK, DAVID, *The Two Irelands, 1912–1939* (Oxford, 1998).

FOLLIS, BRYAN A., *A State Under Siege: The Establishment of Northern Ireland 1920–1925* (Oxford, 1995).

FORREST, Sir GEORGE, *The Life of Lord Roberts, V.C.* (London, 1914).

FOSTER, R. F., *Modern Ireland 1600–1972* (London, 1988).

—— *Paddy and Mr Punch: Connections in Irish and English History* (London, 1993).

FOY, MICHAEL T., 'The Ulster Volunteer Force: Its Domestic Development and Political Importance', Ph.D. thesis, Queen's University, Belfast (1986).

FRASER, PETER, *Lord Esher: A Political Biography* (London, 1973).

FRENCH, DAVID, *British Economic and Strategic Planning, 1905–1915* (London, 1982).

—— *British Strategy and War Aims, 1914–1916* (London, 1986).

—— *The British Way in Warfare, 1688–2000* (London, 1990).

—— *The Strategy of the Lloyd George Coalition, 1916–1918* (Oxford, 1995).

FRENCH, Viscount, *1914* (London, 1919).

FULLER, J. F. C., *Memoirs of an Unconventional Soldier* (London, 1936).

GAILEY, ANDREW, 'King Carson: An Essay on the Invention of Leadership', *Irish Historical Studies*, 30 (1996–7), 66–87.

GALLAGHER, JOHN, *The Decline, Revival and Fall of the British Empire* (Cambridge, 1982).

—— 'Nationalisms and the Crisis of Empire, 1919–22', *Modern Asian Studies*, 15 (1981), 355–68.

GARDNER, NIKOLAS, *Trial by Fire: Command and the British Expeditionary Force in 1914* (Westport and London, 2003).

GERMAINS, VICTOR WALLACE, *The Tragedy of Winston Churchill* (London, 1931).

GILBERT, MARTIN, *Winston S. Churchill*, iv, *1916–1922* (London, 1975); Companion Volumes (London, 1977).

GLEICHEN, Lord EDWARD, *A Guardsman's Memories* (Edinburgh and London, 1932).

GOLLIN, A. M., *Proconsul in Politics: A Study of Lord Milner in Opposition and in Power* (New York, 1964).

GOOCH, GEORGE P., and TEMPERLEY, HAROLD W. (eds.), *British Documents on the Origins of the War*, 11 vols. (London, 1926–38).

GOOCH, JOHN, *Armies in Europe* (London, 1980).

—— 'The Maurice case', in id., *The Prospect of War: Studies in British Defence Policy, 1847–1942* (London, 1981), 146–63.

—— *The Plans of War: The General Staff and British Military Strategy c.1900–1916* (London, 1974).

GOUGH, Sir HUBERT, *Soldiering On* (London, 1954).

GRAUBARD, S. R., 'Military Demobilisation in Great Britain Following the First World War', *Journal of Modern History*, 19 (1947), 297–311.

GRAVES, ROBERT, *Good-Bye To All That* (London, 1929).

GREEN, A. F. U., *Evening Tattoo* (London, 1941).

GREEN, ANDREW, *Writing the Great War: Sir James Edmonds and the Official Histories, 1915–1948* (London, 2003).

GREENHALGH, ELIZABETH, 'Why the British Were on the Somme in 1916', *War in History*, 6/2 (1999), 147–73.

GREGORY, ADRIAN, ' "You might as well recruit Germans": British Public Opinion and the Decision to Conscript the Irish in 1918', in id. and Senia Paseta (eds.), *Ireland and the Great War: 'A War to Unite Us All'?* (Manchester, 2002).

GRIEVES, KEITH, *The Politics of Manpower, 1914–18* (Manchester, 1988).

GRIFFITH, PADDY, *Battle Tactics of the Western Front: The British Army's Art of Attack, 1916–18* (New Haven and London, 1994).

—— 'The extent of Tactical Reform in the British Army', in id. (ed.), *British Fighting Methods in the Great War* (London, 1996), 1–22.

GRIGG, JOHN, *Lloyd George: From Peace to War, 1912–1916* (London, 1985).

GUINN, PAUL, *British Strategy and Politics 1914 to 1918* (Oxford, 1965).

HALDANE, Sir AYLMER, *A Soldier's Saga* (Edinburgh and London, 1948).

HALDANE, RICHARD BURDON, *Before the War* (London, 1920).

HANCOCK, W. K., *Smuts: The Sanguine Years, 1870–1919* (Cambridge, 1962).

—— *Survey of British Commonwealth Affairs*, i, *Problems of Nationality, 1918–1936* (London, 1937).

HANKEY, Lord, *The Supreme Command 1914–1918*, 2 vols. (London, 1961).

—— *The Supreme Control at the Paris Peace Conference 1919* (London, 1963).

HARGREAVES, R. C., 'Field Marshal Sir Henry Wilson', *Rifle Brigade Chronicle for 1922*, 43–9.

HARINGTON, Sir CHARLES, *Tim Harington Looks Back* (London, 1940).

HARRIES-JENKINS, GWYN, *The Army in Victorian Society* (London, 1977).

HART, PETER, 'The Geography of Revolution in Ireland 1917–1923', *Past and Present*, 155 (1997), 142–73; also published in id., *The I.R.A. at War*, 30–61.

—— *The I.R.A. and Its Enemies: Violence and Community in Cork, 1916–1923* (Oxford, 1998).

—— *The I.R.A. at War 1916–1923* (Oxford, 2003).

—— 'Michael Collins and the Assassination of Sir Henry Wilson', *Irish Historical Studies*, 28/116 (Nov. 1992), 150–70; also published in id., *The I.R.A. at War*, 194–220.

HARVEY, BASIL, *The Rifle Brigade* (London, 1975).

HOARE, Sir SAMUEL, *The Fourth Seal: The End of a Russian Chapter* (London, 1930).

HOLMES, RICHARD, *The Little Field-Marshal: Sir John French* (London, 1981).

HONEY, J. R. DE S., *Tom Brown's Universe: The Development of the Victorian Public School* (London, 1977).

HOPKINSON, MICHAEL, *Green Against Green: The Irish Civil War* (Dublin, 1988).

—— *The Irish War of Independence* (Dublin, 2002).

—— (ed.), *The Last Days of Dublin Castle: The Mark Sturgis Diaries* (Dublin, 1999).

HOWARD, MICHAEL, *The Continental Commitment: The Dilemma of British Defence Policy in the Era of Two World Wars* (Harmondsworth, 1972).

HUGUET, VICTOR, *Britain and the War: A French Indictment* (London, 1928).

HUSSEY, JOHN, 'Appointing the Staff College Commandant 1906: A Case of Trickery, Negligence or Due Consideration?', *British Army Review*, 114 (Dec. 1996), 99–106.

—— 'Portrait of a Commander-in-Chief', in Bond and Cave, *Haig*, 12–36.

HUSSEY DE BURGH, U. H., *The Landowners of Ireland* (Dublin, 1878).

INGLIS, BRIAN, *Downstart* (London, 1990).

JACKSON, ALVIN, *Ireland 1798–1998* (Oxford, 1999).

—— *Sir Edward Carson* (Dublin, 1993).

JALLAND, PATRICIA, *The Liberals and Ireland: The Ulster Question in British Politics to 1914* (Brighton, 1980).

JAMES, DAVID, *Lord Roberts* (London, 1954).

JEFFERY, KEITH, 'The British Army and Internal Security 1919–1939', *Historical Journal*, 24/2 (1981), 377–97.

—— *The British Army and the Crisis of Empire, 1918–22* (Manchester, 1984).

—— 'British Security Policy in Ireland 1919–21', in Peter Collins (ed.), *Nationalism and Unionism: Conflict in Ireland, 1885–1921* (Belfast, 1994), 163–75.

—— 'An Introduction to the Papers of Field Marshal Sir Henry Wilson', *Imperial War Museum Review*, 4 (1989), 12–21.

—— *Ireland and the Great War* (Cambridge, 2000).

—— *Ireland and War in the Twentieth Century*, Magdalene College Occasional Paper No. 31 (Cambridge, 2005).

—— 'The Irish Soldier in the Boer War', in John Gooch (ed.), *The Boer War: Direction, Experience and Image* (London, 2000), 141–51.

—— 'Kruger's Farmers, Strathcona's Horse, Sir George Clarke's Camels and the Kaiser's Battleships: The Impact of the South African War on Imperial Defence', in Donal Lowry (ed.), *The South African War Reappraised* (Manchester, 2000), 188–202.

—— 'The Post-war Army', in Ian F. W. Beckett and Keith Simpson (eds.), *A Nation in Arms: A Social Study of the British Army in the First World War* (Manchester, 1985); revised and corrected edn., (London, 1990), 211–34.

—— 'The Second World War', in Wm. Roger Louis and Judith M. Brown (eds.), *The Oxford History of the British Empire*, iv, *The Twentieth Century* (Oxford, 1999), 306–28.

—— 'Sir Henry Wilson and the Defence of the British Empire, 1918–22', *Journal of Imperial and Commonwealth History*, 5/3 (May 1977), 270–93.

—— (ed.), *'An Irish Empire'? Aspects of Ireland and the British Empire* (Manchester, 1996).

—— (ed.), *The Military Correspondence of Field Marshal Sir Henry Wilson, 1918–1922*, Army Records Society, vol. 1 (London, 1985).

—— and HENNESSY, PETER, *States of Emergency: British Governments and Strikebreaking Since 1919* (London, 1983).

JERROLD, DOUGLAS, *The Royal Naval Division* (London, 1923).

JOFFRE, J. J. C., *Memoirs of Marshal Joffre*, 2 vols. (London, 1932).

JONES, THOMAS, *Whitehall Diary*, ed. Keith Middlemas, 3 vols. (London, 1969–71).

KEDOURIE, ELIE, 'Sa'ad Zaghlul and the British', in Albert Hourani (ed.), *St Antony's Papers No. 11* (London, 1961), 139–60.

KENNEDY, JOHN, *The Business of War: The War Narrative of Major-General Sir John Kennedy*, ed. Bernard Fergusson (London, 1957).

KENNEDY, PAUL, 'Great Britain Before 1914', in May (ed.), *Knowing One's Enemies*, 172–204.

KENNEDY, PAUL, *The Rise and Fall of the Great Powers: Economic Change and Military Conflict from 1500 to 2000*, Fontana edn. (London, 1989).

KENNY, KEVIN (ed.), *Ireland and the British Empire* (Oxford, 2004).

KLIEMAN, AARON S., *Foundations of British Policy in the Arab World: The Cairo Conference of 1921* (Baltimore and London, 1970).

LEE, JOHN, *A Soldier's Life: General Sir Ian Hamilton 1853–1947* (London, 2000).

LEE COLE, RICHARD, *History of Methodism in Ireland, 1869–1960* (Belfast, 1960).

LEES-MILNE, JAMES, *The Enigmatic Edwardian: The Life of Reginald, Second Viscount Esher* (London, 1986).

LENTIN, ANTONY, *Lloyd George and the Lost Peace: From Versailles to Hitler, 1919–1940* (Basingstoke, 2001).

—— 'Lloyd George, Clemenceau and the Elusive Anglo-French Guarantee Treaty, 1919 "A disastrous episode"?', in Alan Sharp and Glyn Stone (eds.), *Anglo-French Relations in the Twentieth Century: Rivalry and Co-operation* (London, 2000), 104–19.

LIDDELL HART, B. H., *Foch: Man of Orleans*, 2 vols. (Harmondsworth, 1937).

LLOYD GEORGE, DAVID, *The Truth about the Peace Treaties*, 2 vols. (London, 1938).

—— *War Memoirs*, 2 vols., Odhams edn. (London, n.d. [1938]).

LUVAAS, JAY, *The Education of an Army: British Military Thought, 1815–1940* (London, 1965).

LYNE, GERARD J., *The Lansdowne Estate in Kerry Under the Agency of William Steuart Trench, 1849–72* (Dublin, 2001).

LYTTELTON, NEVILLE, *Eighty Years: Soldiering, Politics, Games* (London, n.d. [1927]).

MCEWAN, J. M. (ed.), *The Riddell Diaries, 1908–1923* (London, 1986).

MACKINTOSH, JOHN P., *The British Cabinet*, 2nd edn. (London, 1968).

MACMILLAN, MARGARET, *The Peacemakers: Six Months that Changed the World*, pbk edn. (London, 2002).

MACPHAIL, ANDREW, *Three Persons* (New York, 1929).

MCQUILLEN, DEIRDRE, *Irish Country House Cooking* (New York, 1994).

MACREADY, Sir GORDON, *In the Wake of the Great* (London, 1965).

MACREADY, Sir NEVIL, *Annals of an Active Life*, 2 vols. (London, 1924).

MADSEN, AXEL, *Coco Chanel: A Biography* (London, 1990).

MALIM, F. B., 'Athletics', in A. C. Benson (ed.), *Cambridge Essays in Education* (London, 1917), 148–67.

MANGAN, J. A., 'Athleticism: A Case Study of the Evolution of an Educational Ideology', in Simon and Bradley, *The Victorian Public School*, 146–67.

—— *Athleticism in the Victorian and Edwardian Public School* (Cambridge, 1981).

MANSERGH, NICHOLAS, *The Unresolved Question: The Anglo-Irish Settlement and Its Undoing, 1912–72* (New Haven, 1991).

MARDER, ARTHUR J. (ed.), *Fear God and Dread Nought: The Correspondence of Admiral of the Fleet Lord Fisher of Kilverstone*, ii, *Years of Power 1904–1914* (London, 1956).

MARSH, EDWARD, *A Number of People: A Book of Reminiscences* (London, 1939).

MARSHALL-CORNWALL, Sir JAMES, *Foch as Military Commander* (London, 1972).

MARTIN, GED, *The Cambridge Union and Ireland, 1815–1914* (Edinburgh, 2000).

MAURICE, NANCY (ed.), *The Maurice Case* (London, 1972).

MAURICE, Sir FREDERICK, *The Life of General Lord Rawlinson of Trent* (London, 1928).

MAY, Sir EDWARD, *Changes and Chances of a Soldier's Life* (London, 1925).

MAY, ERNEST R., 'Cabinet, Tsar, Kaiser: Three Approaches to Assessment', in id. (ed.), *Knowing One's Enemies*, 11–36.

—— (ed.), *Knowing One's Enemies: Intelligence Assessments Before the Two World Wars* (Princeton, 1984).

MEGAHEY, ALAN, *The Irish Protestant Churches in the Twentieth Century* (Basingstoke, 2000).

MIDDLEMAS, KEITH, *Politics in Industrial Society: The British Experience Since 1911* (London, 1979).

MIDLETON, The Earl of (ST JOHN BRODERICK), *Records and Reactions, 1856–1939* (London, 1939).

MILLMAN, BROCK, 'Henry Wilson's Mischief: Field Marshall [*sic*] Sir Henry Wilson's Rise to Power 1917–18', *Canadian Journal of History*, 30 (Dec. 1995), 468–86.

MONROE, ELIZABETH, *Britain's Moment in the Middle East, 1914–56* (London, 1963).

—— *Britain's Moment in the Middle East, 1914–71* (London, 1981).

MONTGOMERY-CUNINGHAME, Sir THOMAS, *Dusty Measure: A Record of Troubled Times* (London, 1939).

MOODY, T. W., MARTIN, F. X., and BYRNE, F. J. (eds.), *A New History of Ireland*, viii, *A Chronology of Irish History to 1976* (Oxford, 1982).

MORGAN, JANE, *Conflict and Order: The Police and Labour Disputes in England and Wales, 1900–1939* (Oxford, 1987).

MORRIS, A. J. A., *The Scaremongers: The Advocacy of War and Rearmament, 1896–1914* (London, 1984).

—— (ed.), *The Letters of Lieut.-Col. Charles à Court Repington CMG, Military Correspondent of* The Times *1903–1918*, Army Records Society, vol. 15 (Stroud, Glos., 1999).

NEAME, Sir PHILIP, *Playing With Strife: The Autobiography of a Soldier* (London, 1947).

NEILSON, KEITH, *Strategy and Supply: The Anglo Russian Alliance 1914–1917* (London, 1984).

NICHOLSON, W. N., *Behind the Lines* (London 1939).

NICOL, GRAHAM, *Uncle George: Field Marshal Lord Milne of Salonika and Rubislaw* (London, 1976).

NICOLSON, HAROLD, *King George V: His Life and Reign* (London, 1952).

NEILLANDS, ROBIN, *The Great War Generals on the Western Front, 1914–18* (London, 1999).

O'BRIEN, CONOR CRUISE, *Passion and Cunning and Other Essays* (London, 1988).

O'FARRELL, PADRAIC, *The Seán MacEoin Story* (Dublin, 1981).

—— *Who's Who in the Irish War of Independence* (Cork, 1980).

O'HALPIN, EUNAN, *The Decline of the Union: British Government in Ireland, 1892–1920* (Dublin, 1987).

—— *Defending Ireland: The Irish State and its Enemies Since 1922* (Oxford, 1999).

—— *Head of the Civil Service: A Study of Sir Warren Fisher* (London, 1989).

O'MALLEY, ERNIE, *The Singing Flame*, pbk. edn. (Dublin, 1978).

OMISSI, DAVID, *Air Power and Colonial Control: The Royal Air Force, 1919–1939* (Manchester, 1990).

ORPEN, Sir WILLIAM, *An Onlooker in France, 1917–1919*, rev. edn. (London, 1924).

—— *Stories of Old Ireland and Myself* (London, 1924).

PAKENHAM, FRANK, *Peace by Ordeal: An Account, from First-hand Sources, of the Negotiations and Signature of the Anglo-Irish Treaty 1921* (London, 1935).

PAKENHAM, THOMAS, *The Boer War*, pbk. edn. (London, 1982).

PEMBERTON, W. BARING, *Battles of the Boer War*, pbk. edn. (London, 1964).

PHILPOTT, WILLIAM JAMES, *Anglo-French Relations and Strategy on the Western Front, 1914–18* (Basingstoke, 1996).

POWELL, GEOFFREY, *Plumer: The Soldier's General* (London, 1990).

PRETE, ROY A., 'Joffre and the Question of Allied Supreme Command, 1914–16', *Proceedings of the Annual Meeting of the Western Society for French History*, 16 (1989), 329–38.

PRIESTLEY, J. B., *Margin Released: A Writer's Reminiscences and Reflections* (London, 1962).

PRIOR, ROBIN, and WILSON, TREVOR, *Command on the Western Front: The Military Career of Sir Henry Rawlinson 1914–18* (Oxford, 1992).

PUTKOWSKI, JULIAN, and SYKES, JULIAN, *Shot at Dawn*, new edn. (London, 1992).

RAMSDEN, JOHN (ed.), *Real Old Tory Politics: The Political Diaries of Robert Sandars, Lord Bayford, 1910–1935* (London, 1984).

RAWLING, BILL, *Surviving Trench Warfare: Technology and the Canadian Corps, 1914–1918* (Toronto, 1992).

REILLY, EILEEN, 'The Wilson Family, 1650–1930', BA dissertation, St Patrick's College, Maynooth (1990).

REPINGTON, CHARLES À COURT, *The First World War*, 2 vols. (London, 1920).

—— *Vestigia* (London, 1919).

REPINGTON, MARY [LADY GARSTIN], *Thanks for the Memory* (London, 1938).

Report of the Committee appointed by the Secretary of State for War to Enquire into the Nature of Expenses incurred by Officers of the Army [Cd 1421], H.C. 1903, x, 535–75.

RIDDELL, Lord, *Lord Riddell's Intimate Diary of the Peace Conference and After, 1918–1923* (London, 1933).

—— *Lord Riddell's War Diary, 1914–1918* (London, n.d. [1933]).

RITTER, GERHARD, *The Sword and the Scepter: The Problem of Militarism in Germany*, ii, *The European Powers and the Whilhelminian Empire 1890–1914* (Coral Gables, Fla., 1970).

ROBBINS, KEITH, *Nineteenth-Century Britain: Integration and Diversity* (Oxford, 1988).

ROBERTSON, Sir W. R., *From Private to Field Marshal* (London, 1921).

—— *Soldiers and Statesmen*, 2 vols. (London, 1926).

ROSKILL, STEPHEN, *Hankey: Man of Secrets*, 3 vols. (London, 1970–4).

ROTHSTEIN, ANDREW, *The Soldiers' Strikes of 1919* (London, 1980).

ROYLE, TREVOR, *The Kitchener Enigma* (London, 1985).

RUBIN, GERRY R., *War, Law and Labour: The Munitions Acts, State Regulation, and the Unions, 1915–1921* (Oxford, 1987).

RYAN, A. P., *Mutiny at the Curragh* (London, 1956).

RYAN, W. MICHAEL, *Lieut.-Col. Charles à Court Repington* (New York and London, 1987).

SATRE, LOWELL J., 'St. John Brodrick and Army Reform, 1901–1903', *Journal of British Studies*, 15/2 (Spring 1976), 117–39.

SCHELLING, THOMAS C., *Choice and Consequence* (London, 1984).

SCOTT, BROUGH, *Galloper Jack: A Grandson's Search for a Forgotten Hero* (London, 2003).

SCOTT, PETER T. (ed.), 'The View from GHQ: The Second Part of the War Diary of Gen. Sir Charles Deedes', *Stand To!*, 11 (Summer 1984), 6–17.

—— (ed.), 'The View from the War Office: A Preliminary Extract from the Previously Unpublished War Diary of Gen. Sir Charles Deedes', *Stand To!*, 10 (Spring 1984), 14–16.

SHARP, ALAN, 'Britain and the Channel Tunnel, 1919–1920', *Australian Journal of Politics and History*, 25 (1979), 210–15.

—— *The Versailles Settlement: Peacemaking in Paris, 1919* (London, 1991).

SHEFFIELD, G. D., 'The Effect of War Service on the 22nd Battalion Royal Fusiliers (Kensington) 1914–18, With Special Reference to Morale, Discipline, and the Officer/Man Relationship', University of Leeds MA thesis (1984).

—— *Forgotten Victory: The First World War: Myths and Realities*, pbk. edn. (London, 2002).

—— and INGLIS, G. I. S. (eds.), *From Vimy Ridge to the Rhine: The Great War Letters of Christopher Stone DSO MC* (Marlborough, 1989).

SIMKINS, PETER, 'Haig and the Army Commanders', in Bond and Cave, *Haig*, 78–106.

—— *Kitchener's Army: The Raising of the New Armies, 1914–16* (Manchester, 1988).

SIMON, BRIAN, and BRADLEY, IAN (eds.), *The Victorian Public School: Studies in the Development of an Educational Institution* (Dublin, 1975).

SMITH, JEREMY, *The Tories and Ireland 1910–1914: Conservative Party Politics and the Home Rule Crisis* (Dublin, 2000).

SMYTHE, DONALD, *Pershing: General of the Armies* (Bloomington, Ind., 1986).

SPIERS, EDWARD, *Haldane: An Army Reformer* (Edinburgh, 1980).

—— *The Late Victorian Army 1868–1902* (Manchester, 1992).

STAFFORD, DAVID, 'Churchill and Intelligence: His Early Life', in K. G. Robertson (ed.), *War, Resistance and Intelligence: Essays in Honour of M. R. D. Foot* (Barnsley, 1999), 151–68.

STEINER, ZARA S., *Britain and the Origins of the First World War* (London, 1977).

—— and NEILSON, KEITH, *Britain and the Origins of the First World War*, 2nd edn. (London, 2003).

STEWART, A. T. Q., *The Ulster Crisis* (London, 1967).

STONE, NORMAN, *The Eastern Front* (London, 1975).

STUART, DENIS, *Dear Duchess: Millicent Duchess of Sutherland* (London, 1982).

STRACHAN, HEW, *The First World War*, i, *To Arms* (Oxford, 2001).

—— *The First World War: A New Illustrated History* (London, 2003).

—— *The Politics of the British Army* (Oxford, 1997).

STROUSE, JEAN, *Morgan: American Financier* (London, 1999).

SUTHERLAND, MILLICENT, *That Fool of a Woman and Four Other Sombre Tales* (London, 1925).

SWINTON, Sir ERNEST, *Eyewitness* (London, 1932).

SYKES, Sir FREDERICK, *From Many Angles: An Autobiography* (London, 1942).

TAYLOR, A. J. P., *English History, 1914–1945* Penguin edn. (Harmondsworth, 1970).

—— (ed.), *Lloyd George: A Diary by Frances Stevenson* (New York, 1971).

TAYLOR, REX, *Assassination: The Death of Sir Henry Wilson and the Tragedy of Ireland* (London, 1961).

TERRAINE, JOHN, *Douglas Haig: The Educated Soldier* (London, 1963).

THEATRE WORKSHOP, *Oh What a Lovely War*, pbk. edn. (London, 1967).

THOMSON, C. B., *Smaranda: A Compilation in Three Parts*, new edn. (London, 1931).

TOWNSHEND, CHARLES, *Britain's Civil Wars: Counterinsurgency in the Twentieth Century* (London, 1986).

—— *The British Campaign in Ireland, 1919–1921: The Development of Political and Military Policies* (London, 1975).

—— *Political Violence in Ireland: Government and Resistance Since 1848* (Oxford, 1983).

TRAVERS, TIM, *The Killing Ground: The British Army, the Western Front and the Emergence of Modern Warfare, 1900–1918* (London, 1987).

TRENCH, CHARLOTTE VIOLET, *The Wrays of Donegal, Londonderry and Antrim* (Oxford, 1945).

ULLMAN, RICHARD H., *Anglo-Soviet Relations, 1917–1921*, 3 vols. (Princeton, 1961–73).

WALKER, BRIAN M. (ed.), *Parliamentary Election Results in Ireland, 1801–1922* (Dublin, 1978).

—— (ed.), *Parliamentary Election Results in Ireland, 1918–92* (Dublin, 1992).

WARD, ALAN J., 'Lloyd George and the 1918 Irish Conscription Crisis', *Historical Journal*, 17/1 (1974), 107–29.

WHITE, TERENCE DE VERE, *The Anglo-Irish* (London, 1972).

WILLIAMSON Jr., SAMUEL R., *The Politics of Grand Strategy: Britain and France Prepare for War, 1904–1914* (Cambridge, Mass., 1969).

WILSON, KEITH M., *Empire and Continent: Studies in British Foreign Policy from the 1880s to the First World War* (London, 1987).

—— 'National Party Spirits: Backing into the Future', in Matthew Hughes and Matthew Seligmann (eds.), *Leadership in Conflict, 1914–1918* (London, 2000), 209–26.

—— 'Over the Top? The Question of Political Aspirations on the Part of the British High Command in the Course of the First World War', *Journal of the Society for Army Historical Research*, 74/298 (1996), 77–89.

—— (ed.), *The Rasp of War: The Letters of H. A. Gwynne to The Countess Bathurst, 1914–1918* (London, 1988).

WILSON, TREVOR (ed.), *The Political Diaries of C. P. Scott, 1911–1928* (London, 1970).

WOODWARD, DAVID R., 'Did Lloyd George starve the British army of Men Prior to the German Offensive of 21 March 1918?', *Historical Journal*, 27/1 (1984), 241–52.

—— *Lloyd George and the Generals* (London, 1983).

—— (ed.), *The Military Correspondence of Field-Marshal Sir William Robertson, Chief of the Imperial General Staff, December 1915–February 1918*, Army Records Society, vol. 5 (London, 1989).

YOUNG, F. W. (ed.), *The Story of the Staff College 1858–1958* (London, 1958).

Index

Note: Henry Wilson is abbreviated as 'HW' and references to illustrations are given in **bold**

Adye, Gen. Sir John 19
Africa, German colonies in 237
  see also South Africa
air power, on western front 170, 214, 225
  see also Royal Air Force
All Souls College, Oxford 54, 62
Allenby, Gen. Sir Edmund (Lord) 145, 152, 167
  dinner with HW 54
  favoured by Clemenceau 212
  GOC 1st Army 163–4
  GOC Egypt 201, 211, 216, 220
  High Commissioner for Egypt 253
Amery, Leopold, MP 26, 30, 34, 108, 228
  and army reform 54, 56
  and conscription 76, 150
  'first glimpse' of HW 37
  friendship with HW 48, 114
  on importance of Middle East 233
  inadequate punting technique 62
  and Supreme War Council 209, 213
  and *The Times* history of the Boer War 54–5
  and Ulster crisis 114, 119, 123–4
  and 'X' committee 223–4, 227
Anderson, Gen. Sir Hastings 70
Anderson, Sir John, civil servant 268
Arabia 249
Ardagh, Gen. Sir John 25 n. 76
Ardnamona House 14–15
Arnold-Forster, Hugh, war minister 56, 59–61, 64, 67, 68
Armytage, Maj. 165
artillery, use of on western front 163–4, 167–8, 214, 225–6
Ash, Bernard:
  absurd prediction about HW's political future 295
  biography of HW (*The Lost Dictator*) 294–5
Askwith, Lord, Marlburian 5
Asquith, Herbert Henry ('Squiff'), Prime Minister 108, 112, 154, 178, 181–2, 260
  and Committee of Imperial Defence 96–7
  dissatisfaction with 173–5, 177
  fall from power 179
  forms coalition government 149
  a 'good' member of the Cabinet 101
  and HW 140–3, 150, 152–3
  and Ireland 117–18, 122–3, 127
  and outbreak of First World War 128, 131–2
  and Supreme War Council 208–9, 217
  war minister 126

Aston, Gen. Sir George 16
Attenborough, Richard 294
Austin, Brig.-Gen. Herbert 62
Australia 273
  Irish community in 198, 222
Austria, Austria-Hungary:
  as German ally 95, 148, 199
  offensives: (1916) 182, (1918) 206, 209
  and outbreak of First World War 127
  sues for peace 227

Baird, John, MP 120
Baker-Carr, C. D., chauffeur 136
Baldwin, Stanley, Prime Minister 295
Balfour, Arthur 75, 124, 218
  in coalition Cabinet 149
  on Irish policy 267
  Prime Minister 48, 56, 62
Ballinalee, County Longford 2, 6, 275
Barker, Maj. J. S. S. 23
Barnett-Baker, Lt.-Col. Randle 164–6
Barrington, Sir Charles, Irish landlord 257
Barrow, Gen. Sir George 81
Barter, Gen. Sir Charles 158, 162–5, 169
Bartholomew, Col. William 137, 291
Barton, Gen. Geoffrey 29
Bates, Richard Dawson, Northern Ireland politician 197
  'a small man in every way' 280
Battenberg, Admiral Prince Louis of 128
Beatty, Admiral Lord 269
Beauchamp, Lord, landowner 11
Beaverbrook, Lord, politician 144
Beckett, Ian, historian 120, 132
Beckett, J. C., historian 1–2
Belfast 114, 127, 296
  HW in 16, 119
  HW's forebears from 2
  'Peace Day' celebration in 258
  Queen's University of 10, 242
Belgium 83
  army 145, 212
  'Belgian scheme' at Staff College 72–4
  as coalition partners 181
  deployment of BEF in 134
  gallant and Catholic 156
  operations in (1917) 195, 199
  and outbreak of First World War 128
  possible Anglo-Belgian alliance 97–8, 101–3
Belin, Gen. 127, 135

Bell, Johannes, German plenipotentiary 239
Bentinck, Maj. Lord Charles ('Daddy') 194
Bernard, Dr J. H., archbishop 257
Berthelet, Gen. 135
Bertie, Lord, diplomat 143
Bethell, Admiral Sir Alexander 96
Bethmann-Hollweg, Theobald von, German
    Chancellor 90
Bethune, Col. Edward 33
Birley, Sir Oswald, painter 296
Birrell, Augustine, politician 175, 297
Bliss, Gen. Tasker H. 211
Bolshevism:
    in the Caucasus 248
    threat from 229, 231–2, 237–8, 277
Bond, Brian, historian 16, 294
    mobilisation of BEF 131
    on Staff College 17, 67, 68 n. 26, 72, 78
Botha, Gen. Louis 29, 31
Bowman, Timothy, historian 172 n. 87
Boyd, Gen. Gerald 268, 273
Brackenbury, Gen. Henry 22, 57
Bredow, Gen. Claus von 71
Brehm, Bruno von, Nazi novelist 286
Briand, Aristide, politician 181, 187, 191
Bridges, Gen. Tom 98, 100–1, 103
British army:
    appointments system 66–7
    attitudes towards politicians 143–4
    cavalry 36
    commitments 232, 247–51
    demobilisation 229–31
    Irish crisis and 116–17
    in Irish war of independence 258–72
    militia and volunteers 44, 46, 63, 75
    post-war requirements 229–30
    reform of 11, 43–7, 55–63, 75–6
    strain of service in Ireland 264–5, 272
    Victorian officer corps 11–13
    see also Staff College; War Office
British army formations:
    First World War divisions: 1st 156, 159; 2nd
        161–3, 165, 173; 3rd 173; 9th (Scottish)
        168–70; 12th (Eastern) 150; 15th
        (Scottish)156, 158–9; 16th (Irish) 156–7,
        159; 'riff raff Redmondites' 158; 23rd
        161–2; 25th 164; 36th (Ulster) 152;
        47th (2nd London) 156–60, 162–4, 168;
        63rd (Royal Naval) 160 n. 25, 169–70
    regiments etc.: Black Watch 171; Durham
        Light Infantry 30, 35–6; Irish Guards
        284; King's Royal Rifle Corps 13, 33;
        London Regiment 160; Longford Militia
        12; Princess Patricia's Royal Canadian
        Regiment 173; Rifle Brigade 12–13, 16,
        19, 21, 30, 35, 49–50, 173; Royal
        Berkshire Regiment 164; Royal Fusiliers

164; Royal Irish Regiment 12; Royal Irish
    Rifles 119; Royal Munster Fusiliers 12,
    283; Scottish Rifles (Cameronians) 33
other formations: Irish Brigade 29–30, 35;
    Light Brigade 27, 29–37; mounted
    infantry 33, 36; Territorial Force 75–7,
    67, 92, 109–10
British Expeditionary Force (BEF) 72–3
    executions in 171–2
    mobilisation and deployment 128–9, 131–4
    organisation of 157
    planning for 63, 85–8, 91–3, 101–2,
        110, 123
    possible need of 44, 46
    size 86, 110, 126, 132, 134–5
    staff deficiencies and high command 136,
        139–42, 178
    training 157, 159–61
British governments:
    Liberal (1906–15) reformist programme
        107–8
    coalition (1915) 149, 177
    Lloyd George coalition: (1916) 179;
        (1918) 230
British navy, *see* Royal Navy
Brodrick, St John:
    on Lord Esher 56
    war minister 43–4, 46–7, 55–6, 86
Brooks's club 18
Brugha, Cathal, compared with HW 289
Buchan, John, writer 10
Buchanan, Sir George, diplomat 127–8
buggery, peacemaking likened to 234
Bulgaria 104, 239
    enemy ally 182, 184, 193, 196, 199, 203–4
    sues for peace 226–7
Buller, Gen. Sir Redvers 27, 29–37, 50
Burke, Edmund 186
Burke, Thomas Henry 287
Burma 13–14
Butt, Dame Clara, singer 54
Byng, Gen. Sir Julian (Lord) ('Bungo') 67,
    162–3

Cadorna, Gen. Luigi 181, 207, 211
Callwell, Gen. Sir Charles 58
    and biography of HW 286, 291
    catastrophic effect on HW's reputation 292
    quoted 13, 33, 55, 74, 159, 213
Cambon, Paul, diplomat 131
Cambridge, Duke of 47
Campbell-Bannerman, Sir Henry, statesman
    44, 62
Canada 273
    Canadian Corps 170, 191
    lecture on 83
    strategic importance of 45–6

Capel, Arthur, lover of Coco Chanel 212
Carrington, Charles, soldier 157, 160 n. 22,
    163
Carson, Sir Edward, politician 1
    and British high command 141
    in coalition Cabinet 149
    on Lloyd George 176
    meetings with HW 174–5
    and HW's political ambitions 196, 198, 279
    and Ulster crisis 117, 120, 123, 127
    and war leadership 177
Castelnau, Gen. de Cuières de 102–3, 184,
    194
Caucasus:
    during First World War 182, 226
    after 1918: 231, 233–4, 247–8, 252
Cavan, Gen. Lord 79 n. 83, 229
    HW's successor as CIGS 278
Cavendish, Lord Frederick 287
Chamberlain, Austen, politician 124, 149, 227
    on HW as MP 279
    meetings with HW 139, 174, 176, 183
    'murderer' 287
Chamberlain, 'Joe', politician 63, 111–12
Chamberlain, Neville, politician 76 n. 65
Chanak crisis (1922) 252
Channel tunnel 237
Chantilly, Allied conference at (1915) 167
Chapman, Gen. Edward 22–3
Charley, Lt.-Col. Harold 281
Charteris, Gen. John 142–3, 153, 214
    reports adversely on IV Corps HQ 165–6
Chetwode, Gen. Sir Philip 124
Churchill, Winston **plate 7** 11, 107–9,
    114–15, 295
    at Admiralty 101
    'alive to the German danger' 102
    Colonial Secretary 251
    and Dardanelles 148–9
    and Egypt 253
    eloquent views on Mesopotamia (Iraq) 250
    and HW 48, 92, 96–100, 134, 205, 240–1,
        293
    and intelligence 99–100
    and Ireland 260–2, 266–7
    and outbreak of First World War 128–9
    praised by HW 101
    review of army expenditure 278
    and Ulster crisis 120
    war minister 230–2, 242, 243–5, 247–50
    and wartime politics 174
civil–military relations 47, 121, 125
    during First World War 132, 199–208,
        216–18
Clarke, Gen. Sir George 56, 59–60
Clemenceau, Georges, statesman 168, 210–11,
    219, 220–1

'furious' with Haig 212
    and peace negotiations 238
Clery, Gen. Sir Francis 17, 24, 26, 29, 31, 36
Clive, Nigel, intelligence from 18
Clive, Gen. Sidney 144, 146–7, 152, 156, 192,
    216
    and HW's farewell from French HQ (1917)
        195
coalition warfare 144–7, 167, 171, 180–1,
    214–16, 220–1
    development of inter-allied machinery
        200–1, 204–9
    see also under individual allied states
Colchester 53–4
Coleraine 114
Collier, Basil, biography of HW (*Brasshat*)
    293–4
Collins, Michael 267, 270, 276, 285, 294, 296
    describes HW as 'a violent Orange partisan'
        280
    little evidence to link him with killing of HW
        284
committee of imperial defence (CID) 57–8,
    86–7, 107, 109, 115, 128
    and Cabinet secretariat 180
    invasion inquiry (1913–14) 110, 126
    meeting of 23 Aug. 1911: 96–7, 101
Congreve, Billy, soldier 147
Congreve, Gen. Sir Walter ('Squibbie') 30,
    147, 194, 253, 277
Connaught, Duke of 20
conscription 44, 108–10
    during First World War 175, 196
    HW on 46, 69, 75–7, 87, 109, 150, 197,
        29–31
    and Ireland 196–7, 222–3
Cooper, Maj. F. E. 50
Coote, Jack 276
Cornabie, Amy, housemaid 286
Cowan, Admiral Sir Walter **plate 3** 40
Cowans, Gen. Sir John ('Jack') 19
    marital problems 24
    in Paris hotel with a Mrs McCalmont 103
Cowling, Maurice, historian 279
Craig, Sir James 175, 296
    'a very second rate man' 280
    HW's advice to 297
    Prime Minister of Northern Ireland 273,
        278–80
Creed, Percy, on commercial value of becoming
    an MP 279
Crewe, Lord, politician 101
Crowe, Sir Eyre, civil servant 94, 128
Cruttwell, Charles, historian 67
Cumming, Mansfield, spy 100
Cunliffe, Lord, banker 237–8
Curragh incident (1914) 121–6

Curzon, Lord, politician 43, 149, 218, 295
  backs HW 189, 193
  expansionist imperial vision in Middle East
    233–4, 247–50
  suggests 'Indian' methods in Ireland 266
  in War Cabinet 180, 199
Cuthbert, Brig.-Gen. Gerald 163

Dale, Arthur, soldier and murderer 172
Danilov, Gen. 185
Davidson, Gen. John 164
Davies, David, MP 196
Davies, Gen. 'Joey' 58, 119, 132
Dawnay, Hugh, soldier 27
  killed, 173
Dawson, Geoffrey, *see* Robinson, Geoffrey
Deedes, Gen. Sir Charles 5, 102, 135
  character appreciation of HW 292–3
Derby, Lord (formerly Lord Stanley) ('Eddie')
    plate 3 127, 225, 265
  ambassador in Paris 223, 240
  and Gallipoli 148
  and HW 193, 198, 217, 242; 'quite mad on
    the subject of Ireland' 274
  and Lloyd George 183
  in South Africa 38–9
  war minister 188, 206, 209–10, 218, 269
de Valera, Eamon 197
  HW wants him handed over to the police
    274
  'your Cuban Jew compatriot' 273
de Vesci, Lord 18
Diaz, Gen. Armando 208
Dill, Field Marshal Sir John, on HW 293
Dillon, Col. Eric **plate 6** 28, 81, 194
Dobbie, Col. William 159
Docherty, John, soldier 171–2
d'Ombrain, Nicholas, historian 39, 85
Douglas, Gen. Sir Charles ('Sunny Jim'):
  Adjutant-General 57–9, 78
  CIGS 123, 126, 128, 132
  premature death 150
Drogheda, Lord, Irish landlord 15
Du Cane, Gen. Sir John ('Johnnie') 118, 149,
    157, 171
Dubail, Gen. Auguste 92–3
Dublin 3, 14, 296
  Alexandra College 257
  Trinity College 4, 242, 257
  University College 257–8
Duff, Col. Beauchamp 39
Dufferin, Lord 278
Duke, H. E., politician 197
Duncannon, Lord, ADC to HW 166, 174,
    193–4
  and HW entering politics 195–6, 198
Dundonald, Gen. Lord 36, 242

Dunne, Reginald (*alias* James Connolly) **plate 11**
  and killing of HW 281–4, 294
Dunsany, Lord 105
Dunsterville, Maj. Lionel ('Stalky') 233
d'Urbal, Gen. 157
Dyer, Brig.-Gen. Reginald, of Amritsar 266–7

École Supérieure de Guerre 73–4, 90
Edmonds, Sir James, historian 25 n. 78, 66, 79,
    171, 291
  and counter-intelligence 100
  'just a spiteful old gossip' 67
Edward VII, King 75, 236, 269
Egerton, Gen. Granville 124
Egypt 25, 49, 63, 234, 244
  Allenby Declaration 253–4
  during First World War 201, 208, 226
  nationalist unrest in 246
  strategic importance of 46, 249, 251–3,
    277–8
Eisenhower, Gen. Dwight D. 221
elections:
  bye (1913) 117
  general: (1906) 62–3, 107; (1910) 108,
    112–13; (1918) 223, 230, 243, 257
  in Ireland (1921) 268–9, 271
Elgin Commission 55–6
Ellison, Gen. Sir Gerald 55–6, 58, 68
Elphinstone, Lady 24
Esher, Lord 171, 192
  high opinion of HW 58, 65, 84, 190
  on HW entering politics 195–6
  on HW's 'Irish blood' 125–6
  pessimistic 178
  and War Office reform 56–60, 68
Estonia 239
Evert, Gen. 186
Ewart, Gen. Sir John Spencer 78, 85, 120,
    122–4
ex-servicemen:
  enlistment into Irish gendarmerie 263
  feared revolutionary threat from 245

Faillières, President 71
Fairholme, Col. William 90, 100
Fanshawe, Gen. 157
Farquhar, Col. 'Fanny' 100
  killed 173
Fay, Sir Sam, wartime bureaucrat 193
  colourful remark about HW 107
Fergusson, Bernard, soldier 293
Fergusson, Gen. Sir Charles 170
Fermoy, IRA attack on soldiers at Methodist
    Church 258
Finland 239
Fisher, Admiral Lord ('Jackie') 56
  criticizes HW 91

Fisher, Sir Warren, civil servant 269
Fitzalan, Lord 296
Fitzgerald, Lt.-Col. Brinsley 200
Fitzgerald, Capt. Evelyn, stockbroker 240
Flameng, François, painter 143
Foch, Marshal Ferdinand **plate 9** 89, 102–3,
    145, 152–3
  and British high command 141, 146, 168,
    192–3, 212
  becomes generalissimo 220–1
  HW critical of 225
  HW predicts Foch will command Allied
    armies 74
  attends HW's funeral 288
  and Lloyd George 176
  and Nivelle 191
  relationship with HW 73–4, 90, 138, 143,
    146, 178, 194, 207, 219, 225, 228, 242
  on size of BEF 86
  tactical views 167–8
  on war with Germany 90
Fontainebleau memorandum (1919) 236–8
Fortesque, Sir John, historian:
  on relationship between height and brain
    development 11
Foster, R. F., historian 9
France:
  and Agadier crisis (1911) 92–3
  Anglo-French war planning 126–7, 129
  coalition relations with Britain 144–7, 167,
    180–2, 206–8, 214, 220–1, 228
  Franco-British alliance 72–3, 79, 83, 85, 90,
    94, 237–8
  Lloyd George says French government is
    'absolutely rotten' 201
  mobilisation 95–6, 131
  mutiny and unrest in army 191, 194
  proposal for unified Allied command (1917)
    187–8
  and peace conference 235–8
Franz Ferdinand, Archduke, assassination of 126
French, David, historian 180, 221 n. 78, 224
French, Field Marshal Sir John (Lord) 12 n. 5,
    39, 90, 96, 107, 174, 189, 291
  CinC, BEF 123, 128–9, 132–52
  CIGS 102–3, 105, 110
  and French allies 144–6, 181
  attends HW's funeral 288
  portrayal in *Oh What a Lovely War* 294
  relations with HW 140–1, 146–7, 151, 198,
    199–200, 242
  and Robertson 199, 205–6
  and Ulster crisis 116–17, 119–20, 122–3, 125
  Viceroy of Ireland 223, 257, 261
  views on war strategy sought by Lloyd
    George 201, 203, 205
Freytag-Loringhoven, Gen. Alexander von 163

Fryers, Lieut. Hubert 16
Furse, Gen. Sir William 76 n. 65, 168, 291

Gailey, Andrew, historian 274
Gaisford, Walter 19
Gardner, Nikolas, historian 135
Garstin, Mary Isabella (née North; later
    Repington) 49–52
Garstin, Sir William 49–51, 53, 76, 120 n. 46
Garvin, J. L., editor 108
gas, use of on western front 169
Gatacre, Gen. Sir William 31
Geddes, Eric, wartime civil servant 179
  and committee on national expenditure 177–8
general staff:
  break-up of (1914) 132
  establishment of in Britain 47, 57–60, 63
George V, King 119, 288, 295
  and British high command 150, 154,
    188–9, 218
  concerns about Ireland 116, 198, 271
  and HW 190
  visit to Staff College 77
Germains, Victor Wallace, writer 97
Germany:
  British occupation forces 239, 246, 252,
    256, 269
  fears of revolution in 229–30
  First World War offensives 139, 163–4, 206,
    209, 220–1, 226
  HW travels to 75, 90
  military training 76
  mobilisation 95–6
  and outbreak of First World War 127–8
  and peace conference 235–40
  sues for peace 227
  threat from 72–3, 75, 83, 95, 99–100, 148,
    226
  see also under War, First World
Girton College, Cambridge:
  HW encounters 'frights' from 103
Gladstone, W. E. 111
Godley, Gen. Sir Alexander ('Alex') 78, 125
Gooch, John, historian and sharp-eyed
    typescript reader x, 57, 60
Gough, Gen. Sir Hubert 173, 220
  'best hated and most useless general we have
    got' 170
  GOC, I Corps 157
  criticises HW 188–9
  criticises John French 150, 154
  HW on 170–1
  and Ulster crisis 121–5
Gough, Brig.-Gen. John 119, 121–2, 124–5
  killed 173
Graves, Robert, Irish schoolboy 6
Greece 252

Green, Brig.-Gen. Arthur 80, 147
Greenwood, Sir Hamar, politician 261,
    267–8, 271
Grenfell, Gen. Sir Francis 49
Grey, Sir Edward, Foreign Secretary 91, 93–4,
    96, 98, 100
    'ignorant & careless' 94
    and outbreak of First World War 128
    qualified praise from HW 101
Grierson, Gen. Sir James ('Jimmy') 57–9, 63,
    85, 100
Griffith, Arthur, politician 285
Griffith, Paddy, historian 169
Grigg, John, historian 177
Guilbert, Yvette, *chanteuse* 23
Guilford, Lady ('Gac'), friendship with HW
    24, 48–52
Guilford, Lord ('Nipper') 24, 48
Guinn, Paul, historian 226
Guinness, Walter, soldier and politician 177
Gwynn, Stephen, writer 287
Gwynne, H. A., editor 108–9, 123–4,
    141, 217

Haig, Field Marshal Sir Douglas (Earl) 39, 65,
    68, 77, 101, 157, 171, 192, 226
    adverse opinion of John French 150, 153–4
    aggressive tactics 162
    attends HW's funeral 288
    becomes CinC, BEF 152
    and BEF 128–9, 135
    and capital sentences 172
    favourable opinion of Robertson 150; less so
        228
    and General Reserve 217, 219–20
    on HW's threat to resign (1917) 192–5
    HW's views of 156, 166 n. 54, 167–8, 198,
        212, 219–20, 242
    ill-served by own staff 214
    low opinion of HW 142–3, 152
    and Lloyd George 176–7, 201, 203–6, 211,
        216, 218
    personal dislike for HW 189–90
    plans for 1917 offensive 195
    relations with HW as CIGS 218, 228
    relations with HW while GOC, IV Corps
        164–6, 169–70, 178
    threat of being put under Nivelle 187–8
    and training 160–1
    and war strategy 199, 201, 203, 213–15
Haking, Gen. Sir Richard 150, 169–70, 177
Haldane, Gen. Sir Aylmer 65
    GOC Mesopotamia 250
    grumpy memoirs 43
    at Staff College with HW 19
Haldane, Richard Burdon (Viscount) 110,
    125, 128

backs HW 101
British 'nation in arms' concept 75–6
and expeditionary force 91–2, 94, 96
opposes Belgian alliance 98
and Staff College 77
war minister 63, 65, 67, 74, 86, 89,
    103, 109
Hale, Col. Lonsdale 89
Hamilton, Hubert 19
    killed 173, 236
Hamilton, Gen. Sir Ian ('Johnnie') 31, 42,
    57–8, 76 n. 65, 82, 128
    on HW and Rawlinson 19
    in South Africa 39
Hamilton-Gordon, Gen. Sir Alex 58
Hankey, Sir Maurice, indispensable bureaucrat
    ('Hanky Panky') **plate 8**
    blames President Wilson for imperial
        troubles 234
    and Cabinet secretariat 180–1, 199, 223–4,
        227
    CID meeting of 23 Aug. 1911: 97
    despatch of BEF 128–9
    development of Supreme War Council 201,
        206–7, 209, 211, 213, 215
    and domestic unrest 245–6
    at Fontainbleau weekend 236–8
    on HW 91, 153, 205
    HW pays tribute to 242
Harington, Gen. Sir Charles ('Tim') 1, 53, 279
    GOC Constantinople 252
Harcourt, Lewis ('Loulou'), politician 101
Harper, Gen. Sir George ('Uncle' or 'Daddy')
    74–5, 101, 194 n. 68
    on uselessness of drink 173
Hart, Gen. Fitzroy 29–30, 37
    a 'perfect disgrace' 35–6
Hart, Peter, historian 284
Hartington, Lord **plate 6** 235
Headlam, Gen. Sir John 164
Henderson, Arthur, politician 149, 180
Henderson, Col. G. F. R. 17, 19
Hickie, Gen. Sir William 158
Hildyard, Gen. Sir Henry 17, 29–30, 34, 55,
    57–8, 65
Hill, Lord Arthur 285
Holland 98
Holland, Gen. Sir Arthur 159
House, Col. Edward M. 211
Howard, Sir Michael, historian 243
Huguet, Col. Victor 129, 194, 242
    ally of HW 143
    and Anglo-French liaison 133, 138, 140,
        144, 147, 181
    assists HW to obtain chef 174
    French military attaché in London 74, 85–7,
        92–3

Hungary 239
Hunter, Charles, MP 108, 139, 174, 176
  and Ulster crisis 113–14, 118, 120
  visits Turkey with HW 104
Hunter, Private William 172
Hussey, John, historian 67

Ignatieff, Count 181
India 253
  Amritsar massacre (1919) 266–7
  defence of 226, 234, 246, 248–9
  HW service in 13, 20
  a 'storm centre' (1919) 244
  strategic importance 45–6, 232–4, 251,
    277–8
Inglis, Brian, Irish schoolboy 6
intelligence:
  HW gathering 74–5, 90, 100–1
  HW's use of 96, 99–100
Iraq, *see* Mesopotamia
Ireland and the 'Irish question' 111–15, 234,
    244, 251, 256–80
  'Bloody Sunday' (1920) 267–8
  British security policy 259–60, 263–9
  conscription 196–8, 222–3
  Easter Rising (1916) 175, 256
  IRA/Sinn Féin split and outbreak of civil
    war 285
  martial law applied 268–9
  nationalism 7–8, 111, 234
  not 'at war' in 1919: 257–8
  parallel with Egypt 253–4; India 266;
    Palestine 253; Turkey 252
  planned summer offensive (1921) 271–3
  recruitment during First World War 156
  threat of civil war 116, 127, 129–30
  truce and treaty 273–4
  Ulster crisis 117–27
  worsening situation in 246, 256 (and,
    inevitably, *passim*)
Ireland, Church of 6
Irish Free State 274, 296
Irish Landowners' Convention 9, 18, 111
Irish Republican Army 257–8, 264, 275
Irish Unionist Alliance 9, 18, 174, 297
Italy 171, 182, 213, 216, 220, 247
  'pigs of organ-grinders' 206
  as wartime ally 181, 183–4, 199, 201, 204,
    207–8, 214, 225

Jameson, Dr Frederick 26
Japan 237
Joffre, Marshal Joseph 127, 133, 191
  1914 battles 135, 137
  and Anglo-French liaison 181
  on British high command 141
  dismissed 187

favours HW 143, 151
French CGS 102–3
relations with John French 138, 145–6
hopes for success 147, 167
Johnson, Revd Henry 275
Johnstone, Lady 240
Jones, Tom, assistant Cabinet secretary 245
Joubert, President 72

Karslake, Lt.-Col. Henry 167
Kell, Vernon, spy 100
Kelleher, Denis, IRA volunteer 283
Kellett, Gen. Richard 165–6
Kelly-Kenny, Gen. Thomas 39, 43, 52, 57
Kemal Atatürk 252
Kennedy, Paul, historian 204
Kenyon, Gen. Edward 161
Kerensky, Alexander, politician 186
Kerr, Philip (Lord Lothian) 236
Kerry, Capt. The Earl of, *see* Lord Lansdowne
Keynes, John Maynard, economist 237
Kiggell, Gen. Sir Launcelot 119
  as DSD 87, 102
  Haig's Chief of Staff 160–2, 190–1, 213
  at Staff College with HW 19; HW suggests
    as Commandant 78
Kirke, Gen. Sir Walter 7, 220
Kitchener, Field Marshal Lord 140, 146, 151,
    183, 288 n. 39
  and BEF 85, 132–4, 137, 144–5
  and British high command 141, 145
  drowned 176
  and HW 78, 133–4, 139, 150, 152–3,
    156
  imperial soldiering 25, 31, 49
  raising of mass army 138–9
  relations with the French 144–5, 180
  as war minister 128–9, 147–8, 150
Knox, Col. Alfred 103, 185–7

labour unrest:
  1911: 94, 108
  1916: 174, 179
  after 1918: 231, 244–7, 264, 271
Ladibat, Gen. Laffort de 90
Lambton, Col. Billy 140
Lanrezac, Gen. 104, 134–5, 137
Lansdowne, Lady 76 n. 65, 183
Lansdowne, Lord (formerly The Earl of Kerry)
  plate 3 15, 40, 124
Lausanne, Treaty of (1923) 252
Law, Andrew Bonar, politician 120, 154, 181,
    248, 288, 295
  Blenheim Palace speech 115
  in Cabinet 149
  and Curragh crisis 123–4
  and HW's political ambitions 197

Law, Andrew Bonar, politician (*cont.*):
  meetings with HW 117, 139, 141, 174–5, 245
  urges HW not to resign 151
  Ulster-Scot family 113–14
  in War Cabinet 179, 193
  and war leadership 173–4, 177, 200
  and war strategy 148
Lawrence, Gen. Herbert 213
Leadenham, Lincs. 183 n. 20
League of Nations 237, 239, 246, 252
Lee, Arthur, politician 108, 123, 151, 166, 174, 176
Leetham, Arthur 74
legislation:
  Act of Union 1, 6, 111, 297
  Daylight Saving Act 179
  Encumbered Estates Act 2
  Government of Ireland Act 259, 268, 272
  Home Rule Bill 111, 114–15, 119, 126, 223
  Irish Church Act 6
  licensing laws 179
  Military Service Bill (1918) 222
  Munitions of War Act 179
  Parliament (or 'Veto') Bill 108, 115
Leitrim, Lord 15
Leo XIII, Pope 7
Leroy Lewis, Col. 192
Lewin, Harry 159, 166
Liddell Hart, Basil, historian 66–7, 137, 143, 167, 214
Littlewood, Joan, and *Oh What a Lovely War* 294
Lloyd George, David, statesman 92–3, 96, 108, 166, 225, 245, 269
  critical of Haig 183, 188, 198
  growing support for 175–6
  and HW 143–4, 177–8, 180, 193–4, 198–202, 210, 236, 240–1, 274–5, 278–9, 293
  HW praises 101
  and HW's death 287–8
  on imperial commitments 248
  and Ireland 197–8, 222–3, 260, 271, 273; backs *sub rosa* police methods 265–6
  meetings with HW 151, 174; consults HW 177
  Minister of Munitions 174–5, 179
  opinion of Robertson 174, 260
  at Paris peace conference 236–40
  People's Budget 107
  and possible Belgian alliance 98
  and post-war reconstruction 230, 243, 245
  Prime Minister 177, 179, 223–4, 227–8
  pro-Greek bias 252
  and royal interference in politics 189, 218
  and Russia 232
  struggle for power over Robertson and Haig 199–208, 216, 217–18

  and Supreme War Council 208–11
  'an underbred swine' 198 n. 88
  'very quick but entirely unreliable' 194
  war minister 176
  war strategy 148, 182–3, 193, 199, 206, 215
Lloyd George, Gwilym **plate 6** 235
Loch, Gen. Douglas (Lord) 139, 142, 170
Locker-Lampson, Geoffrey, MP 174
Long, Col. Charles 29–30
Long, Walter, politician 113–15, 139, 245, 261
Longford, Earl of 47
Lords, House of, limitation of powers 94, 107–8, 111–12
Lovat, Simon, politician 108, 110
Lucan, Lord and Lady 24
Lucas, Col. Cuthbert 187, 188 n. 41, 198
  interrupted fishing trip 264
Lyttelton, Gen. Sir Neville 27, 31–6, 39
  'absolutely incapable' 63
  and HW's appointment to Staff College 64–5, 67
  in War Office 57–61

McCarthy, Justin 8
McCracken, Gen. Frederick 172, 194 n. 68
MacDonald, Ramsay 71
MacDonnell, J. H., solicitor 283
Macdonogh Gen. Sir George 7
  DMI 203
  and intelligence work 100
MacEoin, Gen. Seán, 'Blacksmith of Ballinalee' 3
  HW petition for clemency 275–6
McKenna, Stephen, politician 91–6
  a 'waster' 101
Macmillan, Harold 295
McNeill, Ronald, MP 287
MacPhail, Sir Andrew:
  ludicrous conjecture about HW's killers 286
Macready, Gen. Sir Nevil ('Make-Ready') 136, 203
  attends HW's funeral 288
  and Black and Tans 265–6
  Commissioner of Metropolitan Police 231
  GOC Ireland 260–73; review of policy 262
  on HW as MP 279
  HW defends 271
  and Ireland (1913–14) 118, 120
  on Jack Cowans's conversion 24
  lugubrious but wise epistle to HW 270
  pressed to attack Four Courts after HW's killing 285
  and Seán MacEoin 275–6
  and security in Northern Ireland 280

suggests shooting members of the Dáil 'by mistake' 273
travel advice for HW 296
a 'vain ass' 262
Mahon, Gen. Sir Bryan 12 n. 5
Malleson, Gen. Wilfrid 233
Mangan, J. A., historian 4
Marlborough College 4–5
Marshall-Cornwall, James intelligence officer **plate 6** 235
Marshall-Hall, Edward, barrister 51
Martin, Ged, historian 10
Maude, Gen. Sir Stanley 201
Maurice, Gen. Sir Edward 210
Maxse, Gen. Sir Ivor 127
Maxse, Leo, editor 48, 76
Maxwell, Gen. Sir John ('Conky') 175, 198
May, Gen. Sir Edward ('Edna'):
  on HW and Rawlinson 20
  'worthy but stupid' 65–6
  in War Office 58
Meinertzhagen, Col. Richard **plate 6** 235
Mends, Col. Horatio 50
Mesopotamia (Iraq) 182, 201, 203, 226, 233
  after 1918: 234, 237, 244, 248–50, 252, 271, 277–8
  rebellion (1920) 246, 250, 264
  scheme for control by 'Hot Air, Aeroplanes and Arabs' 251
Messimy, Adolphe, politician 92
Methuen, Gen. Lord 28 n. 3, 29, 31
Miles, Gen. Sir Herbert 65, 91
Millerand, Alexandre, politician 102, 145, 180
Millman, Brock, historian 198
Milne, Gen. Sir George 233, 248
  finds inhabitants of Caucasus 'loathesome' 247
Milner, Sir Alfred (Lord) **plate 3** 76, 128, 154, 194, 212, 217, 221
  and British presence in the Middle East 248–9
  and Egypt 253
  on HW 125, 193, 206, 289; meetings with HW 139, 151, 197
  and Ireland 118, 123, 222
  Mission to Russia 183–4, 187
  political intrigue 176
  and South Africa 27 29, 39
  and Supreme War Council 210–11, 215
  in War Cabinet 180, 199
  war minister 223–4, 227, 230, 242
mining, on western front 162
Monro, Gen. Sir Charles 157–8, 162–7, 177–8
Mons (Belgium) 74
  retreat from 134–6
Montagu, Edwin, politician 236–7
Montgomery-Cunninghame, Col. Sir Thomas 37, 38, 79–80

Morland, Gen. Sir Thomas ('Morlando') 278
Morley, John, politician 101, 122, 125
Morris, Lt.-Col. George, killed 173
Morton, Desmond, ADC 214
Müller, Herman, German plenipotentiary 239
munitions, shortage of (1915) 148–9, 150
Murray, Gen. Sir Archibald ('Archie') **plate 3** 40, 105, 153
  DMT 87, 102
  CGS, BEF 132–3, 135–6, 138–44
  CIGS 150–1, 181
  relations with HW 150–1, 181
muslims, need for good relations with 249–50, 252

Napoleon, Emperor 204
National Service League 76, 108–9, 115, 150
nationalist challenges to empire 234
Neave, Airey, MP 286
Nicholas II, Emperor **plate 5** 185–6
Nicholson, Lt.-Col. Walter 80
Nicholson, Gen. Sir William (Lord) ('Nick' or 'Old Nick') 38, 68
  CIGS 77–8, 87, 89, 102, 107
  and conscription 75
  opposes Belgian alliance 98
  and planning for BEF 91–2, 94, 96, 101
  in War Office 43, 57–8, 61
Nicolson, Sir Arthur, civil servant 88, 90, 127
Nivelle, Gen. Robert:
  attends HW's funeral 288
  French CinC 187–8, 190–2
Norcott, Gen. William 35
Northcliffe, Lord 171
Northern Ireland 273, 278, 289
  and commemoration of HW 296
'Norperforce' 233
Northcott, Maj. H. P. 26
Nugent, Gen. Sir Oliver 12 n. 5

O'Connor, Rory, IRA leader 285
O'Connor, T. P., describes HW as 'typically Irish' 289
oil 233–4, 249, 252
Oliver, Frederick S., draper and editor 108–9, 150, 176, 227, 291
O'Malley, Ernie, IRA volunteer and writer 280
Ommanney, Capt. Rupert, killed 173
Orlando, Vittorio, politician 211
Orpen, Richard Caulfield, architect 14 n. 16
Orpen, Sir William:
  memoir of HW 14
  paints HW 240–1; *see also* **frontispiece**
O'Sullivan, Joseph (*alias* John O'Brien) **plate 11**
  and killing of HW 281–4, 294

Paget, Gen. Sir Arthur 120–2
Paine, Tom 186
Painlevé, Paul, politician 191–3, 208–10
    obliges HW to wait with prostitute 194
Palestine:
    after 1918: 234, 237, 249, 252–3, 277–8
    in First World War 201, 203, 211, 215
Panouse, Lt-Col. Vicomte de la 131–2
Paris peace conference 235–40
    HW's views on 238–9
Pellé, Gen Maurice 181
Pembroke, Beatrice Lady:
    friendship with HW 240
Pembroke, 15th Earl of (formerly Lord Herbert)
    plate 3
Perceval, Spencer, assassinated prime minister
    286
Percival, Col. Edward ('Perks') 71, 74
Percy, Earl 108, 150
    puerile behaviour at Chantilly conference 181
Pershing, Gen. J. J. 213, 221
Persia (Iran) 226, 233–4
    British policy towards 234, 248–9, 250,
    252, 271
Pétain, Gen. Henri-Philippe 167, 191, 226
    194, 219
    and German spring offensive (1918) 220–1
    Pétain strategy, 'do nothing!' 192, 203
    relations with HW 192–3
Pitt Taylor, Maj. W. W. ('P.T.') 239
Plumer, Gen. Sir Herbert (Lord) 25, 195
    GOC Italy 208
    possible CIGS or SWC member 217–18
    suggested as CinC, BEF 212
    in War Office 57–8
Plunket, Archbishop Lord 6
Poincaré, Raymond, politician 127–8, 210,
    221
Poland 103
Portugal:
    empire 278
    troops 221
polo 13, 68, 70, 71
Porro, Gen. 181
potatoes:
    size of 277
    value of to HW 79
Powell, J. Enoch, MP 295
Price-Davies, Mrs Eileen (HW's sister) 294
    attempt to commission fresh biography of
    HW 291–2
Priestley, J. B. 161–2

Queen's University Belfast 10, 242

Radcliffe, Gen. Sir Percy **plate 6** 97, 101, 235
Radko-Dmitriev, Gen. 186

Rattigan, Sir William, MP 44
Rawlinson, Gen. Sir Henry (Lord) ('Rawly')
    247, 260, 272, 274, 277–8
    and battle of the Somme 167–8
    CinC India 251, 262
    commandant of Staff College 55, 62, 64–5,
    68, 79, 89
    critical of John French 153–4
    end of war 227
    estimated length of war 139
    favours Robertson as CIGS 161
    friendship with HW 13, 19–20, 38, 62, 93,
    152
    GOC North Russia 232
    hands over IV Corps to HW 156–7
    and Lord Roberts 20, 38, 76 n. 65, 119
    and *Officers' Note Book* 22
    service overseas 25, 28
    and South African war 27, 31, 36, 38–9
    at Staff College 17, 19–20
    and SWC 217, 218–19
Reading, Lord, politician 220
Redmond, John, politician 62, 116–17,
    156–7, 198, 222
Redmond, 'Willie', MP 158, 197
Repington, Charles à Court:
    and army reform 59–60
    divorce 48–53
    hostility to HW 53, 61, 76, 88–90, 110,
    142, 192
    memoirs 291
    obituary of HW 289–90, 293
    patron for HW 22–3
    quasi-reconciliation with HW 110
    regimental service 21
    and 'shell scandal' 149
    snobbish views 12
Repington, Mrs Mellony 49–51, 53
Rhodes, Cecil, imperialist 26
Ribot, Alexandre, politician 191
Richardson, Gen. Sir George 116
Riddell, Sir George (Lord) **plate 8** 199–201,
    236, 265, 270, 274
Ritter, Gerhard, historian 99
Roberts, Aileen 38, 61
Roberts, Edwina 38, 39, 61
Roberts, Field Marshal Lord **plate 3** 22, 53,
    55, 58, 89, 110, 128, 288
    and BEF 131, 139
    as CinC 44, 47, 57
    and conscription 75–6, 109
    death and funeral 139
    and Foch 74
    'Kindergarten' 39
    patron for HW 20, 38, 42–3, 55, 65–6, 105
    relationship with HW 60–1, 76, 108, 114
    and Repington 52

and South Africa 26–7, 31, 36, 37, 38–40
and Ulster crisis 115–16, 119, 123–4
Roberts, Lt. Freddie 27, 30–1, 38–9, 60
Roberts, Nora Lady 38
Robertson, Field Marshal Sir William ('Wully')
  plate 7 39, 110, 165, 192, 24, 256, 293
  attempt to remove Derby as war minister
    269
  attends HW's funeral 288
  avoids going to Russia 182–3
  and BEF 132, 136 n. 22, 141–2, 144, 181
  CIGS 152–3, 176, 183–4, 188, 198, 207,
    217–18, 227–8
  criticises John French 150–1, 153–4
  desire to be GOC Ireland 260
  'a far sounder man than Wilson' 225
  GOC Eastern Command 218
  HW on 178, 212
  on HW 152–4
  and Lloyd George 183, 198 n. 88, 201–8,
    217
  promotion to field marshal 261
  'quite unfitted to command troops' 218
  relations with HW 78–9, 89, 141–2, 146–7,
    183–4, 189–91, 193, 197, 215–16
  reputed earnings from memoirs 291
  and Staff College 64, 78–84, 88
  and SWC 206–11, 213, 215–18
  and Ulster crisis 119–20
  in War Office 58
  and war strategy 199, 201, 204, 215
Robinson (later Dawson), Geoffrey, editor 89,
  123, 174, 176, 227
Romania 167, 171, 182, 215, 239
Roskill, Stephen, historian 205
Rostron, Maj. R. 164–5, 166 n. 51
Royal Air Force 244, 250–1
Royal Irish Constabulary 222, 258, 261,
  264, 275
  deplorable methods of 'Black and Tans'
    265–7
  reinforcement of 262–3, 265
Royal Military Academy, Sandhurst 11
Royal Military College, Woolwich 11, 78
Royal Navy 45, 244
  joint planning with army 102
  officers at Staff College 68
  war strategy 96–7
Royal Yacht Squadron 276
Rumford, Robert Kennerly, singer 54
Russell, Lt.-Col. A. V. F. 100
Russia 226, 249
  civil war, British intervention in 231–2
  as French ally 95
  HW visits 103
  HW and Allied Mission (1917) 178, 182–7
  and outbreak of First World War 127–8

revolution 190, 230
threat to India 45, 233–4
unpreparedness for war 74, 90
as wartime ally 138, 148, 167, 176–7,
  180–2, 193, 199, 203–4, 207, 211, 215
Ruzski, Gen. 185

Sackville-West, Gen. Sir Charles ('Tit Willow')
  103, 272
  at SWC 209–10, 213, 219–20
Salonika 181, 184, 208, 213, 216
Sarrail, Gen. 197
Saunderson, Edward Aremberg 258
Sclater, Edward, politician 118
Scott, Capt. Herbert ('Sparrow'), killed 173
Seely, J. E. S. ('Jack'):
  and Ulster crisis 120, 122–5
  war minister 109–10
Serbia 127, 181
Sèvres, Treaty of (1920) 252
Sharpe, Maj. A. G. M. 164–5, 167
Shaw, Gen. Sir Frederick 257–8, 261
Shea, Gen. John 169
Sherston, Jack 31
Shore, Capt. 266
Silesia 246, 271, 278
Sinn Féin 197, 222–3, 264–6, 268, 277, 285
Sladen, Brig.-Gen. 157
Smith, T. J., policeman 262
Smith-Dorrien, Gen. Sir Horace 12 n. 5, 77
  commanding II Corps 135, 137
Smuts, J. C., politician 193, 197, 199, 206,
  213
  not at Fontainebleau 236
Snow, Gen. Sir Thomas ('Snowball') 19, 136
South Africa 26–39, 273
  see also under War, Boer
Spain 246
  imperial comparison with England 46
Spears, Gen. Sir Edward 12 n. 5
Spender, J. A., editor 91
Spiers, Edward, historian 86
Spillsbury, Dr Bernard, pathologist 283
'Squiff', *see* Asquith
Staff College 16–20, 55, 62, 64–84, 88
  Draghounds 70
  HW's farewell address at (1921) 278
Stamfordham, Lord, courtier 117, 189–90,
  217–18
Stanford, Charles Villiers, Irish composer 25
Stanley, 'Eddie', *see* Derby, Lord
Stanley, Venetia, prime ministerial confidante
  140
Steel-Maitland, Arthur, MP 195
Stevenson, Frances, secretary and mistress:
  on HW 240–1, 288
Steiner, Zara, historian 96, 99

Stone, Lt. Christopher 160, 173
Stopford, Gen. Sir Frederick 51, 58, 78
    'a 2nd rate ass' 59
Strachan, Hew, historian 144
strategy, British:
    after 1918: 233–4, 244
    'blue water school' 45, 110
    during First World War 148, 167, 171,
        181–4, 192, 199, 201, 211, 221, 225–6
    HW on 45–6, 88, 95–6, 232; 'govern or get
        out' 239, 244, 277
    importance of 115
    post-Boer War reassessment 72
    reviewed by SWC 212–16
Strickland, Gen. Sir Edward 268
Studd, Col. Herbert 213
Sumner, Lord, judge 237–8
Supreme War Council (SWC) 206–17,
    219–20, 221
    after 1918: 245, 269
Sutherland, Millicent Duchess of 194
Swaine, Gen. Leopold 24
Swinton, Ernest, journalist 137
Switzerland 62, 74, 101, 138
Sykes, Gen. Sir Frederick:
    on HW 136
    and possible biography of HW 291
    at SWC 213

tactics:
    in 1918: 226
    in Boer War 29–32, 34–8
    cult of the offensive 82–3
    in IV Corps (1916) 161–2, 168–70
    on the Somme 168, 176
Tansley, Capt. Beaumont 160
Taylor, A. J. P., historian, on HW 284
Taylor, Rex, writer 283, 294
tennis 5, 14, 70
Thompson, Lt. R. G. 160
Thomson, C. B., soldier and politician 71,
    278
Thwaites, Gen. Sir William ('Bill') **plates 6
    and 8**
    CO of 141 brigade 169
    DMI 235
Tirpitz, Admiral Alfred von 90
'Tit Willow', *see* Sackville-West, Charles
trade unions 179
    see also labour unrest; Triple Alliance
Travers, Tim, historian 66, 166
Trench, John Townsend ('Towney') 15
Trench, Leonora ('Little Trench') (later Mrs
    Coote) 48, 62, 236, 276–7, 187
    urges HW to become an MP 279
Trench, Leonora (née Wray) 15, 48
Trenchard, Air Marshal Sir Hugh 250–1

Triple Alliance (of British trade unions) 231,
    246, 271
Tudor, Gen. Hugh
    CRA, 9th Division (1916) 169
    disastrous appointment as Chief of Police in
        Ireland 261–2, 265–6, 270–1, 273, 275
Turkey 226
    British occupation force in 233, 246, 252,
        271, 277–8
    and First World War 148–9, 182, 193, 196,
        199, 201, 203–4, 215
    and Greece 252
    HW visits 104–5
    need for friendly relations with 249–50
    sues for peace 227
Twiss, Maj. 99–100

Ulster Covenant 115
Ulster Special Constabulary:
    HW accused of raising 284
    HW's views on 279–80
Ulster unionism 112–13, 115, 222
    and HW's political ambitions 197
    HW's thoughts on armed resistance 112–13,
        115
    support groups in England 114, 116
    'Ulster crisis' (1914) 119–21
Ulster Volunteer Force (UVF) 116, 118, 120–1
unionism, Irish 8–9, 18, 174, 297
United States of America (USA) 234
    and First World War 191, 203, 211–12,
        214, 216, 221
    as imperial rival 45–6
    Irish in 198, 222
    security guarantee for France 237–8

Venice 103, 278
Versailles, Treaty of (1919), signing 239–40
Victoria, Princess 54–5
Vincent, Col. Berkeley 70
    criticial of HW 82–3

'W.F.' (With France) scheme 91, 129, 173
    see also British Expeditionary Force
Wake, Col. Hereward **plate 3** 40, 213
Walker, Gen. William 162–5
War, American Civil 118–19
War, Boer 26–39
    battles of Colenso 29–31; Spion Kop 32–3;
        Vaal Kranz 34
    lessons of 43, 45, 46–7, 55–6
    relief of Ladysmith 35–6
    The Times history of 54–5
War, First Balkan 103
War, First World 131–228
    battles: Amiens 226; Aubers 147, 149;
        Caporetto 206, 209, 216; Chemin des

Dames (1917) 191–2, (1918) 221;
Dardanelles/Gallipoli 148–9, 150,
180–2; 3rd Gaza 211; German spring
offensive (1918) 220–1; Loos 153;
Marne 137; Messines 195; Neuve
Chapelle 148; Somme 167–9; Vimy
190–1, IV Corps at 161–4, 166, 168–71;
1st Ypres 139; 3rd Ypres 199
casualties 167–9, 172–3, 191, 209; Lloyd
George and 176, 179–80, 209, 211
outbreak 127–8
retreat from Mons 134–6
see also strategy, British
War, Franco-Prussian 71–2
War, Irish, of Independence 256–72
War, Irish Civil 285, 296–7
War, Russo-Japanese 59, 82
war gaming 17, 61, 85, 88, 92, 213–14, 237
War Office:
Directorate of Military Operations 86–8
Intelligence Division 22–3
reform of 43–4, 47, 56–63
war scares:
1906: 63
Agadier crisis (1911) 92–4
Tangier crisis (1905) 85
usefulness of 101
Ward, Dudley (Lord Dorchester), and HW's
sailing accident 276
Warren, Gen. Sir Charles 31–3, 36
Wavell, Gen. Archibald ('Archie') 70, 81, 187
n. 37, 293
Webster, Charles K., historian **plate 6**
sartorially challenged 235
Wedgwood, Josiah MP 150
Weizmann, Chaim, Zionist 252–3
Wellington, Duke of 242
Westminster, Duke of 127
Weygand, Gen. Maxime **plate 9** 104, 211, 215
attends HW's funeral 288
White, Gen. Sir Cyril Brudenell 70
White, Gen. Sir George 27, 29
White, Terence de Vere, writer 5
White's club 18, 26, 119
Wickham, Col. Charles 280
Wigram, Lt.-Col. Clive, courtier 141, 154, 188
Williams, Billy, killed 173
Williams, Nesta 173
Williamson, Samuel L., historian 93, 102, 128
Wilson, Alice (née Taubman) 42
Wilson, Admiral Sir Arthur 96–7
Wilson, Arthur John de Courcy (HW's
brother) 3
employed as land agent 11
tennis doubles partner 14
Wilson, Bridget (HW's niece; later Lady
Blackburne) 81, 242, 258

Wilson, Cecil Mary (née Wray; HW's wife)
plate 1 42, 257, 296
charity work 54, 183
commissioning of HW biography 290–1
domestic life 242
family background 14–16
health 139, 177, 269
influence on HW 21, 38, 118, 290
recriminations after HW's death 287
unionist and conservative politics 15–16,
76, 112, 114, 117–18
wealth at death 290
Wilson, Cecil William ('Tono'; HW's brother)
3
army career 11, 33
personality 38
political work 112
Wilson, Constance Grace Martha (née Hughes;
HW's mother) 3, 42, 83
bitter comments about Lloyd George 288
Wilson, Maj. Cyril (HW's nephew) 294
WILSON, FIELD MARSHAL SIR HENRY HUGHES
(HW) **frontispiece**, **plates 2–3, 5–10**
LIFE AND CHARACTER:
and alcohol 34, 48, 74
attitude towards Catholics 7
birth and early life 2–10
and children 28
cleverness 13
club membership 18
diary **plate 4** 52, 236, 290–1
education 4–5, 11, 12
family background 2–3, 111, 258
fluency in French 103–4
Francophile tendencies 4, 72–3, 79, 99, 101,
131, 137, 153, 189, 207, 225, 228
'Irishness' of 1–10, 16, 62, 83, 98, 125–6,
288–9
marriage and relationship with wife 16–17,
21, 27–8, 38, 40, 42, 48, 118, 134, 147,
177, 269
physique 11, 13, 37, 70–1, 80
personality 5, 13, 16, 28, 37, 49, 62, 80–1,
83, 97, 147, 154, 189, 213, 292–3
pet dog 'Paddles' 48, 55, 61
possible memoirs 290–1
relations with women 240
religious beliefs 6–7
reputation as an intriguer 143, 153–4, 205
MONEY:
end-of-year accounts: (1900) 40; (1906) 67
expenditure on yachts 242–3
family financial help 16, 22, 55
financial position: (1917) 196; (1920) 242
house mortgage 88
legacy from father 68
money-making venture 18

WILSON, FIELD MARSHAL SIR HENRY HUGHES (HW) (*cont.*):
proceeds from house-letting 105, 243 n. 62
wealth at death 243
HOMES:
7 Draycott Place, London 105
36 Eaton Place, London 88, 105, 176, 243, 281–2, 286
Currygrane, Co. Longford 2–3, 8, 11, 24, 48, 175, 242, 258, 297–8; making hay at 18; occupied by Auxiliaries 275; burnt 284
Frascati, Co. Dublin 3, 14, 296
Frimley Lodge 67
Grove End (Bagshot) 18, 67, 197, 242–3
Selwood Park 23–4
Wyndham Place, London 55, 77
RECREATIONS
field sports 13, 18, 24, 53–4, 276
gardening 18, 21, 42, 242, 277
golf 103
hockey 54
polo 13, 68, 71
riding 5, 14, 18, 55
sailing 3, 14, 93, 242–3, 276–7
skiing 62, 88, 90, 102, 105, 127, 236
tennis 5, 14, 71, 269
theatre-going 19, 25, 42, 54, 93
CAREER:
battalion CO 53–4
on BEF staff 131–42, 189
brigade major, 2nd Brigade 25
British representative on SWC 207–16
CIGS 218–79
Director of Military Operations 85–130
enters army 11–13
GOC, IV Corps 156–78, 189, 292–3
GOC, Eastern Command 198
Head of Military Section, British delegation to peace conference 235–40
mission to Russia 178, 182–7
promotions: major general 87, 105; lieutenant general 146, 188; field marshal 241
regimental loyalty 21
service in India and Burma 13–14
service in South Africa 26–40
at Staff College (as student) 17–20; (as commandant) 64–84, 91, 89, 189
in War Office 2–3, 42–63
wartime Anglo-French liaison 137–8, 142, 144–8, 187–95, 224–5
HONOURS AND REWARDS:
baronetcy and grant of £10,000: 242
CB 77
DSO 43, 236

GCB 258
KCB 147
honorary degrees 242
MILITARY MATTERS:
articles on army reform 44–6
imperial defence priorities in order of importance 251–2
and Ireland (1919–22) 256–80; shocked by police methods 265–7; favours martial law 267–70; and Seán MacEoin 275–6
and 'new armies' 138–9, 150, 158, 161–2
and outbreak of First World War 127–30
overextension of British overseas commitments 237, 239, 247–51, 277
and SWC 201, 204, 206–11, 217, 219–20
war strategy 148, 167, 171, 184, 192, 201, 203–5, 213–16, 225–6
POLITICAL MATTERS:
becomes MP 279
political ambitions 195–6, 198–9, 278–9, 295
and politicians 48, 56, 80, 108, 143–4, 149–50
security adviser to N. Ireland government 279–80, 284
'sexual disturbance' caused by proximity to politicians 107
Ulster crisis and Curragh incident 115–28
Unionist and conservative opinions 8, 62–3, 108, 112, 115–17, 222–3, 259, 274, 277, 289, 297
CONTINENTAL TRAVEL:
to École Supérieure de Guerre 73
holidays 62, 73, 88, 102, 105, 246, 269
intelligence-gathering 23, 100–1, 102–3
other visits 19, 71, 74–5, 90, 103–5, 126–7
DEATH:
buried in grave destined for Lord Kitchener 288 n. 39
circumstances of 281–3
myths of: Collins's complicity in 284; and HW's use of sword 285–6
parallel with Phoenix Park murders 287
state funeral 288
POSTHUMOUS REPUTATION:
biographies *see under* Ash, Bernard; Callwell, Charles; Collier, Basil
Memorial Fund 290
memorials to 296
in *Oh What a Lovely War* 294
Wilson, James (HW's father) 2–3, 4, 42
Church of Ireland work 6, 9
health 48
political work and opinions 8–9, 18, 111–12
Wilson, James Mackay ('Jemmy', HW's brother) 3, 4, 11, 176

elegy for old Irish order 297–8
and HW entering politics 196
member of Brooks's 18
money problems 242
political work and opinions 8, 9, 111–12, 114–15, 297
on situation in Ireland (1916) 175, (1917) 197
writes in support of Seán MacEoin 275
Wilson, Keith, historian 97, 198
Wilson, President Woodrow 211, 220, 234, 238
Wolfe Murray, Gen. Sir James ('Sheep') 57–8, 150
Wolseley, Field Marshal Lord 23, 27, 47, 288

Woodroffe, Brig.-Gen. Charles R. 131, 136
Woolcombe, Gen. Sir Charles ('Wooly') 178
Worthington-Evans, Sir Laming, politician 270–4
Wray, Cecil Mary, *see* Wilson, Cecil Mary

'X' committee 223–4

Yarde-Buller, Brig.-Gen. Sir Henry ('Yardie') 13, 19, 36
Yugoslavia 239

Zhilinski, Gen. I. G. 103, 181
Zionism 253